Register Now for (to Your B

SPRINGER PUBLISHING COMPANY
CONNECT™

Your print purchase of *Psychology of Aging,* **includes online access to the contents of your book**—increasing accessibility, portability, and searchability!

Access today at:

http://connect.springerpub.com/content/book/978-0-8261-3729-6 or scan the QR code at the right with your smartphone and enter the access code below.

M55HYVK1

Scan here for quick access.

LS

SPRINGER PUBLISHING COMPANY
View all our products at springerpub.com

Psychology
of Aging

Brian P. Yochim, PhD, ABPP, is board certified in clinical neuropsychology by the American Board of Professional Psychology. He obtained his PhD from Wayne State University and completed an internship in clinical psychology at VA Palo Alto Health Care System in Palo Alto, California. He completed a 2-year postdoctoral fellowship in clinical neuropsychology, with a focus on aging, at VA Northern California Health Care System. In 2006, he became an assistant professor at the University of Colorado at Colorado Springs, where he helped develop a PhD training program in clinical psychology with an emphasis on aging. He next worked as a neuropsychologist at VA Palo Alto Health Care System, where he performed research in the neuropsychology of aging, published the Verbal Naming Test, and supervised postdoctoral fellows, interns, and practicum students in a neuropsychology clinic for older adults. In 2014, he served as the president of the Society of Clinical Geropsychology (Division 12, Section 2 of the American Psychological Association [APA]). He also served as the chair of the Publications and Communications Committee for the Society for Clinical Neuropsychology (Division 40 of the APA) from 2014 to 2017. Since 2006 he has taught graduate courses in the psychology of aging and clinical neuropsychology. In 2016, he returned to his childhood home of St. Louis, Missouri, and accepted a position at the VA St. Louis Health Care System. His professional interests lie in the neuropsychological assessment of older adults, and in teaching and training in psychology of aging and clinical neuropsychology.

Erin L. Woodhead, PhD, is Assistant Professor in the Department of Psychology at San José State University. She completed her undergraduate degree in human development and family studies at the Pennsylvania State University. She completed her master's and doctoral degrees in clinical psychology at West Virginia University. Dr. Woodhead completed postdoctoral fellowships in geropsychology at Rush University Medical Center and at the Geriatric, Research, Education, and Clinical Center (GRECC) at the VA Palo Alto Health Care System. She teaches classes in the areas of life-span development, psychology of aging, addictions, ethical and legal issues for mental health professionals, and clinical psychology. Dr. Woodhead's research is in the areas of age-related differences in mental health services use and age-related differences in the symptoms and outcomes of mental health and substance use disorders.

Psychology of Aging

A BIOPSYCHOSOCIAL PERSPECTIVE

Brian P. Yochim, PhD, ABPP

Erin L. Woodhead, PhD

Editors

SPRINGER PUBLISHING COMPANY

Springer Publishing Company, LLC
11 West 42nd Street
New York, NY 10036
www.springerpub.com

Acquisitions Editor: Sheri W. Sussman
Compositor: Westchester Publishing Services

ISBN: 9780826137289
ebook ISBN: 9780826137296

Instructor's Materials: Qualified instructors may request supplements by emailing textbook@springerpub.com:
Instructor's Manual ISBN: 9780826137326
Instructor's PowerPoints ISBN: 9780826137333

17 18 19 20 21 / 5 4 3 2 1

The author and the publisher of this Work have made every effort to use sources believed to be reliable to provide information that is accurate and compatible with the standards generally accepted at the time of publication. The author and publisher shall not be liable for any special, consequential, or exemplary damages resulting, in whole or in part, from the readers' use of, or reliance on, the information contained in this book. The publisher has no responsibility for the persistence or accuracy of URLs for external or third-party Internet websites referred to in this publication and does not guarantee that any content on such websites is, or will remain, accurate or appropriate.

The contents do not represent the views of the U.S. Department of Veterans Affairs or the United States Government.

Library of Congress Cataloging-in-Publication Data

Names: Yochim, Brian P., editor. | Woodhead, Erin L., editor.
Title: Psychology of aging : a biopsychosocial perspective / Brian P. Yochim, PhD, ABPP,
    Erin L. Woodhead, PhD, editors.
Description: New York, NY : Springer Publishing Company, [2018] | Includes index.
Identifiers: LCCN 2017035270 (print) | LCCN 2017046842 (ebook) | ISBN 9780826137296 (ebook) |
    ISBN 9780826137289 (hard copy : alk. paper)
Subjects: LCSH: Aging—Psychological aspects.
Classification: LCC BF724.55.A35 (ebook) | LCC BF724.55.A35 P7953 2018 (print) | DDC 155.67—dc23
LC record available at https://lccn.loc.gov/2017035270

Contact us to receive discount rates on bulk purchases.
We can also customize our books to meet your needs.
For more information please contact: sales@springerpub.com

Printed in the United States of America by McNaughton & Gunn.

Contents

SECTION IV

Social Aspects of Aging

Contributors

Juliana Baldo, PhD
Research Neuropsychologist
Research Service
VA Northern California Health Care System
Martinez, California

Kyrstle Barrera, PhD
Neuropsychologist
Department of Neuropsychology and
    Rehabilitation Psychology
Assistant Professor
Department of Physical Medicine
    and Rehabilitation
Loma Linda University School of Medicine
Loma Linda, California

Nicholas T. Bott, PsyD
Post-Doctoral Fellow
Clinical Excellence Research Center and
    Department of Neurology and
    Neurological Sciences
Stanford University School of Medicine
Palo Alto, California

Preston Brown, MA
Graduate Student
Department of Psychology
San José State University
San José, California

J. Kaci Fairchild, PhD, ABPP

Center Investigator
Sierra Pacific Mental Illness Research Education
    and Clinical Center
VA Palo Alto Health Care System
Clinical Associate Professor (Affiliated)
Department of Psychiatry and Behavioral Sciences
Stanford University School of Medicine
Palo Alto, California

Sheri Gibson, PhD

Director of Behavioral Health Services
Rocky Mountain Health Care Services
Faculty Affiliate
Gerontology Center
University of Colorado at Colorado Springs
Colorado Springs, Colorado

Kari A. Haws, PhD

Postdoctoral Fellow
VA Northern California Health Care System
Martinez, California

Kimberly E. Hiroto, PhD

Clinical Psychologist
Psychology Service
VA Palo Alto Health Care System
Palo Alto, California

J. W. Terri Huh, PhD, ABPP

Associate Director of Education and Evaluation
Geriatric Research, Education, and Clinical Center
VA Palo Alto Health Care System
Associate Professor (Affiliated)
Department of Psychiatry and Behavioral Sciences
Stanford University School of Medicine
Palo Alto, California

Spring F. Johnson, MA

Graduate Student
Department of Psychology
Loma Linda University
Loma Linda, California

Andrea June, PhD

Assistant Professor
Department of Psychological Science
Central Connecticut State University
New Britain, Connecticut

Victor Kwan, MA

Graduate Student
Department of Psychology
San José State University
San José, California

Magdalene Lim, PsyD

Licensed Clinical Psychologist
UCCS Aging Center
Colorado Springs, Colorado

Meghan A. Marty, PhD

Licensed Clinical Psychologist
Rose City Geropsychology, LLC
Portland, Oregon

Cynthia McQuown, MAEd, PCC-S, LICDC

Cornerstone Psychological and Counseling
Medina, Ohio

Christie Mead, MA

Graduate Student
Palo Alto University
Sierra Pacific Mental Illness Research Education
    and Clinical Center
VA Palo Alto Health Care System
Palo Alto, California

Tyler A. Rickards, PhD

Rehabilitation Neuropsychologist
Division of Neuropsychology
Department of Neurology
The Sandra and Malcolm Berman
    Brain & Spine Institute, LifeBridge Health
Baltimore, Maryland

Rachel L. Rodriguez, PhD, MPH, ABPP

Clinical Psychologist
Psychology Service
Durham VA Health Care System
Durham, North Carolina

Harvey L. Sterns, PhD

Professor of Psychology
Director and Senior Fellow
Institute for Life-Span Development
    and Gerontology
Chair, University Council
The University of Akron
Akron, Ohio
Research Professor of Family and
    Community Medicine
Northeast Ohio Medical University
Rootstown, Ohio

Erin L. Woodhead, PhD

Assistant Professor
Department of Psychology
San José State University
San José, California

Sarah J. Yarry, PhD

Clinical Psychologist
Psychology Service
Albany Stratton VA Medical Center
Albany, New York

Brian P. Yochim, PhD, ABPP

Neuropsychologist
VA St. Louis Health Care System
St. Louis, Missouri

Maya Yutsis, PhD, ABPP

Neuropsychologist
Department of Neurology and Neurological Sciences
Stanford University School of Medicine
Palo Alto, California

Foreword

I am delighted to have the opportunity to welcome readers of this book! Many of us prefer not to think too much about growing older, given its common associations with illness, loss, and eventual death. It is ironic that, as relatively younger people who generally hope to live long lives, we may have somewhat negative feelings about the people we will eventually become (if we are fortunate). Across health care professions, very few people choose to specialize in care of older adults, leading to a crisis in access to competent geriatric health and mental health care services for most older adults in the United States (Institute of Medicine, 2008, 2012) and internationally (Beard & Bloom, 2015; Mateos-Nozal & Beard, 2011).

The aging of our society has profound implications for the economy, health care system, family structures, housing, transportation, business opportunities, and more. No matter what your field of interest, it will be important to have a solid understanding of the aging experience, including strengths, challenges, and the wide diversity of human aging. This text provides an excellent foundation on biological, psychological, and social aspects of aging to inform your clinical training and practice, research, teaching, policy, and/or business activities. If you are pursuing a career in academic and/or clinical psychology, or other health professions, consider this book a core resource to help you address age/cohort as an important component of individual diversity. Even if you choose to address the health/mental health of children, adolescents, or younger adults, older adults will be significant members of family and community systems whose abilities and needs will be important for you to understand.

Drs. Yochim and Woodhead are particularly well-suited to have led the development of this text. They both trained at leading geropsychology doctoral training programs; completed postdoctoral training in geropsychology and/or neuropsychology; have extensive clinical, teaching, and research experience in the field; and have established themselves as respected leaders in service to the geropsychology profession. In addition to writing several chapters, they assembled a talented team of psychologists to contribute chapters. Many contributing authors are early-to-mid career geropsychologists with impeccable academic and/or clinical training who provide current and rigorous perspectives on their topics.

My great hope is that many of you reading this text will be inspired to devote some of your talents and energies to the field of aging. You are needed. As a clinical geropsychologist who has spent more than 20 years in the field to date, I feel very fortunate to have discovered such a meaningful, fascinating, and rewarding line of work. As a clinician, interprofessional team member, teacher, supervisor, researcher, administrator, and frequent collaborator with people who work in geriatric health/ mental health fields, I am inspired daily by the commitment and generosity of people who dedicate their professional lives to improving the quality of care and quality of life for older people. I am grateful to Drs. Yochim and Woodhead for their work in developing this foundational text on the psychology of aging.

Michele J. Karel, PhD, ABPP
Board Certified in Geropsychology
Psychogeriatrics Coordinator
Office of Mental Health and
Suicide Prevention
Veterans Health Administration

REFERENCES

Beard, J. R., & Bloom, D. E. (2015). Towards a comprehensive public health response to population ageing. *Lancet, 385,* 658–661.

Institute of Medicine. (2008). *Retooling for an aging America: Building the health care workforce.* Washington, DC: National Academies Press.

Institute of Medicine. (2012). *The mental health and substance use workforce for older adults: In whose hands?* Washington, DC: National Academies Press.

Mateos-Nozal, J., & Beard, J. R. (2011). Global approaches to geriatrics in medical education. *European Geriatric Medicine, 2,* 87–92.

Preface

OVERALL GOAL OF THE BOOK

Older adults now represent a higher proportion of the world population than at any other time in history. By 2030, there will be more people age 60 and older than age 0 to 9 years. However, the number of mental health clinicians trained to work with older adults is not increasing to meet this surge in demand. With this massive growth in the number of older adults worldwide, there is an increasing need for clinicians from multiple disciplines to receive instruction on the psychological aspects of aging.

In 2006, one of the editors (Brian Yochim) was assigned to teach a graduate-level course on the psychology of aging to a class of students working toward their PhDs in clinical psychology. A search of available textbooks did not arrive at a choice that would fit well with this course. There were books about gerontology in general, handbooks that went into depth on specific topics but did not have the same breadth of coverage as a typical textbook, books focused on certain aspects of aging (e.g., mental health), or books on adult development and aging that included coverage of early and middle adulthood that was beyond the scope of this class. I cobbled together a series of articles for my class to read and opted not to have any textbook. Since that time I hoped to find a textbook to use for a class like this, and eventually Erin Woodhead and I were invited to write it. This book fills a gaping void in the selection of textbooks to use in graduate courses on the psychology of aging.

An instructor for a graduate course on the psychology of aging has the challenge of finding a textbook for this area that is tailored to graduate students. This book was written to fill this gap. This book can serve as a primer for any graduate student who is going to work in a clinical setting with older adults, or in a research lab that studies some aspect of the psychology of aging. In reading any of the chapters, students are provided with the requisite foundational knowledge in a given area, as well as introduced to specific areas in greater depth. For example, a reader of Chapter 4 will be prepared to enter a neuroimaging lab that explores neuroplasticity in older adults. Readers of Chapter 9 will have a solid foundation of neurocognitive disorders that may occur in their future patients. The level of depth provided in these chapters is typically not available in undergraduate textbooks on aging, as textbooks aimed at undergraduates tend to target breadth rather than depth. This book is unique in that it quickly introduces students to the background knowledge needed in order to understand some of the more complex concepts in the psychology of aging. Additionally, this book provides clear explanations of concepts (e.g., genetics of aging research, neuroimaging techniques, understanding of important legal documents for older adults) that, in our experience as instructors for psychology of aging classes, prove to be stumbling blocks for students wanting to learn about aging.

DISTINGUISHING FEATURES

While other textbooks include coverage of adults of all ages, this text is unique in that it focuses solely on older adults, providing in-depth coverage of this burgeoning population. The two editors, Brian Yochim and Erin Woodhead, work in full-time clinical and academic positions, and the content of the book is applicable to future academicians or clinicians. Both editors have taught psychology of aging courses at the graduate and undergraduate levels, and are familiar with the textbooks available to instructors in this area.

One unique feature of this book is the amount of coverage on biological aspects of aging, written in such a manner as to be easily comprehensible to graduate students who are not specializing in this area. When students need important biological concepts explained to them, this book can serve as a useful and user-friendly resource. At the same time, students specializing in biological aspects of aging will find the book to be a useful introduction to the psychology of aging, and research methods and findings from psychology will enhance their research in the biology of aging. The book also provides more coverage on cognitive reserve and neurocognitive disorders than other textbooks in the area. This is balanced by coverage of social aspects of aging that one would not find in books on the biology of aging, such as legal aspects of aging or the aging experience for ethnic and sexual minorities.

Instructors can teach a class with this book as the sole collection of readings or can supplement this text with additional articles. Key references for each chapter are indicated by an asterisk, for instructors looking for further depth of coverage in each chapter. Each chapter ends with Discussion Questions that can be used for discussion in class or essay questions for exams in graduate classes. In support of the text, an Instructor's Manual and PowerPoints are available. **Qualified instructors can request these ancillaries by email: textbook@springerpub.com**.

INTENDED AUDIENCE

This book is intended for graduate students or upper-level undergraduate students in psychology, biology, nursing, counseling, social work, gerontology, speech pathology, psychiatry, and other disciplines who provide services for, or perform research with, older adults. Unlike undergraduate textbooks, this text provides a foundation for graduate students across disciplines who want to embark on research, clinical, or health care careers with older adults. After reading this book, it will serve as a reference that is frequently consulted to provide explanations of many concepts in the field.

BOOK'S ORGANIZATION AND CONTENT

Each chapter in this text was authored by experts in the field to ensure appropriate coverage of the area. An introduction to the field is presented in Section I (Chapter 1), which also covers common research methods in the area. Then Sections II to IV move from the cellular level to larger societal aspects of aging. An understanding of the psychological aspects of aging must begin with a core foundation in biological aspects of aging, and this is covered in Section II. This section includes a chapter on general biological theories of aging, such as the free radical theory of aging. Chapter 3 provides a detailed overview of common physical health problems in older adults, and how these conditions impact the quality of life of older adults. This will help any health professional understand the health problems that older adults are facing. Chapter 4 provides an overview of normal changes that occur to the brain with aging, starting with an overview of neuroimaging methods and ending with an introduction to the exciting area of neuroplasticity.

The book then moves into the largest section, Section III. Changes in personality and emotional development are covered in Chapter 5. A discussion of the unique mental health aspects of aging is presented in Chapter 6. Normal changes in cognitive functioning, and how this applies to driving and mandatory retirement requirements, are presented in Chapter 7. Cognitive reserve and interventions for cognitive decline are presented in Chapter 8. Chapter 9 consists of an up-to-date presentation of neurocognitive disorders in aging, including timely topics such as Alzheimer's disease, delirium, Lewy body disease, frontotemporal dementia, and traumatic brain injuries in older adults. Aging's impact on relationships and families is discussed in Chapter 10. Working in late life and retirement are covered in Chapter 11, with a focus on helping students understand the complexities of medical coverage and retirement options in the current economic climate.

We then move into larger social aspects of aging in Section IV. Death, bereavement, and widowhood are covered in Chapter 12. The aging experience in ethnic and sexual minorities is presented in Chapter 13, with a unique section on intersectionality and how this concept applies to older adults. Lastly, the intersection of aging and the legal system is covered in Chapter 14, with explanations of concepts such as durable power of attorney, advance directives, capacity assessment, and elder abuse.

Thank you for your interest in the psychology of aging. We hope you find this learning journey as fascinating as all the authors of this book have. May this book serve as a solid foundation for a career serving older adults wherever you are.

Acknowledgments

BRIAN YOCHIM

I want to thank my friend and colleague Erin Woodhead, PhD, for coediting this book with me. Without you, this book would not have been completed. I hope you are willing to work on future projects with me. I am very grateful to Sheri Sussman (Editorial Director) and Mindy Chen (Assistant Editor) from Behavioral Sciences at Springer Publishing Company for all your help along the way. Thank you for your guidance and immediate responses whenever we needed assistance.

The broad field of gerontology owes its existence to the thousands of older adults who have donated their time to participate in research. We also are indebted to the researchers who have spent their careers tirelessly performing studies to add to our knowledge base, and to the agencies that fund them. This book is a result of your work. Without you, books such as this would not exist.

Thank you to my friends and colleagues who contributed chapters to this book, and waited for the book to come to completion. I want to thank my friends and colleagues at the University of Colorado at Colorado Springs, at the VA Palo Alto Health Care System, and at the VA St. Louis Health Care System. I have learned a great deal from you about aging, how to be a great colleague, and many other things. You will remain my friends and colleagues throughout my career. Thank you to Katie (Brown) Peever and Morgan Nitta, who provided much assistance in my writing of Chapter 1. Thank you to my mentor, Peter Lichtenberg. You have mentored me since taking me on as a young graduate student, and have been everything I could ask for in a mentor throughout my career.

Thank you to my dear brother Mike, author of four books to date and one of my favorite hiking companions. Thank you to my family and to my wife's family for being so loving and supportive.

Most of all, I thank my dear wife Jill and our son Ellis, who tolerated me spending my weekends and vacation days working on this book. Thank you for reminding me (many times) that life is a highway, Ellis. I look forward to exploring those highways with you and Jill, and I hope they are long and enriching.

ERIN WOODHEAD

Thank you to my coeditor, Brian Yochim, for inviting me to work on this book with him. We helped each other through the process and I look forward to more projects together in the future! We also benefited greatly from the guidance provided by our editors at Springer Publishing Company, who helped us meet our deadlines and shape our materials into a book.

I would also like to thank the mentors I have had over the years at The Pennsylvania State University, West Virginia University, Rush University Medical Center, and the VA Palo Alto Health Care System. I value their mentorship and their assistance with my career path more than I can describe in this section. I am also grateful to my coworkers at San José State University, who have created an environment where balancing work and family life is the norm rather than the exception. They continue to inspire me with their dedication to their research, their students, and their lives outside of academia.

Brian and I also owe a debt of gratitude to all of the clinicians, researchers, and trainees who contributed to this book. They put up with a lot of emails from us and produced excellent work to help train the future generation of gerontologists and geropsychologists.

Finally, I would like to thank my family for supporting my work on this book and my career in higher education and academia. My husband was very helpful in this process, assisting me in managing deadlines and stress while also parenting our 1- and 3-year-old daughters. Watching our daughters grow and develop motivates me every day to work harder at being a good parent, partner, and colleague.

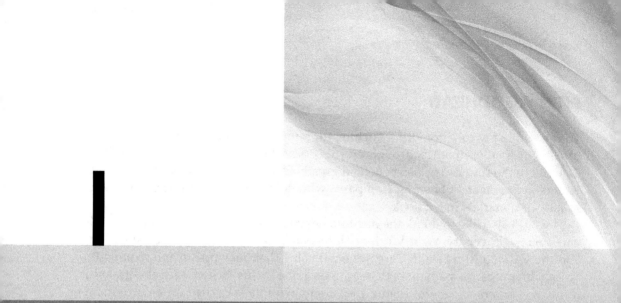

Introduction

1

Introduction to the Psychology of Aging

Brian P. Yochim

In 2017, at age 95, Betty Reid Soskin was the oldest ranger in the National Park System. Born on September 22, 1921, she has lived through racial discrimination, gender discrimination, World War II and other wars, and remains employed full time to tell her story at Rosie the Riveter / World War II Home Front National Historical Park in Richmond, California. Her great-grandmother had been a slave and Betty carried a picture of her when she attended President Barack Obama's inauguration in 2009. She has been interviewed on National Public Radio (NPR) and the Public Broadcasting Service (PBS) and two documentaries are being made about her life (see Box 1.1 at the end of this chapter).

How is the aging experience different for her, as an African American woman? Why is she able to be healthy enough to work into her 90s, whereas other people develop neurocognitive disorders or physical disabilities at a much younger age that prevent them from working? What is her physical health like? Is her brain receiving adequate blood supply? How does past racism affect her life now? Are her cognitive abilities similar to how they were in her 50s? Is she more or less likely to develop mental health problems at her age? Is her personality more likely to be similar or different than how it was in her younger years? At her age, is it necessary for her to be working to support herself? How have her relationships changed in the past several decades? These questions are explored in this textbook.

---

*Key references in the References section are indicated by an asterisk.

DEFINING OLDER ADULTS

At what age would you consider yourself an older adult? There are many factors that go into whom we consider older, and chronological age reflects only one of those components. We might also consider social age, which considers the types of roles the person occupies. We typically think of grandparents as older adults, but what about people who become grandparents in their 30s or 40s? Are these individuals "older adults?" What about functional age? This refers to the idea that some older adults may have "the heart of a 25 year old" in terms of their physiological functioning. Another metric of age might be how old you feel. Research finds that a person's chronological age is similar to their "felt age" in younger adulthood. However, as we start to age, we tend to feel younger than we actually are. This finding is depicted in Figure 1.1, which shows the results of a Pew Research Center survey conducted in 2009 (Pew Research Center, 2009).

In the same 2009 Pew Research Center survey, respondents were asked at which age "old age" begins. Results (as shown in Figure 1.2) suggest that this number is a moving target depending on the age of the respondent. For example, adults between ages 18 and 29 considered age 60 as the start of old age, whereas those who were older than age 65 considered age 74 as the start of old age. This suggests that our conceptualization of aging and older adulthood may change as individuals age.

Typically, the chronological age of 65 is used as the cutoff between middle age and old age. This criterion may have originated in Germany, which was the first country to create a social insurance program for older adults, in 1889. The retirement

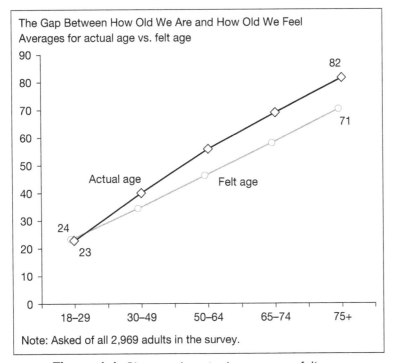

Figure 1.1 Changes in actual age versus felt age.

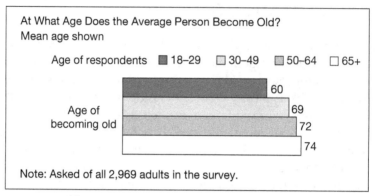

Figure 1.2 What constitutes "old age?"

age was first designated as 70 and was lowered to 65 in 1916. When Social Security was created in the United States in 1935, age 65 was chosen as the retirement age for two main reasons. First, at that time, approximately half of the existing state pension systems used age 65 as the retirement age and half used age 70. The federal Railroad Retirement System was newly created in 1934 and used age 65 as its retirement age. Second, actuarial studies found that a self-sustaining system could be created with small levels of payroll taxation using age 65 (Social Security Administration, 2015).

You might also consider the difference between a 65 year old and a 90 year old. These individuals likely have vastly different abilities and daily experiences, yet we technically consider both of them "older adults." Researchers now typically delineate older adults into three groups based on chronological age: young-old (65–74 years old), old-old (75–84 years old), and the oldest-old (age 85 and older; Neugarten, 1974). This helps counteract the idea that all older adults are alike and have similar concerns or needs.

Who is the typical older adult? You may have certain beliefs about where older adults live, how they spend their time, and other ideas about this population. Based on the Pew Research Center survey described previously (Pew Research Center, 2009), 2% of adults ages 65 to 74 report that they live in an assisted living facility. This percentage increases to 4% of adults ages 75 to 84 and 15% of adults older than 85. As of 2013, about 4% of adults age 65 and older lived in long-term care facilities (e.g., nursing homes). This percentage increases for adults age 85 and older, 15% of whom lived in long-term care facilities (AgingStats.gov, 2016). The majority of older adults live in their own homes or apartments and do not live in assisted living facilities, nursing homes, or senior communities. We refer to this group of older adults who live in their own homes as "community dwelling." Approximately 66% of older adults report that religion is very important to them, compared to 44% of adults ages 18 to 29. Around 76% of older adults report that they are retired with 8% reporting that they are retired but working part time. When asked about their daily activities, most older adults talk with families or friends every day (90%), take at least one prescription medication every day (83%), and drive a car every day (65%). Around a quarter of older adults use the Internet on a daily basis, and 22% engage in vigorous exercise every day. Activity levels tend to decline among older adults in their 70s and 80s, and this age group tends to have higher rates of daily prayer and daily medication use.

What about voting behavior? The extent to which older adults identify as Republican or Democrat tends to correlate with their birth cohort. Cohort effects are a concept that we discuss more later in this chapter. Overall, research suggests that there is a fairly even split among older adults and political party affiliation. In 2014, 47% of the Silent Generation (individuals born between 1937 and 1945) identified as Republican, compared to 41% of Baby Boomers (individuals born between 1946 and 1964), 38% of Generation X (individuals born between 1965 and 1976), and 35% of Millennials (individuals born between 1981 and 2000; Pew Research Center, 2015). Older Baby Boomers, born in the late 1940s and early 1950s, tend to favor Democratic candidates. This cohort came of voting age during the Nixon presidency. Younger Baby Boomers, born in the late 1950s and early 1960s, came of voting age during the Carter and Reagan presidencies and tend to vote Republican. As you can see, many questions that are asked about age are complex and are tied to sociocultural and historical variables that influenced different cohorts. This question is also complex because the characteristics of the Republican and Democratic parties have changed over time.

INTERNATIONAL AND U.S. STATISTICS ON AGING

The world is aging precipitously, which is leading to important economic and social consequences. Older adults currently represent a higher proportion of the world population than at any other time in the history of the world. By 2030, there will be more people age 60 and older than age 0 to 9 years. By 2050, there will be more people age 60 and older than adolescents and youth age 10 to 24 years. This change already occurred in more developed regions in 1998, where older adults represented 23% of the population in 2013. This trend is occurring because of declines in reproductive rates and in child and adult mortalities. Older adults (age 60 and older) comprised 9.2% of the world population in 1990, 12.5% in 2015, and will make up 16.7% of the world population by 2030 (United Nations, 2015). From 2010 to 2040, the proportion of the population of China that is 60 and older will increase from 12.4% to 28.1%, the fastest increase in the world. Japan, Italy, Germany, and Finland had the highest proportions of older adults in their populations in 2015 (United Nations, 2015). China had the highest number of adults age 80 and older, followed by the United States, India, Japan, and Germany. By 2050, China will still have the highest number, at 90 million, distantly followed by India (37 million), the United States, Japan, and Brazil.

There are fewer men compared to women at higher ages, both when considering international and U.S. statistics. In 2015, women comprised 54% of the world population aged 60 years and older, and 61% of the population age 80 or older (United Nations, 2015). In 2013 in the United States, there were 128 women for every 100 men age 65 and older, and 196 women for every man age 85 and older.

By 2050, almost 80% of older adults will live in less developed areas of the world, because the numbers of older adults are growing more rapidly in less developed countries than in more developed countries. According to the United Nations (2015), the percentage of the population age 60 and older varies between developed and less developed countries, as well as within these two categories. More developed countries are aging at rates similar across countries, but within less developed regions there is greater variability, with some countries in a more advanced stage of aging (e.g., Armenia, Argentina, China, Georgia, and Sri Lanka) and other countries with a very small proportion of older adults that is not increasing (e.g., most of sub-Saharan Africa, south-central Asia, southeastern Asia, and western Asia).

While developed countries have populations with the highest *proportions* of older adults, the highest *numbers* of older adults live in developing countries. The number of older adults in the world will more than double from 901 million people in 2015 to more than 2.1 billion in 2050. The numbers of working-age adults per older person, a measure of financial support for older adults, are predicted to continue to decline, which will increase financial strain on support systems for the aging population. In most countries, however, older adults support themselves with their own earnings and income from their assets, in addition to public transfers such as pensions and government-provided health care.

In the United States, older adults are one of the fastest growing and diverse segments of the population. In 1980, 11.3% of the U.S. population was 65 years of age or older (Santos & VandenBos, 1982). In 1990, approximately 3 million people in the United States were 65 or older. By 2008, that number had grown to 35 million, with older adults comprising roughly 13% of the U.S. population. By 2014, 14.1% of the U.S. population was 65 or older (Administration on Aging, 2014), and by 2030 this proportion will increase to more than 20% (Ortman, Velkoff, & Hogan, 2014). Put another way, by 2030, it is expected that one in five people in the United States will be aged 65 or older. Within this older segment of the population, the oldest-old (those age 85 and older) are the most rapidly expanding group, with a growth rate that is twice that of those age 65 or older. The states with the highest numbers of older adults are California, Florida, Texas, New York, and Pennsylvania (Administration on Aging, 2014). In 2013, there were 67,347 Americans age 100 or more.

Older adults will become increasingly ethnically diverse in the United States; the percentage of older Americans that are ethnic minorities will increase from 20.7% in 2012 to 39.1% in 2050 (Ortman et al., 2014). Race and Hispanic origin are treated as two separate entities for U.S. Census records, according to the Office of Management and Budget (OMB) 1997 guidelines. People of Hispanic origin may be of any race, and people in each race group may be Hispanic or non-Hispanic. In 2012, 7.3% of Americans age 65 and older identified as Hispanic. Whites comprised 86% of the older population, 8.8% were Black, 3.8% were Asian, 0.8% were two or more races, 0.6% were American Indian or Alaskan Native, and 0.1% were Native Hawaiian or other Pacific Islander (Ortman et al., 2014). By 2050, these numbers are expected to change to 18.4% Hispanic, 77.3% White, 12.3% Black, 7.1% Asian, 1.8% two or more races, 1.2% American Indian or Alaskan Native, and 0.3% Native Hawaiian or other Pacific Islander.

As mentioned previously, one of the reasons people are living longer is decreased adult mortality, potentially related to improved health care. These changes are reflected in the dramatic changes in life expectancy across the past century. Life expectancy is the mean number of additional years a person can expect to live, assuming that current mortality rates for ages above the person's age were to stay constant for the remainder of that person's life. Life expectancy at birth was 65 years in 1950 in more developed areas of the world and now is estimated to be 78 years in developed areas and 68 in less developed regions. This gap in life expectancy between developed and less developed regions is expected to continue to shrink, so that by 2050 life expectancy will be 83 years in more developed areas and 75 in less developed regions (United Nations, 2015). Gaps in life expectancy exist between men and women and across different races and ethnicities. For example, women born in 2014 have an average life expectancy of 81.2 years, compared to 76.4 years for men (Centers for Disease Control and Prevention [CDC], 2015). African American individuals born in 2014 have an average life expectancy of 75.2 years, compared to 78.8 years for European American individuals and 81.8 years for Hispanic individuals (CDC, 2015). These differences in life expectancy between groups are often tied to access to health care and social resources.

The previous paragraph describes life expectancy at birth. You can also look at life expectancy once a person reaches older adulthood. This number depicts the average number of years the person has left to live. A person who is age 65 in 2014 can expect to live for 19.3 more years, on average. If a person is age 75 in 2014, he or she can expect to live for 12.2 more years, on average (CDC, 2015). This highlights the idea that older adults are already a select group of individuals who have survived various hardships and illnesses in order to reach older adulthood. Individuals who engaged in risky behaviors, or faced multiple illnesses, may have died before reaching older adulthood. Therefore, from a statistical perspective, the longer you live, the more likely you are to keep living.

MEETING THE NEEDS OF AN AGING POPULATION

In contrast to the exploding numbers of older Americans, the number of mental health specialists trained to work with them is extremely low and is barely changing. Only 3% of psychologists work primarily with older adults, although 69% provided some services to older adults (Qualls, Segal, Norman, Niederehe, & Gallagher-Thompson, 2002). In Qualls et al.'s study, only 28% of the sample had completed graduate coursework in aging, and most participants reported their source of geropsychology training to be informal experience (76% of the sample) or on-the-job training (49%). While it was estimated that 5,000 to 7,500 psychologists were needed to meet the needs of older adults' mental health at the time of their writing, Qualls et al. (2002) estimated that approximately 3,000 full-time equivalent (FTE) psychologists were currently providing services to older adults. The number of geriatric psychiatrists is expected to decrease from 1,800 today to 1,650 in 2030, which will be less than one per 6,000 older adults with mental health disorders (Bartels & Naslund, 2013). In 2015, Hoge, Karel, Zeiss, Alegria, and Moye put forth eight recommendations to address the shortage of psychologists with specialized training in aging. These recommendations, outlined in Table 1.1, were written in light of the undersupply of geropsychologists available to accomplish these goals and the awareness that there will likely never be an adequate number of specialists for the mental health needs of older adults.

Table 1.1 Recommendations to Strengthen the Workforce in Psychology for Older Adults

1. Establish a set of core competencies and a minimal amount of graduate training in aging for all psychologists.
2. Incorporate standards of core competency and minimal training requirements into the *Guidelines and Principles for Accreditation* of the American Psychological Association (APA).
3. Increase the amount of content related to older adults on the Examination for Professional Practice in Psychology (EPPP), the licensing exam for the field of clinical psychology.
4. Create and distribute a model curriculum for graduate training in older adults.
5. Create an evidence-based continuing education system in geropsychology for practicing psychologists.
6. Improve the skills of other professions, older adults, and caregivers in the prevention, assessment, and treatment of mental health conditions.
7. Advocate for improved financial incentives (e.g., Medicare) for working with older adults.
8. Perform a supply-and-demand analysis for psychologists qualified to provide services to older adults.

Source: Hoge et al. (2015).

GENERATIONAL INFLUENCES: BABY BOOMERS

Cohorts are groups of people who have similar cultural experiences and values. In the psychology of aging, cohorts are typically defined by the year of birth, which determines the generation to which they belong (Schaie, 1965). Different birth cohorts are often given names that reflect their core traits. For example, the media frequently refers to characteristics of the "Millennials." This cohort is typically defined as individuals born between 1981 and 2000. They are typically labeled as "coddled" by their parents, attached to their digital devices, and highly focused on children and family. Each birth cohort often has many positive and negative labels attached to it, even though many individuals within that cohort may not fit those labels. Being aware of the overall experiences of each cohort can be helpful in working with current and future populations of older adults.

Most of today's older adults are a part of the "Baby Boom" generation. This generation is notable for being the largest, wealthiest, and best-educated generation ever produced in America (Jones, 1980). While the birth rate had declined for 200 years, and continues to decline, a major exception to this occurred after World War II. Births started increasing during World War II, from 1940 to 1943. In 1946, twice as many couples married than in any year before the war. Couples were marrying at younger ages than before the war; the median age of marriage declined from 1940 to 1956 (Jones, 1980). Rather than the increasing birth rate being a temporary increase as soldiers returned home after the war, it continued into the early 1960s, peaking in 1957, when over 4.3 million babies were born. From 1946 to 1964, 76,441,000 babies were born in the United States, and these citizens range from age 53 to 71 as of 2017 (see Figure 1.3). This means that 24% of the current population of the United States was born in those 19 years. The Baby Boom was unique among developed countries such as the United States, Canada, Australia, and New Zealand. While European countries saw increases in numbers of births after the war ended, their birthrates decreased by the end of the 1940s (Jones, 1980; Owram, 1996).

Many long-lasting changes to everyday American life began in the Baby Boom. As much as 83% of the population growth occurred in suburban areas, where 85% of new houses were built from 1948 to 1957. More Americans owned homes than rented them for the first time in history. The automobile became more central to American life, with car registrations jumping from 26 million in 1945 to 40 million in 1950 to 60 million by the end of the 1950s. Television entered the American home and became a part of 98% of homes by 1967; production of television sets increased from 6,000 a year in 1946 to 7 million a year by 1953 (Jones, 1980). Children of this time period thus were the first to be influenced by television commercials. The assassination of John F. Kennedy, a key historical moment in the lives of Baby Boomers, was arguably the first major historical event that almost every American watched on television (Jones, 1980). The Baby Boomers were the first generation to listen to (and purchase) rock music. Fast food became a popular institution in the Baby Boom; for example, Kentucky Fried Chicken increased its number of "restaurants" from 400 in 1964 to 3,317 in 1971 (Jones, 1980).

Every social institution was correspondingly impacted by Baby Boomer development during this period. One of the first social institutions impacted by the Baby Boom was schools. Jones (1980) explained that the Baby Boom was not expected to last long, and schools therefore were slow to expand to make room for growing numbers of students. In 1952, 50,000 new classrooms were built, yet 60% of classes throughout the country were still considered overcrowded (Jones, 1980). In 1958, 62,000 new

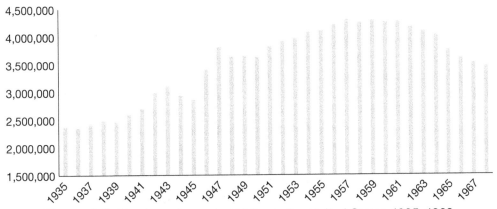

Figure 1.3 Number of reported births in the United States 1935–1968.

classrooms were built. The nation had a shortage of teachers; schools often had half-day sessions in which teachers taught two classes of students for half a day each, and a large number of teachers were underqualified. Because of the perceived threat of nuclear warfare with Russia at the time, school children in this era routinely completed atomic bomb drills in school in which they practiced hiding under furniture to protect themselves in the event of nuclear attack. The Baby Boom led to more U.S. citizens attending college than at any time in history. From 1963 to 1973, enrollment at colleges and universities increased from 4.7 million to 9.6 million (Jones, 1980). The number of college graduates in the population increased from 10 million in 1965 to 19 million in 1980, with a corresponding increase in the proportion of the population with a college degree increasing from 9% to 15%. Now as the Baby Boomers are aging, society will need to meet the older adult housing needs posed by them.

Significant advances in medicine occurred during the era of the Baby Boom. One advancement with a large impact was the development of vaccines. In the 1940s researchers at Boston Children's Hospital began growing viruses in human cell cultures, which led to many vaccine developments over the coming decades (Plotkin & Plotkin, 2008). In 1948, the combination vaccine for diphtheria, tetanus, and pertussis (DTP) first became available (Plotkin & Plotkin, 2008). Jonas Salk licensed a vaccine for polio in 1955 (Salk et al., 1954), and as of 2008 polio was considered eradicated from the Western Hemisphere and has been targeted by the World Health Organization to be eliminated from the world (Plotkin & Plotkin, 2008). Vaccines were developed for measles in the late 1950s (Katz et al., 1960), for mumps in 1967 (Hilleman, Buynak, Weibel, & Stokes, 1968), and for rubella by 1970 (Meyer & Parkman, 1971). As an example of the dramatic impact these vaccinations have had on human health, rubella had caused an estimated 30,000 children to be born with birth defects in the winter of 1963 to 1964 (Jones, 1980), and this disease has since been eliminated from the United States (Plotkin & Plotkin, 2008). A vaccine for varicella was developed in the 1970s (Ueda et al., 1977). The development of vaccines is thought to have had more of an impact on world population growth and reduced mortality than any other development aside from clean water (Plotkin & Plotkin, 2008). Baby Boomers are more likely to use complementary and alternative medicine (CAM) approaches for chronic diseases and pain (43% within the past year) than older adults from the Silent Generation who were born between 1925 and 1945 (35% in the last year; Ho, Rowland-Seymour, Frankel, Li, & Mao, 2014).

In a tragic coincidence of history, the Vietnam War came about just as the largest number of citizens (the Baby Boom generation) entered the age of being draft eligible (Jones, 1980). In 1964, the U.S. Congress approved the Gulf of Tonkin resolution, triggering American military involvement in Vietnam, and in 1964 to 1965, the number of 18-year-olds increased faster than at any time in the nation's history. The military began drafting soldiers in 1965. Although 11 million served in the military, with 1.6 million soldiers seeing combat, this amounted to only 6% of this generation because of its large numbers. A person's chances of being drafted were actually higher during the Korean War. Approximately 58,000 U.S. soldiers were killed in Vietnam, and 153,000 wounded (Jones, 1980). Vietnam Veterans are starting to arrive into old age, and the Veterans' Health Administration (VHA) contains far more Vietnam Veterans than Veterans from the Afghanistan and Iraq wars (see Figure 1.4).

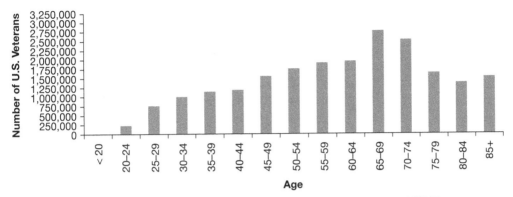

Figure 1.4 Number of U.S. Veterans by age group, as of 2017.
Data obtained from National Center for Veterans Analysis and Statistics, 2017.

WEALTH OF THE BABY BOOMERS

In 2004, 33% of Baby Boomers planned to continue working full time past age 65, which was expected to contribute to economic growth and improved financial security for older adults (Mermin, Johnson, & Murphy, 2007). This percentage may have increased since the recession of the 2000s. Baby Boomers have a considerable amount of wealth that will be transferred as they live into old age and eventually die. It has been estimated that $41 trillion will be transferred from 1998 to 2052, and this is considered a "low-growth" estimate (Havens & Schervish, 2003). Of this, $25 trillion will be inherited by heirs, and the rest will be distributed to estate taxes, charities, and estate settlement expenses. Unfortunately, the crash of the housing market in 2008 caused a large proportion of adults age 55 to 64 to lose all equity they had built up in their homes (Rosnick & Baker, 2010), resulting in a situation in which homeowners ages 55 to 64 lost money in the sale of their homes. As of this writing, it is expected that retiring Baby Boomers will depend more heavily on Social Security for income in retirement than has been expected, as a result of the housing market crash. Baby Boomers are thus thought to be much less well-prepared for retirement than cohorts before them (Rosnick & Baker, 2010).

HISTORY AND THEORY OF THE PSYCHOLOGY OF AGING

The topic of human aging is certainly not new to the current era. In 44 BCE the famous Roman orator Cicero wrote one of the earliest known pieces on human aging, "De Senectitute." This work is notable for addressing many of the same topics we are exploring today in the field and in this book, such as losing sensory acuity (discussed in Chapter 3 of this text), staying actively employed in old age, and being "freed from the bondage of passion." (Changes in emotion are discussed in Chapter 5.) The reader is encouraged to review this work of Cicero to view how conceptualizations of aging in the time of the ancient Romans were strikingly similar to the current era.

One of the earliest modern-era works devoted to this topic was G. Stanley Hall's *Senescence, the Last Half of Life* (1922). In this text, he proposed five stages of life, which included the last two stages, "senescence, which begins in the early forties, or before in women, and . . . senectitude, the post-climacteric or old age proper" (p. vii). Chapters in this text included: "The History of Old Age"; "Literature by and on the Aged"; "Statistics of Old Age and Its Care"; "Medical Views and Treatment of Old Age," which included a "Protest Against the Prepotence of Heredity in Determining Longevity," an early exploration of genetics versus environment in determining longevity; "The Contributions of Biology and Physiology"; a "Report on Questionnaire Returns," which appears to be an overview of results from surveys of older adults conducted by the author; "Some Conclusions," which includes a summary of what was known about psychosocial issues at the time (e.g., "superior powers of the old in perspective and larger views"); and "The Psychology of Death." A case against differentiating between "presenile dementia" and "senile dementia" was made when he wrote, "As to premature senility, in general its symptoms are identical with those of mature senility" (p. 207). Experts would arrive at this same conclusion in later editions of the *Diagnostic and Statistical Manual of Mental Disorders,* and discard the differentiation between "presenile" and "senile." His reference to "memory, the loss of which comes as an advance guard of many symptoms" (p. 206) remains true, as decline in memory often precipitates the cascade of decline that occurs with Alzheimer's disease.

Several other theorists have influenced our knowledge and research into typical aging. Jean Piaget's work (1972) is typically included in texts of human development. His work focused on cognitive changes throughout childhood, adolescence, and early adulthood. He did not explore development in adulthood or older adulthood. His cognitive stages were later expanded to include postformal thought, though this stage is typically applied to emerging adults (individuals between ages 18 and 25). In this chapter we focus on theorists who contributed substantially to our knowledge of the aging process.

ERIK ERIKSON

Erik Erikson (1902–1994) was a prominent developmental theorist. He generated a comprehensive theory of human development and created the term *identity crisis.* He was heavily influenced by psychoanalytic theory and the work of Anna Freud. He proposed that humans progress through various stages in life characterized by specific conflicts (Erikson, 1997). For example, most of adulthood was thought to be characterized by a conflict between "generativity" and "stagnation." Generativity is characterized by procreation, productivity, and creativity. Adults develop an interest in caring for others during this stage, and in the development of the next generation. He proposed that the very last stage of life involves a crisis between "integrity" and "despair." From this conflict humans develop wisdom, which he defines as "informed and detached concern with life itself in the face of death itself" (p. 61). When older adults experience despair, it is often due to a sense of stagnation in life. The despair may also involve mourning for lost time, decreased independence, decreased initiative, lost opportunities for intimacy, and missed opportunities for generativity. He proposed that the last stage of life involves a psychosexual "generalization of sensual modes" (p. 64) that enriches physical and psychological experiences even if sexual functioning declines, as reviewed in Chapter 3. The primary trait involved in this stage is "integrity," or a sense of coherence and wholeness in the face of losses of physical, cognitive, and generative functioning. He concludes his discussion of old age by pointing out: "For individual life is the coincidence of but one life cycle with but one segment of history" (p. 65–66).

In 1997, Joan Erikson published an expanded version of her husband's *The Life Cycle Completed*, which added a discussion about the "ninth stage" of human development, which occurs in one's 80s and 90s. This is further discussed in Chapter 5. Erik Erikson noted: "Lacking a culturally viable ideal of old age, our civilization does not really harbor a concept of the whole of life" (p. 114). Paul Baltes (1997) expressed this same notion, discussed in the next section.

PAUL BALTES: SELECTIVE OPTIMIZATION WITH COMPENSATION

More recently, Paul Baltes (1939–2006) offered a comprehensive theory of human development that included more of a focus on late life. He proposed three principles of human development and aging (Baltes, 1997). First, because natural selection leads to evolution of characteristics that increase the chances of human reproduction, and traits that lengthen the life span into old age are less needed for this purpose, human genes are less likely to protect against diseases and other health problems that can arise in aging. As Baltes notes, throughout most of human history most people died before problematic genes were activated or their negative effects could occur. Baltes terms this the "unfinished architecture" of the human life span.

The second principle of Baltes's (1997) theory is that with age, our need for culture increases, with "culture" defined as the psychological, social, economic, and knowledge resources that humanity has generated throughout our existence. These resources have been transmitted across generations, enable human development, and are needed in increasing amounts as we age. Unfortunately, as the third principle spells out, as we need culture more, the effectiveness of culture simultaneously declines with age. Baltes (1997) proposed that humans assign resources to three areas across the life span: growth, maintenance, and managing losses. Early life development predominantly involves *gains*, and as we develop into middle and old age we experience increasingly higher proportions of *losses*. Thus as we enter old age, we experience less growth and more maintenance and loss management.

Baltes (1997) proposed a model of human development that is particularly relevant to aging: Selective Optimization With Compensation (SOC), outlined in Table 1.2. Selection involves the specification of goals, commitment to goals, and adapting the goal hierarchy when needed. Optimization refers to how one allocates time and resources to the goals that have been selected, and the acquisition and practice of skills necessary for self-development. We engage in compensation when a particular resource is no longer available. Compensation can include increased attentional allocation, increased effort and time, activating unused skills and resources, use of external aids, and help from others.

Table 1.2 Baltes's (1997) Model of Human Development: Examples of Selection, Optimization, and Compensation

Selection	Optimization	Compensation
Elective selection	Attentional focus	Increased time allocation
Specification of goals	Effort/energy	Increased attentional focus
Goal commitment	Time allocation	Increased effort/energy
Loss-based selection	Practice of skills	Activation of unused skills/resources
Focusing on most important goals	Acquiring new skills/resources	Use of external aids/help of others
Search for new goals	Modeling successful others	Therapeutic intervention

The SOC model emphasizes the adaptiveness of older adults in the face of possible declines. Examples of the SOC model are typically applied to age-related health changes. For example, an older adult may reduce time spent in vigorous exercise and instead apply his or her time to studying yoga or another form of less strenuous activity. In this example, the older adult selects physical activity as an important goal and compensates for declines in physical functioning by optimizing his or her performance in other physical activities. Another example of the SOC model comes from a friend of the author who described a decision his aging mother made to optimize her driving. She selected driving as an important goal to her, but realized some of the age-related limitations she was experiencing in her driving ability. To compensate for declines in this area, she optimized her driving skills such that she only made right turns and avoided left turns. She chose this strategy because accidents are more common when making left rather than right turns (discussed in Chapter 7).

Baltes also proposed a way to conceptualize social aging, that is, changes that take place in our environment that may influence our aging process. Baltes (1979) proposed that social influences can include normative history-graded influences, normative age-graded influences, and nonnormative influences. Normative history-graded influences include cultural, political, and social events that impacted a specific generation. For example, most people can tell you where they were when the World Trade Center was destroyed on September 11, 2001. Members of the Baby Boom generation can likely tell you where they were when John F. Kennedy was assassinated or when Neil Armstrong walked on the moon. There are also cultural shifts that are captured in the concept of normative history-graded influences, such as the rise in use of technology and social media. Normative age-graded influences include events that are expected to take place at certain ages, such as obtaining a driver's license, marriage, having children, retiring, and so on. These events typically have socially accepted age norms attached to them, such as marrying in your 20s and having kids in your 30s. Even if these ages are not made explicit, most individuals have a general sense of when these events "should" happen and may experience questions from others if they have not met these milestones. Nonnormative influences are specific to each individual and include unique events that shape development, such as losing a parent, obtaining a new job, or acquiring an illness. Each of these three types of influences shape developmental trajectories in different ways and are often tied to cultural factors, as well as one's birth cohort.

Baltes (1997) proposed that the time of life from age 80 onward be called the "fourth age," and considered this a major area of growth for research and theory development. He challenged developmental scientists to strive to "complete the biological and cultural architecture of the life span" so that the maximization of development (i.e., a positive balance of gains versus losses) could be extended farther into the life span (p. 377). With evolution's lack of focus on old age, however, this challenge will be increasingly difficult into advanced ages.

DEVELOPMENT OF THE PROFESSIONAL FIELD

In 1940, one journal existed devoted to aging, the *Zeitschrift für Altersforschung* (Poon & Welford, 1980). The year 1942 saw the founding of the American Geriatrics Society, and in 1945 the Gerontological Society (now the Gerontological Society of America) and the American Psychological Association's (APA) Division of Maturity and Old Age (Division 20, now known as the Division of Adult Development and Aging) were formed. The International Association of Gerontology was formed in 1950. Research funding for aging became more prominent when the Adult Development and Aging Branch of the National Institute of Child Health and Human Development became the National Institute on Aging in 1975. In that same year, the Department of Veterans Affairs established eight Geriatric Research, Educational, and Clinical Centers (GRECCs) throughout the United States. A summary of the field to date, *Aging in the 1980s: Psychological Issues*, was published by Leonard Poon in 1980 and included sections on: clinical issues; neuropsychological issues; psychophysiological issues: brain evoked potentials; psychopharmacological issues; cognitive issues; stress and coping; environmental issues; interpersonal relations; and methodological issues. It summarized what was known to date in these areas, put forth research directions for the 1980s, and provided a framework for the 1981 White House Conference on Aging.

An important moment in the field occurred in June 1981, when a conference was held in Boulder, Colorado, to address the shortage of psychologists with specialized training in aging and establish training guidelines in the field (Santos & Vanden-Bos, 1982). This conference became known as the "Older Boulder" conference, as a follow-up to the 1949 Colorado Conference on Training in Clinical Psychology in Boulder, which established training guidelines (i.e., the "Boulder" model) for scientist-practitioner clinical psychology training (Raimy, 1950). At that time, only two clinical psychology doctoral training programs with specialized training in aging existed in the United States (Northwestern University and the University of Southern California). Recommendations were made to integrate material on aging into all core psychology courses, to require all psychologists to take at least one course in the psychology of aging, and to increase the number of programs offering specialized training in aging. The importance of instruction in healthy aging in addition to complex problems of aging was emphasized. The conference outlined training goals for the undergraduate and graduate levels, including recommended courses and practicum experiences. The group recommended that the APA develop continuing education courses on aging. The conference made a call for more research to increase the knowledge base of sociopsychological components of aging and biopsychological aspects of aging.

The National Conference on Clinical Training in Psychology: Improving Psychological Services for Older Adults was held in 1992 and came to be known as "Older Boulder II." This conference placed more emphasis on development of clinical services (Knight, Teri, Wohlford, & Santos, 1995), particularly with older adults as an underserved area, similar to children, ethnic minorities, and those with serious mental illnesses. The idea of developing board certification in clinical geropsychology with the American Board of Professional Psychology (ABPP) was discussed. Conference attendees generated sets of recommendations for the APA, National Institute of Mental Health/Center for Mental Health Services, and the U.S. Congress.

One outgrowth of the Older Boulder II conference was the initiative to establish a section on geropsychology within APA's Division 12, the Society of Clinical Psychology. In January 1993, the new section was approved and designated Section II of Division 12 (Abeles, 2015). This section was often referred to as "12-II" and the name was changed to the Society of Clinical Geropsychology (SCG) in 2008. It began operating in 1994 with 213 members (Abeles, 2015). Over the years membership has gone up to over 300 dues-paying members. SCG has provided a forum for members to communicate with each other, share resources, and has provided programming related to aging at the annual meeting of the APA. It has also collaborated with APA Division 20, the Division of Adult Development and Aging, on various aging-related initiatives.

While American psychologists in aging can associate with similar colleagues in SCG and/or Division 20 of the APA, in Europe, geropsychologists can become involved with the Standing Committee on GeroPsychology within the European Federation of Psychologists' Associations (EFPA). Countries within Europe also have national organizations, such as the Portuguese Psychogerontology Association (Ribeiro, Fernandes, Firmino, Simões, & Paul, 2010). In Australia, geropsychologists can find professional opportunities within the Psychology and Ageing Interest Group of the Australian Psychological Society, and in New Zealand geropsychologists can find similar opportunities with the New Zealand Psychologists of Older People (Pachana, 2015).

Shortly after the formation of the SCG, the Ad Hoc Committee on Issues of the Older Adult was formed within the APA in 1996. This eventually became a permanent Committee on Aging within the APA in 1998 and helped in the creation of an Office on Aging within the APA (Abeles, 2015). In 2006, a third conference, the National Conference on Training in Professional Geropsychology, was held in Colorado Springs, Colorado, near Pikes Peak. This conference, known as the Pikes Peak conference, sought to create a comprehensive training model and establish competencies for the practice of professional geropsychology. The primary product of this conference is the listing of the Pikes Peak Competencies in Professional Geropsychology, which are a collection of competencies organized around attitudes, knowledge, and skills needed to work with older adults in addition to training recommendations for those seeking to meet these competencies (Knight, Karel, Hinrichsen, Qualls, & Duffy, 2009). While aspirational in nature, these competencies provide a comprehensive model to assess the training needs of those who work with older adults. It is important to note that the model recognizes that specialized training in geropsychology is not essential for all psychologists who work with older adults; however, as the patient issues become more complex, the need for specific training increases. The competencies are most applicable for those who wish to primarily work with older adults.

In their seminal paper, Knight et al. (2009) define the attitudes, knowledge, and skill competencies for geropsychology practice. The competencies list is meant to be an aspirational list to be used for programs and clinicians seeking training in geropsychology to create and evaluate a plan of training at different levels, including graduate, internship, postdoctoral, and postlicensure levels. Core attitudes include (a) the goal of practicing within one's competence, (b) recognizing how one's attitudes and beliefs about aging will affect her or his work with older adults, (c) being aware of individual diversity in all its forms, and (d) continually increasing one's knowledge, understanding, and skills related to working with older adults. Four domains of knowledge in the Pikes Peak Model include: normal adult development and aging; the interaction of life span development with increased neurological and health problems in later life; assessment methods and tools suitable for assessing older adults; and using knowledge of developmental, cohort, contextual, and systemic issues to inform interventions with older adults. There are six aspects of training that are considered critical parts of a training program for a geropsychologist: (a) understanding of normal aging, (b) supervision by professional geropsychologists, (c) gaining of self-awareness about one's responses to aging that vary by health status, cultural and individual identities, and diverse historical cohort experiences, (d) training in a variety of settings, (e) interprofessional team training, and (f) ethical and legal issues and practice standards that are involved in work with older adults.

TRAINING RESOURCES

Although there have been recent developments to increase the focus on clinical geropsychology training and professional development (Knight et al., 2009), graduate-level educational offerings and practicum experiences do not reflect growing demographic imperatives (Laidlaw & Pachana, 2009). Data from an international survey of training directors indicated that 28.3% of programs in the United States offered a geropsychology course and 37% offered a gerontology course (Pachana, Emery, Konnert, Woodhead, & Edelstein, 2010). Statistics were similar in Canada and Australia, though these countries were more likely to require a course in geropsychology. When courses were offered at the graduate level, they focused on assessment, diagnosis, and/or life span development (Pachana et al., 2010), suggesting a relative lack of training around principles of adult development and aging, and less emphasis on effective interventions for older adults.

Graduate school is an ideal time to obtain training in geropsychology in order to prepare to meet the mental health needs of an aging population. Prior research suggests that there are significant differences in geropsychology training

Table 1.3 Example Items From the Pikes Peak Geropsychology Knowledge and Skill Assessment Tool

DOMAIN: Foundations of Professional Geropsychology Practice		
Knowledge Base—The psychologist or trainee has knowledge of:		
1. Neuroscience of aging	a. The parameters of cognitive changes in normal aging	Rating scale: Novice, Intermediate, Advanced, Proficient, or Expert
	b. Factors that influence levels of cognitive performance in older adults	
2. Functional changes	a. Relationships between age, environment, and functional level	Rating Scale: Novice, Intermediate, Advanced, Proficient, or Expert
	b. Definition and assessment of activities of daily living (ADLs) and instrumental activities of daily living (IADLs)	

experiences available to students depending on the country in which the student is completing graduate training and whether the student is enrolled in a geropsychology specialty track (Woodhead et al., 2013). There are practical resources available online for students and professionals to increase their knowledge of geropsychology, some of which are highlighted at GeroCentral.org, which is a collaborative effort between many organizations involved in geropsychology (www.gerocentral .org/training-career/seminarsce). There are also online courses available through universities that cover topics relevant to mental health and aging. For example, the University of South Florida offers graduate courses on Aging and Mental Disorders, Gerontological Counseling Theories & Practice, and Family Caregiving in Aging and Chronic Illness. These courses can be taken as part of a certificate program or for personal interest (www.usf.edu/cbcs/aging-studies/academics/certificates/ sokclin.aspx). Clinicians and students can assess their competence in working with older adults through regular use of the Pikes Peak Geropsychology Knowledge and Skill Assessment Tool (Karel, Emery, Molinari, & CoPGTP Task Force on the Assessment of Geropsychology Competencies, 2010; see Table 1.3; available online at www.gerocentral.org/competencies).

RESEARCH METHODS IN THE PSYCHOLOGY OF AGING

An exploration of the psychology of aging requires an understanding of how knowledge is acquired in this field. Three variables of interest to researchers in psychology of aging include *age effects, cohort effects,* and *time-of-measurement* effects (Cavanaugh & Blanchard-Fields, 2011). Age effects refer to changes within the person including chronological age, and biological and psychological changes that occur with time, such as changes to the body's structures and functions. Cohort effects refer to differences caused by experiences and circumstances particular to one's generation. For example, the Baby Boom generation was the first to experience television within the home. People born nowadays will always have the Internet available from handheld devices. Lastly, time of measurement effects refer to differences caused by sociocultural or environmental conditions at the time data are obtained from participants. For instance, research on marital relationships may have produced different results before and after the 2015 Supreme Court ruling on same-sex marriage. Research findings on work and retirement vary depending on the state of the economy in the particular country in which the study was conducted. Developmental researchers strive to isolate these three effects, but this is rarely straightforward and often involves the use of complex research designs, some of which are described in the next few paragraphs. Researchers must also distinguish between *age change* and *age difference.* Age change refers to differences that occur in people's behavior over time. People must be observed over time in order to determine age change. Age differences, on the other hand, are found when different people at different ages are compared to each other in a cross-sectional study.

There are several common methods that researchers in aging use to conduct research: longitudinal, cross-sectional, time lag, and sequential designs. *Longitudinal* research involves gathering data from the same participants at two or more time points. For example, the Nun Study has gathered data from Catholic Nuns at multiple time points until death, when brain autopsies were performed. This method is the clearest way to measure change as it occurs and is often considered the "gold standard" of developmental research. Approximately 35% of research studies published between 2000 and 2008 that examined some aspect of the psychology of aging were longitudinal in nature (Bleszner & Sanford, 2010). Longitudinal studies account for the effects of age and time of measurement but not for cohort effects. That is, following one cohort over time allows us to comment on age changes and presents multiple time points to control for time of measurement. However, by following only one cohort, the results that are obtained may be due to cohort effects that would not be seen if we were to follow a different cohort at a different point in time.

Although longitudinal studies are often thought of as the gold standard, there are limitations to longitudinal designs. Practice effects can occur, in which participants improve their performance on various measures (e.g., cognitive tests), simply by taking the measure more than once. This may manifest as improvement on test scores, stable test scores when a decline has actually occurred in the ability being measured, or even decline on test scores that is lower in proportion than the decline occurring in real life. In neuropsychological research, practice effects can be quantified and controlled for (e.g., Duff et al., 2005), but the degree of improvement with practice for many measures is not known.

There is also the need for *measurement invariance.* Measurement invariance implies that each measure relates to the underlying construct in the same way over time, so that the latent construct is defined similarly over time. This also implies that scores on the measure are on the same measurement scale at different points in time. One way to increase the likelihood of measurement invariance is to choose measures that have high reliability and validity for the sample you are using. In many complex longitudinal studies, techniques such as factor analysis, structural equation modeling, or item response theory are used to ensure measurement invariance. This highlights another potential problem with longitudinal designs, which is that measures can be outdated by the time the study is complete. If a researcher chooses a specific measure and uses the same measure for each time point, a new version of the measure may become available during the course of the study. Opting to use the new measure may lead to problems with measurement invariance, as noted above.

Another limitation to longitudinal research is participant dropout, or attrition (Ferrer & Ghisletta, 2011). Reasons for attrition include participants moving and becoming unreachable, participants declining follow-up sessions, participants becoming incapacitated, or death. This can result in lower external validity because the remaining participants may not be representative of the population that was initially sampled. For instance, participants who remain in studies may be healthier than the population from which they are sampled (Ferrer & Ghisletta, 2011). Attrition is a central problem in longitudinal research and must be addressed in any such study. Participants may drop out because of reasons unrelated to the study, with the data considered *missing completely at random (MCAR)*. For example, a person may move to a new location and be unable to participate in the study. This reason for dropping out is unrelated to the outcomes of the study or the variables in the study. Another option is that the data may be missing because of reasons related to the variables that have been measured, which would enable the researchers to account for them in analyses. This is commonly called *missing at random (MAR)*. An example of this is that you may find that women were more likely to complete your study than men. In this case, you can control for gender in your analyses. Unfortunately, often the missing data are related to outcomes of the study but without enough information to explain the reasons for it; these data are considered *not missing at random (NMAR)*. An example of this might be that, in a longitudinal study of physical health, the participants who drop out are the ones who are experiencing the worst health outcomes.

Researchers have used several methods to address the problems posed by missing data. One method has been to simply delete the cases that have missing data and perform analyses only on the participants with complete data. However, this practice causes the omission of large amounts of valuable data, and biased results if the data are not MCAR. Another approach is to compare the characteristics of participants who did and did not complete the study. This would allow you to see whether participants with certain characteristics were less likely to complete the study. In this situation, you could control for those variables in your analyses, as mentioned above.

Statisticians have developed more advanced methods in recent years that do not require the deletion of any participants' data (Ferrer & Ghisletta, 2011). It is important to note that both these methods assume that data are MAR. *Likelihood-based estimation* assumes that a structural model is known and specified correctly, and that the data are MAR. This method produces unbiased estimates if the reasons for missing data are known and included in the analyses. It can produce estimates of what the data would be if every participant had been measured on all variables at all time points. This method puts forth a model for all cases in a dataset. Then the model parameters are calculated using all the available data. This approach has become the most commonly used estimation method in structural equation modeling statistical programs. In *maximum likelihood* or *full-information maximum likelihood*, parameters are calculated for each person in the sample, and each person's misfit from the data likelihood is calculated separately.

The other method involves *imputation* of missing data. This method does not involve a model of the structure of the data, but replaces missing data with estimates of what the data would be if it had been measured (Ferrer & Ghisletta, 2011). In *multiple imputation*, each missing data point is replaced by several possible values. These new data points create multiple datasets and estimates for each parameter can be generated by repeating this procedure.

In addition to the challenge of handling missing data, there are other limitations to longitudinal research. Findings obtained in one cohort in a longitudinal investigation may not generalize to other cohorts. Another practical limitation of longitudinal research is the time and expense required to perform this research. By definition these studies may take years to complete and may require collaboration among several study sites. Nonetheless, longitudinal studies such as the Berlin Aging Study, Seattle Longitudinal study, and the Nun study have yielded a tremendous amount of knowledge for the field.

Cross-sectional research involves gathering data from participants of various ages at one point in time. With this design, researchers can detect age *differences* but not age *change*. This is because different ages are compared, allowing the possibility that the results are age related; however, participants are not followed over time, which means that other variables may be responsible for the age differences. Therefore, this type of design does not account for time of measurement or cohort effects because there is only one time point used and the age differences that are detected may be related to the cohorts that are sampled. For example, differences found between 60- and 80-year-olds may simply represent differences in cohorts rather than changes that occur with age. This design has the advantages of lower cost and increased convenience of being performed, and researchers use this design more than any other. It can generate hypotheses to further explore in longitudinal or sequential studies. However, it has significant limitations, a chief one being the lack of information learned about change over time.

One type of cross-sectional study is the extreme age groups design, which involves adults at young and old extremes. Most commonly, these studies recruit students at universities and older adults from community centers like senior centers or churches. These convenience samples are obviously not representative of the larger populations, so findings from these studies are less likely to generalize to people not represented by these samples. Another limitation frequently encountered in these studies is that age is represented by categorical variables ("young" and "old"), and this gross classification may decrease the power to detect smaller changes that occur with aging. This design also carries the assumption that measures used in one group assess the same variable in other groups. Measures need to have similar reliability and validity in each age group being examined.

In order to address the limitations inherent in both longitudinal and cross-sectional studies, *sequential* designs involve combinations of both of these types. For example, a *time-sequential* study involves cross-sectional data collected at two separate time points. For example, multiple cohorts could be studied at two or more points in time, which allows researchers to examine whether results are due to time of measurement. This design does not rule out the influence of cohort effects since only a limited number of cohorts are studied. In a *cohort-sequential* design, two or more cohorts are followed longitudinally. This design can assess whether effects found in one cohort are specific to that cohort or due to the aging process. Sequential studies provide the most information in developmental psychology, but are also the most difficult and costly.

CONCLUSION

The goal of this chapter was to introduce some of the concepts that are important in the psychology of aging. We started by discussing definitions of older adulthood and some characteristics, as a whole, of older adults. We then reviewed the data on the projected increase in older adults in the United States and internationally. The importance of birth cohort was discussed in this chapter and continues to be an important theme throughout this book. Specifically, we reviewed characteristics of the Baby Boom generation since most of the current generation of older adults were born in that era. Erik Erikson and Paul Baltes are two researchers who have made substantial contributions to the development of aging studies. In future chapters you will learn about other researchers who have contributed valuable theories and insights about older adult development. We then reviewed development of the professional field and training resources that are available to students and professionals. We ended with a discussion of research methods that attempt to untangle the effects of age, cohort, and time of measurement.

BOX 1.1 Betty Reid Soskin

The author of this chapter met with Betty Reid Soskin, at age 95 the nation's oldest National Park ranger, in April 2017. She gives a talk three times a week at Rosie the Riveter World War II Homefront National Historical Park in Richmond, California, and the auditorium is usually filled to capacity. Betty spoke for 40 minutes, without notes or slides, about her experiences as a young African American woman working in World War II.

Afterward, Betty agreed to answer several questions about her life (B. R. Soskin, personal communication, April 29, 2017).

On continuing to work at age 95:

> "It's never been a conscious choice . . . I never really stopped working . . . but then I never had a job that I sought. I've never had a job because I wanted it; I've always been invited in. I've just never been invited out!"

(continued)

BOX 1.1 Betty Reid Soskin (*continued*)

On looking toward the future:

"As long as I have first experiences, a sense of life continually unfolding, I still wake up every morning, expecting newness. There is so much that's novel, that I have a sense that life is continually opening up, so I don't have a sense of completion."

On the mental health needs of women in their 90s:

"There are days when I have a sense that I'm living my life out of context. I've outlived all my peers, and it gives me a sense of being in uncharted waters, because I don't have role models anymore. If I didn't have work that was significant, I'd get lost. People visit from nursing homes, 10 years younger than I am, and that's when I feel out of context. I'm 10 years their senior. But I'm not threatened by the unfamiliar. I have a feeling that I'm in control."

On political activism:

"I went through the 1960s as a political activist. I was fighting for my personal rights and the rights of my children, granted by the Constitution. The Constitution and Bill of Rights are only blueprints with which each generation has to recreate democracy. By participating in it or by not doing so, we determine the outcome."

DISCUSSION QUESTIONS

1. Describe how older adulthood is defined in terms of age and some typical characteristics of older adults.

2. Summarize the information on the projected increase in the aging population both in the United States and internationally.

3. Define what a cohort is, and describe some features of the Baby Boom cohort.

4. Describe Baltes's SOC model and provide an example.

5. Describe the difference between age changes and age effects. How can researchers determine whether results are due to age changes or age effects?

6. Summarize the strengths and weaknesses of cross-sectional and longitudinal research in the study of aging. Describe other research designs that can account for the weaknesses of these two designs.

REFERENCES

Abeles, N. (2015). Historical perspectives on clinical geropsychology. In P. A. Lichtenberg & B. T. Mast (Eds.), *APA handbook of clinical geropsychology: Vol. 1. History and status of the field and perspectives on aging* (pp. 3–18). Washington, DC: American Psychological Association. doi:10.1037/14458-002

Administration on Aging, Administration for Community Living, U.S. Department of Health and Human Services. (2014). A profile of older Americans: 2014. Retrieved from https://www.acl.gov/sites/default/files/Aging%20and%20Disability%20in%20America/2014-Profile.pdf

AgingStats.gov. (2016). Older Americans 2016: Key indicators of well-being. Retrieved from https://agingstats.gov/docs/LatestReport/Older-Americans-2016-Key-Indicators-of-Well Being.pdf

Baltes, P. B. (1979). Life-span developmental psychology: Some converging observations on history and theory. In P. B. Baltes & J. O. G. Brim (Eds.), *Life-span development and behavior* (Vol. 2, pp. 255–279). New York, NY: Academic Press.

Baltes, P. B. (1997). On the incomplete architecture of human ontogeny: Selection, optimization, and compensation as foundation of developmental theory. *American Psychologist, 52*(4), 366–380.

Bartels, S. J., & Naslund, J. A. (2013). The underside of the silver tsunami—Older adults and mental health care. *New England Journal of Medicine, 368*(6), 493–496.

Bleszner, R., & Sanford, N. (2010). Looking back and looking ahead as *Journal of Gerontology: Psychological Sciences* turns 65. *Journals of Gerontology: Psychological Sciences, 65B*, 3–4.

Cavanaugh, J. C., & Blanchard-Fields, F. (2011). *Adult development and aging* (6th ed.). Belmont, CA: Wadsworth.

Centers for Disease Control and Prevention. (2015). *Health, United States, 2015, with special feature on racial and ethnic health disparities*. Retrieved from https://www.cdc.gov/nchs/data/hus/hus15.pdf#015

Duff, K., Beglinger, L. J., Schoenberg, M. R., Patton, D. E., Mold, J., Scott, J. G., & Adams, R. L. (2005). Test-retest stability and practice effects of the RBANS in a community dwelling elderly sample. *Journal of Clinical and Experimental Neuropsychology, 27*(5), 565–575. doi:10.1080/1380 3390490918363

Erikson, E. H. (1997). *The life cycle completed.* (Extended version with new chapters on the ninth stage of development by J. M. Erikson.) New York, NY: W. W. Norton.

Ferrer, E., & Ghisletta, P. (2011). Methodological and analytical issues in the psychology of aging. In K. W. Schaie & S. L. Willis (Eds.), *Handbook of the psychology of aging* (pp. 25–39). Burlington, MA: Academic Press.

Hall, G. S. (1922). *Senescence: The last half of life*. New York, NY: D. Appleton. Retrieved from https://archive.org/details/senescencelastha00halliala

Havens, J. J., & Schervish, P. G. (2003). Why the $41 trillion wealth transfer estimate is still valid: A review of challenges and questions. *Journal of Gift Planning, 7*(1), 11–15, 47–50.

Hilleman, M. R., Buynak, E. B., Weibel, R. E., & Stokes, J. (1968). Live attenuated mumps-virus vaccine. *New England Journal of Medicine, 278*, 227–232.

Ho, T. F., Rowland-Seymour, A., Frankel, E. S., Li, S. Q., & Mao, J. J. (2014). Generational differences in complementary and alternative medicine (CAM) use in the context of chronic diseases and pain: Baby boomers versus the silent generation. *Journal of the American Board of Family Medicine, 27*, 465–473. doi:10.3122/jabfm.2014.04.130238

*Hoge, M. A., Karel, M. J., Zeiss, A. M., Alegria, M., & Moye, J. (2015). Strengthening psychology's workforce for older adults: Implications of the Institute of Medicine's report to Congress. *American Psychologist, 70*(3), 265–278. doi:10.1037/a0038927

Jones, L. Y. (1980). *Great expectations: America and the baby boom generation*. New York, NY: Coward, McCann, & Geoghegan.

Karel, M. J., Emery, E. E., Molinari, V., & CoPGTP Task Force on the Assessment of Geropsychology Competencies. (2010). Development of a tool to evaluate geropsychology knowledge and skill competencies. *International Psychogeriatrics, 22*, 886–896.

Katz, S. L., Kempe, C. H., Black, F. L., Lepow, M. L., Krugman, S., Haggerty, R. J., & Enders, J. F. (1960). Studies on an attenuated measles-virus vaccine. VIII. General summary and evaluation of the results of vaccine. *New England Journal of Medicine, 263,* 180–184.

*Knight, B. G., Karel, M. J., Hinrichsen, G. A., Qualls, S. H., & Duffy, M. (2009). Pikes Peak model for training in professional geropsychology. *American Psychologist, 64*(3), 205–214. doi:10.1037/a0015059

Knight, B. G., Teri, L., Wohlford, P., & Santos, J. (1995). *Mental health services for older adults: Implications for training and practice in geropsychology.* Washington, DC: American Psychological Association.

Laidlaw, K., & Pachana, N. A. (2009). Demographics in older adults. *Professional Psychology: Research and Practice, 40,* 601–608.

Mermin, G. B. T., Johnson, R. W., & Murphy, D. P. (2007). Why do boomers plan to work longer? *Journal of Gerontology: Social Sciences, 62B*(5), S286–S294.

Meyer, H. M., & Parkman, P. D. (1971). Rubella vaccination: A review of practical experience. *Journal of the American Medical Association, 215,* 613–619.

National Center for Veterans Analysis and Statistics. (2017). Veteran population. Retrieved from http://www.va.gov/vetdata/veteran_population.asp

Neugarten, B. L. (1974). Age groups in American society and the rise of the young-old. *Annals of the American Academy of Political and Social Science, 415,* 187–98.

Ortman, J. M., Velkoff, V. A., & Hogan, H. (2014). *An aging nation: The older population in the United States.* Washington, DC: U.S. Census Bureau.

Owram, D. (1996). *Born at the right time: A history of the baby-boom generation.* Toronto, ON, Canada: University of Toronto Press.

*Pachana, N. A. (2015). International trends in geropsychology. In P. A. Lichtenberg & B. T. Mast (Eds.), *APA handbook of clinical geropsychology: Vol. 1. History and status of the field and perspectives on aging* (pp. 421–441). Washington, DC: American Psychological Association. doi:10.1037/14458-017

Pachana, N. A., Emery, E. E., Konnert, C., Woodhead, E., & Edelstein, B. (2010). Geropsychology content in clinical training programs: A comparison of Australian, Canadian and U.S. Data. *International Psychogeriatrics, 22,* 909–918. doi:10.1017/S1041610210000803

Pew Research Center. (2009). Growing old in America: Expectations vs. reality. Overview and executive summary. Retrieved from http://www.pewsocialtrends.org/2009/06/29/growing-old-in-america-expectations-vs-reality

Pew Research Center. (2015). A different look at generations and partisanship. Retrieved from http://www.people-press.org/2015/04/30/a-different-look-at-generations-and-partisanship

Piaget, J. (1972). Intellectual evolution from adolescence to adulthood. *Human Development, 15,* 1–12.

Plotkin, S. L., & Plotkin, S. A. (2008). A short history of vaccination. In S. A. Plotkin, W. A. Orenstein, & P. A. Offit (Eds.), *Vaccines* (5th ed., pp. 1–16). Philadelphia, PA: Saunders Elsevier.

Poon, L. W. (Ed.). (1980). *Aging in the 1980s: Psychological issues.* Washington, DC: American Psychological Association.

Poon, L. W., & Welford, A. T. (1980). A historical perspective. In L. W. Poon (Ed.), *Aging in the 1980s: Psychological issues* (pp. xiii–xvii). Washington, DC: American Psychological Association.

Qualls, S. H., Segal, D. L., Norman, S., Niederehe, G., & Gallagher-Thompson, D. (2002). Psychologists in practice with older adults: Current patterns, sources of training, and need for continuing education. *Professional Psychology: Research and Practice, 33,* 435–442. doi:10.1037/0735-7028.33.5.435

Raimy, V. C. (Ed.). (1950). *Training in clinical psychology.* Englewood Cliffs, NJ: Prentice-Hall.

Ribeiro, O., Fernandes, L., Firmino, H., Simões, M. R., & Paul, C. (2010). Geropsychology and psychogeriatrics in Portugal: Research, education and clinical training. *International Psychogeriatrics, 22*(6), 854–863. doi:10.1017/S1041610210000347

Rosnick, D., & Baker, D. (2010). The impact of the housing crash on the wealth of the baby boom cohorts. *Journal of Aging and Social Policy, 22*(2), 117–128. doi:10.1080/08959421003620848

Salk, J. E., Krech, U., Youngner, J. S., Bennett, B. L., Lewis, L. J., & Bazeley, P. L. (1954). Formaldehyde treatment and safety testing of experimental poliomyelitis vaccines. *American Journal of Public Health, 44*(5), 563–570.

Santos, J. F., & VandenBos, G. R. (Eds.). (1982). Psychology and the older adult: Challenges for training in the 1980s. *Proceedings of the conference on training psychologists for work in aging, Boulder, Colorado.* Washington, DC: American Psychological Association.

Schaie, K. W. (1965). A general model for the study of developmental problems. *Psychological Bulletin, 64,* 92–107.

Social Security Administration. (n.d.). Age 65 retirement. Retrieved from http://www.ssa.gov/history/age65.html

Ueda, K., Yameda, I., Goto, M., Nanri, T., Fukuda, H., Katsuda, M., . . . Takahashi, M. (1977). Use of a live varicella vaccine to prevent the spread of varicella in handicapped or immunosuppressed children including MCLS (muco-cutaneous lymphnode syndrome) patients in hospitals. *Biken Journal, 20*(3–4), 117–123.

*United Nations. (2015). World population ageing 2015: Highlights. Retrieved from http://www.un.org/en/development/desa/population/publications/pdf/ageing/WPA2015_Highlights.pdf

Woodhead, E. L., Emery, E. E., Pachana, N. A., Scott, T. L., Konnert, C. A., & Edelstein, B. A. (2013). Graduate students' geropsychology training opportunities and perceived competence in working with older adults. *Professional Psychology: Research and Practice, 44,* 355–362. doi:10.1037/a0034632

Biological Underpinnings of Aging

2

Biological Theories of Aging

Brian P. Yochim

The media today is full of references to antioxidants and various antiaging treatments. What are antioxidants? What do they have to do with the aging process? Why does the human body experience conditions involving excessive growth (e.g., cancer), and excessive destruction (e.g., Alzheimer's disease)? This chapter addresses these general concepts and more, whereas Chapter 3 addresses specific physical changes and diseases that occur frequently in older adults.

While aging is typically associated with an increased prevalence of disease in humans and other species, there are other organisms that seem to avoid the development of disease. Sequoia and Redwood trees, for instance, live hundreds of years while avoiding disease (Lanner, 1999). The longest-living organism on Earth is the Bristlecone pine tree, which can live more than 4,000 years; one tree is believed to be at least 4,682 years old (Lanner, 1999). These species are mostly free of internal disease processes. When they die, it tends to be due to external factors such as lightning strikes, fire, pest outbreaks, soil erosion, or damage inflicted by humans (Lanner, 1999). Bristlecone pines, Sequoias, Redwoods, and other tree species do not seem to show symptoms of senescence (Lanner, 2002), a topic described in the following section on telomeres. One can ponder a time far into the future in which the prevalence of mortal disease is so low that humans only die from external forces. How is it that these species have evolved to be so resistant to disease, and can we learn from that? A comprehensive account of the psychology of human aging begins at the cellular or genetic level, as events at this level ultimately determine the events of human existence.

---

*Key references in the References section are indicated by an asterisk.

TELOMERES

An important variable that determines how long humans live is the length of telomeres (Aviv, 2011). Telomeres lie at the ends of chromosomes and protect the ends, similar to the plastic coverings on the ends of shoelaces (see Figure 2.1).

After a chromosome has divided, telomeres prevent fragments from reattaching. DNA replication requires telomeres as a place for RNA to attach during replication; without telomeres, cells would not be able to reproduce. Telomeres serve at least three important functions (Yang, Song, & Johnson, 2016): (a) they prevent chromosome ends from degrading; (b) they prevent chromosome ends from being perceived as broken and in need of cessation of division or programmed cell death, and (c) they prevent DNA repair mechanisms that could mistakenly cause problems such as chromosome fusions. As cells reproduce by dividing multiple times over the life span, most predominantly from birth to adulthood, telomeres continue to shorten, resulting in the *end replication problem*. With each reproduction, telomeres become shorter and shorter, until a point at which cells are no longer able to divide. This point is termed *replicative senescence* or *replicative aging* (Shay & Wright, 2011; Yang et al., 2016).

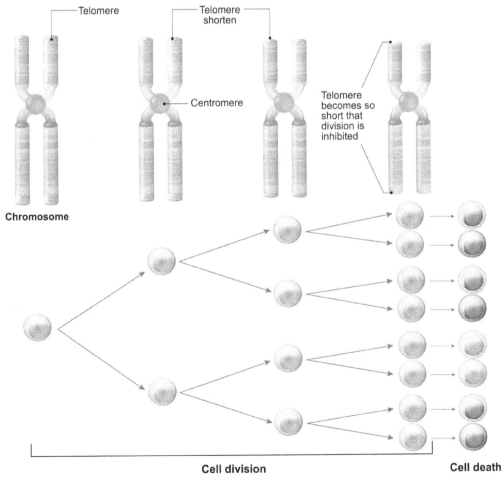

Figure 2.1 Telomeres.

This cessation has been called the *Hayflick limit* (Hayflick, 1965) and places a limit on the life span of mammals (Aviv, 2011). This represents a *biological* clock as opposed to a *chronological* clock. Telomere length is associated with cardiovascular diseases (Fyhrquist, Saijonmaa, & Strandberg, 2013), the reproductive life span of women (Aydos, Elhan, & Tükün, 2005), diabetes mellitus (Zhao, Miao, Wang, Ding, & Wang, 2013), and other age-related conditions. Once a cell can no longer divide, it can remain in a state of *cell senescence* for years, which can lead to telomere shortening, but it eventually goes through programmed cell death, or *apoptosis*. Apoptosis is most common in cell types for which disposal is easy, such as skin or intestine cells. If a cell remains in senescence for prolonged periods (e.g., as in skin moles), it can undergo major changes in its physiology. Radiation can induce cell senescence and shorten telomeres, inhibiting cell growth (Tchkonia, Zhu, Deursen, Campisi, & Kirkland, 2013), which has led to it being used to prevent the growth of cancer, a form of uncontrolled cell growth (Yang et al., 2016).

Cell senescence influences age-related pathology by at least two mechanisms. First, senescent cells have limited ability to create new cells needed for tissue health. Second, senescent cells may also affect their surrounding cells by releasing *senescence-associated secretory phenotype* (SASP), which can lead to inflammation, alter tissue structure, and stimulate growth of malignant cells in old age (Tchkonia et al., 2013). SASP may exhibit *antagonistic pleiotropy*. Antagonistic pleiotropy occurs when genes that may have harmful effects in late life are favored by natural selection if they have beneficial effects earlier in life (Gavrilov & Gavrilova, 2006). Natural selection leads to increased production of genes that benefit an organism during reproductive years even if the gene can cause detrimental effects after the reproductive years. Therefore, although SASP may be harmful in older adults, it may lead to tissue healing in younger people, promoting immune clearance of damaged cells such as in skin wounds.

The enzyme *telomerase* makes telomeres longer and adds new DNA onto them. In human embryonic development, telomerase is active but dissipates in brain and bone tissue after 16 weeks and declines in other tissue during fetal development (Yang et al., 2016). Regenerative tissues in the esophagus, intestines, hair, skin, uterus, sperm, and other tissues show some telomerase activity, but most human tissue contains insufficient levels of telomerase to stop the loss of telomeres that occurs with age (Yang et al., 2016).

Cancer cells have evolved to have the ability to circumvent replicative senescence by preserving telomere lengths, allowing cancer cells to reproduce without limit. Telomerase is found in 90% of malignant tumors (Kim et al., 1994) and enables cancer cells to reproduce indefinitely (Shay & Wright, 2011) but is not present in most human cells except sperm and egg cells. Because of its presence in almost all cancer cells, and because it facilitates the growth of cancer, telomerase is a common target for cancer treatments. Treatments that inhibit telomerase are in various stages of development for pancreatic cancer, breast cancer, lung cancer, and multiple myeloma (Shay & Wright, 2011).

Three factors limit the generalizability of research on telomeres. Most research on telomeres has been conducted with leukocytes (Sutphin & Korstanje, 2016). Leukocytes are also known as white blood cells; they are a colorless cell that circulates in blood and body fluids and reacts to foreign substances and diseases. Leukocytes include lymphocytes, granulocytes, monocytes, and macrophages. It is not known whether leukocyte telomere length is an adequate representation of aging or even telomere length in other cell types (Sutphin & Korstanje, 2016; Yang et al., 2016). Second, similar to the measurement of psychological constructs, different techniques are used to measure telomere lengths and may lead to different findings across studies. Another factor is that correlation does not mean causation. It is still difficult to establish whether shortened telomeres lead to age-related disease, or if age-related diseases shorten human telomeres.

Telomere length varies within and across species. In humans, women tend to have longer telomeres than men (Benetos et al., 2001; Nawrot, Staessen, Gardner, & Aviv, 2004), which may explain why they tend to live longer than men (Aviv, 2011). Other animal species have longer telomeres than humans do. Mice, who are frequent participants in research on aging, have much longer telomeres than humans (Aviv, 2011). The question arises as to why humans have short telomeres compared to other species. In order to understand one important reason, one must recall that long telomeres by definition allow for cells to reproduce multiple times. Unfortunately, the more replications there are, the higher the chances of spontaneous genetic mutations, which can trigger the formation of cancerous tumors. Short telomeres thus may act as a mechanism of preventing the growth of cancer (Sutphin & Korstanje, 2016). Indeed, the inhibition of telomerase from extending telomeres is being investigated as a treatment for cancer. On the other hand, telomeres need to be long enough to prevent *genomic instability*, in which telomeres are too short and diseases such as cancer develop by methods that work around the telomere limitation. Genomic instability can lead to chromosomal rearrangements, including *aneuploidy development*, the development of abnormal numbers of chromosomes in a cell (Shay & Wright, 2011). Evolution may have led to the creation of a "just right" length of telomeres in humans to prevent the development of cancer as much as possible. Natural selection may have led to telomeres that are long enough to allow humans to live into reproductive age and are short enough to prevent humans from developing cancer in reproductive ages (Aviv, 2011).

FREE RADICALS AND AGING

One of the longest-lasting theories of aging has been the free radical theory of aging, put forth by Harman (1956). *Free radicals* are atoms or molecules that have at least one unpaired electron, making them volatile and destabilizing molecules near them. These effects on nearby molecules lead to the formation of more free radicals, causing further instability and cellular damage. Free radicals may arise in connective tissues through chemical reactions involving traces of iron, cobalt, and manganese (Harman, 1956). The predominant type of free radical related to human aging is generated during cellular metabolism involving mitochondria. Mitochondria generate energy within cells. Oxygen is necessary for energy production but this process also leads to the production of reactive oxygen species (ROS) as by-products (Scheibye-Knudsen, Fang, Croteau, Wilson, & Bohr, 2015). ROS are free radicals that contain oxygen molecules, such as OH and HO_2 molecules (Harman, 1956). Mitochondria are the main creators of ROS and are also the main target of them (Ramis, Esteban, Miralles, Tan, & Reiter, 2015). In healthy cells, ROS generation occurs at controlled rates, but ROS production increases in disease states or under high stress (Ramis et al., 2015). ROS lead to many consequences including altered gene expression, genomic instability, genetic mutations, loss of ability to engage in mitosis (cellular reproduction), impaired communication between cells, disorganized tissue, organ dysfunction, and increased vulnerability to stress (Rattan, 2006). ROS lead to cumulative damage to cells, eventually leading to cell death (Scheibye-Knudsen et al., 2015) and death of an organism.

Antioxidants are chemicals that inhibit or eliminate oxidation and thus may protect against free radicals. The antioxidant *resveratrol* has inherent antioxidant characteristics and also prompts the activity of other antioxidant enzymes (Ramis et al., 2015). Resveratrol is a polyphenol (nutrient) found in plants, particularly plants going through environmental stresses. These plants include grapes, raspberries, blueberries, peanuts, and some pine trees. Perhaps the most studied source of resveratrol is red wine, which has been postulated to be responsible for the "French paradox." This term refers to the finding that the French population has a low incidence of cardiovascular disease despite having a diet high in saturated fats (Liu, Zhang, Zhang, & Zhen, 2007); it is thought that the ingestion of red wine offsets the harmful effects of the saturated fats. In one example of a study exploring the potential benefits of resveratrol, Witte, Kerti, Margulies, and Flöel (2014) found that 23 participants given a 26-week treatment with resveratrol improved their delayed recall by two words on the Rey Auditory Verbal Learning Test (AVLT), whereas 23 participants given a placebo did not improve their recall. These results suggest that resveratrol intake may be associated with improved memory. The group given resveratrol treatment also showed increased hippocampal connectivity with the prefrontal cortex. Resveratrol shows promise in the prevention of age-related diseases, but more research is needed to determine its utility in this.

While excessive ROS may harm cells, small levels of ROS may actually lead to an adaptive response. This concept is known as *hormesis*. This idea has stemmed from research showing that: (a) ROS may increase life span in yeast and worms (Mesquita et al., 2010; Van Raamsdonk & Hekimi, 2009), (b) increasing mitochondrial ROS do not always decrease life span in mice (Zhang et al., 2009), and (c) ROS do have important biological roles (Ramis et al., 2015). Small levels of ROS may be implicated in caloric restriction, described next.

CALORIC RESTRICTION

One of the most consistent findings in the biology of aging is that decreasing rats' food intake slows growth and increases their life span, reported as early as 1917 by Osborne, Mendel, and Ferry. During the Great Depression, there were concerns that chronic hunger might shorten the human life span (Kenyon, 2010), but McCay, Crowell, and Maynard (1935) and McCay, Maynard, Sperling, and Barnes (1939) showed that decreased food intake actually lengthened the life span of rats. This is likely due to reduced intake of calories in general rather than reduced intake of a certain nutrient (Masoro, 2005). This reduction in calories has been shown to increase life span in yeast, fruit flies, nematodes, fish, rats, mice, hamsters, and dogs (Ramis et al., 2015). Studies show that reducing calories in numerous species by 30% to 60% increases the life span by 20% to 50% (Kennedy, Steffen, & Kaeberlein, 2007). It reduces the incidence or delays the onset of age-related conditions such as diabetes, cancer, cardiovascular disease, and brain atrophy in rhesus monkeys (Colman et al., 2009), reduces declines in memory in humans (Witte, Fobker, Gellner, Knecht, & Flöel,, 2009), and is associated with improved cognitive functioning and decreased risk of Alzheimer's disease in mice (Halagappa et al., 2007). In contrast, research at the National Institute on Aging (NIA) has not found caloric restriction to be associated with increased life span in primates (Mattison et al., 2012). However, Colman et al. (2014) claim that the control monkeys in the NIA study were actually undergoing what could be considered caloric restriction, based on analysis of their body weights, which would explain the lack of difference between monkeys in the control and experimental conditions. Regardless, caloric restriction has since been conceptualized as a model helping to identify mechanisms of aging and slowing down the aging process (Kennedy et al., 2007). One mechanism by which this works is that caloric restriction slows down the cumulative buildup of cells damaged by ROS with age (Ramis et al., 2015).

Caloric restriction may exert its effects on longevity by increasing the expression of *sirtuins*. Sirtuins are mammalian homologues of the yeast *Silent Information Regulator 2* (Sir2). There are seven homologues of the Sir2 protein, which are sirtuins 1–7 (SIRT1, SIRT2, SIRT3, SIRT4, SIRT5, SIRT6, and SIRT7), and they regulate systems associated with energy metabolism and cell longevity (Ramis et al., 2015). Sirtuins are important contributors to the life span of animals (Ramis et al., 2015). There are seven sirtuins in the human body, which regulate various cellular functions such as apoptosis, tumor suppression, and responses to stress (Covington & Bajpeyi, 2016). Sirtuin activity depends on nicotinamide adenine dinucleotide (NAD). NAD+ is an *oxidizing agent*, accepting electrons from other molecules, offsetting the damage inflicted by free radicals. Genetic overexpression of SIRT1 has been shown to increase longevity in mice (Satoh et al., 2013) and a decrease in SIRT1 in mice hastened the aging process of skin and shortened the life span of mice (Sommer et al., 2006). Another study (Herranz et al., 2010) did not find longer life span related to SIRT1 but found improved glucose tolerance and increased resistance to toxic liver damage related to higher levels of SIRT1. SIRT1 promotes neuronal axon development and dendritic branching, modulates synaptic plasticity, and is involved in protecting against neurodegenerative diseases like Alzheimer's disease, Parkinson's disease, and motor neuron diseases (Herskovits & Guarente, 2014). Kim et al. (2007) found that SIRT1 protected against Alzheimer's disease in mice and prevented neurodegeneration in the hippocampus. SIRT2 plays a role in microtubule function and in the response to stresses placed on microtubules (Covington & Bajpayi, 2016). Caloric restriction increases SIRT1 and SIRT3 activity, maintaining mitochondrial health (Covington & Bajpeyi, 2016). Caloric restriction and exercise have been shown to increase SIRT3 in mice (Palacios et al., 2009). SIRT1, SIRT2, and SIRT6 influence telomere preservation (Covington & Bajpeyi, 2016). In summary, sirtuins have many beneficial effects related to aging, and caloric restriction increases the activity of sirtuins.

If caloric restriction indeed could lengthen the human life span, the feasibility or desirability of engaging in such a restricted dietary regime throughout life is questionable. Researchers have thus sought to identify ways to mimic the effects of caloric restriction, or to find *mimetics* for caloric restriction. Ingestion of the antioxidant resveratrol (discussed previously), a chemical in various foods, can mimic the benefits of caloric restriction (Barger et al., 2008; Baur et al., 2006). Resveratrol increases activation of SIRT1. Sirtuins may be instrumental in creating strategies to mimic the beneficial effects of caloric restriction.

Melatonin is another chemical found in plants that may increase SIRT1 activity. It has antioxidant properties and decreases free radicals. In humans it is released from the pineal gland at night (Ramis et al., 2015). This cycle weakens with age but tends to be preserved in animals undergoing caloric restriction (Reiter, 1992). Melatonin may be involved in cancer reduction by actually inhibiting SIRT1, which is overexpressed in prostate cancer (Jung-Hynes et al., 2011).

Research in the coming decades will continue to explore mimetics of caloric restriction. Next, we review genes pertinent to aging.

GENETICS OF AGING

Hundreds of genes are associated with longevity or with other phenotypes related to aging. It has been thought that prolonging life would simply lead to more people developing diseases that typically develop in old age, such as Alzheimer's disease. On the contrary, genetic mutations that delay the aging process are found to delay age-related diseases as well (Kenyon, 2010).

Research on genetics and aging can be categorized into two types (Kremen & Lyons, 2011): quantitative and molecular. *Quantitative* studies include family, twin, and adoption studies. *Molecular* studies, by contrast, directly investigate specific genetic variations related to specific traits. Genes can exert additive effects, where more than one gene is associated with a trait, and the genes act additively to cause a trait, or they can be nonadditive. *Nonadditive* models occur when one single gene has a large effect or in *epistasis*, in which a genetic interaction occurs and the effects of one gene mask the effects of another gene (Kremen & Lyons, 2011).

Within the realm of *quantitative* genetic studies, the Seattle Longitudinal Study (Schaie, 2013) is one example of a *family* genetic study that has produced valuable data. Investigating parent–child associations and sibling associations has provided evidence for the heritability of most cognitive abilities (Schaie, 2013). *Adoption* studies utilize an already-occurring situation in which participants have the genes of one family but the environment provided by another family (Kremen & Lyons, 2011). This is a powerful method for assessing the effects of genes versus environment on behavioral traits. This approach is rarely used in the field of aging, aside from the Swedish Adoption/Twin Study of Aging (SATSA). The third quantitative method of genetic research has been the area of *twin* studies (Kremen & Lyons, 2011). Dizygotic twins share an average of 50% of their genes, whereas monozygotic twins share 100% of their genes. Studies determine whether monozygotic twins are significantly more similar on a trait than dizygotic twins, which provides evidence of heritability. *Heritability* represents the proportion of variance explained by genetic factors.

Molecular studies primarily consist of genetic association studies. These studies investigate whether particular polymorphisms are related to phenotypes, or the observable traits of someone that are encoded by genes (e.g., one's hair color). A polymorphism is a variation of a DNA sequence inherited by an individual. When a single nucleotide varies across individuals at a certain place on a gene, this is called a *single nucleotide polymorphism (SNP;* see Figure 2.2). A SNP consists of one of the four bases (A, C, G, or T), a sugar, and a phosphate molecule. Such genetic variants must typically exist in at least 1% of the population to be considered a SNP (Kremen & Lyons, 2011). SNPs can consist of substitutions, deletions, or insertions. Approximately 1% to 2% of SNPs are actually found to be *functional* (i.e., to lead to amino acid changes in *translation*). *Translation* is the production of proteins from DNA, and essentially how genetic alterations are manifest.

Researchers search as much of the human genome as possible to find *candidate genes* in *genome-wide association studies (GWAS)*. This approach brings forth the problem, however, of hundreds of thousands of statistical tests and the accompanying need to change the alpha level to avoid Type 1 statistical errors. That is, when performing this many statistical tests, a researcher is bound to find effects just by chance and might conclude a relationship exists when it in fact does not (i.e., a Type 1 error). Thus, large effect sizes are required to determine the presence of significant effects. To complicate this further, most traits related to the psychology of aging are *polygenic*. That is, the majority of psychological traits are associated with multiple genetic and environmental factors, each likely with a small effect size. Researchers attempt as much as possible to specify a priori hypotheses in a candidate gene approach, to guide their analyses and give them support for conclusions that may be drawn from small effect sizes.

In addition to differences in the DNA coding sequence, the *amount* of a given gene also provides genetic diversity. When the number of copies of a gene varies

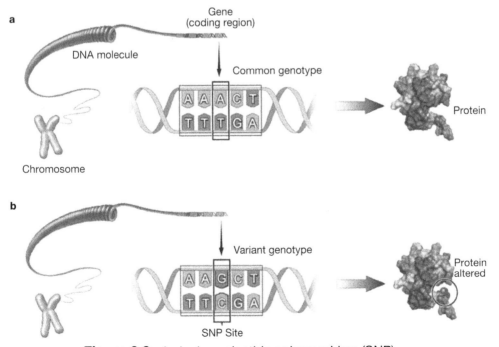

Figure 2.2 A single nucleotide polymorphism (SNP).

among individuals, these are known as *copy number variants (CNVs)*. CNVs have been found to be involved in Alzheimer's and Parkinson's diseases (Lee & Lupski, 2006), for example, and may contribute to genetic diversity more significantly than SNPs.

When studying genes related to aging, it is important to conceptualize each not as simply the gene itself, but as an interaction between the gene and particular environmental conditions. Nongenetic factors (e.g., exposure to carcinogens, diet, degree of stress) can activate or inhibit the expression of genes without changing the underlying DNA structure. These differences are known as *epigenetics*. One aspect of epigenetics involves *DNA methylation*, which occurs when methyl groups combine with DNA and modify it. DNA methylation declines in the brain with aging (Gravina & Vijg, 2009) and may affect memory in the aging process (Liu, van Groen, Kadish, & Tollefsbol, 2009).

Molecular genetic research includes "reverse genetic" and "forward genetic" approaches. In *reverse genetic* approaches, genes are knocked out individually and researchers determine the effect on the life span of the organism. This method has been used with invertebrate organisms with short lives (e.g., *Saccharomyces cerevisiae* [yeast], *Caenorhabditis elegans* [nematodes, or microscopic worms], and *Drosophila melanogaster* [fruit flies]). This work has found hundreds of genes related to life span, including genes related to mitochondrial metabolism, protein homeostasis, and stress resistance (Sutphin & Korstanje, 2016).

In contrast to reverse genetic approaches, *forward genetics* research uses the natural phenotypic variation among genetically diverse populations to identify candidate aging genes. This method can directly identify longevity-related genes among mammals (as opposed to yeast, worms, or fruit flies), increasing the human relevance of findings. These studies include studies on humans, exploring genetic loci among families with notable longevity. Individuals usually have two *alleles* of a gene, one from the mother and one from the father. *Alleles* may be *homozygous* (alike) or *heterozygous* (different) and lead to variation in inherited characteristics.

APOLIPOPROTEIN E (APOE)

The gene for APOE, located on chromosome 19, has consistently been related to longer human life spans. The APOE gene has three possible alleles, ε2, ε3, and ε4, thus leading to six genotypes that one can inherit: ε2/ε2, ε2/ε3, ε2/ε4, ε3/ε3, ε3/ε4, and ε4/ε4. This gene encodes an apolipoprotein that is a large component of very low density lipoproteins (VLDLs), which remove excess cholesterol from blood. Allelic variants of APOE are related to Alzheimer's disease, atherosclerosis, and other pathologies related to aging. Because of its role in metabolizing triglycerides and cholesterol, the ε3/ε4 and ε4/ε4 genotypes have been found to be associated with increased risk of myocardial infarction, whereas the ε2/ε3 genotype is associated with decreased risk (Wang et al., 2015). That is, the ε4 allele may lead to increased cholesterol levels, whereas the ε2 allele may lower cholesterol levels. Apolipoprotein is expressed in many organs and is expressed the most in the liver, followed by the brain (Verghese, Castellano, & Holtzman, 2011). It directs the delivery of lipids from one cell type to another (Verghese et al., 2011). In cerebrospinal fluid, APOE is related to cholesterol and HDL-like lipoproteins; cerebrospinal fluid does not contain LDLs or VLDLs. It is not known whether APOE affects cholesterol or phospholipids in the central nervous system. Thus, APOE's effects on neurological disorders might occur without direct effects on lipid metabolism (Verghese et al., 2011).

The presence of one ε4 allele increases one's risk for developing Alzheimer's disease, and inheriting two alleles causes even greater risk; the ε2 allele, on the other hand, may protect against Alzheimer's disease (Farrer et al., 1997; Verghese et al., 2011). The ε4 allele is also related to slight cognitive decrements in episodic memory and executive functioning in healthy aging (Small, Rosnick, Fratiglioni, & Backman, 2004). The relationship of APOE to Alzheimer's disease is explored further in Chapter 9.

Catechol-o-Methyltransferase (COMT)

The genes related to COMT may impact cognition and affect in older adults. The COMT enzyme catalyzes the degradation of catecholamines (norepinephrine, epinephrine, and dopamine) in neuronal synapses (Das et al., 2014), particularly for dopamine in the frontal lobes (Lee & Song, 2014). It rapidly inactivates these neurotransmitters in the synapse and terminates their action. The gene is located on chromosome 22q (22q11). One common SNP, rs4680 G/A, makes this gene exist in two different forms, or alleles. One allele ("VAL") encodes the amino acid valine (VAL) at position 158 of the amino acid sequence, and the other allele ("MET") encodes the amino acid methionine (MET) at the same place (Das et al., 2014). The enzyme produced by the MET allele catalyzes much less than the VAL allele, so that catecholamine neurotransmitters linger longer at synapses (Das et al., 2014). COMT enzymes lead to half of the dopamine clearance in the frontal lobes, so COMT is particularly important for this part of the brain. This increase in dopamine availability caused by the MET allele may increase the efficiency of information processing (Egan et al., 2001), as suggested by lower brain activation (Egan et al., 2003), and improved executive function and memory performance (Witte & Flöel, 2012). However, other studies have not found a significant association between the COMT VAL158MET genotype and cognitive functions (Witte & Flöel, 2012). While carriers of the MET allele of this gene have been found to experience negative affect more than carriers of the VAL allele, this relationship was not found to be true among older adults (Turan, Sims, Best, & Carstensen, 2016). Turan et al. suggest that older adults may distribute regulatory effort toward affective modulation more than younger adults. The relationship between aging and emotional regulation is discussed in Chapter 5.

COMT does not appear to be related to increased risk of neurodegenerative disease; a meta-analysis did not find any relationship between this gene and Alzheimer's disease (Lee & Song, 2014). Another meta-analysis found that the COMT VaL158Met polymorphism may decrease the risk of Alzheimer's disease among Asians but not among European or American populations (Yan, Zhao, Sun, & Tang, 2016). Despite its importance in the metabolism of drugs used to treat Parkinson's disease, a meta-analysis of 24 studies did not find a relationship between this gene and Parkinson's disease (Jimenez-Jimenez, Alonso-Navarro, Garcia-Martin, & Agundez, 2014).

Brain-Derived Neurotrophic Factor (BDNF)

BDNF increases synaptic plasticity (discussed in Chapter 4) and facilitates learning and memory with the hippocampus (Webster, Herman, Kleinman, & Shannon Weickert, 2006). The BDNF gene on chromosome 11 (11p13) produces it. The common polymorphism of this gene (rs6265 G/A) causes MET to replace VAL at location 66 (VAL66MET). The MET allele leads to less secretion of BDNF (Chen et al., 2004) and lower neuronal survival and synaptic plasticity (Frielingsdorf et al., 2010). This is associated with poor episodic memory, working memory, and hippocampal function (Egan et al., 2003; Ho et al., 2006). However, a meta-analysis by Mandelman and Grigorenko (2012) did not find a relationship between the BDNF VAL66MET polymorphism and cognitive functioning. Studies in this area tend to use different cognitive measures across studies, leading to conflicting results across studies. In addition to their own independent effects on cognition, or perhaps instead of independent effects, COMT and BDNF may interact to affect cognition in older adults (Das et al., 2014).

Peroxisome Proliferator-Activated Receptor-γ (PPARγ)

Another gene that is studied in aging is PPARγ, which regulates adipocyte differentiation, insulin sensitivity, and lipid metabolism (Beaven & Tontonoz, 2006). It suppresses microglial inflammatory responses and inhibits beta amyloid generation by increasing cholesterol outflow from glial cells (Wang et al., 2010). (Beta amyloid is a core component of Alzheimer's disease, discussed in Chapter 9.) However, it does not relate to Alzheimer's disease, according to one meta-analysis (Lee & Song, 2014). A variant of the gene for this may lead to increased insulin sensitivity, lower body mass, and prevention of type 2 diabetes (Tonjes & Stumvoll, 2007).

Kidney and Brain Expressed Protein (KIBRA)

The KIBRA polymorphism may impact memory in older adults. People with the T-allele for this gene have shown stronger episodic memory than people homozygous for the C-allele (Schneider et al., 2010). In the brain, KIBRA exerts its effects mainly in the hippocampus and affects proteins involved with long-term potentiation. Polymorphisms on the gene for dopamine D2 receptors (the DRD2 gene) are associated with better inhibition ability and memory, but there are few studies on this gene to date (Papenberg, Lindenberger, & Bäckman, 2015).

Genes Related to Insulin-Like Growth Factor

Genes related to insulin also play a role in longevity. One pathway that has been found to affect aging in animals has been the *insulin/insulin-like growth factor (IGF) pathway* (Kenyon, 2010; Waterson & Pletcher, 2016). IGF is synthesized by the liver in response to human growth hormone secretion. IGF is similar to insulin in its chemical structure and it stimulates cell growth, DNA synthesis, bone growth, and replication of cancer cells. This pathway plays a major role in metabolic homeostasis. Genetic manipulations that decrease IGF prolong life span across species from worms to mammals. Decreased levels of IGF signaling decrease the incidence of cancer and diabetes (Guevara-Aguirre et al., 2011; Steuerman, Shevah, & Laron, 2011).

Papenberg et al. (2015), in their *resource modulation hypothesis*, propose that genetic variation causes stronger effects on cognition as anatomical and neurochemical brain resources decline in old age. That is, genes that relate to higher cognitive ability may benefit older adults more than younger adults. Papenberg et al. note that most studies on polymorphisms in APOE, BDNF, COMT, KIBRA, and DRD2 find small or no effects of genetic differences on cognitive functioning in younger adults, but that these effects increase in size among older adults.

CHALLENGES IN RESEARCH ON GENETICS RELATED TO AGING

One limitation of behavioral genetics research has been what Kremen and Lyons (2011) term the *construct-measurement fallacy* (p. 102). This refers to the often-erroneous assumption that if a trait is heritable, then any measure of that trait is heritable. However, constructs such as memory or executive functioning can be subdivided into many other constructs. While one measure may tap into one aspect of executive functioning, for example, other measures may tap into other facets or may not be a reliable or valid measure of the construct at all. Likewise, measures of memory include multiple variables and produce multiple scores. Many measures in use today (e.g., the Trail Making test, the Boston Naming test) were created decades ago, before a great deal was learned about the constructs they were purported to measure. Researchers must carefully choose which test variable to include in genetic analyses.

The importance of *broad* or *narrow* phenotypes presents another challenge to researchers in the genetics of aging. Broad phenotypes such as general intelligence tend to show more heritability than specific phenotypes (Kremens & Lyons, 2011) such as visuospatial ability. However, general intelligence, as measured by IQ scores, comprises many different cognitive abilities. People with similar levels of general intelligence may actually have quite different profiles of cognitive strengths and weaknesses, and little is learned about variation in cognitive abilities in studies on the heritability of general intelligence. On the other hand, broad conclusions about cognition should not be drawn when relationships are found between a gene and one particular aspect of cognitive functioning, such as visuospatial ability. Likewise, genetic studies on age-related changes to specific brain structures usually investigate brain volume. Brain volume is a combination of cortical thickness and surface area. While separate genetic influences exert independent effects on these two variables (Panizzon et al., 2009), most studies in this area use general measures of brain volume and may not reveal all the sets of genes involved in this variable. Researchers in genetics and aging must take care to fully understand a phenotype when investigating it, and decide whether to explore broad or narrow measures of the phenotype. Because of this, Kremens and Lyons (2011) point out the importance of continuing to perform twin studies and integrating them with molecular genetic approaches.

CONCLUSION

This chapter provided an introduction to current theories and areas of investigation in the biology of aging. Telomeres are an important determinant of life span, and after a number of cell replications, the end replication problem becomes manifest. Antagonistic pleiotropy is the concept of biological properties that have developed through evolution to increase reproductive capability, even if they cause harm later in life. Free radicals drive the aging process but their effects can be ameliorated with antioxidants. Caloric restriction provides a well-established mechanism for extending the life span, but requires chronic food deprivation. Ways to mimic this effect without requiring starvation, such as through the intake of sirtuins, are being explored. Lastly, this chapter provided an introduction to basic concepts in research on genes related to aging, such as SNPs, and several genes under focus, such as those related to APOE, COMT, and BDNF.

DISCUSSION QUESTIONS

1. What are telomeres and telomerase, and how are they involved in determining longevity?

2. Define antagonistic pleiotropy.

3. What are antioxidants, and how do they impact our biological health?

4. Explain caloric restriction and how it may lead to longer life spans.

5. What is a SNP?

6. Explain the relationship between APOE and Alzheimer's disease.

7. Describe two genes that are heavily researched because of their likely involvement in the aging process.

REFERENCES

Aviv, A. (2011). Leukocyte telomere dynamics, human aging, and life span. In E. J. Masoro & S. N. Austad (Eds.), *Handbook of the biology of aging* (7th ed., pp. 163–176). London, United Kingdom: Academic Press.

Aydos, S. E., Elhan, A. H., & Tükün, A. (2005). Is telomere length one of the determinants of reproductive life span? *Archives of Gynecology and Obstetrics, 272,* 113–116. doi:10.1007/s00404-004 -0690-2

Barger, J. L., Kayo, T., Vann, J. M., Arias, E. B., Wang, J., Hacker, T. A., . . . Prolla, T. A. (2008). A low dose of dietary resveratrol partially mimics caloric restriction and retards aging parameters in mice. *Public Library of Science One, 3*(6), e2264. doi:10.1371/journal.pone.0002264

*Baur, J. A., Pearson, K. J., Price, N. L., Jamieson, H. A., Lerin, C., Kalra, A., . . . Sinclair, D. A. (2006). Resveratrol improves health and survival of mice on a high-calorie diet. *Nature, 444*(7117), 337–342.

Beaven, S. W., & Tontonoz, P. (2006). Nuclear receptors in lipid metabolism: Targeting the heart of dyslipidemia. *Annual Review of Medicine, 57,* 313–329.

Benetos, A., Okuda, K., Lajemi, M., Kimura, M., Thomas, F., Skurnick, J., . . . Aviv, A. (2001). Telomere length as indicator of biological aging: The gender effect and relation with pulse pressure and pulse wave velocity. *Hypertension, 37*(2, Pt. 2), 381–385.

Chen, Z.-Y., Patel, P. D., Sant, G., Meng, C.-X., Teng, K. K., Hempstead, B. L., & Lee, F. S. (2004). Variant brain-derived neurotrophic factor (BDNF) (Met66) alters the intracellular trafficking and activity-dependent secretion of wild-type BDNF in neurosecretory cells and cortical neurons. *The Journal of Neuroscience, 24,* 4401–4411. doi:10.1523/JNEUROSCI.0348-04.2004

*Colman, R. J., Anderson, R. M., Johnson, S. C., Kastman, E. K., Kosmatka, K. J., Beasley, T. M., . . . Weindruch, R. (2009). Caloric restriction delays disease onset and mortality in rhesus monkeys. *Science, 325,* 201–204.

Colman, R. J., Beasley, T. M., Kemnitz, J. W., Johnson, S. C., Weindruch, R., & Anderson, R. M. (2014). Caloric restriction reduces age-related and all-cause mortality in rhesus monkeys. *Nature Communications, 5,* 3557. doi:10.1038/ncomms4557

Covington, J. D., & Bajpeyi, S. (2016). The sirtuins: Markers of metabolic health. *Molecular Nutrition Food Research, 60,* 79–91. doi:10.1002/mnfr.201500340

Das, D., Tan, X., Bielak, A. A. M., Cherbuin, N., Easteal, S., & Anstey, K. J. (2014). Cognitive ability, intraindividual variability, and common genetic variants of *catechol-o-methyltransferase* and *brain-derived neurotrophic factor*: A longitudinal study in a population-based sample of older adults. *Psychology and Aging, 29*(2), 393–403. doi:10.1037/a0035702

Egan, M. F., Goldberg, T. E., Kolachana, B. S., Callicott, J. H., Mazzanti, C. M., Straub, R. E., . . . Weinberger, D. R. (2001). Effect of COMT val108/158 met genotype on frontal lobe function and risk for schizophrenia. *Proceedings of the National Academy of Sciences of the United States of America, 98,* 6917–6922. doi:10.1073/pnas.111134598

Egan, M. F., Kojima, M., Callicott, J. H., Goldberg, T. E., Kolachana, B. S., Bertolino, A., . . . Weinberger, D. R. (2003). The BDNF val66met polymorphism affects activity-dependent secretion of BDNF and human memory and hippocampal function. *Cell, 112,* 257–269. doi:10.1016/S0092-8674(03)00035-7

Farrer, L. A., Cupples, L. A., Haines, J. L., Hyman, B., Kukull, W. A., Mayeux, R., . . . van Duijn, C. M. (1997). Effects of age, sex, and ethnicity on the association between apolipoprotein E genotype and Alzheimer disease: A meta-analysis. *Journal of the American Medical Association, 278*(16), 1349–1356. doi:10.1001/jama.1997.03550160069041

Frielingsdorf, H., Bath, K. G., Soliman, F., Difede, J., Casey, B. J., & Lee, F. S. (2010). Variant brain-derived neurotrophic factor val66met endophenotypes: Implications for posttraumatic stress disorder. *Annals of the New York Academy of Sciences, 1208,* 150–157. doi:10.1111/j.1749-6632.2010.05722.x

Fyhrquist, F., Saijonmaa, O., & Strandberg, T. (2013). The roles of senescence and telomere shortening in cardiovascular disease. *Nature Reviews: Cardiology, 10,* 274–283. doi:10.1038/nrcardio.2013.30

Gavrilov, L. A., & Gavrilova, N. S. (2006). Reliability theory of aging and longevity. In E. J. Masoro & S. N. Austad (Eds.), *Handbook of the biology of aging* (6th ed., pp. 3–42). Burlington, MA: Academic Press.

Gravina, S., & Vijg, J. (2009). Epigenetic factors in aging and longevity. *European Journal of Physiology, 459*(2), 247–258.

Guevara-Aguirre, J., Balasubramanian, P., Guevara-Aguirre, M., Wei, M., Madia, F., Cheng, C.-W., . . . Longo, V. D. (2011). Growth hormone receptor deficiency is associated with a major reduction in pro-aging signaling, cancer, and diabetes in humans. *Science Translational Medicine, 3*(70), 70ra13. doi:10.1126/scitranslmed.3001845

Halagappa, V. K. M., Guo, Z., Pearson, M., Matsuoka, Y., Cutler, R. G., LaFerla, F. M., & Mattson, M. P. (2007). Intermittent fasting and caloric restriction ameliorate age-related behavioral deficits in the triple-transgenic mouse model of Alzheimer's disease. *Neurobiology of disease, 26*(1), 212–20. doi:10.1016/j.nbd.2006.12.019

*Harman, D. H. (1956). Aging: A theory based on free radical and radiation chemistry. *Journal of Gerontology, 11*(3), 298–300.

*Hayflick, L. (1965). The limited in vitro lifetime of human diploid cell strains. *Experimental Cell Research, 37,* 614–636.

Herranz, D., Muñoz-Martin, M., Cañamero, M., Mulero, F., Martinez-Pastor, B., Fernandez-Capetillo, O., & Serrano, M. (2010). Sirt1 improves healthy ageing and protects from metabolic syndrome-associated cancer. *Nature Communications, 1,* 3. doi:10.1038/ncomms1001

Herskovits, A. Z., & Guarente, L. (2014). SIRT1 in neurodevelopment and brain senescence. *Neuron, 81*, 471–483. doi:10.1016/j.neuron.2014.01.028

Ho, B.-C., Milev, P., O'Leary, D. S., Librant, A., Andreasen, N. C., & Wassink, T. H. (2006). Cognitive and magnetic resonance imaging brain morphometric correlates of brain-derived neurotrophic factor val66met gene polymorphism in patients with schizophrenia and healthy volunteers. *Archives of General Psychiatry, 63*, 731–740. doi:10.1001/archpsyc.63.7.731

Jimenez-Jimenez, F. J., Alonso-Navarro, H., Garcia-Martin, E., & Agundez, J. A. G. (2014). COMT gene and risk for Parkinson's disease: A systematic review and meta-analysis. *Pharmacogenetics and Genomics, 24*, 331–339. doi:10.1097/FPC.0000000000000056

Jung-Hynes, B., Schmit, T. L., Reagan-Shaw, S. R., Siddiqui, I. A., Mukhtar, H., & Ahmad, N. (2011). Melatonin, a novel Sirt1 inhibitor, imparts antiproliferative effects against prostate cancer in vitro in culture and in vivo in TRAMP model. *Journal of Pineal Research, 50*(2), 140–149.

Kennedy, B. K., Steffen, K. K., & Kaeberlein, M. (2007). Ruminations on dietary restriction and aging. *Cellular Molecular Life Sciences, 64*(11), 1323–1328.

Kenyon, C. J. (2010). The genetics of ageing. *Nature, 464*, 504–512. doi:10.1038/nature08980

Kim, D., Nguyen, M. D., Dobbin, M. M., Fischer, A., Sananbenesi, F., Rodgers, J. T., . . . Tsai, L.-H. (2007). SIRT1 deacetylase protects against neurodegeneration in models for Alzheimer's disease and amyotrophic lateral sclerosis. *The EMBO Journal, 26*(13), 3169–3179. doi:10.1038/sj.emboj.7601758

Kim, N. W., Pietyszek, M. A., Prowse, K. R., Harley, C. B., West, M. D., Ho, P. L. C., . . . Shay, J. W. (1994). Specific association of human telomerase activity with immortal cells and cancer. *Science, 266*, 2011–2015.

Kremen, W. S., & Lyons, M. J. (2011). Behavior genetics of aging. In K. W. Schaie & S. L. Willis (Eds.), *Handbook of the Psychology of Aging* (7th ed., pp. 93–107). London, United Kingdom: Elsevier.

Lanner, R. M. (1999). *Conifers of California*. Los Olivos, CA: Cachuma Press.

Lanner, R. M. (2002). Why do trees live so long? *Ageing Research Reviews, 1*, 653–671.

Lee, J. A., & Lupski, J. R. (2006). Genomic rearrangements and gene copy-number alterations as a cause of nervous system disorders. *Neuron, 52*, 103–121. doi:10.1016/j.neuron.2006.09.027

*Lee, Y. H., & Song, G. G. (2014). COMT Val158Met and PPARγ Pro12Ala polymorphisms and susceptibility to Alzheimer's disease: A meta-analysis. *Neurological Science, 35*, 643–651. doi:10.1007/s10072-014-1645-4

Liu, B.-L., Zhang, X., Zhang, W., & Zhen, H.-N. (2007). New enlightenment of French Paradox: Resveratrol's potential for cancer chemoprevention and anti-cancer therapy. *Cancer Biology & Therapy, 6*(12), 1833–1836.

Liu, L., van Groen, T., Kadish, I., & Tollefsbol, T. O. (2009). DNA methylation impacts on learning and memory in aging. *Neurobiology of Aging, 30*, 549–560.

Mandelman, S. D., & Grigorenko, E. L. (2012). BDNF val66met and cognition: All, none, or some? A meta-analysis of the genetic association. *Genes, Brain and Behavior, 11*, 127–136. doi:10.1111/j.1601-183X.2011.00738.x

Masoro, E. J. (2005). Overview of caloric restriction and ageing. *Mechanisms of Ageing and Development, 126*, 913–922. doi:10.1016/j.mad.2005.03.012

Mattison, J. A., Roth, G. S., Beasley, T. M., Tilmont, E. M., Handy, A. M., Herbert, R. L., . . . de Cabo, R. (2012). Impact of caloric restriction on health and survival in rhesus monkeys from the NIA study. *Nature, 489*(7415), 318–21. doi:10.1038/nature11432

McCay, C. M., Crowell, M. F., & Maynard, L. A. (1935). The effect of retarded growth upon the length of life and upon the ultimate body size. *Journal of Nutrition, 10*, 63–79.

McCay, C. M., Maynard, L. A., Sperling, G., & Barnes, L. L. (1939). Retarded growth, lifespan, ultimate body size, and age changes in the albino rat after feeding diets restricted in calories. *Journal of Nutrition, 18*, 1–13.

Mesquita, A., Weinberger, M., Silva, A., Sampaio-Marques, B., Almeida, B., Leão, C., . . . Ludovico, P. (2010). Caloric restriction or catalase inactivation extends yeast chronological lifespan by inducing H2O2 and superoxide dismutase activity. *Proceedings of the National Academy of Sciences United States of America, 107*(34), 15123–15128.

Nawrot, T. S., Staessen, J. A., Gardner, J. P., & Aviv, A. (2004). Telomere length and possible link to X chromosome. *Lancet, 363*, 507–510.

Osborne, T. B., Mendel, L. B., & Ferry, E. L. (1917). The effect of retardation of growth upon the breeding period and duration of life in rats. *Science, 45*, 294–295.

Panizzon, M. S., Fennema-Notestine, C., Eyler, L. T., Jernigan, T. L., Prom-Wormley, E., Neale, M., . . . Kremen, S. (2009). Distinct genetic influences on cortical surface area and cortical thickness. *Cerebral Cortex, 19*, 2728–2735. doi:10.1093/cercor/bhp026

*Papenberg, G., Lindenberger, U., & Bäckman, L. (2015). Aging-related magnification of genetic effects on cognitive and brain integrity. *Trends in Cognitive Sciences, 19*(9), 506–514. doi:10.1016/j .tics.2015.06.008

*Ramis, M. R., Esteban, S., Miralles, A., Tan, D.-X., & Reiter, R. J. (2015). Caloric restriction, resveratrol and melatonin: Role of SIRT1 and implications for aging and related-diseases. *Mechanisms of Ageing and Development, 146–148*, 28–41. doi:10.1016/j.mad.2015.03.008

*Rattan, S. I. (2006). Theories of biological aging: Genes, proteins, and free radicals. *Free Radical Research, 40*(12), 1230–1238.

Reiter, R. J. (1992). The ageing pineal gland and its physiological consequences. *Bioessays, 14*(3), 169–75.

Satoh, A., Brace, C. S., Rensing, N., Cliften, P., Wozniak, D. F., Herzog, E. D., . . . Imai, S. (2013). Sirt1 extends life span and delays aging in mice through the regulation of Nk2 homeobox 1 in the DMH and LH. *Cell Metabolism, 18*(3), 416–430. doi:10.1016/j.cmet.2013.07.013

Schaie, K. W. (2013). *Developmental influences on adult intelligence: The Seattle Longitudinal Study* (2nd ed.). New York, NY: Oxford University Press.

Scheibye-Knudsen, M., Fang, E. F., Croteau, D. L., Wilson, D. M., & Bohr, V. A. (2015). Protecting the mitochondrial powerhouse. *Trends in Cell Biology, 25*(3), 158–170. doi:10.1016/j.tcb.2014.11.002

Schneider, A., Huentelman, M. J., Kremerskothen, J., Duning, K., Spoelgen, R., & Nikolich, K. (2010). KIBRA: A new gateway to learning and memory? *Frontiers in Aging Neuroscience, 2*, 1–9. doi:10.3389/neuro.24.004.2010

Shay, J. W., & Wright, W. E. (2011). Role of telomeres and telomerase in cancer. *Seminars in Cancer Biology, 21*, 349–353. doi:10.1016/j.semcancer.2011.10.001

Small, B. J., Rosnick, C. B., Fratiglioni, L., & Backman, L. (2004). Apolipoprotein E and cognitive performance: A meta-analysis. *Psychology and Aging, 19*, 592–600.

Sommer, M., Poliak, N., Upadhyay, S., Ratovitski, E., Nelkin, B. D., Donehower, L. A., & Sidransky, D. (2006). DeltaNp63alpha overexpression induces downregulation of Sirt1 and an accelerated aging phenotype in the mouse. *Cell Cycle, 5*(17), 2005–2011.

Steuerman, R., Shevah, O., & Laron, Z. (2011). Congenital IGF1 deficiency tends to confer protection against post-natal development of malignancies. *European Journal of Endocrinology, 164*, 485–489. doi:10.1530/EJE-10-0859

Sutphin, G. L., & Korstanje, R. (2016). Longevity as a complex genetic trait. In M. Kaeberlein & G. M. Martin (Eds.), *Handbook of the biology of aging* (8th ed., pp. 3–54). London, United Kingdom: Elsevier. doi:10/1016/B978-0-12-411596-5.00001-0

Tchkonia, T., Zhu, Y., Deursen, J. V., Campisi, J., & Kirkland, J. L. (2013). Cellular senescence and the senescent secretory phenotype: Therapeutic opportunities. *Journal of Clinical Investigation, 123*(3), 966–972. doi:10.1172/JCI64098

Tonjes, A., & Stumvoll, M. (2007). The role of the Pro12Ala polymorphism in peroxisome proliferator-activated receptor gamma in diabetes risk. *Current Opinion in Clinical Nutrition and Metabolic Care, 10*(4), 410–414. doi:10.1097/MCO.0b013e3281e389d9

Turan, B., Sims, T., Best, S. E., & Carstensen, L. L. (2016). Older age may offset genetic influence on affect: The *COMT* polymorphism and affective well-being across the life span. *Psychology and Aging, 31*(3), 287–294. doi:10.1037/pag0000085

Van Raamsdonk, J. M., & Hekimi, S. (2009). Deletion of the mitochondrial superoxide dismutase sod-2 extends lifespan in Caenorhabditis elegans. *Public Library of Science Genetics, 5*(2), e1000361. doi:10.1371/journal.pgen.1000361

*Verghese, P. B., Castellano, J. M., & Holtzman, D. M. (2011). Apolipoprotein E in Alzheimer's disease and other neurological disorders. *Lancet Neurology, 10*, 241–252.

Wang, H.-M., Zhao, Y.-X., Zhang, S., Liu, G.-D., Kang, W.-Y., Tang, H.-D., . . . Chen, S.-D. (2010). PPARγ agonist curcumin reduces the amyloid-β-stimulated inflammatory responses in primary astrocytes. *Journal of Alzheimer's Disease, 20*, 1189–1199. doi:10.3233/JAD-2010-091336

Wang, Y.-L., Sun, L.-M., Zhang, L., Xu, H.-T., Dong, Z., Wang, L.-Q., & Wang, M.-L. (2015). Association between Apolipoprotein E polymorphism and myocardial infarction risk: A systematic review and meta-analysis. *FEBS Open Bio, 5,* 852–858. doi:10.1016/j.fob.2015.10.006

Waterson, M. J., & Pletcher, S. D. (2016). The role of neurosensory systems in the modulation of aging. In M. Kaeberlein & G. M. Martin (Eds.), *Handbook of the biology of aging* (8th ed., pp. 161–178). London, United Kingdom: Elsevier.

Webster, M. J., Herman, M. M., Kleinman, J. E., & Shannon Weickert, C. (2006). BDNF and trkB mRNA expression in the hippocampus and temporal cortex during the human lifespan. *Gene Expression Patterns, 6,* 941–951. doi:10.1016/j.modgep.2006.03.009

Witte, A. V., & Flöel, A. (2012). Effects of COMT polymorphisms on brain function and behavior in health and disease. *Brain Research Bulletin, 88,* 418–428. doi:10.1016/j.brainresbull.2011.11.012

Witte, A. V., Fobker, M., Gellner, R., Knecht, S., & Flöel, A. (2009). Caloric restriction improves memory in elderly humans. *Proceedings of the National Academy of Sciences of the United States of America, 106*(4), 1255–1260. doi:10.1073/pnas.0808587106

Witte, A. V., Kerti, L., Margulies, D. S., & Flöel, A. (2014). Effects of resveratrol on memory performance, hippocampal functional connectivity, and glucose metabolism in healthy older adults. *Journal of Neuroscience, 34*(23), 7862–7870. doi:10.1523/jneurosci.0385-14.2014

Yan, W., Zhao, C., Sun, L., & Tang, B. (2016). Association between polymorphism of COMT gene (Val158Met) with Alzheimer's disease: An updated analysis. *Journal of the Neurological Sciences, 361,* 250–255. doi:10.1016/j.jns.2016.01.014

*Yang, T.-L. B., Song, S., & Johnson, F. B. (2016). Contributions of telomere biology to human age-related disease. In M. R. Kaeberlein & G. M. Martin (Eds.), *Handbook of the biology of aging* (8th ed., pp. 205–239). Amsterdam, the Netherlands: Elsevier.

Zhang, Y., Ikeno, Y., Qi, W., Chaudhuri, A., Li, Y., Bokov, A., . . . Van Remmen, H. (2009). Mice deficient in both Mn superoxide dismutase and glutathione peroxidase-1 have increased oxidative damage and a greater incidence of pathology but no reduction in longevity. *Journal of Gerontology: Biological Sciences, 64*(12), 1212–1220. doi:10.1093/gerona/glp132

Zhao, J., Miao, K., Wang, H., Ding, H., & Wang, D. W. (2013). Association between telomere length and type 2 diabetes: A meta-analysis. *Public Library of Science One, 8*(11), e79993. doi:10.1371/journal.pone.0079993

3

The Aging Body and Age-Related Health Conditions

J. Kaci Fairchild, Kari A. Haws, and Christie Mead

Older adults are one of the most diverse segments of the population, yet there are universal physical changes that everyone experiences as they age. In fact, these physical changes are an expected product of the aging process and thus are considered normal. While these physical changes commonly occur, they also increase the risk of developing certain age-related disorders or illnesses that are not considered to be normative aging. This distinction between normative aging and age-related pathophysiology is essential to the care of older adults. Providers must avoid dismissing clinically significant complaints as "old age" while also not overtreating age-associated physical changes as pathophysiology.

The clinical picture of older adults is further complicated by the number of chronic conditions with which older adults may present. Approximately three out of four older adults have at least one diagnosed chronic health condition and a closer examination of that statistic reveals that about 16% of people ages 65 to 79 and 31% of people age 85 or older have at least four diagnosed chronic health conditions (Newman, 2012). These statistics highlight the concept of *multimorbidity*, which is defined as the cooccurrence of two or more chronic health conditions in one person. These multiple physical conditions often interact to create adverse outcomes in this population.

---

*Key references in the References section are indicated by an asterisk.

Aging is largely an unavoidable process and as such, a person's risk for certain illnesses will increase as they grow older. Nonetheless, a growing literature supports the benefit of lifestyle interventions, such as physical activity and diet, that assist with overcoming some of the internal or physical changes that occur with aging, therefore reducing the risk for certain age-related diseases.

The purpose of this chapter is to present a broad and general overview of the structural and physiological changes that occur with aging as well as the underlying pathophysiology of age-related diseases. The body comprises eleven organ systems that include the integumentary, muscular, skeletal, nervous, circulatory, lymphatic, respiratory, endocrine, urinary/excretory, reproductive, and digestive systems. As such, the ensuing sections are arranged by organ system and structured to cover age-related physiological changes and common disorders. We recognize the ambitious nature of this chapter; thus, much of the information provided herein should serve as an overview of this topic. Readers are encouraged to explore the listed references for a more in-depth discussion of this field.

THE INTEGUMENTARY SYSTEM

STRUCTURE OF THE INTEGUMENTARY SYSTEM

The integumentary system is the largest of the organ systems and comprises the skin and its associated structures (e.g., hair, nails, sweat glands, and sebaceous glands). The integumentary system acts as the body's exoskeleton as it is tasked with protecting the body from the outside world. Yet in addition to serving as a physical barrier, the integumentary system also interacts with other organ systems to guard against disease, regulate body temperature, retain bodily fluids, and eliminate waste.

Structurally, the skin has three layers, each of which has a specific function. The outermost layer is the epidermis, which is a thin, yet tough and relatively waterproof layer of the skin. The epidermis is composed of keratinocytes, Langerhans cells, melanocytes, and Merkel cells. Each of these cells assists in protecting the body from the outside world. The majority of cells in the epidermis are keratinocytes, which serve as a barrier against foreign organisms like bacteria, parasites, and viruses (McGrath & Uitto, 2016). Langerhans cells work as part of the skin's immune system in the defense against infection. Melanocytes, located in the deepest layer of the epidermis (also known as the basal layer), produce the pigment melanin (a main contributor to skin color), which filters ultraviolet B (UVB) radiation out of sunlight, thus reducing the risk of skin cancer. Similar to melanocytes, Merkel cells are found in the basal layer of the epidermis. These cells are believed to be associated with tactile sensory perception.

Underneath the epidermis is the dermis, which is the dense fibrous elastic layer of tissue that affords skin's both strength and flexibility while also cushioning the body from stress and strain. The dermis comprises nerve endings, sweat glands, sebaceous oil glands, hair follicles, and blood vessels. The nerve endings found in the dermis work to sense pain, touch, pressure, and temperature. Sweat glands assist with temperature regulation through the production of sweat. As the body is exposed to heat or stress, sweat is produced, which in turn cools the body as it evaporates on the skin. Sebaceous oil glands secrete sebum into the hair follicles. This oily substance conditions the hair while keeping the surrounding skin moist and soft. Hair, which is produced by hair follicles that are found in the dermis, assists with regulating body temperature and also acts as a sensitive touch receptor. The blood vessels in the dermis respond to changes in temperature such that heat causes the blood vessels to expand, which allows the body to release heat, and cold causes blood vessels to contract, which assists the body with preserving heat.

The lowest or deepest layer of the integumentary system is the subcutis. This subcutaneous tissue is a connective layer of fat, which insulates the body from extreme temperatures, provides protective padding, and serves as an energy repository.

AGE-RELATED CHANGES TO PHYSIOLOGY OF THE INTEGUMENTARY SYSTEM

As a person ages, there are structural and functional changes at every level of the skin and in all of the skin's associated structures. The epidermis and dermis layers of the skin grow thinner as does the subcutis layer. In the epidermis layer, the keratinocytes shrink, which reduces skin elasticity. There are also fewer melanocytes, which reduces the skin's ability to filter out UV radiation from sunlight. The skin's immune system is also weakened as there are fewer Langerhans cells, and tactile sensory perception is reduced as the number of Merkel cells also decline with age (Nagaratnam, Nagaratnam, & Cheuk, 2016). In the dermis, sebaceous oil glands produce less sebum, which leads to drier skin. There are also fewer nerve endings, which results in reduced sensation. As the dermis loses blood vessels, the skin is less able to effectively react to temperature change. The cumulative effect of these internally mediated, structural changes is that skin is more easily damaged and slower to heal.

Whereas many of the structural and functional age-related changes that occur to the skin are predetermined by one's genetics, environmental factors often result in premature aging. Specifically, chronic sun exposure has been estimated to account for up to 80% of facial aging as seen in wrinkles, irregular pigmentation, dryness, and blotchy complexion (Uitto, 1997).

COMMON DISORDERS OF THE INTEGUMENTARY SYSTEM

With advanced age, the skin goes through structural and functional changes that make it less resilient and more susceptible to damage. Some of the most common skin disorders include dermatitis and pruritus, shingles, and skin cancer (see Table 3.1).

Dermatitis and Pruritus

Dermatitis and pruritus are two of the most common skin disorders in older adults. Dermatitis, which is also known as eczema, is a collection of disorders that include conditions such as xerosis and seborrheic dermatitis. Xerosis, which is rough or dry skin, is present in most older adults and is the result of reduced production of sebum as well as age-related changes in the surface of the epidermis. If left untreated, xerosis can progress from scales to fissures, inflammation, and infection. Seborrheic dermatitis, also known as dandruff, is a chronic condition that involves red scaly

Table 3.1 Integumentary System: Key Points

Age-Associated Physiological Changes	Common Disorders in Old Age
• Thinning of epidermis, dermis, and subcutis • Reduced elasticity • Reduced ability to filter UV radiation • Weakened skin immune system • Reduced sensation	• Skin diseases frequently occur in older adults • Dermatitis and pruritus are most common complaints in older adults • One in three people age 50 or older will develop shingles • The most frequently occurring skin cancers are basal cell carcinoma, squamous cell carcinoma, and melanoma • Skin diseases in older adults are often due to sun exposure

patches, occurring primarily on the scalp, though they could occur in any area with abundant sebaceous oil glands (Fillit, Rockwood, & Young, 2017). Pruritus is severe skin itching, in the absence of an obvious skin lesion, that is often symptomatic of other ailments including diabetes, anemia, thyroid disease, and drug sensitivity. While dermatitis and pruritus are not life threatening, they are physically uncomfortable and may have a negative psychosocial impact on a person.

Shingles

Shingles, or the herpes zoster virus, is a reactivation of the varicella-zoster virus, which is the same virus that causes chickenpox. Once a person has chickenpox, the varicella virus goes dormant until later reactivated as shingles. The Centers for Disease Control and Prevention (CDC) estimates that over 99% of people age 40 and older have experienced chickenpox, which places virtually all older adults at risk for shingles. After the age of 50, a person's risk of developing shingles increases such that one in three persons will develop shingles at some point in his or her life. Symptoms of shingles include a painful, itchy, red rash, which most commonly appears along a person's trunk. In addition to the pain and discomfort from the rash, older adults are also at risk for postherpetic neuralgia (PHN), which is persistent pain at the site of the rash. As shingles is a virus, there is no cure for it though antiviral medications may shorten its duration and medication may be used to manage pain (Pierwola, Patel, Lambert, & Schwartz, 2017). Persons age 60 and older may choose to be vaccinated against shingles as the vaccine reduces the risk of shingles by 51% and the risk of PHN by 67% (CDC, 2017).

Skin Cancer

Older adults are susceptible to skin cancer due to chronic sun exposure as well as the skin's diminished resiliency and reduced ability to heal that occurs as a person ages. The most common types of keratinocytic skin cancers are basal cell carcinoma, squamous cell carcinoma, and melanoma. Basal cell and squamous cell carcinomas are the most common types of skin cancer, and both are highly curable cancers with low mortality rates. Melanoma represents only 4% of cases of skin cancer though is the most aggressive form of skin cancer with the highest mortality rate. Melanoma occurs more frequently in older adults due to the cumulative effect of UV sun exposure across their life spans (Jemal et al., 2011). Moreover, as men age, their risk for developing melanoma exceeds that of women such that men age 80 and older have three times greater risk than women the same age (American Cancer Society, 2016). There are six types of standard treatment of skin cancer which include surgery, radiation therapy, chemotherapy, photodynamic therapy, biologic therapy, and targeted therapy.

THE MUSCULOSKELETAL SYSTEM

While the integumentary system acts as the body's exoskeleton, the musculoskeletal system serves as its endoskeleton. This system provides the body with movement and mechanical support, protection of soft tissues, and serves as a calcium repository (Fillit et al., 2017). Components of this system include the body's bones, muscles, joints, and the connective tissues (e.g., ligaments, tendons, and cartilage) that support and bind tissues and organs.

AGE-RELATED CHANGES TO THE PHYSIOLOGY OF THE MUSCULOSKELETAL SYSTEM

As a person ages, there are widespread changes throughout the musculoskeletal system. Many of these changes begin in middle age though become much more pronounced in older adulthood. For instance, the total amount of calcium in the skeleton begins to decline in middle age, which results in an overall decrease in bone mass, a process that is greatly accelerated in women postmenopause (Gregson, 2017). The strength of bones is further reduced by microfractures that accumulate in the bone across the passage of time (Todd, Freeman, & Pirie, 1972). This reduction in bone mass coupled with reduced strength results in a weaker, more brittle, and less stable skeleton that is more susceptible to fracture.

Muscle tissue is also greatly affected by the aging process. After the age of 50, the body begins to lose muscle tissue as the amount and the size of the muscle fibers begins to decline at the rate of 1% to 2% a year (Marcell, 2003). By age 60, a person's muscle strength will decline by 20% to 30%. This loss of muscle strength is largely due to microscopic changes in the muscle, which compromise the quality of the muscle fibers (Freemont & Hoyland, 2007). This results in an overall loss of muscle mass and muscle strength, which places increased stress on a person's joints that in turn increases the risk for certain illnesses (e.g., arthritis) and injuries (e.g., falls).

The body composition (i.e., ratio of muscle mass to body fat) also changes with age. While the body's bone density and muscle mass decrease with age, the percent of body fat increases until around age 80, at which point it levels off. In fact, by age 75, a person's muscle mass will be reduced by up to half and the amount of body fat will double (Nagaratnam, 2016). In addition to the change in body composition, people lose height as they age due to changes in skeleton, muscle mass, and connective tissues. This loss of height coupled with changing body composition can lead to in an increase in body mass index (BMI), even in a weight-stable individual (Newman, 2012; Visser & Harris, 2012). Older adults also have less water in the body, which increases the risk of dehydration. This change in body composition coupled with a slowed metabolism increases an older adult's risk for adverse drug reaction as well as their susceptibility to the effects of alcohol. Put another way, older adults' changing body composition (i.e., more fat, less muscle and water in the body) increases their sensitivity to alcohol and certain drugs and medications.

Joints are complex structures that comprise bones, muscles, and connective tissues. Muscles are connected to the body's bones with tendons, which are tough fibrous connective tissues. Ligaments, which are another connective tissue, join the ends of two bones together to form a joint. The ends of the two bones are then covered with cartilage, which is a tissue that reduces friction to promote movement in a joint. As a person ages, each of the structures change in a way that can compromise the overall integrity of the joint. The cartilage grows thinner, and ligaments and tendons become more rigid and brittle. These changes have the overall effect of reducing the joint's resiliency, thereby making it more vulnerable to damage (Beers & Jones, 2004). With age and disuse, joints become stiffer with reduced range of motion, which can then greatly limit a person's mobility.

COMMON DISORDERS OF THE MUSCULOSKELETAL SYSTEM

Musculoskeletal problems are a significant concern for older adults as they can result in substantial pain and functional impairment. The most common disorders of the musculoskeletal system in older adults are osteoporosis and osteoporotic fractures, sarcopenia, and osteoarthritis (see Table 3.2).

Osteoporosis

Osteoporosis is a leading cause of disability in the elderly as it accounts for over 70% of fractures that older adults experience. These fragility fractures, or osteoporotic fractures, happen when an older adult falls from a standing height while engaging in normal activity (Glowacki & Vokes, 2016). The risk for osteoporotic fractures increases with age as the body's bones become less dense and more brittle. The most common osteoporotic fractures are of the hip, vertebrae, and wrist. Osteoporosis is more common in women because they have smaller, thinner bones and have widespread loss of estrogen experienced at menopause. It is estimated that after the age of 50, one

Table 3.2 Musculoskeletal System: Key Points

Age-Associated Physiological Changes	Common Disorders in Old Age
• Reduced bone density • Reduced muscle mass • Reduced height • Thinning of cartilage • Increased rigidity of ligaments and tendons • Stiff joints with reduced range of motion	• Osteoporosis is more common in women than men • After age 50, one in two women will experience an osteoporotic fracture • Sarcopenia affects 20%–30% of older adults • Osteoarthritis is the most common arthritis

in two women will experience an osteoporotic fracture. In a national study of women aged 55 and older, osteoporotic fractures were found to account for 4.9 million hospitalizations over an 11-year period. To put that in perspective, 2.9 million were hospitalized for myocardial infarction, 3 million for stroke, and roughly 700,000 for breast cancer. Thus, osteoporotic fractures accounted for 40% of the hospital admissions in this nationwide sample (Singer et al., 2015). As the effects of osteoporosis are difficult to reverse, much of the focus of the treatments and interventions is on prevention. Such treatment and interventions include exercise, hormone replacement therapy, medication, and a diet rich in calcium and vitamin D (National Osteoporosis Foundation, 2008).

Sarcopenia

Sarcopenia is a disease caused by the slow progressive loss of skeletal muscle mass and function. As the condition progresses, so does the risk for falls and fractures. This is of great concern as 20% to 30% of older adults have sarcopenia. While it is most commonly seen in older adults who are inactive, sarcopenia is most likely due to multiple factors, such as fewer neurons responsible for communication between the brain and muscles; reduction in hormones (e.g., growth factor, testosterone, estrogen); slowed protein synthesis; and restricted caloric intake to support muscle mass (Iannuzzi-Sucich, Prestwood, & Kenny, 2002). The primary treatment for sarcopenia is exercise, with a focus on resistance exercise.

Osteoarthritis

Osteoarthritis is the most common form of arthritis as it is estimated to occur in over 33% of older adults (Lawrence et al., 2008). The joints in the hips, knees, and hands are most frequently affected and the disorder is more common in women than men. Osteoarthritis occurs when the cartilage inside a joint wears down, which results in inflammation, pain, and the eventual loss of cartilage in the affected joint. The causes of osteoarthritis are multifactorial and include aging, overuse, past injury or trauma, and metabolic abnormalities (Fillit et al., 2017). There is also some evidence of a genetic risk (Goldring, 2009). Treatment of osteoarthritis focuses on symptom management through physical activity, weight management, stretching and range of motion exercises, occupational and physical therapy, assistive devices, pain or anti-inflammatory medications, and in severe cases, surgery.

THE NERVOUS SYSTEM

While the integumentary and musculoskeletal systems protect the body, the nervous system is the medium through which the body communicates with the outside world. This system also controls many of the body's inner workings. It comprises two separate systems: (a) the central nervous system that includes the brain, cranial nerves, spinal cord and (b) the peripheral nervous system that includes all other nerves in the body. The nervous system is further divided into the voluntary, or somatic, nervous system, which is all things that are consciously controlled (i.e., moving arms and legs), and the involuntary, or autonomic, nervous system. As the name implies, the involuntary nervous system includes things that are not consciously controlled such as heart rate and breathing. The involuntary nervous system is further divided into three parts: the sympathetic nervous system, the parasympathetic nervous system, and the enteric (i.e., gastrointestinal) nervous system. The central and peripheral nervous systems each has voluntary and involuntary components.

AGE-RELATED CHANGES TO THE PHYSIOLOGY OF THE NERVOUS SYSTEM

As the body ages, the brain and spinal cord lose neurons and begin to atrophy. Neurons are less responsive and may transmit information more slowly. The impact of these age-related changes can be easily seen in the impact on the five senses. The nervous system processes information from the body's sensory organs. There are changes in the structure and functioning of all sensory organs with increasing age, though there is significant variability in the attributes and extent of decline. Potential reasons for the change may be due to decrements in the sensory receptors themselves, but can also be due to changes in the peripheral and central nerve pathways that support these functions (Aiken, 2001). These physiological alterations can lead to changes in the threshold and response time for vision, hearing, taste, and balance. Overall, the declines become more pronounced after age 60, with the average older adult tending to receive, and/or react, to sensory information more slowly. The following sections discuss the age-related sensory changes.

Vision

There are a number of changes that occur through the life span that can contribute to greater visual difficulties with advancing age. Visual acuity begins to decline during middle to late life in part due to decreased ability of the muscle that controls the size of the pupil (Besdine & Wu, 2008). The changes in pupil size result in less light reaching the retina, making it difficult to read written information in lower light. Change in the muscle functioning also results in the eye being slower to constrict and dilate the iris, which can have a negative impact on the eye's ability to adjust to sudden changes in brightness. This change in reactivity for sudden differences in brightness has important implications for increased difficulties when entering or leaving a room, and when going outdoors.

In addition to changes in the reactivity of the pupil, the lens of the eye also shows the effects of age, with yellowing of the lens over time. This change may result in colors looking less vibrant, and greater difficulties distinguishing between colors, especially with the blue spectrum (Salvi, Akhtar, & Currie, 2006). This change creates added difficulty reading letters printed in blue ink, or increased trouble when text appears on a blue background. The change in the transparency of the lens also causes a scattering of light within the eye, thereby creating additional glare. The combination of increased glare and poorer reactivity to changes in light has significant implication for night driving, which can be particularly hazardous.

Another change contributing to poorer vision with age is the hardening of the lenses. Normally the lens will expand or contract in response to visual stimuli in order to focus on the object of interest. Thus, a stiffer lens can make it more difficult to focus on objects or small print close up (Besdine & Wu, 2008).

Hearing

Hearing loss is a common occurrence in later adulthood (Stuck et al., 1999). Due to gradual atrophy of the auditory nerve and damage within the inner ear, hearing acuity exhibits declines starting in early adulthood (Aiken, 2001). These changes can result in greater difficulties hearing sounds (i.e., presbycusis), particularly those in the higher frequency range. Additionally, men tend to experience hearing loss at an earlier age than women, which may be the result of differential exposure to loud noises (Stuck et al., 1999). Unfortunately, many older adults compensate for hearing loss by avoiding social interactions in which hearing is necessary.

Given the common occurrence of hearing problems, and increased isolation for individuals with hearing impairment, there are some general recommendations when communicating with an older adult who has hearing difficulties. While many attempt to speak louder or overarticulate particular words in order to be heard, this approach should be avoided as it can create great distortion in speech sounds, and make it more difficult to be understood (Besdine & Wu, 2008). Instead, it is recommended that one speak in a lower or deeper tone. It is also recommended that background noises be eliminated, in order to decrease the interference from background stimuli.

Smell and Taste

With advancing age, there are significant changes in the olfactory system with one third of older adults suffering from some form of olfactory impairment (Shu et al., 2009) and almost half of those older than the age of 80 having no ability to smell at all (Lafreniere & Mann, 2009). Some of these changes include decreased sensitivity to smells, which can result in a preference for stronger essences and spices, and a decreased awareness of smells that would be unbearable for younger adults including strong body odor and the smell of waste (Aiken, 2001). While increased age has been related to greater olfaction impairment, literature has shown that such changes may be more related to chronic diseases, sinus problems, and medications than age per se (Rawson, 2006). More recent literature has found that healthy older adults with impaired odor identification also showed early signs of Alzheimer's disease (AD), thus indicating that olfactory testing may help identify preclinical AD (Growdon et al., 2015).

Related to changes in olfaction, there are significant changes in taste with age. Some of the changes in taste can be linked to decreases in the number and functioning of taste receptors. Research has shown that in the typical male by the age of 70 there are less than half as many taste buds as in the early 20s (Aiken, 2001). These changes can be present for all taste modalities: sweet, salt, sour, and bitter; however, there appears to be a greater loss for the sensitivity to sweet and salt. With such changes, older adults will also tend to use greater amounts of seasoning (i.e., salt, pepper, and other seasonings) to make up for the changes in taste, which may need to be monitored to avoid worsening health problems (e.g., diabetes and hypertension). Additionally, deficits in taste can also represent a risk factor for nutritional deficiencies and adherence to specific dietary regimens, due to decreased pleasure from food (Schiffman, 1997).

Cutaneous/Skin

The four traditional cutaneous senses are touch, pain, temperature (warm and cold), and pruritic (itch). As previously discussed, touch sensitivity becomes less accurate in older age and is associated with a decline in the number of nerve cells innervating the skin (Aiken, 2001). These losses can comprise an older adult's ability to grasp objects and maintain balance, can change the sensation of pain, and can affect temperature sensitivity. The decrease in the number of nerve cells results in decreased sensitivity to pain (Arehart-Treichel, 1972); however, the change in pain sensitivity is not uniform across the entire body. For example, there is greater loss of pain sensitivity within the hands, feet, and face than within the legs (Wickremaratchi & Llewelyn, 2006). The change in touch sensitivity also has implications for temperature sensitivity. For older adults this change results in decreased ability to adapt or tolerate temperature extremes, especially when coupled with decreased sweat output (Dufour & Candas, 2007). Taken together, these changes can result in older adults having a feeling of discomfort, of being either too hot or too cold, even when the external temperature remains constant. Such changes in the skin have important implications for morbidity and mortality, since impairment in temperature sensitivity and decreased ability to regulate the body's core temperature can cause death due to hyperthermia or hypothermia when in extreme environmental conditions such as cold snaps and heat waves.

Balance/Gait

Beginning by age 50, receptors for the vestibular senses, including cells in the semicircular and otolith organs of the inner ear, which contribute to a sense of balance and posture, show declines with advancing age (Aiken, 2001). These changes result in older adults having more difficulty detecting their body positions and increase the likelihood they will lose their balance. The loss of balance is one of the main factors leading to falls in older adults (Dickin, Brown, & Doan, 2006). Increased risk for falls has implications for quality of life, ability to live independently, and mortality. For example, in 2006 about 1.8 million people were treated for fall-related injuries with 460,000 of those treated needing to be hospitalized (Stevens, Mack, Paulozzi, & Ballestros, 2008). In addition to the potential for hospitalization, in 2005 more than 15,800 people older than the age of 65 were known to have died directly from injuries sustained during a fall (Kung, Hoyert, Xu, & Murphy, 2008).

COMMON DISORDERS OF THE NERVOUS SYSTEM

As the nervous system undergoes widespread change as a result of the aging process, it can be difficult to differentiate normative aging from age-related pathophysiology. Common age-related disorders that affect the sensory organs as well as the brain and peripheral nervous system are described in Table 3.3.

Cataracts, Macular Degeneration, and Glaucoma

A cataract is the clouding of the lens of the eye, which results in visual impairment. Cataracts are very common in older adults; in fact, it is estimated that one in two people age 80 or older will currently have or have had surgery to correct cataracts.

Table 3.3 Nervous System: Key Points

Age-Associated Physiological Changes	Common Disorders in Old Age
• Fewer neurons in brain and spinal cord • Reduced visual acuity • Reduced hearing acuity, particularly higher frequencies • Changes in smell • Reduced number of taste receptors • Reduced accuracy in touch sensitivity • Reduced balance • Overall brain atrophy and reduced volume	• One in two persons age 80 or older has or had cataracts • Macular degeneration is the leading cause of vision loss in older adults • Glaucoma is a group of disorders that damage the optic nerve, resulting in vision loss • Tinnitus (i.e., ringing in ears) affects one in three older adults • Roughly half of people older than age 75 have hearing loss (i.e., presbycusis) • Over 47 million people worldwide have dementia • Peripheral neuropathy is caused by damage to the peripheral nervous system

Cataracts are caused by proteins aggregating on the lens of one or both eyes. This is a gradual process that occurs over time; thus, many older adults may not notice the initial changes. Yet as the proteins build and the cataract grows, vision will grow blurry, thus reducing visual acuity. The biggest risk factor for the development of cataracts is age, though other risk factors include diseases such as diabetes; behaviors such as smoking and alcohol use; and prolonged exposure to sunlight. Treatment for cataracts is informed by the size of the cataract and the severity of its resultant functional impairment. While vision changes due to small cataracts may be helped with assistive devices like glasses or magnification tools, once the cataract grows to a certain size or vision becomes further impaired, surgical removal of the cloudy lens and replacement with an artificial lens is warranted (National Eye Institute, 2015).

Macular degeneration is the leading cause of vision loss in people age 50 and older. It is a type of vision loss that is due to the deterioration of the macula, which is the part of the retina that focuses central vision in the eye and then transmits visual information from the eye through the optic nerve to the brain. Macular degeneration is divided into two types: dry (atrophic) and wet (exudative). It is estimated that the dry type comprises 85% to 90% of cases. The biggest risk factor for macular degeneration is age, though other risk factors include heredity, European American race, and smoking, which doubles a person's risk for developing the disorder. Macular degeneration is incurable, although there are things a person can do to reduce the risk such as physical exercise, avoiding smoking, and eating a balanced, nutrient-rich diet (National Eye Institute, 2015).

Glaucoma refers to a group of disorders that damage the optic nerve and result in visual impairment and blindness. The most common type of glaucoma is known as *open-angle glaucoma*. In this type of glaucoma, a naturally occurring fluid builds up inside the eye, creating excessive pressure that damages the optic nerve. While eye pressure is a leading cause of optic nerve damage in glaucoma, not all persons who have elevated pressure in the eye will develop glaucoma and not all cases of glaucoma are due to elevated pressure in the eye (e.g., normal-tension glaucoma). In the early stages, a person may not realize he or she has glaucoma as there is no pain or visual changes. As the disease progresses, a person will experience peripheral vision loss, which gives the effects of tunnel vision. If glaucoma goes untreated, it can eventually result in blindness. Risk factors for glaucoma include heredity, increased age, and African American race. Unlike macular degeneration, there are treatments for glaucoma, which include medications, laser, and conventional surgery, or a combination of these. Early intervention is essential as the treatments may stop the progression of glaucoma, although they will not correct visual impairment that has already occurred (National Eye Institute, 2015).

Tinnitus and Presbycusis

Tinnitus is persistent abnormal noise when no sound is present and occurs among up to 30% of older adults. Tinnitus may present as a ringing, buzzing, roaring, clicking, or hissing sound that may vary in pitch ranging from a low roar to a high squeal, in one or both ears (Shargorodsky, Curhan, & Farwell, 2010). There are two types of tinnitus: subjective (i.e., audible to only the affected person) and objective (i.e., audible to others in addition to the affected person). Subjective tinnitus can be caused by problems in any part of the ear, auditory nerve, or the auditory pathways in the brain. This type of tinnitus is the brain's response to a lack of auditory stimulation at some juncture in the auditory system and may be associated with neuronal hyperactivity at some point in the auditory pathway. Objective tinnitus is fairly rare, is typically caused by sound being created somewhere in the body, and is usually of vascular or muscular etiology (Moller, 2016). Treatment options for tinnitus are dictated by the severity of the symptoms and may include assistive devices such as hearing aids, and nonpharmacological interventions such as sound therapy or cognitive behavior therapy. There are no recommended medications or supplements for the treatment of tinnitus.

Presbycusis is the gradual loss of hearing that occurs with age. It affects 30% to 35% of people ages 65 to 75 years and the percentage increases to 40% to 50% of people over age 75. This hearing loss is typically for particular frequencies, including the frequencies of sibilants, such as *s, sh,* and *ch,* which are carried over speech frequencies above 3,500 hertz. Older adults may struggle to hear high-pitched sounds and other people's speech may seem slurred. It may also be difficult to hear conversations in situations where the background noise is high, like a restaurant. Presbycusis is often a type of sensorineural hearing loss, which means it is due to damage or impairment in the inner ear. Such damage may be caused by chronic exposure to loud sounds, such as construction, loud music, or any equipment that causes loud noises. It can occur as a result of aging or health conditions such as heart disease, hypertension, or diabetes. Interventions for presbycusis often focus on prevention of damage through the use of ear protection. Once hearing impairment occurs, assistive devices such as hearing aids or assistive listening devices may be helpful (Roth, 2015).

Peripheral Neuropathy

Peripheral neuropathy affects over 20 million people in the United States. It is the result of damage to the peripheral nervous system and includes symptoms such as burning, numbness, and tingling; paresthesia (prickling sensation); allodynia (pain resulting from stimuli that would not normally provoke it); muscle weakness and wasting; and in severe cases, paralysis. Damage to the peripheral nervous system may also impact organ function or result in gland dysfunction, which could impact digestion, sexual function, urination, and sweating. There are over 100 types of peripheral neuropathy and each has its own symptom presentation and prognosis. There are many causes of peripheral neuropathy although the most common include physical causes (e.g., physical trauma or repetitive movements); disease (e.g., endocrine or metabolic disorders, autoimmune disorders, infections, small vessel disease, cancer, kidney dysfunction, or neuromas); or toxic exposure (e.g., medication, environmental, heavy alcohol use). Treatment of peripheral neuropathy is twofold. First, it involves treating the underlying cause, which in some cases is enough to stop the symptoms and allow the nerves to regenerate. Second, symptom management often involves treatment of neuropathic pain through pharmacological (e.g., medications, topical ointments or creams) or nonpharmacological means (e.g., transcutaneous electrical nerve stimulation [TENS]), acupuncture, psychotherapy, or assistive devices; National Institute of Neurological Disorders and Stroke, 2014).

THE CARDIOVASCULAR SYSTEM

The cardiovascular system undergoes progressive, cumulative decline with advancing age, although not all people and not all systems are uniformly affected. Aging of the cardiovascular system is a complex, multifactorial process that is unlikely to be dependent on a single pathway, process, or genetic contribution. With age the cardiovascular system undergoes many physiological changes including alterations in ventricular function, heart rate, cardiac electrophysiology, vascular compliance, and endothelial function.

AGE-RELATED CHANGES TO THE PHYSIOLOGY OF THE CARDIOVASCULAR SYSTEM

Of greatest relevance to aging is the left ventricle of the heart, which is responsible for pumping oxygenated blood out of the heart and into the arteries. Over time this structure loses efficiency, which can contribute to deleterious changes to the entire cardiovascular system. With age, the left ventricle wall becomes thicker, making the heart large and less capable of contracting (Pearson, Gudipati, & Labovitz, 1991). The change to the heart's ventricular wall has the effect of reducing diastolic functioning, meaning there is less blood exiting from the aorta with each contraction of the heart (Nikitin et al., 2006). When coupled with decreased vascular compliance, or the arteries' ability to adjust to changes in blood flow, the arteries become less able to accommodate the flow of blood that the ventricle ejects (Otsuki et al., 2006).

The heart loses some of its resiliency with aging, making the number of heartbeats fewer and more irregular (also known as an arrhythmia, or an abnormal heart rhythm), resulting in a reduction of the blood output volume (Minaker, 2011). In addition, resting heart rate variability, or the variation in the time between one heartbeat and the next throughout a day in response to changes in the environment, has been shown to decrease after the age of 65 when compared to younger individuals across the age spectrum (Umetani, Singer, McCraty, & Atkinson, 1998). This means that with age, the heart beats more slowly, tends to be more irregular, and does not react to the same way to changes in the environment. It also takes longer for the heart of an older individual to return to its normal pumping and beating levels after excitement or exercise (Ogawa et al., 1992).

In addition to changes to the heart, the arteries within the vascular system undergo changes with advancing age, including changes to the distensibility and compliance of the large artery walls. Distensibility reflects the elasticity of the artery, while compliance refers to the buffering capacity, or the ability of the vessel to change in area, diameter, or volume in response to a given change in pressure (McVeigh, Hamilton, & Morgan, 2002; Van Bortel & Spek, 1998).

As the body ages, there is an overall reduction in total body water, thus there is less fluid in the bloodstream. As blood volume also decreases, older adults are at greater risk of dehydration and an increased sensitivity to alcohol when compared to younger adults. There is also a reduction in the number of red blood cells, so older adults do not recover as quickly from blood loss and they can develop anemia. In addition to changes in the number of red blood cells, the blood also has less of certain types of white blood cells, called neutrophils, that reduce the blood's ability to fight off infection (Minaker, 2011).

COMMON DISORDERS OF THE CARDIOVASCULAR SYSTEM

Before discussing some of the diseases that are common in aging, it is important to note that disorders that typically occur in advanced age account for most of the loss of function with advancing age and not age itself (Besdine & Wu, 2008; see Table 3.4).

Hypertension

Essential hypertension is a chronic, age-related condition associated with multiple alterations in the vascular system for which there is no known, single underlying

Table 3.4 Cardiovascular System: Key Points

Age-Associated Physiological Changes	Common Disorders in Old Age
• Thickened left ventricle wall resulting in larger, less efficient heart • Number of heartbeats is reduced and becomes more irregular • Reduced resting heart rate variability • Arteries lose elasticity (i.e., become more stiff) • Reduced body water • Reduced red blood cells and certain white blood cells (e.g., neutrophils)	• Hypertension is defined as a diastolic BP > 90 mm Hg and/or systolic BP > 140 to 160 mmHg • Over half of persons age 70 or older experiences hypertension • Older adults are 10 times more likely to experience CHF than younger adults • Cerebral arteriosclerosis is the hardening of the arteries within the brain, which increases the risk of stroke

BP, blood pressure; CHF, congestive heart failure.

cause (Marin & Rodriguez-Martinez, 1999). While a single underlying factor is not known to cause hypertension, there are a number of factors that appear to be related to its occurrence including diminished compliance of the aorta and large arteries, changes in heart rate, narrowed vessel walls, long-term high sodium intake, obesity, and changes in blood volume, to name a few (see Oparil, Zaman, & Calhoun, 2003 for a comprehensive review). Hypertension is the most prevalent vascular disease in older adults, affecting over 55% of adults aged 70 years and older (Ong, Cheung, Man, Lau, & Lam, 2007). It has been estimated that more than 90% of individuals who are free of hypertension at 65 years of age will develop hypertension during their remaining lifetime (Mosley & Lloyd-Jones, 2009). A diagnosis of hypertension is defined as an average diastolic BP above 90 mm Hg and/or systolic BP above 140 to 160 mmHg with measurements taken over the course of days to months (Chobanian et al., 2003). Hypertension has been shown to be a major risk factor for cerebrovascular disease, increased risk of total mortality, cerebrovascular mortality, coronary heart disease mortality, myocardial infarction, congestive heart failure (CHF), atrial fibrillation, stroke/transient ischemic attack, peripheral vascular disease, and renal failure (Franklin et al., 2001; Haider, Larson, Franklin, Levy, & Framingham Heart Study, 2003; Lewington et al., 2002; Psaty et al., 2001).

Congestive Heart Failure

CHF is a condition in which the heart is unable to pump enough blood to the body's other organs. In CHF, the heart's ability to efficiently pump blood is significantly reduced, which results in blood moving through the heart more slowly. This slowed pace results in greater pressure inside the heart. As the heart works to accommodate this pressure, the walls of the heart may grow weaker, which further compromises the heart's ability to efficiently pump blood. Eventually the tissues being supplied with blood from the heart become congested with fluid. This fluid often builds up in the arms, legs, ankles, feet, lungs, and other organs, causing edema (i.e., swelling). Symptoms of CHF include shortness of breath (due to the collection of fluid within the lungs), chest pain, weakness, and swelling. While many disorders can impact the pumping efficiency of the heart, the most common culprits are coronary artery disease, hypertension, chronic heavy alcohol use, and underlying heart disease (a range of conditions affecting the heart including narrowing of blood vessels, arrhythmia, and congenital heart defects). CHF is primarily a disease of old age as it occurs 10 times more often than in younger adults (Schwartz & Zipes, 2011). Treatment for CHF is often dictated by the underlying cause of the disorder. Common treatments include fluid restriction, reduced sodium intake, diuretics, and medications that improve cardiac performance like angiotensin-converting enzyme (ACE) inhibitors and beta blockers. Other interventions include physical exercise, quitting tobacco use, and management of chronic health conditions that may cause CHF (i.e., hypertension, hyperlipidemia, and diabetes; Ho, Pinsky, Kannel, & Levy, 1993; Schwartz & Zipes, 2011).

Cerebral Arteriosclerosis and Strokes

In addition to the changes noted within the vasculature of the body, there are also diseases related to effects of these vascular changes on the brain. Cerebral arteriosclerosis is defined as the hardening of the arteries within the brain, with onset typically in the mid-60s (Aiken, 2001). Additionally, thickening of the artery walls with advancing age, along with reductions in diameter of the vessels due to accumulation of fatty tissues and calcification, can lead to an interference in the blood circulation to the brain. Without the necessary blood circulation, the brain is depleted of vital nutrients, vitamins, and oxygen, which can increase the probability of blockage or a rupture of the vessels and result in a stroke.

THE IMMUNE SYSTEM

The primary purpose of the immune system is to protect the body from infection and disease. It does this through a complex system of cells that circulate through the body or reside in specific organs. These cells have specific tasks that include detecting problems, interacting with other cells, or performing specific functions. The lymphatic system is part of the body's immune system and is made up of a network of vessels that consists of lymph, extracellular fluid, and lymphoid organs. Lymph is a watery fluid that carries nutrients to cells and waste away from cells. Lymph travels through the lymph nodes, which contain immune cells to help fight infection and filters to remove waste from the lymph. The filtered lymph is then directed back into the bloodstream. Swollen lymph nodes are often a sign of illness as the lymph nodes swell as they work to filter the infection in a process known as lymphadenopathy. Key cells involved in the lymphatic system are found in the bloodstream. These include red blood cells, white blood cells, and platelets as well as plasma, which comprises about 55% of blood (Beers & Jones, 2004). Additional cells are found in the bone marrow, spleen, and thymus.

While the spleen is not part of the lymphatic system per se, it functions in a similar manner. The spleen functions as a filter for blood as it both recycles red blood cells and stores white blood cells and platelets (Beers & Jones, 2004). The thymus is essential to the immune system as it produces thymosin, a hormone that stimulates the production of T cells. Matured T cells are released from the thymus and travel to the lymph nodes where they fight infections and antigens. The function of the thymus is time limited as it is only active until puberty, at which time it begins to shrink and be replaced with fatty tissue. Antibodies are proteins that are produced in the plasma by specialized white blood cells known as B cells, or B lymphocytes. These proteins identify and remove antigens or target viruses and bacteria (Kale, Namita, & Yende, 2014).

AGE-RELATED CHANGES TO THE PHYSIOLOGY OF THE IMMUNE SYSTEM

With advancing age, the immune system becomes less effective in fighting infection due to widespread changes throughout the system. This process is known as immunosenescence (Kale et al., 2014). The immune system is less accurate in distinguishing foreign substances from itself and thus begins to engage in autoimmune responses (i.e., the response of the immune system on its own tissues and cells). There is an overall slowing in the response to infections by specialized cells known as macrophages, which are a type of white blood cell that consumes bacteria and other foreign bodies. The thymus ceases production of T cells at puberty. With age, the remaining T cells respond more slowly, thus inhibiting the body's immune response. Fewer white blood cells are produced by the bone marrow, which further weakens the body's immune response. An important part of the immune system is the complement system, which comprises proteins that work to enhance the ability of the immune system by augmenting the work of antibodies. When faced with infection, older adults produce fewer complement proteins than younger adults. In addition to fewer complement proteins, older adults produce fewer antibodies that are then less able to effectively attach to the antigen. Immunosenescence also impacts the body's receptiveness to vaccinations, although vaccinations are of great importance to older adults (Aspinall et al., 2007). The cumulative effect of immunosenescence is that older adults are more susceptible to infections, those infections tend to be more severe, and vaccines are less effective.

COMMON DISORDERS OF THE IMMUNE SYSTEM

Older adults are much more susceptible to infection due to their weakened immune system. Not only do older adults acquire more infectious diseases, they have worse outcomes once infections manifest, are less likely to return to normal after recovery, and are less likely to respond to vaccination. The most common infections in older adults are respiratory infections (e.g., pneumonia), urinary tract infections (UTIs), and sepsis. In fact, infections account for up to 19% of hospitalizations in the oldest old (85 years old and older). Older adults are also more likely to contract an infection after hospitalization. Infectious diseases have a higher mortality rate in older adults than younger adults. For instance, older adults have a five times greater risk of mortality from a UTI than younger adults (Yoshikawa, 1997).

Older adults have numerous risk factors that, when coupled with their weakened immune systems, increase their risk for infection. For instance, older adults are more likely to live in long-term care (LTC) facilities, which are associated with an increased risk of infection partially due to the number of immune-compromised residents with chronic disease. Other risk factors for infection include chronic disease, malnutrition, polypharmacy, difficulty accessing medical care, and greater use of prosthetic devices and other medical instruments (e.g., catheters; see Table 3.5).

Table 3.5 Immune System: Key Points

Age-Associated Physiological Changes	Common Disorders in Old Age
• Reduced ability to fight off infection • Increased autoimmune responses • Reduced response to vaccinations	• Greater susceptibility to infection and less likely to fully recover from infection • Most common infections are respiratory infections, UTIs, and sepsis • Older adults have numerous risk factors that increase likelihood of infection

UTIs, urinary tract infections.

THE RESPIRATORY SYSTEM

The respiratory system is a group of tissues and organs that work together to facilitate breathing. The main function of the respiratory system is to bring fresh air into the body (i.e., oxygen) and expel waste gases (i.e., carbon dioxide). This system consists of three main parts: the airway, the lungs, and muscles of respiration. These parts are further divided into their subparts. The airway consists of the nose and nasal cavities, the mouth, larynx, trachea, and the bronchi and their branches. The airway is responsible for moving air to the lungs and carrying carbon dioxide out of the lungs. The lungs and associated blood vessels transmit the oxygen to the blood as well as remove carbon dioxide out of the body. The muscles surrounding the lungs work with the lungs to contract and expand to promote breathing. These muscles include the diaphragm, intercostal muscles, abdominal muscles, and the muscles in the neck and collarbone area.

AGE-RELATED CHANGES TO THE PHYSIOLOGY OF THE RESPIRATORY SYSTEM

The respiratory system ages in a similar manner to other organ systems as it becomes less efficient. In addition to the normative aging process, the lungs are also exposed to an accumulation of environmental exposures due to the direct contact with the atmosphere. These exposures result in both structural and functional changes throughout the respiratory system. The lungs experience a decrease in peak air flow and gas exchange, as well as a decrease in vital capacity, which is defined as the greatest amount of air that can be expelled from the lungs after the biggest breath. There is also an overall weakening of the respiratory muscles, which reduces both their strength and endurance. As some of the respiratory muscles grow weaker, this in turn creates an imbalance in the respiratory muscles, which can result in feelings of breathlessness. As the immune system weakens, the lungs are less able to effectively combat pathogens, resulting in more frequent and severe respiratory infections (Davies & Bolton, 2017).

COMMON DISORDERS OF THE RESPIRATORY SYSTEM

The respiratory system experiences structural changes that, when coupled with the body's reduced immune response, can increase an older adult's risk for lung infections like pneumonia and bronchitis. Furthermore, these structural changes to the respiratory system can compound the effects of preexisting cardiovascular or respiratory diseases (see Table 3.6).

Pneumonia

Pneumonia is the second most common infection experienced by older adults. It is an infection or inflammation of one or both lungs that causes the small sacs in the lungs, called alveoli, to fill with pus and fluid, which results in painful labored breathing and reduced oxygen intake. As previously discussed, the higher prevalence of this respiratory infection is due to older adults' weakened immune systems. Cases

Table 3.6 Respiratory System: Key Points

Age-Associated Physiological Changes	Common Disorders in Old Age
• Aging and the cumulative environmental exposures result in structural and functional changes • Reduced peak air flow • Reduced gas exchange • Weakened respiratory muscles • Increased susceptibility to infections	• Pneumonia is the second most common infection in older adults • COPD is the third leading cause of death in the United States • One in 10 older adults has asthma • Lung cancer is the second most common cancer with 2/3 of new cases occurring in older adults

COPD, chronic obstructive pulmonary disease.

of bacterial pneumonia can be effectively treated with antibiotics; however, as viral pneumonia is caused by a virus, antibiotic treatment in these cases is not effective. Treatment of viral pneumonia often focuses on amelioration of the symptoms of the virus rather than the cause of the virus. Severe cases of pneumonia may result in hospitalization. In fact, pneumonia is the second most common cause of hospital admission in the United States, after childbirth. Even after an older adult recovers from pneumonia, there are often long term sequelae like reduced exercise capacity, worsened cardiovascular disease (CVD), cognitive decline, and reduced quality of life. Pneumococcal vaccines are recommended for older adults, although the vaccines may not protect against all types of pneumonia (American Thoracic Society, 2015).

Chronic Obstructive Pulmonary Disease

Chronic obstructive pulmonary disease (COPD) is the progressive restriction of airflow due to emphysema, chronic bronchitis, or both (American Thoracic Society, 1995). COPD affects over 11 million people and is the third leading cause of death in the United States. When a person has COPD, inflammation causes the lungs to thicken and destroys tissue that is responsible for the exchange of oxygen. There is also increased mucus that further tightens the airway. As the flow of air going into and out of the lungs declines, less oxygen is transmitted to the blood and bodily tissues. It also becomes more difficult to remove carbon dioxide from the body. As the COPD progresses, the affected person develops shortness of breath, which results in reduced activity (CDC, 2011b). In addition to shortness of breath, symptoms of COPD include wheezing, chest tightness, and productive cough. COPD is a progressive disorder that worsens over time. Currently there is no cure for COPD although there are treatments and lifestyle changes to manage the symptoms such as stopping smoking and avoidance of lung irritants; dietary intervention and vitamins or nutritional supplements; physical activity; pulmonary rehabilitation; oxygen therapy; medications like bronchodilators, inhaled glucocorticosteroids; and vaccines to prevent other infections like influenza and pneumonia. In severe cases of COPD, surgical interventions such as bullectomy, lung volume reduction, and lung transplant may be beneficial. Cigarette smoking causes up to 50% of COPD cases, followed by air pollution and occupational exposure to irritants like fumes and dust (Salvi & Barnes, 2009).

Asthma

Asthma is a chronic lung disease that causes inflammation and narrowing of the airways. Symptoms of asthma include recurrent wheezing, chest tightness, shortness of breath, and coughing. Approximately 10% of older adults experience asthma. Of those 10%, about half are acquired in late life. Interestingly, up to half of the older adults with asthma have not been diagnosed and of those who have been diagnosed, only a third are treated with inhaled steroids (Enright, McClelland, Newman, Gottlieb, & Lebowitz, 1999). The most common causes of late onset asthma are respiratory infection or virus, exercise, allergens, and air pollution or irritants. Quick-relief medications focus on alleviation of symptoms as they flare up. Long-term control medications work to reduce airway inflammation and prevent chronic symptoms like coughing and shortness of breath. Older adults often take other medications (e.g., beta blockers, aspirin, nonsteroidal anti-inflammatory drugs [NSAIDs]) that may reduce the effectiveness of asthma medications or worsen asthma symptoms; thus it is important for doctors to be aware of all the medications an affected person takes (Hanania & Busse, 2016).

Lung Cancer

Lung cancer is the second most common type of cancer, and accounts for more deaths annually than colon, breast, and prostate cancers combined. Lung cancer mainly affects older adults; fully two out of three new cases are diagnosed in persons age 65 or older (American Cancer Society, 2016). Lung cancer affects not only the lungs, but can metastasize to the liver, bone, brain, and adrenal glands. Older adults often present with bony metastases. The main risk factor for the development of lung cancer is smoking, although 10% to 15% of nonsmokers also develop the disease. Additional risk factors include heredity, exposure to radon, history of radiation therapy, second-hand smoke, environmental exposures, and diseases such as COPD, pulmonary fibrosis, and HIV. Treatment of lung cancer depends on the stage of the disease but may include smoking cessation, chemotherapy, surgery, thoracotomy and radiation therapy, and palliative care (Akgün, Crothers, & Pisani, 2012).

THE ENDOCRINE SYSTEM

The endocrine system plays an important role in regulating the body's organs through hormone secretion. It consists of the major endocrine glands that are the hypothalamus, pituitary gland, thyroid gland, parathyroid gland, adrenal gland, and pineal body, as well as the reproductive organs (e.g., ovaries and testes) and the pancreas. These glands and organs work together to regulate and control bodily functions through the production and secretion of hormones. Hormones are important as they control the functions of certain organs and impact vital processes such as growth and development, reproduction, and expression of sexual characteristics. Furthermore, hormones also influence how the body uses and stores energy.

AGE-RELATED CHANGES TO THE PHYSIOLOGY OF THE ENDOCRINE SYSTEM

As with many other physical functions, certain endocrine functions become more vulnerable to dysfunction or disease with age. This vulnerability arises due to changes in the functions of the endocrine system. For example, with age, there are changes in the responsiveness of tissues, levels of hormone secretion, and hormone release rhythms (Chahal & Drake, 2007). Hormone levels begin to decline around age 30 and continue to decline about 1% a year in subsequent years (Morley & McKee, 2017). Furthermore, as one gets older, changes in the body composition (for example, reduced muscle and increased fat mass) can also affect how the hormones are circulated or metabolized (Anawalt, Kirk, & Shulman, 2013; Chahal & Drake, 2007). The endocrine system relies on many complex systems to be in sync, and when one area is affected, this can cause a ripple effect where many systems are impacted (Chahal & Drake, 2007).

Men and women have similar reductions in reproductive hormones as they grow older. Menopause in women occurs when the ovaries cease production of estrogen. This typically occurs around age 51. Menopause is often preceded by perimenopause, which is a period at which the ovaries produce less estrogen. Perimenopause may occur several years before the onset of menopause. The ensuing widespread loss of estrogen is associated with increased risk of hip fractures as well as decreased quality of life due to the physical side effects of menopause (e.g., hot flashes, night sweats, vaginal dryness, and sexual dysfunction). Older males experience a loss of total testosterone at a rate of 1% a year. Interestingly, it is estimated that half of the decline is due to increased body fat, which occurs as the muscle to body fat ratio shifts with age. The Reproductive System section of this chapter provides greater details on these structural and functional changes that occur after reduced production of reproductive hormones.

In healthy individuals, the pancreas (more specifically, beta cells within the pancreas) produces and releases insulin into the blood stream when blood glucose levels rise. The insulin helps absorb, store, and use glucose for energy. Yet, as part of the aging process, the body can develop *insulin resistance*, which creates a situation in which the body is not able to use insulin effectively and, therefore, requires more insulin to maintain normal blood sugar levels. This requires the pancreas to produce more insulin to accommodate for the insulin resistance; however, when the pancreas cannot produce enough insulin to surmount the insulin resistance, this leads to glucose buildup in the blood and prediabetes and diabetes (National Institutes of Diabetes and Digestive and Kidney Disease [NIDDK], 2014).

Thyroid functioning also changes over the course of the normal aging process. Specifically, human and animal studies have found that thyroid hormone synthesis and secretion both decrease with age. Additionally, of the two thyroid hormones (triiodothyronine or T3 and thyroxine or T4), T3 declines with age. The metabolism and action of thyroid hormones in the body also change with age, with findings suggesting that while T4 secretion is reduced in older adults, the concentrations of T4 remain stable due to decreases in degradation of T4 (Mariotti, Franceshi, Cossarizza, & Pinchera, 1995; Peeters, 2008). In other words, the ability of T4 to catalyze into T3 is reduced. Thyroid-stimulating hormone (TSH) is also known to decrease over the course of healthy aging (Mariotti et al., 1995; Mitrou, Raptis, & Dimitriadi, 2011). These changes, along with other possible factors such as chronic illness or medications, can lead to thyroid problems.

COMMON DISORDERS OF THE ENDOCRINE SYSTEM

Two common endocrine system diseases that can occur with age, diabetes mellitus (DM, type 2) and thyroid dysfunction, will provide examples as to how dysfunction in one system can lead to a host of problems throughout the body (see Table 3.7).

Diabetes

Diabetes is described as a group of metabolic diseases caused by either a *lack of insulin production* by the pancreas or a *reduced ability to use insulin*, which results in high blood sugar levels, or hyperglycemia (NIDDK, 2014; WHO, 2016). Diabetes is divided into two primary categories: type 1 and type 2, or DM.

Type 1 diabetes, which accounts for about 5% to 10% of the diabetic population, is considered an autoimmune disorder and is caused by the destruction of pancreatic-β cells that produce insulin (Atkinson, Eisenbarth, & Michels, 2014; Biessels & Luchsinger, 2009; Bluestone, Herold, & Eisenbarth, 2010; Daneman, 2006). Type 1 diabetes develops earlier in life, with presentation peaking around 5 to 7 years of age and around puberty, with the majority of cases presenting earlier than 18 to 20 years of age (Bluestone et al., 2010; Daneman, 2006). The development of type 1 diabetes has a strong genetic component; however, there may also be an interplay of environmental and unknown factors as there has been a rise in the incidence rates of type 1 diabetes, particularly among children younger than 5 (Atkinson et al., 2014; Bluestone et al., 2010; Daneman, 2006; WHO, 2016). Currently, there is no prevention or cure for type 1 diabetes, though there are effective ways to manage the disease with insulin analogues and monitors (Atkinson et al., 2014; WHO, 2016).

Table 3.7 Endocrine System: Key Points

Age-Associated Physiological Changes	Common Disorders in Old Age
• Changes in body composition impact metabolism and circulation of hormones • Reductions in reproductive hormones • Insulin resistance can increase • Thyroid hormone synthesis and secretion decline	• Type 2 diabetes, or DM, occurs in 30% of older adults • Half of older adults are estimated to have prediabetes • DM is associated with widespread changes in many organ systems • Prevalence of hyperthyroidism (i.e., overactive thyroid) increases with age • Hypothyroidism (i.e., underactive thyroid) is more common in older women • Rates of thyroid cancer have doubled over the past 30 years

DM, diabetes mellitus.

DM (type 2 diabetes) is the most common form of diabetes and is prevalent among older adults, and thus will be the focus of this section. Almost 30% of older adults are estimated to have diabetes, and 50% are estimated to have prediabetes, a state in which blood sugar levels are elevated above normal but below the range classified as diabetes (CDC, 2011a). Studies suggest that the incidence rate will increase substantially (possibly by 4.5 times) in the older adult population (Narayan, Boyle, Geiss, Saaddine, & Thompson, 2006; Strotmeyer & Zgibor, 2015). The cause for this epidemic of DM is thought to be related to increasing rates of obesity that have been observed in Western cultures like the United States. While there are genetic factors that interact with obesity, environmental influences (such as unhealthy eating or overconsumption and lack of physical activity) have strongly impacted rates of obesity. Thus, with the rise of obesity, there has been a related rise in the prevalence of DM (Biessels & Luchsinger, 2009; U.S. Department of Health and Human Services, 2001).

Acute symptoms of DM are due to high blood glucose levels and include polyuria (increased urine production), polydipsia (excessive thirst), weight loss, and blurred vision. In some cases, the person does not experience any symptoms (American Diabetes Association, 2010). While these short-term symptoms may seem harmless, it is essential that these early signs of diabetes are taken seriously, as the long-term damage that occurs over the course of DM is severe and often irreversible. Diabetes slowly damages blood vessels and nerves due to prolonged high blood glucose levels. Although the exact mechanism is not fully understood, complications are associated to the formation of advanced glycation end products (AGEs). AGEs are groups of molecules that are found naturally in humans, as they are formed during sugar reactions; however, in diabetes, the formation of AGEs increases. The accumulation of AGEs is linked to structural changes and complications in vessels and nerves, and the damage can be widespread and life-threatening (Peppa, Uribarri, & Vlassara, 2003). This can include adverse effects to several organs including the brain, heart, eyes, kidneys, and nerves (see Figure 3.1).

In the brain, damage to small blood vessels and fluctuating/high blood glucose levels can lead to cognitive decline and reduced neuronal connectivity. Additionally, narrowing small vessels in the brain significantly increases the risk of stroke (Moheet, Mangia, & Seaquist, 2015). In the heart, DM is highly associated with CVD, which is linked to a host of additional complications including increased risk for heart attack and increased mortality rates (American Heart Association, 2015). In the eyes, damage to blood vessels in the retinal tissue in the back of the eye can lead to a condition called diabetic retinopathy, which can lead to blindness (Biessels & Luchsinger, 2009; Kempen et al., 2004). The kidneys are also affected, as they have more difficulty functioning when blood glucose levels are high, and over time, this can lead to inefficiencies in filtering the blood. As the kidneys begin to fail, buildups of wastes that should be excreted, such as creatinine and urea, cause serious symptoms (e.g., swelling of the legs/ankles or face, vomiting, fatigue, confusion), which may ultimately require dialysis or kidney transplant (American Heart Association, 2015).

Additionally, chronically high blood glucose levels can cause peripheral neuropathy or peripheral artery disease (PAD), caused by blockages or damage to the vessels that supply blood to the parts of the body outside of the heart and brain.

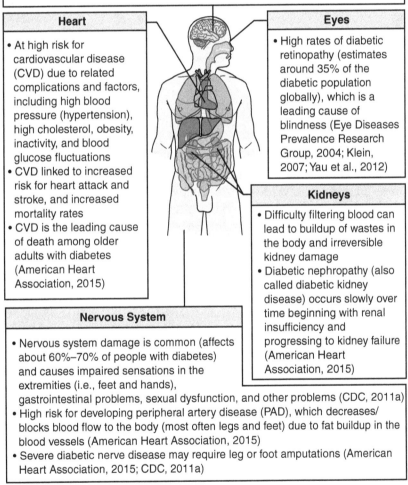

Brain

- Poorer cognitive functioning, particularly in domains of processing speed, memory, attention, and executive functioning (Moheet, Mangia, & Seaquist, 2015)
- Changes in brain structure, increased brain atrophy, and decreased brain connectivity (Cui et al., 2016; Moheet et al., 2015; Musen et al., 2012; Reijmer, Leemans, Brundel, Kappelle, & Biessels, 2013)
- Increased risk for cerebrovascular disease and related complications (i.e., stroke; Karsito, 2008; Lukovits, Mazzone, & Gorelick, 1999)
- Increased risk for dementia and other diseases that affect the brain (including Alzheimer's disease, vascular dementia, and diabetic encephalopathy; Barnes & Yaffe, 2011; Moheet et al., 2015; Soares, Nunes, Reis, & Pereira, 2012)

Heart

- At high risk for cardiovascular disease (CVD) due to related complications and factors, including high blood pressure (hypertension), high cholesterol, obesity, inactivity, and blood glucose fluctuations
- CVD linked to increased risk for heart attack and stroke, and increased mortality rates
- CVD is the leading cause of death among older adults with diabetes (American Heart Association, 2015)

Eyes

- High rates of diabetic retinopathy (estimates around 35% of the diabetic population globally), which is a leading cause of blindness (Eye Diseases Prevalence Research Group, 2004; Klein, 2007; Yau et al., 2012)

Kidneys

- Difficulty filtering blood can lead to buildup of wastes in the body and irreversible kidney damage
- Diabetic nephropathy (also called diabetic kidney disease) occurs slowly over time beginning with renal insufficiency and progressing to kidney failure (American Heart Association, 2015)

Nervous System

- Nervous system damage is common (affects about 60%–70% of people with diabetes) and causes impaired sensations in the extremities (i.e., feet and hands), gastrointestinal problems, sexual dysfunction, and other problems (CDC, 2011a)
- High risk for developing peripheral artery disease (PAD), which decreases/ blocks blood flow to the body (most often legs and feet) due to fat buildup in the blood vessels (American Heart Association, 2015)
- Severe diabetic nerve disease may require leg or foot amputations (American Heart Association, 2015; CDC, 2011a)

Figure 3.1 Long-term problems associated with diabetes mellitus.

Symptoms may include pain and changes in sensation and/or control of their extremities, most often the legs and feet (American Heart Association, 2015; Biessels & Luchsinger, 2009). Damage to these nerves can also lead to autonomic neuropathy, which can cause gastrointestinal problems, sexual dysfunction, and other problems (American Diabetes Association, 2010).

The most common cause of DM is insulin resistance, which is when the body cannot effectively use the insulin it produces (NIDDK, 2014). Diabetes is diagnosed through a blood test, most commonly an A1C test, which provides an average blood glucose measure over the past 3 months (American Diabetes Association, 2010). Normal A1C levels are around 5%. Diabetes is diagnosed when the A1C level is at or greater than 6.5%. Prediabetes, which is often a precursor to the development of diabetes, is diagnosed when A1C levels are between 5.7% and 6.4% (American Diabetes Association, 2010; NIDDK, 2014). People diagnosed with prediabetes are at high risk for the development of DM and other related complications. During this state, however, making healthy lifestyle changes and reducing risk factors can delay or prevent the onset of diabetes (American Diabetes Association, 2010; American Heart Association, 2015).

There are several risk factors for the development of DM. Modifiable risk factors include obesity, physical inactivity, high blood pressure (hypertension), and abnormal cholesterol levels (specifically, low high-density lipoprotein [HDL] and high triglycerides; American Heart Association, 2015; Biessels & Luchsinger, 2009; Mokdad et al., 2003). To provide a sense of the strength of the relationship between these risk factors and DM, the CDC reported that between 2009 and 2010, about 85% of adults with diabetes were obese or overweight, 36% were physically inactive, 57% had hypertension, and 58% had high cholesterol levels (CDC, 2014). Lifestyle changes that help reduce weight and increase physical activity have been shown to adequately manage, or even prevent, DM (Biessels & Luchsinger, 2009). Non-modifiable risk factors for DM include age (being older than the age of 45), racial or ethnic background (people from African American, Asian American, Latino/Hispanic American, or Native American or Pacific Islander decent), family history (first-degree relative with diabetes), and a prior diagnosis of gestational diabetes (American Heart Association, 2015; Biessels & Luchsinger, 2009).

Early detection and management of risk factors are the first steps to preventing or delaying the onset of DM. This includes targeting the modifiable risk factors of obesity, physical inactivity, hypertension, and abnormal cholesterol levels. Weight loss and increased physical activity have been shown across many studies to have positive outcomes of either preventing or delaying the onset of DM or slowing the progression of the disease once acquired (American Diabetes Association and NIDDK, 2002; Biessels & Luchsinger, 2009; Tuomilehto et al., 2001). In patients with cardiovascular risk factors or CVD, management of blood pressure and cholesterol levels is essential. Lifestyle modifications to help with weight loss and increased physical activity can assist with stabilizing blood pressure, although medications are also effective, particularly in controlling cholesterol levels (Grundy et al., 1999). Taking steps to control these cardiovascular risk factors (as well as others, such as smoking) are linked to better prognosis. Glucose monitoring and management is also an important aspect of diabetes management. While weight loss and exercise have beneficial effects on lowering glucose, medications have also been found to be efficacious. Glucose-lowering agents to maintain control of blood sugar levels are essential to preventing long-term consequences of DM (Grundy et al., 1999). The most common DM medications are oral (pill) form, though there are some people with DM who also require insulin injections (CDC, 2011a).

Hyperthyroidism

Hyperthyroidism is a condition where the thyroid synthesizes and secretes too much thyroid hormone (Bahn et al., 2011). The prevalence of hyperthyroidism increases in those older than the age of 60 (frequencies range from 0.5% to 2–3%; Mariotti et al., 1995). Toxic multinodular goiter and Graves's disease are common causes of hyperthyroidism in older adults. Symptoms of hyperthyroidism include appetite loss (or weight loss) and muscle weakness or wasting (Mitrou et al., 2011). There are fewer signs and symptoms in older adults compared to their younger counterparts, which may make it more difficult to detect (Mariotti et al., 1995, 2011). If left untreated, hyperthyroidism can lead to cardiovascular complications, gastrointestinal symptoms (e.g., diarrhea or constipation), insulin resistance, osteoporosis, and neurological symptoms or cognitive impairment (Mitrou et al., 2011). Subclinical hyperthyroidism, which is diagnosed when TSH levels are low but T3 and T4 are within the normal range, is also prevalent among the elderly (ranging from 3% to 8%; Mitrou et al., 2011; Peeters, 2008). Depending on the cause and severity of the hyperthyroidism, treatment may involve radioactive iodine, antithyroid or beta-blocking medications, or thyroidectomy (Bahn et al., 2011; Mitrou et al., 2011).

Hypothyroidism

Hypothyroidism, a condition when the thyroid underproduces thyroid hormones, is also common among older adults (affecting up to 6% of the population older than 65) and is more common in women than men (Mitrou et al., 2011; NIDDK, 2013a). Autoimmune thyroiditis is the most common cause of hypothyroidism in older adults, although treatment (medications or surgeries) for hyperthyroidism can also lead to hypothyroidism (Mitrou et al., 2011; Peeters, 2008). As with hyperthyroidism, hypothyroidism presents slightly differently in older adults and can be difficult to detect. Symptoms may include fatigue, constipation, cold intolerance, CHF, hair loss or dry skin, depression, and cognitive impairment (Mitrou et al., 2011; Peeters, 2008). Subclinical hypothyroidism, which is diagnosed when TSH levels are elevated but T4 remains normal, is also important to detect as it has been correlated with several cardiovascular risk factors and insulin resistance. Hypothyroidism is most commonly treated with the drug levothyroxine, a synthetic thyroid hormone (Mitrou et al., 2011; NIDDK, 2013a; Peeters, 2008).

Thyroid Cancer

The rates of thyroid cancer are reported to have doubled over the past 30 years, and the risk of thyroid cancer increases significantly with age (Davies & Welch, 2006). Estimates have reported up to 50% of people having thyroid nodules by the age of 65. The cause for this increase in thyroid cancer rates is not fully understood, although some studies have suggested that better diagnostic abilities and/or overdiagnosis may be part of the cause (Davies & Welch, 2006, 2014). This is supported by the stability of reported mortality rates from thyroid cancer (reported around 0.5 deaths per 100,000) since the 1970s (Davies & Welch, 2006). The most common type of thyroid cancer is papillary thyroid, followed by follicular thyroid cancer. Most patients with thyroid cancer are treated through a thyroidectomy and radioiodine ablation (Mitrou et al., 2011; Sajid-Crokett & Hershman, 2015).

THE URINARY SYSTEM

The urinary system filters waste and fluid from the blood stream and then removes it from the body. The system includes the kidneys and the urinary tract, which consists of the ureters, bladder, and urethra. Inside the kidneys are filtering units, called nephrons, that filter waste from the blood. The kidneys are capable of filtering 120 to 150 quarts of blood a day to produce 1 to 2 quarts of urine. Each kidney is connected to the bladder by a ureter, which is a thin muscular tube through which urine flows from the kidney to the bladder. The bladder acts as a reservoir and can hold up to two cups of urine. A trio of muscles work together to hold the urine in the bladder. These muscles include the urethra, the internal sphincter, and the pelvic floor muscles. Unlike the kidneys, a person has control over the bladder function. When a person urinates, the brain signals the muscles of the bladder wall to contract and the sphincter to relax, which has the sum effect of pushing urine out of the bladder through the urethra (NIDDK, 2013b).

AGE-RELATED CHANGES TO THE PHYSIOLOGY OF THE URINARY SYSTEM

As the arteries that supply the kidneys with blood grow narrow with advancing age, the kidneys decrease in size. There is also an accompanying decline in the ability of nephrons to filter waste from the blood with age. This has the cumulative effects of slowing the filtering process, although not to a degree that prevents the kidneys from adequate function. However, due to the age-related changes, the kidneys are vulnerable to injury or illness that would further impair kidney function (Minaker, 2011).

While the ureters are fairly immune to the aging process, the bladder and urethra do exhibit age-associated change. The wall of the bladder becomes more rigid causing the bladder to be less elastic, which limits the amount of urine it can store. Bladder muscles also weaken with age, which affects the rate at which urine flows out of the bladder. There may be sporadic contractions of the bladder, which result in instances of urinary incontinence. Older adults may need to urinate more often as the bladder becomes less efficient as it empties, which results in some urine remaining in the bladder. This also increases the risk for UTIs.

There are gender differences in age-related urinary system changes. After menopause, a woman's urethra shortens as its lining grows thinner. The urinary sphincter has less ability to close tightly, thus increasing the risk for urinary incontinence. Men may experience an enlargement of the prostate gland, which may block the urethra. This results in men having the urge to urinate but being unable to effectively void. An untreated enlarged prostate can result in retention of urine and eventually kidney damage (Smith & Kuche, 2017).

COMMON DISORDERS OF THE URINARY SYSTEM

Two of the most common urinary system disorders that affect older adults are UTIs and chronic kidney disease.

Urinary Tract Infections

A UTI is an infection of the urinary system and may involve the lower urinary tract or both the upper and lower tracts. It is highly prevalent in older adults; in fact, it is the most common infection in LTC facilities as it is responsible for one third of infections in that setting (Tsan et al., 2010). UTIs are more common in older women; roughly 10% of women older than age 65 have experienced a UTI in the past year. The prevalence rate increases threefold in women age 85 and older. Risk factors like reduced immune response, exposure to hospital-associated pathogens, and higher rates of comorbidities place older adults at risk for a UTI (Juthani-Mehta & Quagliarello, 2010). With cognitive impairment comes greater challenges in the diagnosis of the infection in older adults. For instance, older adults with an expressive aphasia or severe cognitive impairment may have difficulty communicating with providers as to the presence and nature of their symptoms, possibly preventing early detection and treatment. Nursing home residents are also more likely to present with nonspecific symptoms, which further complicates the diagnostic process (Tsan et al., 2010). Use of antibiotics is the most common treatment for UTIs (see Table 3.8).

Chronic Kidney Disease

Chronic kidney disease is a broad category that includes any condition that damages the kidneys and impairs their function. As the kidneys grow more impaired, a buildup of waste and fluid accumulates in the body, which in turn affects most of the organ systems. Symptoms of chronic kidney disease vary by the stage of the disease. In the early stages of the disease, the symptoms are nonspecific and include anorexia, general malaise, headaches, pruritus, and nausea. As the kidneys grow more damaged, symptoms may include skin discoloration, bone pain, drowsiness or problems concentrating, numbness and swelling in extremities, muscle twitching or cramps, bruising and blood in stool, dehydration and thirst, hiccups, amenorrhea, shortness of breath, sleep problems, and vomiting. Symptoms will worsen over a period of months to years and, as the symptoms progress so slowly, many do not recognize the symptoms until the kidneys are barely functioning. In the final stage of chronic kidney disease, known as end-stage renal disease, the kidneys are no longer

Table 3.8 Urinary System: Key Points

Age-Associated Physiological Changes	Common Disorders in Old Age
• Kidneys grow smaller. • Bladder grows more rigid. • Urinary incontinence may occur due to bladder spasms. • Women are at greater risk of urinary incontinence. • Men may have increased urge to urinate though be unable to due to enlarged prostate.	• UTIs are the most common infection in LTC facilities. • UTIs are more common in women. • Diabetes and hypertension are the two most common causes of chronic kidney disease.

LTC, long-term care; UTI, urinary tract infection.

able to process waste and excess fluid (Abboud & Henrich, 2010). The two most common causes of chronic kidney disease are diabetes and hypertension. Treatments for chronic kidney disease include management of hypertension and hyperlipidemia, as well as lifestyle changes like abstinence from tobacco and physical exercise. Older adults with chronic kidney disease may also work with a dietician to develop a special diet that limits salt, potassium, phosphorous, protein, and fluids (Fogarty & Tall, 2012).

THE REPRODUCTIVE SYSTEM

The primary function of the reproductive system is to produce sex cells and hormones. The female reproductive system consists of the ovaries, fallopian tubes, uterus, cervix, and the vagina. Other parts of the body affect the function of the female reproductive system such as the hypothalamus, pituitary gland, and the adrenal glands. The male reproductive system consists of the penis, scrotum, testes, epididymis, vas deferens, urethra, prostate, and seminal vesicles.

AGE-RELATED CHANGES TO THE PHYSIOLOGY OF THE REPRODUCTIVE SYSTEM

Age-associated changes occur in both the female and male reproductive systems. Women have a finite number of usable eggs. As the usable eggs are depleted, the ovaries stop producing estrogen and progesterone. This results in less frequent menstruation and ovulation. Once a woman has been without a menstrual cycle for a year, she is considered to be in menopause. This typically occurs around age 52. Some symptoms of menopause include irregular menstrual periods, hot flashes, mood changes, irritability, sleep disturbances, night sweats, and difficulty concentrating. These symptoms become less frequent and less severe after menopause, although the reduced estrogen can negatively impact a woman's health. There are other physical changes that are associated with menopause including changes to the reproductive tract such as vaginal atrophy, reduction in the size of sex organs, and reduced libido. The urinary tract also experiences changes as the urethra becomes thinner and shorter, which in turn increases a woman's risk for UTI as well as urinary incontinence. As the body produces less estrogen, the skin will become more thin, dry, and vulnerable to injury. An additional consequence of reduced estrogen is an increased risk of osteoporosis as bones become less dense. Breast tissue may also change with age as the connective tissue in the breast decreases and fibrous tissue is replaced with fat, leading to sagging and less firm breasts. Finally, women may experience increased low-density lipoprotein (LDL) cholesterol, which places them at risk of atherosclerosis and coronary artery disease (Nagaratnam, Nagaratnam, & Cheuk, 2016).

With advanced age, men experience gradual changes in sexual functioning. Some changes include declines in the frequency, duration, and rigidity of the erection. Testosterone also declines with age, which reduces libido. Additional changes include reduced sensitivity in the penis, reduced volume of ejaculation, reduced forewarning of ejaculation, orgasms without ejaculation, more rapid detumescence, and longer refractory periods (Nagaratnam et al., 2016).

COMMON DISORDERS OF THE REPRODUCTIVE SYSTEM

Older men and women experience higher rates of cancer in the reproductive system. The most common cancers of the reproductive system are uterine and ovarian cancer (in females) and prostate cancer (in men; see Table 3.9).

Uterine and Ovarian Cancer

Uterine cancer is a gynecologic cancer that begins when cells in the uterus proliferate and change to form a malignant tumor. This type of cancer is the most common gynecologic cancer as it affects over 60,000 women annually. The disorder affects a large number of older adults as the median age of diagnosis is 60 years old. Uterine cancer is more common in European American women although African Americans are more likely to die from uterine cancer. Symptoms of uterine cancer include unusual vaginal bleeding, difficulty or pain when urinating, pain during intercourse, and pain in the pelvic area. Five-year survival rates for uterine cancer are 82% and 10-year survival rates are 79%, indicating that uterine cancer does respond to treatments that may include surgery, radiation, chemotherapy, and hormone therapy (American Cancer Society, 2016).

Ovarian cancer is a gynecologic cancer that originates in cells in the ovaries, fallopian tube, or the peritoneum. Over 22,000 women in the Unites States are diagnosed with ovarian cancer annually. Survival rates of ovarian cancer are lower than uterine cancer; the 5-year survival rate for women age 65 and older is 28%. Women with a family history of breast or ovarian cancer can develop ovarian cancer, and women with certain genetic conditions (e.g., Lynch syndrome, Peutz–Jeghers syndrome, nevoid basal cell carcinoma, and ataxia-telangiectasia) develop ovarian cancer at higher rates. In addition to age and certain hereditary and genetic conditions, women who are obese have a 50% greater risk of developing ovarian cancer and have a higher mortality risk from the disease. Women of North America, Northern European, and Ashkenazi Jewish heritage have a greater risk of developing ovarian cancer as do women who have not had children or have not taken birth control. As with other cancers, choice of treatment for ovarian cancer is dictated by the stage at which

Table 3.9 Reproductive System: Key Points

Age-Associated Physiological Changes	Common Disorders in Old Age
• Menopause occurs in women around age 52. • Reduced estrogen increases risk of osteoporosis. • Women experience increases in LDL cholesterol. • Testosterone declines in men with age, as does libido.	• Uterine cancer is the most common gynecologic cancer. • Survival rates of ovarian cancer are lower than uterine cancer. • Prostate cancer is the fourth most common disorder in men. • One in 39 men will die from prostate cancer, making it the second most deadly cancer.

LDL, low-density lipoprotein.

the cancer is diagnosed. Recommended treatments include surgery, chemotherapy, hormone therapy, targeted therapy to attack specific cancer cells, and radiation therapy (American Cancer Society, 2016).

Prostate Cancer

Prostate cancer is the fourth most common disorder in men older than age 65 and the second most common cancer in men, after skin cancer. It affects up to 30% of men aged 50 and older and 90% of men at age 90 or older (Nagaratnam et al., 2016). In addition to being highly prevalent, prostate cancer is the second leading cause of cancer death in men as approximately one out of 39 will die from prostate cancer. Prostate cancer occurs primarily in older men; the average age of diagnosis is 66. It is also more common in African American men and Caribbean men of African ancestry. There appears to be a hereditary link with prostate cancer as having an immediate relative (i.e., father or brother) who has it doubles a person's risk for developing it. Affected individuals often do not have symptoms in the early stage of the disease but as it progresses they may experience problems urinating, blood in the urine, erectile dysfunction, bone pain, or weakness or numbness in lower extremities. As with other types of cancer, treatment of prostate cancer is often dictated by the stage of the cancer. Treatments for prostate cancer include active surveillance, surgery, radiation therapy, chemotherapy, cryotherapy, hormone therapy, vaccine treatment, and bone directed treatment. The 5-year relative survival rate for prostate cancer is almost 100% and that only declines slightly to 95% at the 15-year relative survival rate (American Cancer Society, 2016).

THE DIGESTIVE SYSTEM

The digestive system is responsible for ingestion and digestion of food, absorption of nutrients, and discharge of residual waste. The digestive system consists of the digestive tract as well as several organs outside of the digestive tract. The digestive tract comprises the mouth, throat and esophagus, stomach, small intestine, large intestine (or colon), rectum, and anus. Other key organs of the digestive system that lay outside of the digestive tract include the pancreas, the liver, and the gallbladder. The digestive system is also responsible for other functions beyond those listed previously. For instance, organs in the digestive tract produce blood clotting factors and hormones, remove harmful substances from the bloodstream, and metabolize medications.

AGE-RELATED CHANGES TO THE PHYSIOLOGY OF THE DIGESTIVE SYSTEM

With advanced age, there are structural changes throughout the digestive tract and the organs of the digestive system, although many of these changes do not result in functional impairment. Esophageal contractions weaken as does the esophageal sphincter. The lining of the stomach is more susceptible to damage, which increases a person's risk for peptic ulcers. As the stomach becomes less elastic, the amount of food that it can accommodate decreases as does the rate at which the stomach passes food to the small intestine. While the structure of the small intestine undergoes minimal change with aging, changes inside the intestine result in older adults being more vulnerable to lactose intolerance. The colon is resistant to the effects of age, although the rectum enlarges. Organs associated with the digestive system also undergo some age-related changes. Both the liver and the pancreas decrease in weight. The liver also becomes less able to metabolize substances and less resistant to the effects of stress while also recovering more slowly from damage (Feldstein, Beyda, & Katz, 2017).

COMMON DISORDERS OF THE DIGESTIVE SYSTEM

Overall, the digestive system is fairly resistant to the aging process, although aging is a factor in the development of some digestive system disorders. Some of the most common disorders of the digestive system that affect older adults are constipation and gastritis (see Table 3.10).

Constipation

Constipation is a condition where a person has fewer than three bowel movements a week, has small, dry, hard, painful stool, or has bowel movements that are difficult to pass. Constipation is considered chronic when it occurs over several weeks. Constipation is common in older adults for several reasons including reduced physical activity, reduced fluid intake, dietary changes, reduced motility in the large intestine, and drug side effects. Up to one third of persons age 60 or older have at least occasional constipation and the prevalence increases to fully half of LTC facility residents (Bharucha, Pemberton, & Locke, 2013). Treatments for constipation involve lifestyle changes as well as medication. Examples of recommended lifestyle changes include increased fiber intake and increased physical activity. There are different types of medications to treat constipation. These include over-the-counter laxatives as well as prescription medication that increases water in the intestine. Surgery is an option for more severe cases of chronic constipation or if the constipation is due to posterior prolapse, anal fissure, or anal stenosis.

Gastritis

Gastritis is a condition in which the lining of the stomach grows inflamed. Symptoms of gastritis are indigestion, nausea, vomiting, and feelings of fullness in the upper abdomen. Older adults have a heightened risk for gastritis due to the thinning of their

Table 3.10 Digestive System: Key Points

Age-Associated Physiological Changes	Common Disorders in Old Age
• Weakened esophageal contractions and sphincter • Less elastic stomach, which can accommodate less food • Increased vulnerability to lactose intolerance • Enlarged rectum • Lighter liver and pancreas	• Up to one third of older adults experience constipation • Older adults have increased risk of gastritis

stomach lining as well as their reduced immune response. Older adults also have a greater incidence of the bacterial infection *H. pylori* in addition to higher use of pain relievers like aspirin, ibuprofen, and naproxen, both of which increase the risk of gastritis. Other risk factors include chronic heavy alcohol use; stress; and autoimmune disorders. Treatment choice for gastritis is often predicated on the cause. Possible treatments include: antibiotics used to kill bacteria like *H. pylori*; medications that block acid production and promote healing of the gut; medications that reduce acid production; and antacids that neutralize stomach acid (Feldstein et al., 2017).

CONCLUSION

Older adults experience a myriad of physiological changes as they age. While some of these physiological changes are benign, other changes increase the risk of age-associated pathophysiological changes, which can result in significant functional impairment or morbidity. These pathophysiological changes are not to be considered part of the normative aging process. Thus, it is essential that providers distinguish between the two states.

DISCUSSION QUESTIONS

1. State the 11 organ systems that make up the body.

2. Describe why it is important to understand the various physical health conditions that may impact older adults.

3. Describe age-related changes in three of the systems.

4. Describe common age-related disorders in three of the systems.

5. Describe the condition of DM, the risk factors for it, and how it can be prevented.

REFERENCES

Abboud, H., & Henrich, W. L. (2010). Clinical practice. Stage IV chronic kidney disease. *New England Journal of Medicine, 362*, 56–65.

Aiken, L. R. (2001). *Aging and later life: Growing old in modern society*. Springfield, IL: Charles C Thomas.

Akgün, K. M., Crothers, K., & Pisani, M. (2012). Epidemiology and management of common pulmonary diseases in older persons. *The Journals of Gerontology Series A: Biological Sciences and Medical Sciences, 67A*(3), 276–291.

American Cancer Society. (2016). *Cancer facts & figures 2016*. Atlanta, GA: American Cancer Society.

American Diabetes Association. (2010). Diagnosis and classification of diabetes mellitus. *Diabetes Care, 33*(Suppl. 1), S62–S69. doi:10.2337/dc10-S062

American Diabetes Association and National Institute of Diabetes, Digestive, and Kidney Diseases. (2002). The prevention or delay of type 2 diabetes. *Diabetes Care, 25*, 742–749.

American Heart Association. (2015, September). About diabetes. Retrieved from http://www .heart.org/HEARTORG/Conditions/Diabetes/AboutDiabetes/About-Diabetes_UCM_002032 _Article.jsp#.V4vQ31feOOo

American Thoracic Society. (1995). Standards for the diagnosis and care of patients with Chronic obstructive pulmonary disease. *American Journal of Respiratory and Critical Care Medicine, 152,* S77–S121.

American Thoracic Society. (2015). Top 20 pneumonia facts. Retrieved from https://www.thoracic .org/patients/patient-resources/resources/top-pneumonia-facts.pdf

Anawalt, B. D., Kirk, S., & Shulman, D. (2013, May). Factors that affect endocrine function. Retrieved from http://www.hormone.org/hormones-and-health/the-endocrine-system/factors-that -affect-endocrine-function

Arehart-Treichel, J. (1972). How you age. *Science News, 102,* 412–413.

Aspinall, R., Del Giudice, G., Effros, R. B., Grubeck-Loebenstein, B., & Sambhara, S. (2007). Challenges for vaccination in the elderly. *Immunity and Aging, 4,* 9. doi:10.1186/1742-4933-4-9

Atkinson, M. A., Eisenbarth, G. S., & Michels, A. W. (2014). Type 1 diabetes. *The Lancet, 383,* 69–82.

Bahn, R. S., Burch, H. B., Cooper, D. S., Garber, J. R., Greenlee, M. C., Klein, I., . . . American Association of Clinical, E. (2011). Hyperthyroidism and other causes of thyrotoxicosis: management guidelines of the American Thyroid Association and American Association of Clinical Endocrinologists. *Thyroid, 21,* 593–646.

Barnes, D. E., & Yaffe, K. (2011). The projected effect of risk factor reduction on Alzheimer's disease prevalence. *The Lancet Neurology, 10,* 819–828.

Beers, M. H., & Jones, T. V. (2004). *The Merck manual of health & aging.* Whitehouse Station, NJ: Merck Research Laboratories.

Besdine, R. W., & Wu, D. (2008). Aging of the human nervous system: What do we know? *Rhode Island Medical Journal, 91*(5), 129–131.

Bharucha, A. E., Pemberton, J. H., & Locke, G. R., 3rd. (2013). American Gastroenterological Association technical review on constipation. *Gastroenterology, 144,* 218–238.

Biessels, G. J., & Luchsinger, J. A. (2009). Diabetes and the brain. New York, NY: Humana Press.

Bluestone, J. A., Herold, K., & Eisenbarth, G. (2010). Genetics, pathogenesis and clinical interventions in type 1 diabetes. *Nature, 464,* 1293–1300.

Centers for Disease Control and Prevention. (2011a). National diabetes fact sheet: national estimates and general information on diabetes and prediabetes in the United States. Retrieved from https://www.cdc.gov/diabetes/pubs/pdf/ndfs_2011.pdf

Centers for Disease Control and Prevention. (2011b). *Public health strategic framework for COPD prevention.* Atlanta, GA: Author.

Centers for Disease Control and Prevention. (2014, October). Age-adjusted percentage of adults aged 18 years or older with diagnosed diabetes who have risk factors for complications, United States, 2010. Retrieved from http://www.cdc.gov/diabetes/statistics/comp/fig10.htm

Centers for Disease Control and Prevention. (2017). What everyone should know about shingles vaccine. Retrieved from https://www.cdc.gov/vaccines/vpd/shingles/public/index.html

Chahal, H. S., & Drake, W. M. (2007). The endocrine system and ageing. *The Journal of Pathology, 211*(2), 173–180.

Chobanian, A. V., Bakris, G. L., Black, H. R., Cushman, W. C., Green, L. A., Izzo, J. L., Jr., . . . National High Blood Pressure Education Program Coordinating, C. (2003). Seventh report of the Joint National Committee on Prevention, Detection, Evaluation, and Treatment of High Blood Pressure. *Hypertension, 42,* 1206–1252.

*Cui, Y., Li, S. F., Gu, H., Hu, Y. Z., Liang, X., Lu, C. Q., . . . Teng, G. J. (2016). Disrupted brain connectivity patterns in patients with type 2 diabetes. *American Journal of Neuroradiology.* doi:10.3174/ajnr.A4858

Daneman, D. (2006). Type 1 diabetes. *The Lancet, 367,* 847–858.

Davies, G. A., & Bolton, C. E. (2010). Age-related changes in the respiratory system. In H. M. Fillit, K. Rockwood, & K. Woodhouse (Eds.), *Brocklehurst's textbook of geriatric medicine and gerontology* (7th ed., Chapter 17). Philadelphia, PA: Elsevier Saunders.

Davies, L., & Welch, H. G. (2006). Increasing incidence of thyroid cancer in the United States, 1973–2002. *Journal of the American Medical Association, 295,* 2164–2167.

Davies, L., & Welch, H. G. (2014). Current thyroid cancer trends in the United States. *Journal of the American Medical Association Otolaryngology Head and Neck Surgery, 140,* 317–322.

Dickin, D. C., Brown, L. A., & Doan, J. B. (2006). Age-dependent differences in the time course of postural control during sensory perturbations. *Aging and Clinical Experimental Research, 18,* 94–99.

Dufour, A., & Candas, V. (2007). Ageing and thermal responses during passive heat exposure: sweating and sensory aspects. *European Journal of Applied Physiology, 100,* 19–26.

Enright, P. L., McClelland, R. L., Newman, A. B., Gottlieb, D. J., & Lebowitz, M. D. (1999). Under-diagnosis and undertreatment of asthma in the elderly. *Chest, 116,* 603–613.

Feldstein, R., Beyda, D. J., & Katz, S. (2017). Aging and the gastrointestinal system. In H. M. Fillit, K. Rockwood, & J. Young (Eds.), *Brocklehurst's textbook of geriatric medicine and gerontology* (8th ed., pp. 127–132). Philadelphia, PA: Elsevier.

Fillit, H. M., Rockwood, K., & Young, J. (2017). *Brocklehurst's textbook of geriatric medicine and gerontology* (8th ed.). Philadelphia, PA: Elsevier.

Fogarty, D. G., & Tall, M. W. (2012). A stepped care approach to the management of chronic kidney disease. In M. W. Taal, G. M. Chertow, P. A. Marsden, A. Skorecki, A. S. L. Yu, & B. M. Brenner, (Eds.), *Brenner and Rector's the kidney* (9th ed. pp. 2205–2239). Philadelphia, PA: Elsevier Saunders.

*Franklin, S. S., Larson, M. G., Khan, S. A., Wong, N. D., Leip, E. P., Kannel, W. B., & Levy, D. (2001). Does the relation of blood pressure to coronary heart disease risk change with aging? The Framingham Heart Study. *Circulation, 103,* 1245–1249.

Freemont, A., & Hoyland, J. (2007). Morphology, mechanisms and pathology of musculoskeletal ageing. *Journal of Pathology, 211,* 252–259. doi:10.1002/path.2097

Glowacki, J., & Vokes, T. (2016). Osteoporosis and mechanisms of skeletal aging. In F. Sierra & R. Kohanski (Eds.), *Advances in geroscience* (pp. 277–308). New York, NY: Springer.

Goldring, S. R. (2009). Role of bone in osteoarthritis pathogenesis. *Medical Clinics of North America, 93*(1), 25–35.

Gregson, C. (2017). Bone and joint aging. In H. M. Fillit, K. Rockwood, & J. Young (Eds.), *Brocklehurst's textbook of geriatric medicine and gerontology* (8th ed., pp. 120–126.e2). Philadelphia, PA: Elsevier.

*Growdon, M. E., Schultz, A. P., Dagley, A. S., Amariglio, R. E., Hedden, T., Rentz, D. M., . . . Marshall, G. A. (2015). Odor identification and Alzheimer disease biomarkers in clinically normal elderly. *Neurology, 84,* 2153–2160.

Grundy, S. M., Benjamin, I. J., Burke, G. L., Chait, A., Eckel, R. H., Howard, B. V., . . . Sowers, J. R. (1999). Diabetes and cardiovascular disease a statement for healthcare professionals from the American Heart Association. *Circulation, 100,* 1134–1146.

Haider, A. W., Larson, M. G., Franklin, S. S., Levy, D., & Framingham Heart Study. (2003). Systolic blood pressure, diastolic blood pressure, and pulse pressure as predictors of risk for congestive heart failure in the Framingham Heart Study. *Annals of Internal Medicine, 138,* 10–16.

Hanania, N. A., & Busse, P. (2016). Asthma and aging. In F. Sierra & R. Kohanski (Eds.), *Advances in geroscience* (pp. 397–429). New York, NY: Springer.

Ho, K. K., Pinsky J. L., Kannel, W. B., & Levy, D. (1993). The epidemiology of heart failure: The Framingham Study. *Journal of American College of Cardiology, 22*(4, Suppl. A), 6A–13A.

Iannuzzi-Sucich, M., Prestwood, K. M., & Kenny, A. M. (2002). Prevalence of sarcopenia and predictors of skeletal muscle mass in healthy, older men and women. *The Journals of Gerontology: Series A, 57*(12), M772–M777.

Jemal, A., Bray, F., Center, M. M., Ferlay, J., Ward, E., & Forman, D. (2011). Global cancer statistics. *CA: A Cancer Journal for Clinicians, 61,* 69–90. doi:10.3322/caac.20107

Juthani-Mehta, M., & Quagliarello, V. J. (2010). Infectious diseases in the nursing home setting: Challenges and opportunities for clinical investigation. *Clinical Infectious Diseases, 51,* 931–936.

Kale, S. S., Namita, A., & Yende, S. (2012). Aging, infection, and immunity. In A. B. Newman, & J. A. Cauley (Eds.), *The epidemiology of aging* (pp. 237–253). Dordrecht, the Netherlands: Springer.

Karsito, S. D. (2008). Diabetes and stroke. *Acta Medica Indonesiana, 40*(3), 151–158.

Kempen, J. H., O'Colmain, B. J., Leske, M. C., Haffner, S. M., Klein, R., Moss, S. E., . . . Hamman, R. F. (2004). The prevalence of diabetic retinopathy among adults in the United States. *Archives of Ophthalmology, 122,* 552–563.

Klein, B. E. (2007). Overview of epidemiologic studies of diabetic retinopathy. *Ophthalmic Epidemiology, 14*, 179–183.

Kung, H. C., Hoyert, D. L., Xu, J., & Murphy, S. L. (2008). Deaths: Final data for 2005. *National Vital Statistics Report, 56*, 1–120.

Lafreniere, D., & Mann, N. (2009). Anosmia: Loss of smell in the elderly. *Otolaryngologic Clinics of North America, 42*, 123–131, x.

Lawrence, R. C., Felson, D. T., Helmick, C. G., Arnold, L. M., Choi, H., Deyo, R., . . . National Arthritis Data Workgroup. (2008). Estimates of the prevalence of arthritis and other rheumatic conditions in the United States: Part II. *Arthritis & Rheumatism, 58*, 26–35.

Lewington, S., Clarke, R., Qizilbash, N., Peto, R., Collins, R., & Prospective Studies Collaboration. (2002). Age-specific relevance of usual blood pressure to vascular mortality: A meta-analysis of individual data for one million adults in 61 prospective studies. *Lancet, 360*, 1903–1913.

Lukovits, T. G., Mazzone, T. M., & Gorelick, T. M. (1999). Diabetes mellitus and Cerebrovascular Disease. *Neuroepidemiology, 18*, 1–14.

Marcell, T. J. (2003). Sarcopenia: Causes, consequences, and preventions. *The Journals of Gerontology: Series A, 10*(1), M911–M916.

Marin, J., & Rodriguez-Martinez, M. A. (1999). Age-related changes in vascular responses. *Experimental Gerontology, 34*, 503–512.

Mariotti, S., Franceschi, C., Cossarizza, A., & Pinchera, N. (1995). The aging thyroid. *Endocrine, 16*, 686–715.

McGrath, J. A., & Uitto, J. (2016). Structure and function of the skin. In C. Griffiths, J. Barker, T. Bleiker, R. Chalmers, & D. Creamer (Eds.), *Rook's textbook of dermatology* (9th ed.). Hoboken, NJ: John Wiley.

McVeigh, G. E., Hamilton, P. K., & Morgan, D. R. (2002). Evaluation of mechanical arterial properties: Clinical, experimental and therapeutic aspects. *Clinical Science, 102*, 51–67.

Minaker, K. L. (2011). Common clinical sequelae of aging. In L. Goldman & A. I. Schafer (Eds.), *Goldman's Cecil medicine* (24th ed., pp. 104–110). Philadelphia, PA: Elsevier Saunders.

Mitrou, P., Raptis, S. A., & Dimitriadis, G. (2011). Thyroid disease in older people. *Maturitas, 70*, 5–9.

*Moheet, A., Mangia, S., & Seaquist, E. R. (2015). Impact of diabetes on cognitive function and brain structure. *Annals of the New York Academy of Sciences, 1353*, 60–71.

Mokdad, A. H., Ford, E. S., Bowman, B. A., Dietz, W. H., Vinicor, F., Bales, V. S., & Marks, J. S. (2003). Prevalence of obesity, diabetes, and obesity-related health risk factors, 2001. *Journal of the American Medical Association, 289*, 76–79.

Moller, A. R. (2016). Sensorineural tinnitus: Its pathology and probable therapies. *International Journal of Otolaryngology 2016*, 1–13. doi:10.1155/2016/2830157

Mosley, W. J., 2nd, & Lloyd-Jones, D. M. (2009). Epidemiology of hypertension in the elderly. *Clinics in Geriatric Medicine, 25*, 179–189.

*Musen, G., Jacobson, A. M., Bolo, N. R., Simonson, D. C., Shenton, M. E., McCartney, R. L., . . . Hoogenboom, W. S. (2012). Resting-state brain functional connectivity is altered in type 2 diabetes. *Diabetes, 61*, 2375–2379.

Nagaratnam, N., Nagaratnam, K., & Cheuk, G. (2016). *Diseases in the elderly: Age-related changes and pathophysiology*. Cham, Switzerland: Springer.

*Narayan, K. M., Boyle, J. P., Geiss, L. S., Saaddine, J. B., & Thompson, T. J. (2006). Impact of recent increase in incidence on future diabetes burden: U.S., 2005-2050. *Diabetes Care, 29*, 2114–2116.

National Eye Institute. (2015). Facts about cataracts. Retrieved from https://nei.nih.gov/health/cataract

National Institute of Diabetes and Digestive and Kidney Diseases. (2013a, March). Hypothyroidism (underactive thyroid). Retrieved from https://www.niddk.nih.gov/health-information/health-topics/endocrine/hypothyroidism/Pages/fact-sheet.aspx

National Institute of Diabetes and Digestive and Kidney Diseases. (2013b, December). The urinary tract & how it works. Retrieved from https://www.niddk.nih.gov/health-information/urologic-diseases/urinary-tract-how-it-works

National Institute of Diabetes and Digestive and Kidney Diseases. (2014, June). *Insulin Resistance and Prediabetes, 14*, 4893.

National Institute of Neurological Disorders and Stroke. (2014). Peripheral neuropathy fact sheet. Retrieved from https://www.ninds.nih.gov/Disorders/Patient-Caregiver-Education/Fact -Sheets/Peripheral-Neuropathy-Fact-Sheet

National Osteoporosis Foundation. (2008). Osteoporosis: What you need to know. Retrieved from https://cdn.nof.org/wp-content/uploads/2016/02/Osteoporosis-What-you-need-to-know .pdf

Newman, A. B. (2012). Comorbidity and multimorbidity. In A. B. Newman & J. A. Cauley (Eds.), *The epidemiology of aging* (pp. 119–133). Dordrecht, The Netherlands: Springer.

Nikitin, N. P., Loh, P. H., de Silva, R., Witte, K. K., Lukaschuk, E. I., Parker, A., . . . Cleland, J. G. (2006). Left ventricular morphology, global and longitudinal function in normal older individuals: a cardiac magnetic resonance study. *International Journal of Cardiology, 108*, 76–83.

Ogawa, T., Spina, R. J., Martin, W. H., 3rd, Kohrt, W. M., Schechtman, K. B., Holloszy, J. O., & Ehsani, A. A. (1992). Effects of aging, sex, and physical training on cardiovascular responses to exercise. *Circulation, 86*, 494–503.

Ong, K. L., Cheung, B. M., Man, Y. B., Lau, C. P., & Lam, K. S. (2007). Prevalence, awareness, treatment, and control of hypertension among United States adults 1999-2004. *Hypertension, 49*, 69–75.

Oparil, S., Zaman, M. A., & Calhoun, D. A. (2003). Pathogenesis of hypertension. *Annals of Internal Medicine, 139*, 761–776.

Otsuki, T., Maeda, S., Sugawara, J., Kesen, Y., Murakami, H., Tanabe, T., . . . Matsuda, M. (2006). Age-related reduction of systemic arterial compliance relates to decreased aerobic capacity during sub-maximal exercise. *Hypertension Research, 29*, 759–765.

Pearson, A. C., Gudipati, C. V., & Labovitz, A. J. (1991). Effects of aging on left ventricular structure and function. *American Heart Journal, 121*, 871–875.

Peeters, R. P. (2008). Thyroid hormones and aging. *Hormones, 7*, 28–35.

Peppa, M., Uribarri, J., & Vlassara, H. (2003). Glucose, advanced glycation end products, and diabetes complications: What is new and what works. *Clinical Diabetes, 21*, 186–187.

Pierwola, K. K., Patel, G. A., Lambert. W. C., & Schwarz, R. A. (2017). Skin disease and old age. In H. M. Fillit, K. Rockwood, & J. Young (Eds.), *Brocklehurst's textbook of geriatric medicine and gerontology* (8th ed., pp. 789–798). Philadelphia, PA: Elsevier.

Psaty, B. M., Furberg, C. D., Kuller, L. H., Cushman, M., Savage, P. J., Levine, D., . . . Lumley, T. (2001). Association between blood pressure level and the risk of myocardial infarction, stroke, and total mortality: The cardiovascular health study. *Archives of Internal Medicine, 161*, 1183–1192.

Rawson, N. E. (2006). Olfactory loss in aging. *Science of Aging Knowledge Environment: SAGE KE, 2006*(5), pe6.

*Reijmer, Y. D., Leemans, A., Brundel, M., Kappelle, L. J., & Biessels, G. J. (2013). Disruption of the cerebral white matter network is related to slowing of information processing speed in patients with type 2 diabetes. *Diabetes, 62*, 2112–2115.

Roth, T. N. (2015). Aging of the auditory system. *Handbook of Clinical Neurology, 129*, 357–373.

Sajid-Crokett, S., & Hershman, J. (2015). Thyroid nodules and cancer in the elderly. In L. J. De Groot, G. Chrousos, K. Dungan, A. Grossman, J. M. Hershman, C. Koch, M. Korbonits, R. McLachlan, M. New, J. Purnell, R. Rebar, F. Singer, & A. Vinik (Eds.), Endotext [Internet]. Retrieved from https://www.ncbi.nlm.nih.gov/books/NBK278969

Salvi, S. M., Akhtar, S., & Currie, Z. (2006). Ageing changes in the eye. *Postgraduate Medical Journal, 82*, 581–587.

Salvi, S. S., & Barnes, P. F. (2009). Chronic obstructive pulmonary disease in non-smokers. *Lancet, 374*, 733–43.

Schiffman, S. S. (1997). Taste and smell losses in normal aging and disease. *Journal of American Medical Association, 278*, 1357–1362.

Schwartz, J. B., & Zipes, D. P. (2011). Cardiovascular disease in the elderly. In R. O. Bonow, D. L. Mann, D. P. Zipes, & P. Libby (Eds.), *Braunwald's heart disease: A textbook of cardiovascular medicine* (9th ed., pp. 1727–1756). Philadelphia, PA: Elsevier Saunders.

Shargorodsky, J., Curhan, G. C., & Farwell, W. R. (2010). Prevalence and characteristics of tinnitus among US adults. *The American Journal of Medicine, 123*, 711–718.

Shu, C. H., Hummel, T., Lee, P. L., Chiu, C. H., Lin, S. H., & Yuan, B. C. (2009). The proportion of self-rated olfactory dysfunction does not change across the life span. *American Journal of Rhinology and Allergy, 23,* 413–416.

Singer, A., Exuzides, A., Spangler, L., O'Malley, C., Colby, C., Johnston, K., . . . Kagan, R. (2015). Burden of illness for osteoporotic fractures compared with other serious diseases among postmenopausal women in the United States. *Mayo Clinic Proceedings, 90*(1), 53–62.

Smith, P. P., & Kuche, G. A. (2017). Aging of the urinary tract. In H. M. Fillit, K. Rockwood, & J. Young (Eds.), *Brocklehurst's textbook of geriatric medicine and gerontology* (8th ed., pp. 133–137). Philadelphia, PA: Elsevier.

Soares, E., Nunes, S., Reis, F., & Pereira, F. C. (2012). Diabetic encephalopathy: The role of oxidative stress and inflammation in type 2 diabetes. *International Journal of Interferon, Cytokine and Mediator Research, 4,* 75–85.

Stevens, J. A., Mack, K. A., Paulozzi, L. J., & Ballesteros, M. F. (2008). Self-reported falls and fall-related injuries among persons aged>or=65 years—United States, 2006. *Journal of Safety Research, 39,* 345–349.

Strotmeyer, E. S., & Zgibor, J. C. (2015). Diabetes and aging. *Clinical Geriatric Medicine, 31,* xiii–xvi.

*Stuck, A. E., Walthert, J. M., Nikolaus, T., Bula, C. J., Hohmann, C., & Beck, J. C. (1999). Risk factors for functional status decline in community-living elderly people: A systematic literature review. *Social Science and Medicine, 48,* 445–469.

Tajar, A., Forti, G., O'Neill, T. W., Lee, D. M., Silman, A. J., Finn, J. D., . . . Group, E. (2010). Characteristics of secondary, primary, and compensated hypogonadism in aging men: evidence from the European Male Ageing Study. *Journal of Clinical Endocrinology and Metabolism, 95,* 1810–1818.

Todd, R. C., Freeman, M. A. R., & Pirie, C. J. (1972). Isolated trabecular fatigue fractures in the femoral head. *Journal of Bone and Joint Surgery, 54B,* 723–728.

Tsan, L., Langberg, R., Davis, C., Phillips, Y., Pierce, J., Hojlo, C., . . . , Roselle, G. (2010). Nursing home-associated infections in Department of Veterans Affairs community living centers. *American Journal of Infection Control, 38,* 461–466.

Tuomilehto, J., Lindström, J., Eriksson, J. G., Valle, T. T., Hämäläinen, H., Ilanne-Parikka, P., . . . Uusitupa, M. (2001). Prevention of type 2 diabetes mellitus by changes in lifestyle among subjects with impaired glucose tolerance. *New England Journal of Medicine, 344,* 1343–1350.

Uitto, J. (1997). Understanding premature skin aging. *New England Journal of Medicine, 337,* 1419–1428.

Umetani, K., Singer, D. H., McCraty, R., & Atkinson, M. (1998). Twenty-four hour time domain heart rate variability and heart rate: relations to age and gender over nine decades. *Journal of the American College of Cardiology, 31,* 593–601.

U.S. Department of Health and Human Services. (2001). *The Surgeon General's call to action to prevent and decrease overweight and obesity.* Rockville, MD: U.S. Department of Health and Human Services, Public Health Service, Office of the Surgeon General.

Van Bortel, L. M., & Spek, J. J. (1998). Influence of aging on arterial compliance. *Journal of Human Hypertension, 12,* 583–586.

Visser, M., & Harris, T. B. (2012). Body composition and aging. In A. B. Newman & J. A. Cauley (Eds.), *The epidemiology of aging* (pp. 275–292). Dordrecht, The Netherlands: Springer.

Wickremaratchi, M., & Llewelyn, J. (2006). Effects of ageing on touch. *Postgraduate Medical Journal, 82,* 301–304.

World Health Organization. (2016). *Global report on diabetes.* Geneva, Switzerland: WHO Press.

Yau, J. W., Rogers, S. L., Kawasaki, R., Lamoureux, E. L., Kowalski, J. W., Bek, T., . . . Wong, T. Y. (2012). Global prevalence and major risk factors of diabetic retinopathy. *Diabetes Care, 53,* 556–564.

Yoshikawa, T. T. (1997). Perspective: aging and infectious diseases: past, present, and future. *Journal of Infectious Diseases, 176,* 1053–1057.

4

Changes to the Brain: Methods of Investigation, Aging, and Neuroplasticity

Tyler A. Rickards, Juliana Baldo, and Brian P. Yochim

This goal of this chapter is to explore changes that occur to the brain, beginning with an overview of modern technologies that are used to answer questions about brain functioning in older adults. Next we summarize the changes that occur to the brain with normal aging. Finally, we present an overview of neuroplasticity.

PART 1: METHODS OF INVESTIGATING AGE-RELATED CHANGES TO THE BRAIN

Early in the history of investigations into the aging brain, clinicians and researchers had to wait for postmortem data to observe brain changes related to aging. By the 1970s, a revolution in brain imaging began with computed tomography, which allowed an individual's brain to be visualized in vivo (Hounsfield, 1980). This major advance greatly facilitated brain-behavior research in all areas of neurology, because a patient's symptoms/deficits could be assessed and related directly to the presence of current brain changes. CT scanning relies on x-rays to visualize brain tissue, and

---

* Key references in the References section are indicated by an asterisk.

then reconstructs a series of slices to allow for a 3D visualization of the brain. Early CT scans had relatively poor spatial resolution (i.e., produced fuzzy or grainy-looking pictures of the brain that lacked detail), and thus magnetic resonance imaging (MRI; described in the following paragraph) soon became the chosen method for assessing changes associated with aging. CT is still a preferred method of brain imaging in certain instances, however, such as when cost is a concern (CT scans are much cheaper than MRI scans), if rapid scanning is needed, and in cases where MRI is contraindicated (such as when an individual has a pacemaker, metal fragment, or any other implant that is susceptible to magnetic forces).

By the 1980s, MRI technology was developed, which allowed for a much better spatial resolution (and thus crisper brain images) than CT imaging (see Figure 4.1; Sijbers, Scheunders, Bonnet, Van Dyck, & Raman, 1996). In addition, MRI does not expose individuals to the potentially harmful effects of ionizing radiation as in CT scanning. MRI works by placing an individual on a table that slides into a large, powerful magnet. This magnet has the effect of lining up all the protons in the brain (and other parts of the body). Next, a radio frequency pulse is emitted from the scanner, which causes all of the protons to get out of alignment. After the radio frequency pulse stops, the protons start to realign themselves since the magnet is always on. A computer in the scanner records two important bits of information: (a) the time it takes for the protons to get back into alignment and (b) the amount of

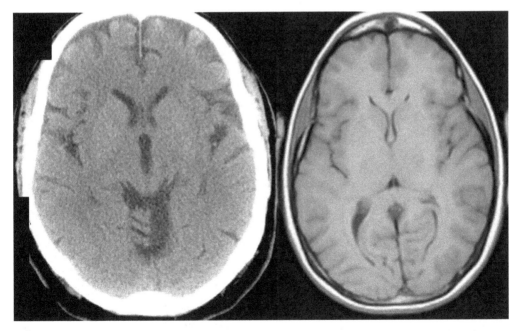

Figure 4.1 Comparison of a CT image (left) and MRI image (right), illustrating the superior spatial resolution of MRI. Prominent features, which are seen in more detail on the MRI, include the gyri and sulci that make up the outer perimeter of the cerebral hemispheres. The MRI image also offers more contrast of the grey matter (the gyri and sulci) from the white matter (the fiber tracts that run deep through the brain). The darker areas on both the CT and MRI images are spaces filled with cerebrospinal fluid (CSF).

energy they release to do so. Based on these two pieces of information, it is possible to deduce the type of tissue or fluid a proton is part of (e.g., bone, blood, cerebrospinal fluid, gray matter, etc.). The computer then "reconstructs" brain images based on this information, producing a series of brain slice images (Weishaupt, Köchli, & Marincek, 2008).

Modern MRI scanners have a spatial resolution on the order of millimeters, which means that the brain images look more like actual brain tissue and are much less fuzzy than CT or early MRI images. Typical MRI scanners used today for clinical purposes (e.g., in a hospital) have a field strength of 1.5 to 3 Tesla (T), and MRI scanners used for research are typically 3 T but may have a field strength up to 7 T. The "T" refers to Tesla or the strength of the magnetic field. A higher magnetic field allows for better spatial resolution and thus, a sharper brain image showing more detail. Such resolution and detail is critical when attempting to identify subtle or statistical changes in brain tissue, for example, in an at-risk group such as individuals with mild cognitive complaints.

Characterizing brain anatomy with MRI typically involves collecting multiple sequences, including T1-weighted, T2-weighted ("T" refers to a "time" constant), and fluid-attenuated inversion recovery (FLAIR) imaging, among others (see Figure 4.2). Each of these MRI sequences emphasizes a different aspect of brain anatomy, depending on the tissue characteristics. For example, T1 and T2 images differ with respect to scanner parameters that vary the relaxation times for protons to return to equilibrium after being perturbed by the radio frequency pulse. These distinct relaxation time parameters result in brain images that vary with respect to signal intensity (e.g., fluid appears dark on T1 images but appears bright on T2 images). With FLAIR sequences, the signal from cerebrospinal fluid is suppressed to allow for more sensitivity to smaller changes/lesions in brain tissue that might otherwise be missed.

Diffusion weighted imaging (DWI) is an additional MR sequence that provides indirect estimates of white matter in the brain (Basser, Pajevic, Pierpaoli, Duda, & Aldroubi, 2000; Kruggel, Masaki, Solodkin, & Alzheimer's Disease Neuroimaging

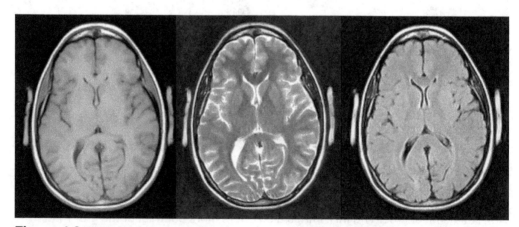

Figure 4.2 MRI slices in the axial plane (i.e., parallel to the ground), showing the distinction in images produced with T1-weighted (left), T2-weighted (middle), and FLAIR (right) sequences.

Initiative, 2017). White matter refers to the brain's bundles of axons (where an axon is the tree trunk-like extension that emanates from the nerve cell body). White matter appears white in the brain because it is covered in a fatty substance, myelin, that helps propagate electrical signals along the axon of the nerve cell. If various brain structures are conceptualized as destinations or cities, the white matter tracts are like the highways or train lines that connect the different cities. Because recent research has shown that the connections between brain regions are as important as the regions themselves in understanding brain function, the development of imaging methods, such as these, that can distinguish these white matter tracts has been invaluable.

Diffusion MRI makes use of the fact that the rate of diffusion of water molecules across axon membranes is not random but rather is constrained by the structure of these axon bundles. When a brain is injured, DWI can highlight areas of abnormal diffusion that reflect changes such as brain edema within minutes (i.e., swelling due to accumulation of fluid). The information provided by DWI can also be used to reconstruct directional information of the diffusion pattern as a proxy for the underlying white matter pathways. This directional information can then be used to generate white matter maps that show colorized reconstructions of distinct white matter pathways in the brain (known as diffusion tractography; see Figure 4.3; Assaf & Pasternak, 2008; Medina & Gaviria, 2008).

Another MRI sequence that has been used in aging research is MRS. MRS does not produce a brain image like T1 or T2 scans but rather provides numeric information about metabolic activity, as indexed by the amount of several different molecules in a given brain region. These molecules include various amino acids, glutamate, and creatine, to name a few, and provide an indication of the health of the brain tissue (Mandal, 2007). These MRS-derived levels are compared between an experimental group of interest (e.g., individuals with mild cognitive complaints or individuals with Alzheimer's disease) and a control group (e.g., age-matched, healthy individuals), and can also be used to track brain changes over time.

After an MRI scan is complete, a series of processing steps can be undertaken in order to quantify and statistically compare brain images across individuals and groups. Early studies in aging and aging-related diseases made use of volumetric analyses, in which brain regions of interest (ROIs) were manually traced on every brain slice (Ikeda et al., 1994; Murphy et al., 1993). These studies showed a clear reduction in cortical volume in normal aging and even more so in dementia. For such volumetric studies, tracing was typically done on T1 MRI scans as they provide good definition of the various cortical and subcortical structures in the brain. By the 1990s, computerized software was readily available that made it possible to directly trace brain structures on an MRI image to facilitate this type of analysis. For example, many aging studies have focused on the size of medial temporal lobe structures such as the hippocampus, and the ROI is traced on every brain slice where it appears. Next, the number of pixels contained in each ROI on each slice is calculated and then multiplied by the slice thickness to obtain the ROI volume (where slice thickness is the number of millimeters captured in each MRI image). Variables such as a patient's overall cranial volume are also calculated and used as corrections in the analyses. Then, the average volume of the ROI (e.g., the hippocampus) can be compared between groups, such as younger versus older individuals, or healthy older adults versus individuals with Alzheimer's disease. These volumetric results can also then be

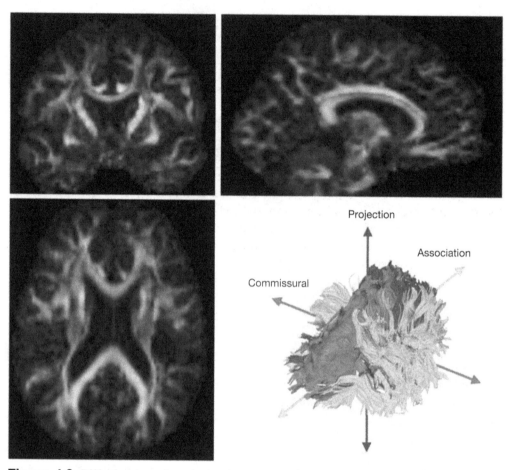

Figure 4.3 Diffusion imaging-derived maps used to reconstruct white matter pathways in the brain.
Figure courtesy of Stephanie Forkel.

correlated with behavioral measures (e.g., memory scores) in order to relate behavioral performance to the quantified MRI data (Golomb et al., 1994).

By the beginning of the 21st century, these slice-by-slice volumetric approaches were updated with automated, computerized methods that were more objective and did not require the painstaking work of manually tracing every ROI on every brain slice (Ashburner & Friston, 2000). These voxel-based morphometry (VBM) techniques involve comparing the volume of gray and white matter structures across two groups (e.g., healthy older individuals and those with mild cognitive impairment) on a voxel-by-voxel basis (a voxel is a 3D pixel). That is, rather than selecting and manually tracing a particular ROI, VBM allows for a statistical, whole-brain comparison. To run VBM analyses, individuals' T1 MRIs are first "normalized" or warped to fit a representative brain template so that all individuals' brains can be directly compared in the same reference frame. A spatial smoothing procedure is also applied in order to blur out small individual differences; this process reduces the spatial resolution of an individual image but facilitates the aggregation of data across a very large number of individuals that is not possible with manual data analyses.

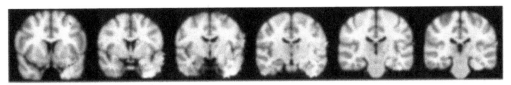

Figure 4.4 Voxel-based morphometry (VBM) map showing significant reductions in temporal lobe gray matter in patients with dementia relative to people without dementia.
Source: Dalton, Weickert, Hodges, Piguet, and Hornberger (2012).

After normalization, each individual brain is then segmented into gray matter, white matter, and cerebrospinal fluid. The resultant VBM map is displayed on an average or standard MRI image, with a scale indicating those regions in which there are statistical differences in volume between the two groups (see Figure 4.4). One can also correlate voxel-wise measures with a variable such as age, in order to study within-group, interindividual differences or to study longitudinal changes within the same individual. For example, VBM studies have been used to show the linear relationship between cognitive decline and reductions in gray matter in normal aging, as well as the neural progression of diseases such as Alzheimer's disease over time.

While the development of *structural* brain imaging techniques such as CT and MRI provide scientists with a snapshot of an individual's brain at a given point in time (analogous to a photograph), *functional* brain imaging methods were developed in the 20th century that allow scientists to measure ongoing regional brain activity (analogous to a video). The earliest of these techniques, electroencephalography (EEG), is a relatively inexpensive and noninvasive technique that measures electrical brain activity by placing recording electrodes on the scalp. Differences in EEG patterns can be discerned between different patient groups (e.g., Alzheimer's versus mild cognitive impairment) or different age groups (e.g., young versus old; Jeong, 2004; Rossini, Rossi, Babiloni, & Polich, 2007). One particular measure that can be derived from the EEG are event-related potentials (ERPs), which measure electrical brain activity that is time-locked to a given event or stimulus (e.g., the pattern of electrical activity produced every time a participant hears an unexpected word or sound; Figure 4.5). EEG data, and thus ERP data, provide very high temporal resolution of brain activity (i.e., they can measure electrical brain changes on the order of milliseconds), but they do not afford good spatial resolution like MRI.

A similar, though not widely used, technique is magnetoencephalography (MEG), which measures small magnetic field changes produced by electrical activity in the brain. Like EEG, MEG offers excellent temporal resolution, on the order of milliseconds; however, given the way that magnetic fields interact with each other and with other layers of tissue, MEG provides better spatial estimates for the location of brain activity than EEG. MEG has been used to identify biomarkers of aging and early changes associated with Alzheimer's disease (Stam, 2010). The drawbacks of MEG are its very high cost and the paucity of MEG centers.

Another set of important functional brain imaging techniques developed in the second half of the 20th century is positron emission tomography (PET), and a related lower-spatial resolution technique, single-photon emission computed tomography

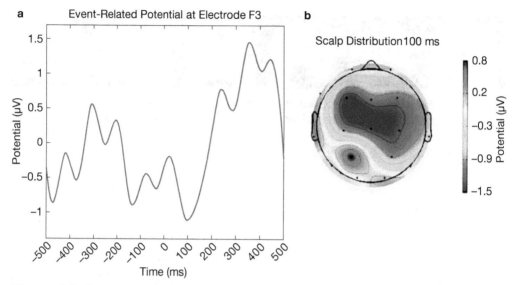

Figure 4.5 Event-related brain potential (ERP) time-locked to hearing a drum beat (shown on left) and scalp distribution of brain potentials at 100 ms after the drum beat (shown on right).

Figure courtesy of Matt Schalles.

(SPECT; Coimbra, Williams, & Hostetler, 2006). For both of these techniques, a radioactively labeled tracer (a molecule that can be "traced") is introduced into the body (e.g., via injection), and the tracer is taken up by active brain regions. In this way, these techniques reflect ongoing, online brain activity that can be recorded while an individual is at rest in the scanner (e.g., lying quietly) or while the individual is engaged in a task (e.g., reading words on a computer screen). Early on, researchers using these functional imaging methods made use of the "subtraction" technique whereby brain activation patterns generated by a baseline task (e.g., reading a series of words) could be "subtracted" from a more complex task (e.g., generating a semantic associate for the same words) in order to identify brain regions specifically "activated" in the cognitive process of interest while controlling for baseline brain activity (Corbetta, Miezin, Shulman, & Petersen, 1993).

The most common PET and SPECT tracers track glucose metabolism (a reflection of synaptic activity) and regional blood flow (an indirect measure of neuronal activity). PET and SPECT have been used to identify differences between groups of individuals (e.g., the finding that older adults show reduced blood flow in limbic and association cortices), as well as differences between different brain regions within a particular patient group (e.g., the finding that glucose metabolism in the temporal lobe is very reduced in Alzheimer's disease, relative to other brain regions). The most commonly used tracer in PET scanning is [¹⁸F]—fluorodeoxyglucose (FDG for short); the accumulation of FDG reflects the amount of synaptic or neuronal activity in a particular brain region. These methods have been used to aid diagnosis, as well as track the progression of aging and disease (Herholz et al., 2002).

PET and SPECT have also been used to study the regional uptake of specific molecules that provide information as to the functioning of particular neurotransmitters and other systems in the aging brain. For example, radioligands (radioactive tracers attached to a molecule) that preferentially bind to cholinergic or dopamine receptors can provide an indication of the integrity of these systems and how they are affected in healthy and diseased aging processes. Perhaps the most important of these for aging research is Pittsburgh Compound-B or PIB (Klunk et al., 2004). PIB was developed in the early 2000s as a PET radioligand that reflects the amount of beta-amyloid deposition in the brain. Beta-amyloid deposition is a hallmark symptom of Alzheimer's disease that previously could only be visualized in postmortem brain tissue. PIB has been used not only as an important diagnostic tool in aging and Alzheimer's research (e.g., differentiating between different types of dementia such as Alzheimer's vs. Lewy body disease), but also to identify early changes in aging that predict later conversion to Alzheimer's disease (Okello et al., 2009).

Another functional brain imaging technique was developed in the early 1990s when it was shown that signals from a standard MRI scanner could be obtained that reflected changes in regional blood oxygenation (blood oxygenation level dependent imaging or BOLD), a proxy for regional neuronal activity. This technique, known as functional MRI (fMRI), has been used widely to study brain activation patterns in both healthy and neurologically impaired individuals (Saykin et al., 1999). Similar to PET, fMRI studies of aging typically made use of the subtraction technique to uncover the neural basis of distinct cognitive processes underlying higher-level tasks and how these processes break down in aging and disease. Unlike PET, fMRI does not require a radioactive tracer and thus does not expose individuals to ionizing radiation. MRI scanners are also more readily available and less expensive to operate than PET scanners. MRI, however, does not currently have clinically available tracers like PIB (used in PET) to quantify abnormalities associated with aging, but such tracers are beginning to be developed for MRI as well.

fMRI studies of aging have reported both under- and overactivity in various parts of the brain (Reuter-Lorenz & Lustig, 2005). A number of reasons for these seemingly contradictory findings have been offered. Depending on the demands of the fMRI task, older participants may not make use of a strategy utilized by younger participants and thus may show underactivity in particular brain regions. On the other hand, overactivity in other brain regions may reflect the fact that the aging brain has to work harder to recruit additional brain regions to do the same thing (i.e., the aging brain becomes less efficient over time; see the HAROLD (Hemispheric Asymmetry Reduction in OLDer adults) and CRUNCH (Compensation-Related Utilization of Neural Circuits Hypothesis) models discussed in Part 2). It has also been suggested that apparent overactivity is actually due to a degradation of inhibitory pathways in the brain, which then appears as excess excitation during task-based fMRI.

A relatively recent development in fMRI research is the analysis of functional connectivity in brain networks when the brain is "at rest" (Gusnard & Raichle, 2001; Fox & Raichle, 2007). Unlike task-based fMRI that requires an individual to actively engage in a task while in the scanner, resting-state fMRI (rs-fMRI) simply requires individuals to lie quietly in the scanner. These so-called "resting-state networks" represent tightly interconnected brain regions that show highly correlated activity in the absence of a task. One of these networks, the default-mode network (DMN), is made up of a number of brain regions including medial prefrontal cortex, the posterior cingulate, and medial temporal lobe regions. Altered activity in the DMN has been reported in aging and Alzheimer's disease, and may be useful as an early biomarker of progressive brain changes (Dennis & Thompson, 2014). Such connectivity approaches have also been applied to task-based fMRI to highlight which brain regions work together to accomplish a particular task (Friston, 2009).

In short, a wide variety of structural and functional brain imaging techniques are available for both clinical and research purposes in the area of aging and disease (Minati, Grisoli, & Bruzzone, 2007). Depending on the types of brain changes being studied and the type of information that is needed, clinicians or researchers focus their investigation on data from the technique that best highlights those changes. A newer "multimodal" imaging approach involves combining different imaging modalities to capitalize, for example, on the temporal resolution of MEG and the spatial resolution of MRI (Polikar, Tilley, Hillis, & Clark, 2010; Zhang et al., 2011). Such approaches require additional statistical analysis techniques to combine the information from multiple modalities. Multimodal imaging approaches, combined with advances in genetic and physiological biomarker technology, promise to provide an increasingly clearer picture of the brain in aging, and ultimately, will lead to improvements in diagnosis and treatment of age-related disorders.

PART 2: CHANGES THAT OCCUR TO THE BRAIN WITH TYPICAL AGING

All the methods described in Part 1 have been used to determine what happens to the brain with age, in the absence of neurological diseases. This section presents research findings on what happens to a normal brain with age. One obvious question that is difficult to answer is: "What is a normal brain?" Most would agree that a brain that has experienced a large stroke is not normal and a person with this history would not be included in a research study on this. The brains of most people, however, undergo some amount of ischemic damage in old age (i.e., damage due to decreased blood supply), and if a study excluded anyone with any evidence of ischemic damage, it would not be representative of most people. Cerebrovascular disease and cardiovascular disease are very common among older adults. Likewise, it would be difficult to find someone who has not sustained any injury to the head, however mild, whether from a car accident, assault, falling, or playing a sport. Is the goal of the research to determine what happens to the brains of most people, or to determine what happens to a brain if it does not undergo any damage in life? Therefore, the choice of whom to include in studies on age-related changes to the brain can be difficult. This has led to differentiation between "normal brain aging" and "healthy brain aging." *Healthy* brain aging is thought to refer to structural and functional preservation of the brain in the absence of pathology and is less common than *normal* brain aging (Lockhart & DeCarli, 2014).

One factor that must be considered in this line of research is whether studies are cross-sectional or longitudinal. In this vein, Fotenos, Snyder, Girton, Morris, and Buckner (2005) found that, in late life, cross-sectional and longitudinal estimates of rates of decline with age were similar. In contrast, Raz et al. (2005) found that longitudinal measures of atrophy surpassed cross-sectional estimates. Another consideration is the age range of the sample. If a researcher were to only include older adults, she or he may conclude that the brain continues a long-term trajectory of volume loss in old age. However, studies examining the life span find a more complicated picture characterized by growth, mild volume loss, and then an increase in the pace of volume loss. Raz et al. (2005) point out the importance of sampling a wide age range of participants in studies in this area, in order to ensure nonlinear patterns of change can be found.

One leading theory of what happens to the brain with age is the premise of "last in, first out." This theory of brain aging proposes that areas of the brain that develop later than other areas are the first to be affected by advanced age. That is, the areas that are late to mature and have thinner myelinated fibers are more vulnerable to age-related declines (Raz et al., 2005). A graphical depiction of the volume of the brain over time shows an inverted-U shape throughout the life span, with increasing volume during young adulthood, stability in middle age, and decline in old age. The mid-50s (Raz et al., 2005) or age 60 (Pfefferbaum et al., 2013) may represent a time point at which the rate of volume loss begins to increase. Although the brain in general shrinks with age, the magnitude and rate of change varies across regions of the brain. In tandem with these losses of volume, the lateral ventricles and Sylvian fissures increase in volume particularly from age 60 on, more so in men than in women (Pfefferbaum et al., 2013).

Some studies have found gender differences in size of the entire brain or parts of the brain. When adjusting for head size, women have a greater mean cerebral volume as a percentage of head size throughout the life span. If not controlling for head size, men have a greater brain volume (DeCarli et al., 2005). Women have been found to have larger frontal lobes and less reduction in their frontal lobes with age than men (DeCarli et al., 2005; Van Velsen et al., 2013). Some individuals, mostly women, retain their brain volume even beyond age 80 (DeCarli et al., 2005). In contrast, Raz et al. (2005) found no relationship between sex and volume loss in the brain. Regardless of gender, having a large brain volume at baseline is largely unrelated to rate of change in volume with age (Raz et al., 2005).

Gray matter includes neural tissue that is dominated by cell bodies, whereas the parts that are enclosed in myelin, which makes the tissue appear white, are known as white matter. White matter volume tends to decline more rapidly with age than gray matter (Lockhart & DeCarli, 2014). White matter grows in volume with increased myelination throughout early adulthood. At the same time, neurons also undergo pruning or elimination if they do not develop connections with other neurons, likely because of lack of environmental need or stimulation. This occurs until approximately age 30, and mild reduction of volume continues to occur until age 60, when volume decrease becomes more rapid (Pfefferbaum et al., 2013).

Fotenos et al. (2005) followed 370 adults age 18 to 97 years (mean age 78) for an average of 1.8 years and found that whole brain volumes, gray matter, and white matter volumes all decreased with advancing age at about 0.45% per year, with the frontal lobes showing the greatest rates of atrophy. White matter volumes tended to increase until approximately age 40 and then began decreasing. Gray matter volume began to decline from an earlier age than was measured in the study. Whole brain volumes began to decrease by age 30.

Bright, or "hyperintense" images often appear on the MRI scans of older adults. These occur in white matter and are known as white matter hyperintensities (WMHs). In normal aging they are often found in the deep white matter or near the ventricles, as in *periventricular* WMHs, particularly the anterior periventricular areas. WMHs may appear brighter because of increased water content and degeneration in damaged white matter. WMHs are associated with age, and with vascular risk factors such as hypertension, diabetes, and smoking (Lockhart & DeCarli, 2014). Pathological studies have shown them to be caused by demyelination, gliosis, and axonal atrophy, and they are generally thought to be caused by ischemic damage of small blood vessels. The descriptions of many clinical MRI scans of patients make mention of "small vessel disease" suggested by the presence of WMHs. WMHs are often surrounded by a "penumbra" of reduced white matter functioning. WMHs are associated with reduced frontal lobe metabolism, possibly because they occur most often near the ventricles, which may disrupt axons connecting the frontal and posterior areas of the brain (Lockhart & DeCarli, 2014). They are associated with decreased attention, processing speed, memory, and executive functioning, likely due to slowing of the transmission of information across cortical networks. It is also normal to have very small brain infarctions found on MRI that are not associated with any discrete clinical event, and their prevalence increases with age. These are known as "lacunar" infarcts. Vascular risk factors are associated with increased rates of atrophy (Debette et al., 2011), even when blood pressure lies in the higher range of normal (Seshadri et al., 2004).

Researchers have investigated cortical thickness, surface area, and volume as measures of size of parts of the brain. Although some research has found the cerebellum to show the greatest rates of change in old age (Raz et al., 2005), the frontal lobes have consistently been found to show the greatest rates of atrophy (DeCarli et al., 2005; Lockhart & DeCarli, 2014; Pfefferbaum et al., 2013). This rate of change increases with advanced age (Raz et al., 2005). The frontal lobes may show two phases of change, with a slow rate of reduction from age 20 to 60, and then accelerated decline after age 60 (Pfefferbaum et al., 2013). Hypertension is associated with greater rate of volume loss in the orbitofrontal cortex (Raz et al., 2005).

After the frontal lobes, the hippocampus shows the second largest reduction in size with age (DeCarli et al., 2005), with the rate of shrinkage increasing in late life (Raz et al., 2005). The rate of atrophy in the hippocampus may stay stable until age 60 (Pfefferbaum et al., 2013) or the mid-50s (Raz et al., 2005), when the rate of atrophy increases. The rate of volume loss in the hippocampus is greater in older adults if they have hypertension (Raz et al., 2005). This indicates that age alone may not be the cause of volume loss, but time spent with hypertension may be the determining factor. The negative impact of hypertension increases with years of having this condition. The hippocampus shows a greater rate of volume decline than the nearby entorhinal cortex, which shows minimal change with normal aging (Raz et al., 2005).

The parietal lobes show less atrophy with age. The occipital lobes, including the calcarine cortex, show the least changes with age, although they too become smaller with age, starting around age 60 (Lockhart & DeCarli, 2014; Pfefferbaum et al., 2013). In a 5-year follow-up study, Raz et al. (2005) also found no change in the volume of the primary visual cortex. The corpus callosum may be the only structure that does not show change with age (Pfefferbaum et al., 2013).

As can be seen, the areas of the brain that change the most with advancing age, such as the hippocampus, are also the areas most susceptible to Alzheimer's disease. That is, they show a *normalcy-pathology homology* (Fjell, McEvoy, Holland, Dale, &

Walhovd, 2014). The vulnerability of these areas to normal age changes, even in the absence of disease, corresponds to their vulnerability to diseases such as Alzheimer's disease. The common underlying factor may be that areas such as the hippocampus show a large degree of plasticity throughout life. This plasticity, which enables the hippocampus to engage in learning and memory, requiring high levels of plasticity throughout life, may make it more vulnerable to decline with age. The decline in age may then make these areas more vulnerable to insults such as Alzheimer's disease. That is, the changes observed with normal aging are not thought to simply represent early signs of Alzheimer's disease. Rather, these areas of the brain change with age, and their loss of integrity makes them more susceptible to Alzheimer's disease.

Given the consistent findings of brain volume loss with age, how does our brain continue to function well? Several models have emerged to explain how the brain reacts to reduced integrity in order to keep functioning. The HAROLD model (Cabeza, 2002) proposes that latent areas contralateral to the areas involved in a task are increasingly recruited as we age in order to continue to complete cognitive tasks effectively. The CRUNCH model (Reuter-Lorenz & Cappell, 2008) proposes that compensation occurs by both increased activation of already-specialized brain regions and through selective recruitment of alternative regions. The Scaffolding Theory of Aging and Cognition (STAC; Goh & Park, 2009) proposes that the aging brain maintains the potential for positive neuroplasticity with new stimulation and learning, and that increased compensatory frontal activation develops from engagement. The HAROLD, CRUNCH, and STAC models are revisited in Chapter 8. We turn now to a review of neuroplasticity and aging.

PART 3: NEUROPLASTICITY

A BRIEF HISTORY OF NEUROPLASTICITY

Ioan Minea is credited as being the first to use the term "plasticity" as it relates to the central nervous system (Jones, 2000; Minea, 1909). The modern conceptualization of brain plasticity may be traced to William James, however, who suggested that plasticity occurs gradually and is related to "habit," or acts which we repeatedly do. James went on to describe how these brain changes are not simply modifications of existing networks but also include the establishment of *new* networks or pathways (Berlucchi & Buchtel, 2009).

> Plasticity, then, in the wide sense of the word means the possession of a structure weak enough to yield to an influence, but strong enough not to yield all at once . . . Organic matter, especially nervous tissue, seems endowed with a very ordinary degree of plasticity of this sort. . . . (James 1890, vol. I, p. 105).

According to Cowan and Kandel (2001), it was Ramón y Cajal (1894) who specified that the connections *between* neurons are important for new learning. This important "space" between neurons was called the "synapse" (Sherrington, 1897). Eugenio Tanzi first hypothesized that use-dependent learning influences communication of messages across the synapse:

. . . conductivity of the nervous system will stand in an inverse relation with the spaces between neurons. To the extent that exercise tends to shorten distances, it increases the conductivity of neurons that is their functional capacity. (Tanzi, 1893, p. 469)

We now know that it is not simply the shortening of the physical space between neurons which undergoes change but the chemical communication(s) between them (among other changes, discussed later). Acknowledging the role of chemical communication between neurons is credited to Ernesto Lugaro (Berlucchi & Buchtel, 2009; Lugaro, 1898). Additionally, Lugaro suggested that different regions of the brain have varying degrees of ability to change, or plasticity, with the more plastic regions being "still capable of further perfection—especially in the cerebral cortex" (Lugaro, 1909, pp. 96–97). In addition to this "perfection" of structural and chemical changes and strengthening of existing neuronal connections, Ramón y Cajal (1911) also suggested that the creation of new pathways of the brain was involved in the development of new behaviors.

Possibly one of the more well-known contributions to the area of brain plasticity, Donald Hebb's *The Organization of Behavior* (1949) highlighted the importance of repetitive firing of correlated synapses and neurons in the process of plasticity (commonly referred to as *Hebb's postulate*; see Bi & Poo, 2001 for a review). This idea of plasticity occurring at the level of the synapse was first discussed in Tanzi's work, which predates Hebb's findings by approximately 50 years. Hebb himself in a personal letter (Berlucchi & Buchtel, 2009) acknowledged Tanzi's work and that Tanzi should get the "credit due to him" for his seminal theory (Berlucchi & Buchtel, 2009, p. 317).

On Naming: The Plasticity of the Term "Neuroplasticity"

Plasticity and neuroplasticity have become ubiquitous in contemporary research findings and when describing observed phenomenon thought to reflect brain change (Jones, 2000). Jacques Paillard (Will, Dalrymple-Alford, Wolff, & Cassel, 2008) identified problems with what he considered to be the loose applications of these terms to phenomenon that may or may not be "plastic" (Berlucchi & Buchtel, 2009). He cautioned that "changes" observed at a given cellular level may actually result from alterations at a lower (molecular) or higher (systems) level. Zatorre, Fields, and Johansen-Berg (2012) more recently echoed this sentiment, stressing the importance of considering systems-level, macrostructural, and microstructural changes and their interactions. Also, Paillard suggested that plasticity can only be demonstrated if a new function is achieved by alterations in underlying internal connectivity or constituent elements. Therefore, the morphologic change—in and of itself—is not sufficient to demonstrate plasticity, accordingly.

Paillard's considerations suggest that structure and function need to be collectively considered when using the term plasticity (Berlucchi & Buchtel, 2009). More contemporary conceptualizations of neuroplasticity include changes in neuronal connectivity, generation of new neurons, as well as neurochemical changes (Fuchs & Flügge, 2014). The neuroimaging techniques described earlier in this chapter have

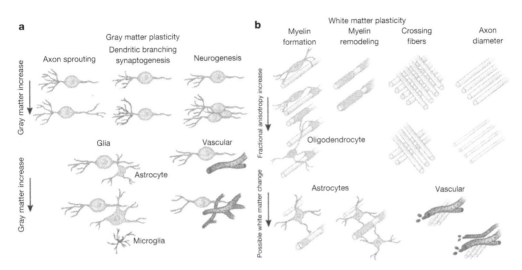

Figure 4.6 Drivers of neuroplasticity.
Source: Zatorre, Fields, and Johansen-Berg (2012, p. 531). Adapted by permission from Macmillan Publishers Ltd.

allowed for the increasingly accurate delineation of the "level" of change more related to the accompanying alteration in function/behavior, with multiple mechanisms observed to have plastic qualities. In addition to different types or "levels" of structural change, location and timing of change are important to consider (Valkanova, Rodriguez, & Ebmeier, 2014). For example, stem cells may require up to 3 months to develop and differentiate (Cummings et al., 2005). Zatorre et al. (2012) describe how these observed plastic phenomena can be organized as being of gray matter, white matter, or as extraneuronal, as illustrated in Figure 4.6. Gray matter changes include the creation of new neurons (neurogenesis), new synapses (synaptogenesis), and changes in neuronal structure, all depicted on the left side of Figure 4.6. White matter changes include myelination, packing density of fibers, and qualities of axons including their trajectories, quantity, diameter, and branching, as depicted on the right side of Figure 4.6. Extraneuronal changes include the formation of new blood vessels (angiogenesis) and increases in glial cell size and quantity, as shown on the bottom of Figure 4.6.

Tanzi (1893) stated that "exercise" (or increased use or habit) drives the increase in "conductivity of neurons" (p. 469), with this sentiment echoed later by Hebb (1949). This concept is generally well understood; however, its practical application for clinical and research purposes necessitates more specific delineation. Kleim and Jones (2008) suggested 10 "principles of experience-dependent plasticity" (p. S227), which consider relevant literature to highlight general themes in behavior that are related to neural plasticity.

In Kleim and Jones's (2008) initial concept of the 10 principles, principle 1, *use it or lose it*, recognizes that, in the absence of use, neural circuits can actually deteriorate and/or become subsumed by other circuits. Functional MRI research has demonstrated this in individuals with visual impairment with activation of their cortical areas typically dedicated to vision during tactile tasks (Sadato et al., 1996), and in individuals who are deaf with activation of auditory cortical areas during visual tasks (Finney, Fine, & Dobkins, 2001). Structural neuroplastic change has been demonstrated following skill training (increased "use") in healthy adults learning how to juggle (Boyke, Driemeyer, Gaser, Buchel, & May, 2008; Draganski, Gaser, Busch, Schuierer, Bogdahn, & May, 2004), and adults poststroke (Gauthier et al., 2008), consistent with the idea of principle 2, *use it and improve it*. In the Gauthier et al. (2008) study, adults with stroke and upper-extremity hemiparesis (between 38 and 87 years of age) who participated in upper-extremity rehabilitation therapy showed improved functioning, which correlated with gray matter volume increases in the hippocampus, as well as sensory and motor areas of both sides of the brain. Importantly, age did not correlate with increases in gray matter volume, suggesting that age was not a factor in driving the observed volumetric change or clinical improvement. Also, these individuals were 3.6 years poststroke on average, and most had participated in some type of physical therapy for their hemiparesis, suggesting that improvement (and brain plasticity) can occur years following an injury and after previous attempts at improvement.

Simple repetition or "use" may not be sufficient in all cases to elicit neural change: Principle 3, the *specificity* of a task, must be considered. Perez, Lungholt, Nyborg, and Nielsen (2004) demonstrated that skilled ankle movements increased corticospinal excitability, whereas simple repeated movement of the ankle did not. Repetition, intensity, and salience matter when evaluating neuroplastic change. Considering *repetition* (principle 4), several days of training have been demonstrated to be necessary to increase synaptic strength (Monfils & Teskey, 2004) and number of synapses or cortical map reorganization (Kleim et al., 2002), in some cases. It follows, then, that a task may require sufficient *intensity* (principle 5) to drive neuroplastic change, as well: Raymer et al. (2008) echoed this sentiment in their review of aphasia rehabilitation. Relatedly, adaptive training paradigms—where intensity must be increased as the "difficulty of the task is adjusted according to individual performance"— may be influential in inducing plasticity, as well (Valkanova et al., 2014, p. 905). In adults following stroke (Gauthier et al., 2008) following an upper-extremity rehabilitation program, gray matter volume increase related to improvement in real-world arm use, not improvement on a laboratory-based measure of maximum ability. This finding further substantiates the theory that neuroplastic change is driven by and is related to tasks of sufficient *salience* (principle 7) and importance (e.g., tasks of real-world arm use), not simply performance on a laboratory-based measure of dexterity and motor speed. This highlights a criticism given in response to negative outcomes or lack of finding neuroplastic change in such research: It is speculated that insufficient importance/ecological validity is often the culprit of the limited or nonexistent observed change (Valkanova et al., 2014).

When considering principle 6, how *time matters*, it has been posited that *Critical Windows* for learning and development exist (Adams et al., 2000), and these periods may create times of high opportunity and vulnerability. In addition to "windows" of chronological age and development, there may be optimal "windows" of time following an insult to the nervous system to capitalize upon neuroplastic potential (Kleim & Jones, 2008). Some research finds rehabilitation to be more efficacious poststroke when initiated at day 5 versus day 30 (Biernaskie, Chernenko, & Corbett, 2004). However, animal models suggest that starting physical activity too quickly following an ischemic infarction can actually *increase* the lesion volume, possibly due to unique characteristics of the recovering brain tissue immediately surrounding the lesion (e.g., cortical hyperexcitability; Risedal, Zeng, & Johansson, 1999). Following a TBI, advanced rates of neurodegeneration ("negative neuroplasticity") may occur, and these changes correlate with poorer cognition and other functions (Tomaszczyk et al., 2014). Possible mechanisms of this negative neuroplasticity may include gliotic scar formation, inflammation, cell death, or other mechanisms (Su, Veeravagu, & Grant, 2016). New therapies with at least some preliminary evidence of effectiveness from animal studies include interventions targeting neurogenesis, reducing inflammation, vascular development (angiogenesis), and synaptic remodeling and formation (Su et al., 2016). Also, an ongoing study of adults with upper-extremity hemiparesis following TBI (Taub & Uswatte, 2015) is examining neuroplastic change in gray matter, white matter, and functional brain activity following an upper-extremity rehabilitation therapy (Shaw et al., 2005).

In considering principle 8, how *age matters*, plastic change in the adult nervous system was long believed to be impossible or nearly so due to both a passing of "windows" of possible change as well as advancing age, in general. According to Lugaro in 1898, "The plasticity of the nervous elements . . . decreases as the years go by . . . declines progressively and reaches an almost complete annulment in a variable time from one individual to the other" (p. 38). Indeed, even Ramón y Cajal suggested that plasticity "decreases in adults and disappears almost completely in old age" (1894, p. 195). Demonstrated generation of neurons in adult animals (Altman & Das, 1965) and in adult humans (Eriksson et al., 1998) helped shift this belief. Indeed, neuroplastic change has been observed in adult humans (Valkanova et al., 2014). Boyke et al. (2008) demonstrated that while only 23% of their older adult sample mastered a juggling skill compared to 100% of younger samples in previous studies (Draganski et al., 2004; Driemeyer, Boyke, Gaser, Büchel, & May, 2008), older adults who did acquire the new skill showed neuroplastic gray matter volume increases. This illustrates that, while possibly more difficult to elicit, neuroplastic processes do occur even in older populations.

Principles 9 *transference* and 10 *interference* refer to the ability of a given circuit to enhance (transference) or disrupt (interference) subsequent plastic change (Kleim & Jones, 2008). Types of transference can include electrical brain stimulation coupled with motor rehabilitation following stroke (Hummel & Cohen, 2006). Additionally, exercise may enhance production of brain-derived neurotrophic factor (BDNF), a protein (discussed in Chapter 2) that promotes neuroplasticity (Gómez-Pinilla, Ying, Roy, Molteni, & Edgerton, 2002; Petzinger et al., 2013). BDNF has also been found to play an important role in neurogenesis in animal models of the effect of exposure to complex environments (Rossi et al., 2006). Interestingly, selective serotonin reuptake inhibitors (SSRIs) have been associated with neurogenesis through various mechanisms (D'Sa & Durman, 2002), with a more recent study finding that SSRIs may enhance neuroplastic effects of transcranial direct current stimulation, a mechanism of directly sending electrical stimulation into the brain (Kuo et al., 2016). A neuroprosthesis—a "device or a system that communicates with specific groups of neurons to restore as much functionality as possible"—has also been explored as a possible means of enhancing functioning of a brain circuit (Fernandez et al., 2005, p. R2). For example, neuroprosthetics have been used to restore hand movement following spinal cord injury (Ajiboye et al., 2017). The interested reader is directed to Patil & Turner (2008) for additional information in this area.

Contrary to *transference*, principle 10, *interference*, includes activities that disrupt subsequent plastic change. Learning to complete a task in a different way following an injury—such as writing with a nondominant hand following a stroke impairing one's dominant hand—may be considered an example of interference. In this way, such compensatory strategies may lead to "bad habits" or the learned disuse or nonuse of an otherwise-available capacity (Mark & Taub, 2004).

CONCLUSION

This chapter explored changes that occur to the brain, beginning with an overview of modern technologies that are used to answer questions about brain functioning in older adults. A brief summary of changes that occur to the brain with normal aging was presented next. Last, an overview of neuroplasticity was presented. Although the human brain clearly loses volume with age, the brain also shows plasticity that can be used to maintain functioning in old age. Research in the coming decades can use the principles of neuroplasticity described previously to enhance the functioning of older adults, whether they are experiencing normal age-related change or damage to the brain following strokes or other neurological events. Neuroimaging methods will continue to be developed that allow us to determine what happens to the brain with age, and in response to neurological events, and how neuroplasticity enables the brain to adjust to such changes.

DISCUSSION QUESTIONS

1. Explain how fMRI works.

2. Explain the differences between spatial and temporal resolution in neuroimaging techniques, and which methods are strong in each category.

3. Describe the inclusion and exclusion criteria you would use for a study on age-related changes to a normal human brain, and why.

4. Explain an overall theory to explain which areas of the brain experience the most volume loss with age, and identify areas that show the most loss in old age.

5. Describe five principles of neuroplasticity, and explain how they might apply to an older adult who experiences loss of language ability and use of her right hand in response to a stroke.

REFERENCES

Adams, J., Barone, S., Jr., LaMantia, A., Philen, R., Rice, D. C., Spear, L., & Susser, E. (2000). Workshop to identify critical windows of exposure for children's health: Neurobehavioral work group summary. *Environmental Health Perspectives, 108*(Suppl. 3), 535.

Ajiboye, A. B., Willett, F. R., Young, D. R., Memberg, W. D., Murphy, B. A., Miller, J. P., . . . Kirsch, R. F. (2017). Restoration of reaching and grasping movements through brain-controlled muscle stimulation in a person with tetraplegia: A proof-of-concept demonstration. *Lancet*, *389*(10081), 1821–1830. doi:10.1016/S0140-6736(17)30601-3

Altman, J., & Das, G. D. (1965). Autoradiographic and histological evidence of postnatal hippocampal neurogenesis in rats. *Journal of Comparative Neurology, 124*, 319–335.

Ashburner, J., & Friston, K. J. (2000). Voxel-based morphometry—The methods. *Neuroimage, 11*, 805–821.

Assaf, Y., & Pasternak, O. (2008). Diffusion tensor imaging (DTI)-based white matter mapping in brain research: A review. *Journal of Molecular Neuroscience, 34*, 51–61.

Basser, P. J., Pajevic, S., Pierpaoli, C., Duda, J., & Aldroubi, A. (2000). In vivo fiber tractography using DT-MRI data. *Magnetic Resonance in Medicine, 44*, 625–632.

Berlucchi, G., & Buchtel, H. A. (2009). Neuronal plasticity: Historical roots and evolution of meaning. *Experimental Brain Research, 192*(3), 307–319.

Bi, G. Q., & Poo, M. M. (2001). Synaptic modification by correlated activity: Hebb's postulate revisited. *Annual Review of Neuroscience, 24*, 139–166.

Biernaskie, J., Chernenko, G., & Corbett, D. (2004). Efficacy of rehabilitative experience declines with time after focal ischemic brain injury. *The Journal of Neuroscience, 24*, 1245–1254.

Boyke, J., Driemeyer, J., Gaser, C., Büchel, C., & May, A. (2008). Training-induced brain structure changes in the elderly. *The Journal of Neuroscience, 28*, 7031–7035.

Cabeza, R. (2002). Hemispheric asymmetry reduction in older adults: The HAROLD model. *Psychology and Aging, 17*, 85–100.

Coimbra, A., Williams, D. S., & Hostetler, E. D. (2006). The role of MRI and PET/SPECT in Alzheimer's disease. *Current Topics in Medicinal Chemistry, 6*, 629–647.

Corbetta, M., Miezin, F. M., Shulman, G. L., & Petersen, S. E. (1993). A PET study of visuospatial attention. *Journal of Neuroscience, 13*, 1202–1226.

Cowan, W. M., & Kandel, E. R. (2001). A brief history of synapses and synaptic transmission. *Synapses*, 1–87.

Cummings, B. J., Uchida, N., Tamaki, S. J., Salazar, D. L., Hooshmand, M., Summers, R., . . . Anderson, A. J. (2005). Human neural stem cells differentiate and promote locomotor recovery in spinal cord-injured mice. *Proceedings of the National Academy of Sciences of the United States of America, 102*, 14069–14074.

Dalton, M. A., Weickert, T. W., Hodges, J. R., Piguet, O., & Hornberger, M. (2012). Impaired acquisition rates of probabilistic associative learning in frontotemporal dementia is associated with fronto-striatal atrophy. *NeuroImage: Clinical, 2*, 56–62. doi:10.1016/j.nicl.2012.11.001

Debette, S., Seshadri, S., Beiser, A., Au, R., Himali, J. J., Palumbo, C., & DeCarli, C. (2011). Midlife vascular risk factor exposure accelerates structural brain aging and cognitive decline. *Neurology, 77*, 461–468. doi:10.1212/WNL.0b013e318227b227

DeCarli, C., Massaro, J., Harvey, D., Hald, J., Tullberg, M., Au, R., & Wolf, P. A. (2005). Measures of brain morphology and infarction in the Framingham Heart Study: Establishing what is normal. *Neurobiology of Aging, 26*, 491–510.

*Dennis, E. L., & Thompson, P. M. (2014). Functional brain connectivity using fMRI in aging and Alzheimer's disease. *Neuropsychology Review, 24*, 49–62.

Draganski, B., Gaser, C., Busch, V., Schuierer, G., Bogdahn, U., & May, A. (2004). Neuroplasticity: Changes in grey matter induced by training. *Nature, 427*, 311–312.

Driemeyer, J., Boyke, J., Gaser, C., Büchel, C., & May, A. (2008). Changes in gray matter induced by learning—revisited. *Public Library of Science One, 3*, e2669.

D'Sa, C., & Duman, R. S. (2002). Antidepressants and neuroplasticity. *Bipolar Disorders, 4*, 183–194.

Eriksson, P. S., Perfilieva, E., Björk-Eriksson, T., Alborn, A. M., Nordborg, C., Peterson, D. A., & Gage, F. H. (1998). Neurogenesis in the adult human hippocampus. *Nature Medicine, 4*, 1313–1317.

Fernandez, E., Pelayo, F., Romero, S., Bongard, M., Marin, C., Alfaro, A., & Merabet, L. (2005). Development of a cortical visual neuroprosthesis for the blind: The relevance of neuroplasticity. *Journal of Neural Engineering, 2*, R1.

Finney, E. M., Fine, I., & Dobkins, K. R. (2001). Visual stimuli activate auditory cortex in the deaf. *Nature Neuroscience, 4*, 1171–1173.

*Fjell, A. M., McEvoy, L., Holland, D., Dale, A. M., & Walhovd, K. B. (2014). What is normal in normal aging? Effects of aging, amyloid and Alzheimer's disease on the cerebral cortex and the hippocampus. *Progress in Neurobiology, 117,* 20–40.

Fotenos, A. F., Snyder, A. Z., Girton, L. E., Morris, J. C., & Buckner, R. L. (2005). Normative estimates of cross-sectional and longitudinal brain volume decline in aging and AD. *Neurology, 64,* 1032–1039. doi:10.1212/01.WNL.0000154530.72969.11

Fox, M. D., & Raichle, M. E. (2007). Spontaneous fluctuations in brain activity observed with functional magnetic resonance imaging. *Nature Reviews Neuroscience, 8,* 700–711.

Friston, K. (2009). Causal modelling and brain connectivity in functional magnetic resonance imaging. *Public Library of Science Biology, 7,* e1000033. doi:10.1371/journal.pbio.1000033

Fuchs, E., & Flügge, G. (2014). Adult neuroplasticity: More than 40 years of research. *Neural Plasticity, 2014,* 541870. doi:10.1155/2014/541870

Gauthier, L. V., Taub, E., Perkins, C., Ortmann, M., Mark, V. W., & Uswatte, G. (2008). Remodeling the brain plastic structural brain changes produced by different motor therapies after stroke. *Stroke, 39,* 1520–1525.

Goh, J. O., & Park, D. C. (2009). Neuroplasticity and cognitive aging: The scaffolding theory of aging and cognition. *Restorative Neurology and Neuroscience, 27,* 391–403.

Golomb, J., Kluger, A., de Leon, M. J., Ferris, S. H., Convit, A., Mittelman, M. S., . . . George, A. E. (1994). Hippocampal formation size in normal human aging: A correlate of delayed secondary memory performance. *Learning & Memory, 1,* 45–54.

Gómez-Pinilla, F., Ying, Z., Roy, R. R., Molteni, R., & Edgerton, V. R. (2002). Voluntary exercise induces a BDNF-mediated mechanism that promotes neuroplasticity. *Journal of Neurophysiology, 88,* 2187–2195.

Gusnard, D. A., & Raichle, M. E. (2001). Searching for a baseline: Functional imaging and the resting human brain. *Nature Reviews Neuroscience, 2,* 685–694.

Hebb, D. O. (1949). *The organization of behaviour. A neuropsychological theory.* New York, NY: John Wiley.

Herholz, K., Salmon, E., Perani, D., Baron, J. C., Holthoff, V., Frölich, L., . . . Zündorf, G. (2002). Discrimination between Alzheimer dementia and controls by automated analysis of multicenter FDG PET. *Neuroimage, 17,* 302–316.

Hounsfield, G. N. (1980). Computed medical imaging. *Medical Physics, 7,* 283–290.

Hummel, F. C., & Cohen, L. G. (2006). Non-invasive brain stimulation: A new strategy to improve neurorehabilitation after stroke? *Lancet Neurology, 5,* 708–712.

Ikeda, M., Tanabe, H., Nakagawa, Y., Kazui, H., Oi, H., Yamazaki, H., . . . Nishimura, T. (1994). MRI-based quantitative assessment of the hippocampal region in very mild to moderate Alzheimer's disease. *Neuroradiology, 36,* 7–10.

James, W. (1890). *Principles of psychology.* London, United Kingdom: MacMillan.

Jeong, J. (2004). EEG dynamics in patients with Alzheimer's disease. *Clinical Neurophysiology, 115,* 1490–1505.

Jones, E. G. (2000). Plasticity and neuroplasticity. *Journal of the History of the Neurosciences, 9,* 37–39.

Kleim, J. A., Barbay, S., Cooper, N. R., Hogg, T. M., Reidel, C. N., Remple, M. S., & Nudo, R. J. (2002). Motor learning dependent synaptogenesis is localized to functionally reorganized motor cortex. *Neurobiology of Learning and Memory, 77,* 63–77.

*Kleim, J. A., & Jones, T. A. (2008). Principles of experience-dependent neural plasticity: Implications for rehabilitation after brain damage. *Journal of Speech, Language, and Hearing Research, 51,* S225–S239.

Klunk, W. E., Engler, H., Nordberg, A., Wang, Y., Blomqvist, G., Holt, D. P., . . . Ausén, B. (2004). Imaging brain amyloid in Alzheimer's disease with Pittsburgh Compound-B. *Annals of Neurology, 55,* 306–319.

Kruggel, F., Masaki, F., Solodkin, A., & Alzheimer's Disease Neuroimaging Initiative. (2017). Analysis of longitudinal diffusion-weighted images in healthy and pathological aging: An ADNI study. *Journal of Neuroscience Methods, 278,* 101–115.

Kuo, H. I., Paulus, W., Batsikadze, G., Jamil, A., Kuo, M. F., & Nitsche, M. A. (2015). Chronic enhancement of serotonin facilitates excitatory transcranial direct current stimulation-induced neuroplasticity. *Neuropsychopharmacology, 41,* 1223–1230.

*Lockhart, S. N., & DeCarli, C. (2014). Structural imaging measures of brain aging. *Neuropsychology Review, 24*, 271–289. doi:10.1007/s11065-014-9268-3

Lugaro, E. (1898). Le resistenze nell'evoluzione della vita. *Rivista moderna di cultura, 1*, 29–60.

Lugaro, E. (1909). *Modern problems in psychiatry.* Manchester, UK: The University Press.

Mandal, P. K. (2007). Magnetic resonance spectroscopy (MRS) and its application in Alzheimer's disease. *Concepts in Magnetic Resonance Part A, 30*, 40–64.

*Mark, V. W., & Taub, E. (2004). Constraint-induced movement therapy for chronic stroke hemiparesis and other disabilities. *Restorative Neurology and Neuroscience, 22*, 317–336.

Medina, D. A., & Gaviria, M. (2008). Diffusion tensor imaging investigations in Alzheimer's disease: The resurgence of white matter compromise in the cortical dysfunction of the aging brain. *Neuropsychiatric Disease and Treatment, 4*, 737–742.

Minati, L., Grisoli, M., & Bruzzone, M. G. (2007). MR spectroscopy, functional MRI, and diffusion-tensor imaging in the aging brain: A conceptual review. *Journal of Geriatric Psychiatry and Neurology, 20*, 3–21.

Minea, I. (1909). *Cercetări experimentale asupra variatiunilor morfologice ale neuronului sensitiv (studiul 'reactiunii plastice').* Bucharest, Romania: Brozer and Parzer.

Monfils, M. H., & Teskey, G. C. (2004). Skilled-learning-induced potentiation in rat sensorimotor cortex: A transient form of behavioural long-term potentiation. *Neuroscience, 125*, 329–336.

Murphy, D. G. M., DeCarli, C. D., Daly, E., Gillette, J. A., McIntosh, A. R., Haxby, J. V., . . . Horwitz, B. (1993). Volumetric magnetic resonance imaging in men with dementia of the Alzheimer type: Correlations with disease severity. *Biological Psychiatry, 34*, 612–621.

Okello, A., Koivunen, J., Edison, P., Archer, H. A., Turkheimer, F. E., Någren, K. U., . . . Rossor, M. N. (2009). Conversion of amyloid positive and negative MCI to AD over 3 years An 11C-PIB PET study. *Neurology, 73*, 754–760.

Patil, P. G., & Turner, D. A. (2008). The development of brain-machine interface neuroprosthetic devices. *Neurotherapeutics, 5*, 137–146.

Perez, M. A., Lungholt, B. K., Nyborg, K., & Nielsen, J. B. (2004). Motor skill training induces changes in the excitability of the leg cortical area in healthy humans. *Experimental Brain Research, 159*, 197–205.

Petzinger, G. M., Fisher, B. E., McEwen, S., Beeler, J. A., Walsh, J. P., & Jakowec, M. W. (2013). Exercise-enhanced neuroplasticity targeting motor and cognitive circuitry in Parkinson's disease. *The Lancet Neurology, 12*, 716–726.

*Pfefferbaum, A., Rohlfing, T., Rosenbloom, M. J., Chu, W., Colrain, I. M., & Sullivan, E. V. (2013). Variation in longitudinal trajectories of regional brain volumes of healthy men and women (ages 10 to 85 years) measured with atlas-based parcellation of MRI. *NeuroImage, 65*, 176–193. doi:10.1016/j.neuroimage.2012.10.008

Polikar, R., Tilley, C., Hillis, B., & Clark, C. M. (2010, August). Multimodal EEG, MRI and PET data fusion for Alzheimer's disease diagnosis. In *Engineering in Medicine and Biology Society (EMBC), 2010 Annual International Conference of the IEEE* (pp. 6058–6061). Retrieved from http://ieeexplore.ieee.org/document/5627621

Ramón y Cajal, S. (1894). La Wne structure des centres nerveux. *Proceedings of the Royal Society of London, 55*, 444–468.

Ramón y Cajal, S. (1911). Histologie du systeme nerveux de l'homme et des vertebres. *Maloine, Paris, 2*, 887–890.

Raymer, A. M., Beeson, P., Holland, A., Kendall, D., Maher, L. M., Martin, N., . . . Altmann, L. (2008). Translational research in aphasia: From neuroscience to neurorehabilitation. *Journal of Speech, Language, and Hearing Research, 51*, S259–S275.

*Raz, N., Lindenberger, U., Rodrigue, K. M., Kennedy, K. M., Head, D., Williamson, A., . . . Acker, J. D. (2005). Regional brain changes in aging healthy adults: General trends, individual differences and modifiers. *Cerebral Cortex, 15*, 1676–1689. doi:10.1093/cercor/bhi044

Reuter-Lorenz, P. A., & Cappell, K. A. (2008). Neurocognitive aging and the compensation hypothesis. *Current Directions in Psychological Science, 17*, 177–182.

Reuter-Lorenz, P. A., & Lustig, C. (2005). Brain aging: Reorganizing discoveries about the aging mind. *Current Opinion in Neurobiology, 15*, 245–251.

Risedal, A., Zeng, J., & Johansson, B. B. (1999). Early training may exacerbate brain damage after focal brain ischemia in the rat. *Journal of Cerebral Blood Flow & Metabolism, 19*, 997–1003.

Rossi, C., Angelucci, A., Costantin, L., Braschi, C., Mazzantini, M., Babbini, F., . . . Caleo, M. (2006). Brain-derived neurotrophic factor (BDNF) is required for the enhancement of hippocampal neurogenesis following environmental enrichment. *European Journal of Neuroscience, 24*, 1850–1856.

Rossini, P. M., Rossi, S., Babiloni, C., & Polich, J. (2007). Clinical neurophysiology of aging brain: From normal aging to neurodegeneration. *Progress in Neurobiology, 83*, 375–400.

Sadato, N., Pascual-Leone, A., Grafman, J., Ibañez, V., Deiber, M. P., Dold, G., & Hallett, M. (1996). Activation of the primary visual cortex by Braille reading in blind subjects. *Nature, 380*, 526–528.

Saykin, A. J., Flashman, L. A., Frutiger, S. A., Johnson, S. C., Mamourian, A. C., Moritz, C. H., . . . Weaver, J. B. (1999). Neuroanatomic substrates of semantic memory impairment in Alzheimer's disease: Patterns of functional MRI activation. *Journal of the International Neuropsychological Society, 5*, 377–392.

Seshadri, S., Wolf, P. A., Beiser, A., Elias, M. F., Au, R., Kase, C. S., & DeCarli, C. (2004). Stroke risk profile, brain volume, and cognitive function: The Framingham Offspring Study. *Neurology, 63*, 1591–1599.

Shaw, S. E., Morris, D. M., Uswatte, G., McKay, S., Meythaler, J. M., & Taub, E. (2005). Constraint-induced movement therapy for recovery of upper-limb function following traumatic brain injury. *Journal of Rehabilitation Research and Development, 42*, 769.

Sherrington, C. S. (1897). The central nervous system. In M. Foster (Eds.), *A text-book of physiology* (Vol. 3, p. 60). London, United Kingdom: Macmillan.

Sijbers, J., Scheunders, P., Bonnet, N., Van Dyck, D., & Raman, E. (1996). Quantification and improvement of the signal-to-noise ratio in a magnetic resonance image acquisition procedure. *Magnetic Resonance Imaging, 14*, 1157–1163.

Stam, C. J. (2010). Use of magnetoencephalography (MEG) to study functional brain networks in neurodegenerative disorders. *Journal of the Neurological Sciences, 289*, 128–134.

Su, Y. S., Veeravagu, A., & Grant, G. (2016). Neuroplasticity after traumatic brain injury. In. D. Laskowitz & G. Grant (Eds.), *Transnational research in traumatic brain injury* (Chapter 8). Boca Raton, FL: CRC Press/Taylor & Francis.

Tanzi, E. (1893). I fatti e la induzioni nell 'odierna istologia del sistema nervoso. *Revista Sperimentale di Freniatria e Medicine Legale, 19*, 419–472.

Taub, E., & Uswatte, G. (2015). *Harnessing neuroplasticity to promote rehabilitation: CI therapy for TBI.* Birmingham: University of Alabama at Birmingham.

Tomaszczyk, J. C., Green, N. L., Frasca, D., Colella, B., Turner, G. R., Christensen, B. K., & Green, R. E. (2014). Negative neuroplasticity in chronic traumatic brain injury and implications for neurorehabilitation. *Neuropsychology Review, 24*, 409–427.

Valkanova, V., Rodriguez, R., & Ebmeier, K. P. (2014). Mind over matter—What do we know about neuroplasticity in adults. *International Psychogeriatrics, 26*, 891–909.

Weishaupt, D., Köchli, V. D., & Marincek, B. (2008). *How does MRI work? An introduction to the physics and function of magnetic resonance imaging.* Berlin, Germany: Springer-Verlag..

Will, B., Dalrymple-Alford, J., Wolff, M., & Cassel, J. C. (2008). The concept of brain plasticity—Paillard's systemic analysis and emphasis on structure and function (followed by the translation of a seminal paper by Paillard on plasticity). *Behavioural Brain Research, 192*(1), 2–7.

*Zatorre, R. J., Fields, R. D., & Johansen-Berg, H. (2012). Plasticity in gray and white: Neuroimaging changes in brain structure during learning. *Nature Neuroscience, 15*, 528–536.

Zhang, D., Wang, Y., Zhou, L., Yuan, H., Shen, D., & Alzheimer's Disease Neuroimaging Initiative. (2011). Multimodal classification of Alzheimer's disease and mild cognitive impairment. *Neuroimage, 55*, 856–867.

III

Psychological Components of Aging

5

Personality and Emotional Development

Erin L. Woodhead

PERSONALITY DEVELOPMENT

In your undergraduate psychology courses, you may remember learning about different ways that personality is conceptualized. In this section of the chapter, we review psychodynamic perspectives on personality, emphasizing Freudian theory as well as Erikson's stages, the trait approach to conceptualizing personality (commonly called the "Big 5"), as well as the coping perspective, which emphasizes how people come to interpret and understand the situations they face. We then review recent research that proposes an overarching model of personality. Finally, we discuss research on the stability of personality traits across the life span.

OVERVIEW OF PERSONALITY THEORIES

Psychodynamic Perspectives

For most people, the name Sigmund Freud comes to mind when considering any type of psychodynamic theory, particularly his focus on the id, ego, and superego. To briefly review, the id focuses on biological instincts, the superego works to control the id by following the conventions of society via internalization of cultural rules, and the ego controls rational thought ("reality principle"). The ego is often equated with one's sense of self and/or personality structure. The ego is also the

---

*Key references in the References section are indicated by an asterisk.

structure that engages defense mechanisms to minimize conflict between the id, ego, and superego. Most of Freud's work on personality development focused on changes occurring in childhood and adolescence. He believed that older adults had personalities that were so rigid that therapy was likely to be useless. Modern psychodynamic perspectives on personality development focus on ego psychology and Erik Erikson's theory of psychosocial development, adult attachment theory, and theories of defense mechanisms. We review each of these in turn.

Erik Erikson's theory of psychosocial development focuses on the successful resolution of eight developmental stages that occur throughout the life span. According to Erikson's theory, individuals have to successfully resolve each crisis before moving onto the next. In middle and older adulthood, the crises are generativity versus stagnation and ego integrity versus despair. It is presumed from Erikson's writings that individuals will face the ego integrity versus despair phase around age 60 or 65, and that individuals need to resolve the earlier stage-related crises in order to contemplate the concepts of ego integrity versus despair (Hannah, Domino, Figueredo, & Hendrickson, 1996). In his late life, Erikson started to revise his view on this, proposing that the outcome of the eighth stage (ego integrity vs. despair) is not necessarily determined by the successful resolution of the prior stages (Erikson, Erikson, & Kivnick, 1986). Erikson's wife, Joan Erikson, added to her husband's work by proposing a ninth stage that was experienced by adults in their 80s and 90s (Erikson & Erikson, 1998). This stage focuses on "gerotranscendence," which is the idea that living into the 80s and 90s is associated with a shift from a materialistic and rational view to a view that goes beyond oneself and into the future (Tornstam, 1996). This ninth stage is conceptualized by other researchers as similar to wisdom, although Joan Erikson did not directly use that term. An individual in the ninth stage might begin to disengage from friends and family and spend more time in quiet reflection.

Research on the eighth and ninth stages in Erikson's model suggests that the level of ego integrity achieved in the 60s is stable into later life, as measured by a 30-item questionnaire about ego integrity (Brown & Lowis, 2003). Example items from this scale include, "I can accept the ups and downs of my past life," and "My life has been a growth process right up to the present" (Lowis & Raubenheimer, 1997). Attempts to measure levels of ego integrity using the Lowis and Raubenheimer (1997) scale prior to age 60 result in very low scores, suggesting that an individual needs to have lived a significant period of time before being able to reflect on her or his life. The finding that scores on the ego integrity measure did not increase with advancing age after age 60 implies that ego integrity stabilizes after it is successfully resolved. In contrast, scores on a measure designed to assess one's level of gerotranscendence, a prominent construct in the proposed ninth stage, continued to increase with increasing age, suggesting that "gerotranscendence" continues to increase into the 80s and 90s. Example items from the measure of gerotranscendence include: "Later life has given me a release from the stresses of life" and "The meaning of life seems more clear to me now" (Brown & Lowis, 2003).

Research also suggests that age is associated with differential experience of generativity, which was included in Erikson's seventh stage (generativity vs. stagnation). Generativity is typically defined as some activity that supports the next generation. Typically this is defined as parenting during middle adulthood, but could also involve volunteering or other ways to give back to younger individuals. Erikson initially proposed that generativity peaks in midlife and then decreases in older adulthood. When examining a composite measure of generativity, composed of four different types of generativity (generative concern, commitment, action, and narration), middle-aged and older adults scored higher on generativity than younger adults although there were no significant differences between middle-aged and older adults (McAdams, de St. Aubin, & Logan, 1993). When examining the four types of generativity separately, middle-aged and older adults reported more generative commitments and generative narration than younger adults, although there was no significant difference in these types of generativity between middle-aged and older adults. Generative commitments were assessed by asking participants to write about personal strivings (i.e., objective or goals participants were trying to accomplish). Generative narration was assessed by asking participants to answer open-ended questions about important life experiences. Taken together, the life-span research on Erikson's stages suggests that individuals continue to develop and change into very late life, although some of the crises (generativity) may continue more into older adulthood than Erikson originally proposed.

The second personality theory rooted in the psychodynamic perspective is adult attachment theory. John Bowlby studied infants' attachment to their primary caregiver and proposed that, through our early experiences with caregivers, we develop internal working models of how relationships should function, which may be carried into romantic relationships in adulthood. If infants feel safe and well-cared for by their primary caregivers, they will display a secure attachment style, with adult relationships characterized by confidence in themselves and the belief that others will treat them well. If infants feel abandoned by their primary caregivers, either literally or emotionally, they may display an anxious attachment style, with adult relationships characterized by clinging to romantic partners due to a fear of abandonment. If infants were neglected, they may display an avoidant attachment style, with adult relationships characterized by an avoidance of closeness. In a study of attachment styles among older African American and Caucasian individuals (Magai et al., 2001), 22% of the sample was classified as securely attached and 78% of the sample was classified as dismissing, which is a variation of the avoidant attachment style. The researchers propose that the adverse events that are often faced by older adults, particularly older adults that are part of an ethnic minority group, may change attachment style over the course of the life span from secure to insecure due to the "adverse background circumstances" (Magai et al., 2001, p. S28) that the adults faced in their emerging adulthood years.

Longitudinal studies suggest that attachment in infancy is associated with attachment in adulthood, with studies showing high stability of attachment ratings up to 20 years later (Waters, Merrick, Treboux, Crowell, & Albersheim, 2000). Attachment style can change based on negative life events, which most often result in a person moving from a secure attachment to an insecure attachment (Waters et al., 2000). These negative life events can include parental divorce, loss of a parent, or other adverse circumstances as noted by the aforementioned study by Magai et al. (2001). Adult attachment style is often associated with the quality of the relationship with one's spouse or partner. Individuals who have a secure adult attachment pattern report higher levels of marital satisfaction compared to individuals with an avoidant or ambivalent adult attachment pattern (Meyers & Landsberger, 2002). Among older adult couples who were married for an average of 40 years, participants who reported secure attachment to their partners also reported fewer depressive symptoms, greater life satisfaction, and less negative affect 2.5 years later. For female participants, secure attachment to one's partner was also associated with better memory functioning 2.5 years later (Waldinger, Cohen, Schulz, & Crowell, 2015). This research suggests a developmental model of attachment theory, such that attachment patterns in infancy are relatively stable into adulthood, and that adult attachment styles are associated with relationship satisfaction and relationship security into older adulthood.

Some researchers have proposed that attachment bonds are also applicable to older adults in the area of caregiving, coping with bereavement and loss, and overall adjustment and well-being (Bradley & Cafferty, 2001). Among individuals who are caring for older adults, a secure infant–mother attachment may promote empathy toward the care recipient (Lechich, 1996). In terms of the care recipient, an insecure attachment style was associated with more paranoid delusions and anxiety among individuals with Alzheimer's disease (Magai & Cohen, 1998). In this study, participants with Alzheimer's disease who had an insecure attachment also had caregivers who reported higher burden from caregiving, supposedly from the challenging behaviors that may result from an insecure versus secure attachment (more expression of negative emotion, and higher premorbid levels of contempt, anger, and inhibition). Secure infant attachment may also predict coping and level of distress following the loss of a spouse among older adults (Sable, 1989). Although this research is dated, it suggests that the association between infant attachment patterns and adult attachment patterns may influence how an individual grieves after losing their spouse.

The third personality theory rooted in the psychodynamic perspective is around the use of defense mechanisms and how the use of certain mechanisms may change with age. Recall from the prior section that defense mechanisms are used by the ego to protect individuals from unacceptable urges and desires that develop in the id. George Vaillant is one of the primary researchers who has examined change in the use of defense mechanisms across the life span. Vaillant proposed that age increases the use of adaptive defense mechanisms and decreases the use of immature defense mechanisms. He viewed altruism, suppression, sublimation, anticipation, and humor as highly adaptive defense mechanisms, whereas immature defense mechanisms included projection, passive aggression, acting out, and denial. Vaillant has studied the use of defense mechanisms across the life span in several longitudinal studies, termed the College Sample and the Core City Sample (Vaillant, 2000). The use of adaptive defense mechanisms between ages 20 and 47 was positively associated with income at midlife, psychosocial adjustment between ages 50 and 65, social support, joy in living, marital satisfaction at midlife, and subjective physical health. Use of adaptive defense mechanisms was a stronger predictor of these outcomes than years of education and scores on a measure of neuroticism (Vaillant, 2000).

Trait Perspectives

Trait theories of personality are typically based on descriptions of an individual based on certain psychological characteristics, often thought to be tied to genetic predispositions. Trait theories assume that personality traits are enduring and stable. The most well-known trait approach is the Five-Factor Model (McCrae & Costa,

2003). The Five-Factor Model proposes that personality is made up of variations on five major traits: openness to experience, conscientiousness, extraversion, agreeableness, and neuroticism. Students often use the acronym OCEAN to remember all five factors. In cross-sectional studies, older adults tend to score higher on agreeableness and conscientiousness than younger adults, and lower on extraversion, neuroticism, and openness to experience than younger adults (McCrae et al., 1999). In a study of age-related differences in the Big 5 personality traits across five countries (Germany, Italy, Korea, Croatia, Portugal), the differences noted previously between younger and older adults were similar (McCrae et al., 1999). Across the five countries, openness to experience was the most stable trait, demonstrated at similar rates across all five countries, whereas neuroticism was the least stable trait. The age-related differences in Big 5 personality traits are thought to exist because of developmental changes that occur in personality prior to age 30. Before age 30, levels of neuroticism, agreeableness, and openness to experience tend to be higher within individuals than after age 30 (Costa & McCrae, 1994). Longitudinal research suggests that there is very little change in levels of the Big 5 after age 30 (McCrae & Costa, 2003). In an upcoming section we review more recent longitudinal studies that examine change or stability in personality traits across the life span.

The extent to which individuals endorse certain personality characteristics is associated with physical and mental health. For example, Kotov, Gamez, Schmidt, and Watson (2010) found that individuals who were high on neuroticism and low on conscientiousness were more likely to be diagnosed with mood, anxiety, and substance use problems. Individuals who were low on extraversion were more likely to be diagnosed with dysthymic disorder and social phobia. Specific to older adults, higher levels of neuroticism were associated with more self-reported medical problems, more visits to a primary care physician, and negative perceptions of one's health status. Positive health behaviors and positive perceptions of one's health were more common among older adults who scored high on extraversion, openness to experience, and agreeableness (Jerram & Coleman, 1999). Levels of the Big 5 are also associated with performance on cognitive tasks among older adults. High levels of extraversion and low levels of neuroticism were associated with better performance on an episodic memory task among healthy adults between ages 68 and 95 (Meier, Perrig-Chiello, & Perrig, 2002). A review study by Curtis, Windsor, and Soubelet (2015) found that older adults who scored higher on openness to experience tended to perform better on cognitive tests, and those high in conscientiousness had slower rates of cognitive decline. Similar results were found by Booth, Schinka, Brown, Mortimer, and Borenstein (2006) who documented a positive association between scores on openness to experience and performance on verbal memory tests and general cognitive ability. These findings are consistent with a large body of research suggesting that individuals high in conscientiousness and openness to experience tend to be in better health, potentially due to a tendency to engage in more preventive care throughout life. In contrast, individuals high in neuroticism tend to experience more physical and mental health difficulties.

Coping Perspectives

How do you cope with stressful situations? Do you try to change the situation or change your thoughts about the situation? The way that you choose to cope with a stressful situation may overlap, or be predicted by, your specific personality traits. However, coping and personality can be thought of as different constructs, with personality representing traits that are stable across time and situations, and coping representing attempts to regulate one's environment that may change depending on the type of stressor an individual faces (Connor-Smith & Flachsbart, 2007). Specifically, coping is defined as efforts to manage stressful situations, which can involve behavioral or cognitive strategies (Ben-Zur, 2009). Personality does not consistently predict coping style (Connor-Smith & Flachsbart, 2007), suggesting that coping style may play an important role in daily functioning and well-being.

Coping styles are typically delineated into problem or emotion focused. Coping can also be categorized as approach or avoidance based. Problem-focused coping typically includes strategies to change the situation whereas emotion-focused coping includes strategies to manage your emotional or physiological reaction to the stressor. Approach coping involves efforts to manage or reduce the problem whereas avoidance coping, as the name implies, includes efforts to avoid the problem (Ben-Zur, 2009). Avoidance coping is characterized by strategies such as avoiding others, venting one's feelings (especially anger) on other people, and/or engaging in unsafe health behaviors to reduce tension (e.g., alcohol misuse). According to these distinctions, problem-focused coping is conceptually similar to approach coping and emotion-focused coping is conceptually similar to avoidance coping. Examples of problem-focused/approach coping include efforts to change or modify the situation, whereas examples of emotion-focused/avoidance coping include efforts such as engaging in other activities to manage emotions. Most people use both strategies and there are aspects of each strategy that can be adaptive. However, emotion-focused/avoidant coping is typically thought of as less adaptive than problem-focused coping and tends to be associated with unsatisfactory outcomes (Folkman, Lazarus, Dunkel-Schetter, DeLongis, & Gruen, 1986).

One way in which avoidance coping may be problematic is through the generation of new negative life events that may increase the likelihood of future stressors. In their study of community-residing adults, Holahan, Moos, Holahan, Brennan, and Schutte (2005) found that baseline avoidance coping was associated with reports of more negative life events 4 years later. Holahan et al. (2005) suggested that, due to their tendency to avoid dealing with difficulties, individuals who engage in avoidance coping may have problems that grow over time and lead to additional stressors. In longitudinal studies, avoidance coping has been associated with other negative outcomes, including problem drinking and suicidal ideation (Brennan, Holland, Schutte, & Moos, 2012; Woodhead, Cronkite, Moos, & Timko, 2014).

Research on age-related differences in coping suggests that older adults engage in less avoidance coping and similar or higher levels of approach coping than other age groups (Aldwin, Sutton, Chiara, & Spiro, 1996; Amirkhan & Auyeung, 2007; Segal, Hook, & Coolidge, 2001; Woodhead et al., 2014). This suggests that older adults are potentially better at coping than other age groups because they engage in more attempts to confront the stressful situation rather than avoid it. It is also possible that older adults have learned that avoidance coping may not be as effective as other strategies and are therefore unlikely to try to escape the problem through unhealthy coping efforts (alcohol and drugs; Aldwin et al., 1996). There is some support for the idea that all types of coping decrease with age (Brennan et al., 2012), especially among old-old adults (over age 80; Aldwin et al., 1996). This may reflect an effort to manage stressors before they happen so that older adults are not presented with stressful situations that require distinct coping strategies. Later in this chapter we discuss this issue more when we review research on age-related differences in emotion regulation strategies.

OVERARCHING MODEL OF PERSONALITY DEVELOPMENT

Researchers have attempted to integrate the different theoretical perspectives on personality into an overarching model. This integrative framework proposes five factors that influence personality development: evolution and human nature, the dispositional signature (i.e., traits), characteristic adaptations (i.e., values, goals, plans, life roles), life narratives constructed to make meaning, and the differential role of culture (McAdams & Pals, 2006). Although personality traits are relatively stable over the life span, as noted in the prior section, there may be considerable variation within and between individuals when considering characteristic adaptations and life narratives. Although there has not been empirical research on this framework, these aspects of personality may change substantially over the life span depending on the situations and roles that the individual is in at different ages. This framework is summarized in Table 5.1.

LONGITUDINAL STUDIES OF PERSONALITY CHANGE IN ADULTHOOD

There have been several studies that have followed adults longitudinally to determine the stability or change of personality across adulthood and into older adulthood. Most of these studies have used the trait approach, assessing the Big 5 personality

Table 5.1 Integrative Framework of Personality Development

Dimension	Description and Examples
Evolution and human nature	Human lives as individual variations on a universal design. Example: Tendencies that lead individuals to compete or cooperate with others
Dispositional traits	Broad individual differences in behaviors, thoughts, and feelings that are consistent across time and situations. Example: Big 5 traits
Characteristic adaptations	Aspects of human individuality that may vary across time and situations. Example: Schemas, strategies, tasks
Integrative life narratives	Evolving life stories that provide meaning and identity. Example: "The redemptive self"—gifted protagonist delivered from suffering
Culture	Behavior as a product of the interaction between person and environment (culture). Example: Collectivist vs. individualist cultures

Source: McAdams and Pals (2006).

traits at different ages. When considering change over time, researchers have to consider both mean-level stability and rank-order stability (Specht, Egloff, & Schmukle, 2011). *Mean-level stability* refers to stability in the overall mean of a trait across a period of time for the whole sample. Studies of mean-level stability examine changes in the mean of a personality trait over the course of adulthood. Changes in mean-level stability are thought to be due to maturational or historical changes experienced by a cohort (Robins, Fraley, Roberts, & Trzesniewski, 2001). *Rank-order stability* focuses on change within an individual and is typically measured by the correlation between personality scores across two time points (Robins et al., 2001). High levels of rank-order stability imply that a person's relative position within the sample distribution remains the same. For example, if one person is higher on a certain trait than another person is, high rank-order stability would hypothesize that the first individual will still be higher on the trait than the second individual several years later, even if they both increase or both decrease on the trait (mean-level stability).

In a 4-year study of individuals ages 16 to 96, Specht et al. (2011) found that age had a complex relationship with the Big 5 personality traits. For example, analyses of mean-level stability found that levels of conscientiousness increased among younger adult participants across the 4 years of the study, steadily declined among participants aged 30 to 70, and declined again after age 70. Levels of agreeableness were higher among older than younger adult participants, while levels of extraversion were lower among older than younger adults. Levels of emotional stability increased until age 30, decreased until around age 60 or 70, and then increased again. With regard to rank-order stability, an inverted U-shaped function was found for emotional stability, extraversion, openness, and agreeableness. That is, these traits were most stable around age 40 to 60 and were less stable in younger and older adulthood. Conscientiousness was the only trait that had a consistently increasing rank-order stability, suggesting that the stability of this trait increases with age, even when the mean level of conscientiousness decreases with age. Results of other longitudinal studies also suggest that personality traits may demonstrate an inverted U pattern of rank-order stability, with traits reaching their peak stability in midlife (Milojev & Sibley, 2014; Wortman, Lucas, & Donnellan, 2012).

In a meta-analysis of mean-level stability, Roberts, Walton, and Viechtbauer (2006) found that mean levels of conscientiousness increased in adulthood up to age 70 and then leveled out. Mean levels of social vitality, a facet of extraversion that includes sociability, positive affect, and gregariousness, decreased significantly between ages 60 and 70. Emotional stability and agreeableness also increased significantly between ages 50 and 60. This study concluded that the majority of personality change occurs between ages 20 and 40. As you may have noticed, some of these results are different than the Specht et al. (2011) study summarized previously. This may be due to different analytic techniques and different samples. Nevertheless, the results on mean-level change in personality strongly suggest that personality continues to change into middle and older adulthood.

In a meta-analysis of rank-order stability across 152 longitudinal studies of personality, test-retest correlations indicated that stability was highest between ages 50 and 70 (correlation coefficient of .74) and lowest during childhood (correlation coefficient of .31). The correlation coefficient during the college years was .54 and was .64 at age 30 (Roberts & DelVecchio, 2000). Although this and other studies have found relatively high rank-order stability at most ages, the research cited previously on the inverted U shape for stability of personality traits contradicts other research suggesting that personality traits are highly stable after age 30 (McCrae & Costa, 2003; Terracciano, McCrae, & Costa, 2010). Taken together, this research suggests that mean levels of personality traits may change with age, although the association is more complex than a linear increase or decrease. Additionally, individual stability of personality traits appears to peak in midlife with less stability at the younger and older ends of the age spectrum.

EMOTIONAL FUNCTIONING IN LATE LIFE

Think about a typical day for you and describe the types of emotions you experienced during that day. This task might seem straightforward, but with further thought you may notice that your emotional experience can vary on multiple dimensions, including the intensity of the emotions (i.e., strength of the emotions), their duration (i.e., how long they lasted), and their frequency (i.e., how often you experienced an emotion). You might also consider how well you were able to regulate your emotions that day, whether there was anything in your day that produced a strong emotion, and how you would describe your overall emotional well-being on that particular day. The goal of this section is to understand how the emotional experiences of older adults compare to other age groups, according to the aforementioned dimensions, as well as whether the structure or function of emotions changes with age.

AGE AND EMOTIONAL WELL-BEING

Early research on age and emotional well-being posited that emotional experience over the life span followed a similar curve as other biological functions (Banham, 1951). This early research attributed these changes in emotional well-being to "limited opportunities of old people for the satisfaction of thwarted needs" as well as to declines in mental and physical health (p. 175). Early research on emotional development proposed that there were increases in emotional well-being through the 20s and then a steady decline through middle and older adulthood (Banham, 1951). Some of the emotional traits attributed to older adults included "feelings of inadequacy, rejection, anxiety, depression, hypochondria, and emotional sensitivity," among others (p. 175).

Modern research suggests that the emotional experience of middle-aged and older adults may not be as negative as outlined previously. In a longitudinal study of adults ages 18 to 43, Galambos, Fang, Krahn, Johnson, and Lachman (2015) found that happiness ratings continued to increase into the 30s. Although there was a modest decrease in happiness at age 43, this study provides some initial data suggesting that happiness continues to increase across adulthood. This study also controlled for several variables typically associated with happiness, such as marital and employment status, physical health, gender, school grades, self-esteem, and parents' educational levels. The increase in happiness across age groups remained even when accounting for these variables.

These results might make you wonder how happiness is measured. Is happiness the same as life satisfaction? These types of questions about how to measure happiness have been debated extensively in the literature (Diener, Suh, Lucas, & Smith, 1999). One approach to thinking about the measurement of happiness is to consider happiness and life satisfaction as different constructs that make up subjective well-being. Studies that examine age-related differences in happiness tend to ask participants how happy they are with their lives in general, with responses ranging from not very happy at all to very happy (Galambos et al., 2015). A different approach is to ask participants to rate their happiness at different points throughout the day, rather than assess global reports of happiness (Stone, Schwartz, Broderick, & Deaton, 2010).

In a study comparing happiness ratings between younger adults (ages 16 to 59) and older adults (older than age 60), levels of happiness did not vary by age with 39.6% of the sample reporting that they were currently "very happy" and only 8.0% reporting that they were "not too happy" (Cooper et al., 2011). In this study, higher ratings of happiness were more likely among those with a social network of more than three people, less dependency on others for activities of daily living, more social capital, and more frequent social participation. When looking only at the older adult participants, additional age differences emerged. For example, more religious attendance and a higher importance placed on religion were associated with higher happiness ratings only among participants older than age 80 and not among those ages 60 to 69 or ages 70 to 79. Being married was associated with higher happiness ratings only among those ages 60 to 69 and not among those who were older than age 70.

Happiness ratings may be influenced by the time period in which an individual was born, which means that these ratings may be subject to cohort effects. However, even when controlling for cohort effects, research suggests that there is a U-shaped curve to happiness across the life span and across different cultures (Blanchflower & Oswald, 2008). Happiness ratings are typically the lowest in middle age, consistent with the study presented previously which found that happiness ratings decreased around age 43 (Galambos et al., 2015). This curve is similar for men and women and for people from developed or developing nations (Blanchflower & Oswald, 2008). There appears to be a shift in happiness ratings and emotional experience around age 50. Prior to this age, global well-being and positive affect decrease slightly with increasing age. Prior to age 50, negative emotions of worry and sadness tend to stay at similar levels whereas stress and anger tend to decrease. After age 50 people tend to report higher global well-being, more positive affect, and less negative affect except for sadness, which does not show much change across age groups (Stone et al., 2010). Overall, Stone et al. (2010) found that stress and anger declined starting in the early 20s, worry stayed elevated throughout middle age and then started to decline, and sadness tended to stay constant.

As you may have noticed, the prior study examined both global measures of happiness and the experience of specific positive and negative emotions. Research on the trajectory of specific emotions across the life span replicates the Stone et al. (2010) study and suggests that the frequency of sadness remains stable across the life span with a slight increase in old age, whereas anger increases during young adulthood and then declines into old age (Kunzmann, Richter, & Schmukle, 2013). When older adults do experience anger, it appears to be experienced less intensely than younger adults whereas sadness is experienced with the same intensity regardless of age (Kunzmann & Thomas, 2014). In an experience-sampling study of adults across a 1-week time period in which they were asked to report on their emotional experience five times per day, a decrease in the frequency of negative emotions was observed for adults between ages 18 and 60, with a leveling out after age 60 (Carstensen, Pasupathi, Mayr, & Nesselroade, 2000; see Figure 5.1). There were no age-related differences in the experience of positive emotion, or in the intensity of both positive and negative emotions. The authors conclude that age is related to a decline in the experience of negative emotions but no changes in the intensity of emotional experiences.

It is possible that happiness ratings and the experience of positive and negative affect with increasing age are different among older adults who are coping with chronic illnesses. Much of the research on happiness and life satisfaction tends to be done with community-dwelling older adults who may be relatively healthy compared to their peers. Some research suggests that older adults maintain similar happiness ratings as younger adults even in the face of declining physical and mental health (Vestergaard et al., 2015). However, specific chronic illnesses may impact daily well-being. In a study of adults older than age 50, individuals with chronic illnesses reported significantly lower quality of life and happiness ratings than those older adults without chronic illnesses (Wikman, Wardle, & Steptoe, 2011). In this sample, approximately half of the participants had a chronic illness. The results suggest that older adults who had a stroke reported the lowest level of happiness and quality of life as well as the most elevated reports of depressed mood. This is consistent with the "vascular depression" hypothesis of late-life depression (Alexopoulos et al.,

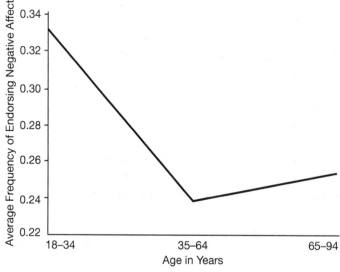

Figure 5.1 Decrease in negative affect with age.
Source: Carstensen et al. (2000).

1997). Reporting two or more chronic illnesses was associated with lower happiness ratings than having only one chronic illness.

This study assessed both happiness ratings and level of depressed mood. We have primarily been reviewing studies that have examined happiness ratings, although you might also wonder whether older adults have lower or higher rates of psychological disorders than other age groups. Generally the prevalence of certain mental health conditions, such as major depressive disorder, declines with age (see Chapter 6; Byers, Yaffe, Covinsky, Friedman, & Bruce, 2010). Additionally, measures of psychological distress, which usually examine symptoms of both depression and anxiety, tend to decrease from the 20s to the 60s (Jorm, Windsor, Dear, & Anstey, 2005). Other research suggests that psychological distress may peak in middle age (45 to 54 years old) and then decline, consistent with the U-shaped happiness curve (Forman-Hoffman et al., 2014).

When thinking about your own emotional experience, you might consider how often you experience both positive and negative emotions in response to the same situation. The experience of greater affective complexity (i.e., experiencing positive and negative emotions in the same moment) has been proposed as an adaptive process that is indicative of healthy emotional development (Carstensen et al., 2000). When this process is examined among adults, results suggest that older adults are more likely to experience situations in which positive and negative emotions co-occur, often referred to as poignancy (Carstensen et al., 2000), although recent research has found no evidence for an increase in affective complexity with age (Grühn, Lumley, Diehl, & Labouvie-Vief, 2013). Examining the occurrence of mixed emotions can be difficult, however, because many studies find that older adults are unlikely to report strong negative emotions on a daily basis (Grühn et al., 2013). It is unclear, however, whether the low variability in the experience of negative emotions among older adults is adaptive or not. For instance, infrequent experience of negative emotions may suggest that older adults are better at avoiding situations that provoke negative affect, which could be positive or negative depending on the context.

ATTENTION TO POSITIVE AND NEGATIVE STIMULI

The research reviewed in the prior section suggests that older adults tend to report either greater or similar emotional well-being than other age groups, and an overall decrease in the experience of negative emotion and psychological distress. Why do we see these findings? Evidence is accumulating that older adults may differentially attend to positive and negative stimuli, leading to a phenomenon known as the *age-related positivity effect* (Reed, Chan, & Mikels, 2014). We first consider evidence for the age-related positivity effect from laboratory studies and then consider evidence from studies that ask older adults to recall and describe positive versus negative memories.

Laboratory-based studies of the age-related positivity effect typically ask participants to view a series of emotional (positive and negative) and neutral images involving both social and nonsocial material. The images are typically presented for a couple seconds. After about a 15-minute delay, participants are asked to write down as much as they can remember about all of the images. In a study of younger, middle-aged, and older adults, Charles, Mather, and Carstensen (2003) found that middle-aged and older adults recalled a greater number of positive than negative images compared to younger adults, who recalled similar numbers of positive and negative images. This suggests that, with age, relatively more positive than negative information was recalled, which may partially explain why older adults show decreases in negative emotions compared to other age groups.

Another strategy for assessing age-related differences in attention to emotional stimuli is by studying how long participants look at emotional images, as opposed to what type of information is recalled. Two methods for assessing attention to emotional images are the dot-probe task and eye tracking. In the dot-probe task, two images are presented (one neutral and one emotional) for a short period of time. Once the images disappear, a dot is presented in place of one of the images, which remains until the participant presses a key to indicate the location of the dot. This produces a bias score, which can tell the researcher whether there were longer reaction times when the dot was in place of the emotional or nonemotional image. A positive bias score indicates a preference for emotional images (Isaacowitz, Wadlinger, Goren, & Wilson, 2006). The eye-tracking paradigm involves tracking the movement of the left eye during presentation of the images. Relative looking times for the two images are compared and calculated into a fixation ratio score. Similar to the dot-probe paradigm, a positive ratio score indicates a preference for the emotional images. Isaacowitz and colleagues (2006), using both the dot-probe task and eye-tracking, found that older adults demonstrated an eye-tracking pattern whereby their gaze was more toward happy faces and away from sad faces. In contrast, younger adults also gazed away from sad faces but did not show a preference toward happy faces like the older adult participants. When considering the data from the dot-probe task, older adults responded more quickly to the location of the dot when it replaced positive stimuli (i.e., happy faces).

One criticism of the research on the age-related positivity effect is that it has been done primarily on U.S. participants. Some researchers suggest that the high value that Americans place on independence and autonomy may lead individuals to seek positive emotional experiences to maintain their sense of optimism and self-esteem (Fung et al., 2008). In contrast, other cultures that are more interdependent (i.e., East Asian cultures) may attune more to negative emotions in order to avoid social mistakes and therefore fit in better with one's social unit. In a study of younger and older adults in Hong Kong (Fung et al., 2008), the older adults in the study gazed longer at fearful than happy faces or sad faces, whereas the younger participants did not show attentional preferences toward any of the stimuli. This suggests that there may not be an age-related positivity bias, per se, but instead a preference for emotionally meaningful information, which may vary across cultures.

Other researchers have studied the age-related positivity effect through the recall of autobiographical memories. The hypothesis here is that older adults may put a positive spin on their memories, recalling more of the positive aspects of an event than the negative ones. For example, Kennedy, Mather, and Carstensen (2004) found that, when asked to recall memories several years after they initially reported them, older adults tended to put a positive spin on the memories. In a study that analyzed spontaneous autobiographical memories from younger and older adults, Schlagman, Schulz, and Kvavilashvili (2006) found that recall of positive memories was relatively equal between younger and older adults, whereas older adults recalled very few negative events relative to younger adults. When older adults did recall negative events, they tended to rate them as either neutral or positive, suggesting that recasting negative life events in positive or neutral terms may be an emotion regulation strategy for older adults. Even in the midst of discussing a disagreement with a spouse, older adults tend to view their spouse's behavior more positively than middle-aged couples and more positively than an objective rater (Story et al., 2007).

In light of this evidence let us return to the idea of the age-related positivity effect. Some researchers have posited that there may be a positivity bias among older adults because they have reduced cognitive abilities to process negative stimuli (MacPherson, Phillips, & Della Sala, 2002). Indeed, research by MacPherson and colleagues (2002) suggests that older adults show a reduced ability to label negative facial emotions relative to younger adults. However, research on the age-related positivity effect has found that similar types of preferences for positive stimuli and emotionally meaningful goals can be induced among younger adults in the face of limited time horizons (e.g., Fung, Carstensen, & Lutz, 1999). This suggests that the shift toward positivity with age is motivated by a desire for emotional gratification (Carstensen & Mikels, 2005), potentially due to limited time horizons for older adults.

Other researchers have posited that there may not necessarily be a positivity bias among older adults, but rather that older adults may attend less to negative information than other age groups (Wood & Kisley, 2006). In a study of younger and older adults, Wood and Kisley (2006) found that younger adults attended more to negative than positive information, consistent with a negativity bias that is often seen among individuals. This means that, on average, individuals tend to pay more attention to negative than positive information. In Wood and Kisley's study (2006) older adults attended equally to negative and positive information, demonstrating no negativity bias but also no positivity bias. This suggests that older adults are able to weigh information more equally than other age groups.

You might be able to think of situations in which turning your attention away from negative information may have caused problems. For example, in decisions related to your health, you may have to attend to negative information in order to make an informed choice about treatments for a serious health condition. Research on the positivity effect in the context of health care decision making suggests that when older and younger adults are asked to decide on a health care plan and physician, older adults tended to review and recall more positive information than younger adults (Löckenhoff & Carstensen, 2007), potentially making a poor decision by not attending to the negative aspects of their decisions. However, this preference for positive information among older adults could be shifted by asking them to focus on the "facts and details" when making their decisions about health care plans and physicians. Specifically, older adults in a control condition reviewed more positive than negative material to come to their decisions, compared to older adults in the "information focused" condition. The results of this study suggest that older adults can potentially override their preferences for positive information when they are specifically cued to consider all information at hand.

AGE-RELATED DIFFERENCES IN EMOTION REGULATION

In the previous section we reviewed research suggesting that one way in which older adults may regulate their emotions is through the age-related positivity effect. That is, older adults may limit their exposure to negative emotions by attending more to positive stimuli and putting a positive spin on autobiographical memories. However, there are other ways in which people may regulate emotions beyond a preference for positive over negative stimuli. For example, consider how you regulate your emotions immediately during and after a negative event. You might talk to yourself to try to calm down or manage strong emotions. Are older adults better able to control their emotions in the moment when faced with a negative event? Additionally, consider your physiological reactivity during an emotional event. You may experience a racing heart, flushed face, and other signs that your body is under stress. How do older adults compare when we examine their emotional reactivity?

Let us start by examining what happens to older adults after they experience a negative event. Research suggests that older adults may employ more passive strategies to regulate their emotions during stressful events, such as walking away, ignoring a situation, or doing nothing. In contrast, younger adults may employ more active strategies, such as cognitively reframing the situation or directly confronting the individual who is causing a conflict (Blanchard-Fields, Mienaltowski, & Seay, 2007). In fact, older adults tend to choose better strategies for solving interpersonal problems than younger adults, suggesting that they are more adept at regulating their emotional reactions in interpersonal relationships characterized by high levels of tension (Birditt, Fingerman, & Almeida, 2005). As an example of this, Charles, Piazza, and Luong (2009) conducted a daily-diary study of adults between ages 25 and 74. Participants were asked to report their daily experiences of having an argument, avoiding an argument, total number of daily stressors, and negative affect. Older participants in the sample reported fewer arguments and fewer avoided arguments than other age groups. Younger participants experienced higher levels of negative affect on days when arguments were avoided, whereas this association was not significant for older adults. When arguments did occur and were not avoided, younger and older participants reported similar levels of negative affect. The authors calculated that for every 10-year increase in age, negative affect in response to avoided arguments decreased by 16%. These results suggest that avoiding arguments is an effective emotion regulation strategy for older but not younger adults, as younger adults' levels of negative affect were still relatively high on days of avoided arguments.

Why does avoiding situations work for older but not younger adults? We can make light of these findings by considering the process model of emotion regulation (Gross, 1998). *Situation selection* allows individuals to control their emotions by selecting the types of situations in which they find themselves. *Situation modification* involves changing the situation. *Attentional deployment* involves attending to other aspects of the situation or redirecting attention to something else. *Cognitive change* is when individuals try to reframe the situation or reappraise it so that the emotional impact is modified. Finally, *response modulation* refers to managing and changing emotions and behavior once the situation is happening, such as through suppressing emotions or displaying a different emotion than is felt internally by the individual.

Urry and Gross (2010) suggested that there are age-related differences in the use of these emotion regulation strategies. The decrease in the quantity of social relationships with age may help with situation selection. That is, older adults tend to have smaller social networks that involve closer relationships (see Chapter 10). Therefore, older adults may select the situations they are in by surrounding themselves with people who are unlikely to elicit frequent negative emotions. Older adults typically do not try to modify the situation, instead preferring to "preserve harmony" in interpersonal relationships (Birditt & Fingerman, 2003). As discussed previously, the age-related positivity effect suggests that older adults may be better at attentional deployment by shifting their focus away from negative situations and toward positive situations. In contrast, older adults may perform less well in the areas of cognitive change and response modulation. Although older adults are better at using positive reappraisal than younger adults, and tend to use it more frequently, some types of cognitive reframing are less effective for older adults, such as detached reappraisal, which involves focusing one's attention on the nonemotional aspects of a situation (Shiota & Levenson, 2009). Additionally, older adults may suppress their outward experiences of emotional states less frequently than younger adults (John

Table 5.2 Age-Related Differences in the Process Model of Emotion Regulation

Domain	Description	Age-Related Differences
Situation selection	Avoid situations that are likely to provoke negative emotions	- Older adults more likely to use situation selection - May be related to having a smaller, closer relationship network - Older adults experience less negative affect than younger adults when avoiding arguments
Situation modification	Change the situation	- Older adults want to preserve harmony in relationships - Younger adults try to change the person or situation
Attentional deployment	Attend to other aspects of the situation or think about something else	- Age-related positivity effect suggests that older adults can divert attention more easily to positive stimuli
Cognitive change	Reframe the situation either positively or as a way to detach from the situation	- Older adults engage in more positive reframing than younger adults - Other cognitive strategies work better for younger than older adults
Response modulation	Suppress or conceal outward emotional expression	- Older adults are less likely to suppress or conceal emotional expressions

& Gross, 2004). Taken together, older and younger adults use different strategies to regulate emotions, with older adults tending to select the situations they are in more strategically than younger adults in order to limit negative interactions (see Table 5.2). Due to this, older adults may be more effective at regulating emotions around interpersonal stressors than other age groups.

MODELS OF EMOTIONAL FUNCTIONING IN LATE LIFE

Let's review the research findings we have discussed so far. Older adults experience fewer negative emotions than younger adults, although when they do experience negative emotions, they are experienced at the same intensity as other age groups. Older adults experience more positive emotions and have an increased ability to attend to positive stimuli, which is accounted for by the age-related positivity effect. Older adults may also recast current and prior negative life events more positively than is warranted by outside evidence. However, when it is necessary to consider negative information, such as in decisions about health care, older adults are able to do so if cued appropriately. Finally, older adults may choose more effective strategies for regulating emotions, particularly in interpersonal situations.

We have hinted at the idea that older adults may experience this type of improved emotional life due to an appreciation of their limited time horizons compared to other age groups (Carstensen & Mikels, 2005). What is meant by "limited time horizons?" Socioemotional selectivity theory (Carstensen, Fung, & Charles, 2003) posits that perceived limitations on the time that an individual has left to live leads to a motivational shift such that emotionally meaningful goals are pursued. The theory posits that goals are always set within a temporal context. When an individual is younger, time is seen as open ended. This leads a younger individual to pursue goals that emphasize the acquisition of knowledge and new experience (expansive goals). These goals may lead to the experience of negative emotions and feeling-states, such as anxiety, failure, and disappointment. As an individual ages, there is a shift in perception about time (termed *future time perspective*). Time horizons become shorter with age, which leads to a shift in goals. Whereas younger adulthood is characterized by information-seeking goals, older adulthood is characterized by emotionally meaningful goals. For example, the immediate positive feelings of connecting with a close friend or family member are prioritized over the desire to try something new such as traveling in order to gain knowledge, which may involve future payoffs (i.e., more knowledge about other cultures) at the expense of current emotional state (i.e., interacting with people you may or may not like, the stress of traveling, the inconvenience of being away from familiar friends and routines). In sum, socioemotional selectivity theory posits that older adults experience a more positive and complex emotional life because their perception that time is "running out" leads them to prioritize emotionally meaningful goals, which limits their exposure to negative emotional states.

A second model that accounts for age-related differences in emotional functioning is the Strength and Vulnerability Integration (SAVI) model (Charles, 2010). This model accounts for the strengths that older adults bring to emotional regulation and well-being, as well as the potential weaknesses. First let us consider the strengths that older adults bring to the area of emotional well-being. The SAVI model considers that the limited time perspective of older adults increases emotional well-being in that it leads to prioritization of emotionally meaningful goals and a focus on the present as opposed to the future, as discussed in the prior section on socioemotional selectivity theory. A second strength that is considered in the SAVI model is that the passage of time leads older adults to have a better understanding of how to keep themselves content and avoid situations that lead to high levels of distress in their daily lives. Therefore, older adults have at least two strengths that contribute to improved emotional well-being.

Older adults also have strengths that lead to improved ability to regulate emotions. First, the age-related positivity effect, discussed earlier in this chapter, leads to an improved ability to shift focus away from negative stimuli. Second, they are more likely to quickly disengage from a negative situation than younger adults. This is done by using the strategies discussed in the emotion regulation section, such as doing nothing or walking away. These types of strategies should not be mistaken for passive–aggressive strategies, as the goal is typically to downplay the negative experience rather than deny that it has happened. This relates to the third strength that older adults have with emotion regulation, which is that they typically downplay the potentially negative sides of an event after it has passed.

The vulnerabilities that are discussed by the SAVI model focus on situations when older adults are unable to escape negative situations, such as when they are unable to extricate themselves from a situation by not entering the situation in the first place, downplaying it, distracting attention away from the negative aspects, or engaging in passive regulation strategies. When older adults are exposed to inescapable negative situations, the vulnerabilities that they face include physiological impacts of sustained emotional arousal, such as reduced physiological flexibility in the cardiovascular system (seen in the decrease in heart rate variability) and

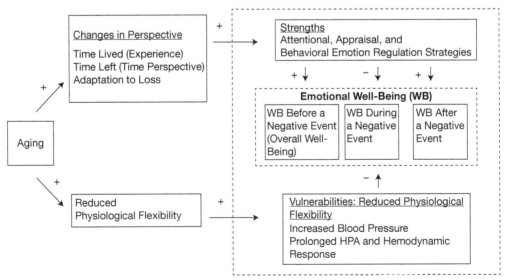

Figure 5.2 Summary of the Strength and Vulnerability Integration (SAVI) model.
HPA, hypothalamic–pituitary–adrenal.
Source: Charles (2010).

neuroendocrine system (seen in the reduced ability to downregulate the activity of the hypothalamic–pituitary–adrenal [HPA] axis). These are all normal age-related physiological changes. However, in the context of prolonged exposure to a negative situation, these physiological changes lead to a more difficult time recovering from a stressful event, both emotionally and physiologically. These changes are not observed in younger adults and are therefore considered vulnerabilities in the context of the SAVI model. Taken together, the SAVI model seeks to combine the literature on age-related differences in emotional well-being and emotion regulation in order to understand a broader picture of emotional development across the life span. The SAVI model is summarized in Figure 5.2.

KEYS TO HAPPY AGING

The age-related positivity effect suggests that older adults are motivated to attend to positive stimuli and avoid attention to negative stimuli as an emotion regulation strategy. Socioemotional selectivity theory suggests that older adults prioritize emotionally meaningful goals as they realize that time is running out. Therefore, older adults may not have to "do" anything per se to experience a better emotional life with age. However, there may be daily activities that increase or decrease happiness ratings among older adults. What else can older adults do to maintain or improve happiness in late life? In a study of retired older adults in the Netherlands ranging in age from 55 to 88, spending more time on physical, social, and cognitive activities was associated with greater daily happiness ratings. In contrast, spending more time on household activities (i.e., chores) was associated with lower daily happiness ratings (Oerlemans, Bakker, & Veenhoven, 2011). Interestingly, older adults in this study were most happy when they combined physical, social, and cognitive activities with restful activities, suggesting that there may need to be recovery time between activities. Therefore, older adults may benefit from encouragement to engage in enjoyable activities that are also stimulating as a way to maintain a positive mood in late life. It is also important to consider individual differences when thinking of types of activities that may increase happiness. For example, not all of the older adults in the aforementioned study benefited from social interaction; those who scored higher on measures of extraversion had high levels of happiness resulting from social interaction whereas those who were introverted tended to not derive happiness from daily social interactions (Oerlemans et al., 2011). Other research suggests that regular interaction with friends has more of a positive impact on happiness and well-being among older adults than interactions with relatives, potentially due to the ability to confide in a friend, as well as less of a sense of obligation among friends than family members (Blieszner, 2014).

CONCLUSION

In this chapter we reviewed age-related changes in personality and emotional functioning. There are several theoretical approaches to studying personality, and most of them have examined the extent to which the theory applies to older adults. For example, Joan Erikson's proposal of a ninth stage of psychosocial development, as well as ways in which attachment processes may be important in late life, and ways in which coping strategies change with age, all represent the application of existing theories to later life. The approach that has the most research is the five-factor model. Although personality function was initially proposed to be fairly stable across the life span, recent longitudinal studies suggest that stability may be greatest in midlife, between ages 40 and 60, with less stability among younger and older adults. Additionally, the extent to which the Big 5 personality traits change with age is complex, with some traits increasing throughout young adulthood, decreasing in middle age, and then increasing again in late life.

The second section of the chapter focused on emotional functioning in late life. Overall happiness and life satisfaction tends to increase with age. The experience of negative emotions tends to decrease with age, with a relative increase in attention to positive stimuli, termed the age-related positivity effect. Older adults also show more effective strategies for regulating emotions, including situation selection and attentional deployment toward more positive features of the situation. Some of these changes can be accounted for through two theoretical models: socioemotional selectivity theory and the SAVI model. Socioemotional selectivity theory posits that the changes seen in the emotional life of older adults are due to a shift in goals toward more emotionally meaningful interactions. The SAVI model integrates the research on emotional development and posits that older adults bring strengths and weaknesses to this process.

DISCUSSION QUESTIONS

1. Summarize the major theories of personality development.

2. Describe age-related changes seen in personality traits, as suggested by results of longitudinal studies.

3. Describe what is meant by the U-shaped curve for happiness across the life span, and factors that may contribute to happiness ratings among older adults.

4. Explain the age-related positivity effect and discuss the cross-cultural findings on this effect.

5. Describe some of the emotion regulation strategies that older adults use and how they fit within Gross's process model of emotion regulation.

6. How does socioemotional selectivity theory account for age-related differences in emotional functioning?

REFERENCES

Aldwin, C. M., Sutton, K. J., Chiara, G., & Spiro, A. (1996). Age differences in stress, coping, and appraisal: Findings from the Normative Aging Study. *The Journals of Gerontology, 51B*, P179–P188. doi:10.1093/geronb/51B.4.P179

Alexopoulos, G. S., Meyers, B. S., Young, R. C., Campbell, S., Silbersweig, D., & Charlson, M. (1997). "Vascular depression" hypothesis. *Archives of General Psychiatry, 54*, 915–922.

Amirkhan, J., & Auyeung, B. (2007). Coping with stress across the lifespan: Absolute vs. relative changes in strategy. *Journal of Applied Developmental Psychology, 28*, 298–317. doi:10.1016/j.app dev.2007.04.002

Banham, K. M. (1951). Senescence and the emotions: A genetic theory. *The Pedagogical Seminary and Journal of Genetic Psychology, 78*, 175–183. doi:10.1080/08856559.1951.10533576

Ben-Zur, H. (2009). Coping styles and affect. *International Journal of Stress Management, 16*, 87–101. doi:10.1037/a0015731

Birditt, K. S., & Fingerman, K. L. (2003). Age and gender differences in adults' descriptions of emotional reactions to interpersonal problems. *The Journals of Gerontology, 58B*, P237–P245. doi:10.1093/geronb/58.4.P237

Birditt, K. S., Fingerman, K. L., & Almeida, D. M. (2005). Age differences in exposure and reactions to interpersonal tensions: A daily diary study. *Psychology and Aging, 20*, 330–340. doi:10.1037/0882-7974.20.2.330

*Blanchard-Fields, F. Mienaltowski, A., & Seay, R. B. (2007). Age differences in everyday problem-solving effectiveness: Older adults select more effective strategies for interpersonal problems. *The Journals of Gerontology, 62B*, P61–P64. doi:10.1093/geronb/62.1.P61

Blanchflower, D. G., & Oswald, A. J. (2008). Is well-being U-shaped over the life cycle? *Social Science and Medicine, 66*, 1733–1749. doi:10.1016/j.socscimed.2008.01.030

Blieszner, R. (2014). The worth of friendship: Can friends keep us healthy and happy? *Generations, 38*, 23–30.

Booth, J. E., Schinka, J. A., Brown, L. M., Mortimer, J. A., & Borenstein, A. R. (2006). Five-factor personality dimensions, mood states, and cognitive performance in older adults. *Journal of Clinical and Experimental Neuropsychology, 28*, 676–683. doi:10.1080/13803390590954209

Bradley, J. M., & Cafferty, T. P. (2001). Attachment among older adults: Current issues and directions for future research. *Attachment and Human Development, 3*, 200–221. doi:10.1080/146 16730126485

Brennan, P. L., Holland, J. M., Schutte, K. K., & Moos, R. H. (2012). Coping trajectories in later life: A 20-year predictive study. *Aging and Mental Health, 16*, 305–316. doi:10.1080/13607863.2011 .628975

Brown, C., & Lewis, M. J. (2003). Psychosocial development in the elderly: An investigation into Erikson's ninth stage. *Journal of Aging Studies, 17*, 415–426. doi:10.1016/S0890-4065(03)00061-6

Byers, A. L., Yaffe, K., Covinsky, K. E., Friedman, M. B., & Bruce, M. L. (2010). High occurrence of mood and anxiety disorders among older adults: The national comorbidity survey replication. *Archives of General Psychiatry, 67*, 489–496. doi:10.1001/archgenpsychiatry.2010.35

Carstensen, L. L., Fung, H., & Charles, S. T. (2003). Socioemotional selectivity theory and the regulation of emotion in the second half of life. *Motivation and Emotion, 27*, 103–123. doi:0146 -7239/03/0600-0103/0

*Carstensen, L. L., & Mikels, J. A. (2005). At the intersection of emotion and cognition: Aging and the positivity effect. *Current Directions in Psychological Science, 14*, 117–121. doi:10.1111/j.0963 -7214.2005.00348.x

*Carstensen, L. L., Pasupathi, M., Mayr, U., & Nesselroade, J. R. (2000). Emotional experience in everyday life across the adult life span. *Journal of Personality and Social Psychology, 79*, 644–655. doi:10.1037/0022-3514.79.4.644

*Charles, S. T. (2010). Strength and vulnerability integration (SAVI): A model of emotional well-being across adulthood. *Psychological Bulletin, 136*, 1068–1091. doi:10.1037/a0021232

Charles, S. T., Mather, M., & Carstensen, L. L. (2003). Aging and emotional memory: The forgettable nature of negative images for older adults. *Journal of Experimental Psychology: General, 132*, 310–324. doi:10.1037/0096-3445.132.2.310

Charles, S. T., Piazza, J. R., & Luong, G. (2009). Now you see it, now you don't: Age differences in affective reactivity to social tensions. *Psychology and Aging, 24*, 645–653. doi:10.1037/a0016673

Connor-Smith, J. K., & Flachsbart, C. (2007). Relations between personality and coping: A meta-analysis. *Journal of Personality and Social Psychology, 93*, 1080–1107. doi:10.1037/0022-3514.93 .6.1080

Cooper, C., Bebbington, P., King, M. Jenkins, R., Farrell, M., Brugha, T., . . . Livingston, G. (2011). Happiness across age groups: Results from the 2007 National Psychiatric Morbidity Survey. *International Journal of Geriatric Psychiatry, 26*, 608–614. doi:10.1002/gps.2570

Costa, P. T., Jr., & McCrae, R. R. (1994). Stability and change in personality from adolescence through adulthood. In C. F. Halverson, G. A. Kohnstamm, & R. P. Martin (Eds.), *The developing structure of temperament and personality from infancy to adulthood* (pp. 139–150). Hillsdale, NJ: Erlbaum.

Curtis, R. G., Windsor, T. D., & Soubelet, A. (2015). The relationship between Big-5 personality traits and cognitive ability in older adults—A review. *Aging, Neuropsychology, and Cognition, 22*, 42–71. doi:10.1080/13825585.2014.888392

Diener, E., Suh, E. M., Lucas, R. E., & Smith, H. L. (1999). Subjective well-being: Three decades of progress. *Psychological Bulletin, 125*, 276–302. doi:10.1037/0033-2909.125.2.276

Erikson, E. H., & Erikson, J. M. (1998). *The life cycle completed* (extended version). New York, NY: W. W. Norton.

Erikson, E. H., Erikson, J. M., & Kivnick, H. Q. (1986). *Vital involvement in old age: The experience of old age in our time.* New York, NY: W. W. Norton.

Folkman, S., Lazarus, R. S., Dunkel-Schetter, C., DeLongis, A., & Gruen, R. J. (1986). Dynamics of a stressful encounter: Cognitive appraisal, coping, and encounter outcomes. *Journal of Personality and Social Psychology, 50*, 992–1003.

Forman-Hoffman, V. L., Muhuri, P. K., Novak, S. P., Pemberton, M. R., Ault, K. L., & Mannix, D. (2014). Psychological distress and mortality among adults in the U.S. household population. Substance Abuse and Mental Health Services Administration. Retrieved from https://www.samhsa.gov/data/sites/default/files/CBHSQ-DR-C11-MI-Mortality-2014/CBHSQ-DR-C11-MI-Mortality-2014.htm

Fung, H. H., Carstensen, L. L., & Lutz, A. M. (1999). Influence of time on social preferences: Implications for life-span development. *Psychology and Aging, 14*, 595–604. doi:10.1037/0882-7974.14.4.595

Fung, H. H., Isaacowitz, D. M., Lu, A. Y., Wadlinger, H. A., Goren, D., & Wilson, H. R. (2008). Age-related positivity enhancement is not universal: Older Chinese look away from positive stimuli. *Psychology and Aging, 23*, 440–446. doi:10.1037/0882-7974.23.2.440

Galambos, N. A., Fang, S., Krahn, H. J., Johnson, M. D., & Lachman, M. E. (2015). Up, not down: The age curve in happiness from early adulthood to midlife in two longitudinal studies. *Developmental Psychology, 51*, 1664–1671. doi:10.1037/dev0000052

Gross, J. J. (1998). Antecedent- and response-focused emotion regulation: Divergent consequences for experience, expression, and physiology. *Journal of Personality and Social Psychology, 74*, 224–237. doi:10.1037/0022-3514.74.1.224

Grühn, D., Lumley, M. A., Diehl, M., & Labouvie-Vief, G. (2013). Time-based indicators of emotional complexity: Interrelations and correlates. *Emotion, 13*, 226–237. doi:10.1037/a0030363

Hannah, M. T., Domino, G., Figueredo, A. J., & Hendrickson, R. (1996). The prediction of ego integrity in older persons. *Educational and Psychological Measurement, 56*, 930–950. doi:10.1177/0013164496056006002

Holahan, C. J., Moos, R. H., Holahan, C. K., Brennan, P. L., & Schutte, K. K. (2005). Stress generation, avoidance coping, and depressive symptoms: A 10-year model. *Journal of Consulting and Clinical Psychology, 73*, 658–666. doi:10.1037/0022-006X.73.4.658

Isaacowitz, D. M., Wadlinger, H. A., Goren, D., & Wilson, H. R. (2006). Is there an age-related positivity effect in visual attention? A comparison of two methodologies. *Emotion, 6*, 511–516. doi:10.1037/1528-3542.6.3.511

Jerram, K. L., & Coleman, P. G. (1999). The big five personality traits and reporting of health problems and health behaviour in old age. *British Journal of Health Psychology, 4*, 181–192. doi:10.1348/135910799168560

John, O. P., & Gross, J. J. (2004). Healthy and unhealthy emotion regulation: Personality processes, individual differences, and life span development. *Journal of Personality, 72*, 1301–1334. doi:10.1111/j.1467-6494.2004.00298.x

Jorm, A. F., Windsor, T. D., Dear, K. B. G., & Anstey, K. J. (2005). Age group differences in distress: The role of psychosocial risk factors that vary with age. *Psychological Medicine, 35*, 1253–1263. doi:10.1017/S0033291705004976

Kennedy, Q., Mather, M., & Carstensen, L. L. (2004). The role of motivation in the age-related positivity effect in autobiographical memory. *Psychological Science, 15*, 208–214. doi:10.1111/j.0956-7976.2004.01503011.x

Kotov, R., Gamez, W., Schmidt, F., & Watson, D. (2010). Linking "big" personality traits to anxiety, depressive, and substance use disorders: A meta-analysis. *Psychological Bulletin, 136,* 768–821. doi:10.1037/a0020327

Kunzmann, U., Richter, D., & Schmukle, S. C. (2013). Stability and change in affective experience across the adult life span: Analyses with a national sample from Germany. *Emotion, 13,* 1086–1095. doi:10.1037/a0033572

Kunzmann, U., & Thomas, S. (2014). Multidirectional age differences in anger and sadness. *Psychology and Aging, 29,* 16–27. doi:10.1037/a0035751

Lechich, M. L. (1996). Empathy and its importance in long-term home health care. *The Journal of Long Term Home Health Care: The PRIDE Institute Journal, 15,* 15–23.

Löckenhoff, C. E., & Carstensen, L. L. (2007). Aging, emotion, and health-related decision strategies: Motivational manipulations can reduce age differences. *Psychology and Aging, 22,* 134–146. doi:10.1037/0882-7974.22.1.134

Lowis, M. J., & Raubenheimer, J. R. (1997). Ego integrity and life satisfaction in retired males. *Counseling Psychology in Africa, 2,* 12–23.

MacPherson, S. E., Phillips, L. H., & Della Sala, S. (2002). Age, executive function and social decision making: A dorsolateral prefrontal theory of cognitive aging. *Psychology and Aging, 17,* 598–609. doi:10.1037/0882-7974.17.4.598

Magai, C., Cohen, C., Milburn, N., Thorpe, B., McPherson, R., & Peralta, D. (2001). Attachment styles in older European American and African American adults. *The Journals of Gerontology, 56B,* S28–S35. doi:10.1093/geronb/56.1.S28

Magai, C., & Cohen, C. I. (1998). Attachment style and emotion regulation in dementia patients and their relation to caregiver burden. *The Journals of Gerontology, 53B,* P147–P154. doi:10.1093/geronb/53B.3.P147

McAdams, D. P., de St. Aubin, E., & Logan, R. L. (1993). Generativity among young, midlife, and older adults. *Psychology and Aging, 8,* 221–230. doi:10.1037/0882-7974.8.2.221

McAdams, D. P., & Pals, J. L. (2006). A new big five: Fundamental principles for an integrative science of personality. *American Psychologist, 61,* 204–217.

McCrae, R. R., & Costa, P. T., Jr. (2003). *Personality in adulthood: A five-factor theory perspective* (2nd ed.). New York, NY: Guilford Press.

*McCrae, R. R., Costa, P. T., Jr., De Lima, M P., Simões, A., Ostendorf, F., Angleitner, A., . . . Piedmont, R. L. (1999). Age differences in personality across the adult life span: Parallels in five cultures. *Developmental Psychology, 35,* 466–477. doi:10.1037/0012-1649.35.2.466

Meier, B., Perrig-Chiello, P., & Perrig, W. (2002). Personality and memory in old age. *Aging, Neuropsychology, and Cognition, 9,* 135–144.

Meyers, S. A., & Landsberger, S. A. (2002). Direct and indirect pathways between adult attachment style and marital satisfaction. *Personal Relationships, 9,* 159–172. doi:10.1111/1475-6811.00010

Milojev, P., & Sibley, C. G. (2014). The stability of adult personality varies across age: Evidence from a two-year longitudinal sample of adult New Zealanders. *Journal of Research in Personality, 51,* 29–37. doi:10.1016/j.jrp.2014.04.005

Oerlemans, W. G. M., Bakker, A. B., & Veenhoven, R. (2011). Finding the key to happy aging: A day reconstruction study of happiness. *The Journals of Gerontology, 66B,* 665–674. doi:10.1093/geronb/gbr040

*Reed, A. E., Chan, L., & Mikels, J. A. (2014). Meta-analysis of the age-related positivity effect: Age differences in preferences for positive over negative information. *Psychology and Aging, 29,* 1–15. doi:10.1037/a0035194

*Roberts, B. W., & DelVecchio, W. F. (2000). The rank-order consistency of personality traits from childhood to old age: A quantitative review of longitudinal studies. *Psychological Bulletin, 126,* 3–25. doi:10.1037/0033-2909.126.1.3

*Roberts, B. W., Walton, K. E., & Viechtbauer, W. (2006). Patterns of mean-level change in personality traits across the life course: A meta-analysis of longitudinal studies. *Psychological Bulletin, 132,* 1–25. doi:10.1037/0033-2909.132.1.1

Robins, R. W., Fraley, R. C., Roberts, B. W., & Trzesniewski, K. H. (2001). A longitudinal study of personality change in young adulthood. *Journal of Personality, 69,* 617–640.

Sable, P. (1989). Attachment, anxiety, and the loss of a husband. *American Journal of Orthopsychiatry, 59,* 550–556. doi:10.1111/j.1939-0025.1989.tb02745.x

Schlagman, S., Schulz, J., & Kvavilashvili, L. (2006). A content analysis of involuntary autobiographical memories: Examining the positivity effect in old age. *Memory, 14,* 161–175. doi:10.1080/09658210544000024

Segal, D. L., Hook, J. N., & Coolidge, F. L. (2001). Personality dysfunction, coping styles, and clinical symptoms in younger and older adults. *Journal of Clinical Geropsychology, 7,* 201–212. doi:10.1023/A:1011391128354

Shiota, M. N., & Levenson, R. W. (2009). Effects of aging on experimentally instructed detached reappraisal, positive reappraisal, and emotional behavior suppression. *Psychology and Aging, 24,* 890–900. doi:10.1037/a0017896

Specht, J., Egloff, B., & Schmukle, S. C. (2011). Stability and change of personality across the life course: The impact of age and major life events on mean-level and rank-order stability of the Big Five. *Journal of Personality and Social Psychology, 101,* 862–882. doi:10.1037/a0024950

Stone, A. A., Schwartz, J. E., Broderick, J. E., & Deaton, A. (2010). A snapshot of the age distribution of psychological well-being in the United States. *PNAS Proceedings of the National Academy of Sciences of the United States of America, 107,* 9985–9990. doi:10.1073/pnas.1003744107

Story, T. N., Berg, C. A., Smith, T. W., Beveridge, R., Henry, N. J. M., & Pearce, G. (2007). Age, marital satisfaction, and optimism as predictors of positive sentiment override in middle-aged and older married couples. *Psychology and Aging, 22,* 719–727. doi:10.1037/0882-7974.22.4.719

Terracciano, A., McCrae, R. R., & Costa, P. T., Jr. (2010). Intra-individual change in personality stability and age. *Journal of Research in Personality, 44,* 31–37. doi:10.1016/j.jrp.2009.09.006

Tornstam, L. (1996). Gerotranscendence—A theory about maturing into old age. *Journal of Aging and Identity, 1,* 37–50.

*Urry, H. L., & Gross, J. J. (2010). Emotion regulation in older age. *Current Directions in Psychological Science, 19,* 352–357. doi:10.1177/0963721410388395

Vaillant, G. E. (2000). Adaptive mental mechanisms: Their role in a positive psychology. *American Psychologist, 55,* 89–98. doi:10.1037/0003-066X.55.1.89

Vestergaard, S., Thinggaard, M., Jeune, B., Vaupel, J. W., McGue, M., & Christensen, K. (2015). Physical and mental decline yet rather happy: A study of Danes aged 45 and older. *Aging and Mental Health, 19,* 400–408. doi:10.1080/13607863.2014.944089

Waldinger, R. J., Cohen, S., Schulz, M. S., & Crowell, J. A. (2015). Security of attachment to spouses in late life: Concurrent and prospective links with cognitive and emotional well-being. *Clinical Psychological Science, 3,* 516–529. doi:10.1177/2167702614541261

Waters, E., Merrick, S., Treboux, D., Crowell, J., & Albersheim, L. (2000). Attachment security in infancy and early adulthood: A twenty-year longitudinal study. *Child Development, 71,* 684–689. doi:10.1111/1467-8624.00176

Wikman, A., Wardle, A., & Steptoe, A. (2011). Quality of life and affective well-being in -aged and older people with chronic medical conditions: A cross-sectional population based study. *Public Library of Science One, 6,* e18952. doi:10.1371/journal.pone.0018952

Wood, S., & Kisley, M. A. (2006). The negativity bias is eliminated in older adults: Age-related reduction in event-related brain potentials associated with evaluative categorization. *Psychology and Aging, 21,* 815–820. doi:10.1037/0882-7974.21.4.815

Woodhead, E. L., Cronkite, R. C., Moos, R. H., & Timko, C. (2014). Coping strategies predictive of adverse outcomes among community adults. *Journal of Clinical Psychology, 70,* 1183–1195. doi:10.1002/jclp.21924

Wortman, J., Lucas, R. E., & Donnellan, M. B. (2012). Stability and change in the Big Five personality domains: Evidence from a longitudinal study of Australians. *Psychology and Aging, 27,* 867–874. doi:10.1037/a0029322

6

Mental Health and Aging

Erin L. Woodhead, Preston Brown, and Victor Kwan

The mental health care needs of an aging population are expected to increase in the coming years. Currently, one in five older adults has a mental health disorder, including dementia (Karel, Gatz, & Smyer, 2012). The number of older adults with mental health conditions is projected to increase, due to the increasing population of older adults in the United States and internationally (Administration on Aging, 2012; Karel et al., 2012; National Institute on Aging, 2011).

Although the overall prevalence of certain mental health conditions, such as major depressive disorder, declines with age (Byers, Yaffe, Covinsky, Friedman, & Bruce, 2010), these disorders are still common among older adults and are often undertreated. The prevalence of mental health conditions among older adults varies by the setting in which the older adult lives. For example, among community-dwelling older adults the prevalence of major depressive disorder ranges from 1% to 5% as compared to 14% to 42% among residents of long-term care facilities and 5% to 10% among medical outpatients (Fiske, Wetherell, & Gatz, 2009). Additionally, as discussed later in this chapter, many older adults may not meet criteria for a *Diagnostic and Statistical Manual of Mental Disorders, Fifth Edition* (*DSM-5*) diagnosis but may still suffer from subclinical symptoms that have a significant impact on functioning (Chachamovich, Fleck, Laidlaw, & Power, 2008).

USE OF MENTAL HEALTH SERVICES BY OLDER ADULTS

Older adults have particularly low rates of psychotherapy use. In one study of community-dwelling adults older than age 65, 65.9% of those with major depressive

---

*Key references in the References section are indicated by an asterisk.

disorder and 72.5% with anxiety did not receive mental health care in the past year (Garrido, Kane, Kaas, & Kane, 2011). Other studies suggest that around 70% of older adults with mental health conditions did not use services in the past year (Byers, Arean, & Yaffe, 2012). Additionally, older adults are significantly less likely to report use of mental health services than younger adults (Karlin, Duffy, & Gleaves, 2008). Use of mental health services among older adults tends to be the lowest among those with mild mood or anxiety disorders and those of racial-ethnic minority status (Byers et al., 2012). This study also found that older adults with the most severe forms of mental illness endorsed a lack of belief in the benefits of professional mental health care.

ACCESS TO MENTAL HEALTH CARE

As noted previously, older adults tend to not receive needed mental health care. This has led some researchers to posit that older adults' use of mental health services is lower than that of other age groups due to differences in beliefs (Lawrence et al., 2006; Switzer, Wittink, Karsch, & Barg, 2006; Wittink, Dahlberg, Biruk, & Barg, 2008) and knowledge (Robb, Haley, Becker, Polivka, & Chwa, 2003) about mental health conditions, as compared to younger adults, as well as stigma around obtaining mental health care (Conner et al., 2010).

BELIEFS ABOUT MENTAL HEALTH CARE

Beliefs held by older adults about depression are more likely to reflect a social model rather than a medical model (e.g., Lawrence et al., 2006). For example, older adults report "loss" and "relationships" as primary sources of depression, compared to younger adults who tend to endorse more biological factors as contributing to their depression (e.g., Zeitlin, Katona, D'Ath, & Katona, 1997). Additionally, older adults may believe that they can handle their problems on their own (Mackenzie, Pagura, & Sareen, 2010). Finally, older adults' knowledge about depression and how to access mental health providers is less than that of younger adults (e.g., Robb et al., 2003). Specifically, compared to younger adults, older adults report that they are less likely to recognize the signs of a mental health problem in a friend or family member, and are less knowledgeable about when it is appropriate to see a mental health professional (Robb et al., 2003).

Despite these beliefs that may limit use of mental health care services, older adults tend to have positive views about mental health care. For example, Byers et al. (2012) found that 60% of their sample stated that professional mental health care would be beneficial and 88% reported that they were willing to see a mental health professional for emotional problems. Approximately a third of participants, however, stated that they would feel embarrassed getting mental health services, suggesting that there may be stigma about receiving mental health services among older adults.

STIGMA

There is mixed research regarding whether older adults experience stigma toward mental health services. Perceived stigma may lead to negative attitudes toward mental health services and therefore deter individuals from seeking needed services. Some research suggests that younger adults have higher levels of perceived stigma (Sirey et al., 2001) and report more barriers to mental health treatment (Pepin, Segal, & Coolidge, 2009) than older adults. However, as noted previously, older adults may feel embarrassed about getting mental health services (Byers et al., 2012) and may be more likely to discontinue treatment than younger adults if they endorse perceived stigma toward treatment (Sirey et al., 2001). There are also data to suggest that older African American adults may endorse more stigma toward mental health services than White older adults (Conner et al., 2010).

More research is needed to determine whether older adults' lower use of mental health services is associated with perceived stigma or other factors such as beliefs about treatment or accessibility of services. It is also possible that low use of mental health services is a cohort effect, as prior research suggests that adults in the old-old age category (80+) may have less positive attitudes toward mental health treatment and be less likely to utilize mental health services than those in a young-old age category (Currin, Hayslip, Schneider, & Kooken, 1998).

DIAGNOSING MENTAL HEALTH CONDITIONS AMONG OLDER ADULTS

MOOD DISORDERS

Mood disorders are among the most common mental illnesses that appear in the United States. These disorders include major depressive disorder, dysthymic disorder, bipolar disorder, and cyclothymia (American Psychiatric Association, 2013). In a worldwide survey conducted by Kessler et al. (2007), 31% of adults were diagnosed with a mood disorder at some point in their lives by the time they reached age 75.

About 11.9% of patients suffering from mood disorders report their symptoms first appearing at age 60 or later (Kessler et al., 2005). Additionally, rates of significant depressive symptoms may vary by setting. Older adults who are medical outpatients, medical inpatients, or residents of long-term care facilities are more likely to express symptoms of major depressive disorder than those living in the community (Fiske et al., 2009).

Aging does seem to affect some symptoms related to depressive disorders. While older adults with depression do not experience higher levels of sadness, they do suffer from increased anhedonia in comparison to younger adults (Wuthrich, Johnco, & Wetherell, 2015). However, older adults also tend to endorse somatic symptoms, such as psychomotor retardation, and cognitive symptoms, such as executive dysfunction. This differential symptom presentation may impact how likely it is that older adults meet *DSM-5* criteria for major depressive disorder (Fiske et al., 2009). For example, the somatic symptoms reported by older adults may be attributed to normal aging, which may cause practitioners to not consider a depression diagnosis among older patients.

Older adults with bipolar disorder do not generally differ in terms of severity of manic symptoms compared to younger patients (Oostervink, Nolen, & Kok, 2015). Age may affect other dimensions of bipolar disorder, with research suggesting that older adults with bipolar disorder (50–65 years of age) perform more poorly than younger adults with bipolar disorder in emotion processing, processing speed, and executive functioning skills (Weisenbach et al., 2014).

ANXIETY DISORDERS

A large proportion of older adults diagnosed with a depressive disorder also suffer from an anxiety disorder. Among patients older than 60 suffering from a major depressive disorder, nearly 40% also suffer from a comorbid anxiety disorder (van der Veen, van Zelst, Schoevers, Comijs, & Voshaar, 2015). It is important to note occurrences of comorbidity, as it may negatively impact treatment outcome in both middle and late adulthood (Andreescu et al., 2007). Prevalence rates of anxiety disorders among older adults vary depending on the methodology used (Wolitzky-Taylor, Castriotta, Lenze, Stanley, & Craske, 2010). Reported figures on diagnosed anxiety disorders in older adults can range from 3.2% to 14.2% (Forsell & Winblad, 1997; Ritchie et al., 2004). Subclinical anxiety must also be noted as these symptoms may affect well-being and health outcomes among older adults (Grenier et al., 2011).

Like mood disorders, there are many anxiety disorders of note, such as phobias, panic disorder, and generalized anxiety disorder (GAD; American Psychiatric Association, 2013). Symptoms of these disorders tend to fluctuate late in age, with longitudinal research suggesting that symptom levels declined until older adults reached their 80s at which point symptoms leveled off (Lee, Gatz, Pedersen, & Prescott, 2016).

Although not a diagnosable condition, older and younger adults may also report different types of worries, which may affect their well-being. Older adults are more likely to worry about health-related concerns while younger adults worry more about work, school, and social issues (Diefenbach, Stanley, & Beck, 2001). Older adults also tend to worry less than younger adults (Hunt, Wisocki, & Yanko, 2003).

PERSONALITY DISORDERS

Personality disorders involve profound patterns of thought and behavior that lead to distress or impairment. These include borderline, obsessive compulsive, avoidant, schizotypal, antisocial, and narcissistic personality disorders (American Psychiatric Association, 2013). Although there is limited research on the prevalence of personality disorders among older adults, early research suggested that personality disorders were diagnosed at a higher rate among younger than older adults (Ames & Molinari, 1994). Among younger and older adults with anxiety, younger adults had greater personality dysfunction than older adults (Coolidge, Segal, Hook, & Stewart, 2000). Among older adults in the study, the most common personality disorders were obsessive-compulsive, schizoid, and avoidant. The high prevalence of personality disorders in this study (61% among the older adult sample) suggests that personality disorders are frequently comorbid with anxiety among older adults.

Overall, symptoms of personality disorders generally lessen as adults mature (Cooper, Balsis, & Oltmanns, 2014). Nevertheless, age affects each personality disorder in different ways. Certain symptoms of personality disorders such as aggressive and impulsive behavior may lessen with age (Moffitt, Caspi, Harrington, &

Milne, 2002). However, symptoms of hypochondria, depression, and medication misuse tend to increase, while others remain stable in severity (van Alphen, Derksen, Sadavoy, & Rosowsky, 2012).

SUICIDALITY

Suicide is a severe and pervasive issue among older adults. In 1980, the rate of suicide was highest for those aged 65 and older at a rate of 17.7 per 100,000. This was markedly high in comparison to the rest of the nation, which held a rate of 11.9 per 100,000 (McIntosh, 1985). A more recent review of data attained from the World Health Organization corroborates this finding, revealing that suicide rates generally increase with age (Shah, 2012). Mental illnesses such as depression and social factors such as family discord are important when considering risk factors for suicide among older adults (Conwell, Duberstein, & Caine, 2002; Legarreta et al., 2015). Additionally, personality traits may contribute to suicidal behavior as well. For example, older adults who are high in openness to experience also have higher rates of suicidal ideation, whereas older adults who are high in extraversion are less likely to have attempted suicide (Duberstein et al., 2000). Medical illness, poor coping strategies toward negative life events, and physical impairments have also been found to increase risk of completed suicide (Heisel, 2006).

SUBSTANCE USE DISORDERS

Substance use disorders (SUDs) do not discriminate by age as older adult populations also suffer from SUDs. However, lack of treatment options and difficult diagnostic criteria can prevent older adults from receiving appropriate diagnosis and treatment. When individuals use illicit drugs during their youth and adolescent years at a high rate, they typically show higher rates of substance use and related health problems as they age (Gfroerer, Penne, Pemberton, & Folsom, 2003).

One particular birth cohort that is transitioning to older adulthood is the Baby Boomers, described in Chapter 1. Due to their birth cohort being exceptionally large coupled with a larger rate of past drug use, prediction models have suggested that we should expect to see an increase in older adults afflicted with SUDs (Colliver, Compton, Gfroerer, & Condon, 2006). Prediction models estimate that by the year 2020, those who misuse illicit drugs and alcohol are expected to reach a total of 4.4 million older adults (see Figure 6.1). Furthermore, the total amount of older adults who need treatment for SUDs is expected to exceed 5.7 million (Han, Gfroerer, Colliver, & Penne, 2009). Conversely, it is estimated that only 7% of treatment facilities in the United States have programs specially designed for older adults (Gfroerer et al., 2003; Han et al., 2009).

Although alcohol is currently one of the most commonly misused substances among older adults, it is expected that misuse of prescription drugs will increase the most in the coming years when compared to other illicit drugs (Colliver et al., 2006; Simoni-Wastila & Yang, 2006). Comorbidity of SUDs in the Baby Boomer generation is much more likely to occur. Despite prediction models warning us about the impending impact on our healthcare system, there is a lack of research on

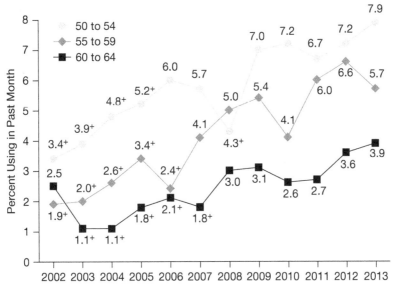

Figure 6.1 Illicit drug use is increasing among older adults.
Source: National Institute on Drug Abuse (2014).

assessment techniques and treatment for substance use disorders among older adults (Simoni-Wastila & Yang, 2006). Although older adults report a high rate of physician visits, individuals with SUDs can be commonly misdiagnosed. This may result in older adults receiving treatment for an outcome of the substance use disorder (i.e., dementia) without being assessed or treated for the SUD that led to this condition (Simoni-Wastila & Yang, 2006).

SLEEP

Understanding the integral role that sleep has in maintaining one's health is critical as disturbances in sleep patterns can be indicators for chronic diseases. However, studying the effects of sleep disturbances on older adults is a difficult task as chronic diseases and other medical conditions are highly prevalent in this population. Further adding to the difficulty of studying sleep disturbances is that common outcomes of sleep disturbances (i.e., daytime sleepiness and cognitive impairment) share similar symptoms with chronic diseases such as cardiovascular ailments, affective disorders, and substance use disorders (Whitney et al., 1998).

Despite overall improvements in older adults' health in the United States, most have at least one major chronic disease (Foley, Ancoli-Israel, Britz, & Walsh, 2004). Furthermore, there have been differences in the subjective quality of sleep observed in older adults of varying ethnicities in the United States. Jean-Louis et al. (2001) investigated the most common sleep complaints in older adults from both U.S.-born European Americans and U.S.-born African Americans. The most common registered reports of sleep-related issues involved initiating sleep, maintaining sleep, or awakening during sleep. Proportionally, 82.1% of U.S.-born European Americans reported either of these complaints compared to 49.2% of U.S.-born African Americans. These differences are potentially explained by the underutilization of health services by various ethnic groups that live in the United States. Additionally, one must also consider the ethnocultural variables that may influence how sleep is perceived. For example, African American older adults may accept sleep problems as part of the aging process and therefore report fewer sleep-related problems than European Americans (Jean-Louis et al., 2001).

These detriments to sleep are not limited to the United States. Kim et al. (2014) investigated sleep problems in a Korean older adult sample and found that chronic diseases also adversely affected sleep. Additionally, Kim et al. (2014) found that all types of sleep disturbances experienced by older Korean adults were significantly related to sleep durations of 6 hours or less. This also holds true for older adult populations in Spain, Taiwan, and Brazil (Almeida, Tamai, & Garrido, 1999; Chen, Su, & Chou, 2013; López-Torres Hidalgo et al., 2012). Almeida et al. (1999) found that within their sample of older Brazilian adults approximately 59.3% reported sleeping difficulties, which included nearly the same complaints registered by older adults in the United States. Also similar to the United States, problems with sleep duration have been associated with morbidity and mortality rates such that those who sleep for shorter durations tend to have higher mortality rates (Kim et al., 2014). For example, sleep durations of 5 hours or less have been associated with cardiovascular disease.

Overall, common problems with sleep in older adult populations have similar trends across the world. The cause for disturbances in sleep is not simply from growing older, but stems from a multitude of physiological and psychological changes as a result of the aging process. However, oftentimes these problems with sleep are labeled as symptoms from other disorders resulting in treatment that does not directly address the sleep disturbances.

SCHIZOPHRENIA

The prevalence of individuals diagnosed with schizophrenia is expected to increase in the coming decades due to increased longevity (Berry & Barrowclough, 2009), although the majority of research on individuals with schizophrenia examines adults younger than age 65. Genetic disposition is a main cause for schizophrenia with an estimated 60% heritability rate (O'Donnell, 2007).

Cognitive impairment is a core feature of schizophrenia. Additional impairments associated with schizophrenia include deficits in sensory processing, attention, verbal and spatial learning, working memory, contextual processing, and eye movements (O'Donnell, 2007). These symptoms have high rates of comorbidity with depression and anxiety (Berry & Barrowclough, 2009). Depression in older adults with schizophrenia has been associated with poor quality of life, smaller social networks, and poor day-to-day functioning (Berry & Barrowclough, 2009).

Among older adults diagnosed with schizophrenia, Friedman et al. (2001) found that mental status and functional ability scores of individuals older than 65 years declined, whereas those younger than 65 showed no change over a 6-year follow-up study. Bowie et al. (2005) found that speech capabilities worsened for individuals older than 75 years of age. Both of these longitudinal studies suggest that cognitive decline in older adults with schizophrenia seems to be more closely related to the aging process. Cognitive deficits that are associated with age-related decline include weaknesses in memory, executive functions, learning of new skills, attention, and psychomotor skills. Furthermore, it can be difficult to decipher whether these cognitive impairments are due to schizophrenia or other types of cognitive impairments (i.e., dementia; Berry & Barrowclough, 2009).

POSTTRAUMATIC STRESS DISORDER

Posttraumatic stress disorder (PTSD) can develop after an individual experiences extreme trauma such as combat or sexual abuse. PTSD is characterized by intrusive memories of the event, such as through episodic flashbacks or nightmares, avoidance of stimuli associated with the event, negative alterations in mood and cognition, and hypervigilance. PTSD in older adult populations can be most clearly categorized into two main causes: early life trauma (i.e., war veterans, prisoner of war [POW] experiences, physical and/or sexual abuse) and late life trauma (i.e., natural disasters and acts of violence; Böttche, Kuwert, & Knaevelsrud, 2012). Much research has focused on those who have experienced combat and/or have been POWs (Rauch, Morales, Zubritsky, Knott, & Oslin, 2006). Averill and Beck (2000) found that older adults who were war veterans had a 3% to 56% prevalence rate of PTSD. Furthermore, research conducted by Kluznik, Speed, van Valkenburg, and Magraw (1986) focused on U.S. soldiers who were POWs nearly 40 years after the conclusion of World War II and found a prevalence rate of nearly 67%.

The history of a formal definition of PTSD has its origins dating back as early as World War I when the term "shell shock" sparked the initial interest in the psychological effects of combat (Weintraub & Ruskin, 1999). During World War II, the term evolved into "combat neurosis," which has a high degree of overlap with our modern symptom criteria of PTSD (Weintraub & Ruskin, 1999). Research focused on both war veterans and nonveteran populations revealed mixed findings pertaining to their symptom severity, especially when compared to younger populations (Böttche et al., 2012; Frans, Rimmö, Åberg, & Fredrikson, 2005; Kessler et al., 2005; Spitzer et al., 2008). Lifetime prevalence of PTSD remains fairly consistent from a global perspective with older adult populations in Sweden reporting a prevalence rate of 3.9%, 3.1% in Germany, and 3.4% in the United States (Frans et al., 2005; Kessler et al., 2005; Spitzer et al., 2008). It is important to understand that not everyone exposed to a traumatic event will develop PTSD. Research suggests that certain characteristics, such as psychosocial support from family and friends, may mitigate PTSD symptoms (Weintraub & Ruskin, 1999). Specifically in older adult populations, PTSD can be a result of either early life or late life trauma. Those with a predisposition to anxiety and depression may be more likely to manifest PTSD symptoms; however, old age alone does not increase the risk of the development of PTSD after experiencing trauma (Weintraub & Ruskin, 1999).

ASSESSMENT OF MENTAL HEALTH CONDITIONS AMONG OLDER ADULTS

In the following sections, we review common self-report instruments for assessing depressive symptoms among older adults. Table 6.1 presents common self-report

Table 6.1   Assessment Instruments for Mental Health Conditions Other Than Depression

Mental Health Condition	Assessment Instruments for Use With Older Adults
Anxiety disorders	Geriatric Anxiety Inventory (GAI; Pachana et al., 2007) Geriatric Anxiety Scale (Segal, June, Payne, Coolidge, & Yochim, 2010) Penn State Worry Questionnaire (PSWQ; Meyer, Miller, Metzger, & Borkovec, 1990)
Suicidality	Reasons for Living—Older Adults (RFL-OA; Edelstein et al., 2009)
Substance use disorders	Michigan Alcoholism Screen Test—Geriatric Version (MAST-G; Blow et al., 1992) Short Michigan Alcoholism Screen Test—Geriatric Version (SMAST-G; Blow, Gillespie, Barry, Mudd, & Hill, 1998)
Sleep disorders	Pittsburgh Sleep Quality Index (PSQI; Buysse, Reynolds, Monk, Berman, & Kupfer, 1989)
Posttraumatic stress disorder (PTSD)	PTSD Checklist (PCL; Weathers et al., 2013)

instruments for other mental health conditions. When selecting an assessment instrument for use with older adults it is important to examine the reliability and validity of the instrument with an older adult population. Assessment instruments that were developed with younger adults may not be psychometrically valid with older adults. Additionally, normative data may not be available for older adults, which may impact the interpretation of scores.

THE CES-D

The Center for Epidemiologic Studies Depression Scale, or CES-D, has been a common and widely used self-report measure for assessing depression in the general population (Radloff, 1977). The primary components of depression symptomology that the CES-D assesses are depressed mood, feelings of guilt and worthlessness, feelings of helplessness and hopelessness, psychomotor retardation, loss of appetite, and disturbances with sleep (Radloff, 1977).

Findings from Lewinsohn, Seeley, Roberts, and Allen (1997) demonstrated that the CES-D had adequate psychometric properties when used with older adult populations. Additionally, this assessment tool has also been successfully used with international populations (Beekman et al., 1995). A shortened version of the CES-D (10 items) has been created for use in older adult communities (Andersen, Malmgren, Carter, & Patrick, 1994). This reduction in length did not adversely affect its psychometric properties. Furthermore, the shortened CES-D has been cross validated in older adult populations in China (Boey, 1999).

THE GERIATRIC DEPRESSION SCALE

The Geriatric Depression Scale (GDS) was developed by Yesavage et al. (1983) to address the lack of adequate depression assessment tools for older adult populations. This scale consists of 30 items specifically tailored toward older adult populations. Each question is responded to in a yes/no format. This assessment tool is helpful for assessing depression severity in older adults due to its ability to differentiate between those who are mildly depressed and severely depressed. However, one drawback of the GDS is that it was originally designed to assess older adults who are independently living in the community; therefore, it may not be an appropriate tool to use for those who are living in a nonindependent/assisted living setting (Montorio & Izal, 1996).

The 15-item version of the GDS has been shown to have adequate psychometric properties (De Craen, Heeren, & Gussekloo, 2003; see Figure 6.2). The GDS has been appropriately validated in countries outside of the United States. Bae and Cho (2004) found that a version of the GDS translated to Korean (GDS-K) and its short version (SGDS-K) were suitable for assessing depression in older Korean adults. Furthermore,

No.	Question	Answer	Score
1.	Are you basically satisfied with your life?	YES / **No**	
2.	Have you dropped many of your activities and interests?	**YES** / No	
3.	Do you feel that your life is empty?	**YES** / No	
4.	Do you often get bored?	**YES** / No	
5.	Are you in good spirits most of the time?	YES / **No**	
6.	Are you afraid that something bad is going to happen to you?	**YES** / No	
7.	Do you feel happy most of the time?	YES / **No**	
8.	Do you often feel helpless?	**YES** / No	
9.	Do you prefer to stay at home, rather than going out and doing new things?	**YES** / No	
10.	Do you feel you have more problems with memory than most people?	**YES** / No	
11.	Do you think it is wonderful to be alive?	YES / **No**	
12.	Do you feel pretty worthless the way you are now?	**YES** / No	
13.	Do you feel full of energy?	YES / **No**	
14.	Do you feel that your situation is hopeless?	**YES** / No	
15.	Do you think that most people are better off than you are?	**YES** / No	
		TOTAL	

Figure 6.2 15-Item Geriatric Depression Scale.
Note: Positive responses are in bold.
Image obtained from Geriatric Depression Scale (2017).

validation of subsequent translations in Chinese, Greek, and Turkish languages all resulted in high measures of internal consistency and reliability (Chan, 1996; Ertan & Eker, 2000; Fountoulakis et al., 1999).

THE PHQ-9

The Patient Health Questionnaire (PHQ) is a self-report questionnaire designed to be completed by the individual without substantial interaction with a clinician. The PHQ-9 corresponds to the nine items within the full PHQ specifically formulated to assess *DSM* symptoms of depression in patients (Kroenke, Spitzer, & Williams, 2001). The PHQ-9 is a commonly used assessment tool and enables clinicians to indicate the severity of symptoms. The scores on the PHQ-9 range from 0 to 27. The cutoff thresholds of 5, 10, 15, and 20 are representative of mild, moderate, moderately severe, and severe depression (Kroenke et al., 2001). The PHQ-9 has been validated for the general population along with older adult populations (Kroenke & Spitzer, 2002; Phelan et al., 2010; Lamers et al., 2008). Furthermore, the PHQ-9 has also been applied in a global context. For example, Han et al. (2008) sought to determine if the accuracy of the PHQ-9 in the assessment of depression remained consistent when assessing older Korean adult populations. Their findings suggest that the PHQ-9 is a suitable tool to be utilized in Korean populations.

THE CORNELL SCALE FOR DEPRESSION IN DEMENTIA

The Cornell Scale for Depression in Dementia (CSDD) was developed in order to effectively detect and assess symptoms of major depression in individuals afflicted with dementia (Alexopoulos, Abrams, Young, & Shamoian, 1988). This measure was created in order to enable clinicians to reliably assess depression among patients with dementia, who may not be able to provide reliable responses. To effectively assess the individual, the CSDD utilizes two semistructured interviews with the patient and an informant. If there are any discrepancies between the informant and the patient, then the clinician performs an additional interview to effectively resolve the differences in information being provided. The CSDD takes approximately 20 minutes to complete.

The CSDD has been administered and validated in older adults from the United States and other countries. For example, Kørner et al. (2006) found that the CSDD was an effective assessment tool for older adults with dementia living in Denmark. Lam et al. (2004) found that the CSDD performed well when used to detect depression in older Chinese patients with dementia.

EMPIRICALLY SUPPORTED TREATMENTS FOR OLDER ADULTS

In this section we review empirically supported treatments for the mental health conditions presented in the prior section. Although we focus primarily on psychological treatments, we offer comments when applicable regarding pharmacotherapy treatments. Table 6.2 summarizes this section by listing empirically supported psychological treatments by diagnosis.

Table 6.2 Overview of Psychological Treatment Options by Diagnosis

Diagnosis	Empirically Supported Psychological Treatments
Mood disorders and suicidality	Cognitive behavioral therapy (CBT), Interpersonal psychotherapy (IPT), Reminiscence therapy
Anxiety disorders	CBT
Personality disorders	Dialectical behavior therapy (DBT)
Substance use disorders	Brief motivational interventions, CBT
Sleep issues/disorders	CBT for insomnia (CBT-I)
Schizophrenia	CBT with social skills training

Note: Treatments for posttraumatic stress disorder (PTSD) not included in this table because of the limited data for older adults.

MOOD DISORDERS AND SUICIDALITY

Mood disorders can be treated through either pharmacotherapy or psychotherapy. Options for pharmacotherapy such as selective serotonin reuptake inhibitors (SSRIs), tricyclic antidepressants, and monoamine oxidase inhibitors have been shown to be highly effective treatments for depression in older adults. The most popular psychotherapy intervention, cognitive behavioral therapy (CBT) has been shown to be comparable in effectiveness to pharmacotherapy treatments (Pinquart, Duberstein, & Lyness, 2006).

The goal of CBT is to modify irrational thoughts and behaviors that contribute to the symptoms of the patient's illness. CBT involves a restructuring of one's thoughts in order to modify appraisals, belief systems, and instrumental behaviors. However, a large challenge that clinicians face is attrition. Unfortunately, many patients drop out of therapy before its completion (Fernandez, Salem, Swift, & Ramtahal, 2015; Pinquart et al., 2006).

Another common intervention that can be used for treatment of mood disorders is interpersonal psychotherapy (IPT). This treatment involves examining and addressing the interpersonal relationships of the patient. Therapists employ a number of techniques in IPT, such as clarification and communication analyses, which attempt to reduce symptoms of depression (Miller & Reynolds, 2007). In general, CBT has demonstrated higher efficacy than IPT interventions in older adults (Pinquart et al., 2006).

A third intervention for mood disorders is reminiscence, also called life review. In reminiscence, the patient reviews events in their past that they deem to be personally significant. This treatment option has been shown to produce significant improvements with large effect sizes in older populations (Pinquart et al., 2006; Pinquart, Duberstein, & Lyness, 2007; Pinquart & Forstmeier, 2012).

ANXIETY DISORDERS

Pharmacotherapy and psychotherapy have been shown to be effective treatments for GAD, which is one of the most common anxiety disorders among older adults. Pharmacotherapy interventions such as benzodiazepines and antidepressants show slightly better outcomes in comparison to psychotherapy (Gonçalves & Byrne, 2012). Again, like mood disorders, CBT is one of the more common interventions available to those suffering from anxiety disorders. Although late-life anxiety is amenable to psychological treatment, comparison studies suggest that CBT may not offer additional benefit beyond what can be obtained from active control groups, such as discussion groups focused on specific worry topics (i.e., memory problems, health concerns) that emphasized validation and supportive listening (Wetherell, Gatz, & Craske, 2003).

PERSONALITY DISORDERS

Two treatment options for personality disorders are dialectical behavior therapy (DBT) and medication plus clinical management. DBT was initially developed to help alleviate suicidal thoughts and behaviors. In this treatment, therapists work with patients to develop skills to help alleviate their symptoms. These skills address mindfulness, interpersonal effectiveness, emotion regulation, and distress tolerance (Linehan & Wilks, 2015). In a study that examined older adults who suffered from comorbid depression and personality disorders, DBT in conjunction with medication was found to be effective in helping patients reach remission, whereas medication alone was not (Lynch et al., 2007).

SUBSTANCE USE DISORDERS

As stated previously, alcohol is among the most commonly misused substances among older adults (Colliver et al., 2006; Simoni-Wastila & Yang, 2006). Additionally, dually diagnosed psychiatric and substance use patients suffer from less desirable outcomes (Prigerson, Desai, & Rosenheck, 2001).

Substance use treatment facilities provide detoxification and pharmacotherapies such as nicotine replacement, methadone, and Vivitrol. Counseling and CBT therapies to treat SUDs are commonly offered at substance use clinics. Unfortunately, substance use treatment facilities specializing in older adults have been found to be lacking (Morgen, Denison-Vesel, Kobylarz, & Voelkner, 2015). Brief interventions based on principles of motivational interviewing are effective for older adults with substance use problems (Barry, Oslin, & Blow, 2001). For example, in a study that combined naltrexone with a psychological treatment based on motivational interviewing, older adults had greater attendance at therapy sessions and greater adherence to the medication (Oslin, Pettinati, & Volpicelli, 2002).

SLEEP DISORDERS

Over 50% of older adults suffer from insomnia (Foley, Monjan, Brown, & Simonsick, 1995). Poor sleep can lead to a number of negative outcomes such as sleepiness during the daytime and increased symptoms of depression and anxiety (Crenshaw, 1996). Pharmacological treatments are available to help combat insomnia. For older adults, use of sleep medications may offer only small benefits that may not be clinically significant (Glass, Lanctot, Hermann, Sproule, & Busto, 2005). Due to this, behavioral treatments such as CBT have been recommended due to their greater efficacy. Specifically, short- and long-term improvements in insomnia may be greater for those receiving CBT treatment for insomnia as compared to those receiving only sleep medication (Sivertsen et al., 2006). Occasionally, medication is combined with CBT in order to combat insomnia (Neikrug & Ancoli-Israel, 2010).

SCHIZOPHRENIA

Common treatment methods for those suffering from schizophrenia include CBT and prescription medication. Unfortunately, there is a lack of research focusing on older adult populations suffering from schizophrenia, as compared to the amount of research focusing on younger adults. However, there are recent advances in treatment techniques specifically for older adult populations. One such treatment intervention focuses on integrating cognitive-behavioral training with social skills interventions. The goal of this type of treatment is to teach social skills while teaching the individuals to address maladaptive thoughts that would normally interfere with community interaction (Granholm et al., 2005, 2007; Granholm, Auslander, Gottlieb, McQuaid, & McClure, 2006; Granholm, McQuaid, Auslander, & McClure, 2004; McQuaid et al., 2000). While this intervention method has shown success with addressing social skills, the treatment does not effectively address other comorbid symptoms (i.e., depression; Berry & Barrowclough, 2009).

Another type of treatment intervention focuses on developing independent living and social skills. This type of intervention occurs throughout the course of a year. Furthermore, it enlists the aide of nurse-specialists who attempt to ensure that the individual's medical needs are met (Bartels, 2004; Pratt, Bartels, Mueser, & Forester, 2008). Participants in this treatment intervention demonstrated improvements in their independent social living skills (Berry & Barrowclough, 2009). Unfortunately, studying and treating older adult populations that are afflicted with schizophrenia is difficult to do because of age-associated declines in cognition and physical ability.

POSTTRAUMATIC STRESS DISORDER

Typical treatments used for adult populations with PTSD include cognitive approaches, exposure approaches, and narrative/writing approaches (Böttche et al., 2012). A pilot study on the use of prolonged exposure therapy with older veterans found that 6 weeks of treatment led to a decrease in clinician-rated and self-reported PTSD symptoms (Thorp, Stein, Jeste, Patterson, & Wetherell, 2012). There is some concern, however, that exposure-based approaches may be contraindicated for older patients with cardiovascular disease due to the strong physiological reactions that may occur during treatment (Böttche et al., 2012). Although there have been case studies and pilot studies published on the use of these three types of treatments with older adults, most with positive results, there are no randomized clinical trials examining whether these treatment approaches are effective with older adults.

CONCLUSION

The current chapter discussed several topics relevant to older adults' mental health including access and use of mental health services, prevalence of common mental health diagnoses, assessment of mental health symptoms, and empirically supported treatments for older adults. Although some topics presented in this chapter need additional research focused specifically on an older adult population, several conclusions can be drawn from the material. First, several studies have documented that older adults use mental health services less frequently than other age groups, although it is unclear why this is the case and likely involves a combination of barriers/access to treatment and stigma. Second, several of the mental health problems discussed in the chapter may present differently among older adults, such as the specific symptoms of depression that older adults endorse. Practitioners need to be cautious to separate physical from mental health symptoms to avoid under- or over-diagnosing mental health problems among older adults. Third, assessment instruments for older adults need to be selected cautiously to ensure that adequate validity and reliability has been established for this population. Finally, empirically supported treatments are available for older adults for many types of mental health problems, although it can be difficult to find practitioners and/or treatment facilities that are familiar with treatment issues and outcome research relevant to an older adult population.

DISCUSSION QUESTIONS

1. Compare the prevalence rate of major depressive disorder among older adults versus younger adults and older adults across different settings.

2. Describe some of the reasons why older adults may use mental health services less frequently than other age groups.

3. Discuss the difference in presentation for depressive symptoms among older and younger adults.

4. Describe factors that may increase the risk of suicide among older adults.

5. Describe common sleep complaints among older adults and factors associated with sleep problems.

6. Summarize the assessment instruments that can be used to assess depressive symptoms among older adults.

7. Describe the psychological treatments that are available for older adults with schizophrenia.

REFERENCES

Administration on Aging. (2012). A profile of older Americans: 2012. Washington, DC: Author. Retrieved from https://www.acl.gov/sites/default/files/Aging%20and%20Disability%20in%20America/2012profile.pdf

Alexopoulos, G. S., Abrams, R. C., Young, R. C., & Shamoian, C. A. (1988). Cornell scale for depression in dementia. *Biological Psychiatry, 23*, 271–284.

Almeida, O. P., Tamai, S., & Garrido, R. (1999). Sleep complaints among the elderly: Results from a survey in a psychogeriatric outpatient clinic in Brazil. *International Psychogeriatrics, 11*, 47–56.

American Psychiatric Association. (2013). *Diagnostic and statistical manual of mental disorders* (5th ed.). Washington, DC: Author.

Ames, A., & Molinari, V. (1994). Prevalence of personality disorders in community-living elderly. *Journal of Geriatric Psychiatry and Neurology, 7*, 189–194. doi:10.1177/089198879400700311

Andersen, E. M., Malmgren, J. A., Carter, W. B., & Patrick, D. L. (1994). Screening for depression in well older adults: Evaluation of a short form of the CES-D. *American Journal of Preventive Medicine, 10*, 77–84.

Andreescu, C., Lenze, E. J., Dew, M. A., Begley, A. E., Mulsant, B. H., Dombrovski, A. Y., . . . Reynolds, C. F. (2007). Effect of comorbid anxiety on treatment response and relapse risk in late-life depression: Controlled study. *The British Journal of Psychiatry, 190*, 344–349. doi:10.1192/bjp.bp.106.027169

Averill, P. M., & Beck, J. G. (2000). Posttraumatic stress disorder in older adults: A conceptual review. *Journal of Anxiety Disorders, 14*, 133–156.

Bae, J. N., & Cho, M. J. (2004). Development of the Korean version of the Geriatric Depression Scale and its short form among elderly psychiatric patients. *Journal of Psychosomatic Research, 57*, 297–305. doi:10.1016/j.jpsychores.2004.01.004

Barry, K. L., Oslin, D. W., & Blow, F. C. (2001). *Alcohol problems in older adults: Prevention and management*. New York, NY: Springer.

Bartels, S. J. (2004). Caring for the whole person: Integrated health care for older adults with severe mental illness and medical comorbidity. *Journal of the American Geriatrics Society, 52*, S249–S257. doi:10.1111/j.1532-5415.2004.52601.x

Beekman, A., Deeg, D., van Tilburg, T., Smit, J. H., Hooijer, C., & van Tilburg, W. (1995). Major and minor depression in later life: A study of prevalence and risk factors. *Journal of Affective Disorders, 36*, 65–75.

*Berry, K., & Barrowclough, C. (2009). The needs of older adults with schizophrenia: Implications for psychological interventions. *Clinical Psychology Review, 29*, 68–76. doi:10.1016/j.cpr.2008.09.010

Blow, F. C., Gillespie, B. W., Barry, K. L., Mudd, S. A., & Hill, E. M. (1998). Brief screening for alcohol problems in elderly populations using the Short Michigan Alcoholism Screening Test-Geriatric Version (SMAST-G). *Alcoholism: Clinical and Experimental Research, 22* (Suppl.), 131A.

Boey, K. W. (1999). Cross-validation of a short form of the CES-D in Chinese elderly. *International Journal of Geriatric Psychiatry, 14*(8), 608–617.

*Böttche, M., Kuwert, P., & Knaevelsrud, C. (2012). Posttraumatic stress disorder in older adults: An overview of characteristics and treatment approaches. *International Journal of Geriatric Psychiatry, 27*, 230–239. doi:10.1002/gps.2725

Bowie, C. R., Tsapelas, I., Friedman, J., Parrella, M., White, L., & Harvey, P. D. (2005). The longitudinal course of thought disorder in geriatric patients with chronic schizophrenia. *American Journal of Psychiatry, 162*, 793–795. doi:10.1176/appi.ajp.162.4.793

Buysse, D. J., Reynolds, C. F., Monk, T. H., Berman, S. R., & Kupfer, D. J. (1989). The Pittsburgh Sleep Quality Index: A new instrument for psychiatric practice and research. *Psychiatry Research, 28*, 193–213.

Byers, A. L., Arean, P. A., & Yaffe, K. (2012). Low use of mental health services among older Americans with mood and anxiety disorders. *Psychiatric Services, 63*, 66–72. doi:10.1176/appi.ps.201100121

Byers, A. L., Yaffe, K., Covinsky, K. E., Friedman, M. B., & Bruce, M. L. (2010). High occurrence of mood and anxiety disorders among older adults: The National Comorbidity Survey Replication. *Archives of General Psychiatry, 67*, 489–496. doi:10.1001/archgenpsychiatry.2010.35

Chachamovich, E., Fleck, M., Laidlaw, K., & Power, M. (2008). Impact of major depression and subsyndromal symptoms on quality of life and attitudes toward aging in an international sample of older adults. *The Gerontologist, 48*, 593–602. doi:10.1093/geront/48.5.593

Chan, A. C. M. (1996). Clinical validation of the geriatric depression scale (GDS) Chinese version. *Journal of Aging and Health, 8*, 238–253.

Chen, H.-C., Su, T.-P., & Chou, P. (2013). A nine-year follow-up study of sleep patterns and mortality in community-dwelling older adults in Taiwan. *Sleep, 36*, 1187–1198. doi:10.5665/sleep.2884

Colliver, J., Compton, W., Gfroerer, J., & Condon, T. (2006). Projecting drug use among aging baby boomers in 2020. *Annals of Epidemiology, 16*, 257–265. doi:10.1016/j.annepidem.2005.08.003

Conner, K. O., Copeland, V. A., Grote, N. K., Koeske, G., Rosen, D., Reynolds, C. F., & Brown, C. (2010). Mental health treatment seeking among older adults with depression: The impact of stigma and race. *American Journal of Geriatric Psychiatry, 18*, 531–543. doi:10.1097/JGP.0b013e3181cc0366

Conwell, Y., Duberstein, P. R., & Caine, E. D. (2002). Risk factors for suicide in later life. *Biological Psychiatry, 52*, 193–204. doi:10.1016/S0006-3223(02)01347-1

Coolidge, F. L., Segal, D. L., Hook, J. N., & Stewart, S. (2000). Personality disorders and coping among anxious older adults. *Journal of Anxiety Disorders, 14*, 157–172. doi:10.1016/S0887-6185(99)00046-8

Cooper, L. D., Balsis, S., & Oltmanns, T. F. (2014). Aging: Empirical contribution: A longitudinal analysis of personality disorder dimensions and personality traits in a community sample of older adults: Perspectives from selves and informants. *Journal of Personality Disorders, 28*, 151–165. doi:10.1521/pedi.2014.28.1.151

Crenshaw, M. C. (1996, August). Sleep and waking cognitive performance in the elderly. *Dissertation Abstracts International, 57*, 1464.

Currin, J. B., Hayslip, B., Schneider, L. J., & Kooken, R. A. (1998). Cohort differences in attitudes toward mental health services among older persons. *Psychotherapy, 34*, 506–518.

De Craen, A. J. M., Heeren, T. J., & Gussekloo, J. (2003). Accuracy of the 15-item geriatric depression scale (GDS-15) in a community sample of the oldest old. *International Journal of Geriatric Psychiatry, 18*, 63–66. doi:10.1002/gps.773

Diefenbach, G. J., Stanley, M. A., & Beck, J. G. (2001). Worry content reported by older adults with and without generalized anxiety disorder. *Aging & Mental Health, 5*, 269–274. doi:10.1080/13607860120065069

Duberstein, P. R., Conwell, Y., Seidlitz, L., Denning, D. G., Cox, C., & Caine, E. D. (2000). Personality traits and suicidal behavior and ideation in depressed inpatients 50 years of age and older. *The Journals of Gerontology: Series B: Psychological Sciences and Social Sciences, 55B*, P18–P26.

Edelstein, B. A., Heisel, M. J., McKee, D. R., Martin, R. R., Koven, L. P., Duberstein, P. R., & Britton, P. C. (2009). Development and psychometric evaluation of the Reasons for Living—Older Adults scale: A suicide risk assessment inventory. *Gerontologist, 49*, 736–745. doi:10.1093/geront/gnp052

Ertan, T., & Eker, E. (2000). Reliability, validity, and factor structure of the geriatric depression scale in Turkish elderly: Are there different factor structures for different cultures? *International Psychogeriatrics, 12*, 163–172.

Fernandez, E., Salem, D., Swift, J. K., & Ramtahal, N. (2015). Meta-analysis of dropout from cognitive behavioral therapy: Magnitude, timing, and moderators. *Journal of Consulting and Clinical Psychology, 83*, 1108–1122. doi:10.1037/ccp0000044

Fiske, A., Wetherell, J. L., & Gatz, M. (2009). Depression in older adults. *Annual Review of Clinical Psychology, 5*, 363–389. doi:10.1146/annurev.clinpsy.032408.153621

Foley, D., Ancoli-Israel, S., Britz, P., & Walsh, J. (2004). Sleep disturbances and chronic disease in older adults: Results of the 2003 National Sleep Foundation Sleep in America Survey. *Journal of Psychosomatic Research, 56*, 497–502. doi:10.1016/j.jpsychores.2004.02.010

Foley, D. J., Monjan, A. A., Brown, S. L., & Simonsick, E. M. (1995). Sleep complaints among elderly persons: An epidemiologic study of three communities. *Sleep: Journal of Sleep Research & Sleep Medicine, 18*, 425–432.

Forsell, Y., & Winblad, B. (1997). Anxiety disorders in non-demented and demented elderly patients: Prevalence and correlates. *Journal of Neurology, Neurosurgery & Psychiatry, 62*, 294–295. doi:10.1136/jnnp.62.3.294

Fountoulakis, K. N., Tsolaki, M., Iacovides, A., Yesavage, J., O'Hara, R., Kazis, A., & Ierodiakonou, C. (1999). The validation of the short form of the Geriatric Depression Scale (GDS) in Greece. *Aging Clinical and Experimental Research, 11*, 367–372.

Frans, Ö., Rimmö, P. A., Åberg, L., & Fredrikson, M. (2005). Trauma exposure and post-traumatic stress disorder in the general population. *Acta Psychiatrica Scandinavica, 111*, 291–299.

Friedman, J. I., Harvey, P. D., Coleman, T., Moriarty, P. J., Bowie, C., Parrella, M., . . . Davis, K. L. (2001). Six-year follow-up study of cognitive and functional status across the lifespan in schizophrenia: A comparison with Alzheimer's disease and normal aging. *The American Journal of Psychiatry, 158*, 1441–1448. doi:10.1176/appi.ajp.158.9.1441

Garrido, M. M., Kane, R. L., Kaas, M., & Kane, R. A. (2011). Use of mental health care by community-dwelling older adults. *Journal of the American Geriatrics Society, 59*, 50–56. doi:10.1111/j.1532-5415.2010.03220.x

Geriatric Depression Scale. (2017). Retrieved from https://web.stanford.edu/~yesavage/GDS.english.short.score.html

Gfroerer, J., Penne, M., Pemberton, M., & Folsom, R. (2003). Substance abuse treatment need among older adults in 2020: The impact of the aging baby-boom cohort. *Drug and Alcohol Dependence, 69*, 127–135. doi:10.1016/S0376-8716(02)00307-1

Glass, J., Lanctot, K. L., Hermann, N., Sproule, B. A., & Busto, U. E. (2005). Sedative hypnotics in older people with insomnia: Meta-analysis of risks and benefits. *British Medical Journal, 331*, 1169.

Gonçalves, D. C., & Byrne, G. J. (2012). Interventions for generalized anxiety disorder in older adults: Systematic review and meta-analysis. *Journal of Anxiety Disorders, 26*, 1–11. doi:10.1016/j.janxdis.2011.08.010

Granholm, E., Auslander, L. A., Gottlieb, J. D., McQuaid, J. R., & McClure, F. S. (2006). Therapeutic factors contributing to change in cognitive-behavioural group therapy for older persons with schizophrenia. *Journal of Contemporary Psychotherapy, 36*, 31–41.

Granholm, E., McQuaid, J. R., Auslander, L. A., & McClure, F. S. (2004). Group cognitive behavioural social skills training for older outpatients with chronic schizophrenia. *Journal of Cognitive Psychotherapy: An International Quarterly, 18*, 265–279.

Granholm, E., McQuaid, J. R., McClure, F. S., Auslander, L. A., Perivoliotis, D., Pedrelli, P., . . . Jeste, D. V. (2005). A randomized, controlled trial of cognitive behavioral social skills training for middle-aged and older outpatients with chronic schizophrenia. *American Journal of Psychiatry, 162*, 520–529.

Granholm, E., McQuaid, J. R., McClure, F. S., Link, P. C., Perivoliotis, D., Gottlieb, J. D., . . . Jeste, D. V. (2007). Randomised controlled trial of cognitive behavioural social skills training for older people with schizophrenia: 12-month follow-up. *Journal of Clinical Psychiatry, 68*, 730–737.

Grenier, S., Schuurmans, J., Goldfarb, M., Préville, M., Boyer, R., O'Connor, K., . . . Hudon, C. (2011). The epidemiology of specific phobia and subthreshold fear subtypes in a community-based sample of older adults. *Depression and Anxiety, 28*, 456–463. doi:10.1002/da.20812

Han, B., Gfroerer, J., Colliver, J., & Penne, M. (2009). Substance use disorder among older adults in the United States in 2020. *Addiction, 104*, 88–96. doi:10.1111/j.1360-0443.2008.02411.x

Han, C., Jo, S. A., Kwak, J. H., Pae, C. U., Steffens, D., Jo, I., & Park, M. H. (2008). Validation of the Patient Health Questionnaire-9 Korean version in the elderly population: The Ansan Geriatric study. *Comprehensive Psychiatry, 49*, 218–223. doi:10.1016/j.comppsych.2007.08.006

Heisel, M. J. (2006). Suicide and its prevention among older adults. *The Canadian Journal of Psychiatry, 51*, 143–154.

Hunt, S., Wisocki, P., & Yanko, J. (2003). Worry and use of coping strategies among older and younger adults. *Journal of Anxiety Disorders, 17*, 547–560. doi:10.1016/S0887-6185(02)00229-3

Jean-Louis, G., Magai, C. M., Cohen, C. I., Zizi, F., von Gizycki, H., DiPalma, J., & Casimir, G. J. (2001). Ethnic differences in self-reported sleep problems in older adults. *Sleep, 24*, 926–933.

*Karel, M. J., Gatz, M., & Smyer, M. A. (2012). Aging and mental health in the decade ahead: What psychologists need to know. *American Psychologist, 67*, 184–198. doi:10.1037/a0025393

*Karlin, B. E., Duffy, M., & Gleaves, D. H. (2008). Patterns and predictors of mental health service use and mental illness among older and younger adults in the United States. *Psychological Services, 5*, 275–294. doi:10.1037/1541-1559.5.3.275

Kessler, R. C., Angermeyer, M., Anthony, J. C., De Graaf, R., Demyttenaere, K., Gasquet, I., . . . Bedirhan Ustun, T. (2007). Lifetime prevalence and age-of-onset distributions of mental disorders in the world health organization's world mental health survey initiative. *World Psychiatry, 6,* 168–176.

Kessler, R. C., Berglund, P., Demler, O., Jin, R., Merikangas, K. R., & Walters, E. E. (2005). Lifetime prevalence and age-of-onset distributions of DSM-IV disorders in the national comorbidity survey replication. *Archives of General Psychiatry, 62,* 593–602. doi:10.1001/archpsyc .62.6.593

Kim, W.-H., Kim, B.-S., Kim, S.-K., Chang, S.-M., Lee, D.-W., Cho, M.-J., & Bae, J.-N. (2014). Sleep duration and associated factors in a community sample of elderly individuals in Korea. *Psychogeriatrics : The Official Journal of the Japanese Psychogeriatric Society, 15,* 87–94. doi:10.1111/ psyg.12072

Kluznik, J. C., Speed, N., van Valkenburg, C., & Magraw, R. (1986). Forty-year follow-up of United States prisoners of war. *American Journal of Psychiatry, 143,* 1443–1446.

Kørner, A., Lauritzen, L., Abelskov, K., Gulmann, N., Marie Brodersen, A., Wedervang-Jensen, T., & Marie Kjeldgaard, K. (2006). The Geriatric Depression Scale and the Cornell Scale for Depression in Dementia. A validity study. *Nordic Journal of Psychiatry, 60,* 360–364. doi:10.10 80/08039480600937066

Kroenke, K., & Spitzer, R. L. (2002). The PHQ-9: A new depression diagnostic and severity measure. *Psychiatric Annals, 32,* 509–515. doi:10.3928/0048-5713-20020901-06

Kroenke, K., Spitzer, R. L., & Williams, J. B. W. (2001). The PHQ-9: Validity of a brief depression severity measure. *Journal of General Internal Medicine, 16,* 606–613. doi:10.1046/j.1525-1497 .2001.016009606.x

Lam, C. K., Lim, P. P. J., Low, B. L., Ng, L.-L., Chiam, P. C., & Sahadevan, S. (2004). Depression in dementia: A comparative and validation study of four brief scales in the elderly Chinese. *International Journal of Geriatric Psychiatry, 19,* 422–428. doi:10.1002/gps.1098

Lamers, F., Jonkers, C. C. M., Bosma, H., Penninx, B. W. J. H., Knottnerus, J. A., & van Eijk, J. T. M. (2008). Summed score of the Patient Health Questionnaire-9 was a reliable and valid method for depression screening in chronically ill elderly patients. *Journal of Clinical Epidemiology, 61,* 679–687. doi:10.1016/j.jclinepi.2007.07.018

*Lawrence, V., Murray, J., Banerjee, S., Turner, S., Sangha, K., Byng, R., . . . Macdonald, A. (2006). Concepts and causation of depression: A cross-cultural study of the beliefs of older adults. *The Gerontologist, 46*(1), 23–32.

*Lee, L. O., Gatz, M., Pedersen, N. L., & Prescott, C. A. (2016). Anxiety trajectories in the second half of life: Genetic and environmental contributions over age. *Psychology and Aging, 31,* 101–113. doi:10.1037/pag0000063

Legarreta, M., Graham, J., North, L., Bueler, C. E., McGlade, E., & Yurgelun-Todd, D. (2015). DSM–5 posttraumatic stress disorder symptoms associated with suicide behaviors in veterans. *Psychological Trauma: Theory, Research, Practice, and Policy, 7,* 277–285. doi:10.1037/tra0000026

Lewinsohn, P. M., Seeley, J. R., Roberts, R. E., & Allen, N. B. (1997). Center for Epidemiologic Studies Depression Scale (CES-D) as a screening instrument for depression among community-residing older adults. *Psychology and Aging, 12*(2), 277–287. doi:10.1037/0882-7974.12.2.277

Linehan, M. M., & Wilks, C. R. (2015). The course and evolution of dialectical behavior therapy. *American Journal of Psychotherapy, 69,* 97–110.

López-Torres Hidalgo, J., Navarro Bravo, B., Párraga Martínez, I., Andrés Pretel, F., Téllez Lapeira, J., & Boix Gras, C. (2012). Understanding insomnia in older adults. *International Journal of Geriatric Psychiatry, 27,* 1086–1093. doi:10.1002/gps.2834

Lynch, T. R., Cheavens, J. S., Cukrowicz, K. C., Thorp, S. R., Bronner, L., & Beyer, J. (2007). Treatment of older adults with co-morbid personality disorder and depression: A dialectical behavior therapy approach. *International Journal of Geriatric Psychiatry, 22,* 131–143. doi:10.1002/gps.1703

Mackenzie, C. S., Pagura, J., & Sareen, J. (2010). Correlates of perceived need for and use of mental health services by older adults in the collaborative psychiatric epidemiological surveys. *American Journal of Geriatric Psychiatry, 18*(12), 1103–1115. doi:10.1097/JGP.0b013e3181dd1c06

McIntosh, J. L. (1985). Suicide among the elderly: Levels and trends. *American Journal of Orthopsychiatry, 55,* 288–293. doi:10.1111/j.1939-0025.1985.tb03443.x

McQuaid, J. R., Granholm, E., McClure, F. S., Roepke, S., Pedrelli, P., Patterson, T. L., & Jeste, D. V. (2000). Development of an integrated cognitive-behavioural and social skills training intervention for older patients with schizophrenia. *Journal of Psychotherapy Practice Research, 9,* 149–156

Meyer, T. J., Miller, M. L., Metzger, R. L., & Borkovec, T. D. (1990). Development and validation of the Penn State Worry Questionnaire. *Behaviour Research and Therapy, 28,* 487–495.

Miller, M. D., & Reynolds, C. I. (2007). Expanding the usefulness of Interpersonal Psychotherapy (IPT) for depressed elders with co-morbid cognitive impairment. *International Journal of Geriatric Psychiatry, 22,* 101–105. doi:10.1002/gps.1699

Moffitt, T. E., Caspi, A., Harrington, H., & Milne, B. J. (2002). Males on the life-course-persistent and adolescence-limited antisocial pathways: Follow-up at age 26 years. *Development and Psychopathology, 14,* 179–207. doi:10.1017/S0954579402001104

Montorio, I., & Izal, M. (1996). The Geriatric Depression Scale: A review of its development and utility. *International Psychogeriatrics, 8,* 103–112. doi:10.1017/S1041610296002505

Morgen, K., Denison-Vesel, K., Kobylarz, A., & Voelkner, A. (2015). Prevalence of substance use disorder treatment facilities specializing in older adult and trauma care: N-SSATS data 2009 to 2011. *Traumatology, 21,* 153–160. doi:10.1037/trm0000038

National Institute on Aging. (2011). *Global health and aging.* Washington, DC: Author. Retrieved from http://www.who.int/ageing/publications/global_health.pdf

National Institute on Drug Abuse. (2014). Drug facts: Nationwide trends. Retrieved from https://www.drugabuse.gov/sites/default/files/drugfactsnationwidetrends.pdf

*Neikrug, A. B., & Ancoli-Israel, S. (2010). Sleep disorders in the older adult—A mini-review. *Gerontology, 56,* 181–189. doi:10.1159/000236900

O'Donnell, B. F., (2007). Cognitive impairment in schizophrenia: A life span perspective. *American Journal of Alzheimer's Disease and Other Dementias, 22,* 398–405.

Oostervink, F., Nolen, W. A., & Kok, R. M. (2015). Two years' outcome of acute mania in bipolar disorder: Different effects of age and age of onset. *International Journal of Geriatric Psychiatry, 30,* 201–209. doi:10.1002/gps.4128

Oslin, D. W., Pettinati, H., & Volpicelli, J. R. (2005). Alcoholism treatment adherence: Older age predicts better adherence and drinking outcomes. *American Journal of Geriatric Psychiatry, 10,* 740–747.

Pachana, N., Byrne, G., Siddle, H., Koloski, N., Harley, E., & Arnold, E. (2007). Development and validation of the Geriatric Anxiety Inventory. *International Psychogeriatrics, 19,* 103–114. doi:10.1017/S1041610206003504

Pepin, R., Segal, D. L., & Coolidge, F. L. (2009). Intrinsic and extrinsic barriers to mental health care among community-dwelling younger and older adults. *Aging & Mental Health, 13,* 769–777.

Phelan, E., Williams, B., Meeker, K., Bonn, K., Frederick, J., Logerfo, J., & Snowden, M. (2010). A study of the diagnostic accuracy of the PHQ-9 in primary care elderly. *BioMed Central Family Practice, 11,* 63. doi:10.1186/1471-2296-11-63

Pinquart, M., Duberstein, P. R., & Lyness, J. M. (2006). Treatments for later-life depressive conditions: A meta-analytic comparison of pharmacotherapy and psychotherapy. *The American Journal of Psychiatry, 163,* 1493–1501. doi:10.1176/appi.ajp.163.9.1493

*Pinquart, M., Duberstein, P. R., & Lyness, J. M. (2007). Effects of psychotherapy and other behavioral interventions on clinically depressed older adults: A meta-analysis. *Aging & Mental Health, 11,* 645–657. doi:10.1080/13607860701529635

Pinquart, M., & Forstmeier, S. (2012). Effects of reminiscence interventions on psychosocial outcomes: A meta-analysis. *Aging & Mental Health, 16,* 541–558. doi:10.1080/13607863.2011.651434

Pratt, S. I., Bartels, S. J., Mueser, K. T., & Forester, B. (2008). Helping older people experience success: An integrated model of psychosocial rehabilitation and health care management for older adults with serious mental illness. *American Journal of Psychiatric Rehabilitation, 11,* 41–60. doi:10.1080/15487760701853193

Prigerson, H. G., Desai, R. A., & Rosenheck, R. A. (2001). Older adult patients with both psychiatric and substance abuse disorders: Prevalence and health service use. *Psychiatric Quarterly, 72,* 1–18. doi:10.1023/A:1004821118214

Radloff, L. (1977). The CES-D scale a self-report depression scale for research in the general population. *Applied Psychological Measurement, 1,* 385–401. doi:10.1177/014662167700100306

Rauch, S. A., Morales, K. H., Zubritsky, C., Knott, K., & Oslin, D. (2006). Posttraumatic stress, depression, and health among older adults in primary care. *American Journal of General Psychiatry, 14,* 316–324. doi:10.1097/01.JGP.0000199382.96115.86

Ritchie, K., Artero, S., Beluche, I., Ancelin, M. L., Mann, A., Dupuy, A. M., . . . Boulenger, J. P. (2004). Prevalence of DSM-IV psychiatric disorder in the French elderly population. *The British Journal of Psychiatry, 184,* 147–152. doi:10.1192/bjp.184.2.147

Robb, C., Haley, W. E., Becker, M. A., Polivka, L. A., & Chwa, H. J. (2003). Attitudes toward mental health care in younger and older adults: Similarities and differences. *Aging and Mental Health, 7,* 142–152.

Segal, D. L., June, A., Payne, M., Coolidge, F. L., & Yochim, B. (2010). Development and initial validation of a self-report assessment tool for anxiety among older adults: The Geriatric Anxiety Scale. *Journal of Anxiety Disorders, 24,* 709–714. doi:10.1016/j.janxdis.2010.05.002

Shah, A. (2012). Suicide rates: Age-associated trends and their correlates. *Journal of Injury and Violence Research, 4,* 79–86.

Simoni-Wastila, L., & Yang, H. K. (2006). Psychoactive drug abuse in older adults. *American Journal Geriatric Pharmacotherapy, 4,* 380–394. doi:10.1016/j.amjopharm.2006.10.002

Sirey, J., Bruce, M. L., Alexopoulos, G. S., Perlick, D. A., Raue, P., Friedman, S. J., & Meyers, B. S. (2001). Perceived stigma as a predictor of treatment discontinuation in young and older outpatients with depression. *American Journal of Psychiatry, 3,* 479–481. doi:10.1176/appi.ajp.158.3.479

Sivertsen, B., Omvik, S., Pallesen, S., Bjorvatn, B., Havik, O. E., Kvale, G., . . . Nordhus, I. H. (2006). Cognitive behavioral therapy vs zopiclone for treatment of chronic primary insomnia in older adults: A randomized controlled trial. *Journal of the American Medical Association, 295,* 2851–2858.

Spitzer, C., Barnow, S., Völzke, H., John, U., Freyberger, H. J., & Grabe, H. J. (2008). Trauma and posttraumatic stress disorder in the elderly: Findings from a German community study. *Journal of Clinical Psychiatry, 69,* 693–700

Switzer, J. F., Wittink, M. N., Karsch, B. B., & Barg, F. K. (2006). Pull yourself up by your bootstraps: A response to depression in older adults. *Qualitative Health Research, 16,* 1207–1216.

Thorp, S. R., Stein, M. B., Jeste, D. V., Patterson, T. L., & Wetherell J. L. (2012). Prolonged exposure therapy for older veterans with posttraumatic stress disorder: A pilot study. *The American Journal of Geriatric Psychiatry, 20,* 276–280. doi:10.1097/JGP.0b013e3182435ee9

van Alphen, S., Derksen, J., Sadavoy, J., & Rosowsky, E. (2012). Features and challenges of personality disorders in late life. *Aging & Mental Health, 16,* 805–810. doi:10.1080/13607863.2012.667781

van der Veen, D. C., van Zelst, W. H., Schoevers, R. A., Comijs, H. C., & Voshaar, R. C. (2015). Comorbid anxiety disorders in late-life depression: Results of a cohort study. *International Psychogeriatrics, 27,* 1157–1165. doi:10.1017/S1041610214002312

Weathers, F. W., Litz, B. T., Keane, T. M., Palmieri, P. A., Marx, B. P., & Schnurr, P. P. (2013). The PTSD Checklist for DSM-5 (PCL-5). Retrieved from www.ptsd.va.gov

Weintraub, D., & Ruskin, P. E. (1999). Posttraumatic stress disorder in the elderly: A review. *Harvard Review of Psychiatry, 7,* 144–52.

Weisenbach, S. L., Marshall, D., Weldon, A. L., Ryan, K. A., Vederman, A. C., Kamali, M., . . . Langenecker, S. A. (2014). The double burden of age and disease on cognition and quality of life in bipolar disorder. *International Journal of Geriatric Psychiatry, 29,* 952–961. doi:10.1002/gps.4084

Wetherell, J. L., Gatz, M., & Craske, M. G. (2003). Treatment of generalized anxiety disorder in older adults. *Journal of Consulting and Clinical Psychology, 71,* 31–40. doi:10.1037/0022-006X.71.1.31

Whitney, C. W., Enright, P. L., Newman, A. B., Bonekat, W., Foley, D., & Quan, S. F. (1998). Correlates of daytime sleepiness in 4578 elderly persons: The Cardiovascular Health Study. *Sleep, 21,* 27–37.

Wittink, M. N., Dahlberg, B., Biruk, C., & Barg, F. K. (2008). How older adults combine medical and experiential notions of depression. *Qualitative Health Research, 18,* 1174–1183.

Wolitzky-Taylor, K. B., Castriotta, N., Lenze, E. J., Stanley, M. A., & Craske, M. G. (2010). Anxiety disorders in older adults: A comprehensive review. *Depression and Anxiety*, 27, 190–211. doi:10.1002/da.20653

Wuthrich, V. M., Johnco, C. J., & Wetherell, J. L. (2015). Differences in anxiety and depression symptoms: Comparison between older and younger clinical samples. *International Psychogeriatrics*, 27, 1523–1532. doi:10.1017/S1041610215000526

Yesavage, J., Brink, T. L., Rose, T. L., Lum, O., Huang, V., Adey, M., & Leirer, V. O. (1983). Development and validation of a geriatric depression screening scale: A preliminary report. *Journal of Psychiatric Research*, 17, 37–49. doi:10.1016/0022-3956(82)90033-4

Zeitlin, D., Katona, C., D'Ath, P., & Katona, P. (1997). Attitudes to depression in primary care attenders: Effects of age and depressive symptoms. *Primary Care Psychiatry*, 3, 17–20.

7

Cognition and Aging

Spring F. Johnson, Kyrstle Barrera, and Brian P. Yochim

As explained earlier in this book, older adults are an important and rapidly growing segment of the population. Longer life expectancy unfortunately raises the risk of neurodegeneration and cognitive decline due to the natural aging of the brain. With the expectation of this population continuing to grow, it is important to understand how cognitive abilities change with age. But what constitutes the normal cognitive changes with aging? Some commonly reported problems are forgetfulness, slower cognitive speed, and difficulty learning new tasks. The *common cause hypothesis* suggests that cognitive changes occur with age because of an overall weakening of the integrity of the brain and the nervous system (Vance & Crowe, 2006) based on studies showing a decline in cognitive abilities related to declines in other systems, such as motor and sensory functioning (Christensen, MacKinnon, Korten, & Jorm, 2001). It is also important to be mindful of the fact that some cognitive change is normal with age, and is not a pathognomonic sign of a neurodegenerative process.

BASIC COGNITIVE FUNCTIONING

To understand basic cognitive functioning, it is important to explore the various domains, which include the following:

- Motor skills—the ability to initiate gross motor, fine motor, and facial motor actions, including both speed and dexterity

- Attention and concentration—the ability to focus on a given task, concentrate until a task is completed, and the ability to shift awareness when needed

---

*Key references in the References section are indicated by an asterisk.

- Processing speed—the speed at which cognitive tasks can be completed

- Language—the ability to communicate fluently and comprehend in both oral and written formats

- Visuospatial skills—the ability to understand, categorize, and reproduce what is seen

- Learning and memory—working memory, or one's ability to rapidly take in and modify information in real time (this overlaps with attention), and one's ability to learn, store, recognize, and recall new information. Semantic memory, or memory for information learned long ago, is also included in this domain

- Executive functions—higher order cognitive functioning such as planning, organizing, problem solving, evaluating, and conceptualizing. Social skills are also included in this domain, and are also included in their own domain

Normal aging can bring about changes within these domains and it is through cognitive/neuropsychological assessment that these changes can be evaluated within the context of comparison to normal aging processes. More specific changes in each domain as a result of normal aging are described in this chapter.

INTELLIGENCE: FLUID AND CRYSTALLIZED

Cognitive functioning has traditionally been summarized as the concept of "intelligence." One way that intelligence has been conceptualized is by breaking it down into two categories. In 1963, Cattell (later refined by Horn in 1966 and 1982) hypothesized that intelligence could be divided into crystallized and fluid intelligence. Crystallized intelligence refers to learned knowledge and experience, and fluid intelligence refers to the ability to change, adapt, and learn within a novel experience. In normal aging, age-related cognitive change can differentially affect the patterns of crystallized and fluid intelligence.

To explain further, crystallized intelligence is the result of cumulative learning across the life span becoming solidified over time, and is based on life experience. Essentially, it is knowledge that becomes solidified, hence the name crystallized. Tests of vocabulary and factual information assess crystallized intelligence as they rely on accumulated knowledge.

As can be expected, based on the makeup of crystallized intelligence, this form of intelligence typically remains stable over time and can even gradually improve throughout an individual's 60s and 70s as more information is accumulated with age. More specifically, older adults can even outperform younger adults in tasks involving crystallized intelligence. As age increases so does crystallized intelligence (Harada, Natelson Love, & Treibel, 2013).

In comparison, fluid intelligence relates to novel experiences and the ability to perform in the moment. It includes the ability to apply logic, solve problems, and identify patterns within a new experience. Fluid intelligence, as its name suggests, is flexible and adaptive and is necessary in novel situations. It is the capability to adapt to new situations independently of what has been learned in the past. For example, solving a puzzle for the first time, driving, and learning how to use new technology, all require the ability to adapt and perform in a new or changing environment and utilize fluid intelligence. Unfortunately, this fluid ability to adapt and learn in new situations shows an inverse correlation with age, specifically demonstrating a peak in the 30s and then declining at an estimated rate of −0.02 standard deviation per year (Harada et al., 2013). Effectively, older adults tend to struggle more in response to novel situations and in their ability to gather and organize new learning as compared to their younger counterparts.

INTELLIGENCE: MULTIPLE COMPONENTS

Another way of conceptualizing cognitive functioning has been to move away from the concept of general intelligence and to further break down cognition into multiple abilities. Initial inquiry into cognitive functioning focused primarily on evaluating cognition as a single construct, such as "intelligence" or general intellectual functioning (Spearman's *g*). What was previously seen as a unitary construct is now well known to include many different cognitive functions such as attention, visuospatial skills, memory, and more (Lezak, Howieson, Bigler, & Tranel, 2012). While it was initially thought that intelligence increased over the initial developmental period of life and declined with biological compromise of the brain's functioning, more careful attention was paid to the area and size of damage to the brain and its effect on overall intelligence. Over time, it was seen that overall intelligence did not necessarily correlate highly with extent of brain damage, which called into question the utility of using a single score to denote one's functioning. As knowledge of the complexities of brain functioning has increased, the concept of a unitary construct to describe the totality of an individual's functioning has fallen out of favor (Lezak et al., 2012). Cognitive functioning can be broken down into five key abilities (attention, visuospatial skills, language, memory, and executive functioning), six key abilities, such as in the *Diagnostic and Statistical Manual of Mental Disorders, Fifth Edition (DSM-5;* the five mentioned before plus another domain of social cognition), or even more subdomains of cognition. Furthermore, each of these domains can be further subdivided. Executive functioning, for example, probably includes more subdomains than any other cognitive ability.

SEATTLE LONGITUDINAL STUDY

One of the landmark longitudinal studies in aging has been the Seattle Longitudinal Study, conducted by K. Warner Schaie and colleagues. The study initially began as Schaie's doctoral dissertation at the University of Washington (in Seattle) in 1956 with the hopes of creating a longitudinal study that would address the discrepancies between cross-sectional and longitudinal findings in studying adult intellectual development. He designed a follow-up study in 1963 that ultimately became its own research program given the methodological and theoretical questions that grew from the original study (Schaie & Willis, 2010). Perhaps the most compelling aspects of the research program include its ability to assess cohort differences, their impact on adult cognition, and individual and differential change. These data have then been extrapolated to create and implement cognitive interventions for older adults based on these findings.

The study has evaluated its participants initially ranging in age from 22- to 70-years-old in 7-year intervals since 1956, with new participants included each year. Previous participants are also invited to join again. In later years of the study, the breadth of the participant pool expanded to include siblings of the main participants to evaluate familial similarities and the impact of genetics (Schaie & Willis, 2010).

The Seattle Longitudinal Study initially focused on five major questions. First, it sought to assess intelligence through adulthood, with the hopes of evaluating whether it changes uniformly throughout or if there are different patterns of change among various abilities over time. They found that there was no uniform pattern of change across all intellectual abilities, and that evaluating intellectual ability as a whole (i.e., general IQ) was not sufficient in elucidating the nuances of change with age. Specifically, their data suggested that fluid abilities tend to decline earlier than crystallized abilities, with decrements in fluid abilities occurring earlier in adulthood and crystallized abilities exhibiting a steeper decline in the late 70s and onward.

Second, the study aimed to evaluate whether there was a reliable age at which cognition declines, and at what magnitude. They found that there was a reliable decline in cognition at age 60 and older in some abilities, and that reliable declines were found for all abilities by age 74. Third, they sought to evaluate the pattern and magnitude of generational differences. They conclusively demonstrated that there are substantial cohort differences that vary in magnitude and direction, which indicated that cross-sectional studies would not accurately assess cognitive aging. These findings also indicated that the differences varied in magnitude and direction by ability, and that using a composite IQ variable washed out these nuances.

Fourth, Schaie and colleagues investigated the etiology of individual differences in age-related change. They found that the absence of cardiovascular risk factors, high socioeconomic status, involvement in a complex and intellectually stimulating environment, a flexible personality style, a high cognitive ability of one's spouse, and maintenance of high levels of processing speed reduced the risk of cognitive decline in adulthood. They found that these results were perhaps the most powerful and unique contribution of the longitudinal data collection method, which allows for evaluation of individual differences in variables that lead to early cognitive decline.

Lastly, Schaie and colleagues sought to evaluate whether or not intellectual decline with age could be reversed by educational intervention. They found that cognitive training resulted in significant improvement in approximately two thirds of their experimental sample, and about 40% of those who exhibited cognitive decline returned to their predecline level posttraining (Schaie & Willis, 2010). This speaks to the importance of encouraging cognitively stimulating activity in all older adults, not just those that exhibit a decline. The Seattle Longitudinal Study remains one of the classic research programs in this area. We turn now to discussion of changes that occur to specific cognitive abilities with age.

ATTENTION

Attention is one domain affected by normal aging and it encompasses the ability to attend to and concentrate on specific tasks. Attention can be divided into the categories that are shown in Table 7.1 (Glisky, 2007).

Sustained attention, also known as vigilance, is the ability to focus and attend to specific stimuli over time. This is a basic component of information processing, and is often a stepping stone for other cognitive processes and encapsulates what is at the forefront of awareness. It is the maintaining of focus for a prolonged amount of time. However, this level of attention can be difficult to maintain without becoming distracted; therefore, this ability can vary from person to person. In addition, there are three stages of sustained attention, attention getting, attention holding, and attention releasing, and a key feature is the ability to refocus on a task after becoming distracted. Without this ability, an individual is unable to adapt and attend to environmental demands such as playing a video game or listening to a lecture.

Selective attention is the filter of the brain allowing an individual to focus on important or salient environmental information and ignore the nonessential information. Current research considers attention as a limited resource that is divided to allow for processing of selected environmental stimuli. Selective attention makes it possible to watch a show while ignoring the phone ringing, or participate in a conversation at a bar while filtering out the other conversations of people around you.

Divided attention or multitasking is the ability to pay attention to two or more activities at once. This is the act of splitting attention while trying to do two or more things simultaneously. Typically divided attention is something that can only be successfully employed for activities that are familiar or routine. Much research has been devoted to the concept of divided attention and the prevailing idea is that the attentional system is limited and performance typically suffers when divided. For example, driving performance is typically worse when the driver is engaged in tasks other than just driving (Salvucci & Taatgen, 2008).

Working memory is the brain's ability to hold onto and manipulate temporary information before it is stored in long-term memory, and is considered to have a limited capacity of 7 plus or minus 2 bits of information (Miller, 1956). According to

Table 7.1 Different Subtypes of Attention

Sustained	The ability to attend to a stimulus for an extended amount of time such as being able to continue reading through a difficult passage in a textbook
Selective	The ability to attend to a stimulus despite competing stimulus such as being able to complete a work project in a busy office while others are talking and working on other tasks
Divided	The ability to attend to two tasks at the same time such as driving while engaging in conversation
Working Memory	The ability to keep information in mind long enough to perform a task such as remembering a number long enough to dial it

Baddeley & Hitch (1974), working memory comprises the central executive (directing allocation of attention), the phonological loop (brief storage of rehearsed language), and the visuospatial sketchpad (brief storage of visual and spatial information). Remembering a phone number by repeated rehearsal, using directions while driving, and cooking using a recipe are all examples of working memory. Everyday examples of activities that require attention and processing speed are listed in Table 7.2.

Difficulties in attention can present as taking longer to accomplish a task, needing to double check work, and being able to think and concentrate more easily when other things in the environment are not competing for attention. Normal aging research shows that working memory is affected by age (Brown, 2016). This effect can be conceptualized through the idea of the visuospatial sketchpad proposed by Baddeley and Hitch (1974). The visuospatial sketchpad provides a virtual environment within the mind to manipulate and think about information as it is initially processed, often referred to as a "mental chalkboard." Older adults display marked decline in spatial working memory (Jenkins, Myerson, Joerding, & Hale, 2000; Moffat, Zonderman, & Resnick, 2001), therefore inhibiting their ability to utilize the visuospatial sketchpad in comparison to their younger counterparts.

In addition, there is a noticeable age-related effect on selective and divided attention. Older adults may have some difficulty quickly recalling brief auditory instructions, and have a harder time focusing on a single stimulus when there are distractors competing for their attention. An example of this would be attending to a conversation at a loud or crowded event and being able to retain the message of the conversation while ignoring the distraction of surrounding stimuli. Some of these deficits could be explained by the *inhibitory deficit hypothesis* (Hasher & Zacks, 1988; Hasher, Zacks, & May, 1999; Zacks & Hasher 1997), which is viewed as a major source of cognitive decline. This theory posits that aging can affect an individual's ability to employ attentional discrimination and can explain the inability for older adults to suppress unnecessary information leading to higher levels of distractibility, reduced working memory capacity, and poor retrieval of details (Lustig, Hasher, & Zacks,

Table 7.2 Examples of Everyday Activities That Involve Attention and Processing Speed

- Reading
- Participating in a conversation
- Comprehending and following the plot of a movie or story
- Driving
- Following directions for how to get to a destination
- Keeping up with automated telephone operating systems
- Avoiding an accident or a fall
- Using a computer, tablet, or smartphone
- Counting out change
- Cooking a complex meal
- Crossing a street
- Parking a car

2007). The inhibitory deficit can also lead to greater proactive interference, or difficulty with learning something new due to old learning interfering with the new information being encoded. In addition, attention and inhibition ability seem to also impact speech perception in older adults. In a study by Getzmann, Golob, and Wascher (2016), deficits in preparation and allocation of attention led to an overall decline and delay in speech perception processing in older adults exposed to an adverse listening condition such as a cocktail party.

In addition, older adults struggle more with multitasking or attending to multiple tasks simultaneously in comparison to younger adults. This can impair the ability to carry on a conversation with another person while texting or more commonly the ability to carry on a conversation while driving. Older adults also show a decline in working memory on tasks that involve manipulating information while it is being stored in memory, and an example of this is being able to recall and modify steps in a recipe and even remembering directions or instructions (Salthouse, Fristoe, Lineweaver, & Coon, 1995). Furthermore, older adults have a decreased ability to refocus after being disrupted from a task, making any form of multitasking very difficult. Essentially, interruptions impair an older adult's performance on a task more so than a younger adult's, and multitasking leads to significant working memory disruption (Clapp, Rubens, Sabharwal, & Gazzaley, 2011).

PROCESSING SPEED

Processing speed is another form of fluid intelligence impacted by normal aging and corresponds to the speed at which cognitive activities are performed as well as the speed of motor responses. The ability to make quick decisions and rapid responses to changing road conditions while driving is an example of processing speed. Unfortunately, aging impacts this ability and declines in processing speed begin in the 30s and continue on throughout the life span (Harada et al., 2013). As such, older adults are slower in completing tasks, responding to questions, and responding to stimuli in their environment. Salthouse's (1996) foundational processing speed theory posits that older adults struggle in two main mechanisms (limited time and simultaneity) that affect their processing speed, and these two mechanisms cause functional problems. Limited time is the notion that older adults struggle to perform later operations because a majority of their processing time is spent on earlier operations, and this therefore limits and/or restricts their time for total processing of information. For example, an older adult may struggle with understanding and comprehending the plot of a fast-paced action movie. The simultaneity mechanism is the inability to hold onto earlier processing information to be used to complete later processing. Essentially that information may decay or become displaced, and therefore may not be available when it is needed. An example of this is being able to calculate the tip on a restaurant bill because tip calculation requires being able to hold a number in working memory without decay long enough to be able to perform multiple calculation all in one's mind. Brinley plots are a great way to visualize the difference in processing speed between older and younger adults. In a Brinley plot, the mean response times of older adults and younger adults are placed on a scatterplot, and a regression line is then fitted to the data. Overall, the use of Brinley plots shows that older adults display significantly slower processing speed times in comparison to younger adults (Maylor & Rabbitt, 1994).

LANGUAGE

Language utilizes both crystallized and fluid intelligence and encompasses the mechanics of communication, linguistic and lexical knowledge, word-finding and verbal fluency, and production and comprehension. Examples of everyday activities that involve language are listed in Table 7.3. Overall language ability remains intact within the normal aging process, and older adults even show improvement in narrative discourse. For example, older adults are often credited with telling more interesting stories and exhibiting more extensive vocabularies than younger adults, even though word-finding difficulties might increase or physical changes like hearing loss might impact communication abilities (Glisky, 2007). Word-finding ability and fluency tend to be negatively impacted with age, and as such, it is common to observe older adults struggling to find the words they want to use to express themselves as well as having difficulty speaking extemporaneously (La Rue, 1992). Because older adults have typically smaller working memory spans, their levels of language processing decline with age. Additionally, working memory is associated with language production and affects older adults' capacities for temporary maintenance of information (Engle, Tuholski, Laughlin, & Conway, 1999). More specifically, three general factors of processing speed, working memory, and inhibition (suppression of incorrect or inappropriate verbal information) affect language processing in older adults (Van der Linden et al., 1999). This decreased ability in language processing can lead to difficulty in understanding spoken language and finding words, and can

Table 7.3 Examples of Everyday Activities That Involve Language Skills

- Reading and comprehension
- Initiating and sustaining conversations
- Maintaining interpersonal relationships
- Placing orders
- Discussing healthcare needs and making appointments
- Participating in social groups
- Reading food and medication labels
- Creating a grocery list
- Naming objects
- Talking on the phone
- Participating in therapy (including psychotherapy, occupational therapy, physical therapy, and of course speech therapy)
- Recalling words, stories, names, etc.
- Explaining directions
- Asking for help

lead to low self-confidence in their abilities to communicate, thereby decreasing their desires to verbally engage with others (Hummert, Garstka, Ryan, & Bonnesen, 2004).

VISUOSPATIAL SKILLS

Visuospatial skills incorporate the ability to accurately perceive and manipulate visual information in the environment, as well as the ability to understand the physical relationships between multiple stimuli in two- and three-dimensional space. At its most elemental level, visual perception involves the ability to simply perceive visual information accurately in the environment. Examples of everyday activities that involve these skills are listed in Table 7.4. In general, these abilities tend to remain relatively intact with normal aging (Harada et al., 2013), consistent with the occipital lobes showing very little change with age, as described in Chapter 4.

MEMORY

Memory can be broken down into different stages, and deficits at any stage of memory can negatively impact overall memory functioning. The greatest effect of age can be seen in the domain of memory and can be related to a number of factors including the slowing of processing speed, reduction in the ability to selectively attend to stimuli, and decreased use of methods to improve learning and memory (Harada et al., 2013). These factors may be seen as "building blocks" of memory and the foundation upon which memory sits. They contribute to successful learning/acquisition,

Table 7.4 Examples of Everyday Activities That Involve Visuospatial Skills

- Reading
- Fixing household objects or a car or other machines
- Assembling a new piece of furniture or other new purchase
- Arranging a room or garage or kitchen or closet efficiently
- Wrapping presents
- Cooking a complex meal
- Organizing a pillbox
- Packing a suitcase or car for a trip
- Finding things in the kitchen/house
- Navigating with a map
- Driving or using public transportation
- Finding the car in a parking lot or finding a particular building/location
- Recognizing people or things from far away
- Crossing a street
- Navigating in a grocery store and finding an item on a grocery shelf
- Parking a car
- Using stairs

Table 7.5 **Types of Memory**

Type	Definition	Example
Episodic	Memory for personal events that occurred at a specific time	• Remembering where you parked your car • Remembering what you ate for dinner yesterday • Remembering where you left your keys • Remembering your wedding day • Remembering your graduation
Semantic	Memory for general world knowledge and factual information	• Remembering the names and locations of cities • Remembering authors of specific books or actors in specific movies • Remembering the meaning of words
Procedural	Memory for skills and procedures, "muscle memory"	• Remembering how to ride a bike • Remembering how to type on a keyboard • Remembering how to shift gears on a manual-transmission car
Prospective	Memory for things that need to be done in the future	• Remembering to attend a doctor's appointment • Remembering to pay your bills • Remembering to stop by a store after work or school

which maximizes the amount of information available for later recall. When these building block functions are compromised, information is not learned to its fullest extent and as a result, may not be available for later recall. In other words, if information is not initially learned, one cannot be expected to remember it.

In general, memory can be divided into *declarative* and *nondeclarative* memory. Declarative memory can be broken down into *episodic* and *semantic* memory. Nondeclarative memory includes procedural learning, priming, and classical conditioning. *Prospective* memory, or remembering to do something in the future, is another type of memory investigated in older adults. Episodic, semantic, procedural, and prospective memory are described in Table 7.5.

Within normal aging, episodic memory and semantic memory are the most affected (Harada et al., 2013). Episodic memory (autobiographical memory) is defined as the memory of personally experienced events in a specific place and time. Episodic memory includes memories such as what one did last weekend, or a trip taken several years ago. Declines in episodic memory with age are well-documented (Nyberg & Bäckman, 2011). Emotionally salient memories, often referred to as "flashbulb memories" like remembering one's wedding or the day one learned of a family member's death are more resistant to change. It is theorized that older adults may have deficiencies in encoding, storage, or retrieval processes, which contribute to the loss of ability in this area. Most older adults believe that their memory for more distant events is better than their memory for more recent events (Glisky, 2007), and this pattern is found in adults with Alzheimer's disease (see Chapter 9).

Semantic memory houses the general fund of information and includes knowledge of language and factual knowledge (crystallized knowledge), as opposed to personal experience. Semantic memory shows decline specifically in old age, and some experts feel that declines in word-finding are due to semantic memory declines (Rönnlund, Nyberg, Bäckman, & Nilsson, 2005). While semantic and episodic memory both decline with normal aging, research suggests that episodic memory declines gradually over the lifetime whereas semantic memory declines most significantly in late life (Harada et al., 2013).

Procedural memory, one type of nondeclarative memory, is the memory for how to do things, and is often cultivated outside of an individual's awareness (Harada et al., 2013). It is often referred to as "muscle memory" and includes physically based memory such as remembering how to bounce a basketball or tie one's shoelaces. These are often abilities that are difficult to verbalize, and are often completed automatically. Research suggests that this type of information accumulates with time and is relatively unaffected in normal aging (Harada et al., 2013).

Prospective memory involves remembering to do something in the future, and is relatively new to the memory literature (Glisky, 2007). It is critical in independent living and involves tasks such as remembering an upcoming doctor's appointment, remembering to go to the grocery store, and remembering to pay bills each month. Research suggests that older adults may perform just as well as their younger counterparts on these tasks (Einstein & McDaniel, 1990; Glisky, 2007).

EXECUTIVE FUNCTIONING

Executive functions are higher-order cognitive skills that encompass a broad range of abilities that include planning, organization, cognitive control, set shifting/mental flexibility, multitasking, concept formation, problem solving, and abstract reasoning. It also includes the ability to control behavior and resist impulsive actions, resulting in appropriate social interaction. This requires higher-level cognitive processing such as the ability to self-monitor, reason, solve problems, maintain cognitive flexibility, organize, and plan. Executive functions form the basis of many cognitive, emotional, and social skills, and involve four component abilities of volition, planning, purposive action, and effective performance (Lezak et al., 2012). Volition encompasses the will to decide on and commit to a course of action and requires self-awareness, motivation, and an awareness of the surrounding environment. Planning is the ability to make choices to direct activity and take steps to achieve a goal. Purposive action is the decision to act independently and with purpose and to move a plan forward into action, and requires self-regulation and programming of behavior. Effective performance is the ability to self-correct and regulate behaviors in relation to others while interacting interpersonally and utilizes the ability to process and respond correctly to feedback. A depiction of executive functioning is presented in Figure 7.1. Declines in executive functioning can result in reductions in judgment such as inhibiting inappropriate behaviors or questions, or falling prey to phone and email scams; dressing inappropriately for the weather or different types of meetings; and poor short-term and long-term planning of events such as meals, or birthday parties. Examples of everyday activities that require executive functioning are listed in Table 7.6.

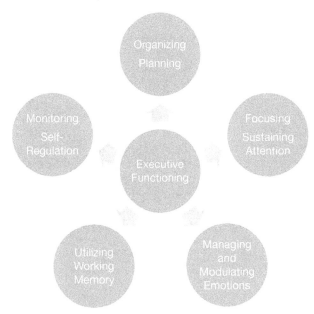

Figure 7.1 Components of executive functioning.

Table 7.6 Examples of Everyday Activities That Involve Executive Functioning

- Behaving and speaking appropriately in social settings
- Following social norms
- Adhering to a budget
- Solving problems
- Creating a shopping list
- Emotional stability
- Having insight into one's own motivations and the motivations of others
- Controlling emotions and expressing them appropriately
- Planning a dinner party
- Dressing appropriately for the weather
- Maintaining interpersonal relationships
- Planning and starting a home improvement project
- Keeping track of time
- Finishing a task on time
- Asking for help when needed
- Participating in social groups

This type of functioning requires a level of fluidity that can be categorized under fluid intelligence, and it is this area of fluid intelligence that shows some of the most significant decline in relation to age. Executive functioning has been shown to decline with age, and significant age-related effects can be seen in the fifth to sixth decade of life as older adults tend to think more concretely than younger adults. In

BOX 7.1 Wisdom and Aging

Older adults are frequently perceived as possessing wisdom gained through their many years of life experience. However, research in this area has found that (a) wisdom is very difficult to operationally define, and concepts of it vary across cultures, and (b) there is little evidence for a relationship between wisdom and age. Baltes and Staudinger (2000), summarizing their research in this area, described three factors that relate to wisdom: (a) general personal characteristics, including cognitive ability, (b) specific conditions of expertise, including mentoring or practice, and (c) life contexts that facilitate acquisition of wisdom, including education or leadership experience. While these conditions do require the passage of time, growing old itself is not necessarily correlated with the acquisition of wisdom.

addition, older adults have a harder time suppressing automatic responses in novel situations. This decline in executive functioning most commonly affects an individual's working memory and ability to plan strategically and shift mental sets (Janssen, Aken, De Mey, Witteman, & Egger 2014).

Structurally, the frontal lobes are generally considered to be essential for executive functioning, and it is this area of the aging brain that shows significant changes and atrophy in comparison to other areas of the brain (see Chapter 4). These observed structural changes led to the development of the frontal aging hypothesis (Dempster, 1992), which posits that many observed changes in cognitive functioning can be explained by age-related volume and function changes in the frontal lobes, specifically affecting the areas of working memory, attention, and executive functioning (Rodríguez-Aranda & Sundet, 2006). These changes in volume of the frontal lobes can be associated with an older adult's inability to inhibit undesired actions, such as talking excessively about a topic that is irrelevant to the conversation at hand or making socially inappropriate comments (Pushkar et al., 2000). This decline of inhibition in older adults has also been found to possibly contribute to excessive rumination leading to late-onset depression, and gambling problems among some older adults (von Hippel, 2007).

Alternatively, changes in executive functioning in older adults can also have some positive effects. Older adults tend to have a better ability to attend to positive emotions more so than younger adults, and this is even shown in reduced responding in the amygdala to negative events but not positive events (Carstensen & Mikels, 2005). Additionally, older adults may be more capable of solving some social problems than younger adults because they are more likely to incorporate contextual strategies with emotion-regulation strategies in the face of immediate needs (Blanchard-Fields, 2007). The possibility of increased wisdom late in life is discussed in Box 7.1. However, overall changes in executive functioning for older adults can lead to unintended social changes affecting an individual's overall quality of life.

POTENTIAL FUNCTIONAL CONSEQUENCES OF COGNITIVE CHANGES WITH AGING

DRIVING

The rate of traffic accidents is higher among drivers ages 16 to 19 than for any other age group. Per mile driven, drivers ages 16 to 19 are nearly three times more likely than drivers aged 20 and older to be in a fatal crash (Centers for Disease Control and Prevention [CDC], 2017). Older adult drivers represent the second age group most likely to be involved in accidents. In 2015, more than 40 million older adults possessed a driver's license (Federal Highway Administration, 2016). For older adults, the ability to drive is paramount to independence and mobility; however, the risk of being injured or killed in a motor vehicle accident increases with age, due both to increased crash risk and greater physical frailty when exposed to a crash (Boot, Stothart, & Charness, 2014). Older adults can optimize their driving safety if they work to avoid high-risk driving situations, but many older adults are not able to accurately judge their own driving abilities (Horswill, Sullivan, Lurie-Beck, & Smith, 2013). Situations involving making turns across opposing traffic at intersections, merging from a yield lane, and changing lanes on a highway are particularly dangerous for older drivers (Staplin, Lococo, Martell, & Stutts, 2012). This increased risk for driving accidents can be related to the cognitive domains that are affected by the normal aging process. Age-related declines in visual attention/processing, visual perception, executive functioning, and memory can affect an individual's ability to drive safely (Wagner, Muri, Nef, & Mosimann, 2011). For example, overall slowing of processing speed for older adults can impact the ability to respond in time to avoid an accident. Declines in visual attention and processing speed could affect the ability to change lanes while driving. This is likely to be increasingly difficult on busy streets or streets with a high number of visual distractors (e.g., billboards, businesses, multiple intersecting streets, etc.). Older adults' abilities to divide attention between a central location and the periphery decline with age, resulting in a smaller *useful field of view* (Boot et al., 2014). In addition, as executive function declines, so does the ability to respond fluidly to rapidly changing stimuli, which would prove difficult when adjusting to rapidly changing road conditions or even the behavior of other drivers. The normal aging process of the brain can contribute greatly to an older adult's ability to drive, although it is important to keep in mind that these changes do not affect all older adults in the same way and at the same time, and many older adults are able to drive safely into older age. Therefore, it is important to continually monitor this ability to keep older adults safe on the road while still respecting their right to independence and mobility.

Although there is an increased safety risk for older adults who are driving, there are also a number of protective factors significant to older adults that aid in their abilities to drive safely. For example, older adults are more likely to wear their seatbelts in comparison to younger adults (National Highway Traffic Administration, 2012). Older drivers tend to curtail their driving during bad weather and at night, and they also tend to drive fewer miles than younger drivers (Bauer, Adler, Kuskowski, & Rottunda, 2003). Furthermore, older adults have the lowest rates of accidents involving driving under the influence of alcohol and only 6% of drivers age 65 and older involved in fatal accidents had a blood alcohol level at .08 (the legal limit) or higher (National Highway Traffic Administration, 2012).

While cessation of driving for at-risk older adults may seem an obvious solution, it comes at substantial cost to older adults and society as a whole. Cessation of driving leads to increased transportation burdens on families and caregivers. This is especially problematic in rural areas that do not have public transportation. The cessation of driving also leads to negative outcomes among individual older adults. Longitudinal studies have shown poorer health trajectories, higher rates of depression and institutionalization, increased mortality, and decreased levels of behavioral activation outside of the home in older adults who have had to stop driving (Curl, Stowe, Cooney, & Proulx, 2014). Furthermore, a 2003 research study commissioned by Clarity and The EAR Foundation found that older adults fear the loss of independence even more than they fear death (Marketing Charts, 2007). It is important to take this into account when reviewing the abilities of older adults to drive safely.

Driving exercises/programs that focus on enhancing processing speed and improving divided attention can prolong an older adult's ability to drive (Ross et al., 2016; see also Box 7.2). For example, through Speed of Processing Training (SPT), a computerized, process-based, training program, initial processing speed performance for complex amounts of visual information can be improved (Ball, Edwards, & Ross, 2007). Furthermore, SPT has been shown to prolong driving mobility and increase driving frequency (Ross et al., 2016). Therefore, older adults have the potential to improve their driving skills and prolong their abilities to drive through training programs that focus on improving processing speed. Modifications to roadways such as improved lighting of signs, street signs placed a certain distance before a roadway, increased text size of signs, and modified perception-action time estimates (e.g., how long to make a yellow light last) can increase the safety of roadways for older drivers (Boot et al., 2014). Other transportation interventions for older adults include ensuring safe areas for pedestrians and bicyclists, especially for people who cease driving. Self-driving cars will eventually preclude the need for older adults to drive, while still providing mobility and independence.

BOX 7.2 Selection, Optimization, and Compensation Applied to Driving

Paul Baltes's theory on selection, optimization, and compensation applies to older adults maintaining the ability to drive. One older adult, aware that her driving abilities have declined, understood that a large percentage of accidents occur when making left turns. She selected this aspect of her driving as an area of focus, and decided to completely avoid making left turns. She optimizes her ability to continue driving by arranging her trips in such a way that she does not need to make left turns, even if it involves making three right turns to get where she needs to go. This form of compensation has ensured her safety and enabled her to remain independent.

Mandatory Retirement Ages

In addition to driving, cognitive changes with age have led some professions to impose mandatory retirement ages. Although the Age Discrimination in Employment Act of 1967 (ADEA) prohibits forced retirement for those older than the age of 40, there are a few professions that are not able to employ older adults indefinitely, because of public safety concerns. These professions include pilots, air traffic controllers, and federal law enforcement officers. More specifically, some mandatory retirement ages are 65 for airline pilots, 56 (with exceptions up to age 61) for air traffic controllers, and 57 for federal law enforcement officers (or later if less than 20 years of service). These mandatory retirement exceptions are specifically aimed at professions that are considered to require high levels of physical and mental skill and/or are highly dangerous. It is assumed that normal cognitive aging affects the level of processing speed necessary for these jobs to be performed safely. However, mandatory retirement laws are controversial as they do not allow for individual variability and are typically based on limited scientific data (Gokhale, 2004). Most older adults can enjoy the independence and mobility that having a job affords them. Older adult employment and mandatory retirement ages are explored further in Chapter 11.

CONCLUSION

This chapter reviewed the typical changes in cognitive functioning that occur with aging. An overview of the concept of crystallized and fluid intelligence was presented. More recently, intelligence has been conceptualized as consisting of multiple abilities, not adequately represented by a general quotient. The Seattle Longitudinal Study was the first major longitudinal study of cognitive changes with age. We next discussed changes in specific cognitive abilities with age. The inhibitory deficit hypothesis was presented as an explanation for changes with attention with age. One consistent finding has been that processing speed declines with advancing age. Visuospatial and language abilities remain fairly stable compared to other abilities. Memory comprises several types of memory, which are affected differentially by aging. Executive functioning also consists of several separate skills, affected differently by aging. Lastly, two important implications of cognitive changes with age, driving and mandatory retirement ages, were discussed.

DISCUSSION QUESTIONS

1. Explain the concepts of fluid and crystallized intelligence, and how each is affected by age.

2. Describe some of the principal findings from the Seattle Longitudinal Study.

3. Explain the inhibitory deficit hypothesis and its relation to changes in attention with age.

4. Summarize the cognitive abilities that remain the most stable with advancing age.

5. Describe the different forms of memory presented in this chapter. Explain which types are affected by aging and which are more preserved.

6. Describe some specific driving situations that are hazardous for older adults.

7. Compare the safety of older drivers to that of other ages, and describe some ways in which their safety can be improved.

REFERENCES

Baddeley, A. D., & Hitch, G. (1974). Working memory. *Psychology of Learning and Motivation, 8,* 47–89.

Ball, K. E., Edwards, J. D., & Ross, L. A. (2007). The impact of speed of processing training on cognitive and everyday functions. *The Journals of Gerontology. Series B, Psychological Sciences and Social Sciences, 62*(1), 19–31.

*Baltes, P. B., & Staudinger, U. M. (2000). Wisdom: A metaheuristic (pragmatic) to orchestrate mind and virtue toward excellence. *American Psychologist, 55,* 122–136.

Bauer, M. J., Adler, G., Kuskowski, M. A., & Rottunda, S. (2003). The influence of age and gender on the driving patterns of older adults. *Journal of Women & Aging, 15*(4), 3–16.

Blanchard-Fields, F. (2007). Everyday problem solving and emotion: An adult developmental perspective. *Current Directions in Psychological Science, 16,* 26–31.

Boot, W. R., Stothart, C., & Charness, N. (2014). Improving the safety of aging road users—A mini-review. *Gerontology, 60*(1), 90–96. doi:10.1159/000354212

Brown, L. A. (2016). Spatial-sequential working memory in younger and older adults: Age predicts backward recall performance within both age groups. *Frontiers in Psychology, 4*(7), 1–11.

Carstensen, L. L., & Mikels, J. A. (2005). At the intersection of emotion and cognition: Aging and the positivity effect. *Current Directions in Psychological Science, 14,* 117–121.

Cattell, R. B. (1963). Theory of fluid and crystallized intelligence: A critical experiment. *Journal of Educational Psychology, 54*(1), 1–22. doi:10.1037/h0046743

Centers for Disease Control and Prevention. (2017). Teen drivers: Get the facts. Retrieved from https://www.cdc.gov/motorvehiclesafety/teen_drivers/teendrivers_factsheet.html

Christensen, H., Mackinnon, A. J., Korten, A., & Jorm, A. F. (2001). The "common cause hypothesis" of cognitive aging: Evidence for not only a common factor but also specific associations of age with vision and grip strength in a cross-sectional analysis. *Psychology and aging, 16*(4), 588.

Clapp, W. C., Rubens, M. T., Sabharwal, J., & Gazzaley, A. (2011). Deficit in switching between functional brain networks underlies the impact of multitasking on working memory in older adults. *Proceedings of the National Academy of Sciences of the United States of America, 108*(17), 7212–7217. doi:10.1073/pnas.1015297108

*Curl, A. L., Stowe, J. D., Cooney, T. M., & Proulx, C. M. (2014). Giving up the keys: how driving cessation affects engagement in later life. *Gerontologist, 54*(3), 423–433. doi:10.1093/geront/gnt037

Dempster, F. N. (1992). The rise and fall of the inhibitory mechanism: Toward a unified theory of cognitive development and aging. *Developmental Review, 12,* 45–75.

Einstein, G. O., & McDaniel, M. A. (1990). Normal aging and prospective memory. *Journal of Experimental Psychology: Learning, Memory, and Cognition, 16*(4), 717–726.

Engle, R. W., Tuholski, S. W., Laughlin, J. E., & Conway, A. A. (1999). Working memory, short-term memory, and general fluid intelligence: A latent-variable approach. *Journal of Experimental Psychology: General, 128*(3), 309–331. doi:10.1037/0096-3445.128.3.309

Federal Highway Administration. (2016). Highway Statistics 2015. Washington, DC: Author. Retrieved from https://www.fhwa.dot.gov/policyinformation/statistics/2015/dl20.cfm

Getzmann, S., Golob, E. J., & Wascher, E. (2016). Focused and divided attention in a simulated cocktail-party situation: ERP evidence from younger and older adults. *Neurobiology of Aging, 41,* 138–149. doi:10.1016/j.neurobiolaging.2016.02.018

Glisky, E. L. (2007). Changes in cognitive function in human aging. In D. R. Riddle (Ed.), *Brain aging: Models, methods, and mechanisms* (pp. 3–20). Boca Raton, FL: CRC Press/Taylor & Francis.

Gokhale, J. (2004). Mandatory retirement age rules: Is it time to re-evaluate? (Testimony of Jagadeesh Gokhale). Retrieved from https://www.cato.org/publications/congressional-testimony/mandatory-retirement-age-rules-is-it-time-reevaluate

*Harada, C. N., Natelson Love, M. C., & Triebel, K. (2013). Normal cognitive aging. *Clinics in Geriatric Medicine, 29*(4), 737–752. doi:10.1016/j.cger.2013.07.002

Hasher, L., & Zacks, R. T. (1988). Working memory, comprehension, and aging: A review and a new view. In G. H. Bower & G. H. Bower (Eds.), *The psychology of learning and motivation: advances in research and theory* (Vol. 22, pp. 193–225). San Diego, CA: Academic Press. doi:10.1016/S0079-7421(08)60041-9

Hasher, L., Zacks, R. T., & May, C. P. (1999). Inhibitory control, circadian arousal, and age. In D. Gopher, A. Koriat, D. Gopher, & A. Koriat (Eds.), *Attention and performance XVII: Cognitive regulation of performance: Interaction of theory and application* (pp. 653–675). Cambridge, MA: The MIT Press.

Horn, J. L., & Cattell, R. B. (1966). Refinement and test of the theory of fluid and crystallized general intelligences. *Journal of Educational Psychology, 57*(5), 253–270. doi:10.1037/h0023816

Horn, J. L., & Cattell, R. B. (1982). Whimsy and misunderstanding of gf–gc theory: A comment on Guilford. *Psychological Bulletin, 91*(3), 623–633. doi:10.1037/0033-2909.91.3.623

Horswill, M. S., Sullivan, K., Lurie-Beck, J. K., & Smith, S. (2013). How realistic are older drivers' ratings of their driving ability? *Accident Analysis & Prevention, 50*, 130–137. doi:10.1016/j.aap.2012.04.001

Hummert, M. L., Garstka, T. A., Ryan, E. B., & Bonnesen, J. L. (2004). The role of age stereotypes in interpersonal communication. In J. F. Nussbaum, J. Coupland, J. F. Nussbaum, & J. Coupland (Eds.), *Handbook of communication and aging research* (pp. 91–114). Mahwah, NJ: Lawrence Erlbaum Associates.

Janssen, G., Aken, L. V., De Mey, H., Witteman, C., & Egger, J. (2014). Decline of executive function in a clinical population: Age, psychopathology, and test performance on the Cambridge Neuropsychological Test Automated Battery (CANTAB). *Applied Neuropsychology: Adult, 21*(3), 210–219. doi:10.1080/09084282.2013.793191

Jenkins, L., Myerson, J., Joerding, J. A., & Hale, S. (2000). Converging evidence that visuospatial cognition is more age-sensitive than verbal cognition. *Psychology of Aging, 15*, 157–175. doi:10.1037/0882-7974.15.1.157

La Rue, A. (1992). *Aging and neuropsychological assessment cognition in normal aging.* New York, NY: Plenum Press.

Lezak, M. D., Howieson, D. B., Bigler, E. D., & Tranel, D. (2012). *Neuropsychological assessment* (5th ed.). New York, NY: Oxford University Press.

*Lustig, C., Hasher, L., & Zacks, R. T. (2007). Inhibitory deficit theory: Recent developments in a "new view." In D. S. Gorfein, C. M. MacLeod, D. S. Gorfein, & C. M. MacLeod (Eds.), *Inhibition in cognition* (pp. 145–162). Washington, DC: American Psychological Association. doi:10.1037/11587-008

Marketing Charts. (2007). Seniors fear loss of independence, nursing homes more than death. Retrieved from https://www.marketingcharts.com/demographics-and-audiences/boomers-and-older-2343

Maylor, E. A., & Rabbitt, P. A. (1994). Applying Brinley plots to individuals: Effects of aging on performance distributions in two speeded tasks. *Psychology and Aging, 9*(2), 224–230. doi:10.1037/0882-7974.9.2.224

Miller, G. A. (1956). The magical number seven, plus or minus two: Some limits on our capacity for processing information. *Psychological Review, 63*, 81–97.

Moffat, S. D., Zonderman, A. B., & Resnick, S. M. (2001). Age differences in spatial memory in a virtual environment navigation task. *Neurobiology of Aging, 22*, 787–796. doi:10.1016/S0197-4580(01)00251-2

National Highway Traffic Administration. (2012). Traffic safety facts 2010: Older population. Retrieved from http://www-nrd.nhtsa.dot.gov/Pubs/811640.pdf

*Nyberg, L., & Bäckman, L. (2011). Memory changes and the aging brain: A multimodal imaging approach. In K. W. Schaie & S. L. Willis (Eds.), *Handbook of the psychology of aging* (7th ed., pp. 121–132). London, United Kingdom: Academic Press. doi:10.1016/B978-0-12-380882-0.00008-5

Pushkar, D., Basevitz, P., Arbuckle, T., Nohara-LeClair, M., Lapidus, S., & Peled, M. (2000). Social behavior and off-target verbosity in elderly people. *Psychology and Aging, 15*, 361–374.

*Rodríguez-Aranda, C., & Sundet, K. (2006). The frontal hypothesis of cognitive aging: Factor structure and age effects on four frontal tests among healthy individuals. *Journal of Genetic Psychology, 167*(3), 269–287.

*Rönnlund, M., Nyberg, L., Bäckman, L., & Nilsson, L. (2005). Stability, growth, and decline in adult life span development of declarative memory: cross-sectional and longitudinal data from a population-based study. *Psychology and Aging, 20*(1), 3–18. doi:10.1037/0882-7974.20.1.3

Ross, L. A., Edwards, J. D., O'Connor, M. L., Ball, K. K., Wadley, V. G., & Vance, D. E. (2016). The transfer of cognitive speed of processing training to older adults' driving mobility across 5 years. *Journals of Gerontology Series B: Psychological Sciences & Social Sciences, 71*(1), 87–97. doi:10.1093/geronb/gbv022

*Salthouse, T. A. (1996). The processing-speed theory of adult age differences in cognition. *Psychological Review, 103*(3), 403–428. doi:10.1037/0033-295X.103.3.403

Salthouse, T. A., Fristoe, N. M., Lineweaver, T. T., & Coon, V. E. (1995). Aging of attention: does the ability to divide decline? *Memory and Cognition, 23*, 59–71.

Salvucci, D. D., & Taatgen, N. A. (2008). Threaded cognition: An integrated theory of concurrent multitasking. *Psychological Review, 115*(1), 101–130. doi:10.1037/0033-295X.115.1.101

*Schaie, K. W., & Willis, S. L. (2010). The Seattle Longitudinal Study of adult cognitive development. *Bulletin of the International Society for the Study of Behavioral Development, 37*, 24–29.

Staplin, L., Lococo, K. H., Martell, C., & Stutts, J. (2012). Taxonomy of older driver behaviors and crash risk. DOT HS 811 468A. Retrieved from www.nhtsa.gov/staticfiles/nti/pdf/811468a.pdf

*Vance, D. E., & Crowe, M. (2006). A proposed model of neuroplasticity and cognitive reserve in older adults. *Activities, Adaptation & Aging, 30*(3), 61–79.

Van der Linden, M., Hupet, M., El Ahmadi, A., Feyereisen, P., Schelstraete, M.-A., Bestgen, Y., . . . Seron, X., (1999). Cognitive mediators of age-related differences in language comprehension and verbal memory performances. *Aging Neuropsychology and Cognition, 6*, 32–55.

von Hippel, W. (2007). Aging, executive functioning, and social control. *Current Directions in Psychological Science, 16*(5), 240–244. doi:10.1111/j.1467-8721.2007.00512.x

Wagner, J., Müri, R., Nef, T., & Mosimann, U. (2011). Cognition and driving in older persons. *Swiss Medical Weekly, 140*, w13136. doi:10.4414/smw.2011.13136

Zacks, R., & Hasher, L. (1997). Cognitive gerontology and attentional inhibition: A reply to Burke and McDowd. *The Journals of Gerontology: Series B: Psychological Sciences and Social Sciences, 52*(6), P274–P283. doi:10.1093/geronb/52B.6.P274

8

Cognitive Reserve and Cognitive Interventions

Nicholas T. Bott and Maya Yutsis

THE CONCEPT OF COGNITIVE RESERVE

WORKING DEFINITION(S)

The notion of cognitive reserve (CR) refers to the protection, or reserve, afforded to some individuals in the face of neurological insult, whether organic or acquired. In other words, individuals with greater CR demonstrate less functional or cognitive impairment in the face of the same amount of brain pathology. Thus, CR provides an explanation for the individual differences observed in how people process tasks with some compensating better than others with developing brain pathology (Stern, Albert, Tang, & Tsai, 1999). Researchers have proposed various constructs of reserve. Christensen et al. (2007) postulated a brain reserve hypothesis, differentiating between variables related to CR (e.g., intelligence, education) and those associated with brain reserve (e.g., brain and intracranial volume). Similarly, Valenzuela (2008) also hypothesized that reserve is a holistic construct of brain reserve based on tangible "day-to-day observable facts related to complex mental activity" (p. 297). Regardless of the particular "reserve" construct, all CR models share a common concern for how to operationalize and measure the underlying variables/proxies of reserve (e.g., mental activity, education, intelligence). This chapter focuses largely on the concept of CR based on Stern's conceptualization.

---

*Key references in the References section are indicated by an asterisk.

CR is a more active conceptualization of "reserve," which differs somewhat from "brain reserve," the latter being a more passive conceptualization involving neuro-anatomical differences including brain size and volume, head circumference, and synaptic and dendritic count, which are largely inherited (Katzman, 1993). These quantifiable differences can explain heterogeneity in clinical presentation from similar neural insults. Brain reserve models assume a predefined threshold or cutoff score in accumulated brain pathology beyond which functional decline occurs for everyone. Situated within the concept of brain reserve, neural reserve describes the structural variability in neural networks responsible for cognitive task performance. Neural networks with greater capacity, efficiency, or flexibility may be able to sustain function in the face of more neuropathology than networks with less reserve (Stern, 2009). Along with neural reserve, Stern (2009) describes neural compensation, sometimes described as scaffolding, as the functional recruitment of nonstandard brain structures and networks in the face of pathological disruption of standard processing networks in order to improve or maintain cognitive performance. While the concepts of brain reserve, neural reserve, and neural compensation are involved in CR, the CR model is more active as it postulates that the brain is continuously attempting to compensate using preexisting cognitive processes or new compensatory techniques in order to deal with ongoing pathology (Stern, 2002).

History and Significance

The term *reserve* may have first been introduced to the scientific literature by F. A. Pickworth in 1932, who commented with respect to the effect of pathology on clinical presentation that "no clinical abnormality is noticed unless the damage is quantitatively so great as to exceed the reserve" (p. 635). Toward the end of the 20th century Katzman and colleagues (1988) posited that those individuals, who remained nondemented during life, might have had larger brains, and as a result, more neurons, which afforded them reserve against Alzheimer's disease (AD) pathology during life. The language of reserve, or CR, has continued to the present, but observations of interindividual variability in the face of neuropathology can be seen throughout the 20th century. In 1964, Kay, Beamish, and Roth (1964) posited that the pathology present within the brain, "seems therefore to be only one of several factors determining the threshold at which dementia appears" (p. 146). Similarly, Blessed, Tomlinson, and Roth (1968) commented, "occasionally, the brains of individuals who have never become demented have been found to show quite marked changes" (p. 797).

As a construct, CR was first posited as an explanation for the presence of neuropathological findings of AD at autopsy in individuals who did not show symptoms of cognitive impairment during life (Roe, Xiong, Miller, & Morris, 2007). Since then, CR has been applied across various forms of neurological insult including traumatic brain injury, substance abuse, and neurodegenerative disease (Bigler & Stern, 2015; Pedrero-Perez et al., 2014; Stern, 2012; Xu, Yu, Tan, & Tan, 2015). As the construct of CR has grown to include various forms of neuropathology, so too has the nuance in the underlying construct. CR includes both active and passive components. Passive components of CR include the quantifiable material properties of brain reserve, such as brain size and neuronal count (Stern, 2009). As the name suggests, brain reserve refers to the extent or amount of insult the brain can sustain and continue to support normal function. Differences in brain size and neural density between individuals explain the heterogeneity in clinical expression of the same amount of brain damage. These aspects of CR are considered passive due to their static and structural nature. A uniform and quantifiable amount of brain damage is required for functional deficits to emerge, and differences in individual brain capacity explain whether an insult crosses the threshold of brain reserve capacity. Whereas passive models of CR focus on static and structural factors, active models of CR posit dynamic and functional factors associated with compensatory processes (Stern, 2002). As a result, active models of CR do not posit thresholds beyond which functional impairments occur; rather, they suggest brain processes allowing for neural recruitment or compensation in the face of brain damage that allow for the maintenance of cognitive function (see Figure 8.1). Second, many proxy variables of CR are said to be dynamic and directly impact the brain structure. For example, physical activity is related to neuronal plasticity, production of brain-derived neurotrophic factor (BDNF), and resistance to cell death (Nascimento et al., 2015; Zoladz & Pilc, 2010). Others studies have further demonstrated that children with higher IQs have larger brain volume (Willerman, Schultz, Rutledge, & Bigler, 1991).

The concept of CR, as formulated by Stern and colleagues in 1999, was formed based on the observations that the rate at which patients with AD declined on the selective reminding test (SRT) reflected their educational and occupational background (Stern et al., 1999). The Buschke's SRT is a test of word list memory that asks

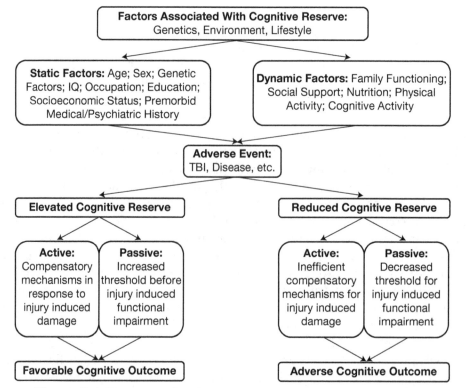

Figure 8.1 Factors and pathways of cognitive reserve on outcome.
TBI, traumatic brain injury.

subjects to learn and remember a list of 12 unrelated words over six trials. On trials two through six, a subject is only reminded of the words that the subject missed during the previous trial and asked to recall as many words as possible from the entire list (Buschke, 1973). The overall score is based on the sum of all six trials. Stern et al. (1999) found that patients with higher CR continued to outperform same-aged peers and showed later onset of memory decline. Furthermore, when matched for dementia severity, patients with higher CR had greater pathology (as measured by regional cerebral blood flow [rCBF]) than patients with lower CR, arguing that CR mitigated the clinical impact of AD pathology (Scarmeas et al., 2003). Since these relatively early descriptions, investigators have sought to isolate the effects of intellectual and related forms of brain activity that most closely reflect CR from the quantifiable neuronal aspects of brain reserve such as brain size and volume and brain networks recruitment (Barulli & Stern, 2013; Stern, 2012). Overall, while CR has been most widely studied in the context of AD, a similar concept has been demonstrated with other neurologic, psychiatric, and acquired injuries including Parkinson's disease (Glatt et al., 1996), traumatic brain injury (Kesler, Adams, Blasey, & Bigler et al., 2003), human immunodeficiency virus (Farinpour et al., 2003), psychiatric disorders (Barnett, Salmond, Jones, & Sahakian, 2006), and multiple sclerosis (Sumowski, Chiaravalloti, & Deluca, 2009).

NEUROPSYCHOLOGICAL PROXY OF CR

Regardless of the model of "reserve" (Christensen et al., 2007; Stern, 2002; Valenzuela, 2008) being referenced, all models of reserve share the common concern for how it is best operationalized and measured (e.g., mental activity, education, intelligence). However, operationalizing CR and its underlying constructs is difficult for at least three reasons. Historically, CR is a theoretical construct in itself. In addition, proxy variables are often used to define CR in order for research to be conducted, but proxies—by definition—are not equivalent to CR. Finally, the clinical outcomes expressed as cognitive and functional decline seen on neuropsychological testing or based on a clinical diagnosis are also not absolute quantifiable measures. Given that direct measures of pathology, for example, amyloid imaging, are not routinely available, it is difficult to quantify the amount of brain pathology and then predict which theoretical construct would predict this "invisible" factor. With this in mind, we describe the most commonly used proxies for CR.

PROXIES OF CR

The most common proxies are years of formal education, occupational achievement level, linguistic skills, literacy, participation in leisure activity, social engagement, socioeconomic status, measures of IQ (Barulli & Stern, 2013; Bennett, Arnold, Valenzuela, Brayne, & Schneider, 2014; Manly, Touradji, Tang, & Stern, 2003; Snowdon et al., 1996), bilingualism (Craik, Bialystok, & Freedman, 2010), and musical background (Gooding, Abner, Jicha, Kryscio, & Schmitt, 2013). However, most of the aforementioned variables are related to environmental factors such as nutrition, living situation, access to educational resources and health care, and cultural background. The difference in these environmental factors could explain the difference in findings between the studies examining the impact of these proxy variables on cognitive decline associated with normal aging, incident rates of dementia, level of pathological burden, rate of decline, and mortality after dementia diagnosis (Sanders, Hall, Katz, & Lipton, 2012; Van Gerven, Van Boxtel, Ausems, Bekers, & Jolles, 2012).

Literacy

In some populations, the degree of literacy may be a more accurate proxy of CR than years of education because literacy level better reflects the quality of education (Manly et al., 2003; Manly, Schupf, Tang, & Stern, 2005). Linguistic ability (i.e., idea content and grammar complexity) is also a potential proxy of CR. Snowdon and colleagues (1996) first published on aspects of language abilities as part of the Nun study. They examined cognitive function of 93 nuns aged 75 to 79, with 14 of these participants with a neuropathologic diagnosis of AD confirmed at the time of death at ages 76 to 96. Two aspects of linguistic ability, content and grammar, were studied based on the autobiographies written by these participants at a mean age of 22 years. The results showed that both lower content density and lower grammar complexity in the autobiographies were related to poorer performance on the neuropsychological tests later in life, with lower content density a stronger predictor of lower scores. Furthermore, at the time of death, all 14 sisters with confirmed AD had low content density in their autobiographical writings at the age of 22.

Premorbid Estimation of General Intelligence

Others suggest that a premorbid estimate of IQ (crystallized intelligence measure) may be a better proxy of CR (Albert & Teresi, 1999; Alexander et al., 1997). As we mentioned earlier, the concept of premorbid IQ as a proxy for higher CR is solely based on cognitive testing. Across cognitive tests, people with higher premorbid IQ perform better on most neuropsychological tests. As such, using premorbid IQ as a proxy may simply serve as a confounder between the results and the outcome, where those with lower IQ would show poorer performances on most cognitive tests including memory tasks, which may not necessarily represent a decline, compared to the individual's baseline level of performance.

Cognitive Activity

Others have focused on quantifying the impact of participation in mental activities as a proxy for CR. While some have studied activities that involve cognitive stimulating activity only, others have shown that engaging in any mental and/or leisure activity may be helpful regardless of its cognitive component (Stern et al., 2012; see review Valenzuela and Sachdev, 2005). These leisure activities are varied and include reading, playing games, participation in classes/workshops, participation in social events, managing independent activities of daily living (e.g., bills, mortgage), speaking a nonnative language, writing for pleasure, listening to music, playing a musical instrument, and volunteering.

Multidomain Proxy of Cognitive Reserve

Finally, Satz, Cole, Hardy, and Rassovsky (2010) have proposed a way to conceptualize and integrate several models of "reserve" and the associated proxy measures. They have provided a conceptual four-factor model of different domains and the associated measures that encompass brain and CR concepts (see Table 8.1).

Table 8.1   A Four-Factor Model of Cognitive Reserve With Associated Proxy Variables and Measures Underlying Each Construct

Factors/Proxy Domains	Measures/Variables
Intelligence "g"	**Crystallized Intelligence** • NAART (Stern et al., 2005) • WRAT-4 (Wilkinson, 1993) • WTAR (Whitney, Shepart, Mariner, Mossbarger, & Herman, 2010) • Vocabulary subtest on WAIS-III/IV (Wechsler, 1997, 2008) • Peabody Picture Vocabulary Test (Dunn & Dunn, 1997) **Fluid Intelligence** • Matrix Reasoning subtest of WAIS-III/IV • Working Memory measures (e.g., arithmetic subtest on WAIS III/IV)
Mental Activity	**Self-Report Questionnaires** • Cognitive Abilities Scale • Activities Scale (Scarmeas et al., 2003) • Lifetime of Experiences Questionnaire (Valenzuela & Sachdev, 2007) • CR Questionnaire (Rami et al., 2011) • Premorbid Cognitive Abilities Scale (Apolinario et al., 2013) • CR Scale (Leon, Garcia, & Roldan-Tapia, 2011) **Demographics/Psychosocial Variables** • Occupation • Literacy • Education • Social Networks
Processing Resources	• Measures of Processing Speed (e.g., Trail Making Test A [Reitan, 1958], Digit Symbol Coding subtest on WAIS-III/IV) • Measures of Working Memory (e.g., Digit Span, Arithmetic subtests of WAIS-III/IV) • Measures of Divided Attention (Trail Making Test B)
Executive Function	• Measures of Verbal and Nonverbal Reasoning (e.g., Similarities and Matrix Reasoning subtests of WAIS-III/IV) • Measures of Cognitive Switching and Inhibition (e.g., Stroop Task, Trail Making Test B, Wisconsin Card Sorting Test) • Measures of Error Monitoring and Selective Attention (e.g., Digit Vigilance Test) • Measures of Fluency (e.g., DKEFS Verbal and Design Fluency (Delis, Kaplan, & Kramer, 2001)

CR, cognitive reserve; DKEFS, Delis Kaplan Executive Function System; NAART, North American Adult Reading Test; WAIS-III/IV, Wechsler Adult Intelligence Scale III/ IV; WRAT-4, Wide Range Achievement Test 4; WTAR, Wechsler Test of Adult Reading.

Adapted from Satz et al. (2011).

Overall, some studies have shown that each of the aforementioned proxies could cumulatively contribute to the overall CR (Evans et al., 1993; Mortel, Meyer, Herod, & Thornby, 1995; Stern et al., 1994; Stern, Tang, Denaro, & Mayeux, 1995). For example, Richards and Sacker (2003) showed that childhood IQ, educational achievement level, and adult occupational level separately and uniquely contributed to predicting an estimated IQ at age 53 (Richards & Sacker, 2003). Interestingly, all of the aforementioned proxy variables including educational attainment, occupational achievement level, lifetime experience, and/or amount of leisure activity could be dynamic and change over the course of someone's life. Consequently, CR is not a static variable, as it is based on the constellation of the nature and quantity of the aforementioned exposures at any specific time when it is measured.

Most importantly, whenever we discuss proxy variables of CR, we should acknowledge the limitations associated with some of the cognitive measures used in this literature. Cognitive or neuropsychological performances may differ not just because of the underlying CR mechanism. For example, education or number of formal years completed may be related to all neuropsychological performances in older adults for several reasons, namely that: (a) it reflects "reserve," (b) it is confounded by age, which alternatively impacts both education and test performance, (c) childhood IQ or academic affinity may influence the amount of formal education a person receives, (d) it reflects socioeconomic or cultural factors that impacted the amount of formal education someone receives. As you see, the reasons underlying the impact of education on test performance could be diverse and not necessarily related to "reserve" alone. Similarly, literacy level may also simply reflect the underlying difference in access to, quality of, and importance of academic achievement that could differ between population subgroups based on socioeconomic, cultural, racial, and gender backgrounds (Jones, 2003). Furthermore, the correlation between literacy and neuropsychological performance may reflect the effect of educational quality (school quality) versus the amount of formal years of education (Manly, Jacobs, Touradji, Small, & Stern, 2002).

CR AND COGNITIVE DEBT

While this section has focused on proximal measures of CR, it is important to point out that more recently Marchant and Howard (2015) have proposed the concept of cognitive "debt" in relationship to AD to describe cognitive processes that can independently deplete CR, thereby increasing one's susceptibility to clinical impairment as a result of AD pathology. Whereas measures of CR, whether passive or active, represent factors that confer protection against clinical deficits, measures of cognitive debt are thought to reduce the amount of CR an individual has—be that great or small. The cognitive debt hypothesis suggests that the increased risk of AD present in individuals reporting depression, anxiety, sleep disorders, neuroticism, life stress, or posttraumatic stress disorder (PTSD) finds a unifying factor in repetitive negative thinking (RNT). RNT is defined as self-relevant, persistent thoughts that elaborate on negative themes, whether ruminative (past directed) or worrisome (future directed). If Marchant and Howard's hypothesis is supported, interventions aimed at remediating RNT may provide another means by which to reduce the risk of AD or other mental health conditions in older adults.

EPIDEMIOLOGIC EVIDENCE FOR CR

Because the concept of CR is so closely linked with the initial observations seen in patients with AD, the epidemiology of CR also parallels the course of AD. Researchers have hypothesized that AD pathology begins perhaps decades before the clinical, cognitive, and behavioral manifestations are observed (Schmitz, Spreng, & ADNI Initiative, 2016). AD pathology gradually increases over the years, becomes more pronounced, and consequently results in observable symptoms used by clinicians to make a clinical diagnosis of dementia. Consequently, the incidence rate of dementia should be lower in those with higher CR, despite the same or even greater pathology. This prediction is based on the CR hypothesis, postulating that there will be individual differences in the amount of pathology needed to demonstrate clinical symptoms and subsequent diagnosis of dementia. More specifically, persons with higher CR might be diagnosed at a later age, as a greater amount of pathology (amyloid-β, white matter disease, etc.) will be needed when dementia is diagnosed (see Figure 8.2). Valenzuela and Sachdev (2005) reviewed 22 cohort-based studies to comment on the potential effects of education, occupation, premorbid IQ, and participation in leisure activities on incidence rates of dementia. The majority of studies showed evidence for protective effects of education, occupational achievement, premorbid IQ, and active participation in leisure activities. The authors concluded that higher CR, defined by the educational and occupational level, higher premorbid IQ, and active mental activity were related to a 46% reduction of incidence rates (i.e., a new diagnosis) of dementia.

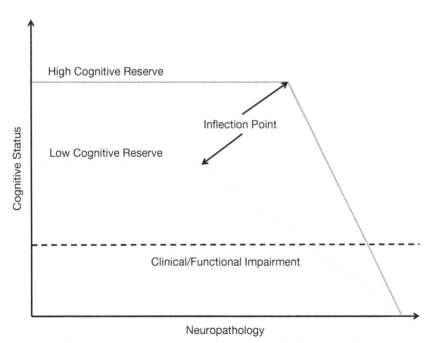

Figure 8.2 Effect of cognitive reserve on onset of clinical/functional impairment.

EFFECTS OF CR ON DISEASE COURSE

The CR hypothesis includes two assumptions: (a) The onset of accelerated cognitive decline appears nearer to the time of clinical diagnosis of dementia in those with a higher level of education and estimated IQ, and (b) The time from the diagnosis of dementia to complete loss of function (i.e., progression of dementia) will be shorter in those with higher CR (Stern et al., 1994, 1999; Stern, 2002, 2007). Both assumptions are based on the underlying belief that persons with higher CR can maintain normal cognition despite accumulating pathology and only show cognitive impairment once the severity of pathology is high (i.e., disease is in the advanced stages). In other words, those with lower CR experience cognitive and memory impairment earlier when the severity of pathology is not as pronounced. Consequently, among patients with dementia (either due to AD, vascular, or other pathology) of comparable clinical severity, memory decline should be more rapid in those with higher CR. Because advanced neurodegenerative pathology (e.g., amyloid-β) is associated with greater mortality, the CR model also assumes that patients with higher CR diagnosed with dementia will have a more accelerated rate to death following the diagnosis (Stern et al., 1995).

Cognitive Reserve and Accelerated Cognitive Decline

With respect to the first assumption of the CR hypothesis, Stern and colleagues examined the incident rates of dementia in 593 community-based nondemented participants aged 60 years or older (Stern et al., 1994). After 1 to 4 years of follow-up among 106 participants who were diagnosed with dementia, the incidence of dementia was 2.2 times higher in participants with lower education level (less than 8 years of education) compared to those with 8 to 11 years or more than 12 years of education. Similarly, in those with lifelong low occupational level, the incidence of dementia was increased by 2.25 times. Low occupational level included jobs such as a skilled trade, unskilled/semiskilled employment, or clerical/office work, while higher occupational level included managerial positions, business/government work, or professional/technical jobs (Stern et al., 1994). Risk of dementia diagnosis was highest in participants with both lower education and low occupational achievement levels (relative risk, 2.87 95% confidence interval [CI], 1.32 to 3.84). Finally, participation in leisure activities (i.e., the environmental proxies for CR over time) was associated with a 38% reduction of risk for developing dementia (Scarmeas, Levy, Tang, Manly, & Stern, 2001). These leisure activities included reading, playing games, participation in classes/workshops, and participation in social events.

Finally, literature on age-related cognitive decline also offers some support for the CR model. Manly and colleagues (2005) examined the impact of literacy (assumed to be related to higher educational achievement level) on cognition in a nondemented sample of ethnically diverse older adults. Manly and colleagues found that increased literacy was correlated with slower decline in cognition (i.e., memory, executive skills, and language). Multiple other studies of normal aging show a similar pattern of slower functional and cognitive decline in older persons with higher educational achievement level (Albert et al., 1995; Butler, Ashford, & Snowdon, 1996; Chodosh, Reuben, Albert, & Seeman, 2002; Snowdon, Ostwald, & Kane, 1989; Lyketsos, Chen, & Anthony, 1999). Overall, findings from these studies support the notion that persons with higher educational level may be better able to cope with cognitive deficits associated with both normal aging as well as dementia.

Cognitive Reserve and Compressed Morbidity

In contrast, the evidence is more limited in support of the second assumption of the CR hypothesis, postulating that higher CR is related to faster cognitive and functional decline once dementia is diagnosed. A series of studies demonstrated that AD patients with higher educational and/or occupational achievement level and equivalent clinical severity of symptoms at the time of initial examination died sooner (Stern et al., 1995) and showed faster cognitive decline (Stern et al., 1999; Scarmeas, Albert, Manly, & Stern, 2006) than those with lower CR. However, until 2007 there was still a lack of epidemiologic evidence that supported the second assumption behind the CR hypothesis. Hall et al. (2007) examined memory performance on the SRT task collected at 12-month intervals from 117 healthy older adults enrolled into the Bronx Aging Study between 1980 and 1983 (mean age at the time of entry into the longitudinal study was 81 years) who were later diagnosed with dementia. The median number of years to dementia diagnosis was 5.6. Half of the subjects (61 participants) followed were diagnosed with possible or probable AD, 20% with vascular dementia, and 7% with other types of dementia. For those with 4 years or fewer of formal education, the median time to accelerated memory decline was 6.35 years before the dementia diagnosis. For those with 12 or more years of education, the accelerated rate of memory decline started 3.82 years prior to the diagnosis. In other words, those with lower estimated CR experienced cognitive decline for almost double the time compared to peers with higher CR. The corresponding estimated annual incidence rate of memory decline in participants diagnosed with dementia was 2.03 for those with 4 or fewer years of education and 3.22 for those with more than 12 years of education. Hall and colleagues provided evidence for the CR model by demonstrating that, for people with higher educational attainment, the onset of cognitive and memory decline was delayed prior to the dementia diagnosis, but the rate of decline was faster after the diagnosis. Figure 8.3 shows a graphical representation of trajectories of memory decline on the SRT memory test based on individuals' educational achievement levels.

Cognitive Reserve and Age

Given that the concept of CR is heavily dependent on cognitive tests used as a proxy for CR, one should also examine whether age could impact the difference in performances on such tasks. Each cognitive test differs in its level of complexity, with age impacting the ability to efficiently perform on the test depending on its complexity. In 2007, Stern wrote that on any cognitive test, any condition, especially age, could impact the overall capacity and efficiency of the individual's neural network and how it is activated during test performance. For example, regardless of age, the same neural network would be activated during a learning phase on a verbal memory test. In regard to the efficiency of the neural network, remembering a list of three words may be easier for a 20-year-old compared to a 65-year-old. Therefore, this task will be less demanding and consequently would require less neural activation for younger adults, rendering the network more efficient. In other words, the neural network will be less efficient due to greater demand of the task, resulting in increased level of

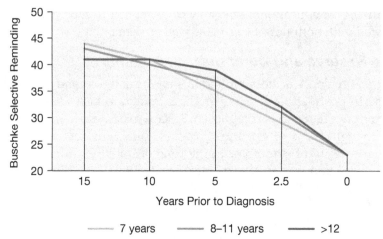

Figure 8.3 Memory decline based on time prior to dementia diagnosis in 117 Bronx Aging Study participants by years of education.

activation in the older adults, while the overall performance (the overall number of words learned after three trials) may be the same regardless of age. Thus in younger adults, greater activation would be seen on a 16-word memory task, as remembering 16 words is more difficult than remembering 3 words only and may require use of additional compensatory strategies that could be developed with age. As such, with greater task demand, greater activation might be seen in young subjects than in the old. All in all, on the same type of a memory test with varying levels of complexity (i.e., 3- vs. 16-item word list), the level of neural activation would be different based on age. In order to further explore the effect of age on CR, it is crucial to determine whether older and younger adults use the same or different brain networks during similar tasks. Imaging studies could be helpful in illuminating brain network recruitment differences.

NEUROANATOMICAL CORRELATES OF COGNITIVE RESEARCH

As mentioned previously, the concept of brain reserve posits that brain size—and neural density by proxy—provides a threshold up to which pathological damage can be sustained before clinical presentation. This passive model of reserve treats the brain as a single entity, with larger brains able to sustain greater amounts of damage. Stern's CR construct also includes the active processes of neural reserve and neural compensation, providing a basis from which to investigate neuroanatomical correlates of CR.

HEMISPHERIC ASYMMETRY REDUCTION IN OLDER ADULTS (HAROLD)

The HAROLD model, originally proposed by Cabeza (2002), posits increased activation in contralateral hemispheric brain regions among older adults during task completion. This effect is particularly present in the prefrontal cortex. Berlingeri and colleagues (2013) have challenged the HAROLD theory, suggesting that a more generalized compensation-related utilization of neural circuits hypothesis (CRUNCH) model accounts for the recruitment of additional brain regions to facilitate successful task completion. Within the larger CR construct, both models can be interpreted as a form of neural compensation providing for successful task completion, evidencing less neural efficiency when compared to younger subjects.

Scaffolding Theory of Aging and Cognition (STAC)

Similar to the CRUNCH model, the scaffolding theory of aging and cognition (Goh and Park, 2009) provides an explanation for neuroplasticity that coheres well with Stern's conceptualization of CR. In fact, Barulli and Stern (2013) identify STAC as a more generalized theory of neural compensation, with CR representing a factor mediating the success of neural compensation. As the name suggests, STAC explains the process of aging and cognition as one whereby the brain reacts to deficient or inefficient neural activity through the recruitment of additional brain regions to achieve satisfactory function. For example, Steffener and colleagues (2009) investigated working memory performance in older adults and found that only older adults demonstrated increased activation in secondary neural networks as working memory load increased. While this result is in keeping with the STAC hypothesis, the question of whether this recruitment represents neural compensation remains a topic of debate (Park & Reuter-Lorenz, 2009).

Imaging and CR

Imaging of CR has grown substantially over the past decade. Stern's early work incorporating imaging into the study of CR included rCBF among severity-matched patients with AD. Higher education was associated with more depleted flow in areas typically affected in AD (parietotemporal). In other words, patients with higher education were able to tolerate more AD pathology than those with lower education while remaining similar in clinical presentation (Stern, 2009). Given the roles neural reserve and neural compensation play within Stern's model of CR, structural and functional neuroimaging studies examining the correlates of CR compare old and young individuals' use of specific brain networks to mediate task performance in order to draw conclusions about the capacity and efficiency of those networks (Zarahn, Rakitin, Abela, Flynn, & Stern, 2007).

FDG-PET and PIB-PET

PET imaging has been used to investigate aspects of the CR construct. Yasuno and colleagues (2015) reported levels of amyloid-β deposition in cognitively normal older adults with varying levels of completed education using Pittsburgh Compound B (PIB) PET imaging. Older adults who completed more education showed less cortical amyloid-β deposition than those wither fewer years of education. In another study, Ewers and colleagues (2013) found that higher education in older adults with amyloid-β deposition—an indication of preclinical AD—was associated with lower fludeoxyglucose PET. This finding suggests that greater CR supports compensatory functioning in the presence of early AD pathology.

Magnetic Resonance Imaging

Studies using MRI have also investigated the neuroanatomical correlates of CR. Pettigrew and colleagues (2016) examined the role of CR (education, reading, and vocabulary) on structural MRI measures of cortical thickness in cortical regions affected by AD pathology in healthy older adults. CR was associated with cortical thinning up to 7 years from baseline. These results suggest that greater CR compensates for cortical thinning during the early progression of AD. Stern (2016) understands CR as a potential moderator of cognitive task-related brain activation, which can be investigated using functional MRI (fMRI) paradigms.

Network Connectivity

Models of neurodegenerative disease understand the spread of neuropathology to be driven by specific functional networks within the brain (Seeley, Crawford, Zhou, Miller, & Greicius, 2009). More recent investigations into the neuroanatomical basis of CR have posited the role of functional network connectivity associated with greater CR. Marques and colleagues (2016) reported that higher levels of CR (defined by greater number of years of completed education) was associated with greater functional connectivity in specific brain regions (occipital and inferior temporal gyrus) and greater global brain network efficiency. The authors concluded that higher CR facilitates more concentrated neural processing, while also facilitating more efficient information processing.

While the cost of imaging presents a barrier for its widespread use in clinical care, imaging studies may provide unique opportunities to quantify CR. Interventions aimed at preventing cognitive decline or promoting increased task efficiency could be measured more precisely with neuroimaging techniques, offering a more substantial outcome measure. Imaging of CR may also prove useful in more precisely staging disease and providing more accurate prognosis. One can imagine a database that allows clinicians to match clinical severity by means of cognitive and functional measures with an imaging database that allows for interindividual comparison of structural and functional measures. These data could then be correlated with clinical trajectories of similarly matched patients.

COGNITIVE INTERVENTIONS AS MEDIATORS OF CR

HISTORY OF COGNITIVE INTERVENTIONS FOR OLDER ADULTS

Cognitive interventions include various types of treatments aimed at restoring or compensating for declines in cognitive functioning as a result of illness or injury. While there is increasing interest in surgical and pharmacological methods of cognitive enhancement, cognitive interventions have traditionally been nonpharmacological and nonsurgical (Prigatano, 2005). Cognitive rehabilitation was born out of techniques focused on remediating cognitive deficits associated with brain injury and stroke (Parente & Stapleton, 1996), and has since grown to include disease-specific methods, as well as preventative interventions. In addition to injury severity, age is a significant factor contributing to the efficiency and efficacy of cognitive interventions (Flanagan, Hibbard, & Gordan, 2005).

Cognitive interventions to reduce cognitive decline in older adults came from early work that identified a "performance-potential" divide associated with cognitive function in older adults. This divide raised questions about the potential modifiability of cognitive performance among older adults, and the underlying mechanism for this modifiability was dubbed brain plasticity (Verhaeghen, 2000). Baltes and Willis (1982) described plasticity as "the range of intellectual aging under conditions not normally existent in either the living ecology of older persons or in the standard assessment situation provided by classical test of psychometric intelligence" (pp. 355–356). Early interventions for older adults focused on teaching strategies to improve task performance, but as the construct has matured strategy use as an intervention has waned in light of the lack of generalizability to real world task performance, as well as the challenges associated with strategy instruction.

COGNITIVE INTERVENTIONS AS PRIMARY PREVENTION

There is growing evidence that a diverse set of risk factors is associated with risk of cognitive decline in adults. These include: diabetes, obesity or hypertension in middle age, low physical activity, depression, smoking, and low educational level. Together, these seven risk factors have been estimated to account for 28% of the risk of developing AD (Shatenstein, Berberger-Gateau, & Mecocci, 2015). As a result, cognitive interventions are increasingly being utilized to prevent or delay the onset of cognitive decline or impairment in healthy and at-risk populations of older adults (Wilson et al., 2002).

In fact, early experiments investigated the efficacy of cognitive interventions for the remediation of cognitive declines in healthy older adults. Schaie and Willis (1986) found that among older adults experiencing decline over a 14-year period, two thirds receiving cognitive training improved their cognitive functioning. Forty percent of those showing improvement demonstrated performance at a predecline level. Longitudinal investigation of performance gains found that the benefits remained 7 years after training in comparison to controls (Schaie, Willis, & O'Hanlon, 1994). More recently, the Advanced Cognitive Training for Independent and Vital Elderly (ACTIVE) study has shown the efficacy of cognitive interventions in healthy older adults. The ACTIVE study was a randomized, controlled single-blind trial ($n=2,832$) with three intervention groups and a no-contact control group to determine the effects of cognitive training on cognitive abilities and everyday function over a 10-year period. Each intervention group received an intervention targeting a specific cognitive domain: processing speed, memory, or reasoning. When postintervention performance was analyzed, all groups showed declines from baseline. Participants who received training in reasoning and processing speed, however, showed fewer declines than those in the memory and control groups. These performances remained after 10 years as reported by Rebok and colleagues (2014), with participants in the reasoning and processing speed intervention groups demonstrating greater frequency of at or above baseline performance levels. Memory performance was similar between the intervention and control groups after 10 years. With respect to functional abilities, individuals in each of the three intervention groups endorsed less subjective difficulty with instrumental activities of daily living (IADLs) than control participants, although objective measure of functional abilities was comparable across intervention and control groups. The relative success of the ACTIVE trial provides support for preventative cognitive interventions in the healthy older adult population. Interventions that extend healthy cognitive aging trajectories could reduce the economic costs associated with cognitive decline and impairment.

Increasingly, multidomain approaches for the prevention of cognitive decline are being tested and implemented. This is likely due in part to the multifactorial nature of cognitive decline and dementia (Richard et al., 2012). The most promising results to date have come from the Finnish Geriatric Intervention Study to Prevent Cognitive Impairment and Disability (FINGER), which provides longitudinal support for the efficacy of multidomain intervention targeting a number of lifestyle-related risk factors associated with subclinical cognitive deficits (Ngandu et al., 2015). Several other randomized clinical trials are employing multi-domain approaches, including the U.S. ENLIGHTEN (Exercise and NutritionaL Interventions for coGnitive and Cardiovascular HealTh ENhancement) trial, the Prevention of Dementia by Intensive Vascular Care (preDIVA) study, and the Healthy Aging Through Internet Counseling in Elderly (HATICE) program, which focuses on the management of modifiable risk factors in older people using an Internet-based platform (Shatenstein et al., 2015).

COGNITIVE INTERVENTIONS AS SECONDARY PREVENTION

In addition to older adults without measurable declines in cognition, interventions have also been employed in populations with objective cognitive impairment. Mild cognitive impairment (MCI) is the term used to describe cognitive decline more significant than those due to typical cognitive aging but without the functional impairments associated with dementia (Huckans et al., 2013). The prevalence of MCI among older adults is estimated between 3% and 42% (Ward, Arrighi, Michels, & Cedarbaum, 2012). Importantly, between 14% and 40% of those diagnosed with MCI return to normal cognitive functioning (Ganguli, Dodge, Shen, & DeKosky, 2004), with others maintaining functioning without further cognitive decline (Manly et al., 2008).

The frontline approach to address cognitive impairment in individuals with MCI is cognitive training aimed at remediating cognitive deficits. This is usually accomplished through the utilization of structured and repeated practice of specific cognitive tasks and mental exercises (Huckans et al., 2013). Cognitive tasks are tailored to the domain(s) of impairment and the individual's ability level. Structured cognitive training aims to restore or maintain cognitive functioning through the generalization of performance gains beyond performance on the specific training task. For example, Gagnon and Belleville (2012) reported that individuals with single-domain MCI (executive dysfunction) benefited from an attentional control cognitive intervention. Similarly, Belleville and colleagues (2006) demonstrated that episodic memory strategy instruction improves memory performance in individuals with MCI. On the other hand, the extent of generalizability of cognitive performance gains in individuals with MCI remains debated (O'Sullivan, Coen, O'Hora, & Shiel, 2015).

In addition to task repetition, performance gains can be observed through the adoption of information processing strategies. Information processing strategies include storytelling, visual imagery, chunking information, and use of acronyms to more effectively manipulate information. In some cases, information processing strategies incorporate structured problem solving, planning, and mindfulness techniques (Huckans et al., 2013; O'Sullivan et al., 2015). Beyond information processing strategies, cognitive interventions used in this population frequently include the use of "cognitive prostheses" to aid with task performance. These include external aids (e.g., calendars, planners, personal notebooks) as well as navigation devices for visuospatial support (Kurz, Pohl, Ramsenthaler, & Sorg, 2009).

Information about lifestyle practices, including risk (e.g., smoking, heavy substance use) and protective factors (e.g., diet, exercise, and cognitively stimulating activities) can be addressed in combination with cognitive training or through motivational interviewing (Huckans et al., 2013; Kurz et al., 2009). While mood and lifestyle factors can be seen as adjunctive components to cognitive interventions in the MCI population (Attix & Welsch-Bohmer, 2006), increasingly, interventions targeting lifestyle factors such as exercise represent effective means of improving cognition (Ströhle et al., 2015). Insofar as specific neuropsychiatric symptoms can contribute to cognitive difficulties, psychotherapeutic interventions can be utilized to augment treatment. These can include cognitive-behavioral interventions, relaxation exercises, and deep breathing (Kurz et al., 2009; O'Sullivan et al., 2015; Huckans et al., 2013). In summary, cognitive retraining, compensatory strategies, modification of lifestyle interventions, and psychotherapy can each play a role in a comprehensive treatment model to improve cognitive function as well as overall quality of life in patients with MCI.

COGNITIVE INTERVENTIONS IN DEMENTIA

Given the progressive nature of neurodegenerative disease, the efficacy (and ethics) of cognitive interventions among older adults diagnosed with dementia remains debatable. Marshall (2005) proposed its unique value when the goal is to improve quality of life as opposed to the return to a previous level of cognitive ability, or the prevention of future decline. The treatment should be patient centered, recognizing the clinical course of the patient, and help support coping. Thus, interventions in this population are focused on optimization of current cognition, and compensation for further cognitive losses, whether through problem solving or environmental optimization (Mountain, 2005).

Interventions for older adults with more severe cognitive impairments are limited to therapies such as reminiscence therapy and reality orientation therapy, among others. The former encourages individuals to recall past life events and experiences, often by means of salient stimuli such as photos or music, in an effort to cue memories. Often, reminiscence therapy is conducted in a group setting to promote social engagement around shared themes (Mountain, 2005). The latter is a technique that presents orientation information (e.g., time, place, social location) with the goal of improving quality of life through increasing a sense of control in individuals with dementia. Bianchetti and Trabucchi (2001) found reality orientation therapy delayed entry into long-term care and slowed further cognitive decline in older adults with mild to moderate dementia.

CONCLUSION

The evidence is growing to support the model of CR and its mediating quality between brain pathology and clinical manifestations of related functional and cognitive decline. While passive models of brain reserve assume that the same amount of brain pathology will inevitably lead to functional decline in all individuals at the same time, the CR model has been deemed more "active" in its conceptualization of reserve. The CR model postulates that people with higher abilities to cope and compensate for developing brain pathology will be able to tolerate greater amounts of pathology than those with lower CR and will develop functional decline later in the disease stage. This model further differentiates between the amount of preexisting within-individual difference in cognitive processing (i.e., neural reserve) and the ability to compensate following the development of disease (i.e., neural compensation). Both the passive and active forms of CR play an important role within this model.

While the differentiation between active versus passive models of reserve was stressed more in the earlier years of this research, recently this delineation does not appear as clear. Physiologically, and from the brain networks perspective, there should be structural and functional changes that underlie the differences in preexisting cognitive processing (i.e., in neural reserve). This difference should incorporate some aspects of the "passive" reserve model that account for differences at the neuronal level. Thus, rather than conceptualizing brain reserve and CR models as separate passive versus active models of reserve, it is more likely that these models complement and supplement one another to allow for more effective compensation in the face of developing pathology.

Imaging studies continue to provide evidence for the complementarity of brain reserve and CR models, although specific theories of regional and network activation remain debated. Investigations of the neuroanatomical correlates of CR indicate a protective role in the face of developing pathology, as well as a role in maintaining cognitive function after the onset of pathology. The clinical utility of imaging CR remains largely unrealized to date, but offers the potential to more precisely quantify the amount of CR present within an individual, and holds promise for more accurate staging and prognosis of pathological decline.

As the demand for cognitive rehabilitation in older adult populations has grown, so too has the interest and development of novel interventions. These interventions include primary and secondary disease prevention, as well as interventions aimed at extending healthy aging cognitive trajectories. Increasingly, the value of cognitive intervention in older adults transcends the clinical benefits afforded to patients; extending the course of healthy cognitive aging trajectories or stabilizing cognition in older adults experiencing cognitive decline is associated with significant societal economic savings. For example, total payments for health care, long-term care, and hospice for persons with dementia in 2016 are estimated at $236 billion, with costs rising to over $1 trillion in 2050 (Alzheimer's Association, 2016). Even modest extension of intact cognitive aging trajectories will result in significant economic savings.

DISCUSSION QUESTIONS

1. Describe the ways in which "reserve" has been defined in the literature (i.e., passive vs. active models).

2. What are some proxy variables for measuring CR?

3. Describe the effects of CR on the incidence and progression of dementia.

4. Describe cognitive interventions that have been used as primary prevention and those that have been used as secondary prevention.

5. Describe the results of studies on cognitive interventions.

REFERENCES

Albert, M. S., Jones, K., Savage, C. R., Berkman, L., Seeman, T., Blazer, D., & Rowe, J. W. (1995). Predictors of cognitive change in older persons: MacArthur studies of successful aging. *Psychology and Aging, 10*, 578–589. [PubMed: 8749585].

Albert, S. M., & Teresi, J. A. (1999). Reading ability, education, and cognitive status assessment among older adults in Harlem, New York City. *American Journal of Public Health, 89*, 95–97. [PubMed: 9987476]

Alexander, G. E., Furey, M. L., Grady, C. L., Pietrini, P., Mentis, M. J., & Schapiro, M. B. (1997). Association of premorbid function with cerebral metabolism in Alzheimer's disease: Implications for the reserve hypothesis. *American Journal of Psychiatry, 154*, 165–172. [PubMed: 9016263]

Apolinario, D., Brucki, S. M. D., Ferretti, R. E. L., Farfel, J. M., Magaldi, R. M., Busse A. L., & Jacob-Filho, W. (2013). Estimating premorbid cognitive abilities in low-educated populations. *Public Library of Science One, 8*, e60084.

Attix, D. K., & Welsh-Bohmer, K. A. (Eds.). (2006). *Geriatric neuropsychology: Assessment and intervention*. New York, NY: Guilford Press.

*Baltes, P. B., & Willis, S. L. (1982). Plasticity and enhancement of intellectual functioning in old age: Penn State's Adult Development and Enrichment Project ADEPT. In F. I. M. Craik & S. E. Trehub (Eds.), *Aging and cognitive processes* (pp. 353–389). New York, NY: Plenum Press.

Barnett, J. H., Salmond, C. H., Jones, P. B., & Sahakian, B. J. (2006). Cognitive reserve in neuropsychiatry. *Psychological Medicine, 36*, 1053–1064. [PubMed: 16854246]

Barulli, D., & Stern, Y. (2013). Efficiency, capacity, compensation, maintenance, plasticity: Emerging concepts in cognitive reserve. *Trends in Cognitive Sciences, 17*, 502–509.

Belleville, S., Gilbert, B., Fontaine, F., Gagnon, L., Ménard, E., & Gauthier, S. (2006). Improvement of episodic memory in persons with mild cognitive impairment and healthy older adults: Evidence from a cognitive intervention program. *Dementia, Geriatrics, and Cognitive Disorders, 22*, 486–499.

Bennett, D. A., Arnold, S. E., Valenzuela, M. J., Brayne, C., & Schneider, J. A. (2014). Cognitive and social lifestyle: Links with neuropathology and cognition in late life. *Acta Neuropathologica, 127*, 137–50.

Berlingeri, M., Danelli, L., Bottini, G., Sberna, M., & Paulesu, E. (2013). Reassessing the HAROLD model: Is the hemispheric asymmetry reduction in older adults a special case of compensatory-related utilisation of neural circuits? *Experimental Brain Research, 224*, 393–410.

Bianchetti, A., & Trabucchi, M. (2001). Reality orientation therapy to delay outcomes of progression in patients with dementia. A retrospective study. *Clinical Rehabilitation, 15*, 471–478.

Bigler, E. D., & Stern, Y. (2015). *Traumatic brain injury and reserve* (Vol. *128*). Waltham, MA: Elsevier.

Blessed, G., Tomlinson, B. E., & Roth, M. (1968). The association between quantitative measures of dementia and of senile change in the cerebral grey matter of elderly subjects. *British Journal of Psychiatry, 114*, 797–811.

Buschke, H. (1973). Selective reminding for analysis of memory and learning. *Journal of Verbal Learning Verbal Behavior, 12*, 543–550.

Butler, S. M., Ashford, J. W., & Snowdon, D. A. (1996). Age, education, and changes in the Mini-Mental State Exam scores of older women: Findings from the Nun Study. *Journal of the American Geriatrics Society, 44*, 675–681. [PubMed: 8642159]

Cabeza, R. (2002). Hemispheric asymmetry reduction in older adults: The HAROLD model. *Psychology of Aging, 17*, 85–100.

Chodosh, J., Reuben, D. B., Albert, M. S., & Seeman, T. E. (2002). Predicting cognitive impairment in high-functioning community-dwelling older persons: MacArthur Studies of Successful Aging. *Journal of the American Geriatrics Society, 50*, 1051–1060. [PubMed: 12110065]

*Christensen, H., Anstey, K. J., Parslow, R. A., Maller, J., Mackinnon, A., & Sachdev, P. (2007). The brain reserve hypothesis, brain atrophy and aging. *Gerontology, 53*, 82–95.

Craik, F. I., Bialystok, E., & Freedman, M. (2010). Delaying the onset of Alzheimer disease: Bilingualism as a form of cognitive reserve. *Neurology, 75*, 1726–1729.

Delis, D., Kaplan, E., & Kramer, N. (2001). Delis–Kaplan executive function system. Odessa, FL: Psychological Assessment Resources.

Dunn, L. M., & Dunn, L. M. (1997). *Examiner's manual for the Peabody Picture Vocabulary Test* (3rd ed.). Circle Pines, MN: American Guidance Service.

Evans, D. A., Beckett, L. A., Albert, M. S., Hebert, L. E., Scherr, P. A., Funkenstein, H. H., & Taylor, J. O. (1993). Level of education and change in cognitive function in a community population of older persons. *Annals of Epidemiology, 3*, 71–77. [PubMed: 8287159]

Ewers, M., Insel, P. S., Stern, Y., Weiner, M. W., & Alzheimer's Disease Neuroimaging, I. (2013). Cognitive reserve associated with FDG-PET in preclinical Alzheimer disease. *Neurology, 80*, 1194–1201.

Farinpour, R., Miller, E. N., Satz, P., Selnes, O. A., Cohen, B. A., Becker, J. T., . . . Visscher, B. R. (2003). Psychosocial risk factors of HIV morbidity and mortality: Findings from the Multicenter AIDS Cohort Study (MACS). *Journal of Clinical and Experimental Neuropsychology, 25*, 654–670. [PubMed: 12815503]

Flanagan, S. R., Hibbard, M. R., & Gordan, W. A. (2005). The impact of age on traumatic brain injury. *Physical Medicine and Rehabilitation Clinics of North America, 16*, 163–177.

Gagnon, L. G., & Belleville, S. (2012). Training of attentional control in mild cognitive impairment with executive deficits: Results from a double-blind randomized controlled study. *Neuropsychological Rehabilitation, 22*, 809–835.

Ganguli, M., Dodge, H. H., Shen, C., & DeKosky, S. T. (2004). Mild cognitive impairment, amnestic type: An epidemiologic study. *Neurology, 63*, 115–121.

Glatt, S. L., Hubble, J. P., Lyons, K., Paolo, A., Troster, A. I., Hassanein, R. E., & Koller W. C. (1996). Risk factors for dementia in Parkinson's disease: Effect of education. Neuroepidemiology, *15*, 20–25. [PubMed: 8719045]

Goh, J. O., & Park, D. C. (2009). Neuroplasticity and cognitive aging: The scaffolding theory of aging and cognition. *Restorative Neurology and Neuroscience, 27*, 391–403.

Gooding, L. F., Abner, E. L., Jicha, G. A., Kryscio, R. J., & Schmitt, F. A. (2014). Musical training and late-life cognition. *American Journal of Alzheimer's Disease and Other Dementias, 29*, 333–343.

Hall, C. B., Derby, C., LeValley, A., Katz, M. J., Verghese, J., & Lipton, R. B. (2007) Education delays accelerated decline on a memory test in persons who develop dementia. *Neurology, 69*, 1657–1664. [PubMed: 17954781]

Huckans, M., Hutson, L., Twamley, E., Jak, A., Kaye, J., & Storzbach, D. (2013). Efficacy of cognitive rehabilitation therapies for mild cognitive impairment (MCI) in older adults: Working toward a theoretical model and evidence-based interventions. *Neuropsychology Review, 23*, 63–80.

Jones, R. (2003). Racial bias in the assessment of cognitive functioning of older adults. *Aging & Mental Health, 7*, 83–102. [PubMed: 12745387]

Katzman, R. (1993). Education and the prevalence of dementia and Alzheimer's disease. *Neurology, 43*(1, Pt. 1), 13. doi:10.1212/WNL.43.1_Part_1.13

Katzman, R., Terry, R., DeTeresa, R., Brown, T., Davies, P., Fuld, P., . . . Peck, A. (1988). Clinical, pathological, and neurochemical changes in dementia: A subgroup with preserved mental status and numerous neocortical plaques. *Annals of Neurology, 23,* 138–144.

Kay, D. W. K., Beamish, P., & Roth, M. (1964). Old age mental disorders in Newcastle upon Tyne. *British Journal of Psychiatry, 110,* 146–148.

Kesler, S. R., Adams, H. F., Blasey, C. M., & Bigler, E. D. (2003). Premorbid intellectual functioning, education, and brain size in traumatic brain injury: An investigation of the cognitive reserve hypothesis. *Applied Neuropsychology, 10,* 153–162. [PubMed: 12890641]

Kurz, A., Pohl, C., Ramsenthaler, M., & Sorg, C. (2009). Cognitive rehabilitation in patients with mild cognitive impairment. *International Journal of Geriatric Psychiatry, 24,* 163–168. doi:10.1002/gps.2086

Leon, I., Garcia, J., & Roldan-Tapia, L. (2011). Development of the scale of cognitive reserve in Spanish population: A pilot study. *Revista De Neurologia, 52,* 653–660.

Lyketsos, C. G., Chen, L. S., & Anthony, J. C. (1999). Cognitive decline in adulthood: An 11.5-year follow-up of the Baltimore Epidemiologic Catchment Area Study. *American Journal of Psychiatry, 156,* 58–65.

Manly, J. J., Jacobs, D. M., Touradji, P., Small, S. A., & Stern, Y. (2002). Reading level attenuates differences in neuropsychological test performance between African American and White elders. *Journal of the International Neuropsychological Society, 8*(3), 341–348.

Manly, J. J., Schupf, N., Tang, M. X., & Stern, Y. (2005). Cognitive decline and literacy among ethnically diverse elders. *Journal of Geriatric Psychiatry & Neurology, 18,* 213–217.

Manly, J. J., Tang, M. X., Schupf, N., Stern, Y., Ronsattel, J. P., & Mayeux, R. (2008). Frequency and course of mild cognitive impairment in a multiethnic community. *Annals of Neurology, 63,* 494–506.

Manly, J. J., Touradji, P., Tang, M. X., & Stern, Y. (2003). Literacy and memory decline among ethnically diverse elders. *Journal of Clinical and Experimental Neuropsychology, 5,* 680–690. [PubMed: 12815505]

Marchant, N. L., & Howard, R. J. (2015). Cognitive debt and Alzheimer's disease. *Journal of Alzheimer's Disease, 44*(3), 755–770.

Marshall, M. (2005). *Perspectives on rehabilitation and dementia.* London, United Kingdom: Jessica Kingsley.

Mortel, K. F., Meyer, J. S., Herod, B., & Thornby, J. (1995). Education and occupation as risk factors for dementia of the Alzheimer and ischemic vascular types. *Dementia, 6,* 55–62. [PubMed: 7728220]

Mountain, G. (2005). Rehabilitation for people with dementia: Pointers for practice from the evidence base. In M. E. Marshall (Ed.), *Perspectives on rehabilitation and dementia* (pp. 50–70). London, United Kingdom: Jessica Kingsley.

Nascimento, C. M., Pereira, J. R., Pires de Andrade, L., Garuffi, M., Ayan, C., Kerr, D. S., . . . Stella, F. (2015). Physical exercise improves peripheral BDNF levels and cognitive functions in mild cognitive impairment in the elderly with different BDNF Val66Met genotypes. *Journal of Alzheimer's Disease, 43,* 81–91.

Ngandu, T., Lehtisalo, J., Solomon, A., Levalahti, E., Ahtiluoto, S., Antikainen, R., . . . Kivipelto, M. (2015). A 2 year multidomain intervention of diet, exercise, cognitive training, and vascular risk monitoring versus control to prevent cognitive decline in at-risk elderly people (FINGER): A randomised controlled trial. *Lancet, 385,* 2255–2263.

O'Sullivan, M., Coen, R., O'Hora, D., & Shiel, A. (2015). Cognitive rehabilitation for mild cognitive impairment: Developing and piloting an intervention. *Aging, Neuropsychology and Cognition, 22,* 280–300.

Parente, R., & Stapleton, M. (1996). History and systems of cognitive rehabilitation. *Neurorehabilitation, 8,* 3–11.

*Park, D. C., & Reuter-Lorenz, P. (2009). The adaptive brain: Aging and neurocognitive scaffolding. *Annual Review of Psychology, 60,* 173–196.

Pedrero-Perez, E. J., Rojo-Mota, G., Ruiz-Sanchez de Leon, J. M., Fernandez-Mendez, L. M., Morales-Alonso, S., & Prieto-Hidalgo, A. (2014). Cognitive reserve in substance addicts in treatment: Relation to cognitive performance and activities of daily living. *Revista De Neurologia, 59*, 481–489.

Pettigrew, C., Soldan, A., Zhu, Y., Wang, M. C., Moghekar, A., Brown, T., . . . Team, B. R. (2016). Cortical thickness in relation to clinical symptom onset in preclinical AD. *NeuroImage: Clinical, 12*, 116–122.

Prigatano, G. P. (2005). A history of cognitive rehabilitation. In P. W. Halligan & D. T. Wade (Eds.), *Effectiveness of rehabilitation for cognitive deficits* (pp. 3–10). New York, NY: Oxford University Press.

Rami, L., Valls-Pedret, C., Bartres-Faz, D., Caprile, C., Sole-Padulles, C., Castellvi M., . . . Molinuevo, J. L. (2011). Cognitive reserve questionnaire. Scores obtained in a healthy elderly population and in one with Alzheimer's disease. *Review Neurology, 52*, 195–201.

Rebok, G. W., Ball, K., Guey, L. T., Jones, R. N., Kim, H. Y., King, J. W., Marsiske, M., . . . Willis, S. L. (2014). Ten-year effects of the advanced cognitive training for independent and vital elderly cognitive training trial on cognition and everyday functioning in older adults. *Journal of the American Geriatrics Society, 62*, 16–24.

Reitan, R. M. (1958). Validity of the Trail Making test as an indicator of organic brain damage. *Perceptual and Motor Skills, 8*, 271–276.

Richard, E., Andrieu, S., Solomon, A., Mangialasche, F., Ahtiluoto, S., Moll van Charante, E. P., . . . Kivipelto, M. (2012). Methodological challenges in designing dementia prevention trials— The European Dementia Prevention Initiative (EDPI). *Journal of Neurological Science, 322*, 64–70.

Richards, M., & Sacker, A. (2003). Lifetime antecedents of cognitive reserve. *Journal of Clinical and Experimental Neuropsychology, 25*, 614–624. [PubMed: 12815499]

Roe, C. M., Xiong, C., Miller, J. P., & Morris, J. C. (2007). Education and Alzheimer disease without dementia: Support for the cognitive reserve hypothesis. *Neurology, 68*, 223–228.

Sanders, A. E., Hall, C. B., Katz, M. J., & Lipton, R. B. (2012). Non-native language use and risk of incident dementia in the elderly. *Journal of Alzheimer's Disease, 29*, 99–108.

Satz, P., Cole, M., Hardy, D., & Rassovsky, Y. (2010). Brain and cognitive reserve: Mediator(s) and construct validity, a critique. *Journal of Clinical and Experimental Neuropsychology, 22*, 121–130. doi:10.1080/1380395.2010.493151

Scarmeas, N., Albert, S. M., Manly, J. J., & Stern, Y. (2006). Education and rates of cognitive decline in incident Alzheimer's disease. *Annals of Neurology, 77*, 308–318.

Scarmeas, N., Levy, G., Tang, M. X., Manly, J., & Stern, Y. (2001). Influence of leisure activity on the incidence of Alzheimer's disease. *Neurology, 57*, 2236–2242. [PubMed: 11756603]

Scarmeas, N., Zarahn, E., Anderson, K. E., Habeck, C. G., Hilton, J., Flynn, J., . . . Stern, Y. (2003). Association of life activities with cerebral blood flow in Alzheimer's disease: Implications for the cognitive reserve hypothesis. *Archives of Neurology, 60*, 359–365.

Schaie, K. W., & Willis, S. L. (1986). Can decline in adult intellectual functioning be reversed? *Developmental Psychology, 22*, 223–232.

Schaie, K. W., Willis, S. L., & O'Hanlon, A. M. (1994). Perceived intellectual performance change over seven years. *Journal of Gerontology: Psychological Sciences, 49*, 108–118.

Schmitz, T. W., Spreng, R. N., & ADNI Initiative. (2016). Basal forebrain degeneration precedes and predicts the cortical spread of Alzheimer's pathology. *Nature Communications, 7*, 13249.

Seeley, W. W., Crawford, R. K., Zhou, J., Miller, B. L., & Greicius, M. D. (2009). Neurodegenerative diseases target large-scale human brain networks. *Neuron, 62*, 42–52.

Shatenstein, B., Barberger-Gateau, P., & Mecocci, P. (2015). Prevention of age-related cognitive decline: Which strategies, when, and for whom? *Journal of Alzheimer's Disease, 48*, 35–53.

Snowdon, D. A., Kemper, S. J., Mortimer, J. A., Greiner, L. H., Wekstein, D. R., & Markesbery, W. R. (1996). Linguistic ability in early life and cognitive function and Alzheimer's disease in late life. Findings from the Nun Study. *Journal of the American Medical Association, 275*, 528–532.

Snowdon, D. A., Ostwald, S. K., & Kane, R. L. (1989). Education, survival and independence in elderly Catholic sisters, 1936–1988. *American Journal of Epidemiology, 130*, 999–1012. [PubMed: 2816907]

Steffener, J., Brickman, A. M., Rakitin, B. C., Gazes, Y., & Stern, Y. (2009). The impact of age-related changes on working memory functional activity. *Brain Imaging & Behavior, 3*, 142–153.

*Stern, Y. (2002). What is cognitive reserve? Theory and research application of the reserve concept. *Journal of the International Neuropsychological Society, 8*, 448–460. [PubMed: 11939702]

Stern, Y. (2007). Imaging cognitive reserve. In Y. Stern (Ed.), *Cognitive reserve: Theory and applications* (pp. 251–264). New York, NY: Taylor & Francis.

*Stern, Y. (2009). Cognitive reserve. *Neuropsychologia, 47*, 2015–2028.

*Stern, Y. (2012). Cognitive reserve in ageing and Alzheimer's disease. *Lancet Neurology, 11*, 1006–1012.

Stern, Y. (2016). An approach to studying the neural correlates of reserve. *Brain Imaging & Behavior, 11*, 410–416.

Stern, Y., Albert, S., Tang, M. X., & Tsai, W. Y. (1999). Rate of memory decline in AD is related to education and occupation cognitive reserve? *Neurology, 53*, 1942–1957. [PubMed: 10599762]

Stern, Y., Gurland, B., Tatemichi, T. K., Tang, M. X., Wilder, D., & Mayeux, R. (1994). Influence of education and occupation on the incidence of Alzheimer's disease. *Journal of the American Medical Association, 271*, 1004–1010. [PubMed: 8139057]

Stern, Y., Habeck, C., Moeller, J., Scarmeas, N., Anderson, K. E., Hilton, H. J., . . . van Heertum, R. (2005). Brain networks associated with cognitive reserve in healthy young and old adults. *Cerebral Cortex, 15*, 394–402. [PubMed: 15749983]

*Stern, Y., Tang, M. X., Denaro, J., & Mayeux, R. (1995). Increased risk of mortality in Alzheimer's disease patients with more advanced educational and occupational attainment. *Annals of Neurology, 37*, 590–595. [PubMed: 7755353]

Ströhle, A., Schmidt, D. K., Schultz, F., Fricke, N., Staden, T., Hellweg, R., . . . Rieckmann, N. (2015). Drug and exercise treatment of Alzheimer's Disease and Mild Cognitive Impairment: A systematic review and meta-analysis of effects on cognition in randomized controlled trials. *American Journal of Geriatric Psychiatry, 23*, 1234–1249.

Sumowski, J. F., Chiaravalloti, N., & Deluca, J. (2009). Cognitive reserve protects against cognitive dysfunction in multiple sclerosis. *Journal of Clinical and Experimental Neuropsychology, 31*, 913–926. [PubMed: 19330566]

Valenzuela, M. J. (2008). Brain reserve and the prevention of dementia. *Current Opinion in Psychiatry, 21*, 296–302.

Valenzuela, M. J., & Sachdev, P. (2005). Brain reserve and dementia: A systematic review. *Psychological Medicine, 35*, 1–14.

Valenzuela, M. J., & Sachdev, P. (2007). Assessment of complex mental activity across the lifespan: Development of the Lifetime of Experiences Questionnaire (LEQ). *Psychological Medicine, 37*, 1015–1025.

Van Gerven, P. W., Van Boxtel, M. P., Ausems, E. E., Bekers, O., & Jolles, J. (2012). Do apolipoprotein E genotype and educational attainment predict the rate of cognitive decline in normal aging? A 12—year follow up of the Maastricht Aging Study. *Neuropsychology, 26*, 459–472.

Verhaeghen, P. (2000). The interplay of growth and decline: Theoretical and empirical aspects of plasticity of intellectual and memory performance in normal old age. In R. D. Hill, L. Bäckman, & N. S. Neely (Eds.), *Cognitive rehabilitation in old age* (pp. 3–22). New York, NY: Oxford University Press.

Ward, A., Arrighi, H. M., Michels, S., & Cedarbaum, J. M. (2012). Mild cognitive impairment: Disparity of incidence and prevalence estimates. *Alzheimer's & Dementia, 8*, 14–21.

Wechsler, D. (1997). *Wechsler Memory Scale–Third Edition: Administration and scoring manual*. San Antonio, TX: The Psychological Corporation.

Wechsler, D. (2008). *Wechsler Memory Scale–Fourth Edition: Administration and scoring manual*. San Antonio, TX: The Psychological Corporation.

Whitney, K. A., Shepart, P. H., Mariner, J., Mossbarger, B., & Herman, S. (2010). Validity of the Wechsler Test of Adult Reading (WTAR): Effort considered in a clinical sample of U.S. military veterans. *Applied Neuropsychology: Adult, 17*, 196–204.

Wilkinson, G. (1993). *Wide range achievement test*. Wilmington, DE: Wide Range.

Willerman, L., Schultz, R., Rutledge, J. N., & Bigler, E. D. (1991). In vivo brain size and intelligence. *Intelligence, 15*, 223–228.

Wilson, R. S., Mendes De Leon, C. F., Barnes, L. L., Schneider, J. A., Bienias, J. L., Evans, D. A., & Bennett, D. A. (2002). Participation in cognitively stimulating activities and risk of incident Alzheimer's disease. *Journal of the American Medical Association, 287,* 742–748.

Xu, W., Yu, J. T., Tan, M. S., & Tan, L. (2015). Cognitive reserve and Alzheimer's disease. *Molecular Neurobiology, 51,* 187–208.

Yasuno, F., Kazui, H., Morita, N., Kajimoto, K., Ihara, M., Taguchi, A., . . . Kishimoto, T. (2015). Low amyloid-beta deposition correlates with high education in cognitively normal older adults: A pilot study. *International Journal of Geriatric Psychiatry, 30,* 919–926.

Zarahn, E., Rakitin, B., Abela, D., Flynn, J., & Stern, Y. (2007). Age-related changes in brain activation during a delayed item recognition task. *Neurobiology of Aging, 28,* 784–798. [PubMed: 16621168]

Zoladz, J. A., & Pilc, A. (2010). The effect of physical activity on the brain derived neurotrophic factor: From animal to human studies. *Journal of Physiology and Pharmacology, 61,* 533–541.

9

Neurocognitive Disorders in Late Life

Brian P. Yochim

M ost people will retain intact cognitive functioning throughout their lifetimes, at least into the late stages of a terminal illness. Although the cognitive abilities of someone in their 90s are not as strong as they were in their 30s or 60s, most adults remain able to live independently (see Chapter 1). Extrapolating from prevalence data (Plassman et al., 2007), 95% of people ages 71 to 79, 76% of people ages 80 to 89, and 63% of people age 90 or more years do not have dementia. A minority of people, however, develop impairment in their cognitive abilities that is severe enough to interfere with their abilities to live independently. Cognitive decline that is significant enough to interfere with independent living is known as dementia, and the *Diagnostic and Statistical Manual of Mental Disorders, Fifth Edition (DSM-5)* introduced the term *major neurocognitive disorder* to refer to this condition. This chapter explains these concepts, as well as mild cognitive impairment (MCI) or mild neurocognitive disorder, and the transient condition of delirium.

Neurocognitive disorders are not unique to late life. Children can be born with neurological problems causing intellectual disability. Children and adults of all ages can also experience strokes and traumatic brain injuries (TBIs). Indeed, TBIs are most common among children and older adults (Faul, Xu, Wald, & Coronado, 2010). However, strokes occur most often among older adults, and conditions such as Alzheimer's disease that cause neurocognitive impairment are also most common among older adults. Before we discuss chronic causes of neurocognitive disorders,

---

*Key references in the References section are indicated by an asterisk.

such as Alzheimer's disease, it is important to understand the more temporary and treatable condition of delirium.

DELIRIUM

A frequent occurrence among hospitalized older adults, which has also likely been experienced by any reader of this textbook at some point in life, is delirium. The nature of delirium (i.e., being delirious) is a rapid decline in cognitive functioning in response to a substantial change in one's physical condition. If you have had surgery with general anesthesia, you have likely been delirious upon awakening. The *DSM-5* diagnostic criteria for delirium include an impairment in attention and orientation that develops rapidly and is caused by a medical condition (American Psychiatric Association, 2013). Impairment is shown in at least one other area of cognitive functioning, such as memory, language, or visuospatial skills. Symptoms fluctuate throughout the day; in an extreme example, a person can be extremely agitated and disoriented 1 hour and be pleasant and well-oriented the next hour. Patients may drift in and out of sleep throughout a conversation. Common causes of delirium include infections, metabolic abnormalities, and changes in medications. While the delirium can resolve by addressing the underlying condition, the effects of delirium can linger long after the cause has been established and treated.

Clinicians are often asked to determine whether a person's cognitive decline is due to dementia, delirium, or both. A useful thought process is to consider someone's cognitive decline as *delirium unless proven otherwise*. Delirium tends to have a more rapid onset that dementia, occurring over the span of days, whereas dementia tends to develop over months or years. Acute medical conditions (e.g., infections, changes in medications, acute withdrawal from excess use of alcohol or other drugs) lead to delirium, and thus the cognitive and behavioral state is closely associated with a change in medical condition, whereas dementia occurs more independently of changes in one's medical condition. Patients with delirium often experience hallucinations, usually of a visual nature. Patients can also experience *illusions*, which are misperceptions of actual visual stimuli, such as seeing characters move in a painting on the wall, or misperceiving spots on the floor as bugs. Patients are frequently disoriented and benefit from frequent reminders of the current place and time. For example, patients may state that they are in the hospital when in fact they have been discharged to a rehabilitation facility. Deficits in orientation and language may lead patients to answer orientation questions incorrectly; for example, when asked what year it is, they may answer with the year they were born or their current age. Patients may show socially inappropriate behaviors they would not normally exhibit, such as aggression toward medical staff, rude statements, or removing clothing. Patients may also show emotional disturbances such as excessive anxiety or crying. The sleep–wake cycle is very often disrupted, such that patients wake up in the middle of the night ready to start the day, and then may sleep throughout the daytime.

Common clinical lore holds that the most common cause of delirium among older adults is urinary tract infections (UTIs). However, few studies have directly explored this relationship. In their review, Chae and Miller (2015) found that 19.4% of patients with delirium had a UTI. They also found that 11.2% of patients with dementia had UTIs and suggested that UTIs can precipitate or exacerbate an onset of dementia. Chae and Miller suggested that one mechanism for this relationship could involve the immune system. When one's body is infected with an agent that is similar to a host autoantigen, yet different enough to cause an inflammatory response, the immune system attacks both the infectious agent and the host autoantigens. This can lead to neurological tissue damage. Balogun and Philbrick (2014) found that patients with delirium had rates of UTI ranging from 25.9% to 32%, compared to 13% of hospitalized patients without delirium. Among patients with UTIs, rates of delirium ranged from 30% to 35%, and among hospitalized patients without UTIs, rates ranged from 7.7% to 8%. Balogun and Philbrick assert that the risk of delirium in the context of a UTI may in fact be similar to the risk of delirium in other conditions such as dementia, depression, heart failure, chronic kidney disease, psychotropic medications or multiple medications, and advanced age. They add that, if a urinalysis in a patient with delirium finds evidence of a UTI, the search for additional causes should continue. It is also important to note that, in rare situations, antibiotic treatment for a UTI can itself cause manic behaviors (Chae & Miller, 2015).

While it is important to rule out delirium when diagnosing dementia, it is also important to note that the weakened state of the brain that leads to dementia also increases one's risk of delirium (American Psychiatric Association [APA], 2013). Often, people who were starting to show mild cognitive deficits experience a steep decline in functioning after a major medical procedure such as surgery with general anesthesia. This is often experienced as delirium immediately after surgery, with decreased memory that is slow to improve or never improves. Lingehall et al. (2017) found that 26.3% of patients age 70 and older, undergoing cardiac surgery, developed dementia within 5 years after surgery. Among those who had developed dementia, 87% had experienced delirium after their surgeries. Lower cognitive functioning before surgery and delirium after surgery was highly associated with eventual development of dementia. This illustrates the close relationship between delirium and dementia. We turn now to discussion of neurocognitive disorders, also known as dementia and MCI.

NEUROCOGNITIVE DISORDERS: DIAGNOSTIC TERMINOLOGY

The most recent terms used to describe these conditions have been major or mild neurocognitive disorder, dementia, and MCI. It is important to understand that all these terms refer to a constellation of cognitive and behavioral symptoms, and that these symptoms have a variety of underlying causes. Unlike most other mental health disorders, a great deal is known about the underlying neurological causes of neurocognitive disorders. Thus, a comprehensive evaluation and diagnosis includes an attempt to pinpoint the underlying cause. The *DSM-5* includes specifiers of "probably due to" or "possibly due to" to reflect the probabilistic nature of specifying likely causes.

The term "dementia" has classically referred to an impairment in one's cognitive functioning that is a *decline* from a prior level and is severe enough to *interfere with one's ability to live independently*. The term has typically been associated with Alzheimer's disease, but it is important to understand that Alzheimer's disease is only one of many conditions that can cause dementia. Formal diagnostic criteria were published in 2011 by the National Institute on Aging (NIA) and Alzheimer's Association (AA; McKhann et al., 2011). When the *DSM-5* was published in 2013, the term *neurocognitive disorder* was intended to replace the term *dementia*, to acknowledge that conditions other than Alzheimer's disease can cause this syndrome of cognitive impairment.

It is important to establish that a patient is indeed demonstrating a *decline* when diagnosing dementia or neurocognitive disorder. Patients with a history of intellectual disability, for example, may show impairment that interferes with their ability to live independently, but a neurocognitive disorder would not be diagnosed until decline is occurring. People with Down's syndrome frequently develop Alzheimer's disease if they live long enough (Krinsky-McHale & Silverman, 2013), and clinical diagnosis of this condition is therefore very challenging. Likewise, people with high levels of cognitive functioning sometimes show decline (e.g., from a high average to a low average level of cognitive functioning) that resembles a pattern seen in Alzheimer's disease, but dementia is not diagnosed until the impairment is severe enough to interfere with the *ability to live independently. Decline* and *impairment* are two different concepts, and one can experience one without the other. Both must be present to be diagnosed with a neurocognitive disorder.

In the 1980s and 1990s it was realized that patients experience a mild cognitive decline before they have cognitive impairment severe enough to be called dementia. Various labels used to represent this state have included "MCI," "cognitive impairment, not dementia (CIND)," "mild neurocognitive disorder," and "cognitive disorder not otherwise specified (NOS)." The term *MCI* emerged as the preferred term, and in 2011 the NIA and AA published their diagnostic criteria for MCI due to Alzheimer's disease (Albert et al., 2011). This set of criteria expanded awareness that (a) one can have Alzheimer's disease but not have symptoms severe enough to be considered dementia, and (b) other conditions in addition to Alzheimer's disease can cause MCI as well as dementia. The criteria also make it known that, while memory decline is typically the first observable symptom, sometimes patients first show decline in other areas such as language or visuospatial ability (discussed later in the sections on Alzheimer's disease and frontotemporal dementia). *Amnestic MCI* refers to the more typical condition of decline in memory, whereas *nonamnestic MCI* refers to decline in other cognitive domains. The cognitive decline may be in one domain ("single-domain MCI") or more than one cognitive domain ("multidomain MCI"). This also reflects the fact that one can have impairment in more than one cognitive domain but it is not considered to be dementia until the cognitive impairment interferes with everyday living.

MCI continues to be a major focus of research. As treatments for Alzheimer's disease or other causes of MCI become developed, they may be given as early as possible in the course of the disease, such as when one starts to show symptoms of MCI. Patients and their families also usually appreciate being informed about this condition and what it means. The term MCI has become highly associated with Alzheimer's disease, and it can be difficult to know what diagnosis to apply to someone who is showing mild cognitive decline due to a stroke, a TBI, or other conditions such as Parkinson's disease. Recognizing this, the *DSM-5* incorporated the term *mild neurocognitive disorder* to refer to cognitive decline from any neurological problem that is not severe enough to interfere with daily functioning.

The *DSM-5* criteria differentiate between major and mild neurocognitive disorder based on the degree to which the cognitive decline interferes with independence in everyday functioning, such as managing finances or medications. Note that impairment in only one domain may be sufficient for the disorder to be considered "major," unlike prior criteria (e.g., McKhann et al., 2011) that required impairment in two or more domains. The exception is that, in order to be diagnosed with *major* neurocognitive disorder due to Alzheimer's disease, impairment must be demonstrated in two or more domains.

PREVALENCE OF DEMENTIA

The prevalence of dementia in the United States due to any cause increases with advancing age, from 5% among individuals ages 71 to 79 years, to 24% in ages 80 to 89, and 37% of people age 90 and older (Plassman et al., 2007). Throughout the world, dementia is estimated to occur in 5% to 7% of adults age 60 and older, with higher prevalence in Latin American countries (8.5%) and lower levels in sub-Saharan Africa (2%–4%; Prince et al., 2013). The higher prevalence in Latin America may result from a low average educational attainment and high prevalence of vascular risk factors. Low educational level is well known to be associated with increased risk of dementia, and is associated with high risk of obesity, sedentariness, diabetes, and hypertension, all of which increase the risk of dementia (Rizzi, Rosset, & Roriz-Cruz, 2014). An estimated 35.6 million people throughout the world had dementia in 2010, and this number is expected to double every 20 years, so that by 2030, 65.7 million people will have dementia, and 115.4 million will have it by 2050 (Prince et al., 2013). While these numbers illustrate the expected rise in *numbers* of people with dementia, there is evidence that the actual *prevalence* of dementia is remaining stable and may even be declining (Wu et al., 2017). Prince et al. note that 58% of people with dementia resided in low- or middle-income countries in 2010, and this proportion is expected to rise to 63% in 2030 and 71% in 2050. (For more information about the proportion of the populations of low-, middle-, and high-income countries that are age 60 and older, and expected changes in the coming decades, see Chapter 1.) Table 9.1 displays prevalence data by region of the world, from Prince et al. (2013). In a review article examining the prevalence rate among indigenous populations in Australia, Brazil, Canada, and the United States (Souza-Talarico, Carvalho, Brucki, Nitrini, R., & Ferretti-Rebustini, 2016), the prevalence rate of dementia was found to vary from 0.4% to 26.8%. Souza-Talarico et al. found that decreased education level and increased number of health conditions was associated with increased risk of dementia.

CAUSES OF NEUROCOGNITIVE DISORDERS

Many, if not most, patients with a major neurocognitive disorder (NCD) have more than one etiology (Thal, Walter, Saido, & Fändrich, 2015). Autopsies of patients with a history of an NCD typically find more than one etiology for the disorder. For

Table 9.1 Estimated Prevalence of Dementia by Regions of the World Where It Was Possible to Perform a Quantitative Meta-Analysis

Region	Age 60–64	Age 65–69	Age 70–74	Age 75–79	Age 80–84	Age 85–89	Age 90+
Australasia	1.8	2.8	4.5	7.5	12.5	20.3	38.3
Asia-Pacific, high income	1.0	1.7	2.9	5.5	10.3	18.5	40.1
East Asia	0.7	1.2	3.1	4.0	7.4	13.3	28.7
South Asia	1.3	2.1	3.5	6.1	10.6	17.8	35.4
Southeast Asia	1.6	2.6	4.2	6.9	11.6	18.7	35.4
Western Europe	1.6	2.6	4.3	7.4	12.9	21.7	43.1
United States	1.1	1.9	3.4	6.3	11.9	21.7	47.5
Latin America	1.3	2.4	4.5	8.4	15.4	28.6	63.9

Data reproduced from Prince et al. (2013).

example, in one autopsy study, 25% of patients with Alzheimer's were also found to have cerebrovascular disease, and another 20% of patients with Alzheimer's disease were found to also have Parkinson's disease (Gearing et al., 1995). In another study (Schneider, Arvanitakis, Bang, & Bennett, 2007), more than half of the individuals with dementia were found to have multiple etiologies, and only 30% had Alzheimer's disease alone. In reality, it is common for a person with an NCD to have more than one disease causing it. Therefore, a diagnostic evaluation can be considered a way of ruling out various possible causes until two or more possibilities cannot be ruled out. Symptoms of a disease process may not emerge until a certain amount of brain tissue is lost, and it may take the additive effect of two or more diseases before symptoms become noticeable.

A discussion of etiologies of neurocognitive disorders begins with TBIs, which can occur at any age but are particularly common among older adults.

TRAUMATIC BRAIN INJURIES

Although commonly associated with younger people, TBIs are also a common problem among older adults. Adults age 65 and older, children ages 0 to 4 years, and adolescents aged 15 to 19 years are the most likely to experience TBIs. The highest rates of TBI-related hospitalizations and death occur among adults age 75 years and older (Faul et al., 2010). Among all age groups, males are thought to have higher rates of TBI than females do (Faul et al., 2010), but another study found that females accounted for 62% of people age 65 and older hospitalized for TBI (Albrecht et al., 2015). Rates of TBI increase with advancing age, with the highest rates among adults age 85 and older (Chan, Zagorski, Parsons, & Colantonio, 2013). The evaluation of older adults with cognitive changes should always incorporate gathering information about possible TBIs.

In addition, modern treatment for acute brain injuries has preserved the lives of many people with TBIs who would have perished at the time of injury in the past. This will result in more people who have suffered severe TBIs living into old age with the deficits that accompany the TBI. Often people had TBIs at younger ages, before our current knowledge about TBIs, and this history is not elicited until late life. The brain damage experienced by a person earlier in life may lead to particular areas of the brain being more susceptible than other areas to future insults. For example, a patient reported a vague history of injury to the left side of his head sometime in his early 20s, along with being hospitalized for 2 weeks afterward and being feverish and unable to speak for a few days. This patient, 60 years later, became severely delirious when given a strong painkiller medication and showed symptoms of aphasia, which can result from damage to the left hemisphere. The patient's left hemisphere may have been particularly susceptible to various insults to the brain because of an injury long ago.

Occasionally authors will include TBIs, strokes, and other causes of injury such as brain tumors in a general category of *brain injuries*, whereby TBIs are different because of the traumatic nature of the situation in which they occurred. The most common causes of TBIs among older adults are falls (Chan et al., 2013), and the leading cause of death from TBI is motor vehicle-traffic injuries (Faul et al., 2010). Falls cause 60.7% of TBIs among adults age 65 and older, followed by 7.9% of injuries caused by motor vehicle traffic accidents (Faul et al., 2010). Being on ladders, walking on ice, intake of alcohol, and having conditions that impair one's balance all increase one's risk for falls. The number of fall-related TBIs has increased over time (Faul et al., 2010). When part of the head suddenly strikes something, the opposite side of the brain also can sustain damage. For example, if someone falls backwards off a ladder, their occipital lobe may suffer damage. Their brain will also recoil off the back of the skull, causing damage to the frontal lobes. This concept of damage to the opposite part of the brain than the part that was struck is known as *contracoup* damage.

TBIs also can occur in the context of other incidents; for example, a person may have a stroke and suddenly lose the ability to use her leg, causing her to fall down steps and strike her head. Likewise, older patients who suffer TBIs have a high rate of suffering intracranial hemorrhages or thromboembolic strokes while hospitalized and within a year after discharge (Albrecht et al., 2015). This rate decreases sharply within 4 months after the TBI and then continues to decrease over the year after the TBI, but the risk of stroke after TBI remains higher than before a TBI. Common *nontraumatic* causes of brain injury among older adults include brain tumors (the most common) and anoxia (deprivation of oxygen; Chan et al., 2013).

We turn now to causes of neurocognitive disorders that are more unique to old age and that tend to develop more gradually.

ALZHEIMER'S DISEASE

Alzheimer's disease is the most common cause of neurocognitive disorders among older adults. The hallmark neuropathological features of Alzheimer's disease include the development of plaques, composed mainly of *amyloid (Aβ)*, and neurofibrillary tangles, consisting mainly of *tau*. These lead to cerebral atrophy, or degeneration, and loss of synapses. Amyloid plaques occur between neurons as byproducts of neuronal degeneration, and hinder communication between neurons. Cognitive decline and impairment are more associated with the number of neurofibrillary tangles than plaques (Nelson et al., 2012). When the microtubules transporting substances from a neuronal cell body to the end of the axon become twisted, the twisted microtubules form into neurofibrillary tangles. Neurons lose their structural integrity as a result. The tangles occur in the hippocampus, entorhinal cortex, and other parts of the temporal lobe, before spreading to other parts of the brain, including the nucleus basalis of Meynert in the forebrain (Boller & Duykaerts, 2003). The nucleus basalis of Meynert contributes to the production of acetylcholine, and as this area degenerates, the depletion of acetylcholine also leads to impaired memory (Lezak, Howieson, Bigler, & Tranel, 2012).

Because of this impact on acetylcholine, current pharmacological treatments attempt to prevent the breakdown of acetylcholine. Acetylcholinesterase, or cholinesterase, is an enzyme that breaks down acetylcholine. By inhibiting cholinesterase, the amount of acetylcholine is increased, which should improve memory functioning. Cholinesterase inhibitors such as donepezil, galantamine, and rivastigmine are commonly prescribed for patients suspected of having Alzheimer's disease. Another medication, memantine, works as an N-methyl-D-aspartate (NMDA) receptor antagonist that is meant to decrease glutamate activity. Both these classes of medications may lead to small improvements in functioning in patients with dementia, but cholinesterase inhibitors have side effects including weight loss and syncope in older adults (Buckley & Salpeter, 2015).

Alzheimer's disease cannot be diagnosed definitively until autopsy of the affected individual's brain, because of the obvious risk in obtaining a biopsy of brain tissue in a living person. Therefore, clinicians make diagnoses such as "major NCD probably due to Alzheimer's disease" or "dementia of the Alzheimer's type" when Alzheimer's disease seems the most likely etiology. At least three sets of criteria gauge the severity of Alzheimer's disease in a deceased person's brain. The Braak and Braak (1991) criteria track a progression of the disease from the transentorhinal cortex (stages I and II) to the hippocampus (stages III and IV) and ending with involvement throughout the neocortex (stages V and VI). The Consortium to Establish a Registry for Alzheimer's Disease (CERAD) also proposed criteria for staging the disease (Gearing et al., 1995). After Ronald Reagan died from complications related to Alzheimer's disease, the NIA–Reagan Institute criteria (Newell, Hyman, Growdon, & Hedley-Whyte, 1999) were developed. The NIA-Reagan criteria provide a high, intermediate, or low likelihood that a person's dementia was due to Alzheimer's disease. Many people who are cognitively intact throughout life are nonetheless found to have the neuropathologic features of Alzheimer's disease in their brains at autopsy (Thal et al., 2015; Vinters, 2015). One may have the disease while not having cognitive impairment. When working with patients, it can be difficult to determine how to answer the question: "So do I have Alzheimer's disease or not?"

Amyloid plaques also develop in the arteries and capillaries of the brain, which is known as *amyloid angiopathy*. Amyloid angiopathy occurs in as many as 85% to

95% of people with Alzheimer's disease (Vinters, 2015). Amyloid angiopathy can cause intracerebral hemorrhages to occur, and it can also cause the gradual development of cerebral microinfarctions (Vinters, 2015).

A small proportion of patients develop Alzheimer's disease through a mutation in one of three genes: the amyloid precursor protein (APP) gene on chromosome 21, presenilin 1 (PSEN1) on chromosome 14, and presenilin 2 (PSEN2) on chromosome 1. PSEN2 mutations rarely occur. These genetic mutations lead to eventual development of the disease, as early as a patient's 40s or 50s. The ε4 form of apolipoprotein E (ApoE ε4) increases the probability of developing Alzheimer's disease, but does not ensure that one will develop it. Neither the *DSM-5* (APA, 2013) nor the NIA/AA diagnostic criteria (McKhann et al., 2011) require genetic information for a diagnosis. The NIA/AA criteria note that an "increased level of certainty" (p. 266) is found with genetic mutations in APP, PSEN1, or PSEN2, but ApoE ε4 is not in this category because it is not considered specific enough. Many people with the ApoE ε4 gene do not develop Alzheimer's disease, and many people without the gene do develop Alzheimer's disease. The *DSM-5* stipulates that ApoE ε4 is a risk factor but neither necessary nor sufficient for Alzheimer's disease to occur.

Research efforts are prioritizing the search for biomarkers of Alzheimer's disease and other neurological conditions. A *biomarker* is anything that serves as a quantifiable representation or marker of a specific pathophysiological disease process. Common examples include neuroimaging findings (e.g., MRI or PET scan results) or levels of a chemical in cerebrospinal fluid (CSF) samples. Neuropsychological tests are also considered a biomarker of Alzheimer's disease (Vinters, 2015). Five well-known biomarkers of Alzheimer's disease include structural MRI, amyloid PET, fluorodeoxyglucose (FDG)-PET, CSF levels of Aβ, and CSF levels of tau. Atrophy in the medial temporal lobe as depicted on MRI is particularly common in Alzheimer's disease (Jagust, 2013). Neuroimaging with Pittsburgh compound B (PiB) can show the amount of Aβ in the brain. CSF levels of Aβ and tau are obtained through lumbar punctures (also known as spinal taps), in which a needle is inserted between two lumbar vertebrae. The NIA/AA criteria place the biomarkers for Alzheimer's disease into two categories: (a) biomarkers of *Aβ protein deposition*, including low CSF levels of Aβ (caused by high levels of Aβ protein deposition in brain tissue) and positive PET amyloid imaging, and (b) biomarkers of "downstream" *neuronal degeneration or injury*, such as elevated CSF tau (including total tau and phosphorylated tau), decreased FDG uptake on PET in temporoparietal cortex, and disproportionate atrophy in the temporal and parietal cortex shown on structural MRI. While the NIA/AA criteria state that biomarkers increase the certainty of Alzheimer's disease as an etiology of dementia, they do not currently promote the use of biomarker tests for diagnosis.

> There are several reasons for this limitation: (1) the core clinical criteria provide very good diagnostic accuracy and utility in most patients; (2) more research needs to be done to ensure that criteria that include the use of biomarkers have been appropriately designed; (3) there is limited standardization of biomarkers from one locale to another; and (4) access to biomarkers is limited to varying degrees in community settings (McKhann et al., 2011, p. 266).

Declines in memory are usually the first symptom of Alzheimer's disease, because the hippocampus is impacted early in the disease process. Patients or their caregivers will often report that the patient's "long-term" memory is intact but that their "short-term" memory is poor. They often will report that the patient can remember events from prior years without difficulty, but that they forget conversations within minutes. This parallels the neuropathology that is occurring in the patient's brain; as the hippocampus deteriorates, the brain's ability to form new memories declines. However, memories or knowledge already established years ago remain unaffected by the disease until late in its course. (For explanation of different types of memory, refer to Chapter 7.) Likewise, procedural memory is preserved late into the disease course, so patients can still engage in activities involving this type of memory, such as using tools and kitchen utensils, playing musical instruments, or completing yardwork. Caregivers can capitalize on a patient's remaining skills while preventing deficits from interfering; for example, a patient may still be able to make an omelet but may need a reminder to turn the stove off when done. Social functioning often remains intact, so that relationships can continue to enrich one's life. Intact social functioning often enables the patient to compensate for memory loss (e.g., by talking around a question asked, rather than answering it, when they do not know the answer), which can mask the symptoms of this and prevent loved ones or acquaintances from noticing a decline in the patient's memory.

Memory problems progress insidiously, and a concerning event may surprise the patient and/or their family members. They may travel out of town and find themselves unable to learn how to find their hotel room. Patients may find themselves becoming lost when driving in an unfamiliar area. They may go to an appointment and return home several hours later after receiving assistance in finding their way home. In this sense, their driving per se (i.e., the procedural memory of operating a motor vehicle) may be intact, but memory impairment interferes with their navigation. Their spouses may notice the patient frequently repeats questions and forgets recent events, such as a conversation or a movie from the prior day. They may be unable to learn how to operate a new appliance because of inability to remember instructions given to them. Neuropsychologists look for whether these symptoms are occurring by presenting patients with a set of information, such as a list of words, short stories, or simple diagrams, and then asking the patient to recall the stimuli immediately after presentation and then some time later, usually 20 to 30 minutes after initial presentation.

After entering the medial temporal area, Alzheimer's disease typically then spreads to nearby neuroanatomical areas, such as the lateral temporal lobes and frontal lobes. This leads to accompanying declines in language abilities, such as finding words in daily conversation. Patients often use *circumlocutions* when they cannot recall a word, using other words or phrases to convey the desired word. Patients can also make *paraphasic* errors in their speech, saying a word semantically (e.g., "rain cover") or phonologically (e.g., "umbilical") similar to the target word (e.g., "umbrella"). Impaired word-finding manifests in neuropsychological testing as poor performance on confrontation naming tests, in which individuals are "confronted" with a stimulus, usually a picture, and asked to name the item.

As the disease spreads to the frontal lobes, patients show behavioral changes in response to damage to this area, such as poor social comportment (e.g., swearing, rude statements they would not have said before), poor planning (e.g., difficulty planning a meal or a set of errands), poor decision making (e.g., making poor financial decisions), or impulsivity (e.g., engaging in extramarital affairs). One patient described making impulsive online purchases, and then forgetting that items had been purchased when they arrived at her doorstep. These abilities are typically considered elements of *executive functioning*. The NIA/AA criteria (McKhann et al., 2011), as well as the *DSM-5*, place poor social behavior into its own domain of cognitive functioning (social cognition), whereas planning and decision-making are considered a part of executive functioning.

Alzheimer's disease eventually intrudes into the posterior temporal lobes and parietal and occipital lobes. Patients may misperceive important visual stimuli, such as picking up a television remote when the phone is ringing, or failing to notice the item they wanted to purchase in the grocery store. They may not be able to quickly process changes in their visual environment, such as when driving or walking. (For review of cognitive changes related to driving, see Chapter 7.) Reading may become laborious, and loved ones may wonder why the patient has "lost interest" in this activity. Decreased reading may also result from finding that they cannot remember what they have read. Visual perceptual problems may lead to difficulty entering information correctly in a checkbook or noticing that their bathroom is dirty.

Every person with Alzheimer's disease has a different trajectory of the disease process and thus will experience a different set of symptoms at various points in time. If the pathology develops first in areas other than the medial temporal lobes, then symptoms resulting from damage to those parts of the brain are the first to manifest. This leads to syndromes, which may be named after the area affected (e.g., posterior cortical atrophy) or the resulting symptoms (e.g., primary progressive aphasia [PPA]). PPA is most often caused by the same pathology that causes frontotemporal degeneration, and is described in the section on frontotemporal dementia. Posterior cortical atrophy is typically caused by Alzheimer's disease.

Occasionally Alzheimer's disease develops first in places like the occipital lobe or posterior temporal lobe, causing *posterior cortical atrophy*. This atrophy is most often caused by Alzheimer's disease (Crutch et al., 2017). Degeneration of the occipital lobes leads to deficits in visuospatial skills. Early symptoms can include difficulty recognizing faces, finding things in the kitchen, house, or grocery store, or difficulty assembling new furniture. One patient described an inability to associate the names and faces of new neighbors that moved in next door. Visuospatial skills are described more in Chapter 7. Deficient visuospatial skills are also a common symptom of Lewy body disease, described next.

LEWY BODY DISEASE

Another common cause of neurocognitive disorders is Lewy body disease. Lewy body disease and Parkinson's disease are intertwined; cognitive impairment in people with Parkinson's disease results from the accumulation of *Lewy bodies*. While the two syndromes differ in their timing of motor symptoms and cognitive symptoms, both syndromes and their underlying pathologies become similar with time. If cognitive symptoms develop before the onset of motor symptoms, the condition is known as Lewy body disease.

In 1912, Frederick Lewy discovered small circular bodies found in the cells of the substantia nigra in patients with Parkinson's disease. These cell bodies are now thought to be the second-most common neuropathological finding in patients with dementia. Lewy bodies are found in the brains of patients with Parkinson's disease, in patients with *multiple system atrophy,* and in those with dementia due to suspected Lewy bodies. Lewy bodies are composed of alpha-synuclein (α-synuclein). This pathology is associated with loss of neurons. Whether Lewy bodies have a neuro-protective or neurotoxic role, and the extent to which they cause the clinical symp-toms of Lewy body disease, is not yet known (Walker, Possin, Boeve, & Aarsland, 2015). Some people with no history of clinical symptoms nonetheless have signifi-cant α-synuclein pathology found at autopsy.

Lewy bodies may develop first in the reticular formation, followed by the brain-stem, the limbic system, and then the neocortex (Braak et al., 2003), with other patterns of progression possible. One biomarker for Lewy body disease may be the amount of α-synuclein in CSF; this has been found to be lower in people with Lewy body disease than in people with Alzheimer's disease, but similar to levels found in people with Parkinson's disease (Lim, Yeo, Green, & Pal, 2013). (It is lower in the CSF because it has accumulated in the tissue of the brain.) Structural neuroimaging, such as MRI, has not been found to be effective in differentiating Lewy body disease from other causes of dementia (Walker et al., 2015). However, patients with Lewy body disease show less metabolism in the occipital area on perfusion single photon emission CT and metabolic PET, compared with healthy control participants or patients with Alzheimer's disease (Walker et al., 2015). This finding is listed as a supportive biomarker in the diagnostic criteria for dementia due to Lewy body disease (McKeith et al., 2017) and it has high sensitivity and specificity. Another indicative biomarker is low dopa-mine transporter uptake in the basal ganglia, as seen on single photon emission CT or PET. The ApoE ε4 allele occurs more among people with Lewy body disease than among controls, but not as common as among people with Alzheimer's disease (Tsuang et al., 2013). Dementia due to Lewy body disease is thought to be underdi-agnosed. Symptoms of Lewy body disease are often misdiagnosed as Alzheimer's disease.

Patients with Lewy body disease often experience well-formed visual halluci-nations of people or animals. Clinicians may address these symptoms by prescrib-ing antipsychotic medications. However, patients with dementia with Lewy bodies can have problematic reactions to antipsychotic medications (Weintraub & Hurtig, 2007). Lewy body disease and Parkinson's disease involve a reduced level of dopa-mine, thus antipsychotic medications that are designed to reduce levels of dopa-mine would be expected to worsen symptoms caused by a shortage of dopamine. Clinicians must be aware that a new onset of visual hallucinations in older adults commonly results from Lewy body symptoms rather than a psychotic process.

People with Lewy body disease commonly have impairments in visuospatial skills and executive functioning. Tiraboschi et al. (2006) found that including visuo-spatial impairment as a core diagnostic criterion would improve sensitivity to the disease. Lewy body disease is also associated with fluctuations in cognition, and this is a core diagnostic feature. Ferman et al. (2004) specified this further, finding that daytime sleep of 2 or more hours, staring into space for long periods, daytime drowsiness and lethargy, and episodes of disorganized speech occurred much more often in people with Lewy body disease than in people with Alzheimer's disease or participants with no neurological disorder.

Lewy body disease is associated with a specific sleep disorder. During rapid eye movement (REM) sleep, the body is typically paralyzed, so that we do not move while we are dreaming. In contrast, people with REM sleep behavior disorder act out their dreams and may yell, scream, wave their limbs, punch, or kick during the REM sleep phase. The dreams in which this occurs often involve a perceived attacker such as a person, animal, or insect. Up to 70% to 90% of patients with REM sleep behavior disorder develop dementia, usually due to Lewy bodies, or Parkinson's disease within 15 years of onset (Howell & Schenck, 2015). It is thought to develop from insults to the brainstem areas involved in the control of REM sleep, such as the reticular formation. These areas may be affected by Lewy body disease earlier than other parts of the brain, which would account for REM sleep behavior disorder occurring years before the manifestations of Lewy body disease (Walker et al., 2015).

There are currently no effective medications for Lewy body disease. Patients with Lewy body disease have a high risk of problematic side effects of medications, which further complicates pharmacological treatment. Medications that address hallucinations might worsen motor symptoms, and medications for motor symptoms might worsen hallucinations, also posing a challenge to treatment. Donepezil and rivastigmine, used for treating Alzheimer's disease, have also been shown to improve cognition and activities of daily living in patients with dementia due to Lewy body disease or Parkinson's disease (Walker et al., 2015). The digestive system contains many acetylcholine receptors, and acetylcholinesterase inhibitors increase the activity of acetylcholine in the digestive system, frequently resulting in diarrhea. This is problematic for some but also can be beneficial to the large numbers of patients who experience constipation related to Lewy body disease and parkinsonism.

PARKINSON'S DISEASE

Neurocognitive disorders can occur in the late stages of Parkinson's disease. The first symptoms of Parkinson's are typically a mild tremor while the hands are at rest, muscular rigidity, and slowing of movements. Eventually patients show poor balance, frequent falls, and difficulty walking. A person's gait may become characterized by short, shuffling steps without lifting the feet very much (a "magnetic gait"). Their face may show less expression and they may appear to have a *masked face*. Handwriting becomes small and difficult to decipher. Parkinson's disease is caused by the atrophy of neurons that produce dopamine in the substantia nigra of the brain. Neurocognitive disorder due to Parkinson's disease is diagnosed when the disease is clearly established, and the cognitive symptoms are similar to those found in Lewy body disease. If motor symptoms have not yet developed, then Lewy body disease is listed as the possible or probable cause. Parkinson's disease can lead to impairments in attention, visuospatial skills, memory, and executive functioning. Litvan et al. (2012) published diagnostic criteria for MCI due to Parkinson's disease. Although Parkinson's disease is thought to result in a "subcortical" profile of neuropsychological test performance, as opposed to the "cortical" pattern found in Alzheimer's disease, in reality both patient groups often show similar performance (Emre et al., 2007).

VASCULAR DISEASE

A buildup of vascular damage in the brain may interfere with cognitive functioning to the extent that a person may be diagnosed with NCD due to vascular disease. Risk factors for this condition include a history of cigarette smoking, type 2 diabetes, poorly controlled hypertension, and atrial fibrillation (Blumenfeld, 2010). This condition involves atherosclerotic plaques building up in the cerebral arteries, interfering with adequate blood supply. Eventually, arteries may become completely blocked, leading to a shortage or lack of blood supply to nearby areas of the brain, a condition called *ischemia*. Neuroimaging often shows multiple ischemic lesions in these patients, typically bordering the cerebral ventricles (i.e., "periventricular") and expanding outward from the ventricles. The arteries first to become blocked tend to be smaller arteries, followed by arteries of increasing size. One example of small arteries that are prone to narrowing are the lenticulostriate arteries, which supply the basal ganglia (Blumenfeld, 2010). Ischemia in this region can cause slower speed of processing. Hence, some of the first deficits seen in these patients are in processing speed.

Other patients may stay cognitively intact until a large infarction occurs. An *infarction* is the death of brain tissue due to sudden lack of blood supply. Infarctions most often are caused by an artery completely closing off, as in ischemia. Ischemic strokes can be caused by a *thrombus*, or a blood clot within a cerebral artery, or blood clots can break off from another artery in the body and become stuck in a cerebral artery, causing an *embolic* stroke. Embolic strokes can occur suddenly, whereas thrombotic strokes may take longer to become manifest. Approximately 13% of strokes are cerebral hemorrhages, or a breakage in an artery, with blood spilling out (Beal, 2010). Strokes vary in size from large-vessel infarcts to small-vessel infarcts. Clinical descriptions of MRI or CT scans may refer to "small-vessel disease," which refers to evidence of ischemia in the small blood vessels of the brain. These are also commonly referred to as "lacunar" infarcts due to their resemblance to small lakes when viewed on neuroimaging or at autopsy. The most common site of large infarctions is the left or right middle cerebral artery, which supplies a large part of the lateral cerebral cortex. Typically patients show some degree of recovery in the weeks after a stroke, but the stroke may have caused enough damage that the patient is left with a permanent NCD.

The cognitive presentation of cerebrovascular disease varies to a large extent, depending on the location of ischemic damage (O'Brien & Thomas, 2015). If patients develop the disease slowly and gradually, they may show declines in processing speed and executive functioning. Significant strokes can cause sudden impairment in language, visual perception, attention, executive functioning, and/or processing speed. If an infarction occurs in the left middle cerebral artery, the patient may suddenly develop *aphasia*, or a disturbance in his or her ability to produce and/or understand language. Strokes in the areas fed by the right middle cerebral artery can cause left inattention, also known as left neglect or hemineglect, a condition in which patients fail to attend to any stimuli (visual, tactile, auditory, etc.) in the left side of space. Patients with right hemisphere damage may also develop *anosognosia* ("not knowing that one does not know"), a condition in which patients are not aware, or do not believe, that they have impairments. This condition interferes substantially with rehabilitation and recovery.

FRONTOTEMPORAL DEMENTIA

Frontotemporal dementia refers to several types of dementia that result from damage to the frontal and/or temporal lobes. The actual damage may result from several different neuropathologies. Most cases of frontotemporal lobar degeneration are caused by the microtubule-associated protein tau (*MAPT*), the transactive response (TAR) DNA-binding protein with molecular weight 43 kDa (*TDP-43*), or the fused-in sarcoma (*FUS*) protein (Bang, Spina, & Miller, 2015). The resulting syndromes may be called frontotemporal dementia or may be a description of the clinical syndrome, as in *PPA*. Symptoms tend to develop in the late 50s, with diagnosis typically occurring in the late 50s to the late 60s (Hodges, Davies, Xuereb, Kril, & Halliday, 2003). A proportion of patients with this condition also develop motor neuron diseases such as *amyotrophic lateral sclerosis (ALS)*, in which patients become unable to engage in any form of voluntary muscle movements.

Frontotemporal dementia typically occurs as the *behavioral variant* subtype (Box 9.1) or the *language variant* subtype. It is thought to be the third most common type of dementia among people younger than 65 (Vieira et al., 2013). The disorder is most common among ages 45 to 64, with 60% of cases diagnosed in this age group. It is often mistaken as a new-onset psychiatric disorder because of the significant behavioral changes and the assumption that neurodegenerative diseases start much later in life. Arnold Pick is thought to have been the first to describe a patient with frontotemporal dementia, in 1892. In 1911, Alois Alzheimer named the syndrome "Pick's disease," and "Pick's disease" and "frontotemporal dementia" have often been used interchangeably.

BOX 9.1 Loss of Behavioral Initiative

Patients with the behavioral variant of frontotemporal dementia may show lack of initiative, such as needing prompting to bathe and put dirty clothes in the laundry, or to solve problems suddenly presented to them. For instance, one patient left a stove burner on, resulting in a small fire on the stovetop. His wife and grandchildren promptly extinguished the fire, and the patient went to take a nap rather than help clean up the resulting mess of burned food and fire extinguisher foam. The same patient would forget to feed his dog, despite the dog barking repeatedly near his food dish. He also showed an inability to choose his clothes to wear for the day, and his wife needed to choose his clothes in order to make it to an appointment on time.

In the *behavioral variant* of frontotemporal dementia, patients gradually develop behavioral changes that interfere with social and occupational functioning, such as inability to inhibit socially inappropriate behaviors. They may say derogatory comments about strangers within hearing distance of them. They may start to purchase pornographic materials for the first time in their adult lives. Patients may engage in risky financial expenditures and their partners may not learn about it until significant amounts of money have been lost. Patients may lose the initiative to complete basic activities of daily living such as bathing or brushing teeth and may need prompts to do so. People who have been faithful to their spouses throughout their lives may suddenly engage in extramarital affairs. Other abnormal behaviors have included leaving the house unclothed, completing tasks at odd times of the day (e.g., yard work in the middle of the night), or changing one's diet to extreme. Possibly the most tragic component of this syndrome is that patients are usually unaware that their behavior has changed.

PPA is a progressive language disorder in which profound impairments in language are the first symptoms to manifest. The syndrome is currently categorized into three subtypes (Gorno-Tempini et al., 2011), but diagnostic guidelines for this condition have changed considerably in recent times and are likely to change again as more knowledge is acquired about this rare condition. Table 9.2 presents the diagnostic criteria put forth by Gorno-Tempini et al. (2011). Note that the criteria include specific *impairments* as well as skills that remain *intact*.

Table 9.2 **Symptoms, Neuroanatomical Correlates, and Commonly Associated Neuropathology for the Three Variants of Primary Progressive Aphasia**

Nonfluent/Agrammatic PPA	Semantic PPA	Logopenic PPA
At least one of the following two: Effortful, halting speech OR Agrammatism in language production At least two of the following three: Impaired comprehension of complex sentences Spared single-word comprehension Spared object knowledge	Both: Impaired confrontation naming Impaired single-word comprehension At least three of the following four: Impaired object knowledge Impaired reading and writing of irregularly spelled words Spared repetition Spared speech production	Both: Impaired word retrieval in speech and naming Impaired repetition of sentences At least three of the following four: Phonologic errors in speech and naming Spared object knowledge and word comprehension Spared motor speech Absence of agrammatism
Left posterior frontal lobe involvement	Anterior temporal lobe involvement	Left posterior perisylvian or parietal involvement
FTLD neuropathology	FTLD pathology	Alzheimer's disease

FTLD, frontotemporal lobar degeneration; PPA, primary progressive aphasia.

Adapted from Gorno-Tempini et al. (2011).

One can think of the nonfluent/agrammatic variant of PPA as a slowly developing Broca's aphasia, which is usually caused by strokes in Broca's area. *Agrammatism* refers to impairment in grammar, including verb conjugation, appropriate word order in sentences, and the use of function words such as articles and prepositions. The semantic variant, previously known as "semantic dementia," can be conceptualized as a loss of semantic knowledge. This loss of knowledge leads to impaired ability to name things and to describe objects when confronted with them (i.e., in "confrontation naming" tasks). This also leads to an inability to read or spell "irregularly" spelled words such as "people," "hour," "said," or "two." The deficit results from loss of the knowledge of that concept, as opposed to loss of ability to associate letters and sounds. The logopenic subtype is the most recently described and is usually caused by Alzheimer's disease. Thus, a given *syndrome* (i.e., PPA) can be caused by different *etiologies* (e.g., Alzheimer's disease or the forms of pathology that cause frontotemporal degeneration). Recall that *posterior cortical atrophy* can be caused by Alzheimer's disease or other neurodegenerative conditions.

ALCOHOL-RELATED DEMENTIA

It is generally thought that light to moderate use of alcohol may actually protect against development of Alzheimer's disease and other causes of dementia. Definitions of *light* and *moderate* vary across culture and time. In the United States, moderate use is considered to be up to one drink per day for women and up to two drinks per day for men, with a *drink* defined as 12 ounces of beer or 5 ounces of wine (U.S. Department of Agriculture & U.S. Department of Health and Human Services, 2015). Sometimes people develop neurocognitive disorders after lengthy histories of excessive alcohol use. The *DSM-5* includes the term alcohol-induced neurocognitive disorder to refer to this condition. It is unique compared to conditions like Alzheimer's disease because it is thought to be less progressive than other causes of neurocognitive disorder. Patients may even show improvements in their functioning after as little as 1 week of sobriety and over ensuing years of sobriety, although older age is related to poorer recovery (Ridley, Draper, & Withall, 2013).

The damage to the brain that results in dementia might be due to direct toxic effects of ethanol (ETOH), to a deficiency of thiamine, or to a combination of both factors. Thiamine is also known as vitamin B1, which is not to be confused with vitamin B_{12}. Alcohol interferes with thiamine metabolism, and excessive alcohol use is often associated with unhealthy diets, leading to inadequate thiamine intake. Ethanol may affect neuronal integrity directly through oxidative stress, disruption of neurogenesis, and glutamate excitotoxicity (Ridley et al., 2013). Wernicke's encephalopathy represents an acute condition caused by deficient thiamine levels, and involves a combination of ophthalmoplegia (paralysis of an eye muscle), ataxia (uncoordinated movements), and confusion. Korsakoff's syndrome is more of a long-term condition of severe memory impairment related to hippocampal damage.

It is difficult to establish a clear relationship between specific levels of lifetime alcohol intake and development of cognitive impairment, because of variability in types of alcoholic drinks, definitions of what is a standard drink, and definitions of normal intake and excessive intake. To add to this, lifetime patterns of excessive use, periods of no alcohol use, and periods of light use vary from person to person. People with a history of alcohol abuse are also more likely to have histories of head injuries, use of other substances, and vascular risk factors, which complicate the establishment of a direct relationship. Alcohol-related dementia tends to have a younger age of onset. Studies have found variable rates of alcohol-related dementia, with prevalence rates ranging from 1% up to 24% of cases of dementia, with its larger prevalence rates to be found among younger patients with dementia (Ridley et al., 2013).

Excessive alcohol use has been found to be associated with volume loss in the frontal lobes, hippocampus, cerebellum, and corpus callosum (Ridley et al., 2013). Increased cognitive impairment has been associated with multiple episodes of binge drinking and periods of withdrawal. Prolonged abstinence, however, may restore myelin in white matter and result in improved cognition and motor abilities. Patients with alcohol-induced neurocognitive disorder tend to show impairment on measures of visuospatial skills and executive functioning, and severe memory impairment (Ridley et al., 2013).

OTHER CAUSES OF NEUROCOGNITIVE DISORDERS

Other, less common causes of neurocognitive disorders in late life that are beyond the scope of this chapter include corticobasal degeneration, multiple system atrophy, and progressive supranuclear palsy. Adults of all ages can develop neurocognitive disorders caused by Huntington's disease, HIV infection, infection from other diseases such as hepatitis C, prion disease, and many other causes.

CONCLUSION

This chapter reviewed the most common causes of neurocognitive disorders in older adults. We began with a discussion of delirium, which should be ruled out whenever an older adult is showing signs of cognitive decline. Next, an overview of the current diagnostic terminology was presented, including MCI, dementia, and the *DSM-5* diagnoses of mild neurocognitive disorder and major neurocognitive disorder. We next reviewed TBIs, Alzheimer's disease, Lewy body disease, Parkinson's disease, vascular disease, frontotemporal degeneration, which includes a behavioral variant and a language variant, and alcohol-related dementia.

As a final note, it can be helpful to conceptualize the symptoms of any neurocognitive disorder as what would be expected from damage to a specific part of the brain, whatever the cause of the damage. For example, both Alzheimer's disease and herpes simplex encephalitis tend to strike the medial temporal area. Thus, the deficits one would expect from damage to the medial temporal area (i.e., memory deficits) occur with either disease. In the unusual circumstance that Alzheimer's disease strikes the occipital lobes first, then the corresponding symptoms are profound visuospatial deficits. Likewise, sometimes strokes happen in the basal ganglia, leading to motor deficits that typically occur in Parkinson's disease, which also involves degeneration of the basal ganglia. This condition is known as "vascular Parkinsonism" (Thanvi, Lo, & Robinson, 2005). We typically associate particular diseases with a constellation of symptoms, but these associations are based on what parts of the brain are most often affected by these disease processes. Neuropsychologists can evaluate the symptoms that would be expected from damage to particular parts of the brain, whatever the cause, and help patients and their families adjust to these profound changes in their lives.

DISCUSSION QUESTIONS

1. Give approximate prevalence rates for delirium among patients with UTIs and what proportion of cases of delirium may be caused by UTIs.

2. You are asked to determine whether an older adult is experiencing delirium or dementia. Describe how you would approach this.

3. State the *DSM-5* diagnostic criteria for major and mild neurocognitive disorder, and differentiate between the two. Indicate how many cognitive domains must be impaired for each to be diagnosed.

4. A patient of yours has been diagnosed with mild neurocognitive disorder possibly due to Alzheimer's disease. They ask you, "so does this mean I have Alzheimer's disease?" Describe how you might answer their question.

5. Describe the two categories of biomarkers of Alzheimer's disease, as put forth in the NIA/AA diagnostic criteria.

6. List the diagnostic criteria for probable and possible Lewy body disease. Explain the symptoms of fluctuating cognition and REM sleep behavior disorder, and describe the relationship between REM sleep behavior disorder and Lewy body disease.

7. Describe the two variants of frontotemporal dementia.

REFERENCES

*Albert, M. S., DeKosky, S. T., Dickson, D., Dubois, B., Feldman, H. H., Fox, N. C., . . . Phelps, C. H. (2011). The diagnosis of mild cognitive impairment due to Alzheimer's disease: Recommendations from the National Institute on Aging–Alzheimer's Association workgroups on diagnostic guidelines for Alzheimer's disease. *Alzheimer's & Dementia, 7,* 270–279. doi:10.1016/j.jalz.2011.03.008

Albrecht, J. S., Liu, X., Smith, G. S., Baumgarten, M., Rattinger, G. B., Gambert, S. R., . . . Zuckerman, I. H. (2015). Stroke incidence following traumatic brain injury in older adults. *Journal of Head Trauma Rehabilitation, 30*(2), E62–E67. doi:10.1097/HTR.0000000000000035

American Psychiatric Association. (2013). *Diagnostic and statistical manual of mental disorders* (5th ed.). Arlington, VA: American Psychiatric Publishing.

Balogun, S. A., & Philbrick, J. T. (2014). Delirium, a symptom of UTI in the elderly: Fact or fable? A systematic review. *Canadian Geriatrics Journal, 17*(1), 22–26. doi:10.5770/cgi.17.90

*Bang, J., Spina, S., & Miller, B. L. (2015). Frontotemporal dementia. *Lancet, 386,* 1672–1682.

Beal, C. C. (2010). Gender and stroke symptoms: A review of the current literature. *Journal of Neuroscience Nursing, 42,* 80–87.

Blumenfeld, H. (2010). *Neuroanatomy through clinical cases* (2nd ed.). New York, NY: Oxford University Press.

Boller, F., & Duykaerts, C. (2003). Alzheimer's disease: Clinical and anatomic issues. In T. E. Feinberg & M. J. Farah (Eds.), *Behavioral neurology and neuropsychology* (2nd ed., pp. 515–544). New York, NY: McGraw-Hill.

Braak, H., & Braak, E. (1991). Neuropathological staging of Alzheimer related changes. *Acta Neuropathology, 82*, 239–259.

Braak, H., Del Tredici, K., Rüb, U., de Vos, R. A. I., Jansen Steur, E. N., & Braak, E. (2003). Staging of brain pathology related to sporadic Parkinson's disease. *Neurobiology of Aging, 24*,197–211.

Buckley, J. S., & Salpeter, S. R. (2015). A risk-benefit assessment of dementia medications: Systematic review of the evidence. *Drugs & Aging, 32*, 453–467. doi:10.1007/s40266-015-0266-9

Chae, J. H. J., & Miller, B. J. (2015). Beyond urinary tract infections (UTIs) and delirium: A systematic review of UTIs and neuropsychiatric disorders. *Journal of Psychiatric Practice, 21*(6), 402–411. doi:10.1097/PRA.0000000000000105

Chan, V., Zagorski, B., Parsons, D., & Colantonio, A. (2013). Older adults with acquired brain injury: A population based study. *BioMed Central Geriatrics, 13*, 97. Retrieved from http://www.biomedcentral.com/1471-2318/13/97

Crutch, S. J., Schott, J. M., Rabinovici, G. D., Murray, M., Snowden, J. S., van der Flier, W. M., . . . Fox, N. C. (2017). Consensus classification of posterior cortical atrophy. *Alzheimer's & Dementia, 13*, 870–884. doi:10.1016/j.jalz.2017.01.014

Emre, M., Aarsland, D., Brown, R., Burn, D. J., Duyckaerts, C., Mizuno, Y., . . . Dubois, B. (2007). Clinical diagnostic criteria for dementia associated with Parkinson's disease. *Movement Disorders, 22*(12), 1689–1707. doi:10.1002/mds.21507

Faul, M., Xu, L., Wald, M. M., & Coronado, V. G. (2010). *Traumatic brain injury in the United States: Emergency department visits, hospitalizations and deaths 2002–2006.* Atlanta, GA: Centers for Disease Control and Prevention, National Center for Injury Prevention and Control. Retrieved from https://www.cdc.gov/traumaticbraininjury/pdf/blue_book.pdf

Ferman, T. J., Smith, G. E., Boeve, B. F., Ivnik, R. J., Petersen, R. C., Knopman, D., . . . Dickson, D. W. (2004). DLB fluctuations: Specific features that reliably differentiate DLB from AD and normal aging. *Neurology, 62*(2), 181–187.

Gearing, M., Mirra, S. S., Hedreen, J. C., Sumi, S. M., Hansen, L. A., & Heyman, A. (1995). The Consortium to Establish a Registry for Alzheimer's Disease (CERAD). Part X. Neuropathology confirmation of the clinical diagnosis of Alzheimer's disease. *Neurology, 45*, 461–466.

*Gorno-Tempini, M. L., Hillis, A. E., Weintraub, S., Kertesz, A., Mendez, M., Cappa, S. F., . . . Grossman, M. (2011). Classification of primary progressive aphasia and its variants. *Neurology, 76*, 1006–1014.

Hodges, J. R., Davies, R., Xuereb, J., Kril, J., & Halliday, G. (2003). Survival in frontotemporal dementia. *Neurology, 61*, 349–354. doi:10.1212/01.WNL.0000078928.20107.52

Howell, M. J., & Schenck, C. H. (2015). Rapid eye movement sleep behavior disorder and neurodegenerative disease. *Journal of the American Medical Association Neurology, 72*, 707–712.

Jagust, W. (2013). Biomarkers and brain connectivity. *Journal of the American Medical Association Neurology, 70*, 1233–1234.

Krinsky-McHale, S. J., & Silverman, W. (2013). Dementia and mild cognitive impairment in adults with intellectual disability: Issues of diagnosis. *Developmental Disabilities Research Reviews, 18*, 31–42. doi:10.1002/ddrr.1126

Lezak, M. D., Howieson, D. B., Bigler, E. D., & Tranel, D. (2012). *Neuropsychological assessment* (5th ed.). New York, NY: Oxford University Press.

Lim, X., Yeo, J. M., Green, A., & Pal, S. (2013). The diagnostic utility of cerebrospinal fluid alpha-synuclein analysis in dementia with Lewy bodies—a systematic review and meta-analysis. *Parkinsonism and Related Disorders, 19*, 851–858.

Lingehall, H. C., Smulter, N. S., Lindahl, E., Lindkvist, M., Engström, K. G., Gustafson, Y. G., & Olofsson, B. (2017). Preoperative cognitive performance and postoperative delirium are independently associated with future dementia in older people who have undergone cardiac surgery: A longitudinal cohort study. *Critical Care Medicine, 45*(8), 1295–1303. doi:10.1097/CCM.0000000000002483

Litvan, I., Goldman, J. G., Tröster, A. I., Schmand, B. A., Weintraub, D., Petersen, R. C., . . . Emre, M. (2012). Diagnostic criteria for mild cognitive impairment in Parkinson's disease: Movement

Disorder Society task force guidelines. *Movement Disorders, 27*(3), 349–356. doi:10.1002/mds
.24893

*McKeith, I. G., Boeve, B. F., Dickson, D. W., Halliday, G., Taylor, J.-P., Weintraub, D., . . . Kosaka, K.
(2017). Diagnosis and management of dementia with Lewy bodies: Fourth consensus report
of the DLB Consortium. *Neurology, 89*, 88–100.

*McKhann, G. M., Knopman, D. S., Chertkow, H., Hyman, B. T., Jack, C. R., Kawas, C. H., . . . Phelps,
C. H. (2011). The diagnosis of dementia due to Alzheimer's disease: Recommendations
from the National Institute on Aging—Alzheimer's Association workgroups on diagnostic
guidelines for Alzheimer's disease. *Alzheimer's & Dementia, 7*, 263–269. doi:10.1016/j.jalz
.2011.03.005

*Nelson, P. T., Alafuzoff, I., Bigio, E. H., Bouras, C., Braak, H., Cairns, N. J., . . . Beach, T. G. (2012).
Correlation of Alzheimer disease neuropathologic changes with cognitive status: A review
of the literature. *Journal of Neuropathology and Experimental Neurology, 71*, 362–381. doi:10.1097
/NEN.0b013e31825018f7

Newell, K. L., Hyman, B. T., Growdon, J. H., & Hedley-Whyte, E. T. (1999). Application of the
National Institute on Aging (NIA)—Reagan Institute criteria for the neuropathological
diagnosis of Alzheimer disease. *Journal of Neuropathology and Experimental Neurology, 58*,
1147–1155.

*O'Brien, J. T., & Thomas, A. (2015). Vascular dementia. *Lancet, 386*, 1698–1706.

Plassman, B. L., Langa, K. M., Fisher, G. G., Heeringa, S. G., Weir, D. R., Ofstedal, M. B., . . .
Wallace, R. B. (2007). Prevalence of dementia in the United States: The Aging, Demographics,
and Memory Study. *Neuroepidemiology, 29*, 125–132. doi:10.1159/000109998

Prince, M., Bryce, R., Albanese, E., Wimo, A., Ribeiro, W., & Ferri, C. P. (2013). The global prevalence of dementia: A systematic review and metaanalysis. *Alzheimer's & Dementia, 9*, 63–75.

Ridley, N. J., Draper, B., & Withall, A. (2013). Alcohol-related dementia: An update of the evidence.
Alzheimer's Research and Therapy, 5(3). Retrieved from http://alzres.com/content/5/1/3

Rizzi, L., Rosset, I., & Roriz-Cruz, M. (2014). Global epidemiology of dementia: Alzheimer's and
vascular types. *BioMed Research International, 2014*. doi:10.1155/2014/908915

Schneider, J. A., Arvanitakis, Z., Bang, W., & Bennett, D. A. (2007). Mixed brain pathologies account
for most dementia cases in community-dwelling older persons. *Neurology, 69*, 2197–2204.

Souza-Talarico, J. N., Carvalho, A. P., Brucki, S. M. D., Nitrini, R., & Ferretti-Rebustini, R. E.
L. (2016). Dementia and cognitive impairment prevalence and associated factors in indigenous populations: A systematic review. *Alzheimer's Disease and Associated Disorders, 30*(3),
281–287.

Thal, D. R., Walter, J., Saido, T. C., & Fändrich, M. (2015). Neuropathology and biochemistry of Aβ
and its aggregates in Alzheimer's disease. *Acta Neuropathology, 129*, 167–182. doi:10.1007/s00
401-014-1375-y

Thanvi, B., Lo, N., & Robinson, T. (2005). Vascular Parkinsonism—an important cause of Parkinsonism in older people. *Age and Ageing, 34*(2), 114–119. doi:10.1093/ageing/afi025

Tiraboschi, P., Salmon, D. P., Hansen, L. A., Hofstetter, R. C., Thal, L. J., & Corey-Bloom, J. (2006).
What best differentiates Lewy body from Alzheimer's disease in early-stage dementia? *Brain,
129*, 729–735.

Tsuang, D., Leverenz, J. B., Lopez, O. L., Hamilton, R. L., Bennett, D. A., Schneider, J. A., . . .
Zabetian, C. P. (2013). ApoE ε4 increases risk for dementia in pure synucleinopathies. *JAMA
Neurology, 70*(2), 223–228. doi:10.1001/jamaneurol.2013.600

U.S. Department of Agriculture & U.S. Department of Health and Human Services. (2015).
2015–2020 Dietary guidelines for Americans (8th ed., Appendix 9). Retrieved from http://health
.gov/dietaryguidelines/2015/guidelines/appendix-9

Vieira, R. T., Caixeta, L., Machado, S., Silva, A. C., Nardi, A. E., Arias-Carrion, O., & Carta, M. G.
(2013). Epidemiology of early-onset dementia: A review of the literature. *Clinical Practice &
Epidemiology in Mental Health, 9*, 88–95.

*Vinters, H. V. (2015). Emerging concepts in Alzheimer's disease. *Annual Review of Pathology: Mech-
anisms of Disease, 10*, 291–319. doi:10.1146/annurev-pathol-020712-163927

*Walker, Z., Possin, K. L., Boeve, B. F., & Aarsland, D. (2015). Lewy body dementias. *Lancet, 386*,
1683–1697.

Weintraub, D., & Hurtig, H. I. (2007). Presentation and management of psychosis in Parkinson's disease and dementia with Lewy bodies. *American Journal of Psychiatry, 164*(10), 1491–1498. doi:10.1176/appi.ajp.2007.07040715

Wu, Y. T., Beiser, A. S., Breteler, M. M. B., Fratiglioni, L., Helmer, C., Hendrie, H. C., . . . Brayne, C. (2017). The changing prevalence and incidence of dementia over time—current evidence. *Nature Reviews Neurology, 13*(6), 327–339. doi:10.1038/nrneurol.2017.63

10

Relationships, Families, and Aging: Changes in Roles With Aging

Rachel L. Rodriguez and J. W. Terri Huh

A long with the global population aging phenomenon, there has been an increase in the diversity of family structures and households across the globe. Several additional factors contribute to the shifting family structures and households, such as improvements in medicine and life expectancy, decreasing rates of fertility, later-life marriages, and increasing rates of divorce, remarriage, cohabitation, lone parenthood, and stepfamily formation. Such growth in the diversity of family structure has also led to changes in the manner in which intergenerational, spousal, sibling, and other kinship relationships function. This in turn affects the way in which older adults receive care and support. Gone is the "pyramid" family structure, with large numbers of people in the younger generations and few in the older generations, only to be replaced with the more vertical, "beanpole" family structure with fewer people in the younger generations and more in the older generations (Bengtson & Silverstein, 1993; Silverstein & Giarusso, 2010). The importance of social factors and relationships on health status has strong support in the literature. Furthermore, the impact of social support for positive health outcomes or providing a buffer from poor health indicates that understanding social networks and relationship status is essential to determining how to promote health in the aging population. This chapter seeks to delve into these societal trends and examine how they are affecting the

---

* Key references in the References section are indicated by an asterisk.

physical health and well-being of the globally aging population. The first section looks into trends in nuptial and relationship status and the impact this has on physical and psychological health of older adults. This is followed by a discussion of the impact of living arrangements for older adults. The chapter concludes with an examination of the impact of caregiving on the psychological well-being of older adults.

NUPTIAL AND RELATIONSHIP STATUS: PREVALENCE AND DEMOGRAPHICS

According to the United Nations report on World Population Ageing (2015), the marital status of older persons varies little across development region (more developed to least developed). The overall proportion of married individuals for both sexes among individuals ages 60 and older in less developed regions is 64%, and approximately 60% in the more developed regions. Regardless of development region, the proportion of married men is much higher (approximately 80%) than for women (slightly below 50%) in this age demographic. A number of factors contribute to this gender difference in marital status, including the fact that older male spouses are more likely to die before their wives, and that men tend to marry younger women (United Nations, Department of Economic and Social Affairs, Population Division, 2015). This then translates into lower remarriage probabilities for older women than for older men, partly because of the reduced availability of men in similar or older age ranges (United Nations, Department of Economic and Social Affairs, Population Division, 2015).

If approximately 60% of the older population is married, then there is a significant portion (~40%) of older adults more than the age of 60 across the world that is not married. The group of unmarried older individuals includes those who are widowed, divorced, or never married. According to U.S. Census data, in 2015 a higher percentage of women aged 65 and older were widowed (34%) compared to their male counterparts (12%). Moreover, 5% of women and 5% of men in this age group fell into the never married category. Divorced and separated (including married/spouse absent) older persons represented only 15% of Americans more than the age of 65 in 2015. However, this percentage has increased since 1980, when approximately 5.3% of the older population were divorced or separated/spouse absent.

Divorce rates—the number of persons divorced per 1,000 married persons—among older men and women have been noticeably increasing over the past decades, especially in the United States. For the more than 50 age group, this is due in part to the aging of the Baby Boomer population (those individuals born between 1946 and 1964). Baby Boomers were the first cohort to divorce and remarry in large numbers during young adulthood. Given that remarriages are more likely than first marriages to end through divorce, this foreshadows that a growing number of older adults may experience divorce (Sweeney, 2010). Indeed, the proportions ever divorced, currently divorced, and married at least twice are highest among individuals aged 50 and older (Kreider & Ellis, 2011).

Another interesting trend among today's unmarried aging population is the increasing rates of dating and cohabitation (a state in which unmarried couples live together in a long-term relationship resembling marriage) among this group. Using data from the 2005 to 2006 National Social Life, Health, and Aging Project, Brown and Shinohara (2013) found that roughly 14% of older single Americans were in a dating relationship. Looking at these rates further, there are significant gender differences in how men and women approach dating relationships later in life. Older men tend to be more interested in formalizing these relationships through marriage than older women (McWilliams & Barrett, 2014; Stevens, 2002). However, both genders report that remarriage can be stressful (de Jong Gierveld, 2002). Older women tend to prefer the companionship of dating as opposed to remarriage, as it allows them to avoid the potential burden of caregiving that marriage can entail in old age (Dickson, Hughes, & Walker, 2005). Maintaining autonomy is also a reason many older women cite for the choice of not entering into a cohabiting relationship or marriage (Dickson et al., 2005; Stevens, 2002). Although older widowed women's interest in remarriage declines with age, the likelihood of having a male companion does not seem to decline (Moorman, Booth, & Fingerman, 2006).

While cohabitation is still relatively rare among older adults, it is accelerating rapidly among older single adults (Brown, Bulanda, & Lee, 2012). While the global prevalence rate of cohabitation among older adults is not known, combining data from Census 2000 and the 1998 Health and Retirement Study (HRS), Brown et al. (2012) estimated that approximately 4% of the unmarried, older adult population in the United States cohabitated. This same study also constructed a portrait of cohabitating older adults in the United States that suggests that more men tend to enter into a cohabitating relationship, and those who choose to cohabitate have lower incomes (particularly women) and are less likely to own their homes than are remarried persons (Brown et al., 2012). Cohabitation is also more common among Blacks and Hispanics than among non-Hispanic Whites (Raley, 1996; Wherry & Finegold, 2004). As these minority groups continued to increase as a proportion of the older population, it is logical to assume that rates of cohabitation among older adults will continue to rise in kind.

EFFECTS OF NUPTIAL AND RELATIONSHIP STATUS ON PHYSICAL AND PSYCHOLOGICAL HEALTH

A large research literature shows that relationships, especially marriage, have an important protective role in supporting physical and psychological health. Studies demonstrate that relationships and social supports can promote health (Clouston & Quesnel-Vallée, 2012), reduce mortality (Gove, 1973; Trovato, 1987; Trovato & Lauris, 1989), maintain function (Clouston, Lawlor, & Verdery, 2014; Unger, McAvay, Bruce, Berkman, & Seeman, 1999), and promote psychological well-being (Thoits, 2011). This section examines the quality of different relationships as a mediator of health and mental health outcomes. The first section reviews marital relationships, on which much research endeavors have focused. This section also includes a review of the role that dissolution of marital unions and other union-level characteristics may play in physical and psychological well-being in late life. The remaining sections include a discussion of other types of relationships, that is, cohabitated unions, sibling relationships, and friendships, and how these relationships may impact physical and psychological health.

Marital Quality and the Effects of Marriage on Physical and Psychological Health

The protective effects of marriage for physical and emotional well-being are widely documented (Carr & Springer, 2010). Married individuals typically display better physical and emotional health while also having longer life spans than unmarried individuals (Holt-Lunstad, Birmingham & Jones, 2008; Pienta, Hayward, & Jenkins, 2000; Waite & Gallagher, 2000). Research repeatedly finds lower rates of chronic illness, physical limitations, disability, and mortality in married individuals when compared to nonmarried counterparts. Studies have often looked to the role of marital quality to determine the protective effects of marriage. Marital quality refers to a married person's assessment of his or her marriage in terms of marital happiness and satisfaction, marital conflict and disagreement, marital interactions, attitudes, and behaviors.

Marriages reporting higher marital happiness and overall better quality are associated with fewer psychological and physical health problems (Choi & Marks, 2008; Kiecolt-Glaser & Newton, 2001; Whisman, 2007). Those reporting poor marital quality also report worse physical health and mental health (Birditt & Antonucci, 2008; Umberson, Williams, Powers, Liu, & Needham, 2006). Data from the 20-year Marital Instability Over the Life Course Study (Booth, Johnson, Amato, & Rogers, 2003) found that respondents in relationships with a low marital quality trajectory had the lowest levels of psychological well-being over time (Dush, Taylor, & Kroeger, 2008).

A recent meta-analysis of 126 published empirical articles over the past 50 years in 11 countries examined the association between marital relationship quality and physical health in over 72,000 individuals and found that greater marital quality was related to better physical health regardless of study design, marital quality measure, and publication year (Robles, Slatcher, Trombello, & McGinn, 2014). Objective health measures included markers of cardiovascular disease and blood pressure, among others. Greater marital quality was associated with better subjective health ratings and better self-rated health and/or lower self-rated symptoms (excluding pain). Moreover, the effects of this meta-analysis demonstrated that poorer marital quality is a risk factor for poorer health outcomes.

This same meta-analysis showed similar effects for the relationship between marital quality and psychological health (Robles et al., 2014). Indeed, greater marital quality was related to greater psychological well-being on a number of indicators including depressive and/or anxiety symptoms, self-esteem, life satisfaction, and happiness. Additionally, diagnosed depression was related to lower marital satisfaction.

There are three main accepted explanations of "how" and "why" marital quality affects health: (a) social, (b) biological/physiological, and (c) social selection. First, social explanations highlight the emotional support and health-enhancing support exchanged in high quality marriages (e.g. Umberson et al., 2006). For example, spouses in high-quality, happy marriages are more likely to encourage each other in engaging in positive healthy behaviors and the avoidance of unhealthy behaviors.

They may encourage better eating habits, physical exercise, compliance with medication, and reduction of smoking and alcohol consumption. On the other hand, those in poorer-quality, unhappy marriages exhibit poorer eating habits, erratic sleep patterns, and higher rates of smoking and substance use (Miller, Hollist, Olson, & Law, 2013). Higher-quality marriages may also buffer the potential negative health effects of life stressors such as work strains, unemployment, and illness (Cohen & Willis, 1985). This is especially important as couples face the physical challenges of aging.

A second explanation focuses on the responses of biological/physiological pathways to close and nurturing relationships. These pathways often affect multiple physiological systems, including cardiovascular, endocrine, immune, metabolic, and sympathetic nervous systems (Robles et al., 2014). For example, negative interactions, such as marital strain and hostility, have been linked with elevated blood pressure, elevated heart rate, and excretion of stress hormones compromising both the cardiovascular and immune systems (Robles & Kiecolt-Glaser, 2003).

Finally, social selection explanations posit that marital quality and health may be mutually influential and that poor physical and mental health may color both one's own and one's spouse's assessment of marital quality (Carr & Pudrovska, 2015). For example, physical or mental health problems may affect one's ability to contribute to the household financially due to inability to maintain employment and/or contribute effectively in the form of completing household chores. Similarly, physical or mental health problems may also inhibit one's ability to provide emotional support central to a good marriage. Indeed, several studies have demonstrated an elevated risk of divorce in couples where one or both spouses have a serious physical or mental health condition (Butterworth & Rodgers, 2006).

While it is clear that marital quality impacts physical and psychological health, it is less clear if these effects vary by gender or race and ethnicity. Research is equivocal in terms of gender, with clinical and laboratory-based studies showing greater female vulnerability to marital strain; however, larger population-based studies detect few if any gender differences (Umberson & Williams, 2005). Surprisingly, not only are there few studies examining racial and ethnic differences in marital quality, there is also little research examining the impact of race and ethnicity on marital quality and health. While some scholars have proposed that the well-documented racial health disparities gap can be partly explained by the fact that Blacks are less likely than Whites to be married, little is known about the impact that marital quality has on these outcomes (Carr & Pudrovska, 2015).

On the other hand, there is growing evidence that the protective effects of marital quality on health vary over the life course. In particular, the deleterious effects of marital stress on health have been shown to intensify with age (Umberson et al., 2006). Henry, Berg, Smith, and Florsheim (2007) hypothesized that unlike other social relationships in which older adults may minimize or leave negative interactions, they are less likely to leave their long-term marital partners. This finding suggests that because older adults are more likely to stay in marriages even with high degrees of marital stress, they remain in a pattern of negative emotions and stressful interactions, which then can create or intensify already-existing health problems.

WHEN MARRIAGE ENDS: IMPACT ON HEALTH AND PSYCHOLOGICAL OUTCOMES

The literature consistently shows that divorced and widowed persons have poorer physical and mental health than their married counterparts. These effects have been documented for a range of outcomes including self-rated health, mortality, cardiovascular disease, chronic illness, smoking-related cancers, functional limitations, depression, and substance use (Hughes & Waite, 2009; Zhang & Hayward, 2006). Moreover, it has been shown that the transition out of marriage, be it through divorce or widowhood, undermines the health of men more than women (Williams & Umberson, 2004). However, the negative health outcomes for marital dissolution are impacted by the quality of the marriage that has ended. Several studies examining the long-term impact of dissolved troubled marriages found gains for physical health and psychological well-being, and health decrements for those who remained married (Hawkins & Booth, 2005; Williams & Umberson, 2004). Similarly, research on widowhood shows that the emotional toll varies based on the quality of the marriage. Those with higher-quality marriages, as measured by warmth, conflict, and dependence experienced worse grief symptoms (Carr et al., 2000). In addition, a recent study looking at the role of marital status and physical function found that large social networks (i.e., having three or more individuals in one's family network) may be enough to offset some of the negative physical consequences of being single, although this study did not differentiate this effect on those who were single due to divorce, becoming widowed, or never married (Clouston et al., 2014).

COHABITATION

Though cohabitation is becoming more common among single adults aged 60 and older, the research into its effects on health and well-being is just beginning. At present, the predominant view is that cohabitation is associated with greater advantages for overall well-being relative to being nonpartnered, but provides fewer economic, psychological, and health benefits relative to being married (Brown et al., 2012; Carr & Springer, 2010; Liu & Reczek, 2012). This finding appears to be especially true for women (Brown et al., 2012). The mechanisms through which this occurs has not yet been fully investigated; however, the underlying theoretical framework is thought to be similar to that proposed for marital unions and described previously.

OTHER SIGNIFICANT RELATIONSHIPS IN LATE LIFE

Marital and romantic partnerships are not the only important relationships during adulthood. Sibling relationships and friendships are also important to physical and psychological well-being, especially in middle and late life. However, unlike marital and romantic relationships that are readily measured in census and other national surveys, investigations of the prevalence and interaction patterns in these relationships are reserved for specialized studies.

Sibling Relationships

Perhaps the longest lasting relationship of an individual's life is the one with his or her surviving sibling(s). It is one of the few adult relationships that can last from childhood to late adulthood, and involves a shared cultural, family, and biological history. Research has shown that many older adults do have contact with their siblings and report these relationships to be meaningful (Bedford, 1997; Connidis & Campbell, 2001). Additionally, the literature states that relationships with siblings can contribute to life satisfaction, higher morale, fewer depressive symptoms, psychological well-being, and a greater sense of emotional security in old age (Cicirelli, 1995).

Though considered second in priority to marital and parent–child relationships, sibling networks are important and a dramatic increase in sibling exchange is often seen in later life (White, 2001). Factors influencing the extent of sibling contact and the importance of the relationship include geographic proximity, being without a partner, and a decrease in contemporaries who can share life review activities. Additionally, the literature suggests that siblings offer more psychological support (companionship, advice, or encouragement) than instrumental support (household assistance, shopping, or financial assistance) in late life. Moreover, relatively few individuals report depending on a sibling for day-to-day needs in old age although they list them as a source of social and emotional support. Cicirelli (1995) found that 60% of respondents said they would help a sibling if their sibling needed their assistance, yet only 7% had actually turned to a sibling as a primary source of assistance during their own time of crisis. It is possible that sibling relations in later life may be viewed as a secondary source of support, available should immediate support resources be limited.

Research has shown that the gender of siblings significantly impacts the emotional closeness of sibling pairs and the extent of contact between siblings. Sister-to-sister and sister-to-brother relationships show greater emotional closeness and more frequency of contact than brother-to-brother relationships (Connidis & Campbell, 2001). Moreover, the closeness of the bond to a sister (by both men and women) was related to reports of less depressive symptoms (Cicirelli, 1989). At the same time, however, more conflict is reported between sister-to-sister relationships than other sibling combinations, which is also related to increased reports of depressive symptoms.

Friendships

Research on friendship in late life is growing both in size and sophistication. Research indicates that although the number of close friendships tends to decrease with age, friendships provide multiple and key sources of support to older adults, including instrumental and emotional support (Blieszner & Roberto, 2004). Friendships across the life span are often characterized by caring, self-disclosure, trust, loyalty, and shared interests, values, and pleasant events (Adams, Blieszner, & De Vries, 2000). Furthermore, while there is variation in the patterns of support received across the life span, strains in friendships tend to decrease over time and levels of positive support tend to remain stable or increase (Birditt, Jackey, & Antonucci, 2009; Newsom, Rook, Nishishiba, Sorkin, & Mahan, 2005). This finding is likely due to the greater tendency among older adults to end nonfamily relationships that are overly negative (Henry et al., 2007).

Close friendships may also evolve into fictive kinship (i.e., considered to be "like family" even though there are no blood or legal ties). When viewed in this way, emotional bonds may be tighter than in other friendships and expectations and obligations greater. These fictive kin friendships play important roles for many older adults who may not have blood relations available to provide support. For example, Chatters and colleagues (1994) note that fictive kin play important roles for older African Americans by extending their family networks. Fictive kin are also of vital importance to gay, lesbian, bisexual, and transgender persons, as well as never-married heterosexual women, all of whom must depend more on friends than relatives for providing social, psychological, and instrumental support (Blando, 2001; Grossman, D'Augelli, & Hershberger, 2000; McDill, Hall, & Turell, 2006).

Whether fictive kin or not, friends contribute to the physical and psychological well-being of older adults in both positive and negative ways. For example, friends can positively affect health by promoting positive health behaviors in terms of diet and exercise, providing information in shared health experiences, and even driving to medical appointments (Gallant, Spitze, & Prohaska, 2007; Moreman, 2008; Roberto & Husser, 2007). On the flip side, however, they can also interfere with health by encouraging negative dietary habits and discouraging exercise.

LIVING ARRANGEMENTS

Living arrangements are often determined by cultural norms regarding coresidence, intergenerational relationships, and family support systems. Most noninstitutionalized older adults fall into one of the following categories: living alone, living with a partner/spouse only, living with a spouse and others, and living with others only. Several factors affect living arrangements among older adults including demographic change, economic resources, and personal preference. As noted previously, in today's more "beanpole" society there are fewer children and grandchildren in the younger generations with whom the older adult may live. Thus, there are fewer multigenerational households and more older individuals living independently, either alone or with a spouse (United Nations, Department of Economic and Social Affairs, Population Division, 2015).

Statistically, at the global level, 40% of the world's population lives independently, with no significant difference by sex (United Nations, Department of Economic and Social Affairs, Population Division, 2015). Almost 50% of women living independently live alone, while only a minority of older men live alone (United Nations, Department of Economic and Social Affairs, Population Division, 2012; United Nations, 2012; United Nations Population Fund & HelpAge International, 2012). However, when looking at the gap in the proportion of individuals living independently based on the development status of the country, the findings are remarkable. Older persons living independently represent approximately 75% of all older individuals in developed countries, but just over 10% in least developed countries and 25% in the less developed regions. In sum, living independently is the dominant living arrangement in developed countries, but is rare among older people in developing countries

(United Nations, Department of Economic and Social Affairs, Population Division, 2015). However, as the world's population continues to age, it is logical to assume that these percentages will likely stay the same or even rise in number.

It should be noted that, depending on the individual older person, living independently may or may not be the desired situation. For example, in developing countries, where the older person may have access to limited resources to sustain themselves and must rely heavily on familial support, living independently or alone could be a disadvantage or even an indication of neglect (United Nations, Department of Economic and Social Affairs, Population Division, 2015). However, in a more developed society where the older adult has sufficient economic resources and/or access to public support, the ability to live independently may be considered a badge of honor, a sign of economic self-sufficiency and overall independence.

One question then worthy of asking is: If older adults are not living independently, are they living in the homes of others or have others moved into their homes? By looking at the reported *Head of Household* in survey and census data on a global scale, it was determined that 15% of older men and 31% of older women live in households in which neither themselves nor their spouses are heads of the households (United Nations, Department of Economic and Social Affairs, Population Division, 2015). This in turn can mean that these older adults are "subordinate" to others (often younger members) within the household, meaning that they do not control resources or make decisions regarding the household. The positive news is that only a minority of older persons are subordinate to younger household members (United Nations, Department of Economic and Social Affairs, Population Division, 2015). However, when household subordinate relationships develop, the data show that: (a) women are more likely to be subordinate to men (45% vs. 13%, respectively), and (b) subordination is greater in less developed regions as compared to more developed regions (28% vs. 9%; United Nations, Department of Economic and Social Affairs, Population Division, 2015).

The next logical questions then are: If older adults are not living independently, with whom are they living? Who are the others in the household? These questions are difficult to answer as they will depend on a variety of factors, ranging from the needs of the older adult to the country of residence's level of economic development, political structure, and cultural norms. For example, in the United States, economic challenges from the recent Great Recession have led to an overall rise in multigenerational households from 12% in 1980 to 16% in 2008 (Pew Research Center, 2010). Moreover, those aged 65 and older in a multigenerational household have increased from 17% in 1980 to 20% in 2008 (Pew Research Center, 2010). These economic challenges also led to a similar rise in the proportion of shared households from 17% in 2007 to 18.7% in 2010 (Mykyta & Macartney, 2012). Kim, Links, and Waite (2016) examined the rise in multigenerational households using a nationally representative data base of community-dwelling older adults (aged 57–85) in the United States. The authors found that while 48.5% of respondents lived with their spouses and 27.6% lived alone, 11% lived in a household that included other members. The substantial majority (90%–99%) of individuals living with the older adults were siblings, other relatives including adult children, other in-laws, and friends.

Taking marital status into consideration, older unmarried women and men are increasingly likely to live with their own children. But older women are more likely to do so than older men. According to the Pew Research Center, in 2014, 15% of older women were unmarried and living with their children, compared with 5% of older men (Stepler, 2016). Moreover, this share has increased by 3 percentage points for women and 2 points for older men since 1990. The share of unmarried older adults living with relatives (other than children) or nonrelatives has also grown slightly, from 6% in 1990 to 8% in 2014. And once again, reasons driving this increase in multigenerational households are complex and dependent on a number of sociocultural factors.

CAREGIVING PATTERNS AND OUTCOMES

With the increasing numbers of older adults living well into their 80s and 90s, the number of health-related challenges they face also increases, many of them impairing the individual's ability to independently care for himself or herself. This has subsequently given rise to informal caregiving as part of the health care landscape for many older adults. Informal caregiving is defined as the act of providing unpaid assistance and support to family members or acquaintances who may have physical, psychological, or developmental needs. There are two general functional domains of caregiving that have been identified: instrumental and emotional. Caregiving is defined by assistance with activities of daily living (ADLs) such as bathing, toileting, transporting from one place to another; and assistance with instrumental ADLs such as managing finances, medications, appointments, shopping, preparing meals, and accessing different services. Caregiving also involves significant emotional support such as listening, counseling, and companionship, and providing behavioral support such as managing challenging behaviors.

While in many cases, particularly when the caregiver is a family member, caregiving is considered "unpaid," the true costs as calculated in terms of hours of care provided is estimated to be $470 billion (Reinhard, Feinberg, Choula, & Houser, 2015). However, there are other costs in terms of both physical and mental health outcomes of caregivers, who themselves need significant supports to maintain their abilities to provide care to older adults. This section focuses on the general trends in caregiving in aging, then describes adult children as caregivers, followed by spouses as caregivers, and then grandparents as custodial caregivers. The impact on caregiving has been studied using theoretical frameworks such as Pearlin's stress process theory (Pearlin, Mullan, Semple, & Skaff, 1990), which indicates that caregivers' characteristics such as gender, race/ethnicity, age, and social roles are important components that influence the caregivers' experience of stress and burden, which may then result in depression, anxiety, and declining physical health. Each subsection therefore reviews characteristics and factors that may lead to different health and mental health outcomes in the various types of caregivers focusing primarily on family caregivers.

GENERAL TRENDS IN CAREGIVING

There are approximately 43.5 million caregivers who provide care to an individual with significant disability, and 34.2 million of them care for an adult who is 50 years or older (AARP Public Policy Institute, 2015). More than 15 million caregivers provide care to an individual with dementia or other neurocognitive disease (Alzheimer's Disease Facts and Figures, 2014). Although the rate of caregiving for individuals with dementia is a relatively minor proportion compared to those providing care to an adult or child with only physical impairments, the duration (as amounts of years and numbers of hours per week) of providing care is significantly higher for caregivers of individuals with dementia. Forty three percent of caregivers of individuals with Alzheimer's disease or other neurocognitive disorders provide 1 to 4 years or more of care compared to 33% of other caregivers (Alzheimer's Disease Facts and Figures, 2014). In terms of hours of care provided per week, one study found that caregivers of patients with dementia provided on average 17 hours per week versus 12.4 hours per week provided by caregivers of other medical problems (Ory, Hoffman, Yee, Tennstedt, & Schulz, 1999). Individuals with dementia require significantly more care of all types, which may vary through the course of the disease but, generally, the degree of care increases exponentially as the care recipient declines in all aspects of their functioning.

Consistent within the literature is the finding that more women tend to provide care than men (Ory et al., 1999; Pinquart & Sörensen, 2003). However, a recent study (Pedersini & Annunziata, 2015) from the 2013 National Health and Wellness Survey of eight countries suggests that the gender gap may be closing, as this study found that half of identified caregivers were men (Pedersini & Annunziata, 2015). In terms of relationship to the older care recipient, the majority of caregivers tend to be spouses and adult children, with a 2003 meta-analysis reporting relatively even numbers of spouses (45.8%) and adult children (43.8%; Pinquart & Sörensen, 2003). Rates of caregiving by ethnicity seem to follow similar patterns with 62% of White, 13% of Black, 12% of Hispanic, and 6% of Asian Americans providing care (AARP Public Policy Institute, 2015). In terms of ethnocultural variations in caregiving characteristics, a meta-analysis (Pinquart & Sörensen, 2005) comparing three ethnic minority groups (African American, Hispanic, and Asian) to White found that ethnic minority caregivers were younger, were less likely to be a spouse, and were more likely to have lower levels of education and income. These results suggest that there are larger proportions of adult child caregivers among ethnic minority groups than in White groups.

In terms of custodial grandparents, according to the U.S. Census Bureau 2010 report, 3% of U.S. households have both grandparents and grandchildren living in the same house (Ellis & Simmons, 2014). Therefore, approximately 64 million grandparents live with grandchildren in their homes, and the U.S. Census Bureau identified that 42% (or 27 million) are primary caregivers for their grandchildren. Of the grandparents living with grandchildren, 54% of American Indian and Alaskan Native, 48% of African American, 43% of non-Hispanic White, 31% of Hispanic, 30% of Native Hawaiian and Pacific Islander, and 15% of Asian Americans were primary caregivers. A review by Hayslip and Kaminski (2005) reported that custodial grandparenting was most common among White grandparents (51%) but followed very closely by African American grandparents (38%). Furthermore, 33% of grandparents who were responsible for raising their grandchildren were raising them without the parents present. Custodial grandparents who were heads of the households were more likely to be married and less likely to be divorced, with 66% of them married, and 2% of them living with a cohabitating partner. Head of household custodial grandparents (20%) were also more likely to live in poverty compared to grandparents living in parent-maintained households (17%). This is likely due to the statistics showing that 44% of grandparents who were heads of the households did not work in the past year but also did not live with additional family members who were working to provide financial assistance (Ellis & Simmons, 2014; U.S. Census Bureau, 2015).

PHYSICAL, PSYCHOLOGICAL, AND EMOTIONAL IMPACTS OF CAREGIVING

There are high rates of reported emotional stress in caregivers, which tend to be highest when providing care for a close relative, such as a spouse or parent (45% and 44%, respectively; AARP Public Policy Institute, 2015). Approximately 17% of all caregivers report fair or poor health in the report published by the AARP Policy Institute, which is higher than that reported by the general public in the Centers for Disease Control and Prevention/National Center for Health Statistics (CDC/NCHS), National Health Interview Survey (Clarke, Ward, Freeman, & Schiller, 2015). Providing more hours of care, caring for someone with mental health issues, coresiding with care recipients, and providing medical/nursing tasks were noted to elevate risk for negative health (AARP Public Policy Institute, 2015). It is therefore not surprising that individuals caring for someone with dementia may be particularly at risk for negative health and mental health outcomes.

Studies demonstrate that caregivers of individuals with dementia experience more stress, and worse physical and mental health effects compared to other caregivers of individuals with other care needs or noncaregivers of the same age (Ory et al., 1999; Pinquart & Sörensen, 2003). These studies also support the finding that caregivers experience more burden due to behavior problems compared to physical and cognitive impairments (Pinquart & Sörensen, 2003). There have been many studies comparing spouses to adult children as caregivers with results suggesting that spouses might experience higher rates of burden (Ott, Sanders, & Kelber, 2007; Rinaldi et al., 2005) and other studies showing that adult child caregivers may experience more burden (Andren & Elmstahl, 2007; Chappell, Dujela, & Smith, 2014). However, rates of mental health issues when they develop may be similar regardless of the relationship between caregivers and care recipients (Covinsky et al., 2003; Pinquart & Sörensen, 2003). Caregivers seem to develop depression (Covinsky et al., 2003) or anxiety (Mahoney, Regan, Katona, & Livingston, 2005) when the care recipient is younger age with greater disease severity, which encompasses ADL function and behavioral symptoms. Caregiver characteristics that seem to predict development of depression or anxiety were being female, being a spouse or adult child, perceived poor health of the caregiver, low levels of financial resources, more hours caregiving, and functional impairment of the caregiver (Covinsky et al., 2003).

ADULT CHILDREN AS CAREGIVERS

Caregivers who are adult children often face the situation in which they are likely to have both family and nonfamily responsibilities, which can affect their health over time. Two theories have been developed referring to the possible impact of having multiple roles on the mental health of middle-aged caregivers. The first refers to role strain or role conflict perspective, which posits that multiple roles (employee, caregiver, spouse, etc.) may result in more challenges with restricted time and resources of the individual (Mui, 1992) and therefore the adult child caregiver may experience more depressive symptoms. The second theory is the role enhancement perspective, which posits that there may be positive consequences from holding multiple roles, such as status security and status enhancement, which may be protective against depression. This second theory posits that different roles may give purpose, meaning, and direction in the adult child caregiver's life (Thoits, 1983). Several studies have looked at employment, being married, and coresiding with children as factors that may determine which of these theories may best explain how depression may or may not develop in adult child caregivers.

In general, studies support the finding that adult child caregivers tend to have more depression compared to similar aged individuals who are not caregivers (Barnett, 2015; Chumbler, Pienta, & Dwyer, 2004; Reid & Hardy, 1999). However, based on the theories described previously, there may be different pathways toward developing depression in these caregivers based on the types of additional roles ascribed. There have been mixed findings of employment and being a caregiver, with some studies suggesting that such a combination could lead to higher levels of depression (Stoller & Pugliesi, 1989), supporting the role conflict theory, and others reporting lower levels of depression (measured as emotional strain related to caregiving; Williams et al., 2008) for those who were employed, supporting the role enhancement theory. It is possible that gender may play a moderating role between employment and caregiving, in that female caregivers spend more hours on care and are more likely to provide personal assistance (Pinquart & Sörensen, 2006), and therefore the balance between caregiving and employment may become more strained for women. However, one study looking at the relationship between employment status and caregiving suggests that long-term patterns are more supportive of better psychological and physical health for married and employed caregivers (Barnett, 2015) regardless of gender. Chumbler et al. (2004) showed that gender may indeed have a role but in terms of the gender of the care recipient. The adult child caregiver seemed to experience more depression when they were caring for their father or father-in-law. The study by Chumbler et al. (2004) also showed that being employed and married decreased depressive symptoms, which seems to also support the previously described protective role of marriage in depression. As a whole, these studies seem to provide more support for the role enhancement theory and that being married and employed may mitigate the potential strain of caregiving and therefore reduce depression for these caregivers.

According to the *Caregiving in the U.S. 2009 Report* (National Alliance for Caregiving & AARP, 2009), approximately 13% of caregivers also live with grown children and some studies describe that 36% to 50% of adult children caregivers coreside with children (Barnett, 2015). A popular view in the U.S. culture is that of the "sandwich generation." This is the idea that adult child caregivers are experiencing further stress due to their dual caregiving roles of caring for children and parents. Some studies of middle-aged parents with coresiding children suggest that these middle-aged adults indeed have worse mental health outcomes (Evenson & Simon, 2005;

Mitchell, 2000). These studies are supportive of the role strain hypothesis. If adult children, prior to becoming caregivers, had mental health problems, adding the role of caregiver to an aging parent could lead to even worse mental health outcomes. However, a recent study was inconclusive as to whether having coresiding children relates to lower mental health of caregivers (Barnett, 2015). In addition, several studies seem to show that having children while also being a caregiver to an older parent does not significantly lead to depression (Dautzenberg, Diederiks, Philipsen, & Tan, 1999; Dautzenberg et al., 2000; Martin 2000; Chumbler et al., 2004). The more influential factor regardless of whether there was a coresiding child seems to be employment and marital status, in that being employed and married seem to confer better mental health.

As noted earlier, the caregivers of older adults from ethnic minority groups are more likely to be younger and more likely to be an adult child than White caregivers. Studies of health and mental health in these groups show that 27% of Hispanic caregivers report poorer health compared to 15% of White caregivers and 15% of Asian American caregivers (National Alliance for Caregiving & AARP, 2009). However, a meta-analysis (Pinquart & Sörensen, 2005) found higher levels of subjective well-being and perceived uplifts of caregiving in ethnic minority caregivers compared to White caregivers, although the effects were small. In addition, the study found lower levels of burden but slightly worse physical health in ethnic minority caregivers, but again the effects were noted to be small. Medium-sized effects were found in filial obligation beliefs, which involves a sociocultural expectation or sense of duty to care for one's parents, with stronger beliefs reported by ethnic minority caregivers. These filial obligation beliefs may mitigate the negative impacts of caregiving and explain the differences between ethnic minority and White caregivers in terms of higher subjective well-being and perceived uplifts from caregiving. When looking at mental health, different levels of depression were found among different ethnic minority caregivers, with lower depression found in African American caregivers but higher rates of depression in Hispanic and Asian American caregivers compared to White caregivers. The higher rates of perceived uplifts seem to be carried primarily by African American and Hispanic Caregivers since results showed that Asian American caregivers had similar findings as White caregivers. It appears, therefore, that having a minority status seems to provide both advantages and disadvantages to caregivers, which vary according to ethnic groups.

OLDER ADULTS AS CAREGIVERS

Much of the research focus in the area of mental health outcomes of caregiving has been on spouse caregivers of patients with dementia. More than two thirds of dementia caregivers are spouses or longtime partners (Alzheimer's Association, 2014). As mentioned in an earlier section, spouses may experience more caregiving burden but similar rates of depression as adult child caregivers (Pinquart & Sörensen, 2003). Burden is typically defined as perceived stress related to caregiving that can lead to many negative physical and emotional consequences, whereas depression is defined as significant clinical symptoms that lead to functional impairment. Spouses themselves are older and have their own health problems and related functional impairments, which may impact their abilities to provide care and lead to the perception of more burden. The results of the meta-analysis on caregivers' stress showed that the care recipients' impairments and caregivers' involvement had stronger effects on burden than on depression (Pinquart & Sörensen, 2003). This was thought to indicate that burden tapped into caregiving-specific factors, whereas depression may be suggestive of low levels of general subjective well-being, which is influenced by many other variables not entirely dependent on caregiving. This seems to suggest that although spouse caregivers are impacted by caregiving responsibilities, there may be other characteristics that serve as protective factors against depression in spouse caregivers.

There seem to be some gender differences in the negative impacts of caregiving, with wives experiencing more adverse impacts than husbands. Another meta-analysis by Pinquart and Sörensen (2006) looking at gender differences showed that wives experienced more burden and depression compared to husbands but the effects were noted to be small. They also found differences in physical health with poorer health in wives compared to husbands. However, subjective well-being did not differ between the groups. The findings were also explained by the lower levels of social support experienced by women, which contributed to the variance in the differences on burden and depression.

Not all caregivers have a completely negative appraisal of their caregiving role, and the stress or burden that is perceived is not all-encompassing or a guarantee of developing mental health problems. Studies indicate that not all caregivers will experience mental health problems despite high rates of stress and feelings of burden, although rates of mental health issues in caregivers are still higher than seen in the average community-dwelling older adult population. Studies indicate a range of 10% to 32% of caregivers in their samples reporting symptoms of depression (Covinsky et al., 2003; Jennings et al., 2015; Mahoney et al., 2005). Pinquart and Sörensen (2003) report caregivers who perceived positive aspects of caregiving, such as feeling useful or experiencing closeness to the care recipient, had lower levels of burden and depression. Given the minority of caregivers who are found with depression and anxiety, these findings suggest that many caregivers perceive that there can be benefits to being in a caregiving role such as improvements in problem-solving abilities, self-understanding, and self-efficacy. These reports also show support for the role enhancement theory. Perhaps theories of marital quality may provide additional explanation, although caregiving literature has not looked specifically at marital quality as a modifying variable to understand how depression may develop in spouse caregivers.

Grandparents as Custodial Caregivers

Similar to spouse caregivers of older care recipients, grandparents serving as custodial caregivers face challenges due to experiencing poor health and fewer resources. In addition, the challenges facing grandparents taking on the role of custodial caregiving are colored by various societal markers such as substance use, incarceration, teen pregnancy, emotional problems, and parental death of the child care recipient (Fuller-Thomson, Minkler, & Driver, 1997; Jendrek, 1994; Pearson, Hunter, Cook, Ialongo, & Kellam, 1997; Pinson-Millburn, Fabian, Schlossberg, & Pyle, 1996). These complex reasons through which grandparents become custodial caregivers may have unique contributions to the physical and mental health consequences of custodial caregiving. Given some of the reasons that grandparents may become custodial caregivers, most studies report elevated rates of negative physical and mental health outcomes. Oftentimes, the children are at high risk of exhibiting emotional and behavioral problems. Furthermore, there is likely to be intrafamily conflicts and strain that suggests reduced social supports for grandparents becoming custodial caregivers (Musil, Warner, Zauszniewski, Jeanblanc, & Kercher, 2006). Many studies point to the negative personal, interpersonal, and economic consequences, as well as reduced physical and mental health status of grandparents in custodial caregiving roles (Butler & Zakari, 2005; Hayslip, Shore, Henderson, & Lambert, 1998; Minkler & Fuller-Thomson, 1999). A study by Minkler and Fuller-Thompson (1999) found that significantly more custodial caregivers (32%) compared to non-caregiving grandparents (25%) were likely to have limitations in at least one or more ADLs, and reported lower satisfaction with health and lower self-rated health status. In a small study of 17 custodial caregivers by Butler and Zakari (2005), 35% of custodial grandparents reported that their health was worse than it was 5 years prior to becoming a custodial caregiver and 47% reported high total stress scores due to anxiety related to child rearing. Minkler, Fuller-Thomson, Miller, & Driver (2000) found greater incidence of depression, diabetes, hypertension, and insomnia in custodial caregivers compared to noncaregivers of the same age (Minkler et al., 2000).

The importance of social support may be critical in considering the factors that may particularly emphasize or alleviate the negative consequences of custodial caregiving (Gerard, Landry-Meyer, & Roe, 2006; Hayslip & Kaminski, 2005). Social isolation can enhance or contribute to the risk for depression (Musil, 1998). By the same token, when social supports are in place, custodial caregivers report elevated well-being, role satisfaction, and self-rated health, and less parental role strain (Emick & Hayslip, 1999). For custodial caregivers raising children with problems, more social support was associated with increased tolerance of a grandchild's disruptive or irritating behavior (Hayslip et al., 1998). Therefore, support can be a critical crutch or alleviate the physical and mental health consequences of caregiving, although these results are based on small, convenience samples of grandparent custodial caregivers.

There is also a cultural context that sheds light on the critical role of social supports. Pruchno (1999) reported that Black custodial grandmothers were more likely to be coresiding with peers, and to have been raised in families where multiple generations were living together compared to White custodial grandmothers (Pruchno, 1999). Research also demonstrates that grandparent custodial caregivers who avail themselves of extended family for help and who participate in special programs have better overall outcomes than those who do not use such resources (Lumpkin, 2008). Another study by Musil, Warner, Zauszniewski, Wykle, and Standing (2009) explored the role of resourcefulness (i.e., coping skills or the capacity to deal with stresses), and social support (i.e., in the form of instrumental or emotional support (Musil et al., 2009). Musil et al. (2009) found that both factors held important protective roles by mitigating depression or the impact of other stressors such as intra-family strain. The protective role of resourcefulness and social support also seemed to hold across the cultural groups included in the sample (66% White, 30% Black, 0.4% American Indian or Alaskan Native, 3% Hispanic or Latino, and 2.5% multiracial).

CONCLUSION

The world's rapidly aging population is the result of a confluence of factors, including declining rates of fertility and improvements in mortality. This demographic trend is reconstructing families and relationships across the life span. Indeed, today's older adults experience much more diversity in terms of relationships, roles, and living arrangements than past cohorts. Studies from multiple sources point to strong associations between social and interpersonal factors, that is, familial and other relationships, with health, well-being, and mental health, across the age spectrum. The association of these factors and their impact in late life takes on additional complex roles and hold important implications for health care policies.

Several theoretical viewpoints on relationships, supported by various research studies and population surveys, seem to all infer a protective role that relationships can provide toward well-being and mental health in late life; married or cohabitating individuals, having sibling relationships, or development of fictive kin relationships all show protection from depression or minimize effects of depression. The rising rates of dating and cohabitation among single older adults suggest more promising health and mental health outcomes for some single older adults. Furthermore, studies indicate that the quality of these relationships is a decisive factor resulting in better health and mental health outcome. Considering that there are still relatively high rates of marriage in today's society, and that many older adults tend to retain high-quality relationships in late life, it is perhaps not so surprising that rates of mental health disorders in late life tend to be low, approximately 3% to 10% in the community. The protective role of high-quality relationships also shows up when looking at caregiving relationships. While caregivers do have higher rates of mental health problems than same-aged peers who are not caregivers, the type and quality of relationships between the caregiver and the care recipient as well as the social supports available to the caregiver can alleviate some of the negative consequences of becoming a caregiver.

The findings of this review call for the need to consider policy changes to enhance and ensure the well-being and quality of life for the aging population. First, the overwhelmingly positive impact of social support networks for both physical and mental health outcomes in late life cannot be denied. Unfortunately, there remain millions of older adults who do not have the benefit of these social networks or relationships. Older adults with limited resources, or without strong social networks, or both, can find themselves in a catastrophic situation when also faced with multiple health problems and their concomitant physical, cognitive, or functional decline. For example, older adults who may need assistance with ADLs, but do not have adequate financial resources or social support networks, may need to become dependent on government assistance programs. As noted previously, many more older women than men are placed in this vulnerable position.

The second finding that calls for a change to current sociopolitical policy lies with the impact of caregiving. Studies exploring factors that led to worse outcomes for caregivers showed that those who were unemployed or unmarried had the worst mental and physical health outcomes. This suggests the need to develop or enhance community resources to aid these caregivers and potentially buffer and/or address caregivers' physical and mental health concerns. Additional findings from the review implicate the need for more policy changes to support working caregivers through, for example, provision of additional community and government assistance services, improving leave policies, and more flexible work schedules. In terms of future research directions, there is a particular dearth of research on ethnic, cultural, and other diversity variations in cohabitation or kinship networks, which would significantly move the literature forward in understanding more nontraditional social networks as possible sources of support. There is also a need for understanding of relationship quality in the caregiving literature, which may contribute to improvements in interventions for caregivers with greater mental health needs. Finally, there is not enough known about the social and mental health needs of older adults who provide care for their adult children due to disability, physical health conditions, mental health conditions, or for other reasons.

In conclusion, this chapter identified multiple exciting and interesting movements in the dynamic shifts in family structure, households, and living arrangements. These changes in turn have been impacting the way relationships, family structure, and social networks may alter mental and physical health particularly later in life. The primary take-home message from this chapter is that high-quality relationships are important factors in maintaining physical and mental health, and function later in life. These findings further implicate the need to bolster the social networks that exist, and particularly to find adequate means to support similar functions when social networks are in short supply or nonexistent.

DISCUSSION QUESTIONS

1. Provide three possible explanations of how marital quality affects health.

2. Describe two theories about the mental health of caregivers who are adult children.

3. Describe trends in nuptial and relationship status among older adults.

4. Discuss how the dissolution of marriage, through either divorce or widowhood, impacts the physical and emotional well-being of the older adult.

5. Compare two specific ways that caregiving burden might differ for caregivers of patients with dementia versus caregivers of patients with other conditions.

6. Identify three culture specific factors that may impact caregiving stress or depression.

REFERENCES

AARP Public Policy Institute. (2015, June). *Caregiving in the U.S. 2015 report*. Retrieved from http://www.aarp.org/content/dam/aarp/ppi/2015/caregiving-in-the-united-states-2015-report-revised.pdf

Adams, R. G., Blieszner, R., & De Vries, B. (2000). Definitions of friendship in the third age: Age, gender, and study location effects. *Journal of Aging Studies, 14*, 117–133. doi:10.1016/s0890-4065(00)80019-5

Alzheimer's Association. (2014). Alzheimer's disease facts and figures. *Alzheimer's & Dementia, 10*(2), 1–75.

Andren, S., & Elmstahl, S. (2007). Relationships between income, subjective health and caregiver burden in caregivers of people with dementia in group living care: A cross-sectional community-based study. *International Journal of Nursing Studies, 44*, 435–446. doi:10.1016/j.ijnurstu.2006.08.016

Barnett, A. E. (2015). Adult child caregiver health trajectories and the impact of multiple roles over time. *Research on Aging, 37*, 227–252. doi:10.1177/0164027514527834

Bedford, V. (1997). Sibling relationships in middle adulthood and old age. In R. M. Blieszner & V. H. Bedford (Eds.), *Handbook on aging and the family* (pp. 201–222). Westport, CT: Greenwood.

Bengtson, V. L., & Silverstein, M. (1993). Families, aging, and social change: Seven agendas for 21st-century researchers. *Annual Review of Gerontology and Geriatrics, 13*, 15–38.

Birditt, K. S., & Antonucci, T. C. (2008). Life sustaining irritations? Relationship quality and mortality in the context of chronic illness. *Social Science and Medicine, 67*(8), 1291–1299.

Birditt, K. S., Jackey, L. M. H., & Antonucci, T. C. (2009). Longitudinal patterns of negative relationship quality across adulthood. *Journals of Gerontology Series B: Psychological Sciences & Social Sciences, 64B*, 55–64. doi:10.1093/geronb/gbn031

Blando, J. A. (2001). Twice hidden: Older gay and lesbian couples, friends, and intimacy. *Generations, 25*, 87–89.

*Blieszner, R., & Roberto, K. A. (2004). Friendship across the life span: Reciprocity in individual and relationship development. In F. R. Lang & K. L. Fingerman (Eds.), *Growing together: Personal relationships across the lifespan* (pp. 159–182). Cambridge, United Kingdom: Cambridge University Press.

Booth, A., Johnson, D., Amato, P., & Rogers, S. (2003). *Marital instability over the life course: A six-wave panel study, 1980, 1983, 1988, 1992–1994, 1997, 2000.* (Version 1) [Data file]. Ann Arbor, MI: Interuniversity Consortium for Political and Social Research.

Brown, S. L., Bulanda, J. R., & Lee, G. R. (2012). Transitions into and out of cohabitation in later life. *Journal of Marriage and Family, 74*, 774–793. doi:10.1111/j.1741-3737.2012.00994.x

Brown, S. L., & Shinohara, S. K. (2013). Dating relationships in older adulthood: A national portrait. *Journal of Marriage and Family, 75*, 1194–1202. doi:10.1111/jomf.12065

Butler, F. R., & Zakari, N. (2005). Grandparents parenting grandchildren: Assessing health status, parental stress, and social supports. *Journal of Gerontological Nursing, 31*, 43–54.

Butterworth, P., & Rodgers, B. (2006). Concordance in the mental health of spouses: Analysis of a large national household panel survey. *Psychological Medicine, 36*, 685–697.

Carr, D., House, J. S., Kessler, R. C., Nesse, R. M., Sonnega, J., & Wortman, C. (2000). Marital quality and psychological adjustment to widowhood among older adults: a longitudinal analysis. *Journals of Gerontology Series B: Psychological Sciences and Social Sciences, 55B*, S197–S207.

Carr, D., & Pudrovska, T. (2015). Marital quality & health. In J. D. Wright (Ed.), *International Encyclopedia of the Social & Behavioral Sciences* (2nd ed., Vol. 14). Oxford, United Kingdom: Elsevier, 512–517.

Carr, D., & Springer, K. W. (2010). Advances in families and health research in the 21st century. *Journal of Marriage and Family, 72*, 743–761. doi:10.1111/j.1741-3737.2010.00728

Chappell, N. L., Dujela, C., & Smith, A. (2014). Spouse and adult child differences in caregiving burden. *Canadian Journal on Aging, 33*, 462–472. doi:10.1017/S0714980814000336

Chatters, L. M., Taylor, R. J., & Jayakody, R. (1994). Fictive kinship relations in black extended families. *Journal of Comparative Family Studies, 25*, 297–312.

Choi, H., & Marks, N. F. (2008). Marital conflict, depressive symptoms, and functional impairment. *Journal of Marriage and Family, 20*, 377–390.

Chumbler, N. R., Pienta, A. M., & Dwyer, J. W. (2004). The depressive symptamatology of parent care among the near elderly. The influence of multiple role commitments. *Research on Aging, 26*, 330–351.

Cicirelli, V. G. (1989). Feelings of attachment to siblings and well-being in later life. *Psychology and Aging, 4*, 211–218.

Cicirelli, V. G. (1995). *Sibling relationships across the life span*. New York, NY: Plenum Press.

Clarke, T. C., Ward, B. W., Freeman, G., & Schiller, J. S. (2015, September). Early release of selected estimates based on data from the January–March 2015 National Health Interview Survey. Retrieved from https://www.cdc.gov/nchs/data/nhis/earlyrelease/earlyrelease201509.pdf

Clouston, S., Lawlor, A., & Verdery, A. M. (2014). The role of partnership status on late-life physical function. *Canadian Journal on Aging, 33*, 413–425.

Clouston, S., & Quesnel-Vallée, A. (2012). The role of defamilialization in the relationship between partnership and self-rated health: A cross-national comparison of Canada and the United States. *Social Science & Medicine, 75*, 1342–1350.

Cohen, S., & Wills, T. A., (1985). Stress, social support and the buffering hypothesis. *Psychological Bulletin, 98*, 10–57.

Connidis, I. A., & Campbell, L. D. (2001). Closeness, confiding, and contact among siblings in middle and late adulthood. In A. Walker, M. Manoogian-O'Dell, L. McGraw, & D. L. White (Eds.), *Families in later life* (pp. 149–155). Thousand Oaks, CA: Pine Forge Press.

Covinsky, K. E., Newcomer, R., Fox, P., Wood, J., Sands, L., Dane, K., & Yaffe, K. (2003). Patient and caregiver characteristics associated with depression in caregivers of patients with dementia. *Journal of General Internal Medicine, 18*, 1006–1014.

Dautzenberg, M. G. H., Diederiks, J. P. M., Philipsen, H., Stevens, F. C. J., Tan, F. E. S., & Vernooij-Dassen, M. J. F. J. (2000). The competing demands of paid work and parent care: Middle-aged daughters providing assistance to elderly parents. *Research on Aging, 22*, 165–87.

Dautzenberg, M. G. H., Diederiks, J. P. M., Philipsen, H., & Tan, F. E. S. (1999). Multigenerational caregiving and well-being: Distress of middle-aged daughters providing assistance to elderly parents. *Women & Health, 29*, 57–74.

de Jong Gierveld, J. (2002). The dilemma of repartnering: Considerations of older men and women entering new intimate relationships in later life. *Ageing International, 27*, 61–78. doi:10.1007/s12126-002-1015-z

Dickson, F. C., Hughes, P. C., & Walker, K. L. (2005). An exploratory investigation into dating among later-life women. *Western Journal of Communication, 69*, 67–82. doi:10.1080/10570310 500034196

Dush, C. M. K., Taylor, M. G., & Kroeger, R. A. (2008). Marital happiness and psychological well-being across the life course. *Family Relations, 57*, 211–226.

Ellis, R. R., & Simmons, T. (2014, October). Coresident grandparents and their grandchildren: Population characteristics. *US Census*. Retrieved from http://www.census.gov/content/dam/Census/library/publications/2014/demo/p20-576.pdf

*Emick, M. A., & Hayslip, B., Jr. (1999). Custodial grandparenting: Stresses, coping skills, and relationships with grandchildren. *International Journal of Aging and Human Development, 48*, 35–61.

Evenson, R. J., & Simon, R. (2005). Clarifying the relationships between parenthood and depression. *Journal of Health and Social Behavior, 46*, 341–358.

Fuller-Thomson, E., Minkler, M., & Driver, D. (1997). A profile of grandparents raising grandchildren in the United States. *Gerontologist, 37*, 406–411.

Gallant, M. P., Spitze, G. D., & Prohaska, T. R. (2007). Help or hindrance? How family and friends influence chronic illness self-management among older adults. *Research on Aging, 29*, 375–409. doi:10.1177/0164027507303169

Gerard, J. M., Landry-Meyer, L., & Roe, J. G. (2006). Grandparents raising grandchildren: The role of social support in coping with caregiving challenges. *International Journal of Aging and Human Development, 62*, 359–383.

Gove, W. (1973). Sex, marital status, and mortality. *American Journal of Sociology, 79*, 45–67.

Grossman, A. H., D'Augelli, A. R., & Hershberger, S. L. (2000). Social support networks of lesbian, gay, and bisexual, adults 60 years of age and older. *Journal of Gerontology: Psychological Sciences, 55B*, P171–P179.

Hawkins, D., & Booth, A. (2005). Unhappily ever after: Effects of long-term, low-quality marriages on well-being. *Social Forces, 84*, 445–465.

*Hayslip, B., Jr., & Kaminski, P. L. (2005). Grandparents raising their grandchildren: A review of the literature and suggestions for practice. *Gerontologist, 45,* 262–269.

Hayslip, B., Jr., Shore, R. J., Henderson, C. E., & Lambert, P. L. (1998). Custodial grandparenting and the impact of grandchildren with problems on role satisfaction and role meaning. *Journals of Gerontology Series B: Psychological Sciences and Social Sciences, 53,* S164–S173.

Henry, N. J. M., Berg, C. A., Smith, T. W., & Florsheim, P. (2007). Positive and negative characteristics of marital interaction and their association with marital satisfaction in middle-aged and older couples. *Psychology and Aging, 22,* 428–441.

Holt-Lunstad, J., Birmingham, W., & Jones, B. Q. (2008). Is there something unique about marriage? The relative impact of marital status, relationship quality, and network social support on ambulatory blood pressure and mental health. *Annals of Behavioral Medicine, 35,* 239–244. doi:10.1007/s12160-008-9018-y

Hughes, M. E., & Waite, L. J. (2009). Marital biography and health at midlife. *Journal of Health and Social Behavior, 50,* 344–358.

Jendrek, M. P. (1994). Grandparents who parent their grandchildren: Circumstances and decisions. *Gerontologist, 34,* 206–216.

Jennings, L. A., Reuben, D. B., Evertson, L. C., Serrano, K. S., Ercoli, L., Grill, J., . . . Wenger, N. S. (2015). Unmet needs of caregivers of individuals referred to a dementia care program. *Journal of the American Geriatrics Society, 63,* 282–289. doi:10.1111/jgs.13251

Kiecolt-Glaser, J. K., & Newton, T. L. (2001). Marriage and health: His and hers. *Psychological Bulletin, 127,* 825–839.

Kim, J., Links, A., & Waite, L. J. (2016). Complex households and the distribution of multiple resources in later life: Findings from a national survey. *Research on Aging, 38,* 150–77. doi:10.1177/0164027515581421

Kreider, R. M., & Ellis, R. (2011). *Number, timing, and duration of marriages and divorces: 2009 (Current Population Reports, P70-125).* Washington, DC: U.S. Census Bureau.

Liu, H., & Reczek, C. (2012). Cohabitation and U.S. adult mortality: An examination by gender and race. *Journal of Marriage and Family, 74,* 794–811. doi:10.1111/j.1741-3737.2012.00983.x

Lumpkin, J. R. (2008). Grandparents in a parental or near-parental role. *Journal of Family Issues, 29,* 357–372.

Mahoney, R., Regan, C., Katona, C., & Livingston, G. (2005). Anxiety and depression in family caregivers of people with Alzheimer disease: The LASER-AD study. *American Journal of Geriatric Psychiatry, 13,* 795–801. doi:10.1176/appi.ajgp.13.9.795

Martin, C. D. (2000). More than the work: Race and gender differences in caregiving burden. *Journal of Family Issues, 21,* 981–1005.

McDill, T., Hall, S. K. & Turell, S. C. (2006). Aging and creating families: Never-married heterosexual women over forty. *Journal of Women & Aging, 18,* 37–50.

McWilliams, S., & Barrett, A. E. (2014). Online dating in middle and later life: Gendered expectations and experiences. *Journal of Family Issues, 35,* 411–436.

Miller, R. B., Hollist, C. S., Olson, J., & Law, D. (2013). Marital quality and health over 20 years: A growth curve analysis. *Journal of Marriage and Family, 75,* 667–680.

Minkler, M., & Fuller-Thomson, E. (1999). The health of grandparents raising grandchildren: Results of a national study. *American Journal of Public Health, 89,* 1384–1389.

Minkler, M., Fuller-Thomson, E., Miller, D., & Driver, D. (2000). Grandparent caregiving and depression. In B. Hayslip & R. Goldberg-Glen (Eds.), *Grandparents raising grandchildren: Theoretical, empirical, and clinical perspectives* (pp. 207–220). New York, NY: Springer.

Mitchell, B. A. (2000). The refilled "nest": Debunking the myth of families in crisis. In E. M. Gee & G. M. Guttman (Eds.), *The overselling of population aging: Apocalyptic demography, intergenerational challenges, and social policy* (pp. 80–99). Toronto, Ontario, Canada: Oxford University Press.

*Moorman, S. M., Booth, A., & Fingerman, K. L. (2006). Women's romantic relationships after widowhood. *Journal of Family Issues, 27,* 1281–1304. doi:10.1177/0192513X06289096

Moreman, R. D. (2008). Best friends: The role of confidantes in older women's health. *Journal of Women & Aging, 20,* 149–167.

Mui, A. C. (1992). Caregiver strain among black and white daughter caregivers: A role theory perspective. *Gerontologist, 32*(2), 203–212.

Musil, C. M. (1998). Health, stress, coping, and social support in grandmother caregivers. *Health Care for Women International, 19,* 441–455. doi:10.1080/073993398246205

Musil, C. M., Warner, C. B., Zauszniewski, J. A., Jeanblanc, A. B., & Kercher, K. (2006). Grandmothers, caregiving, and family functioning. *Journals of Gerontology Series B: Psychological Sciences and Social Sciences, 61,* S89–98.

Musil, C., Warner, C., Zauszniewski, J., Wykle, M., & Standing, T. (2009). Grandmother caregiving, family stress and strain, and depressive symptoms. *Western Journal of Nursing Research, 31,* 389–408. doi:10.1177/0193945908328262

Mykyta, L., & Macartney, S. (2012). Sharing a household: Household composition and economic well-being: 2007–2010. *Current Population Report* (pp. 60–242). Washington, DC: U.S. Census Bureau.

National Alliance for Caregiving & AARP. (2009). *Caregiving in the U.S.: 2009* (pp. 1–72). Retrieved from http://www.caregiving.org/data/Caregiving_in_the_US_2009_full_report.pdf

Newsom, J. T., Rook, K. S., Nishishiba, M., Sorkin, D. H., & Mahan, T. L. (2005). Understanding the relative importance of positive and negative social exchanges: Examining specific domains and appraisals. *Journal of Gerontology: Psychology Science, 60B,* 304–312. doi:10.1093/geronb/60.6.P304

Ory, M. G., Hoffman, R. R., 3rd, Yee, J. L., Tennstedt, S., & Schulz, R. (1999). Prevalence and impact of caregiving: A detailed comparison between dementia and nondementia caregivers. *Gerontologist, 39,* 177–185.

Ott, C. H., Sanders, S., & Kelber, S. T. (2007). Grief and personal growth experience of spouses and adult-child caregivers of individuals with Alzheimer's disease and related dementias. *Gerontologist, 47,* 798–809.

*Pearlin, L. I., Mullan, J. T., Semple, S. J., & Skaff, M. M. (1990). Caregiving and the stress process: An overview of concepts and their measures. *Gerontologist, 30,* 583–594.

Pearson, J. L., Hunter, A. G., Cook, J. M., Ialongo, N. S., & Kellam, S. G. (1997). Grandmother involvement in child caregiving in an urban community. *Gerontologist, 37,* 650–657.

Pedersini, R., & Annunziata, K. (2015). Cross-country profile of adult caregivers. *Value Health, 18,* A739. doi:10.1016/j.jval.2015.09.2838

Pew Research Center. (2010). *The return of the multi-generational family household.* Washington, DC: Pew Research Center.

Pienta, A. M., Hayward, M. D., & Jenkins, K. R. (2000). Health consequences of marriage and retirement years. *Journal of Family Issues, 21,* 559–586.

*Pinquart, M., & Sörensen, S. (2003). Associations of stressors and uplifts of caregiving with caregiver burden and depressive mood: A meta-analysis. *Journals of Gerontology Series B: Psychological Sciences and Social Sciences, 58,* P112–P128.

*Pinquart, M., & Sörensen, S. (2005). Ethnic differences in stressors, resources, and psychological outcomes of family caregiving: A meta-analysis. *Gerontologist, 45,* 90–106.

Pinquart, M., & Sörensen, S. (2006). Gender differences in caregiver stressors, social resources, and health: An updated meta-analysis. *The Journals of Gerontology, 61B,* P33–P45.

Pinson-Millburn, M., Fabian, E., Schlossberg, N., & Pyle, M. (1996). Grandparents raising grandchildren. *Journal of Counseling and Development, 74,* 548–554.

Pruchno, R. (1999). Raising grandchildren: The experiences of black and white grandmothers. *Gerontologist, 39,* 209–221.

Raley, R. K. (1996). A shortage of marriageable men? A note on the role of cohabitation in black–white differences in marriage rates. *American Sociological Review, 61,* 973–983.

Reid, J., & Hardy, M. (1999). Multiple roles and well-being among midlife women: Testing role strain and role enhancement theories. *Journals of Gerontology Series B: Psychological Sciences and Social Sciences, 54,* S329–S338.

Reinhard, S. C., Feinberg, L. F., Choula, R., & Houser, A. (2015). Valuing the Invaluable. *Insight on the Issues, 104,* 1–25.

Rinaldi, P., Spazzafumo, L., Mastriforti, R., Mattioli, P., Marvardi, M., Polidori, M. C., . . . Mecocci, P. (2005). Predictors of high level of burden and distress in caregivers of demented patients: Results of an Italian multicenter study. *International Journal of Geriatric Psychiatry, 20,* 168–174. doi:10.1002/gps.1267

Roberto, K. A., & Husser, E. K. (2007). Social relationships: Resources and obstacles to older women's health adaptations and well-being. In T. J. Owens & J. J. Suitor (Eds.), *Advances in life course research: Interpersonal relations across the life* (pp. 383–410). New York, NY: Elsevier Science.

Robles, T. F., & Kiecolt-Glaser, J. K. (2003). The physiology of marriage: Pathways to health. *Physiology & Behavior, 79*, 409–416.

Robles, T. F., Slatcher, R. B., Trombello, J. M., & McGinn, M. M, (2014). Marital quality and health: A meta-analytic review. *Psychological Bulletin, 140*, 140–187. doi:10.1037/a0031859

Silverstein, M., & Giarrusso, R. (2010). Aging and family life: A decade review. *Journal of Marriage and Family, 72*, 1039–1058.

Stepler, R. (2016, February). *Smaller share of women ages 65 and older are living alone: More are living with spouse or children.* Washington, DC: Pew Research Center.

Stevens, N. (2002). Re-engaging: New partnerships in late-life widowhood. *Ageing International, 27*, 27–42. doi:10.1007/s12126-002-1013-1

Stoller, E. P., & Pugliesi, K. L. (1989). Other roles of caregivers: Competing responsibilities or supportive resources. *The Journals of Gerontology: Series B, 44*, S231–S238.

Sweeney, M. M. (2010). Remarriage and stepfamilies: Strategic sites for family scholarship in the 21st century. *Journal of Marriage and Family, 72*, 667–684.

Thoits, P. A. (1983). Multiple identities and psychological well-being: A reformulation and test of the social isolation hypothesis. *American Sociological Review, 48*, 174–187.

Thoits, P. A. (2011). Mechanisms linking social ties and support to physical and mental health. *Journal of Health and Social Behavior, 52*, 145–161. doi:10.1177/0022146510395592

Trovato, F. (1987). A longitudinal analysis of divorce and suicide in Canada. *Journal of Marriage and the Family, 49*, 193–203.

Trovato, F., & Lauris, G. (1989). Marital status and mortality in Canada: 1951-1981. *Journal of Marriage and the Family, 51*, 907–922.

Umberson, D., & Williams, K., 2005. Marital quality, health, and aging: Gender equity? [Special Issue II] *Journal of Gerontology Series B: Psychological Sciences and Social Sciences, 60B*, 109–112.

Umberson, D., Williams, K., Powers, D. A., Liu, H., & Needham, B. (2006). You make me sick: Marital quality and health over the life course. *Journal of Health and Social Behavior, 47*, 1–16. doi:10.1177/002214650604700101

Unger, J. B., McAvay, G., Bruce, M. L., Berkman, L., & Seeman, T. (1999). Variation in the impact of social network characteristics on physical functioning in elderly persons: MacArthur Studies of Successful Aging. *The Journals of Gerontology Series B: Psychological Sciences and Social Sciences, 54*, S245–S251.

United Nations, Department of Economic and Social Affairs, Population Division. (2012). Population ageing and development: Ten years after Madrid. Population Facts. No. 2012/4. Retrieved from http://www.un.org/en/development/desa/population/publications/pdf/popfacts/popfacts_2012-4.pdf

United Nations, Department of Economic and Social Affairs, Population Division. (2015). *World Population Ageing 2015* (ST/ESA/SER.A/390). Retrieved from http://www.un.org/en/development/desa/population/publications/pdf/ageing/WPA2015_Report.pdf

United Nations Population Fund & HelpAge International (2012). *Ageing in the twenty-first century: A celebration and a challenge.* United Nations Population Fund (UNFPA), New York, NY, and HelpAge International, London, UK.

U.S. Census Bureau. (2015). *Current population survey, annual social and economic supplement, Table A1. Marital status of people 15 years and over, by age, sex, and personal earnings.* Washington, DC: U.S. Census Bureau.

Waite, L. J. & Gallagher, M. (2000). *The case for marriage.* New York, NY: Broadway Books.

Wherry, L., & Finegold, K. (2004). Marriage promotion and the living arrangements of black, Hispanic, and white children. In *New federalism: National survey of America's families* (Publication No. B-61). Washington, DC: The Urban Institute. Retrieved from https://www.urban.org/sites/default/files/publication/57786/311064-Marriage-Promotion-and-the-Living-Arrangements-of-Black-Hispanic-and-White-Children.PDF

Whisman, M. A. (2007). Marital distress and DSM-IV psychiatric disorders in a population-based survey. *Journal of Abnormal Psychology, 116*, 638–643.

White, L. K. (2001). Sibling relationships over the life course: A panel analysis. *Journal of Marriage and the Family, 63,* 555–568.

Williams, K., & Umberson, D., (2004). Marital status, marital transitions, and health: A gendered life course perspective. *Journal of Health and Social Behavior, 45,* 81–98.

Williams, S. W., Williams, C. S., Zimmerman, S., Munn, J., Dobbs, D., & Sloane, P. D. (2008). Emotional and physical health of informal caregivers of residents at the end of life: The role of social support. *Journals of Gerontology, Series B, Psychological Sciences and Social Sciences, 63*(3), S171–S183.

Zhang, Z., & Hayward, M. (2006). Gender, the marital life course, and cardiovascular disease in late midlife. *Journal of Marriage and Family, 68,* 639–657.

11

Aging, Work, and Retirement

Harvey L. Sterns and Cynthia McQuown

W ork plays a major role in our lives. It provides an organizing force in our activities and helps form our self-concept. Who we are and how we see ourselves
is influenced by our work. The study of aging focusing on the employment and
retirement issues of middle-aged and older workers is called industrial gerontology
(Sterns & Alexander, 1987). The aging of the work force creates such issues as choosing to work longer, early retirement by choice or imposed, career patterns, finances,
and health and disability. This chapter addresses many of these issues.

DEFINING WORK

Before a discussion of retirement, a discussion of work is in order. Work is intertwined with all aspects of a person's development. Intellectual, emotional, social,
and physical factors affect one's work and work can affect every aspect of a person's
life (Papalia, Sterns, Feldman, & Camp, 2007). It is important to understand that a
job can be any activity performed for pay and may be temporary or transient, whereas
occupation may refer to a regular or relatively permanent field of work or means of
livelihood. A profession typically refers to an occupation that requires college or postgraduate training, usually comprising a life's work at its end (Papalia et al., 2007). In
summary, a person's work life may consist of a series of jobs, or it may be appropriate to talk about a person's career or careers. Jobs end but work is always present.
There are household chores such as doing laundry, cleaning the house, mowing the

---

* Key references in the References section are indicated by an asterisk.

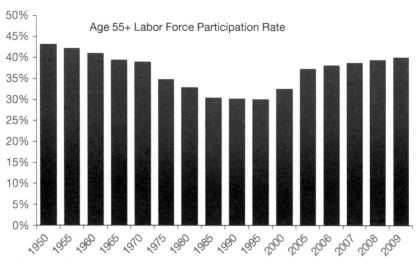

Figure 11.1 Participation rate at older ages levels off and begins to rise.
Source: Bureau of Labor Statistics, http://data.bls.gov/PDQ/outside.jsp?survey=ln

lawn, and so forth. These work activities continue all through life (Sterns & Huyck, 2001).

Many adult and older adult workers are continuing to work and have stated as a group for some time that they plan to work longer (see Figure 11.1; Sterns & Sterns, 1995, 2013).

This desire to work longer has been tracked through a gradual evolution in the approaches to writings on aging, work, and retirement (Czaja & Sharit, 2009; Hedge, Borman, & Lammlein, 2006; Rothwell, Sterns, Shultz & Adams, 2007; Spokus, & Reaser, 2008; Sterns & Alexander, 1987; Sterns & Doverspike, 1988; Sterns & Huyck, 2001). For organizations, it is important for managers to have a clear understanding of what the aging workforce means in terms of planning, training, and past history knowledge management. It is critical that management and executives have a clear understanding of the legal obligations to workers in terms of equal access to training, objective evaluation, and promotion. For some individuals, disabilities that co-occur with age may become more common, such as arthritis or cardiovascular disease. Nonnormative changes, as discussed in Chapter 1, may result in potential overlap between the Americans With Disabilities Act (ADA, 1990) and the Age Discrimination in Employment Act (ADEA, 1967, 1978, and 1986). Such changes are more severe than normative age related changes, and may include issues regarding mobility following a stroke, visual changes due to macular degeneration, or a major loss of hearing. Organizational management must not be driven by stereotypes, but rather have a clear understanding of the specific approaches that will take advantage of the embedded knowledge of adult and older adult workers, retaining the best workers, and retraining workers to ensure they are fully competent and have the requisite skills to maximally perform. Organizations must also address ergonomic alterations to support worker success.

AGEISM

It is of utmost importance that older adults are not treated as one homogeneous age group. The life-span perspective emphasizes the unique development of each individual and this is especially true of health. There is greater variability in the older population compared to the younger population. Reporting older workers as a single group can distort the reality of health and aging. Today's view of aging and work gives the impression that workers have many choices in how they carry out their work; however, there is a great deal of evidence that ageism persists in employment situations and the most insidious is when those ageist ideas are internalized by older adults themselves (Levy & Banaji, 2002).

Any examination of aging and work must address the role of ageism. Ageism is a term first coined by Robert Butler in 1969: "Ageism can be seen as a process of systematic stereotyping of and discrimination against people because they are old, just as racism and sexism accomplished this with skin color and gender" (Butler, 1973, p. 12). Butler further delineates three distinguishable yet interrelated aspects of ageism: "1. Prejudicial attitudes toward older people, old age, and the aging process, which also includes the attitudes that older adults hold of themselves; 2. Discriminatory practices against older people; and 3. institutional practices and policies that perpetuate stereotypes about older people that reduce their opportunity for life satisfaction, and undermine their personal dignity" (p. 249). An example of one of the most pervasive types of ageism is through language and word use. Wilkinson and Ferraro (2002) identify from 30 years of ageism research that the word "ageism" reveals much about societal perceptions of older people. Another example is that the *Journals of Gerontology* and *The Gerontologist* have adopted an editorial policy regarding the use of terms such as elderly or aged. Instead, language that emphasizes personhood such as older person or adult and older adult worker is seen as more appropriate. This has bearing on the world of work because the way in which managers and younger coworkers communicate with older adult workers may have the potential of being demeaning, with less care taken to remain age neutral.

Negative perceptions of aging predate even Butler's observations. Ageist ideas remain prevalent in both the world of work and in the beliefs of older workers themselves. Such negative thinking is harmful to older workers' opportunities at work and their health (Levy & Banaji, 2002; Robbins, 2015). Ageism is a type of prejudice for all groups: women, minorities, lesbian, gay, bisexual, transgender, questioning, (LGBTQ), and disabled. All will age and face the impact of ageism. Palmore (2005) developed the *Facts on Aging Quiz*. Data from the use of this survey suggest that most people know little about aging and their perceptions about older people are negative (Palmore, 2005). Holding these ageist notions affects employer attitudes regarding advancing, training, retaining, and hiring older adults (Lahey, 2008; Posthuma & Campion, 2009).

How we talk about older workers has changed over time. How an older worker is defined may vary depending on the perspective taken. There are six unique ways of defining who is an older worker: chronological, functional, psychosocial, organizational, life-span developmental, and psychology of work (Sterns & Doverspike, 1988; Sterns & Miklos, 1995; Sterns & Sterns, 2013).

Chronological age is the earliest and most common approach of defining older workers. The ADEA (1967) and its amendments (1978, 1986) define an older worker as any individual 40 and older who is still an active worker (Snyder & Barrett, 1988; Sterns & Doverspike, 1988; Sterns, Doverspike, & Lax, 2005). Chronological age has been favored by courts in the assessment of individual performance capacity. Chronological age has consistently been used as a way to evaluate job performance when it is believed that there are no other specific means of accurately measuring performance. Commercial airline pilots, for example, are still subject to mandatory retirement, now at 65 raised from 60, based on their chronological age.

Functional age focuses on the individual's performance to define the person's age. Functional age is presented as a single index that combines assessments based on biological and psychological changes. These changes take into account the range of abilities as well as the changes in skill, wisdom, and experience (Birren & Stafford, 1986). These changes may either increase or decrease in the individual. The index is an indication of how the person performs compared to the average individual of a given age. For example, a 50-year-old individual who can run a mile as fast as the average 25-year-old has a functional age of 25. Two examples of functional age approaches are physical abilities analysis and functional capacity assessment, discussed later in the chapter.

Psychosocial definitions of older workers focus on three issues: (a) the age at which society perceives an individual to be older, (b) the social attitudes regarding older workers, and (c) possible implications in employment settings when labeling a worker as "older." When a worker is perceived as older, either by others or oneself, the attitudes others have toward older workers and the impact of labeling a worker as "older" are central issues. How a worker is viewed may be a function of his or her longevity in the organization, and changes within the organization that no longer use the older worker's skill set or render the worker's skill set as irrelevant. In recent decades, there has been considerable change in organizations' views about how older workers are perceived, both positive and negative. Research in the 1970s and 1980s found that negative perceptions about older workers included being regarded as more difficult to train, less receptive to technological changes, more accident prone, less promotable, and less motivated (Schwab & Heneman, 1978). On the positive side, older adults were perceived as more dependable, cooperative, conscientious, consistent, and knowledgeable (Schwab & Heneman, 1978). In the 1990s, perceptions changed such that a sizeable minority of older workers desired to continue working (Sterns & Sterns, 1995). Most recently, older workers are perceived as likely to continue working, due in equal parts to a desire to be active and financial necessity (Rix, 2011). The stereotypes of older workers remain (Posthuma & Campion, 2009). Older workers today are still viewed as having less flexibility, less energy, lack of interest in training, and greater health problems. They are also positively stereotyped as more loyal and reliable (Sterns & Miklos, 1995). The pychosocial view would suggest that negative perceptions can harm an older worker and contribute to age discrimination and ageism.

The organizational approach is the aging perspective that focuses on understanding the roles of individuals in an organization and the impact of the mix of ages of personnel on the organization as a whole. This perspective emphasizes expertise, seniority, and tenure rather than age. An organization is considered old when the average age of its members is older. For example a start-up software company may have an average age in the 30s with tenures of employees less than 1 year, whereas an established manufacturing company may have an average age of 45 and tenures of 15 years or more. As the average age of personnel increases, attitudinal and financial demands on the organization may change. This approach is most concerned with the nature and interactions of the organization. The mix of cognitive and physical requirements determined by the activities of the personnel as a whole is an important consideration when examining the impact of aging on workers in an organization. For the start-up, software languages and programming are likely changing quickly, whereas in manufacturing environments the change is likely much more gradual, with rare discontinuous sudden changes.

The life-span orientation combines each of the aforementioned approaches with an understanding that people are dynamic and that behavioral change occurs over the entire working life of individuals. The emphasis in this approach is the recognition of substantial individual differences as people age (Baltes, Reese, & Lipsitt, 1980; Bowen, Noack, & Staudinger, 2011; Sterns, 1986). As discussed in Chapter 1, individuals are influenced by normative age-graded, biological, and environmental influences (physical and cognitive changes as one ages), normative history-graded factors (generational events), and nonnormative influences unique to every individual. These normative and nonnormative influences interact to influence and steer an individual's career path. Over time, they determine the strengths and limitations, the skills and experience that an individual brings to their organizational role. Each worker begins with different potentials and each person will improve and decline uniquely.

Finally, the psychology of work perspective (Blustein, Kenna, Gill, & DeVoy, 2008) goes beyond the traditional approaches of industrial/organizational and vocational psychology. It formally considers the impact of social barriers that prevent individuals from fully achieving their potentials. It focuses on the realities of individual working lives as they are experienced regardless, or perhaps specifically because, they are not pursuing a hierarchical self-managed career. This perspective is particularly helpful for understanding those individuals who are challenged by a poor regional economy, disability or addictions, or work limitations due to care of children, a spouse, or older loved ones.

These six definitions of older workers increase our understanding of how the potential impact of future technological changes, employment opportunities, and incentives to remain in the work force are understood and interpreted. Also to be considered is whether an individual has a career track or experiences a disconnected series of jobs over their lifetime of work. Individuals with more education have better abilities to adapt and succeed financially over their working lifetimes.

THE ADULT AND OLDER ADULT WORKFORCE

The phenomenon of the increasing numbers of older individuals in the United States has been forecast for decades. In particular, low-wage older workers, those making $10 per hour or less, often minorities, now represent 38.1% of those ages 35 to 64, up from 30% in 1979 (Schmitt & Jones, 2012). For a summary of changes in workforce participation rates see Table 11.1 (BLS, 2012). Social policy planners have used these demographic changes over time to modify the protections, entitlements, services, and benefits received by this large and growing group. With the leading edge of the Baby Boom generation reaching 65, the challenges of its impact on work force participation, role in continued work and retirement, and representation in entitlement programs, has become a mainstream issue.

Equally important is the perspective of the worker who is now fully responsible for self-managing both career and retirement. Since the 1970s, organizations have moved away from paternalism and maternalism, and workers are increasingly responsible for themselves (Hall & Mirvis, 1996; Sterns & Kaplan, 2003). That means that issues such as career updating, training to maintain expertise, and decisions to change careers are individual decisions alone. How a person experiences his or her work role and how work life continues to evolve for the person's life span determine the meaningfulness of work or how self-relevant work is (Carstensen, 2009). In particular, the positive work experiences impact decisions to continue working. Individual experiences in their work life are now being explored and are important elements in understanding individual decisions about employment (Sterns & Chang, 2010; Sterns & Kaplan, 2003).

There is a significant body of literature outlining age-related deficits that older workers have to overcome in order to successfully remain in the workforce (Rothwell et al., 2008). Some of these adverse stressors include changes in cognitive capacity, sensory decline, musculoskeletal decline, and motor deficits. Older workers must also contend with their changing roles in the workforce as well as potentially confounding roles at home, such as caregiver. Changes in the work environment may also increase levels of adversity for the older worker. Not only can the physical environment pose stressors but attitudes of supervisors and coworkers also have an effect. Negative attitudes can be reflected in offering updating and training only to younger staff, not considering older workers for new assignments, or allowing stereotypes about older workers to influence management decisions instead of valid assessment relevant to the work to be performed.

The ADEA of 1967, amended in 1978 and 1986, marked the beginning of protecting workers older than 40 from discrimination in the workplace and afforded most workers the ability to decide when to exit the workforce. Before the adoption of the age discrimination and employment act, the expected age to exit the workforce was late 50s or early 60s. Given the average life span of adult men and women to be 84.3 and 86.6, respectively (Social Security Administration, 2016), the issue of how long to work, how, when, and whether to leave the workforce has become increasingly diverse. Whereas retirement has been viewed as a particular stage in the life of the career, retirement may now be part of a complex set of decisions facing an older worker, which may be as unique as the individual himself or herself.

ADEA has provided a legal basis for older workers to remain in the work force as long as they are able and choose to do so, except for in the occurrence of a bona fide occupational qualification (BFOQ). The BFOQ affords the opportunity to establish an age limit, if the case can be made that certain age-related changes would impair an employee's ability to perform the required skills of the job. Sterns (1986) proposed a model of career development that is not linked to age, which is consistent with the finding that there is little support for career change linked to age (Sterns & Miklos, 1995).

Another reason people are working longer is that the Social Security Act was amended in 1983 to a gradual increase in "full retirement age" from 65 years of age if born 1937 or earlier in annual increments to 67 for those born 1960 or later. This approach of raising the age for the full retirement benefit was to preserve the solvency of the Social Security Trust Funds. This change was in recognition of the fact that people are living longer and many are in better health. It was felt that people could remain in the workforce for longer periods of time. Individuals can choose to retire as early as 62 with a reduction in payment to offset the longer time they will receive payments. Individuals can delay retirement after their "full retirement age" and receive increased payments (see Social Security website: www.ssa.gov). However, the age for signing up for Medicare remains 65 and waiting longer may lead to higher costs for Part B and Part D. Even if a person is still employed and has health insurance, he or she must sign up at 65 to lock in his or her benefits. Social Security will need to be further amended; however, if no changes are made, benefits may be 75% of current benefits under the worst estimates. Possible approaches to solve future shortfall include having people pay Federal Income Contribution Act (FICA) tax on all income received, means testing, and adjustment to the Cost of Living Index. Social Security was never intended to be the only income in retirement. It was expected that people would have pensions and savings as well.

These changes in Social Security's benefit calculation rules now allow workers to delay receiving benefits, with the incentive of receiving more benefits if they wait (Wheaton & Crimmins, 2013). The steady shift from companies providing defined benefits plans (pension based on years of service and retirement salary level, now available to about 22% of workers) to offering defined contribution plans (pension based on money contributed by the worker with some level of contribution by employer) and the expectation that retirees will bear the costs of their health care insurance have also extended the average person's work life and changed how and when that person will retire. The world of work has evolved from one that incentivized early retirement to one that, in many cases, discourages it. Presently, the future of Social Security has become a national concern. Worries about the ability of this entitlement to sustain future generations is a matter of evolving changes within government policy.

According to Pitt-Catsouphes, Smyer, Matz-Costa, and Kane (2007) from the Sloan Center on Aging & Work, one of the dimensions in which workers can be viewed is through the generational lens. Each cohort is not only similar in age but has also been exposed to significant historical events that may alter their views or values expressed in the workplace. Examples may include the technological savvy of the Millennials (born between 1981 and 1999) as they grew up with easy access to computers and the Internet, or the Baby Boomers (born between 1946 and 1964) being exposed to significant loss and turmoil during the Vietnam War. Adversity may be encountered by (a) an individual misusing the generational lens and overgeneralizing certain characteristics of a "generation" to all members of the cohort instead of treating each employee as an individual or (b) different views, values, or work ethic causing conflict during work responsibilities requiring team interaction and collaboration. The relational pattern of resilience is easily applied here as the older worker must count on positive peer interactions and support to maintain a successful work environment. As retirement evolves into a process rather than an event, it becomes harder to examine why people retire and what factors may influence it.

HISTORY OF RETIREMENT

A number of recent books address the complexity and richness of the history and major trends in career, work, and retirement (Blustein, 2013; Hedge & Borman, 2012; Wang, 2013; Wang, Olson, & Shultz, 2013). Several historical changes have significantly influenced the nature of retirement (Quinn, 2010; Zickar, 2013). In most countries, the idea of retirement is of recent origin, introduced during the late 19th and early 20th centuries. Previously, low life expectancy and the absence of pension arrangements meant that most workers continued to work until death. Germany was the first country to introduce retirement, in 1889.

At one time, companies depended on a large and loyal workforce and, to that end, provided defined benefits plans and health care in retirement. The assurance of wealth and continued health care ensured that older workers would be willing to leave the workforce (Wang, 2012). Retirement took hold in many industrialized countries during the late 19th and early 20th centuries, but in less developed countries most people still work until they are no longer physically able. A brief history of retirement in the United States illustrates the continual evolution of this life transition (Sterns & Kaplan, 2003). Through the 1700s and 1800s retirement was uncommon. Older adults were valued for wisdom and experience, and forced retirement would have been contrary to the social ideology of the time.

The emergence of retirement in the late 19th century was influenced by the rise of labor unions, which sought worker privileges based on seniority. Management's response was that older workers were less able and more expensive. Prevailing theories of older adults as worn out and useless reinforced policies that assumed older adults were incompetent to work. Mandatory retirement became a mechanism for removing older workers so as to provide job opportunities for younger workers. The economic depression of the 1930s was the impetus for the Social Security system that, together with company-sponsored pension plans often negotiated by labor unions, led to the almost universal retirement at age 65. The Social Security Act of 1935 was passed with age 65 based on the need to help older adults in poverty and the resources available to fund the program at the time of its inception (Papalia et al., 2007; Richardson 1993). During World War II benefits packages including health care and pension were developed when wages were required to be held constant, due to the Stabilization Act of 1942.

Ideas regarding retirement have been evolving over the past eight decades, often influenced by the advancing knowledge in life-span development and gerontology. The ADEA (1986) also changed the nature of retirement, by eliminating a mandatory retirement age for all but a few select occupations. Under the act, anyone older than 40 is defined as belonging to a protected class. Further, the ADA (1990) required that a workplace provide "reasonable accommodation" for disabled workers, to enable them to remain in the workplace.

The ADEA and its revisions (1967, 1978, 1986) have, for the most part, eliminated mandatory retirement in the United States. The ADEA legislation in 1967 created a protected class of people ages 40 and older, but maintained mandatory retirement at age 65. In the revisions of 1978, mandatory retirement age was raised to 70 and was removed for federal workers. In the 1986 revisions, all mandatory retirement was eliminated with specific exceptions, known as BFOQs, for commercial airline pilots, air traffic controllers, safety officers (fire fighters and law enforcement officers), tenured college faculty, age authenticity in actors, the military, diplomatic core, certain elected and appointed officers, and individuals in key leadership positions with pensions greater than $44,000 per year (Sterns et al., 2005). Since that time airline pilots' BFOQs changed from 60 to 65, there is no mandatory retirement for tenured faculty, and retirement age for police and fire fighters depends on the jurisdiction. Today there is an emphasis on testing and on objective evaluation of performance, not age based. Instead of a BFOQ, actual direct assessment of job relevant skills, like the ability to climb ladders and carry the fire hose and related equipment, are the measures that most accurately assess job performance. Certain aspects of the job environment can result in age bias. Areas of the work environment that are vulnerable to age bias include selection, interviewing, retention and training, and performance appraisal. Many work places utilize testing to determine a worker's skills and abilities. Where testing is involved it is important to consider the relevance of the test to the actual performance of the job, whether or not standard tests used for placement are normed on age groups similar to those taking the tests or not, and how the test relates to job performance.

WHAT IS RETIREMENT?

Definitions of retirement vary based on the current trends of retirement, age cohort, and economic fluctuations. Atchley, in 1976, defined retirement from a sociological perspective as "a condition in which an individual is forced or allowed to be employed less than full-time and in which his [sic] income is derived at least in part from a retirement pension earned through prior years of service as a job holder" (p. 1). Atchley (1976) was one of the first to propose that retirement was a life event that progressed and changed over the course of the person's life span. He proposed the phases of preretirement, honeymoon, immediate retirement routine, rest and relaxation, disenchantment, reorientation, retirement routine, and termination of retirement, as "concepts that can be used to organize ideas about the issues people face in taking up, playing, and relinquishing the retirement role" (Atchley & Barusch, 2004, p. 258). He posited that adjustment to retirement may be more a function of time after the retirement event, than of the event itself. Moen (1996) summarizes the utility of a life-span perspective for conceptualizing the impact of retirement: "Part of the difficulty in assessing the impact of the retirement transition on well-being is that it constitutes both a positive and negative change and is both voluntary and involuntary. Thus the circumstances surrounding the retirement transition as well as how individuals perceive their retirement become extremely consequential" (Moen, 1996, p.139).

Retirement age is chosen by the individual, based on his or her preferences and needs, and no longer by a mandated age or company incentives. Warner, Hayward, and Hardy (2010), in their update of age-graded regularities of the U.S. retirement life course found that at age 50 men can expect to spend half of their remaining lives working for pay, while women can expect to spend one third. Half of all men had left the workforce by age 63 and half of all women by age 61; the majority of those exits were final. The authors also observed that there is great variability in the retirement process: Nearly one third of men and women who had retired later resumed some type of employment. It must be kept in mind that much of the impetus for these changes took place because of changing gerontological knowledge in the 1980s and the willingness of House and Senate committees to change policies. It was realized that ageism needed to be addressed.

Retirement is increasingly identified as much more than a one-time event and is instead conceptualized as a life-span/life course transition to which an individual adjusts and to which adjustment may have a variable nonlinear course. The life span/life course perspective has been suggested as ideal to capture the entirety of the retirement transition experience (Sterns & Huyck, 2001; Sterns & Subich, 2005). The transition to retirement changes from full-time employment to any one of a full range of retirement options available to today's older worker. This transition may also range from uneventful to disabling crisis. Retirement has become more individualized and has evolved from the idea of a total withdrawal from the workforce to a gradual retreat, often accompanied by continued active involvement in the world of work. Whether one refers to this phase of life as a period of "renewment" (Bratter & Dennis, 2008), "revitalizing retirement" (Schlossburg, 2010), or reinvention (Merrill Lynch Wealth Management, 2013), the nature, timing, and appearance of retirement have changed. Dychtwald, Erickson, and Morrison (2008) argue that it is time to retire the concept of retirement. As Hedge and Borman (2012) observe: "Retirement is typically defined as later-life withdrawal from the workforce, but it has become an increasingly 'phased' phenomenon, involving multiple exits from and re-entries into paid and unpaid work. This increasingly 'blurred' definition speaks to both the complexity of the retirement decision and the concept itself" (p. 692).

In 2012, the American Association of Retired Persons and the Society for Human Resource Management surveyed 1,004 adults age 50 and older who were either employed full or part time or looking for work. They found that 77% of employed workers planned to remain in their current jobs until they stopped working completely, while 9% planned to change jobs but stay in the same field (Brown, 2012). Six percent hoped to find work in a different field, and another 6% intended to start their own business (Brown, 2012). For those 50 and older, working longer may be related to financial circumstances or a desire to remain productive (Brown, 2012; Sterns & Sterns, 1995, 2013). This desire to work longer has been evident throughout the literature on aging, work, and retirement (Czaja & Sharit, 2009; Feldman, 2007; Feldman & Beehr, 2011; Hedge et al., 2006; Rothwell et al., 2008; Shultz & Adams, 2007; Sterns & Huyck, 2001; Wang et al., 2013). The workplace is changing to attract and accommodate these aging workers. A 2011 study (Forbes, 2011) found that nearly one of three firms expected to have a significantly higher proportion of older workers (+65) in the next 5 years, and 43% reported that retention and development of talent is a priority. Seventy-two percent offered diversity and inclusion programs focused on age.

RETIREMENT PATTERNS AND OPTIONS

Retirement at one time in history was a distinct departure from the world of work into a life characterized by leisure pursuits. While retirement was perceived as an abrupt life transition, "the final exit from employment," or "the movement from the midlife to old age" (Kim & Moen, 2001), changes in the workforce, economic and social shifts, and increased longevity have resulted in retirement being a concept that describes a variety of changes in a person's work life for which many options are available. Retirement may be less an exit from the workforce and more of a process that is phased, complex, and dynamic. The type of retirement experience is as varied as the individual who chooses it. Individual characteristics, both work and nonwork related, affect retirement choices (Moen, 2012).

Multiple exit patterns have replaced the traditional, one-time transition (Mutchler, Burr, Pienta, & Massagli, 1997). Patterns of exit from the workforce have emerged and been defined. Mutchler et al. (1997), in a now classic study, examined the frequency and antecedents of different exit patterns in a sample of 2,226 White and Black men aged 55 to 74 who had reported at least 6 months of continuous work history at some time during their lives. Using data from the 1984 panel of the Survey of Income and Program Participation (SIPP), researchers divided subjects into four categories, reflecting different patterns of exit from the workforce. They defined a single exit from full-time work or career as a "crisp" exit pattern, while a "blurred" pattern was described as a worker who reported two or more transitions between labor-force participation and nonparticipation. This could include periods of employment and unemployment as well as periods of employment and labor-force exit followed by reentry to the work force (Mutchler et al., 1997). Identifying 65 as the typical retirement age may no longer be appropriate, as many individuals may retire, initiate blurred transitions, or receive Social Security and pension income prior to this age or later (Cornman & Kingson, 1996; Mutchler et al., 1997).

Crisp and blurred transitioners were also found to differ in terms of age, financial resources, and health status. Crisp transitioners tended to be younger than 65. Although not associated with any particular age group, blurred transitions were rare past the age of 68. In contrast to crisp exiters, blurred transitioners were more likely to have limited financial resources, such as pensions and nonwage income. Inadequate income seemed to prompt those individuals to continue to work, although somewhat sporadically. Lastly, individuals with poor health were more likely to be blurred transitioners than continuous workers. Those with the poorest health, however, were more likely to either exit crisply or not work at all during the period studied.

Others may choose an option of taking a "bridge employment opportunity," rather than a total withdrawal from the workforce. Bridge employment involves a person leaving a primary career role and entering into another paid employment position, although one that is unrelated to his or her primary career role. Cahill, Giandrea, and Quinn (2006) examined retirement patterns based on longitudinal data from the Health and Retirement Study (HRS) during 1992 and 2002, which included 12,600 individuals, aged 51 to 61. They found that a majority of older workers appeared to take a phased approach to retirement, in which those who left full-time career jobs moved first to a bridge job, rather than directly out of the labor force. Older workers without defined benefit pension plans and those at the lower and upper ends of the wage distribution took bridge jobs more than others. Bridge employment can be beneficial to older workers, in that they can remain productive and make money (Doeringer & Terkla, 1990), although according to Wang and Shultz (2010) bridge employment only has a positive impact on mental health if the person remains in the same career field. Zhan, Wang, Liu, and Shultz (2009) found that individuals who engaged in bridge employment reported better physical health than individuals who were fully retired, and individuals pursuing career bridge employment also indicated better mental health.

Another option for today's workforce may be to end one career and venture into a second or third career. Freedman (2007, 2017) describes what he refers to as the "encore career": a 10- to 15-year career in which the person follows traditional career success with work of greater significance that may not last as long, but is more important or gratifying than the first career. Freedman examined major trends that influenced Baby Boomers' (born between 1945 and 1965) decision to seek a different type of work in mid- to later life, including (a) insecurity about future retirement income; (b) cost and availability of health coverage; (c) a shift from company-defined benefit plans to defined-contribution plans, which are more subject to the vagaries of a changing economic market; and (d) the opportunity to remain active and involved.

Van Yperen and Wortler (2016) have coined the term "blended working" to describe a combination of on-site and off-site working through the use of information and communication technologies, which affords a worker the ability to maintain as much or as little access to job relevant information as is desired. This form of work may suit any worker at any age and may be ideal for the individualized needs of the older worker and an organization seeking to capitalize on the knowledge, skills, and abilities of an experienced person.

As retirement evolves into a process rather than an event, it becomes harder to examine why people retire and what factors may influence the process (Sterns & Kaplan, 2003). For example, the economic downturn of 2007 led some individuals to continue to delay retirement, while others sought work without success, and still others, the so-called "discouraged workers," stopped searching and retired by default. Factors related to the decision about when to retire are both financial and nonfinancial. In a national survey of 1,024 adults ages 50 and older, financial resources was the most commonly cited factor in determining time of retirement, endorsed by 69% of respondents (Benz, Sedensky, Tompson, & Agiesta., 2013). However, health and continued ability to perform one's job extremely or very well were also important factors in their decision. Quality of life factors that respondents cited as influential on timing of retirement included job satisfaction, wanting more free time, and time with spouses or partners. Half of the survey respondents reported that most or almost all of their friends and family that are around their age were still working (Benz et al., 2013).

FACTORS RELATED TO THE DECISION TO RETIRE

Decisions about how and when to reduce one's participation in the workforce or to exit it completely are often examined in terms of financial readiness and health status. Many people choose to retire when they feel they have enough financial resources. These may include eligibility for private or public pension benefits, although some are forced to retire when physical conditions no longer allow the person to work any longer (by illness or accident) or as a result of legislation concerning their position.

ROLE OF HEALTH

Health status has been a frequent theme examined in studies on leaving the work force. It is widely found that individuals in poor health generally retire earlier than those in better health (Sterns & Sterns, 1995; Wang, 2012). This does not necessarily imply that poor health status leads people to retire earlier. One way of looking at this finding could be that a person may emphasize health-related concerns to justify their decision to retire. This justification bias, however, is likely to be small. In general, declining health over time, as well as the onset of new health conditions, is positively related to earlier retirement. Some of the health conditions that can influence someone to retire include hypertension, diabetes mellitus, sleep apnea, joint diseases, and hyperlipidemia. The development of these health issues may make individuals more aware of the realities of their aging (Sterns & Huyck, 2001).

Mental health issues may influence decisions to exit the workforce, whether completely or temporarily, or to move to part-time employment. Doshi, Cen, and Polsky (2008) studied six biennial waves (1992 to 2002) of the HRS and found that the presence of active depression in late middle-aged workers significantly increased the likelihood of retirement for both men and women. In addition, depressed workers were more likely to retire completely than nondepressed workers. For women, subthreshold depression was also a predictor of retirement. Doshi et al. (2008) point out that a primary concern raised by these findings is the subsequent adverse impact on financial well-being and access to appropriate health care and treatment, as most of these retirees will not qualify for Social Security benefits until age 62 or Medicare benefits until age 65.

Calvo, Sarkisian, and Tomborini (2013) also used data from the HRS and found that early retirement can have a negative impact on both physical and emotional health. For instance, a depressed worker may conclude that retirement is his or her only choice. Mandal and Roe (2008) found that the voluntariness of one's departure from the workforce is a predictor of adjustment: Involuntary job loss worsens mental health, and reemployment can reverse the decline.

ROLE OF FINANCES

One of the ways that health care influences retirement decision making is in its impact on the cost of living in retirement. The decision to exit the workforce, continue working, or engage in a different manner of workforce participation may be driven by financial needs and a worker's preparedness for the cost of exiting the workforce. Many have suggested that those who will fill the ranks of the future retired are not adequately financially prepared to maintain the lifestyle to which they are accustomed, nor are they prepared for how to manage medical uncertainties. Willet (2008) examined retirement preparedness and identified specific needs for intervention for today's worker planning for retirement. Current workers' perceptions of financial need in retirement may be an inaccurate reflection of the experienced financial need of actual retirees. Willet's study found that 50% of workers surveyed thought they would need 70% or less of their preretirement income to live comfortably in retirement and only one of 12 thought that they would need 95% or more of their preretirement income. In contrast, only 36% of retirees said they actually lived on 70% or less of their preretirement income and more than 55% stated that they lived on 95% or more of their preretirement income (Willett, 2008).

Benz et al. (2013) identified the impact of financial security on anxiety about retirement. Only 30% of those who felt financially insecure about retirement expected that they were unlikely to work in retirement, compared to half of those who felt secure about their finances. The amount of money saved is also a factor in anxiety about retirement savings. People aged 50 and older with less than $50,000 saved felt significantly more anxious about their retirement savings and those who had a pension felt more secure about retirement finances.

Suggestions have been provided about how to help individuals prepare for the current and future financial retirement scenario (Hoagland, 2016; Munnell, 2016; Pew Charitable Trusts, 2017; Polivka, 2012). Munnell (2016) offers a five-part proposal to support resolving the impending financial crisis of retirement income: maintaining Social Security, making personal pension plans like 401K plans fully automatic, ensuring that all workers have access to an employer-based retirement plan, using home equity for retirement income, and promoting longer worker lives. The Pew Charitable Trusts (2017) report addresses how policy makers could increase the degree to which private sector workers save for retirement. Given that more than 40% of full-time employees do not have access to an employer-sponsored defined contribution plan, like a 401K, details on what would encourage small- and medium-sized businesses to offer them is key. The survey found that when workers have access to retirement plans, the vast majority will participate. About one third of employers surveyed indicated that they would be incentivized to provide these retirement plans to employees if they had an increase in profits or received financial incentives like tax credits, as well as if there were an increased demand from employees for such programs. Hoagland (2016) suggests two ideas to help with the financial challenge of an aging and retiring workforce and to increase family income. First, he suggests increasing the workforce by delaying retirement for current workers and increasing immigration, especially for high skilled technical workers. Second, he suggests an increase in worker productivity through skill development, training and retraining, and education. More skilled immigrants increase the workers who are paying into Social Security. Staying in the workforce longer delays the distribution of the Social Security benefit and possibly reduces the number of years the benefit is collected.

Changes in the economy and changes in the demographics of older adults are having a large impact on labor force participation rates and the typical strategy for retirement income: the "three-legged stool" of Social Security benefits, retirement savings, and pension. Demographically there is a significant decline in the number of younger workers entering the job market and a very large number of older workers who are in the process of or who have already left the workforce (see Table 11.1). The result of this is fewer individuals contributing to the buildup of Social Security funds at a time when larger numbers than ever will be ready to collect their Social Security benefits. This is the current landscape that workers of all ages face. Changes are needed to offset potential financial hardship for those who need the Social Security income and for future workers to have this as a source of support when they prepare to leave the workforce. In many ways, the changes that have taken place in Social Security have already begun to change the nature of leaving the workforce. The increase in the age to collect full benefits of Social Security may be a factor in remaining in the workforce longer, although currently many do choose to begin collecting their benefits earlier.

Making decisions about work and retirement are particularly challenging for those who are unemployed or underemployed. It has become extremely clear that many older workers who did not have a position a year ago have not been able to find new employment over the period of a year (Rix, 2011). Both those working and not working are experiencing a new awareness of their financial challenges as they consider the end game of their careers. It is apparent that they are forming new expectations and reforming the assumptions required to plan for the coming decades. With the considerations of health care, retirement savings, pension solvency, and general economic conditions, many people are reporting they are planning to remain in the workforce considerably longer than in the recent past. It may be more difficult to find a job or reenter the work force for older adults. Workers 55 and older averaged 35.5 weeks of joblessness compared with 23.3 weeks for the 16- to 24-year-old age group and 30.3 weeks for the 25- to 54-year age group (U.S. Bureau of Labor Statistics, 2008). Two thirds of those in the 55- to 64-age range who took new jobs after retirement earned, on average, 18% less (Ralphaelon, 2013). Between ages 55 and 64 about two thirds of Americans are in the labor force (Rix, 2013). The reemployment rate for this age group was 47%, but dropped to only 24% after age 64. (Bureau of Labor Statistics, 2012). According to the AARP Public Policy Institute, between 60% and 80% of workers expect to work in retirement, yet only a little over 18% of people older than 65 were currently working (Ralphaelon, 2013).

Those older adults living at or near the poverty line have considerably less freedom in choosing to work. They may work because they require the income to cover basic needs for shelter, heat, food, and medicine (Blustein et al., 2008). Poverty disproportionately affects older women and minorities (Taylor & Geldhauser, 2007). Historically, there have always been more women living in poverty than men. The median income for women 65 and older is just over $12,000 per year, which is only $3,000 over the Census Bureau standard for living in poverty (Beedon & Wu, 2005).

Those living at the bottom of the economic ladder are much more reliant on Social Security payments although Social Security was never intended to be the sole source of financial support for an individual, but as a supplement to income, savings, or employer-sponsored savings plans. Taylor and Geldhauser (2007) examined older Hispanic adults and found that over 75% of their sample relied on Social Security for 50% or more of their total income. Social security income kept 33% of older Hispanics from falling into poverty (Taylor & Geldhauser, 2007).

Older workers at lower income levels are more likely to experience additional barriers to better paying jobs because they are the least likely to have the education, information skills, and training that are advantageous in the world of work (Sterns & Sterns, 2013; Taylor & Geldhauser, 2007). Those without a choice to continue working, due to social disadvantage or oppression (racism, sexism, ageism, etc.) are addressed by the psychology-of-working perspective. This perspective provides a framework to address such barriers, not by the traditional career guidance approaches, but through practical support, providing connection with financial planning and skills

Table 11.1 Civilian Labor Force Participation Rate, by Age, Gender, Race, and Ethnicity, 1994, 2004, 2014, and Projected 2024 (in Percent)

Group	Participation Rate				Percentage-Point Change			Annual Growth Rate		
	1994	2004	2014	2024	1994–2004	2004–2014	2014–2024	1994–2004	2004–2014	2014–2024
Total, 16 years and older	66.6	66.0	62.9	60.9	−0.6	−3.1	−2.0	−0.1	−0.5	−0.3
16 to 24	66.4	61.1	55.0	49.7	−5.3	−6.1	−5.3	−0.8	−1.0	−1.0
16 to 19	52.7	43.9	34.0	26.4	−8.8	−9.9	−7.6	−1.8	−2.5	−2.5
20 to 24	77.0	75.0	70.8	68.2	−2.0	−4.2	−2.6	−0.3	−0.6	−0.4
25 to 54	83.4	82.8	80.9	81.2	−0.6	−1.9	0.3	−0.1	−0.2	0.0
25 to 34	83.2	82.7	81.2	81.3	−0.5	−1.5	0.1	−0.1	−0.2	0.0
35 to 44	84.8	83.6	82.2	81.7	−1.2	−1.4	−0.5	−0.1	−0.2	−0.1
45 to 54	81.7	81.8	79.6	81.0	0.1	−2.2	1.4	0.0	−0.3	0.2
55 and older	30.1	36.2	40.0	39.4	6.1	3.8	−0.6	1.9	1.0	−0.2

(continued)

Table 11.1 Civilian Labor Force Participation Rate, by Age, Gender, Race, and Ethnicity, 1994, 2004, 2014, and Projected 2024 (in Percent) *(continued)*

Group	Participation Rate				Percentage-Point Change			Annual Growth Rate		
	1994	2004	2014	2024	1994–2004	2004–2014	2014–2024	1994–2004	2004–2014	2014–2024
55 to 64	56.8	62.3	64.1	66.3	5.5	1.8	2.2	0.9	0.3	0.3
55 to 59	67.7	71.1	71.4	74.2	3.4	0.3	2.8	0.5	0.0	0.4
60 to 64	44.9	50.9	55.8	58.8	6.0	4.9	3.0	1.3	0.9	0.5
60 to 61	54.5	59.2	63.4	67.1	4.7	4.2	3.7	0.8	0.7	0.6
62 to 64	38.7	44.4	50.2	53.2	5.7	5.8	3.0	1.4	1.2	0.6
65 and older	12.4	14.4	18.6	21.7	2.0	4.2	3.1	1.5	2.6	1.6
65 to 74	17.2	21.9	26.2	29.9	4.7	4.3	3.7	2.4	1.8	1.3
65 to 69	21.9	27.7	31.6	36.2	5.8	3.9	4.6	2.4	1.3	1.4
70 to 74	11.8	15.3	18.9	22.8	3.5	3.6	3.9	2.6	2.1	1.9
75 to 79	6.6	8.8	11.3	14.4	2.2	2.5	3.1	2.9	2.5	2.5
75 and older	5.4	6.1	8.0	10.6	0.7	1.9	2.6	1.2	2.7	2.9

Source: Employment Projections program, U.S. Bureau of Labor Statistics, 2015.

training support, in the context of public programming and the policy to support and implement such programs. Several researchers have made specific policy recommendations that include education of social workers and career counselors (Blustein et al., 2008), and the implementation of financial planning and skills training for older workers (Sterns & Sterns, 2013; Taylor & Geldhauser, 2007).

Financial support in retirement is a factor related to the decision-making process regarding retirement. Various options of retirement income are considerations that are most successfully managed through planning for the eventual exit from work.

RETIREMENT PLANNING

Retirement planning begins when individuals first create "imagined futures" involving retirement (Feldman & Beehr, 2011; Sterns & Kaplan, 2003), but may evolve into a plan with clear and long-term future goals. Although early planning for retirement is encouraged, multiple lines of research have noted the lack of retirement planning that occurs well ahead of immediate retirement (Dennis & Fike, 2012). Even among retired individuals in later life, planning for known and expected future-care needs (such as making an advance directive) may only be done by a slim majority of the population. Nonetheless, retirement education is vital to facilitate planning and has evolved from the time of employer-sponsored pension programs. One of the first types of retirement planning services grew from the need for discussions between the employer and the employee about benefits and insurance. Woodrow Hunter of the University of Michigan initiated the first retirement planning program for the United Auto Workers in 1948. His materials included educational program approaches that addressed financial as well as psychosocial issues pertinent to retirement (Hunter, 1976). Hunter's materials remain relevant in assisting in the development of preretirement education programming and in assisting workers in examining financial needs, leisure planning, health and living arrangements, sexuality and aging, and surviving death of loved ones.

Over time, retirement education programs became part of consistent human resource programming for larger companies. Companies shifted from entirely company financed, defined benefit pensions to more employee-defined contribution plans. By the 1990s, many organizations began trimming their labor force size and workers were pushed to be more active in their own planning for their future employment, financial well-being, and future retirement.

Planning for retirement and voluntary retirement seem to improve early adjustment to the retirement transition (Reitzes & Mutran, 2004). This effect may be time-limited, however. Reitzes and Mutran (2004) followed a group of older adults over a 24-month period during their transition to retirement. By 24 months the beneficial impact of preretirement planning had become less important to retirement adjustment. Salami (2010) examined the relationship of retirement context and psychological factors to well-being and found that retirement status (whether voluntary or involuntary), job challenges, financial situation, physical health, activity level, and social support each separately predicted psychological well-being in retirement. In addition, preretirement expectations, self-efficacy, perceived stress, and optimism separately predicted psychological well-being. Targeting preretirement expectations in preretirement counseling to help people develop more realistic expectations about lifestyle adjustments, importance of building social supports, and managing health care may be helpful in promoting well-being in retirement (Salami, 2010). Bender and Jivan (2005) examined what contributes to retiree happiness, using the 2000 wave of the HRS, and found that economic well-being increased overall well-being. The effect was small, however, and those who had a defined-benefits plan experienced greater well-being than those with only a defined-contribution plan or no pension. In addition, retirees who were healthier and who said that they had voluntarily retired had greater well-being than those who reported poorer health and involuntary retirement. Finally, the authors report that about 60% of retirees were very satisfied with their retirement; another 32.4% were moderately satisfied, while about 8% were not satisfied.

Individual retirement financial preparation is more important than ever. The life span of a person in retirement has increased from 13 years in 1960, to about 20 years today (Ellis, Munnell, & Eschtruth, 2014). Preparing financially for this increased amount of time will require new ways of financial planning. Changes in financing retirement has shifted from a company pension or defined benefit, to more individual defined contribution plans. Changes in the Social Security System may provide less for future retirees. Ellis et al. (2014) cite three factors that contribute to the reduction of Social Security income replacement rates for the average worker. First, the rise in the Social Security program's full retirement age from 65 to 67 years old cuts benefits across the board. For those who retire before their full retirement age, their benefit is lower and those who wait until their full benefit age, in theory, have fewer years to receive the benefit. Second, Medicare premiums are increasing at a faster rate than Social Security benefits and the premiums come directly out of Social Security benefits. Lastly, the Social Security benefit received will be subject to taxation under personal income tax due to tax thresholds not being indexed for inflation or wage growth.

Overall, income after retirement can come from state pensions, occupational pensions, private savings and investments (private pension funds, owned housing), donations (e.g., by children), and social benefits. On a personal level, the rising cost of living during retirement is a serious concern to many older adults, as is the cost of health care.

CONCLUSION

As the population ages, the nature of work and retirement need to adjust accordingly. There is a greater need than in times past for nations to develop policies and workplaces to identify strategies to maximize the value of an aging workforce, and for individuals to plan for what work life and retirement pathways best suit their needs. The combination of changing demographics and an increasingly sophisticated workplace puts greater emphasis on ergonomic and technological interventions in workspaces' design to extend the work life of older adults who desire to participate in the work force. Programs that facilitate planning for one's work life across the life span would aid in individual preparation for the various options available to extend one's work life and to determine one's retirement course. Planning will continue to be instrumental in preparing individuals for the financial and care needs that exist with changes in one's work life. More empirical research in this area is greatly needed in order to understand and meet the needs of an aging workforce.

DISCUSSION QUESTIONS

1. Describe the six ways of defining older workers: chronological, functional, psychosocial, organizational, life-span developmental, and psychology of work.

2. Describe some characteristics of older workers.

3. Summarize what the Age Discrimination in Employment Act is and what impact it has on older adult workers.

4. Describe different patterns of retirement presented in this chapter.

5. Summarize financial ways that adults can plan for retirement.

6. Describe how health may influence retirement.

7. Summarize how the notion of retirement has changed over the years.

8. Describe how ageism may impact older workers and their plans for retirement.

REFERENCES

Age Discrimination in Employment Act, 29 U.S.C. Sec. 621 et seq. (1967 & Supp V. 1978 & 1986).

Americans With Disabilities Act of 1990, Pub.L. No. 101-336, Sec.1211, 9 (1990).

Atchley, R. C. (1976). *The sociology of retirement*. New York, NY: Schenkman.

Atchley, R. C., & Barusch, A. S. (2004). *Social forces & aging: An introduction to social gerontology*. Belmont, CA: Wadsworth/Thomson Learning.

Baltes, P. B., Reese, H. W., & Lipsitt, L. P. (1980). Life-span developmental psychology. *Annual Review of Psychology, 31*, 65–110.

Beedon, L., & Wu, K. (2005, October). Women age 65 and older: Their sources of income. AARP Public Poverty Institute. Retrieved from http://www.aarp.org

Bender, K. A., & Jivan, N. A. (2005). What makes retirees happy? *An Issue in Brief: Center for Retirement Research at Boston College, 28*, 1–9.

Benz, J., Sedensky, M., Tompson, T., & Agiesta, J. (2013). Working longer: Older Americans' attitudes on work and retirement. The Associated Press-NORC Center for Public Affairs Research. Retrieved from http://www.apnorc.org/projects/Pages/working-longer-older-americans-attitudes-on-work-and-retirement.aspx

Birren, J. E., & Stafford, J. I. (1986). Changes in the organization of behavior with age. In J. E. Birren & J. Livingston (Eds.), *Age, health, and employment* (pp. 93–113). Englewood Cliffs, NJ: Prentice-Hall.

Blustein, D. L. (2013). *The Oxford handbook of the psychology of working*. New York, NY: Oxford University Press.

*Blustein, D. L., Kenna, A. C., Gill, N., & DeVoy, J. E. (2008). The psychology of working: A new framework for counseling practice and public policy. *The Career Development Quarterly. 56*, 294–308.

*Bowen, C. E., Noack, M. G., & Staudinger, U. M., (2011). Aging in the work context. In K. W. Schaie & S. L. Willis (Eds.), *Handbook of Psychology of Aging* (7th ed., pp. 263–277). Boston, MA: Academic Press.

Bratter, B., & Dennis, H. (2008). *Project renewment: The first retirement model for career women*. New York, NY: Scribner.

Brown, S. K. (2012). *What are older workers seeking? An AARP/SHRM survey of 50+ workers.* Washington, DC: AARP.

Bureau of Labor Statistics. (2012). The Editor's Desk. Employment status of displaced workers. Retrieved from http://www.bls.gov/opub/ted/2012/ted_20120828.htm

Butler, R. (1973). *Why survive? Being old in America.* New York, NY: Harper & Row.

Cahill, K. E., Giandrea, M. D., & Quinn, J. F. (2006). Retirement patterns from career employment. *The Gerontologist, 46*, 514–523.

Calvo, E., Sarkisian, N., & Tamborini, C. R. (2013). Causal effects of retirement timing on subjective physical and emotional health. *The Journals of Gerontology. Series B, The Psychological Sciences and Social Sciences, 68*, 73–84.

Carstensen, L. (2009). *A long bright future.* New York, NY: Broadway Books.

Cornman, J. M., & Kingson, E. R. (1996). Trends, issues, perspectives and values for the aging of the baby boom cohorts. *The Gerontologist, 36*, 15–26.

Czaja, S. J., & Sharit, J. (2009). *Aging and work: Issues and implications in a changing landscape.* Baltimore, MD: The Johns Hopkins University Press.

Dennis, H., & Fike, A. T. (2012). Retirement planning: New context, process, language, and players. In J. W. Hedge & W. C. Borman, (Eds.), *The Oxford handbook work and aging* (pp. 538–548). New York, NY: Oxford University Press.

Doeringer, P. B., & Terkla, D. G. (1990). Business necessity, bridge jobs, and the nonbureaucratic firm. In P. B. Doeringer (Ed.), *Bridges to retirement: Older workers in a changing labor market* (pp. 146–171). Ithaca, NY: ILR Press.

*Doshi, J. A., Cen, L., & Polsky, D. (2008). Depression and retirement in late middle-aged U.S. workers. *Health Services Research, 43*, 693–713.

Dychtwald, K., Erickson, T., & Morrison, B. (2004, March). It is time to retire retirement. *Harvard Business Review, 82*, 48–57.

Ellis, C., Munnell, A., & Eschtruth, A. (2014). *Falling short: The coming retirement crisis and what to do about it.* New York, NY: Oxford University Press.

Feldman, D. C. (2007). Career mobility and career stability among older workers. In K. S. Shultz & G. A. Adams (Eds.), *Aging and work in the 21st century* (pp. 179–197). Mahwah, NJ: Lawrence Erlbaum Associates.

Feldman, D. C., & Beehr, T. A. (2011). A three-phase model of retirement decision making. *American Psychologist, 66*, 193–203.

Forbes. (2011). *Fostering innovation through a diverse workforce.* New York, NY: Forbes Insight. Retrieved from https://images.forbes.com/forbesinsights/StudyPDFs/Innovation_Through_Diversity.pdf

*Freedman, M. (2007). The social-purpose encore career: Baby boomers, civic engagement, and the next stage of work. *Generations, 4*, 43–46.

*Freedman, M. (2017). The encore Life: A generation of experienced workers is ready to serve. *Generations, 40*(4), 74–78.

*Hall, D. T., & Mirvis, P. H. (1996). The new protean career: Psychological success and the path with a heart. In D. T. Hall (Ed.), *The career is dead—long live the career: A relational approach to careers* (pp. 15–45). San Francisco, CA: Jossey-Bass.

Hedge, J. W., & Borman, W. C. (2012). *The Oxford handbook of work and aging.* New York, NY: Oxford University Press.

Hedge, J. W., Borman, W. C., & Lammlein, S. E (2006). *The aging workforce: Realities, myths, and implications.* Washington, DC: American Psychological Association.

Hoagland, G. W. (2016). The economic, fiscal, and financial, implications, of an aging society. *Generations, 40*(4), 22.

Hunter, W. W. (1976). *Preparation for retirement* (3rd ed.). Ann Arbor: Institute of Gerontology, University of Michigan–Wayne State University.

Kim, J. E., & Moen, P. (2001). Moving into retirement: Preparation and transitions in late midlife. In M. E. Lachman (Ed.), *Handbook of midlife development* (pp. 487–527). New York, NY: John Wiley.

Lahey, J. (2008). Age, women, and hiring: An experimental study. *The Journal of Human Resources, 43*(1), 30–56.

Levy, R., & Banaji, M. R. (2002). Implicit ageism. In T. D. Nelson (Ed.), *Ageism: Stereotyping and prejudice against older persons*. Cambridge: Massachusetts Institute of Technology Press.

Mandal, B., & Roe, B. (2008). Job loss, retirement and the mental health of older Americans. *Journal of Mental Health Policy Economics*, *11*, 167–76.

Merrill Lynch Wealth Management (2013). Americans' perspectives on new retirement realities and the longevity bonus: A 2013 Merrill Lynch retirement study, conducted in partnership with Age Wave. Merrill Lynch Wealth Management, Bank of America Corporation. Retrieved from https://mlaem.fs.ml.com/content/dam/ML/Articles/pdf/AR111544.pdf

Moen, P. (1996). A life course perspective on retirement, gender, and well-being. *Journal of Occupational Health Psychology*, *1*, 131–144.

*Moen, P. (2012). Retirement dilemmas and decisions. In J. W. Hedge and W. C. Borman (Eds.), *The Oxford handbook on work and aging* (pp. 549–569). New York, NY: Oxford University Press.

Mutcher, J. E., Burr, J. A., Pienta, A. M., & Massagli, M. P. (1997). Pathways to labor force exit: Work transitions and work instability. *Journal of Gerontology: Social Sciences*, *52B*, s252–s261.

Munnell, A. H. (2016). Restoring public confidence in retirement income. *Generations*, *40*(4), 23–29.

Palmore, E. (2005). Three decades of research on ageism. *Generations*, *3*, 87–90.

Papalia, D. E., Sterns, H. L., Feldman, R. D., & Camp, C. J. (2007). *Adult Development and Aging* (3rd ed.). Boston, MA: McGraw-Hill.

Pew Charitable Trusts. (2017). *Retirement plan access and participation across generations*. Issue Brief. Retrieved from http://www.pewtrusts.org/en/research-and-analysis/issue-briefs/2017/02/retirement-plan-access-and-participation-across-generations

Pitt-Catsouphes, M., Smyer, M. A., Matz-Costa, C., & Kane, K. (2007). *The national study report: Phase II of the national study of business strategy and workforce development* (Research Highlight No. 04). Chestnut Hill, MA: The Center on Aging & Work/Workplace Flexibility.

Polivka, L. J. (2012). A future out of reach? The growing risk in the U.S. retirement security system. *Generations*, *2*, 12–17.

*Posthuma, R. A., & Campion, M. A. (2009). Age stereotypes in the workplace: Common stereotypes, moderators, and future research directions. *Journal of Management*, *35*, 158–188.

Quinn, J. F. (2010). Work, retirement, and the encore career: Elders and the future of the American workforce. *Generations*, *34*, 45–55.

Ralphaelon, E. (2013, September 7). Working after you retire has its hurdles. *The Akron Beacon Journal*.

Reitzes, D. C., & Mutran, E. J. (2004). The transition to retirement: Stages and factors that influence retirement adjustment. *International Journal of Aging and Human Development*, *59*, 63–84.

Richardson, V. E. (1993). *Retirement counseling: A handbook for gerontology practitioners*. New York, NY: Springer Publishing.

Rix, S. E. (2011). *Recovering from the Great Recession: Long struggle ahead for older Americans*. Insight on the Issues. Washington, DC: AARP Public Policy Institute.

Rix, S. E. (2013). The employment situation. January 2013: Jobs added to the economy but unemployment for older workers holds fast. AARP Public Policy Institute Fact Sheet. Retrieved from https://www.aarp.org/content/dam/aarp/research/public_policy_institute/econ_sec/2013/the-employment-situation-january-2013-AARP-ppi-econ-sec.pdf

Robbins, L. A., (2015). The pernicious problem of ageism. *Generations*, *39*(3), 6–9.

Rothwell, W. J., Sterns, H. L., Spokus, D., & Reaser, J. M. (2008). *Working longer: New strategies for managing, training, and retaining older workers*. New York, NY: American Management Association.

Salami, S. O. (2010). Retirement context and psychological factors as predictors of well-being among retired teachers. *Europe's Journal of Psychology*, *6*(2), 47–64.

Schlossberg, N. K. (1981). A model for analyzing human adaptation to transition. *The Counseling Psychologist*, *9*, 2–18.

Schlossburg, N. K. (2010). *Revitalizing retirement: Reshaping your identity, relationships, and purpose*. Washington, DC: American Psychological Association.

Schmitt, J., & Jones, J. (2012). *Low-wage workers are older and better educated than ever.* Issue Brief. Retrieved from http://cepr.net/documents/publications/min-wage3-2012-04.pdf

Schwab, D. P., & Heneman, H. G. (1978). Age stereotyping in performance appraisal. *Journal of Applied Psychology, 63,* 573–578.

Shultz, K. S., & Adams, G. A. (2007). *Aging and work in the 21st century.* Mahwah, NJ: Erlbaum.

Snyder, C. J. & Barrett, G. V. (1988). The age discrimination in employment act: A review of court decisions. *Experimental Aging Research, 14,* 3–55.

Social Security Administration. (2016). Calculators: Life expectancy. Retrieved from https://www.ssa.gov/planners/lifeexpectancy.html

Sterns, H. L. (1986). Training and retraining adult and older worker. In J. E. Birren & J. Livingston (Eds.), *Age, health, and employment* (pp. 93–113). Englewood Cliffs, NJ: Prentice-Hall.

Sterns, H. L., & Alexander, R. A. (1987). Industrial gerontology: The aging individual and work. In K. W. Schaie (Ed.), *Annual review of gerontology and geriatrics* (pp. 93–113). New York, NY: Springer Publishing.

Sterns, H. L. & Chang, B. (2010). Workforce issue and retirement. In J. C. Cavanaugh, & C. K. Cavanaugh (Eds.), *Aging in America* (Vol.3, pp. 81–105). Santa Barbara, CA: Praeger.

Sterns, H. L., & Doverspike, D. (1988). Training and developing the older worker: Implications for human resource management. In H. Dennis (Ed.), *Fourteen steps in managing an aging workforce* (pp. 97–110). New York, NY: Lexington.

Sterns, H. L., Doverspike, D., & Lax, G. (2005). The age discrimination in employment act. In F. S. Landy (Ed.), *Employment discrimination litigation: Behavioral, quantitative, and legal perspectives* (pp. 256–293). San Francisco, CA: Josey-Bass.

Sterns, H. L., & Huyck, M. H. (2001). Midlife and work. In M. E. Lachman (Ed.), *Handbook of midlife development* (pp. 447–486). New York, NY: John Wiley.

Sterns, H. L., & Kaplan, J. (2003). Self-management of career and retirement. In G. Adams & T. Beehr (Eds.), *Retirement: Reasons, processes and results* (pp. 188–213). New York, NY: Springer Publishing.

Sterns, H. L., & Miklos, S. (1995). The aging worker in a changing environment: Organizational and individual issues. *Journal of Vocational Behavior, 47,* 248–268.

Sterns, H. L. & Sterns, A. A. (1995). Age, health, and employment capability of older Americans. In S. Bass (Ed.), *Older and active* (pp. 10–34). New Haven, CT: Yale University Press.

Sterns, H. L., & Sterns, A. A. (2013). Approaches to aging and working. In D. L. Bluestein (Ed.), *The Oxford handbook of the psychology of working* (pp. 160–184). New York, NY: Oxford University Press.

Sterns, H. L., & Subich, L. M. (2005). Counseling for retirement. In S. D Brown & R. W. Lent (Eds.), *Career development and counseling handbook: Putting theory and research to work* (pp. 506–521). New York, NY: John Wiley.

Taylor, M. A., & Geldhauser, H. A. (2007). Low income older workers. In K. S. Shultz & G. A. Adams (Eds.), *Aging and work in the 21st century* (pp. 25–49). Hillsdale, NJ: Erlbaum.

U.S. Bureau of Labor Statistics. (2008, July). BLS spotlight on older workers. Retrieved from https://www.bls.gov/spotlight

Van Yperen, N. W. & Wortler, B. (2016). Blended working and the employability of older workers, retirement timing, and bridge employment. *Work, Aging, and Retirement, 3,* 102–108.

Wang, M. (2012). Health and fiscal and psychological well-being in retirement. In J. W. Hedge & W. C. Borman (Eds.), *The Oxford handbook of work and aging* (pp. 570–586). New York, NY: Oxford University Press.

Wang, M. (2013). *The Oxford handbook of retirement.* New York, NY: Oxford University Press.

Wang, M., Olson, D. A., & Shultz, K. S. (2013). *Mid and later career issues: An integrative perspective.* New York, NY: Routledge.

Wang, M., & Shultz, K. S. (2010). Employee retirement: A review and recommendations for future investigation. *Journal of Management, 36,* 172–206.

Warner, D. F., Hayward, M. D., & Hardy, M. A. (2010). The retirement life course in America at the dawn of the 21st century. *Population Research and Policy Review, 29,* 893–919.

Wheaton, F., & Crimmins, E. M. (2013). The demography of aging and retirement. In M. Wang (Ed.), *The Oxford handbook retirement* (pp. 22–41). New York, NY: Oxford University Press.

Wilkinson, J. A., & Ferraro, K. F. (2002). *Thirty years of ageism research in T.D. Nelson, Ed. Ageism: Stereotyping and prejudice against older persons.* Cambridge: Massachusetts Institute of Technology Press.

Willet, M. (2008). A new model for retirement education and counseling. *Financial Services Review, 17,* 105–130.

Zhan, Y., Wang, M., Lui, S., & Shultz, K. S. (2009). Bridge employment and retirees' health: A longitudinal investigation. *Journal of Occupational Health Psychology, 14,* 374–389.

Zickar, M. J. (2013). The evolving history of retirement within the United States. In M. Wang (Ed.), *The Oxford handbook of retirement* (pp. 10–21). New York, NY: Oxford University Press.

IV

Social Aspects
of Aging

12

Death and the Dying Process, Bereavement, and Widowhood

Andrea June and Meghan A. Marty

The topic of death has tremendous biopsychosocial complexity. We discuss it under the social aspects of aging because familial, societal, and cultural norms provide the context for understanding the how, when, and where of our deaths as well as our experiences of bereavement and grief. And yet, near the end of life, it is important to note that each person prepares for and faces the challenges differently. The varying illnesses and physical conditions combined with the individual uniqueness that we bring to the dying and bereavement processes create this biopsychosocial complexity. The challenge of our legal, health care, and community systems is to meet these diverse individual needs while evolving with society's changing norms. These topics are globally relevant as they impact all of humanity, and yet it is important to note that any discussion of these topics is also inherently bound by one's cultural perspective. As such, we acknowledge a primary and limited focus on the multicultural American society in our discussion of end-of-life issues.

---

*Key references in the References section are indicated by an asterisk.

DYING IN AMERICA TODAY

DEFINITION AND CAUSES OF DEATH

The legal and medical communities have long contended with how to determine when someone has died. Previously defined as the absence of heartbeat and respiration, advances in medical technology have blurred the definitive moment at which the transition from life to death takes place (Rosenberg, 2009). The Uniform Declaration of Death Act drafted in 1980 to provide guidance to state law makers offered an expansion to the definition. Approved by the American Medical Association and American Bar Association and still used today, the determination of death can also be made when the function of the entire brain, including brain stem and neocortex, ceases (Keely et al., 1980). Nonetheless, this well-established additional definition that includes the neocortex continues to be controversial among philosophers and scientists (Capron, 2001; LiPuma & DeMarco, 2013; Miller & Truog, 2010; Veatch, 2009).

Life expectancy and the leading causes of death have shifted in the past 100 years due to medical advances, improved disease prevention, and health promotion. Without antibiotics, acute infections could not be cured; death occurred rapidly and throughout the life course in the early 1900s. The most recent data from 2012 indicate that life expectancy has continued a long-term rising trend and reached a record high of 78.8 years (Murphy, Kochanek, Xu, & Heron, 2015). The age-adjusted death rate showed that about seven Americans died per 1,000, a record low amid significant decreases almost yearly since 1980. Survival of more Americans into late life also means that older adults make up the majority of those dying each year (Murphy et al., 2015). The leading causes of death in the United States in 2012 were chronic conditions such as heart disease and cancer, accounting for 46.5% of all deaths; chronic respiratory disease and stroke were third and fourth. In contrast, acute infections (influenza and pneumonia) are listed as eighth. For non-Hispanic identifying Black and White men and women, heart disease and cancer are ranked as the first and second leading causes of death, respectively. Among Asians, American Natives, and identifying Hispanic populations, these two causes are reversed in primacy. Greater variation in ranking is noted when other leading causes of death are examined by gender and race (Heron, 2015).

INSTITUTIONALIZATION OF DEATH

Increased life expectancy and advances in medicine have not only changed the causes of death, but also the context of death and dying. Prior to 1900, the multigenerational family assumed responsibility for all activities surrounding death and the majority of people died at home (Corr, Nabe, & Corr, 2009). Over time, Americans have turned this responsibility over to paid professionals. By 1949, nearly 50% of deaths occurred in a health care institution (Corr et al., 2009). More recent data show that approximately 43% of all U.S. deaths between 1999 and 2013 occurred in medical facilities (Centers for Disease Control and Prevention, National Center for Health Statistics, 2015). An additional 22% of U.S. deaths occurred in a nursing home or long-term care facility compared to the 25% who died at home.

DEATH TRAJECTORIES

Understanding the different trajectories of dying associated with the leading causes of death is important because of the impact of expected survival on quality of life, care decisions, and family concerns (Kwak, Allen, & Haley, 2011). In *Time for Dying* Glaser and Strauss (1968) proposed several common dying trajectories found in American hospitals based on their field observations: gradual slant, downward slope, peaks and valleys, and descending plateaus.

Lunney, Lynn, and Hogan (2002) later modified the theory to four modal trajectories based on Medicare claims data: sudden death, terminal illness, organ failure, and frailty. The terminal illness category is found among certain types of cancer and is characterized by individuals maintaining a high functional status that rapidly declines. Individuals with chronic obstructive pulmonary disease or congestive heart failure would be in the organ failure group, who experience gradually decreasing functional ability including periods of increased symptom intensity and disability. The frailty trajectory involves slow decline of functional ability with steadily progressive disability as a result of such illnesses as neurocognitive disorders. However, as with any research aggregated to a group level, these identified trajectories do not preclude individual variation of symptoms or functional decline within a given disease process (Gott et al., 2007).

ACTIVE DYING

As death nears, there are some common occurrences near the very end of life as bodily systems begin to shut down. Often there is loss of appetite and thirst. The dying individual, even if not comatose, may be fatigued, sleeping much of the time. Dying individuals are likely to exhibit weakness, confusion, and disorientation. There may be changes in the color and frequency of urine as well as a loss of bowel and urinary control (Doka, 2014). As the circulatory system begins to fail, hands, arms, feet, or legs may be cool to the touch. Some parts of the skin may become blue-colored or mottled. Breathing may seem labored or shallower. There may be times when the person does not breathe for many seconds. Some people may hear a "death rattle," which is likely because the person is no longer able to reabsorb or swallow the normal fluids in the chest and throat, causing a rattling or gurgling noise (Grey, 2015). However, as suggested previously, such predictions of nearing death are difficult to make. Individuals may rally and stabilize for a while or bodily systems may take longer to shut down than expected. After death, there may still be a few shudders or movements of the arms or legs. There could even be an uncontrolled cry because of muscle movement in the voice box (Kolsky, 2008).

ATTITUDES TOWARD DEATH

Research supports the notion that fear of death is a universal human phenomenon (Lehto & Stein, 2009). Our awareness of the inevitability of death and dying creates apprehension and anxiety (Becker, 1973). Despite conflicting findings about the peak age of death anxiety, multiple studies have shown that death anxiety decreases over adulthood (Cicirelli, 2006; Depaola, Griffin, Young, & Neimeyer, 2003; Neimeyer,

Wittkowki, & Moser, 2004; Russac, Gatfliff, Reece, & Spottswood, 2007). The research on gender differences is inconsistent, with some finding no differences, whereas others report higher levels of death anxiety among women (Eshbaugh & Henninger, 2013; Fortner, Neimeyer, & Rybarczeck, 2000; Russac et al., 2007). Much of the research studying the relationship between religiosity and fear of death has sought to test a *buffering hypothesis* in which those with more certainty in the reality of an afterlife have more confidence in being rewarded with a better life after death (Wink & Scott, 2005). Reaching conflicted conclusions, some have found that highly religious people fear death less than those with little to no faith (Daaleman & Dobbs, 2010; Harding, Flannelly, Weaver, & Costa, 2005) while others report the opposite finding—as religiosity increases so does the fear of death (Power & Smith, 2008). Definitive findings with regard to the relationship between death anxiety and ethnicity are again elusive; some research suggests that older White and African Americans express different forms of death anxiety (Cicirelli, 2000; Depaola et al., 2003). The literature supports the hypothesis that more physical and psychological problems are predictive of higher death anxiety (Fortner & Neimeyer, 1999). In contrast, death anxiety appears to decrease from exposure and understanding of the death process (Hamama-Raz, Solomon, & Ohry, 2000; McClatchey & King, 2015; Quinn-Lee, Olson-McBride, & Unterberger, 2014). After a half-century of research in this area, it is clear that the relationship of death anxiety with many demographic and life-experience variables is often complex and intertwined (Neimeyer et al., 2004).

Attitudes toward an individual's own impending death have also been an important subject of scientific inquiry. Although not the first effort to seek to understand the experience of dying individuals, Kübler-Ross's (1969) *On Death and Dying* resonated with the public and scientific communities when she posited that dying persons went through a series of five stages: *denial, anger, bargaining, depression,* and *acceptance.* Evaluation of her theory of stages has revealed many criticisms (see, for example, Corr, 1993) and yet, the articulation of her theory served a pivotal role in the development of the field. Several contemporary theories merit mention as they have evolved to reflect current trends in the illness experience. Building upon the work of his predecessors, Rando (2000) discussed the concept of *anticipatory mourning* as the diverse reactions and coping processes of individuals and families experienced during the course of a life-limiting illness, including the anticipation of future losses. Doka (1993, 1995) extended previous works to highlight the role of various phases in the illness experience (e.g., diagnosis, recovery), where each phase presents an individual and their family with unique tasks. Finally, Tornstam's (2005) term *gerotranscendence* may be helpful to understand the process of an older adult with advanced physical illness. Describing a level of ego development experienced by many older adults, it refers to a complex interpersonal, emotional, and spiritual process by which an individual may experience increased withdrawal to contemplate meaning from a less material-based perspective (Strada, 2011).

ADVANCE CARE PLANNING

This relatively new, prolonged, and possibly anticipated process of dying that characterizes many end-of-life experiences has created new opportunities and choices including the opportunity to say goodbye or the choice of how to use life-sustaining treatments (e.g., mechanical ventilation, artificial nutrition, antibiotics). Advance care planning is a broad term describing various processes by which an individual communicates choices about future end-of-life decisions (Allen, Eichorst, & Oliver, 2013). These choices can be communicated informally through discussion and/or formally through documented advance directives to health care providers, biological or chosen family, friends, or spiritual guides. The most common advance directives include completion of a living will or a do-not-resuscitate order, and appointment of a durable power of attorney. Because most people nearing the end of life are not physically, mentally, or cognitively able to make their own decisions about care, advance care planning is essential to ensure that individuals receive care reflecting their values, goals, and preferences (Institute of Medicine, 2014).

Legislature requiring that individuals are educated about their choices was established by the Patient Self-Determination Act (PSDA; Omnibus Budget Reconciliation Act, 1990), which applied to all health care institutions receiving federal funds such as Medicare. Specifically, individuals have the right to facilitate their own health care decisions, accept or refuse medical treatments, and execute an advance directive. The PSDA also requires institutions to inquire about whether an individual has completed an advance directive and to document its presence in the medical record.

Despite the available provisions to make these choices known in advance, individuals and families in death averse societies often wait until a medical crisis is imminent before considering preferences. Discussions regarding the potential for death tend to occur very late in a disease process, if such discussions occur at all (Bailey et al., 2012; Dy et al., 2011). Similar to findings in previous studies, Rao and colleagues (2014) analyzed data from the 2009 and 2010 wave of the HealthStyles Survey and found that only 26.3% of 7,946 respondents aged 18 years and older had an advance directive. Focusing on older adults specifically, Hopp (2000) examined data from a community-dwelling sample that completed the Asset and Health Dynamics Among the Oldest Old (AHEAD) survey and found that only 37.2% had an advance directive.

Research on predicting completion of advance directives reveals that factors are complex and involve patient, health provider, and location factors (Lovell & Yates, 2014). Advance directives are more common among individuals receiving any type of long-term care (Jones, Moss, & Harris-Kojetin, 2011). However, older age is associated with completion of advance directives across all health institutions (Chang, Huang, & Lin, 2010; Lovell & Yates, 2014). The literature also identifies significant differences by race and ethnicity across health care institutions in which African American, Hispanic, Native American, and Asian individuals are less likely to have a documented advance care plan or to know about advance directives (Degenholtz, Arnold, Meisel, & Lave, 2002; Guo et al., 2010; Levy, Fish, & Kramer, 2005; Wagner, Riopelle, Steckart, Lorenz, & Rosenfeld, 2010). This may reflect differences in a preference for more aggressive care, a historically based distrust in the health care system to provide quality care, a preference for family to communicate wishes rather than using a written document, a belief that one's God controls the timing and nature of death, a cultural taboo against openly discussing or planning for a death, or a lower level of health literacy among minority populations (Carr, 2011; Crawley et al., 2000; Johnson, Kuchibhatla, & Tulsky, 2008; Matsumura et al., 2002; Waite et al., 2013).

The presence of a mental illness, such as depression and schizophrenia, is also an important patient-provider factor in understanding decreased completion rates (Foti, Bartel, Van Citters, Merriman, & Fletcher, 2005; Ganzini, Lee, Heintz, Bloom, & Fenn, 1994). Regarding factors of the health provider, studies have highlighted the role of uncertainty of when, where, and who should initiate conversations about advance directives as well as discomfort with the process in limiting completion of advance directives (Lovell & Yates, 2014).

PALLIATIVE AND HOSPICE CARE

The founding of St. Christopher's Hospice in the United Kingdom in 1967 by Dr. Cicely Saunders is generally credited with having provided the catalyst for the development of the modern hospice care movement with its emphasis on meeting the holistic needs of individuals with a life-limiting illness. The definition and scope of palliative care—a broader term—evolved from this care movement, which focused on the distinction between the prolongation of life and the prolongation of death. The World Health Organization (2015) offers a definition of palliative care as an approach that improves the quality of life of patients and their families by focusing on assessment and treatment of physical, psychosocial, and spiritual needs. However, this definition does not provide clarity as to the difference between hospice and palliative care with regard to treatment options. Indeed, these terms are so frequently referred to as one entity that many people do not realize there is a distinction in many countries. Palliative care is focused on treatment of any conditions that are life-limiting at any point in the disease trajectory without limiting curative approaches, whereas hospice care refers to a special type of comprehensive palliative care provided during the past 6 months of life when an individual has chosen to forgo aggressive, life-prolonging treatments and focus on quality of life (Hiroto & Kasl-Godley, 2013). Figure 12.1 shows a representation of the proposed model of care for those with life-limiting illness that helps distinguish the two types of care.

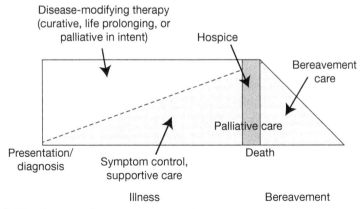

Figure 12.1 Continuum of care.

Source: EPEC (Education for Physicians on End-of-Life Care) Participant's Handbook. The Robert Wood Johnson Foundation/American Medical Association. © The EPEC Project, 1999. Reprinted with permission of Northwestern University.

Palliative care in hospital settings is most often provided by a consult team of health care workers comprised of a physician, nurse, social worker, and chaplain. However, with increasing frequency, palliative care consult teams and hospice teams have expanded to include other professionals such as psychologists, pharmacists, dietitians, occupational or physical therapists, and volunteers (Haley, Larson, Kasl-Godley, Neimeyer, & Kwilosz, 2003). Typically, the needs of individuals with advanced illness and their families are extensive, requiring the expertise and training of more than one discipline (Camartin, 2012). Beyond the required core, the professionals included in any given team may be limited by federal reimbursement guidelines. Medicare, the primary source of insurance for older adults, charges a bundled rate to which all providers must be paid from that single check, and organizations may not be willing to pay for the "extra" discipline-specific or more expensive services as it may limit profit (Twillman & Lewis, 2011). The degree of interdisciplinary integration among the team members and degree of success in meeting client needs may also depend on the system where care is provided, the type of team, and the dynamics of the team (Kasl-Godley & Kwilosz, 2011).

Empirical studies have lent credence to the concerns of professionals in the health care system invested in improving end-of-life care through palliative services. Research has documented dying individuals and their families enduring unnecessary and invasive physical interventions, multiple and prolonged hospitalizations, and economic burdens. Individuals also experienced unrelieved physical and psychological symptoms including pain, fatigue, sleep problems, delirium, depression, anxiety, constipation, and breathing difficulties (Conill et al., 1997; Emanuel, Fairclough, Slutsman, & Emanuel, 2000; Hall, Schroder, & Weaver, 2002). In contrast, evidence suggests that when terminally ill individuals and their families are under the care of a palliative or hospice team, outcomes are improved. Utilization is associated with reduced symptom burden, higher well-being and dignity, decreased intensity of treatment nearing the end of life, and increased family satisfaction with care (Bükki et al., 2013; Connor, Teno, Spense & Smith, 2005; Miller, Mor, Wu, Gozalo, & Lapane, 2002).

Despite the positive outcomes cited for these quality-of-life care options for terminally ill individuals and their families, hospice and palliative care services are underutilized. As with understanding completion rates for advance directives, the possible factors explaining this underutilization are multifaceted. Providers and families may be reluctant to discuss it, believing that a referral to palliative or hospice care symbolizes "giving up" on the individual and that there is no hope (Brickner, Scannell, Marquet, & Ackerson, 2004; Feeg & Elebiary, 2005; Le et al., 2014). Indeed, the underutilization of palliative care is often compounded by misinformation about how it differs from hospice. Palliative care consult teams often spend significant time educating individuals, families, and providers about the ability to continue curative treatment before being accepted by them (Hiroto & Kasl-Godley, 2013). Other factors that may influence utilization include lower health care literacy, experience of discriminatory health care practices and behaviors (based on age, race, ethnicity, gender, or sexual orientation), beliefs that suffering in death is part of a divine plan, and unequal or poor access to medical care (Addis, Davies, Greene, MacBride-Stewart, & Sheperd; 2009; Born, Greiner, Sylvia, Butler, & Ahluwalia, 2004; Crawley, 2002; Francoeur, Payne, Raveis, & Shim, 2006; Krakauer, Crenner, & Fox, 2002).

HASTENING DEATH POLICIES

A discussion about hastening death policies must first start with a distinction between physician-assisted suicide and euthanasia. In physician-assisted suicide, a physician provides the means to enable an individual to end his or her life. In contrast, euthanasia is the deliberate termination of life carried out by a physician. Globally, euthanasia is less likely to be legal or be socially supported than physician-assisted suicide. Euthanasia is not legal in the United States. Physician-assisted suicide is legal or tolerated in many countries and although there are no federal laws in the United States permitting physician-assisted suicide, several states have enacted laws allowing and regulating it.

Oregon voters passed the first physician-assisted suicide legislation in 1994 with the Death With Dignity Act that went into effect in 1997. This legislation permits adult Oregon residents to voluntarily end their lives with self-administration of lethal medication prescribed from a licensed Oregon physician provided certain specifications are met. The Oregon resident must be deemed by the prescribing and consulting physician to have a terminal illness and less than 6 months to live. The physicians must also determine that the resident is capable of making an informed health care decision and is acting voluntarily. The physicians are required to discuss all health care alternatives to physician-assisted suicide with the resident including hospice and palliative care. If either physician believes the resident's judgment is impaired by a mental disorder, he or she must be referred for a psychological evaluation. Finally, residents must request physician-assisted suicide twice verbally separated by at least 15 days and once in writing signed in the presence of two witnesses. The voters of Washington passed a similar law in 2008—Initiative 1000—which was implemented in 2009 after no credible legal challenges. In 2013, Vermont lawmakers enacted the first act passed through legislation— Patient Choice at End of Life—which went into effect immediately. According to the Death With Dignity National Center, 25 legislations plus the District of Columbia have considered Death With Dignity legislation in the 2015 legislative season. Current statuses for each state are listed on the website www.deathwithdignity.org/advocates/national.

As required by law, each year, the Oregon Department of Human Services and Washington State Department of Health publish information about their residents' usage of these acts. As of February 2015, 1,327 people have had prescriptions written and 859 patients have died from ingesting medications prescribed under the Oregon Law since 1997. Most individuals who died had a diagnosis of cancer and were aged 65 years or older. Decedents are commonly White (97%) and had at least some college education (72%). Frequency by sex is split with slightly more males having died (52.7%). Ninety percent were enrolled in hospice. Median duration of patient–physician relationship is 13 weeks and median duration between first request and death is 47 days (Oregon Public Health Division, 2015). In Washington as of March 2015, 725 people have had prescriptions written and 712 have died from ingesting medications prescribed since 2009. The demographic characteristics of Washington residents who died from ingesting the lethal medication are similar to that of Oregon residents (Washington State Department of Health, 2015). Many are interested to see if the data from Vermont reveal the same as it becomes publicly available.

Criticism about the physician-assisted suicide laws range from moral outrage to concerns about the safeguards in the laws as written. Leaders from various religious traditions, from Judeo-Christian sects to Islam, vehemently oppose any law that violates the sanctity of life and questions the sovereignty of their deity. The American Medical Association (n.d.) asserts that physician-assisted suicide is "fundamentally incompatible with the physician's role as a healer" and should instead focus on providing optimal treatment at end of life (Policy No. H-140.952). Many physicians also cite the Hippocratic Oath to "do no harm" as an ethical conflict with physician-assisted suicide laws (Lagay, 2003). Other professionals scrutinize elements of the Oregon law that other states are using as model legislation. In her analysis of the individual clauses of the law, Canetto (2011) raises thoughtful questions about the lack of specificity and inconsistencies in the proposed safeguards of the law. For example, current mental health standards indicate that articulated suicidal intent is a signal of diminished capacity and obligates the provider to intervene by working to remove lethal means. Under Oregon law, the response to intent could be to provide the lethal means, which creates ambiguity about suicidal ideation as a symptom to be resolved or a choice to be supported.

Advocates of the physician-assisted suicide laws argue that it should be respected as a health care choice among many others that Americans are currently afforded (Compassion & Choices, n.d.). Available data suggest that the law has psychological benefits, as individuals with life-limiting illnesses take comfort in knowing that this option exists (Cerminara & Perez, 2000). Advocates argue that the meticulous record keeping by Oregon and Washington provide evidence that the safeguards in the law are effective (Brock, 2000; Chin, Hedberg, Higginson, & Fleming, 1999). Moreover, ethical codes have always provided professional guidance when laws are vague. And, despite opposition from some professional health care organizations, others at the national and state levels assert that the issue is complex and have remained neutral (e.g., American Psychological Association, Oregon Medical Association). One could argue that the oath to do no harm also applies to actively preventing capable individuals from executing a health care choice. Indeed, the current laws allow for physicians to participate or refer patients to another provider. Regarding the position that society should instead focus on building better access to hospice and palliative care, a recent study by Wang and colleagues (2015) showed that Oregon residents had the highest quartile of hospice use of all the states suggesting these are not mutually exclusive.

BEREAVEMENT

DEFINITIONS OF BEREAVEMENT, GRIEF, AND MOURNING

Bereavement refers to the objective situation of having recently lost a significant person through death (Stroebe, Hansson, Stroebe, & Schut, 2001). The emotional reaction to bereavement is typically referred to as *grief* and includes a wide range of cognitive, social, behavioral, physiological, and somatic manifestations (Stroebe et al., 2001), as well as the active process of dealing and coping with loss (Röcke & Cherry, 2002). The term *mourning* is sometimes used interchangeably with grief, and often refers to the "social expressions or acts expressive of grief that are shaped by the practices of a given society or cultural group" (Stroebe et al., 2001, p. 6).

Common Reactions to Bereavement

As noted in the beginning of the chapter, any understanding of the reaction to bereavement will be entangled with culture. The social constructions of any culture will influence if, how, when, and where grief is expressed, felt, and understood. Cultural sensitivity and awareness are necessary in understanding common group reactions as well as within group individual diversity to bereavement, making the "typical" experience elusive. Important scholarship efforts are developing a substantial literature on the connections of culture and grief to bring about a greater global awareness and readers are strongly encouraged to seek out such resources (see, for example, Rosenblatt, 2001, 2008). The summary of the literature that follows is based in the Western perspective of reactions to bereavement.

Psychological reactions are typically most intense in early bereavement and may be identified by four dimensions: affective, behavioral, cognitive, and physiological (Stroebe et al., 2001). Affective reactions to bereavement may include depression, despair and dejection, anxiety, guilt, anger and hostility, anhedonia, and loneliness. Behavioral reactions to bereavement may include agitation, fatigue, crying, and social withdrawal. Cognitive reactions to bereavement may include preoccupation with thoughts of the deceased, lowered self-esteem, self-reproach, helplessness and hopelessness, a sense of unreality, and problems with memory and concentration. Finally, physical reactions to bereavement may include loss of appetite, sleep disturbance, energy loss and exhaustion, somatic complaints, physical complaints similar to those the deceased had endured, changes in drug intake, and susceptibility to illness and disease. Spiritual manifestations of grief may also exist, including a change in religious activity or a sense of anger or betrayal (Strada, 2011).

Bereavement and Mental Health Disorders

As indicated previously, common or "typical" reactions to bereavement may encompass a wide range of symptoms and experiences. These symptoms and experiences may also be criteria for the diagnosis of a variety of mental health disorders. One systematic review examining the incidence of mental health disorders in the first year of widowhood found approximately 22% of the widowed met diagnostic criteria for major depressive disorder (MDD), almost 12% met diagnostic criteria for post-traumatic stress disorder (PTSD), and this group was at higher risk for developing panic disorder and generalized anxiety disorder (Onrust & Cuijpers, 2006). Professionals working with bereaved older adults should carefully consider the presence of other mental health conditions in addition to a normal response to a significant loss, while exercising clinical judgment and noting the bereaved individual's history and cultural norms for the expression of distress in the context of loss (American Psychiatric Association, 2013). In addition to discussing several considerations for differential assessment in the text, core symptom differences are summarized in Table 12.1.

Table 12.1 Differentiating Symptoms of Bereavement and Other Clinical Diagnoses

	Uncomplicated Bereavement	Major Depressive Episode	Posttraumatic Stress Disorder	Persistent Complex Bereavement Disorder
Affect	Sadness, emptiness, and loss; can experience positive emotions	Depressed; inability to experience positive emotions; pervasive guilt	Fear; anger; horror; shame; inability to experience positive emotions; guilt focused on the cause or consequences of the traumatic event	Sadness; intense sorrow and emotional pain; guilt focused on interactions with the deceased or circumstances of the death
Intensity	Decreases over days to weeks; occurs in waves with increases often associated with reminders of the deceased	Persistent; not necessarily tied to specific triggers	Increases associated with reminders of the traumatic event; usually specific to the event; avoidance of stimuli related to the event	Increases are more pervasive and unexpected; severe symptoms >12 months; avoidance of situations and people related to reminders of the loss
Thought content	Preoccupation with thoughts and memories of the deceased	Self-critical; pessimistic rumination	Persistent and exaggerated negative beliefs about oneself, others, or the world	Preoccupation with yearning and longing for the deceased and/or circumstances of the death
Self-esteem	Typically preserved	Worthlessness; self-loathing	May worsen in response to negative beliefs and expectations about oneself	Self-blame; confusion about one's role in life; diminished sense of identity
Thoughts of death	If present, generally focused on the deceased and joining the deceased	Focused on ending one's life because of feeling worthless, undeserving of life, unable to cope	May be associated with reckless or self-destructive behavior	Desire to die to be with the deceased; sense that life is meaningless or empty without the deceased

Grief and MDD share several common symptoms, such as intense feelings of sadness, rumination, insomnia, poor appetite, weight loss, and difficulties with concentration (American Psychiatric Association, 2013). However, grief can be distinguished from MDD such that with grief the predominant affect is feelings of emptiness and loss, rather than depressed mood or anhedonia, and may be accompanied by positive emotions and humor. The intensity of dysphoria in grief tends to decrease over days to weeks and often occurs in waves, typically triggered by thoughts or reminders of the deceased, whereas MDD is characterized by pervasive unhappiness and misery, with an inability to anticipate happiness or pleasure. Thought content in grief generally features a preoccupation with thoughts and memories of the deceased, self-esteem is generally preserved, and if self-derogatory ideation is present, it typically involves perceived failings with regard to the deceased (e.g., not telling the deceased how much he or she was loved). In grief, thoughts of death and dying are generally focused on the deceased and possibly about "joining" the deceased, rather than ending one's life because of feeling worthless, undeserving of life, or unable to cope with the pain of depression. One notable change in the most recent edition of the *Diagnostic and Statistical Manual of Mental Disorders, Fifth Edition (DSM-5)* is the removal of the bereavement exclusion from the MDD diagnostic criteria, which was met with some controversy (Wakefield, 2013). Previous editions of the manual advised clinicians to refrain from diagnosing MDD in individuals within the first 2 months following the death of a loved one. The current MDD diagnostic criteria indicate MDD may occur in the context of early bereavement and that clinicians should carefully consider the presence of both.

The development of PTSD in a bereaved individual is more likely when the loss of life has been massive or the nature of the deaths horrific (Stroebe, Schut, & Stroebe, 2007). In such cases, *complex bereavement* (see the following additional information) should also be considered in the differential diagnosis. PTSD is often triggered by exposure to actual or threatened death of the individual. The primary emotion is fear or horror, nightmares are common, painful reminders are linked to the specific traumatic event, and there is a persistent inability to experience positive emotions (American Psychiatric Association, 2013). In contrast, bereavement is triggered by the loss of a significant person through death. Here, the primary emotion is sadness accompanied by yearning/longing for the deceased, nightmares are rare, painful reminders of the deceased and the relationship with the deceased are more pervasive and unexpected, and the ability to experience positive emotions typically remains intact.

COMPLEX BEREAVEMENT

There is burgeoning evidence for the existence of *complex bereavement*, also referred to as *complicated grief, pathological grief, prolonged grief,* or *traumatic grief.* This type of grief response deviates from the normal grief experience in time course and/or intensity symptoms, taking into consideration cultural and societal norms (Stroebe et al., 2007). Estimated rates of complex bereavement range from 9% to 20% among grieving adults, depending on the diagnostic criteria used (Stroebe et al., 2007). The *DSM-5* included persistent complex bereavement disorder (PCBD) as a condition for further study, indicating the proposed criteria are not meant for clinical use, but future research on the condition is encouraged (American Psychiatric Association, 2013). The current conceptualization of PCBD is characterized by intense longing for the deceased, and preoccupation with the deceased as well as the circumstances surrounding the death. Reactive distress to the death includes extreme difficulty accepting the death; disbelief, emotional numbness, bitterness, or anger related to the loss; maladaptive appraisals about oneself in relation to the deceased or the death; and excessive avoidance of reminders of the loss. Social and identity disruption includes a desire to die in order to be with the deceased, difficulty trusting others, feeling alone or detached, feeling that life is meaningless or empty, confusion about one's role in life, and reluctance to pursue interests since the loss or to plan for the future.

Associated features supporting the presence of PCBD in a grieving individual may include auditory or visual hallucinations of the deceased, diverse somatic complaints (including symptoms experienced by the deceased), and suicidal ideation. These proposed PCBD criteria indicate the symptoms must be experienced by the grieving individual more days than not, to a clinically significant degree, for a period of at least 12 months after the death (American Psychiatric Association, 2013). Confirmed prospective risk factors for developing complex bereavement across all age groups include low social support, anxious/avoidant/insecure attachment style, discovering or identifying the body (in cases of violent death), being the spouse or parent of the deceased, high predeath marital dependence, and high neuroticism (Burke & Neimeyer, 2012). Other research indicates that lower level of education and higher level of cognitive impairment may be associated with higher prevalence of complex bereavement among older adults (Newson, Boelen, Hek, Hofman, & Tiemeier, 2011). Measures of PCBD are currently under development to facilitate further research into the construct (Lee, 2015).

THEORETICAL MODELS OF ADJUSTMENT TO BEREAVEMENT

Traditional models of coping with bereavement stemmed from the psychoanalytic tradition, and posited that confronting the reality of a loss and relinquishing the bond to the deceased were essential for overcoming bereavement (Stroebe & Schut, 2001). Also growing out of the psychoanalytic tradition was the concept of *grief work*, characterized by reviewing the past, including events that occurred before and at the time of death, focusing on memories, and working toward detachment from the deceased (Stroebe & Schut, 2001). This concept was also incorporated into the attachment theory perspective of coping with bereavement, which posited that working through grief takes place through a sequence of overlapping, flexibly occurring phases: shock, yearning and protest, despair, and recovery (Stroebe & Schut, 2001).

In spite of the widely accepted notion that natural response to the death of a loved one involves discrete orderly stages that results in resolution, this concept has also received much critical examination among contemporary bereavement researchers and there is surprisingly little empirical support for the concept. For example, in a sample of primarily White older women who lost a loved one from natural causes, Maciejewski and colleagues (2007) found disbelief peaked at 1 month postloss, yearning peaked at 4 months postloss, anger peaked at 5 months postloss, and depression peaked at 6 months postloss. However, in contrast to stage model predictions, they also found that acceptance of the death was the most frequently endorsed experience initially and increased throughout the study period (1 to 24 months postloss). Additionally, anger and denial occurred at relatively low levels throughout the first 2 years of adjustment. Thinking about the grieving process as phases or stages may be useful as a general orientation to which reactions are likely involved in the experience of grief; however, many variables including situational, personal, and environmental factors are likely to determine the individual grieving process of older adults (Röcke & Cherry, 2002).

One contemporary model of coping with bereavement, the Dual Process Model (DPM), proposes adaptive grieving is characterized by a dynamic process of both focusing on the loss ("loss-orientation") and attending to the everyday consequences of the loss ("restoration-orientation"; Stroebe & Schut, 2010). As shown in Figure 12.2, loss-orientation entails engagement with stimuli that serve as reminders of the loss (e.g., looking through old photos or sharing stories of the deceased), whereas restoration-orientation entails withdrawing from the loss and turning toward everyday life functions (e.g., finances, household tasks) and building a future without the deceased (e.g., finding new sources of social and emotional support). Central to the DPM is the notion that adaptive grieving involves a normative oscillation between these two orientations. The duration of time spent in either orientation may vary, although difficulties may arise if the griever becomes "stuck" in either one. There is mounting empirical support for the tenets and clinical utility of the DPM (Stroebe & Schut, 2010).

Another contemporary approach to understanding coping with bereavement is the *continuing bonds* perspective, which is rooted in attachment theory (Field, Gao, & Paderna, 2005). This perspective highlights the ways in which a connection to the deceased following the death of a significant other may be maintained and, in contrast to the earlier notion of grief work, this continued connection to the deceased is

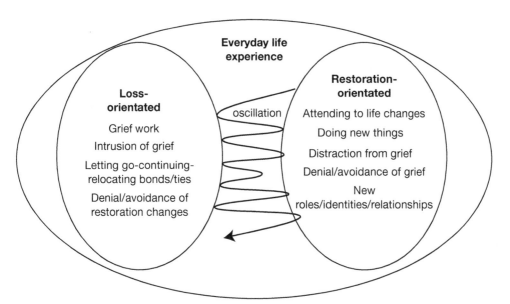

Figure 12.2 The dual process model of coping with bereavement.
Source: Stroebe and Strut (2001).

seen as largely normative. Continuing bonds may be maintained though experiences such as imaginary conversation with the deceased, thinking of good memories of the deceased, or a sense that the deceased is guiding, watching over, or comforting the grieving individual. The current consensus among bereavement researchers is that it is neither generally adaptive for bereaved people to continue their bonds with deceased loved ones, nor to relinquish them, and it is important to attend to individual differences as well as underlying processes in continuing or relinquishing bonds (Stroebe, Schut, & Boerner, 2010).

A final contemporary model for coping with bereavement focuses on the adaptive process of reaffirming or reconstructing a world of meaning that is challenged by the loss of a loved one (Neimeyer, 2001). This meaning-making, narrative approach to coping with bereavement emphasizes processing both the story of the death and the story of the relationship with the deceased, such that grief is integrated into a changed self-narrative. One study of older widowed individuals found those who struggled to find meaning in early bereavement showed greater grief and depression across the first few years of the loss (Coleman & Neimeyer, 2010). In contrast, the widowed individuals who succeeded in making sense of the loss in early bereavement demonstrated considerable resilience, including higher levels of pride, joy, and well-being, 4 years later.

Intervention for Bereaved Individuals

The most basic issue regarding professional intervention for bereaved individuals is whether it should be offered at all. Most reactions to bereavement are not complicated (Bonanno et al., 2002) and for most bereaved people, family and friends, religious and community groups, and various societal resources provide the necessary support (Stroebe et al., 2007). Additionally, a review of the empirical research on the concept of *grief work* found no evidence that emotional disclosure facilitates adjustment to loss in normal bereavement (Stroebe, Schut, & Stroebe, 2005). Primary prevention (i.e., services targeting everyone who has lost a loved one) can be helpful when the initiative is left with the bereaved individual; however, there is no indication that all bereaved people will benefit from intervention (Stroebe et al., 2007). The general consensus among bereavement scholars is that professional intervention should be targeted at high-risk individuals, including those with a debilitating experience of complicated bereavement or bereavement-related depression and other mental health disorders (Stroebe et al., 2007).

Evidence suggests therapy for complicated grief or bereavement-related depression and stress disorders leads to substantial and lasting results (Stroebe et al., 2007). Intervention strategies borrowing from diverse theoretical psychotherapy models may be useful in the treatment of complex bereavement in later life, including behavioral activation, emotion regulation, challenging dysfunctional thinking, retelling the narrative of the death, reconstructing meaning, reworking the continuing bond, life review, goal work, and expressive arts approaches (Neimeyer & Holland, 2015). Developed specifically for individuals with complex bereavement reactions, Complicated grief therapy (CGT) involves a combination of modified in vivo and imaginal exposure focusing on processing traumatic symptoms related to the death, and promotes a sense of connection with the deceased loved one and restoring life in the face of a changed reality. Randomized clinical trials have shown CGT produces greater improvement in complex bereavement and depressive symptoms than grief-focused interpersonal psychotherapy among bereaved individuals across the life span (Shear, Frank, Houck, & Reynolds, 2005) and older adults (Shear et al., 2014).

There is very little empirical evidence supporting the use of psychotropic medication to treat grief-related symptoms. A pharmacological treatment approach for normal bereavement is not indicated. The results of a few small randomized control trials investigating the effectiveness of antidepressant medication in treating grief-related symptoms indicated improvement in depressive symptoms among bereaved individuals, but little effect on grief itself (Cacciatore & Thieleman, 2012). In addition, benzodiazepines have been trialed for treating bereavement, with the evidence indicating no effect (Cacciatore & Thieleman, 2012). Some case series and open-label trials have suggested antidepressant medication may help symptoms associated with complex bereavement; however, until further evidence from controlled trials is gathered, the role of pharmacotherapy in treating complex bereavement is unclear (Jordan & Litz, 2014). Critics of using a pharmacological treatment approach caution against the "medicalization" of grief (Neimeyer & Holland, 2015).

LATE-LIFE SPOUSAL LOSS

GENERAL CHARACTERISTICS

The loss of a spouse or long-term partner is a common occurrence in later life: The majority of persons become widow/ers when they are in their early 70s (Naef, Ward, Mahrer-Imhof, & Grande, 2013). Much of the existing empirical knowledge of late-life spousal loss is based on the experiences of heterosexual couples and since women are affected more often, at a younger age, and for longer time periods than men, we see even more of a focus in the literature on the experiences of older heterosexual women. Common emotions after late-life spousal loss include shock, sadness, pain, numbness, turmoil, remorse, self-blame, regret, and feelings of betrayal and anger (Naef et al., 2013). Sleep disturbance, fatigue, lack of energy, loss of appetite, and nausea are common health concerns (Naef et al., 2013). As with other types of bereavement, most widow/ers find the intensity of grief decreases over time (Naef et al., 2013).

A pervasive sense of loneliness in daily life following the loss of a life companion is common; studies show that older widowed persons experience times in a day or a year that are particularly difficult (e.g., mealtimes, bedtime, anniversaries; Naef et al., 2013). The extent of participation in leisure activities fluctuates; however, most older widow/ers keep or increase social contacts (Naef et al., 2013). Relationships with family, friends, neighbors, and other widow/ers are a resource in late-life spousal bereavement and continued engagement with their lost partners may also serve as a source of comfort (e.g., through sensing the presence of the deceased, reliving the past through memories and dreams, by taking up an activity of the deceased; Naef et al., 2013). Some may have difficulty appearing in public alone and socializing as a single person, but some also find their new status to be a chance to experience self-growth, learn new skills, and assume new roles (Naef et al., 2013).

IMPACT OF SPOUSAL LOSS ON PARTNER MORTALITY

The premature or early death of a widowed person shortly after that individual is widowed is often referred to as the *widowhood effect*. Although the cause of this phenomenon is likely multifactorial, the findings of most longitudinal studies, which controlled for several confounding variables, indicate an excess risk of mortality in the first 6 months during bereavement (Stroebe et al., 2007). Other studies indicate the death of a partner significantly increases the mortality rate of the survivor, with a strong effect during the first 2.5 years (van den Berg, Lindeboom, & Portrait, 2011). As compared with married people, widow/ers have very high rates of accidental and violent causes of death, including completed suicide, and alcohol-related diseases, and moderate rates for chronic ischemic heart disease and lung cancer (Stroebe et al., 2007). Widow/ers have a greater occurrence of physical health complaints (including physical pain) compared with matched controls, with some indication of reduced use of health services for those with intense grief (Stroebe et al., 2007).

IMPACT OF GENDER AND AGE

Results of studies investigating the effect of gender on older widow/ers who are coping with loss are not entirely consistent (Röcke & Cherry, 2002); however, most findings indicate that widowers are at relatively more excessive risk of mortality than widows (Stroebe et al., 2007). Findings also indicate a greater mortality risk for younger than for older bereaved individuals who have lost their spouses; however, there should be caution in interpreting these results since institutionalized individuals (e.g., those residing in nursing homes, residential mental hospitals, etc.) are sometimes excluded from large-scale samples, potentially artificially inflating the relative survival rates of elderly populations as compared with younger people (Stroebe et al., 2007). There is a general trend that implies that older adults generally show less negative and less intense reactions of grief upon losing a spouse or significant other than do younger adults, which may be explained by the concept that widowhood represents an off-time and, therefore, critical and nonnormative life event for young adults (Röcke & Cherry, 2002). Other studies indicate a different age trend, such that very young and very old adults show the greatest difficulty in coping with the loss, perhaps because the younger someone is, the more sudden and unexpected the loss will appear, and for very old persons problems may arise from feelings of being left behind shortly before dying oneself and experiencing concurrent losses outside of bereavement (Röcke & Cherry, 2002).

BEREAVEMENT AFTER CAREGIVING

Late-life spousal bereavement is often preceded by an extended period of chronic illness or disability during which family members take on caregiving tasks. Research investigating the impact of the caregiving experience on bereavement indicates most caregivers benefit from anticipation prior to the loss (e.g., thinking about the impending death and the caregiver's life afterwards). Additionally, caregivers experience stress relief following bereavement, with rapid decreases in depression and grief symptoms within a year after the death (Boerner & Schulz, 2009). However, a sizeable minority (up to 30%) do experience continued high levels of stress and mental health difficulties, as well as complex bereavement, after the death (Boerner & Schulz, 2009). Complex bereavement symptoms may begin before the care recipient's death as well. One study showed that family caregivers younger than 60 years old had higher levels of predeath complex grief symptoms than those 60 and older, but emotional difficulties were present in both groups (Tomarken et al., 2008). The same study found significant associations between predeath complex grief symptoms, pessimistic thinking, and number of moderate-to-severe stressful life events, suggesting these factors should be monitored closely in family caregivers. Notably, some research indicates the positive, rewarding preloss aspects of the caregiving experience (that may provide the caregiver with a sense of meaning and/or achievement) may also be associated with postloss depression and grief, demonstrating the importance of attending to both positive and negative aspects of caregiving in prediction of caregivers' responses to the death of the person for whom they cared (Boerner, Schultz, & Horowitz, 2004).

SAME-SEX PARTNER LOSS

The literature on the grieving process of same-sex partners in late life is sparse; much of the existing research is based on gay men who lost partners or good friends from HIV-related illness. Within the bereavement literature, it is often discussed under the heading of *disenfranchised grief*, although the term is not specific to the sexual minority community. Disenfranchised grief is a term used to describe when an individual's grief is not openly acknowledged, socially validated, or publicly mourned (Doka, 2008). One qualitative study exploring the experiences of midlife heterosexual and gay widowers found many similarities; for example, both groups had difficulties in their efforts to seek emotional support from others (O'Brien, Forrest, & Austin, 2002). However, the gay widowers perceived less societal and familial recognition of the depths of their relationships with their deceased partners and experienced inequities in access to family medical and bereavement leave from work. Additionally, the negative stigma of AIDS was present whether or not the partner died from AIDS, complicating the grief process for all of the gay widowers. Another qualitative study, examining the experiences of mid- to late-life lesbian widows, indicated negative support (e.g., ongoing legal battles, being shut out of a hospital room, lack of recognition of the relationship) was related to less resolution of their own grief (Bent & Magilvy, 2006). Other complicating factors stemmed from whether or not the couple had disclosed the nature of their relationship to others and situational difficulties, such as privileges being given to the biological family regarding decisions about burial or cremation and access to the body of the partner while dying or after death.

OTHER RELATIONSHIP LOSSES

In addition to the loss of a spouse or long-time partner, older adults may be faced with the deaths of other loved ones, including siblings, adult children, and grandchildren. Unfortunately this topic has received very little research or clinical attention.

With regard to the death of a sibling, there is almost no research on this topic, perhaps related to the expectation that the spouse and adult child of the deceased would be more affected than a bereaved sibling. However, there is some indication that the functional and cognitive status of bereaved siblings does not differ significantly from those who have lost a spouse (Moss, Moss, & Hansson, 2001). The findings of studies investigating the impact of losing an adult child are mixed. Some research suggests the loss of a child elicits more intense grief reactions, whereas other research suggests no differences from loss of a spouse (Moss et al., 2001). The impact may, in part, depend on how active or involved the adult child had been in the elderly person's life. Additionally, it is not clear how the age of the elderly parent is a factor in bereavement (Moss et al., 2001). Finally, most studies investigating the impact of losing a grandchild are qualitative in nature, and suggest that this type of loss is life- changing and complex, given that grandparents often try to support their adult children while grieving themselves, and grandparents can experience difficulty finding an outlet for their own grief (Fry, 1997; Gilrane-McGarry & O'Grady, 2011; Youngblut, Brooten, Blais, Kilgore, & Yoo, 2015). Some research indicates grandparents may experience survivor guilt, wishing that they had died instead of their grandchild (Fry, 1997). One quantitative study examining the health and functioning of bereaved grandparents within one year of their grandchild's death found high rates of clinical depression, PTSD, physical illness, hospitalizations, and medication changes (Youngblut et al., 2015). The same study found symptom severity depended on whether the grandparent had provided childcare for the deceased grandchild and the racial/ethnic background of the grandparent.

CONCLUSION

This chapter aimed to introduce readers to the tremendous biopsychosocial complexity of understanding death and loss, in consideration of the diversity found among older adults. This review of the literature suggests our ever-evolving understanding of these concepts is both a product of and a reaction to societal norms and systems (i.e., medical, economic, family, technology). While advances in technology and health prevention have created longer life expectancies, it also helped shape a society with high death aversion. Our longer life spans have raised important questions about quality of life as we age and how a "good death" may be defined differently for each of us. Nevertheless, death and dying continue to remain negatively valenced events for individuals and their loved ones. The experience of grief is highly individualized, but differentiating common grief experiences from clinical manifestations allows us to provide additional support to those who need it.

DISCUSSION QUESTIONS

1. Describe some common physical events that occur near death.

2. Consider preparing your own advance directives at this time. After researching this on your own, describe some of the decisions you need to make in this process.

3. Compare and contrast palliative and hospice care. Draw a diagram if this is helpful.

4. Compare euthanasia and physician-assisted suicide, and describe some characteristics of people who have engaged in physician-assisted suicide.

5. Describe some of the psychological reactions in early bereavement.

6. Describe some differences between uncomplicated bereavement and MDD.

7. Describe the Dual Process model of bereavement.

8. What is disenfranchised grief?

REFERENCES

*Addis, S., Davies, M., Greene, G., MacBride-Stewart, S., & Sheperd, M. (2009). The health, social care and housing needs of lesbian, gay, bisexual, and transgender older people: A review of the literature. *Health and Social Care in the Community, 17*, 647–658. doi:10.1111/j.1365-2524 .2009.00866.x

Allen, R. S., Eichorst, M. K. & Oliver, J. (2013). Advance directives: Planning for the end-of-life. In J. L. Werth, Jr. (Ed.) *Counseling clients near the end of life* (pp. 53–74). New York, NY: Springer Publishing.

American Medical Association. (n.d.). *Physician assisted suicide H-140.952*. Retrieved from https:// policysearch.ama-assn.org/policyfinder/search/physician%20assisted%20suicide%20 H-140.952/relevant/1

American Psychiatric Association. (2013). *Diagnostic and statistical manual of mental disorders* (5th ed.). Arlington, VA: American Psychiatric Publishing.

Bailey, F. A., Allen, R. S., Williams, B. R., Goode, P. S., Granstaff, S., Redden, D. T., & Burgio, K. L. (2012). Do-not-resuscitate orders in the last days of life. *Journal of Palliative Medicine, 15*(7), 751–759. doi:10.1089/jpm.2011.0321

Becker, E. (1973). *The denial of death*. New York, NY: Free Press.

Bent, K. N., & Magilvy, J. K. (2006). When a partner dies: Lesbian widows. *Issues in Mental Health Nursing, 27*, 447–459. doi:10.1080/01612840600599960

Boerner, K., & Schulz, R. (2009). Caregiving, bereavement, and complicated grief. *Bereavement Care, 28*(3), 10–13. doi:10.1080/02682620903355382

Boerner, K., Schultz, R., & Horowitz, A. (2004) Positive aspects of caregiving and adaptation to bereavement. *Psychology and Aging, 19*(4), 668–675. doi:10.1037/0882-7974.19.4.668

Bonanno, G. A., Wortman, C. B., Lehman, D. R., Tweed, R. G., Haring, M., Sonnega, J., . . . Nesse, R. M. (2002). Resilience to loss and chronic grief: A prospective study from preloss to 18-months postloss. *Journal of Personality and Social Psychology, 83*(5), 1150–1164. doi:10.1037// 0022-3514.83.5.1150

Born, W., Greiner, K. A., Sylvia, E., Butler, J., & Ahluwalia, J. S. (2004). Knowledge, attitudes, and beliefs about end-of-life care among inner-city African Americans and Latinos. *Journal of Palliative Medicine, 7*, 247–256. doi:10.1089/109662104773709369

Brickner, L., Scannell, K., Marquet, S., & Ackerson, L. (2004). Barriers to hospice care and referrals: Survey of physicians' knowledge, attitudes, and perceptions in a health maintenance organization. *Journal of Palliative Medicine, 7*(3), 411–418. doi:10.1089/1096621041349518

Brock, D. W. (2000). Misconceived sources of opposition to physician-assisted suicide. *Psychology, Public Policy, And Law, 6*(2), 305–313. doi:10.1037/1076-8971.6.2.305

Bükki, J., Scherbel, J., Stiel, S., Klein, C., Meidenbauer, N., & Ostgathe, C. (2013). Palliative care needs, symptoms, and treatment intensity along the disease trajectory in medical oncology outpatients: A retrospective chart review. *Supportive Care in Cancer, 21*(6), 1743–1750. doi:10 .1007/s00520-013-1721-y

Burke, L. A., & Neimeyer, R. A. (2012) Prospective risk factors for complicated grief: A review of the empirical literature. In M. S. Stroebe, H. Schut, J. van der Bout, & P. Boelen (Eds.), *Complicated grief: Scientific foundations for healthcare professionals* (pp. 145–161). New York, NY: Routledge.

Cacciatore, J., & Thieleman, K. (2012). Pharmacological treatment following traumatic bereavement: A case series. *Journal of Loss and Trauma, 17*, 557–579. doi:10.1080/15325024.2012.688699

Camartin, C. (2012). [Case report—interprofessional teamwork in palliative care]. *Therapeutische Umschau. Revue Thérapeutique, 69*(2), 110–113. doi:10.1024/0040-5930/a000261

Canetto, S. S. (2011). Physician-assisted suicide in the United States: Issues, challenges, roles, and implications for clinicians. In S. H. Qualls, J. E. Kasl-Godley, S. H. Qualls, & J. E. Kasl-Godley (Eds.), *End-of-life issues, grief, and bereavement: What clinicians need to know* (pp. 263–284). Hoboken, NJ: John Wiley

Capron, A. M. (2001). Brain death: Well settled yet still unresolved. *New England Journal of Medicine, 344*, 1244–1246. doi:10.1056/NEJM200104193441611

Carr, D. (2011). Racial differences in end-of-life planning: Why don't Blacks and Latinos prepare for the inevitable? *Omega: Journal of Death and Dying, 63*(1), 1–20. doi:10.2190/OM.63.1.a

Centers for Disease Control and Prevention, National Center for Health Statistics. (2015). Underlying cause of death 1999-2013. Retrieved from http://wonder.cdc.gov/ucd-icd10.html

Cerminara, K. L., & Perez, A. (2000). Therapeutic death: A look at Oregon's' Law. *Psychology, Public Policy, and Law, 6*, 503–525.

Chang, Y., Huang, C.-F., & Lin, C.-C. (2010). Do not resuscitate orders for critically ill patients in intensive care. *Nursing Ethics, 17*, 445–455. doi:10.1177/0969733010364893

Chin, A. E., Hedberg, K., Higginson, G. K., & Fleming, D. W. (1999). *Oregon's Death with Dignity Act: The first year's experience.* Portland: Oregon Health Division.

Cicirelli, V. G. (2000). Older adults' ethnicity, fear of death, and end-of-life decisions. In A. Tomer & A. Tomer (Eds.), *Death attitudes and the older adult: Theories, concepts, and applications* (pp. 175–191). New York, NY: Brunner-Routledge.

Cicirelli, V. G. (2006). Fear of death in mid-old age. *Journal of Gerontology: Psychological Science, 61B*(2), P75–P81. doi:10.1093/geronb/61.2.P75

Coleman, R. A., & Neimeyer, R. A. (2010). Measuring meaning: Searching for and making sense of spousal loss in late-life. *Death Studies, 34*, 804–834. doi:10.1080/07481181003761625

Compassion & Choices. (n.d.). Death with dignity. Retrieved from https://www.compassionand choices.org/death-with-dignity

Conill, C., Verger, E., Henríquez, I., Saiz, N., Espier, M., Lugo, F., & Garrigos, A. (1997). Symptom prevalence in the last week of life. *Journal of Pain and Symptom Management, 14*(6), 328–331. doi:10.1016/S0885-3924(97)00263-7

Connor, S. R., Teno, J., Spence, C., & Smith, N. (2005). Family evaluation of hospice care: Results from voluntary submission of data via website. *Journal of Pain and Symptom Management, 30*, 9–17. doi:10.1016/j.jpainsymman.2005.04.001

Corr, C. A. (1993). Coping with dying: Lessons that we should and should not learn from the work of Elisabeth Kübler-Ross. *Death Studies, 17*(1), 69–83. doi:10.1080/07481189308252605

*Corr, C. A., Nabe, C. M., & Corr, D. M. (2009). *Death and dying, life and living* (6th ed.). Belmont, CA: Wadsworth.

Crawley, L., Payne, R., Bolden, J., Payne, T., Washington, P., & Williams, S. (2000). Palliative and end-of-life care in the African American community. *Journal of the American Medical Association, 284*(19), 2518–2521. doi:10.1001/jama.284.19.2518

Daaleman, T. P., & Dobbs, D. (2010). Religiosity, spirituality, and death attitudes in chronically ill older adults. *Research on Aging, 32*, 224–243.

Degenholtz, H. B., Arnold, R. A., Meisel, A., & Lave, J. R. (2002). Persistence of racial disparities in advance care plan documents among nursing home residents. *Journal of the American Geriatrics Society, 50*(2), 378–81. doi:10.1046/j.1532-5415.2002.50073.x

Depaola, S. J., Griffin, M., Young, J. R., & Neimeyer, R. A. (2003). Death anxiety and attitudes toward the elderly among adults: The role of gender and ethnicity. *Death Studies, 27*(4), 335–354. doi:10.1080/07481180302904

Doka, K. J. (1993). *Living with life-threatening illness: A guide for patients*, their families, and caregivers. Lexington, MA: Lexington Books.

Doka, K. J. (1995). Coping with life threatening illness: A task based approach. *Omega: The Journal of Death and Dying, 32*, 111–122.

*Doka, K. J. (2008). Disenfranchised grief in historical and cultural perspective. In M. S. Stroebe, R. O. Hannson, H. Schut, & W. Stroebe (Eds.), *Handbook of bereavement research and practice: Advances in theory and intervention* (pp. 207–222). Washington, DC: American Psychological Association.

Doka, K. J. (2014). *Counseling individuals with life-threatening illness* (2nd ed.) New York, NY: Springer Publishing.

Dy, S. M., Asch, S. M., Lorenz, K. A., Weeks, K., Sharma, R. K., Wolff, A. C., & Malin, J. L. (2011). Quality of end-of-life care for patients with advanced cancer in an academic medical center. *Journal of Palliative Medicine, 14*(4), 451–457. doi:10.1089/jpm.2010.0434

Emanuel, E. J., Fairclough, D. L., Slutsman, J., & Emanuel, L. L. (2000). Understanding economic and other burdens of terminal illness: The experience of patients and their caregivers. *Annals of Internal Medicine, 132*(6), 451–459. doi:10.7326/0003-4819-132-6-200003210-00005

Eshbaugh, E., & Henninger, W. (2013). Potential mediators of the relationship between gender and death anxiety. *Individual Differences Research, 11*(1), 22–30.

Feeg, V. D., & Elebiary, H. (2005). Exploratory study on end-of-life issues: Barriers to palliative care and advance directives. *American Journal of Hospice & Palliative Medicine, 22*(2), 119–124. doi:10.1177/104990910502200207

Field, N. P., Gao, B., & Paderna, L. (2005). Continuing bonds in bereavement: An attachment theory based perspective. *Death Studies, 29*, 277–299. doi:10.1080/07481180590923689

Fortner, B. V., & Neimeyer, R. A. (1999). Death anxiety in older adults: A quantitative review. *Death Studies, 23*(5), 387–411

Fortner, B. V., Neimeyer, R. A., & Rybarczeck, B. (2000). Correlates of death anxiety in older adults: A comprehensive review. In A. Tomer (Ed.), *Death attitudes and the older adult* (pp. 95–108). Philadelphia, PA: Brunner Routledge.

Foti, M. E., Bartels, S. J., Van Citters, A. D., Merriman, M. P., & Fletcher, K. E. (2005). End-of-life treatment preferences of persons with serious mental illness. *Psychiatric Services, 56*(5), 585–591. doi:10.1176/appi.ps.56.5.585

Francoeur, R. B., Payne, R., Raveis, V. H., & Shim, H. (2006). Palliative care in the inner city: Patient religious affiliation, underinsurance, and symptom attitude. *Cancer, 109*, 425–434. doi:10.1002/cncr.22363

Fry, P. S. (1997). Grandparents' reactions to the death of a grandchild: An exploratory factor analytic study. *Omega: Journal of Death and Dying, 35*, 119–140.

Ganzini, L., Lee, M. A., Heintz, R. T., Bloom, J. D., & Fenn, D. S. (1994). The effect of depression treatment on elderly patients' preferences for life-sustaining medical therapy. *The American Journal of Psychiatry, 151*(11), 1631–1636. doi:10.1176/ajp.151.11.1631

Gilrane-McGarry, U., & O'Grady, T. (2011). Forgotten grievers: An exploration of the grief experiences of bereaved grandparents. *International Journal of Palliative Nursing, 17*(4), 170–176.

Glaser, B. G., & Strauss, A L. (1968). *Time for dying*. Chicago, IL: Aldine Publishing.

Gott, M., Barnes, S., Parker, C., Payne, S., Seamark, D., Gariballa, S., & Small, N. (2007). Dying trajectories in heart failure. *Palliative Medicine, 21*(2), 95–99. doi:10.1177/0269216307076348

Grey, A. (2015). *What to expect when someone important to you is dying: A guide for carers, families and friends of dying people*. London, United Kingdom: The National Council for Palliative Care.

Guo, Y., Palmer, J. L., Bianty, J., Konzen, B., Shin, K., & Bruera, E. (2010). Advance directives and do-not-resuscitate orders in patients with cancer with metastatic spinal cord compression: Advanced care planning implications. *Journal of Palliative Medicine, 13*(5), 513–517. doi:10.1089/jpm.2009.0376

Haley, W. E., Larson, D. G., Kasl-Godley, J., Neimeyer, R. A., & Kwilosz, D. M. (2003). Roles for psychologists in end-of-life care: Emerging models of practice. *Professional Psychology: Research and Practice, 34*, 626–633. doi:10.1037/0735-7028.34.6.626

Hall, P., Schroder, C., & Weaver, L. (2002). The last 48 hours of life in long-term care: A focused chart audit. *Journal of the American Geriatrics Society, 50*(3), 501–506.

Hamama-Raz, Y., Solomon, Z., & Ohry, A. (2000). Fear of personal death among physicians. *Omega: Journal of Death and Dying, 41*(2), 139–149. doi:10.2190/7G35-4CH6-KDRG-MH38

Harding, S. R., Flannelly, K. J., Weaver, A. J., & Costa, A. J. (2005). The influence of religion on death anxiety and death acceptance. *Mental Health, Religion & Culture, 8*, 253–261.

Heron, M. P. (2015). *Deaths: Leading causes for 2012* (Report No. 2014–1120). Hyattsville, MD: National Center for Health Statistics. Retrieved from http://stacks.cdc.gov/view/cdc/33949

Hiroto, K., & Kasl-Godley, J. (2013). Health care teams working with people near the end of life. In J. L. Werth, Jr. (Ed.), *Counseling clients near the end of life* (pp. 75–100). New York, NY: Springer Publishing.

Hopp, F. P. (2000). Preferences for surrogate decision makers, informal communication, and advance directives among community-dwelling elders: Results from a National Study. *The Gerontologist, 40*(4), 449–457. doi:10.1093/geront/40.4.449

Institute of Medicine. (2014). *Dying in America: Improving quality and honoring individual preferences near the end of life.* Washington, DC: National Academies Press.

Johnson, K. S., Kuchibhatla, M., & Tulsky, J. A. (2008). What explains racial differences in the use of advance directives and attitudes toward hospice care? *Journal of the American Geriatrics Society, 56*(10), 1953–1958. doi:10.1111/j.1532-5415.2008.01919.x

Jones, A. L., Moss, A. J., & Harris-Kojetin, L. D. (2011). *Use of advance directives in long-term care populations* (NCHS Data Brief No. 54). Hyattsville, MD: National Center for Health Statistics.

Jordan, A. H., & Litz, B. T. (2014). Prolonged grief disorder: Diagnostic, assessment, and treatment considerations. *Professional Psychology: Research and Practice, 45*(3), 180–187.

Kasl-Godley, J. E., & Kwilosz, D. (2011). Health-care teams. In S. H. Qualls & J. E. Kasl-Godley (Eds.), *End-of-life issues, grief, and bereavement: What clinicians need to know* (pp. 201–228). Hoboken, NJ: John Wiley

Keely, G. C., McGill Gorsuch, A., McCabe, J. M., Wood, W. H, King Hill, M., Pierce, W. J., & Langrock, P. F. (1980). *Uniform determination of Death Act.* Presented at the meeting of the National Conference of Commissioners on Uniform State Law, Kauai, Hawaii.

Kolsky, K. (2008). *End of life: Helping with comfort and care.* Bethesda, MD: National Institute on Aging.

Krakauer, E., Crenner, C., & Fox, K. (2002). Barriers to optimum end of life care for minority patients. *Journal of the American Geriatrics Society, 50*, 182–190. doi:10.1046/j.1532-5415.2002.50027.x

Kübler-Ross, E. (1969). *On death and dying.* New York, NY: Macmillian.

Kwak, J., Allen, J. Y., & Haley, W. E. (2011). Advance care planning and end-of-life decision making. In P. Dilworth-Anderson & M. H. Palmer (Eds.), *Annual review of gerontology and geriatrics: Pathways through the transitions of care for older adults* (Vol. 31, pp. 143–165). New York, NY: Springer Publishing.

Lagay, F. (2003). Physician-assisted suicide: The law and professional ethics. *The Virtual Mentor: VM, 5*(1). doi:10.1001/virtualmentor.2003.5.1.pfor1-0301

Le, B. C., Mileshkin, L., Doan, K., Saward, D., Spruyt, O., Yoong, J., & . . . Philip, J. (2014). Acceptability of early integration of palliative care in patients with incurable lung cancer. *Journal of Palliative Medicine, 17*(5), 553–558. doi:10.1089/jpm.2013.047

Lee, S. A. (2015). The persistent complex bereavement inventory: A measure based on the *DSM-5. Death Studies, 39*, 399–410. doi:10.1080/07481187.2015.1029144

Lehto, R. H., & Stein, K. F. (2009). Death anxiety: An analysis of an evolving concept. *Research and Theory for Nursing Practice: An International Journal, 23*(1), 23–41. doi:10.1891/1541-6577.23.1.23

Levy, C. R., Fish, R., & Kramer, A. (2005). Do-not-resuscitate and do-not-hospitalize directives of persons admitted to skilled nursing facilities under the Medicare benefit. *Journal of the American Geriatrics Society, 53*(12), 2060–2068. doi:10.1111/j.1532-5415.2005.00523.x

LiPuma, S. H., & DeMarco, J. P. (2013). Reviving brain death: A functionalist view. *Journal of Bioethical Inquiry, 10*(3), 383–392. doi:10.1007/s11673-013-9450-y

Lovell, A., & Yates, P. (2014). Advance care planning in palliative care: A systematic literature review of the contextual factors influencing its uptake 2008-2012. *Palliative Medicine, 28*(8), 1026–1035. doi:10.1177/026921631453131

Lunney, J. R., Lynn, J., & Hogan, C. (2002). Profiles of older Medicare decedents. *Journal of the American Geriatrics Society, 50*(6), 1108–1112. doi:10.1046/j.1532-5415.2002.50268.x

Maciejewski, P. K., Zhang, B., Block, S. D., & Prigerson, H. G. (2007). An empirical examination of the stage theory of grief. *Journal of the American Medical Association, 297*(7), 716–723.

Matsumura, S., Bito, S., Liu, H., Kahn, K., Fukuhara, S., Kagawa-Singer, M., & Wenger, N. (2002). Acculturation of attitudes toward end-of-life care: A cross-cultural survey of Japanese Americans and Japanese. *Journal of General Internal Medicine, 17*(7), 531–539. doi:10.1046/j.1525-1497.2002.10734.x

McClatchey, I. S., & King, S. (2015). The impact of death education on fear of death and death anxiety among human services students. *Omega: Journal of Death and Dying, 71*(4), 343–361. doi:10.1177/0030222815572606

Miller, F. G., & Truog, R. D. (2010). Decapitation and the definition of death. *Journal of Medical Ethics, 36*(10), 632–634. doi:10.1136/jme.2009.035196

Miller, S. C., Mor, V., Wu, N., Gozalo, P., & Lapane, K. (2002). Does receipt of hospice care in nursing homes improve the management of pain at the end of life? *Journal of the American Geriatrics Society, 50*, 507–515. doi:10.1046/j.1532-5415.2002.50118.x

Moss, M. S., Moss, S., Z., & Hansson, R. O. (2001). Bereavement in old age. In M. S. Stroebe, R. O. Hannson, W. Stroebe, & H. Schut (Eds.), *Handbook of bereavement research: Consequences, coping, and care* (pp. 241–260). Washington, DC: American Psychological Association.

Murphy, S. L., Kochanek, K. D., Xu, J. Q., & Heron, M. (2015). *Deaths: Final data for 2012* (Report No. 2015–1120). Hyattsville, MD: National Center for Health Statistics.

*Naef, R., Ward, R., Mahrer-Imhof, R., & Grande, G. (2013). Characteristics of the bereavement experience of older persons after spousal loss: An integrative review. *International Journal of Nursing Studies, 50*, 1108–1121. doi:10.1016/j.ijnurstu.2012.11.026

Neimeyer, R. A. (Ed.). (2001). *Meaning reconstruction and the experience of loss.* Washington, DC: American Psychological Association.

Neimeyer, R. A., & Holland, J. M. (2015). Bereavement in later life: Theory, assessment, and intervention. In P. A. Lichtenberg & B. T. Mast (Eds.), *APA handbook of clinical geropsychology: Vol. 2. Assessment, treatment, and issues of later life* (pp. 645–666). Washington, DC: American Psychological Association.

Neimeyer, R. A., Wittkowski, J., & Moser, R. P. (2004). Psychological research on death attitudes: An overview and evaluation. *Death Studies, 28*, 309–340. doi:10.1080/07481180490432324

Newson, R. S., Boelen, P. A., Hek, K., Hofman, A., & Tiemeier, H. (2011). The prevalence and characteristics of complicated grief in older adults. *Journal of Affective Disorders, 132*, 231–238. doi:10.1016/j.jad.2011.02.021

O'Brien, J. M., Forrest, L, & Austin, A. M. (2002). Death of a partner: Perspectives of heterosexual and gay men. *Journal of Health Psychology, 7*(3), 317–328. doi:10.1177/1359105302007003224

Omnibus Budget Reconciliation Act, Pub. L. 101–508, 104 Stat. 143 (1990).

Onrust, S. A., & Cuijpers, P. (2006). Mood and anxiety disorders in widowhood: A systematic review. *Aging and Mental Health, 10*(4), 327–334. doi:10.1080/13607860600638529

Oregon Public Health Division. (2015). *Oregon's death with Dignity Act—2014.* Retrieved from http://public.health.oregon.gov/ProviderPartnerResources/EvaluationResearch/DeathwithDignityAct/Documents/year17.pdf

Power, T. L., & Smith, S. M. (2008). Predictors of fear of death and self mortality: An Atlantic Canadian perspective. *Death Studies, 32*, 253–272. doi:10.1080/07481180701880935

Quinn-Lee, L., Olson-McBride, L., & Unterberger, A. (2014). Burnout and death anxiety in hospice social workers. *Journal of Social Work in End-of-Life & Palliative Care, 10*(3), 219–239. doi:10.1080/15524256.2014.938891

Rando, T. A. (Ed.). (2000). *Clinical dimensions of anticipatory mourning: Theory and practice in working with the dying, their loved ones, and their caregivers.* Champaign, IL: Research Press.

Rao, J. K., Anderson, L. A., Lin, F., & Laux, J. P. (2014). Completion of advance directives among U.S. consumers. *American Journal of Preventive Medicine, 46*(1), 65–70. doi:10.1016/j.amepre.2013.09.008

Röcke, C., & Cherry, K. E. (2002). Death at the end of the 20th century: Individual processes and developmental tasks in old age. *International Journal of Aging and Human Development, 54*(4), 315–333.

*Rosenberg, R. N. (2009). Consciousness, coma, and brain death. *Journal of American Medical Association, 301*(11), 1172–1174. doi:10.1001/jama.2009.224

Rosenblatt, P. C. (2001). A social constructionist perspective on cultural differences in grief. In M. S. Stroebe, R. O. Hannson, W. Stroebe, & H. Schut (Eds.), *Handbook of bereavement research: Consequences, coping, and care* (pp. 285–300). Washington, DC: American Psychological Association.

*Rosenblatt, P. C. (2008). Grief across cultures: A review and research agenda. In M. S. Stroebe, R. O. Hannson, H. Schut, & W. Stroebe (Eds.), *Handbook of bereavement research and practice: Advances in theory and intervention* (pp. 207–222). Washington, DC: American Psychological Association.

Russac, R. J., Gatliff, C., Reece, M., & Spottswood, D. (2007). Death anxiety across the adult years: An examination of age and gender effects. *Death Studies, 31*(6), 549–561. doi:10.1080/074811 80701356936

Shear, K., Frank, E., Houck, P. R., & Reynolds, C. F., 3rd. (2005). Treatment of complicated grief: A randomized controlled trial. *Journal of the American Medical Association, 293*(21), 2601–2608.

Shear, K., Wang, Y., Skritskaya, N., Duan, N., Mauro, C., & Ghesquiere, A. (2014). Treatment of complicated grief in elderly persons: A randomized clinical trial. *Journal of the American Medical Association Psychiatry, 71*(11), 1287–1295. doi:10.1001/jamapsychiatry.2014.1242

Strada, E. A. (2011). Health-care teams. In S. H. Qualls & J. E. Kasl-Godley, (Eds.), *End-of-life issues, grief, and bereavement: What clinicians need to know* (pp. 43–63). Hoboken, NJ: John Wiley.

*Stroebe, M. S., Hansson, R. O., Stroebe, W, & Schut, H. (2001). Introduction: Concepts and issues in contemporary research on bereavement. In M. S. Stroebe, R. O. Hannson, W. Stroebe, & H. Schut (Eds.), *Handbook of bereavement research: Consequences, coping, and care* (pp. 3–22). Washington, DC: American Psychological Association.

Stroebe, M. S., & Schut, H. (2001). Models of coping with bereavement: A review. In M. S. Stroebe, R. O. Hannson, W. Stroebe, & H. Schut (Eds.), *Handbook of bereavement research: Consequences, coping, and care* (pp. 375–403). Washington, DC: American Psychological Association.

*Stroebe, M. S., & Schut, H. (2010). The dual process model of coping with bereavement: A decade on. *Omega: Journal of Death and Dying, 61*(4), 273–289. doi:10.2190/OM.61.4.b

Stroebe, M. S., Schut, H., & Boerner, K. (2010). Continuing bonds in adaptation to bereavement: Toward theoretical integration. *Clinical Psychology Review, 30*, 259–268. doi:10.1016/j.cpr .2009.11.007

*Stroebe, M. S., Schut, H., & Stroebe, W. (2007). Health outcomes of bereavement. *Lancet, 370*, 1960–1973.

Stroebe, W., Schut, H., & Stroebe, M. S. (2005). Grief work, disclosure and counseling: Do they help the bereaved? *Clinical Psychology Review, 25*, 395–414. doi:10.1016/j.cpr.2005.01.004

Tomarken, A., Holland, J., Schachter, S., Vanderwerker, L., Zuckerman, E., Nelson, C., . . . Prigerson, H. (2008). Factors of complicated grief pre-death in caregivers of cancer patients. *Psychooncology, 17*(2), 105–111.

Tornstam, L. (2005). *Gerotranscendence: A developmental theory of positive aging.* New York, NY: Springer.

Twillman, R. K., & Lewis, M. M. (2011). Health-care teams. In S. H. Qualls, J. E. Kasl-Godley, S. H. Qualls, & J. E. Kasl-Godley (Eds.), *End-of-life issues, grief, and bereavement: What clinicians need to know* (pp. 201–228). Hoboken, NJ: John Wiley.

van den Berg, G. J., Lindeboom, M., & Portrait, F. (2011). Conjugal bereavement effects on health and mortality at advanced ages. *Journal of Health Economics, 30*, 774–794. doi:10.1016/j.jheal eco.2011.05.011

Veatch, R. M. (2009). The impending collapse of the whole-brain definition of death. In J. P. Lizza, J. P. Lizza (Eds.), *Defining the beginning and ending of life: Readings on personal identity and bioethics* (pp. 483–497). Baltimore, MD: The Johns Hopkins University Press

Wagner, G. J., Riopelle, D., Steckart, J., Lorenz, K. A., & Rosenfeld, K. E. (2010). Provider communication and patient understanding of life-limiting illness and their relationship to patient communication of treatment preferences. *Journal of Pain and Symptom Management, 39*(3), 527–534. doi:10.1016/j.jpainsymman.2009.07.012

Waite, K. R., Federman, A. D., McCarthy, D. M., Sudore, R., Curtis, L. M., Baker, D. W., & . . . Paasche-Orlow, M. K. (2013). Literacy and race as risk factors for low rates of advance directives in older adults. *Journal of the American Geriatrics Society, 61*(3), 403–406. doi:10.1111/jgs.12134

Wakefield, J. C. (2013). The *DSM-5* debate over the bereavement exclusion: Psychiatric diagnosis and the future of empirically supported treatment. *Clinical Psychology Review, 33,* 825–845. doi:10.1016/j.cpr.2013.03.007

Wang, S., Aldridge, M. D., Gross, C. P., Canavan, M., Cherlin, E., Johnson-Hurzeler, R., & Bradley, E. (2015). Geographic variation of hospice use patterns at the end of life. *Journal of Palliative Medicine, 18*(9), 771–780. doi:10.1089/jpm.2014.0425

Washington State Department of Health. (2015). *Washington State Department of Health 2014 Death with Dignity Act Report Executive Summary* (Report No. 422–109). Retrieved from http://www.doh.wa.gov/portals/1/Documents/Pubs/422-109-DeathWithDignityAct2014.pdf

Wink, P., & Scott, J. (2005). Does religiousness buffer against the fear of death and dying in late adulthood? Findings from a longitudinal study. *Journals of Gerontology: Series B, 60,* 207–214.

World Health Organization. (2015). WHO definition of palliative care. Retrieved from http://www.who.int/cancer/palliative/definition/en

Youngblut, J. M., Brooten, D., Blais, K., Kilgore, C., & Yoo, C. (2015). Health and functioning in grandparents after a young grandchild's death. *Journal of Community Health, 40,* 956–966. doi:10.1007/s10900-015-0018-0

13

Cultural Differences in Aging Experiences of Ethnic and Sexual Minority Older Adults

Kimberly E. Hiroto and Sarah J. Yarry

Working with older adults involves being part historian, part investigator, and part student. It involves developing an appreciation for the sociohistorical context within which older adults live including understanding the zeitgeist of the times, the social mores, and the watershed events that shaped a cohort's experiences. It also involves investigating individual and collective cultures and traditions that shaped the person's or the group's life experiences. Working with older adults requires a dose of humility to learn about one's unique and shared experiences, including the regional, local, and personal experiences that affected their lives.

The aging population is a heterogeneous group. Like any other population, this diverse group consists of multiple cultural, cohort, and age groups with a variety of life experiences, varying access to socioeconomic resources and living conditions, different ways of expressing their gender and sexual orientation, and a range of physical and cognitive abilities. In this chapter we discuss the wealth of diversity within older adults, focusing specifically on ethnic diversity, sexual orientation, and gender expression. Our aim is to provide a general overview of the themes that may arise when working with diverse older adults, knowing that each person and group

---

*Key references in the References section are indicated by an asterisk.

has their own story and collection of life experiences that may or may not be captured here. Specifically, we focus on three major themes: cohort effects, health disparities and cultural stressors, and factors contributing to resiliency and growth.

Before discussing specific populations, we wish to start with an exercise. Consider your own personal experiences of being discriminated against for aspects of your identity beyond your control (e.g., age, gender, orientation, ethnicity). How did you feel during that moment? How did others seem to view and treat you? If you have not experienced this or did not have to think of this until now, why might that be? Imagine how different your life would be if your job, income, and even physical safety—privileges not earned through meritocracy or bestowed through egalitarianism—were dependent on society's acceptance of your gender, ethnicity, or sexual orientation.

ETHNIC MINORITY OLDER ADULTS

Ethnic minority populations are expected to continue rising in the coming decades, with a relative boom in the number of older adults. As seen in Figure 13.1, the number of ethnic minority adults aged 65 years and older is expected to increase through 2050 (U.S. Census Bureau, 2012).

Multiple factors explain these anticipated shifts in population demographics, including changes to immigration trends, increased life expectancies across groups, and the general increase in racial and ethnic minorities in the United States (Ortman, Velkoff, & Hogan, 2014). Similar changes in aging demographics are anticipated globally as well (Department of Economic and Social Affairs Population Division, 2015), which is discussed in Chapter 1. These anticipated shifts in the coming decades reflect growing needs for services catering to the aged including, for example, medical

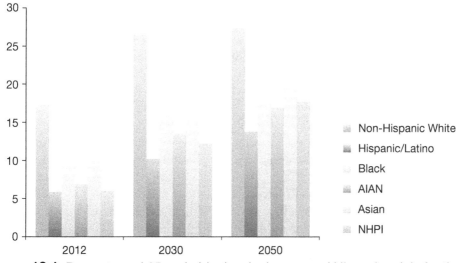

Figure 13.1 Percent aged 65 and older by single race and Hispanic origin for the United States. AIAN, American Indian and Alaska Native; NHPI, Native Hawaiian and Other Pacific Islander.
Source: U.S. Census Bureau, 2012 Population Estimates and 2012 National Projections.

care, mental health care, housing options, in-home support services, and a host of bilingual or polylingual service providers who can accommodate the linguistic and cultural needs of adults.

Cohort Effects

As defined elsewhere, cohorts are groups of people (not necessarily the same age) with shared cultural experiences and values (e.g., Sinnott & Shifren, 2001). For example, the cohorts who lived during World War II differ significantly from the cohorts who lived during the Vietnam War. More specifically, the cohorts within specific time periods differ depending on their own cultural experiences. During and following the Vietnam War, the experiences of enlisted and drafted veterans differed significantly from civilians. Furthermore, one's race, gender and cultural identity may have differentially altered their experiences during this time of civil rights uprising and protest. Within group differences add to the complexity, highlighting the importance of serving as historian, investigator, and student to better understand and appreciate an individual's or cohort's experiences.

Take a moment and consider your own cohort's experiences to date. Which of these watershed moments in your lifetime have affected your experiences and outlook on life: the terrorist attacks on 9/11/2001; the election of Barack Obama as the first African American president; the Occupy Movement of 2011; the Black Lives Matter movement; the 2017 Women's March on Washington; and the ongoing racial tensions in the United States? How have these experiences shaped your cohort, your culture, and you as a person? How might you have experienced these events differently compared to someone of a different racial or ethnic background? Part of working with older adults involves being curious about their lived experiences, and understanding how your own experiences and theirs may shape your interactions.

Views of Aging

Sociocultural factors affect one's view of aging, race, and ethnicity including beliefs, assumptions, and interpersonal interactions. Within our youth-oriented culture are deeply embedded antiaging sentiments that affect individuals in profound ways (Levy, 2003). Ageism remains one of the few remaining acceptable "-isms" in society. Think of the plethora of birthday cards making fun of aging, placing older adults in demeaning situations (e.g., lacking self-awareness or dignity), or equating aging with a sense of purposelessness. Similar public sentiments about race, gender, or sexual orientation would cause an outcry of righteous fury yet similarly derogatory statements about aging are socially condoned if not celebrated (e.g., "over the hill" birthday parties, suggesting a downward trajectory after age 50).

Exposure to ageist stereotypes in early childhood often continues into later adulthood and can affect older adults' views of aging and themselves (e.g., Levy, 2003). Stereotypes serve as cognitive shortcuts, allowing for quick and efficient processing of information (MacCrae, Milne, & Bodenhausen, 1994). However, the downside is the tendency to cling to these stereotypes despite evidence to the contrary. For example, negative ageist stereotypes (e.g., older adults are slow learners) differentially affect individuals' perceptions of their work productivity (e.g., Van Dalen &

Henkens, 2010). When encountering a particularly productive aging adult, this person is seen as an exception to the rule (Levy & Banaji, 2002). Furthermore, negative ageist stereotypes increase the frequency of recalling more negative traits of aging than positive ones, predisposing individuals to view aging within a more pessimistic frame (Levy & Banaji, 2002). When working with older adults, individuals must be acutely aware of their own beliefs and values about aging and its intersection with race and ethnicity. Implicit ageist biases exist and it behooves individuals to be aware of these biases without judgment or blame and remain cognizant of them lest they become a potentially caustic blind spot.

Research on extensions of implicit bias and stereotype threat demonstrate the deleterious effects of underlying ageist attitudes on both patients and health care providers alike. Implicit bias refers to past experiences that affect attitudes and behaviors at a level below self-awareness (see Greenwald & Banaji, 1995), whereas stereotype threat refers to the confirmation of a group's negative stereotype when receiving mild, sometimes subliminal, reminders of this stereotype (see Steele & Aronson, 1995). For example, when presented with positive or negative stereotypes of aging, the performance of older adults improves with positive stereotypes and decreases when presented with negative ones (Levy & Leifheit-Limson, 2009). Indeed, internalized ageism can affect older adults' performance on tests of cognition (Levy, Zonderman, Slade, & Ferrucci, 2012) and physical performance (Levy, Slade, & Kasl, 2002) and even reduce survival (Levy, et al., 2002). Furthermore, health care providers' negative beliefs and attitudes about aging can also affect patient care, manifesting as delayed treatment (Levy & Meyers, 2004), lowered expectations for improvement (Lamberty & Bares, 2013), and assumptions that older adults are too old to change (Kane, 2004).

Sue and colleagues (2007) use the term "microaggressions" to reflect subtle statements or behaviors that (often unintentionally) imply ignorance, negative sentiment, and/or hostility toward a particular group. They define microaggressions in terms of racism, but this concept applies to age and the intersection of both. Examples may include speaking to an older adult using infantilizing language (i.e., elderspeak; Williams, 2004) similar to how one might speak to an infant or toddler.

Elderspeak often involves slowed rate of speech, simplified language, use of collective pronouns when singular pronouns are more accurate, and fluctuating intonations (e.g., "Are *we* ready to shower?" (Williams, 2004, 2006). This type of verbal and nonverbal communication (e.g., hands on hips, finger pointing) typically implies an exaggerated degree of dependency or inability to make basic choices that undermines the older adults' autonomy (e.g., "You want some dinner now, don't you?"). Not intended to be malign, recipients of elderspeak often report feeling infantilized and disrespected. The use of elderspeak constitutes a form of ageism due to its assumption that older adults need these language accommodations to compensate for presumed cognitive and/or sensory deficits. This pattern of communication, which often occurs in long-term care facilities, has significant proximal and distal adverse effects on older adults' emotional, psychological, and physical health, even in those with advanced dementia, and often contributes to difficulties in care provision (Williams, 2004, 2006). Efforts to educate care staff on elderspeak have been beneficial and demonstrated improvements in care and communication (Williams, 2006; Williams, Herman, Gajewski, & Wilson, 2009). Other examples of ageist microaggressions include speaking loudly and slowly to an older adult without evidence of hearing impairment or language difficulties. Similar to elderspeak, this behavior implies assumptions that an older adult has cognitive impairment without evidence of such. Other examples include helping an older adult complete a task without asking permission, a microaggression also commonly experienced by persons with disabilities.

HEALTH DISPARITIES AND CULTURAL STRESSORS

Health disparities in health care refer to "racial or ethnic differences in the quality of healthcare that are not due to access-related factors or clinical needs, preferences, or appropriateness of interventions" (Smedley, Stith, & Nelson, 2003, p. 3–4). Factors including socioeconomic status (SES), access to health care, health literacy, and ethnic minority status contribute to health inequalities. Indeed, racial and ethnic minority adults in general have premature morbidity rates across the life span suggesting complex, multifactorial contributions to health disparities. Often SES, race, and ethnicity are related to factors including residential segregation with differential access to resources (e.g., medical care, senior centers, healthy food options, transportation, education) and differential exposure to risk (e.g., crime, poor quality housing, pollution; e.g., Hill, Pérez-Stable, Anderson, & Bernard, 2015). As a result, some researchers propose that interventions should target the social context rather than the racial or ethnic group to improve health inequity (Thorpe et al., 2015; Thorpe et al., 2014). For example, developing community gardens in lower-income neighborhoods increases access to organic, nutritious foods that might not otherwise be available or affordable. Moreover, access to healthy, natural food can help mitigate rates of multiple chronic health conditions (e.g., diabetes, hypertension, high cholesterol), especially those related to diet and health behaviors with disparate morbidity rates by SES and ethnic minority status (Smedley et al., 2003). Similarly ride-share services through community organizations (churches, senior centers) can help families and individuals with limited accessibility to attend health care appointments and run errands while still maintaining their sense of independence.

In addition, the legacy of institutionalized discrimination against certain groups continues to play a critical role in health disparities and cannot be discounted. For example, the mass incarceration of African Americans is gaining more media attention (for more information, see Michelle Alexander's [2012] book, *The New Jim Crow: Mass Incarceration in the Age of Colorblindness*). These discussions highlight how legacies of systemic discrimination (e.g., slavery) evolve and continue to oppress disenfranchised and marginalized groups (e.g., incarcerating more African American men than non-African American men). After being released from incarceration, adults of historically oppressed groups face an uphill battle (e.g., housing and job discrimination, lack of income, increased fees for legal and imprisonment costs) with limited institutional support. These barriers often further restrict opportunities for upward mobility. Consider the lasting effect of such legacies across generations.

The concept of social reproduction (originally coined by Karl Marx) in more contemporary terms refers to the "structures and activities that transmit social inequality from one generation to the next" (Doob, 2015, p.10). This concept speaks to the ways in which systemic factors ("social-stratification systems") keep groups of people in the same class across generations. Doob proposes that four forms of capital (financial, cultural, human, social) contribute to whether people remain in the same social-stratification system and perpetuate social reproduction. Each form of capital is briefly described here with explanations for how they contribute to health disparities and cultural stressors.

Capital generally refers to the resources one has to promote upward mobility (Doob, 2015). Financial capital involves one's wealth and access to purchase resources that represent his or her social class (e.g., high-end technology, membership to elite health clubs, high-quality clothing). Cultural capital encompasses the worldviews, values, knowledge, skills, and behaviors (e.g., traditions, language) adopted across generations. Of course, the type of cultural capital inherited also depends on the other forms of capital. An individual raised within a low-income urban community would likely develop a different type of cultural capital than an individual raised in an affluent suburban community. Certain types of cultural capital may lend themselves to higher social status than others. Financial and cultural capital often contribute to one's human capital or the knowledge base and skills one has that affects their social value (e.g., education from elite institutions, expertise in computer programming). Understandably, in developed countries like the United States, access to educational resources is often necessary to develop human capital. Related to all prior forms of capital is social capital, referring to one's social network and access to highly valued individuals or groups.

The confluence of financial, cultural, human, and social capital contributes to one's standing in society. For example, a personal connection to the CEO of a high-powered company (social capital) may lead to employment opportunities (human capital) with good social mobility (financial capital), which may expose the person to a different type of social etiquette and network (cultural and social capital). However, a person with limited income (financial capital) due to economic and sociohistorical factors may have strong values promoting resiliency, perseverance, and loyalty (cultural capital) but have limited access to resources or social networks (social capital) due to factors like institutional racism and disenfranchisement, which limits employment options (human capital) and opportunities for upward social mobility (social capital). These intersecting forms of capital can help articulate how privilege facilitates movement in the social-stratification system. However, it also elucidates how legacies of disenfranchisement and health disparities develop. As historian, investigator, and student, it behooves you to consider how these factors may affect the lives of the older adults you serve. Indeed, the conflation of ethnic minority status with these forms of capital may help explain the health disparities and cultural stressors experienced by racial and ethnic minority older adults.

The term *minority stress* refers to the increased prevalence of mental health disorders within minority groups attributed to the chronic stressors commonly experienced by members of disenfranchised and stigmatized minority groups based on factors of their identity (e.g., race, ethnicity, gender; Meyer, 2003). Although initially applied to lesbian, gay, and bisexual populations, this concept generalizes to other minority groups as well. Furthermore, this model highlights how this type of stress can accumulate across generations with lasting effects. While low SES contributes to minority stress, improvements in capital do not necessarily unburden someone from these stressors. For example, a wealthy, older Latina woman with secure financial, cultural, human, and social capital may still experience minority stress due to factors including her age, ethnicity, and gender. Additionally, generations of racism and discrimination may have imbued her with cultural capital that both enhance her resiliencies while also instilling a sense of guardedness for having to justify her success and sense of belonging.

Importantly, the stressors experienced by many ethnic minority older adults carry significant physical and mental health effects as well. Ethnic minority adults, especially older adults, tend to have relatively more chronic health conditions than their non-Hispanic White counterparts (Gilbert, Elder, Lyons, Kaphingst, Blanchard, & Goodman, 2015; Williams & Mohammed, 2009). A lifetime of segregation and minority stress may contribute to the development of chronic health problems among ethnic minority older adults, reflecting the effect of psychological stress on important health factors. For example, research evaluating the role of social location demonstrated higher probability of hypertension among African American males living and working in segregated locations compared to those who did not (Gilbert, et al., 2015). Furthermore, research demonstrates the effect of chronic stress on physical and cognitive health (Juster, McEwen, & Lupien, 2009), placing disadvantaged and lower SES older adults at greater risk for health problems and potentially less access to care compared to peers with more resources. However, other research proposes that health literacy (i.e., general understanding of health information to guide medical decisions) helps explain the relationship between race and health disparities (Bennett, Chen, Soroui, & White, 2009). Such findings reflect the complexity of this issue when considering the intersection of demographic factors (e.g., race, age, SES, cohort).

Older adults tend to underutilize medical and mental health services. This trend is even more pronounced within ethnic minority aging populations. As an example, consider the underutilization of mental health resources. Research on disparities in mental health services use by ethnic minority older adults, which controls for issues of access (i.e., financial capital), proposes that cultural values and health literacy (i.e., cultural capital) may relate to this trend. For example, research on the mental health services use of African American and Latino older adults compared to non-Hispanic White counterparts found that African American and Latino older adults were less likely to initiate mental health care than their White counterparts (Jimenez, Cook, Bartels, & Alegría, 2013). Results cannot be explained by lower prevalence rates of mental illness in ethnic minority aging populations. In fact, higher rates of mental illness exist in ethnic minority older adults than non-Hispanic Whites (Jimenez, Alegría Chen, Chan, & Laderman, 2010). Reasons for these findings of health disparities are likely multifactorial and may relate to the factors described previously, including minority stress and living within a social-stratification system that often promotes social reproduction. However, research is also emerging investigating the factors contributing to resiliencies in ethnic minority older adults (e.g., Becker & Newsom, 2005; Knight & Sayegh, 2010; Kwong, Du, & Xu, 2015).

RESILIENCY AND GROWTH

Of the many models and definitions of resilience, Aldwin and Igarashi's Ecological Model of Resilience in Late Life (2012) eloquently integrates sociocultural, contextual, and individual factors that contribute to resilience in older adults. Following a brief description of this model, we apply it to the concept of resilience in ethnic minority older adults.

Aldwin and Igarashi's (2012) ecological model of resilience articulates how sociocultural, contextual, and individual resources interact to create "generalized resistance resources" (GRR), which contributes to coping. Sociocultural resources include social and/or political policies, institutional practices, and historical events. Examples include policies creating Medicare, low-income housing assistance, and social security. Grass roots advocacy groups also contribute to sociocultural resources. For example, Chicago's Coalition of Limited English Speaking Elderly (CLESE; www.clese.org) came about through collaborations with leaders of ethnic organizations following an assessment of needs among immigrant, refugee, and migrant older adults in Chicago. This resource helps older adults connect to services that were otherwise inaccessible due to cultural and language barriers. Some groups may have fewer sociocultural resources available to them, prompting reliance on other factors to foster resilience. Contextual resources include community characteristics and the social and built environments available locally in which older adults reside. For example, older adults living in a retirement community with formal community features (e.g., activity calendars, paid employees who provide assistance with basic daily tasks like cleaning, bathing, and meal preparation) have a certain degree of formalized contextual resources. However, community-dwelling older adults may have informal contextual resources made of networks (family, friendships, church organizations) that naturally developed similar instrumental (cleaning, transportation) and emotional support systems (friendship, community engagement, sense of inclusion). These types of resources may sound akin to social and cultural capital described previously (Doob, 2015). Informal contextual resources may be naturally occurring over time through the social capital developed within a neighborhood, whereas others may move to specific settings to seek out formalized resources. Finally, individual resources relate to one's personal characteristics including personality, education, health, and economic well-being.

The aforesaid types of resources interact to influence one's GRR, which refers to the coping methods used to navigate stressful life experiences (Aldwin & Igarashi, 2012). The GRR encompasses one's resilience to adapt to changes and ability to cope with specific stressors, which are also influenced by posttraumatic growth and stress-related growth. The former generally refers to personal growth fostered from trauma (e.g., military combat exposure) while stress-related growth refers to intrapersonal growth garnered through daily stressors (e.g., poverty, minority stress). From adversity comes strength. The cultural capital developed across generations may contribute to the GRR. You can see similarities across Doob's (2015) and Aldwin and Igarashi's (2012) models and how these constructs, when organized and framed in certain ways, can explain both the positive and negative sides of posttraumatic and stress-related growth. Indeed much like social reproduction, it is the transaction between Aldwin and Igarashi's resources, rather than each factor alone, that contributes to one's resilience.

The ecological model of resilience may help account for the degree of resilience described within ethnic minority aging groups, exemplified in the caregiving literature. Studies of caregivers to persons with dementia demonstrate that African

American caregivers tend to report less burden than non-Hispanic White caregivers (Haley et al., 2004; Pinquart & Sörensen, 2005). The relationship between the caregiver and care recipient (e.g., adult child vs. spouse) may have influenced these trends, in addition to groups' positive reappraisal of stressors. Akin to Aldwin and Igarashi's model (2012), while non-Hispanic White caregivers tended to use formal sociocultural resources (e.g., health care services), African American caregivers tended to demonstrate relatively stronger individual and possibly contextual resources. For example, likely related to cultural capital and the need to develop coping resources for stress, African American caregivers tend to demonstrate more positive reappraisal of stressors compared to their White counterparts (Haley et al., 2004; Pinquart & Sörensen, 2005). Additionally, individual resources like religious coping and prayer played a significant role in African American caregivers' ability to find personal gain (vs. burden) in their caregiving role (Knight & Sayegh, 2010). However, ethnic minority caregivers also tended to have poorer health factors than non-Hispanic White counterparts, possibly related to the long-term health effects of minority stress coupled with institutional limitations to resources.

Cultural capital appears to play a significant role in the resiliencies of ethnic minority groups to persevere through obstacles, including chronic illness. For example, Becker and Newsom (2005) interviewed 38 African American older adults across a 10-year span to understand cultural values that influenced participants coping with chronic illness. Themes of religiosity, racism, independence, and resilience emerged as organizing principles that helped participants find meaning in their illness experience. The hardships endured personally and collectively seemed tied to these cultural values, including strong determination to assert one's independence, freedom and control, and belief that God would care for them. Indeed, it appears that research examining the coping resources used by aging ethnic minority adults facing health-related hardships (chronic illness, caregiving) tend to include cultural values and the ability to find personal growth despite adversity (Becker & Newsom, 2005; Haley et al., 2004; Knight & Sayegh, 2010; Pinquart & Sörensen, 2005).

SEXUAL AND GENDER MINORITY OLDER ADULTS

The lesbian, gay, bisexual, and transgender (LGBT) aging community is growing in numbers and prominence, although remains highly disenfranchised and underrepresented (e.g., Fredriksen-Goldsen, Hoy-Ellis, Goldsen, Emlet, & Hooyman, 2014). A paucity of research exists on this heterogeneous group, whose health needs are often collapsed together. There are a number of identities associated with sexual orientation and gender identity, which are defined in Table 13.1. Even less research exists on older adults identifying as transgender. The Institute of Medicine (IOM, 2011), recognizing the lack of information on the LGBT community, recommended increased research within these populations to better understand the health care needs of various groups and provide appropriate services.

Even basic information about census data of LGBT older adults remains limited. Estimates suggest populations exceeding 2.4 million LGBT older adults (defined as older than 50 years old; Choi & Meyer, 2016) in the United States with expectations that by year 2030 the population will double to 5 million (Fredriksen-Goldsen, Kim,

Table 13.1 Definitions of Sexual Orientation and Gender Identity Terms

Term	Definition
Biological sex	The unique biological makeup of an individual including sexual hormones, genetics, chromosomes, and genitals
Bisexual	A person who experiences sexual and emotional attachments to both women and men
Cisgender	A person whose binary gender assigned at birth is concordant with his or her sense of identity
Gay	Men who experience their primary sexual and emotional attachments to other men
Gender identity	The extent to which a person identifies on a spectrum of masculine and feminine traits
Lesbian	Women who experience their primary sexual and emotional attachments to other women
Queer	A sociopolitical umbrella term that may be associated with all levels of exploring one's nonbinary sexuality and gender identity
Sexual orientation	The directionality of persons' orientation regarding the gender to which they are attracted, with whom they engage in sexual behaviors, and how they identify themselves
Transgender	An umbrella term to describe an array of identities that do not conform to the pervasive bipolar gender system of most cultures

Shiu, Goldsen, & Emlet, 2014). Other data estimate that LGBT older adults older than age 60 number between 1.75 and 4 million (Administration for Community Living, n.d.). Approximately 5% of older adults report having same-sex partners (Fisher, 2010). This number has risen in recent years, with a diversity of older adults identifying as gay (3%), lesbian (less than 1%), or bisexual (1%). These percentages appear to be consistent across ethnic identities (Fisher, 2010). Most older adults identifying as lesbian women report being "completely" or "mostly" out to their friends (76%) and family (61%, MetLife, 2010), with similar rates for older gay men (74% and 57%, respectively). However, bisexual men and women report a lower percent of disclosure to friends (16%) and family (24%) while transgender older adults report disclosing at a slightly higher frequency (39% to friends and 42% to family; MetLife, 2010). Furthermore, one of the largest studies of transgender adults across the life span found that the overwhelming majority (97%) of those age 65 years and older reported transitioning at age 55 or older (Cook-Daniels, 2015; Grant et al., 2011). These statistics suggest that, for various reasons, older adults transition later in their lives after having established decades of life as their assigned sex. Imagine if you felt prohibited to keep a critical aspect of your identity hidden for fear of discrimination or violence, and the amount of courage needed to disclose later in life.

COHORT EFFECTS

Many of today's older adults identifying as LGBT grew up prior to the 1969 Stonewall Inn Riots, often considered the start of the Gay Liberation Movement (Choi & Meyer, 2016; Fredriksen-Goldsen & Muraco, 2010). This pre-Stonewall era criminalized homosexuality and considered it a mental illness, resulting in many families rejecting their kin. Whether forced or voluntary, upon disclosing their sexual orientation, adults from this cohort often faced consequences including psychiatric institutionalization, electric shock therapy, ostracism from their families of origin and communities, homelessness, religious conversion therapy or individual therapy to change their sexual orientation. Your roles as historian, investigator, and student will be helpful when thinking of LGBT older adults.

A review of the LGBT rights movement exceeds the scope of this chapter; however, some of the lesser known but equally critical moments in history are described here to provide some sociopolitical context. Executive Order 10450, signed into law by President Eisenhower in 1953, required dismissal of government employees deemed to be threats to national security. Such groups included those with mental illness whose judgment may be adversely affected (at the time, homosexuality was deemed a mental disorder) and those who engaged in "any criminal, infamous, dishonest, immoral, or notoriously disgraceful conduct, habitual use of intoxicants to excess, drug addiction, or sexual perversion" (National Archives, 2016). Identifying mental illness and "sexual perversion" as threats to national security resulted in hundreds of LGBT adults losing their jobs.

Three years later, Evelyn Hooker presented groundbreaking research demonstrating no differences in the mental health of heterosexual and homosexual adults. This research played a critical role in the removal of homosexuality as a mental health diagnosis, *nearly 20 years later*. Indeed not until 1962, and only in Illinois, was it legal to engage in private same-sex activity with another consenting adult and not until 1973 in Michigan was there any substantial law protecting LGB adults from discrimination (Fitzgerald, 2013). Only in 1993 did Minnesota establish laws protecting people identifying as transgender. However, stigma remained strong, at times institutionalized through powerful organizations (e.g., the Centers for Disease Control and Prevention [CDC] naming AIDS the gay-related immunodeficiency disease [GRID] until other groups contracted it; Herek & Capitanio, 1999). The connection between AIDS and the LGBT community linked gay life with illness and provided a vehicle for discriminating against sexual and gender minorities. The relative youth of laws and policies protecting LGBT communities and their civil rights, coupled with ongoing discrimination and prejudice, may be a sobering reminder of why many older adults may be reticent to disclose their sexual or gender identities.

On the other hand, some of the older adults you work with may have been among the courageous, dedicated people advocating for LGBT rights in the face of intense discrimination, violence, and fear. The aging cohort who bore witness to these historical events also bears the scars. It is our responsibility as providers to create safe, welcoming, and culturally sensitive environments so adults may feel comfortable with us, whether they disclose aspects of their identity or not. It also behooves us to appreciate the level of progress made for LGBT communities while recognizing the distance we still have to go.

As historian, investigator, and student, we encourage you to consider how current LGBT communities are viewed today. While homophobia and transphobia certainly still exist, think of the openly gay or transgender celebrities embraced by the public, and celebrity advocates who celebrate sexual and gender diversity. Consider that a couple of decades after removing homosexuality from the American Psychiatric Association's Diagnostic and Statistical Manual (the primary mental health diagnostic manual used in the U.S.), the American Psychological Association developed guidelines for working with gay, lesbian, bisexual, transgender, and gender nonconforming adults (American Psychological Association, 2015). And consider that today there are television shows focused on LGBT protagonists portrayed with dignity, respect, and a complexity of human character that does not diminish them to just their gender or sexual orientation. While there is still much progress needed, these advances would not be possible without the current aging cohort who courageously raised their voices, sacrificed their safety and sometimes their lives, to create a more equitable and accepting society.

The changing landscape of federal and state laws has impacted the current cohort of LGBT older adults. From *Lawrence v. Texas*, a 2003 U.S. Supreme Court decision striking down the Texas sodomy law and by extension sodomy laws in 13 other states, to the 2012 challenge to Section 3 of the Defense of Marriage Act in *United States v. Windsor*, the LGBT community has had a windfall of legal rights in recent years. Of particular note is the movement toward open service in the military for LGBT individuals since 41% of bisexual men and transgender older adults served in the military (Fredriksen-Goldsen et al., 2013). The history of discrimination that many older adults faced in their military service, such as World War I–era veterans facing court martial for sodomy and World War II–era veterans being denied entrance for "homosexual proclivities" and dishonorable discharge if found out to be gay, has been replaced with a move toward open service with the repeal of Don't Ask, Don't Tell in 2011. Despite recent efforts to be more LGBT-inclusive (Kauth, Shipherd, Barrera, Ortigo, & Jones, 2016), this represents a massive shift for older adults and they may continue to be wary of such services due to very real historical needs for distance from these institutions.

Health Disparities and Cultural Stressors

Older LGBT adults face more limitations accessing care than their cisgender heterosexual peers (IOM, 2011). Overall, LGBT adults have poorer health and higher rates of disability (47%) compared to the general population (Fredriksen-Goldsen et al., 2011; Wallace, Cochran, Durazo, & Ford, 2011). Nearly half of LGBT older adults report having a disability and one third of LGBT report depression (Brennan-Ing, Karpiak, S. E., & Seidel, 2011). As noted in The National Gay and Lesbian Task Force, "Health disparities and economic insecurity are compounded over the course of a lifetime and have devastating effects on LGBT older adults" (Fitzgerald, 2013 p. 1). For example, examining systemic discrimination reveals cruel ripple effects of prejudice: employment discrimination, limited health care coverage, heterosexism, gender stereotyping, and overt discrimination by health care providers lacking cultural humility or awareness. Many LGBT adults subsequently avoided seeking health care services, partly contributing to significant health disparities today. One can see how minority stress can contribute to disproportionate rates of health disparities in LGBT populations (Meyer, 2003).

The accumulation of minority stress over decades has compounding effects on the mental and physical health status of LGBT older adults (Foglia & Fredriksen-Goldsen, 2014; Fredriksen-Goldsen, Hoy-Ellis, et al., 2014). One of the first national studies of LGBT older adults found over 30% of LGBT older adults reported clinically significant depressive symptoms, with relatively higher rates in transgender older adults than lesbian, gay, or bisexual peers (Fredriksen-Goldsen et al., 2011). Studies report similar rates of depression in this population with a consensus that older LGBT adults generally report higher rates of depression than non-LGBT older adults (e.g., IOM, 2011). Furthermore, older LGBT adults report higher rates of attempted suicide than non-LGBT older adults, with higher risk associated with histories of abuse and trauma (IOM, 2011). Fredriksen-Goldsen and colleagues' (2011) study of older LGBT adults documented that nearly 40% of respondents reported seriously considering suicide at some point in their lives, and over 70% of older transgender adults seriously considered suicide at some point in their lives. Other studies note that over 50% of transgender older adults have reported a lifetime prevalence of thinking, planning, and attempting suicide (IOM, 2011). Within these groups, higher rates of depression (and suicidality) were linked to psychological and physical abuse. Additional factors affecting the mental health of older LGBT participants in Fredriksen-Goldsen's (2011) study included loneliness and neglect, reflecting the degree of perceived and actual emotional, social, and instrumental support.

Regarding physical health, older LGBT adults generally have higher rates of chronic health conditions compared to non-LGBT adults (Fredriksen-Goldsen et al., 2011; Fredriksen-Goldsen et al., 2012; IOM, 2011). For example, gay, bisexual, and transwomen older adults have higher rates of prostate cancer than heterosexual and/ or cisgender men for various reasons, some of which are hypothesized to relate to issues of minority stress (IOM, 2011). Indeed, transgender women who fully transitioned often maintain their prostate. However, research on the prevalence rate of prostate cancer within gay, bisexual, and transwomen is lacking. Additionally, men who have sex with men (MSM) tend to have higher rates of anal human papillomavirus (HPV) infections, a significant risk factor for anal cancer. Moreover, partly due to poor health behaviors (e.g., obesity, tobacco use, lower frequency of pap smears and mammograms), lesbian women tend to have higher rates of breast cancer than heterosexual women (Dean, et al., 2000; IOM, 2011). Unfortunately, limited research exists on lesbian, gay, bisexual, and especially transgender older adults. Some literature finds higher rates of chronic heart failure, diabetes, asthma, and obesity within the transgender aging community than the LGB community, often related to the direct (e.g., discrimination) and indirect (e.g., tobacco and alcohol use to cope with stressors) effects of minority stress (Dean et al., 2000; IOM, 2011).

HIV and AIDS remains another chronic health condition differentially afflicting the LGBT community with the overlay of particularly devastating stigma (e.g.,

CDC, 2016). Recent studies found that gay and bisexual men constituted 67% of HIV cases across gender and sexual orientations, and 83% within the male population alone (CDC, 2014, 2016). Of the 55% of new HIV cases within gay and bisexual men, 17% are among men aged 50 and older (CDC, 2016), and over half (56%) of those living with AIDS identify as gay or bisexual men (CDC, 2014, 2016).

The Baby Boomers living with HIV and AIDS, independent of sexual orientation or gender identity, are one of the first generations to age with these illnesses. Indeed, just over a quarter of all adults living with HIV are 55 years old and older (CDC, 2014). Many older adults remain sexually active (Lindau et al., 2007), but unique age- and cohort-related factors place them at risk of contracting/transmitting HIV. Many older adults are less likely to practice safe sex due to less concern for pregnancy risks, low health literacy for risk factors, and difficulty with condom use due to erectile dysfunction (Brooks, Buchacz, Gebo, & Mermin, 2012). Sexually active LGBT older adults at risk for HIV, AIDS, and other sexually transmitted diseases may be reticent to disclose their identities to providers for fear of unequal treatment (Foglia & Fredriksen-Goldsen, 2014). Furthermore, age-related dryness and thinning of vaginal tissue in postmenopausal women can increase the risk of HIV infection through microabrasions during sexual activity (Brooks et al., 2012; CDC, 2016).

Detecting risk factors for HIV and AIDS remains challenging. Older adults may be less comfortable discussing sexual habits or drug use than younger adults and may attribute HIV symptoms to less serious problems (Brooks et al., 2012; CDC, 2016). Similarly, providers are less likely to ask about these topics (CDC, 2014, 2016) and/or may hold nonconscious heteronormative biases that prevent them from considering other risk factors (e.g., unsafe sexual activity, sexual orientation; Foglia & Fredriksen-Goldsen, 2014). As a result, older adults are more likely to be diagnosed with HIV or AIDS later in the disease course, which can affect prognosis and exacerbate preexisting health conditions (CDC, 2014).

Utilization patterns of LGBT older adults demonstrate a tendency to delay or avoid use of formal health care services, often for fear of discrimination (e.g., Choi & Meyer, 2016; Dean et al., 2000; Fitzgerald, 2013). Fredriksen-Goldsen and colleagues (2011) examined factors contributing to health disparities in older transgender adults. They found that transgender older adults reported on average eleven lifetime experiences of discrimination and/or victimization, with denial of or inferior health care being among the top forms (40%), compared to an average of six for cisgender LGB older adults. Furthermore, LGBT older adults are less likely to have health insurance and have greater likelihood of facing financial barriers to health care services relative to their cisgender, heterosexual peers (Fredriksen-Goldsen et al., 2011).

Only recently has the health of LGBT populations garnered more attention. The landmark report by the IOM (2011) addressed the overall health of LGBT populations. Their recommendations involved supporting the National Institute on Health to develop a research agenda focusing on the LGBT health (demographics, social supports, health inequities and interventions, transgender health needs). This includes adding sexual orientation and gender identity to federally funded surveys through the Department of Health and Human Services, including such identifiers in electronic health records, and developing research training and protocols focused on LGBT health. In response to the IOM recommendations, in late 2016 the National Institute on Minority Health and Health Disparities (NIMHD) identified "sexual and gender minorities as a health disparity population for research purposes" (NIMHD, 2016). Similarly, the American Geriatrics Society Ethics Committee (2015) issued a position statement on LGBT older adults. Their vision for the care of LGBT older adults included the creation and evaluation of policies to offset health inequalities, education for health care providers on age-related LGBT health concerns and the effect of minority stress on health, emphasis on cultural considerations when working with LGBT older adults, and increased research funding on LGBT health and the effect of discrimination on health. While these recommendations and visions are encouraging and ambitious, actualizing these policy shifts and research agendas requires that the government administration invest in these initiatives.

Even if access to health care gradually improves, financial instability remains burdensome to many older adults, especially for sexual and gender minority groups. Estimates find higher poverty rates for gay and bisexual men and women than their straight peers (Albeda, Badgett, Schneebaum, & Gates, 2009), while transgender adults are four times more likely to live in poverty (Grant et al., 2011). Furthermore, older adult same-sex marriages generally result in increased poverty rates compared to decreased rates for opposite-sex couples (Albelda et al., 2009). Same-sex couples' ineligibility for federal benefits, even after same-sex marriage came into law, may partly explain this finding. Unlike opposite-sex marriages, same-sex couples were barred from benefits including Social Security, Medicaid, long-term care, and retirement plans until the 2013 *U.S. vs. Windsor* case (Choi & Meyer, 2016). Even still, couples unable to travel to states that legalized same-sex marriage remained barred from accessing the federal benefits afforded their opposite-sex couples until the 2015 Supreme Court decision on marriage equality. However, for some older adults for whom marriage is not an option due to cultural or personal preferences, they remain disenfranchised from federal benefits. This can be particularly destabilizing when one partner dies, leaving the unmarried survivor without the benefits afforded a married couple.

RESILIENCY AND GROWTH

While the majority of research on LGBT older adults focuses on health disparities, only a paucity of research examines factors contributing to resiliency and growth (e.g., Fredriksen-Goldsen et al., 2011). Existing research in this area largely addresses the health behaviors and social support networks that help LGBT older adults cope with the compounding effects of minority stress and aging. Some studies describe the importance of belonging to a larger LGBT community to increase their sense of empowerment and offset the history of discrimination and victimization experienced (Fredriksen-Goldsen et al., 2011; Fredriksen-Goldsen, Kim, et al., 2014; Van Wagenen, Driskell, & Bradford, 2013). However, the degree of social support may differ by age group (Fredriksen-Goldsen, Kim et al., 2014) and gender identity (Fredriksen-Goldsen, et al., 2013) with some of the oldest adults and transgender adults reporting the least sense of community.

A qualitative study focusing on the resilience of transgender older adults identified various themes that facilitated the aging process (McFadden, Frankowski, Flick, & Witten, 2013). Emerging themes included nurturing one's spiritual self, exercising one's sense of agency (e.g., determining when and how to transition, managing finances for a secure future, engaging in healthy coping to prevent illness), practicing self-acceptance, maintaining caring relationships, engaging in advocacy and activism, and enjoying an active and healthy life. Similar themes of self-acceptance, life engagement, and financial planning surfaced in another survey of transgender-bisexual older adults (Witten, 2016). Some respondents reflected on the personal growth experienced by overcoming adversity, while still acknowledging the fears of increased vulnerability to institutional and interpersonal discrimination that often comes with age for LGBT older adults (e.g., worries about receiving respectful care in nursing homes). Nonetheless, further research is needed in this area to understand factors contributing to the resilience evidenced within many LGBT older adults.

INTERSECTIONALITY

Intersectionality theory originated through U.S. Black feminist writings, which argued that examining women's experiences through gender alone did not sufficiently capture the experiences of African American women (e.g., Viruell-Fuentes, Miranda, & Abdulrahim, 2012). Instead, intersectionality theorists propose that the combined effect of gender, race, *and* class contribute significantly to oppression and inequality. This theory has been applied to health equity in various domains, primarily related to the experiences of marginalized groups. We focus on intersectionality here because issues of age, race, gender identity, and sexual orientation do not exist independent of each other. To fully understand individuals' experiences, we must consider the combined effect of these aspects in all their complexity.

The Health Equity Promotion Model (Fredriksen-Goldsen, Simoni et al., 2014) takes a life-span developmental perspective, focusing on how intersectionality influences health equity. The authors explain that the model ". . . acknowledges both the inter- and intragroup variability, and that an individual's development of health potential can vary within a group of individuals who share a similar life course" (Fredriksen-Goldsen, Simoni et al., 2014, p. 5). This model focuses on how "(a) *social positions* (socio-economic status, age, race/ethnicity) and (b) *individual and structural environmental context* (social exclusion, discrimination, and victimization), intersect with (c) *health-promoting and adverse pathways* (behavioral, social, psychological, and biological processes) to influence the continuum of health outcomes in LGBT communities" (p. 6). The model eloquently acknowledges how these factors affect both health equity and resiliency within the aging population of racial, sexual, and gender minorities. Each facet of this model is described here.

Social positions refers to the multiple layers of one's cultural identity and how these intersect to create further health disparities as well as resilience (Fredriksen-Goldsen, Simoni et al., 2014). Individual aspects of identity (e.g., SES, age, race, sexual and gender identity) carry various burdens and privileges; however, their intersection can contribute to increased marginalization and disenfranchisement while also possibly strengthening a group's resolve to persevere. The whole is greater than the sum of its parts and these aspects of one's identity provide context for other environmental factors described here. For example, studies of aging African American LGB women find increased isolation, discrimination, and invisibility compared to heterosexual peers (e.g., Woody, 2015). Qualitative research by Woody (2015) suggests that in African American culture the term *lesbian* holds negative connotations leading to a sense of otherness. Instead, many African American women report preference for other terms including *same gender loving*. As another example, some American Indian and Alaskan Native (AIAN) cultures refer to sexual and gender minority persons as "two spirits," a reverent term adopted in 1990 to describe persons who embody both male and female spirits (Balsam, Huang, Fieland, Simoni, & Walters, 2004). Traditional AIAN cultures typically viewed two spirits with deep reverence. However, over time, and with the effects of colonialization, this reverence transformed into homophobia and transphobia among mainstream society and even within some native communities. While AIAN individuals generally have higher rates of physical and mental health problems (including trauma) than non-AIAN individuals, AIAN individuals who identify as two spirits report even poorer mental and physical health and higher rates of trauma throughout their lives (Balsam et al., 2004). However, some American Indian individuals viewed their two spirit identity as a source of resilience and advocacy, allowing them to align with other Native groups, embrace an indigenous cultural perspective, and create a safe space to explore their identities (Walters, Evans-Campbell, Simoni, Ronquillo, & Bhuyan, 2006).

Individual and structural environmental contexts refer to the effect of both individual and systemic discrimination, prejudice, and exclusion on the health of LGBT individuals. Not surprisingly, studies consistently find that experiences of interpersonal microaggressions, overt discrimination, and physical assaults at the individual level adversely affect the physical and mental health of sexual and gender minorities (Fredriksen-Goldsen, et al., 2012; Meyer, 2003). At the systemic level, policies that exclude LGBT individuals or place barriers to accessing care (e.g., hospital visitation rights restricted to family/spouses) create further health inequity and at times even reduce the likelihood that some LGBT individuals seek care (Fredriksen-Goldsen, Simoni, et al., 2014). As Fredriksen-Goldsen, Simoni, and colleagues (2014) explain, "Structural and contextual factors create a context of marginalization and oppression, including laws and policies that unfairly treat sexual and gender minorities as well as cultural and institutional oppressions, widespread societal stigma, and religious intolerance and persecution" (p. 8). Such factors can directly affect the mental and physical health of LGBT adults (e.g., Fredriksen-Goldsen, et al. 2012; Fredriksen-Goldsen, et al. 2011).

A study of transgender bisexual adults across the life span found a preponderance of respondents sharing their fears of growing older and the potential for institutional discrimination and interpersonal prejudice and violence (Witten, 2016). Many shared their concerns for systemic discrimination in institutional settings (e.g., nursing homes) and their fears that their gender identities would not be respected should they lose their abilities to communicate health care needs. However, some also reflected on the resiliencies they developed by overcoming adversity, processes aided by social and intrapersonal factors including long-term partnership and psychological health (Williams & Fredriksen-Goldsen, 2014). Furthermore, institutional factors promoting inclusion can also affect general health status, including the recent legalization of gay marriage (Goldsen, Bryan, Kim, Muraco, Jen, & Fredriksen-Goldsen, 2017).

As evidenced previously, social positions and environmental contexts interact to affect various pathways to health, specifically behavioral, social, psychological/

cognitive, and biological health factors (Fredriksen-Goldsen, Simoni, et al., 2014). As described earlier, health behaviors for coping with adversity (e.g., smoking vs. exercise) can affect one's health status. Examples discussed earlier included higher rates of obesity and asthma within lesbian women and higher rates of prostate cancer and risk of anal cancer within LGB and transwomen (Dean et al., 2000; IOM, 2011). Health behavior factors including tobacco, drug, and alcohol use can contribute to these factors in addition to limited help seeking possibly due to systemic discrimination in health care settings (Dean et al., 2000; IOM, 2011).

Social processes can also affect health outcomes, with relative emphasis on the quality over quantity of social networks (Antonucci, 2001; Fredriksen-Goldsen, Simoni et al., 2014). Among aging LGBT adults, a sense of belonging within the larger community can serve as a protective factor against adversity (Fredriksen-Goldsen, et al., 2011; Fredriksen-Goldsen, Kim, et al., 2014; Van Wagenen et al., 2013). However, some old-old adults (85+ years old) and transgender older adults more broadly report less sense of community, placing them at higher risk for adverse health outcomes (Fredriksen-Goldsen et al., 2013; Fredriksen-Goldsen, Kim, et al., 2014). Many older adults identifying as transgender bisexual shared concerns about being unable to care for themselves in old age with uncertainty for who may serve as a caregiver (Witten, 2016). Indeed, the support network of many LGBT older adults consists of similar-aged peers (Witten, 2009). While this affords unique opportunities for shared experiences, this also creates the challenge of lateral caregiving (peer caregivers) compared to the more traditional vertical caregiving (e.g., adult children caring for aging parents; Witten, 2009). As LGBT adults age with their support networks, there may come a time when their respective needs prohibit mutual caregiving, raising their concerns for who will care for them and fears for the type of treatment they may receive (Witten, 2016).

Psychological, cognitive, and biological factors, as influenced by social positions and environmental contexts also affect health outcomes (Fredriksen-Goldsen, Simoni, et al., 2014). Basic factors including cognitive health and adaptive approaches to coping influence health outcomes in general (e.g., Rowe & Kahn, 1998). However, when considering the complexity of intersectionality, factors including internalized stigma (ageism, racism, homophobia, and transphobia) and victimization increase in salience (Fredriksen-Goldsen et al., 2012). The impact of internalized stigma and externalized discrimination can affect mental health, including rates of depression and suicide (e.g., Fredriksen-Goldsen et al., 2012; IOM, 2011; Witten, 2016). More broadly, the biological response to chronic stress adversely affects health outcomes, including cognition (e.g., Juster, et al., 2009). Considering the prevalence of lifetime discrimination and victimization among older LGBT adults (e.g., Fredriksen-Goldsen et al., 2012; IOM, 2011), these factors must be considered when discussing the overall health of diverse ethnic, sexual, and gender minority older adults.

CONCLUSION

This chapter aimed to discuss the cohort effects, health disparities and cultural stressors, and factors contributing to the resiliency and growth of ethnic, sexual, and gender minority older adults. Being part historian, student, and investigator can help clarify how these multifaceted aspects of identity affect the experiences of older adults in your personal and professional lives. The intersectionality of these factors makes for complex, inspiring, and sometimes distressing stories about overcoming adversity, achieving new heights, and at times sitting with the pain and frustration of discrimination and prejudice. The diversity within older adult populations also affords invaluable research opportunities to improve our knowledge of aging and enhance our provision of care. Moreover, developing a greater appreciation for older adults, including their strengths and hard-fought battles, can help us appreciate the privileges and civil rights we often take for granted. We stand on the shoulders of giants, and it can be humbling and empowering to acknowledge the experiences and advocacy of those who came before.

DISCUSSION QUESTIONS

1. How might race and cohort factors affect your work with older adults (e.g., language use, historical events)?

2. What are common ageist microaggressions? What types of communication patterns can you keep watch for and try to avoid when working with older adults?

3. What are common factors to consider when working with an older adult identifying as LGBT?

4. What resiliencies might you look for when working with older adults?

REFERENCES

Administration for Community Living. (n.d.). Diversity and cultural competency. Retrieved from https://www.acl.gov/programs/strengthening-aging-and-disability-networks/diversity-and-cultural-competency

Albeda, R., Badgett, M. V. L., Schneebaum, A., & Gates, G. J. (2009). Poverty in the lesbian, gay, and bisexual community. Retrieved from https://williamsinstitute.law.ucla.edu/wp-content/uploads/Albelda-Badgett-Schneebaum-Gates-LGB-Poverty-Report-March-2009.pdf

*Aldwin, C., & Igarashi, H. (2012). An ecological model of resilience in late life. *Annual Review of Gerontology and Geriatrics, 32*, 115–130.

Alexander, M. (2012). *The new Jim Crow: Mass incarceration in the age of colorblindness.* New York, NY: The New Press.

American Geriatrics Society Ethics Committee. (2015). American Geriatrics Society care of lesbian, gay, bisexual, and transgender older adults position statement. *Journal of the American Geriatrics Society, 63*, 423–426. doi:10.1111/jgs.13297

American Psychological Association. (2015). Guidelines for psychological practice with transgender and gender nonconforming people. *American Psychologist, 70*, 832–864. doi:10.1037/a0039906

*Antonucci, T. C. (2001). Social relations an examination of social networks, social support. In J. E. Birren & K. W. Schaie (Eds.), *Handbook of the psychology of aging* (pp. 427–453). San Diego, CA: Academic Press.

Balsam, K. F., Huang, B., Fieland, K. C., Simoni, J. M., & Walters, K. L. (2004). Culture, trauma and wellness: A comparison of heterosexual, and lesbian, gay, bisexual, and two-spirit Native Americans. *Cultural Diversity and Ethnic Minority Psychology, 10*, 287–307. doi:10.1037/1099-9809.10.3.287

Becker, G., & Newsom, E. (2005). Resilience in the face of serious illness among chronically ill African Americans in later life. *Journal of Gerontology B: Psychological Sciences and Social Sciences, 60*, S214-S223. doi:10.1093/geronb/60.4.S214

Bennett, I. M., Chen, J., Soroui, J. S., & White, S. (2009). The contribution of health literacy to disparities in self-rated health status and preventive health behaviors in older adults. *Annals of Family Medicine, 7*, 204–2011. doi:10.1370/amf.940

Brennan-Ing, M., Karpiak, S. E., & Seidel, L. (2011). *Health and psychosocial needs of LGBT older adults.* Retrieved from http://www.centeronhalsted.org/SAGE.pdf

Brooks, J. T., Buchacz, K., Gebo, K. A., & Mermin, J. (2012). HIV infection and older Americans: The public health perspective. *American Journal of Public Health, 102*, 1516–1526. doi:10.2015/AJPH.2012.300844

Centers for Disease Control and Prevention. (2014). *HIV surveillance report.* Retrieved from https://www.cdc.gov/hiv/library/reports/hiv-surveillance.html

Centers for Disease Control and Prevention. (2016). HIV among people aged 50 and older. Retrieved from https://www.cdc.gov/hiv/pdf/group/age/olderamericans/cdc-hiv-older-americans.pdf

Choi, S. K., & Meyer, I. H. (2016). LGBT aging: A review of research findings, needs, and policy implications. Retrieved from https://williamsinstitute.law.ucla.edu/wp-content/uploads/LGBT-Aging-A-Review.pdf

Cook-Daniels, L. (2015). Transgender aging: What practitioners should know. In Orel, N. A. & Fruhauf, C. A. (Eds.), *The lives of LGBT older adults: Understanding challenges and resilience* (pp. 193–215). Washington, DC: American Psychological Association.

Dean, L., Meyer, I. H., Robinson, K., Sell, R. L., Sember, R., Silenzio, V., . . . Tierney, R. (2000). Lesbian, gay, bisexual, and transgender health: Findings and concerns. *Journal of the Gay and Lesbian Medical Association, 4*, 101–151.

Department of Economic and Social Affairs Population Division. (2015). *World Population Ageing 2015.* Retrieved from http://www.un.org/en/development/desa/population/publications/pdf/ageing/WPA2015_Report.pdf

Doob, C. B. (2015). *Social inequality and social stratification in US society.* New York, NY: Routledge.

Fisher, L. L. (May 2010). *Sex, romance, and relationships: AARP Survey of Midlife and Older Adults.* Retrieved from http://assets.aarp.org/rgcenter/general/srr_09.pdf

Fitzgerald, D. (2013). *No golden years at the end of the rainbow: How a lifetime of discrimination compounds economic and health disparities for LGBT older adults.* Retrieved from http://www.thetaskforce.org/static_html/downloads/reports/reports/no_golden_years.pdf

*Foglia, M. B., & Fredriksen-Goldsen, K. I. (2014). Health disparities among LGBT older adults and the role of nonconscious bias. *Hastings Center Report, 44*, S40–S44. doi:10.1002/hast.369

*Fredriksen-Goldsen, K. I., Cook-Daniels, L., Kim, H-J., Erosheva, E. A., Emlet, C. A., Hoy-Ellis, C. P., . . . Muraco, A. (2013). Physical and mental health of transgender older adults: An at-risk and underserved population. *The Gerontologist, 54*, 488–500. doi:10.1093/geront/gnt021

Fredriksen-Goldsen, K. I., Emlet, C. A., Kim, H-J., Muraco, A., Erosheva, E. A., Goldsen, J., & Hoy-Ellis, C. P. (2012). The physical and mental health of lesbian, gay male, and bisexual (LGB) older adults: The role of key health indicators and risk and protective factors. *The Gerontologist, 53*, 664–675. doi:10.1093/geront/gns123

*Fredriksen-Goldsen, K. I., Hoy-Ellis, C. P., Goldsen, J., Emlet, C. A., & Hooyman, N. R. (2014). Creating a vision for the future: Key competencies and strategies for culturally competent practice with lesbian, gay, bisexual, and transgender (LGBT) older adults in the health and human services. *Journal of Gerontology Social Work, 57*, 80–107. doi:10.1080/01634372.2014.890690

Fredriksen-Goldsen, K. I., Kim, H-J., Emlet, C. A., Muraco, A., Erosheva, E. A., Hoy-Ellis, C. P., . . . Petry, H. (2011). *The aging and health report: Disparities and Resilience among lesbian, gay, bisexual and transgender older adults.* Retrieved from http://depts.washington.edu/agepride/wordpress/wp-content/uploads/2012/10/Full-report10-25-12.pdf

Fredriksen-Goldsen, K. I., Kim, H-J., Shiu, C., Goldsen, J., & Emlet, C. A. (2014). Successful aging among LGBT older adults: Physical and mental health-related quality of life by age group. *The Gerontologist, 55*, 1–15. doi:10.1093/geront/gnu081

Fredriksen-Goldsen, K. I., & Muraco, A. (2010). Aging and sexual orientation: A 25-year review of literature. *Research on Aging, 32*, 372–413. doi:10.1177/0164027509360355

Fredriksen-Goldsen, K. I., Simoni, J. M., Kim, H-J., Lehavot, K., Walters, K. L., Yang, J., Hoy Ellis, C. P. (2014). The Health Equity Promotion Model: Reconceptualization of lesbian, gay, bisexual, and transgender (LGBT) health disparities. *American Journal of Orthopsychiatry, 84,* 653–663. doi:10.1037/ort0000030

Gilbert, K. L., Elder, K., Lyons, S., Kaphingst, K., Blanchard, M., & Goodman, M. (2015). Racial composition over the life course: Examining separate and unequal environments and the risk for heart disease for African American men. *Ethnicity & Disease, 25,* 295–304. doi:10.18865/ed.25.3.295

Goldsen, J., Bryan, A. E. B., Kim, H-J., Muraco, A., Jen, S., & Fredriksen-Goldsen, K. I. (2017). Who says I do: The changing context of marriage and health and quality of life for LGBT older adults. *The Gerontologist, 57,* S50–S62. doi:10.1093/geront/gnw174

Grant, J. M., Mottet, L. A., Tanis, J., Harrison, J., Herman, J. L., & Keisling, M. (2011). *Injustice at every turn: A report of the national transgender discrimination survey.* Retrieved from http://www.thetaskforce.org/static_html/downloads/reports/reports/ntds_full.pdf

Greenwald, A. G., & Banaji, M. R. (1995). Implicit social cognition: Attitudes, self-esteem, and stereotypes. *Psychological Review, 102,* 4–27.

Haley, W. E., Gitlin, L. N., Wisniewski, S. R., Mahoney, D. F., Coon, D. W., Winter, L., . . . Ory, M. (2004). Well-being, appraisal, and coping in African-American and Caucasian dementia caregivers: Findings from the REACH study. *Aging & Mental Health, 8*(4), 316–329. doi:10.1080/1360780410001728998

Herek, G. M., & Capitanio, J. P. (1999). AIDS stigma and sexual prejudice. *American Behavioral Scientist, 42,* 1126–1143. Retrieved from http://psc.dss.ucdavis.edu/faculty_sites/rainbow/html/abs99_sp.pdf

Hill, C. V., Pérez-Stable, E. J., Anderson, N. A., & Bernard, M. A. (2015). The National Institute on Aging health disparities research framework. *Ethnicity & Disease, 25,* 245–254. doi:10.18865/ed.25.3.245

Institute of Medicine. (2011). *The health of lesbian, gay, bisexual and transgender people: Building a foundation for better understanding.* Washington, DC: National Academies Press.

Jimenez, D. E., Alegría, M., Chen, C-N, Chan, D., & Laderman, M. (2010). Prevalence of psychiatric illnesses in older ethnic minority adults. *Journal of the American Geriatrics Society, 58,* 256–264. doi:10.1111/j.1532-5415.2009.02685.x

Jimenez, D. E., Cook, B., Bartels, S. J., & Alegría, M. (2013). Disparities in mental health service use among racial/ethnic minority elderly. *Journal of the American Geriatrics Society, 61,* 18–25. doi:10.1111/jgs.12063

Juster, R. P., McEwen, B. S., & Lupien, S. J. (2009). Allostatic load biomarkers of chronic stress and impact on health and cognition. *Neuroscience & Behavioral Reviews, 35,* 2–16. doi:10.1016/j.neurobiorev.2009.10.002

Kane, M. N. (2004). Ageism and intervention: What social work students believe about treating people differently because of age. *Educational Gerontology, 30,* 767–784. doi:10.1080/0360127490498098

Kauth, M. R., Shipherd, J. C., Barrera, T. L., Ortigo, K., & Jones, K. R. (2016). Trainees' perceptions of the Veterans Health Administration interprofessional psychology fellowships in lesbian, gay, bisexual, and transgender health. *Training and Education in Professional Psychology, 10,* 165–170. doi:10.1037.tep0000123

*Knight, B. G., & Sayegh, P. (2010). Cultural values and caregiving: The updated sociocultural stress and coping model. *The Journals of Gerontology, 65B,* 5–13. doi:10.1093/geronb/gbp096

Kwong, K., Du, Y., & Xu, Q. (2015). Healthy aging of minority and immigrant populations: Resilience in late life. *Traumatology, 21,* 136–144. doi:10.1037/trm0000034

Lamberty, G. L., & Bares, K. K. (2013). Neuropsychological assessment and management of older adults with multiple somatic symptoms. In L. D. Ravdin & H. L. Katzen (Eds.), *Handbook on the neuropsychology of aging and dementia* (pp. 121–134). New York, NY: Springer.

Levy, B. R. (2003). Mind matters: Cognitive and physical effects of aging self-stereotypes. *Journal of Gerontology, 58,* P203–P211. doi:10.1093/geronb/58.4.P203

*Levy, B. R., & Banaji, M. R. (2002). Implicit ageism. In T. Nelson (Ed), *Ageism: Stereotypes and prejudice against older persons,* (pp. 49–75). Cambridge, MA: MIT Press.

Levy, B. R., & Leifheit-Limson, E. (2009). The stereotype-matching effect: Greater influence on functioning when age stereotypes correspond to outcomes. *Psychology and Aging, 24*, 230–223. doi:10.1037/a0014563

*Levy, B. R., & Meyers, L. M. (2004). Preventive health behaviors influenced by self-perceptions of aging. *Preventive Medicine, 39*, 625–629. doi:10.1016/j.ypmed.2004.02.029

Levy, B. R., Slade, S., & Kasl, S. (2002). Longitudinal benefit of positive self-perceptions of aging on functional health. *Journal of Gerontology: Psychological Science, 57*, 409–417. doi:10.1093/geronb/57.5.P409

Levy, B. R., Zonderman, A. B., Slade, M. D., & Ferrucci, L. (2012). Memory shaped by age stereotypes over time. *Journal of Gerontology: Psychological Sciences, 67*(4), 432–436. doi:10.1093/geronb/gbr120

Lindau, S. T., Schumm, P., Laumann, E. O., Levinson, W., O'Muircheartaigh, C. A., & Waite, L. J. (2007). A study of sexuality and health among older adults in the United States. *The New England Journal of Medicine, 357*, 762–774. doi:10.1056/NEJMoa067423

MacCrae, C. N., Milne, A. B., & Bodenhausen, G. B. (1994). Stereotypes as energy saving devices: A peek inside the cognitive toolbox. *Journal of Personality and Social Psychology, 66*, 37–44.

McFadden, S. H., Frankowski, S., Flick, H., & Witten, T. M. (2013). Resilience and multiple stigmatized identities: Lessons from transgender persons' reflections on aging. In J. D. Sinnott (Ed.), *Positive psychology: Advances in understanding adult motivation* (pp. 247–268). New York, NY: Springer.

MetLife. (2010). Still out, still aging: The MetLife study of lesbian, gay, bisexual, and transgender baby boomers. Retrieved from https://www.metlife.com/assets/cao/mmi/publications/studies/2010/mmi-still-out-still-aging.pdf

*Meyer, I. H. (2003). Prejudice, social stress, and mental health in lesbian, gay, and bisexual populations: Conceptual issues and research evidence. *Psychological Bulletin, 129*, 674–697. doi:10.1037/0033-2909.129.5.674

National Archives. (2016). Executive orders. Retrieved from https://www.archives.gov/federal-register/codification/executive-order/10450.html

National Institute on Minority Health and Health Disparities. (2016). Sexual and gender minorities formally designated as a health disparity population for research purposes. Retrieved from https://www.nimhd.nih.gov/about/directors-corner/message.html

Ortman, J. M., Velkoff, V. A., & Hogan, H. (2014). An aging nation: The older population in the United States. *Current Population Reports*, 25–1140. Retrieved from https://www.census.gov/prod/2014pubs/p25-1140.pdf

*Pinquart, M., & Sörensen, S. (2005). Ethnic differences in stressors, resources, and psychological outcomes of family caregiving: A meta-analysis. *The Gerontologist, 45*, 90–106.

Rowe, J. W., & Kahn, R. L. (1998). *Successful aging*. New York, NY: Pantheon.

Sinnott, J. D., & Shifren, K. (2001). Gender and aging. Gender differences and gender roles. In J. E. Birren & K. W. Schaie (Eds.), *Handbook of Psychology and Aging* (5th ed., pp. 454–476). New York, NY: Academic Press.

Smedley, B. D., Stith, A. Y., & Nelson, A. R. (2003). *Unequal treatment. Confronting racial and ethnic disparities in health care*. Washington DC: The National Academies Press.

*Steele, C. M., & Aronson, J. (1995). Stereotype threat and the intellectual test performance of African American. *Journal of Personality and Social Psychology, 69*, 797–811.

*Sue, D. W., Capodilupo, C. M., Torino, G. C., Bucceri, J. M., Holder, A. M. B., Nadal, K. L., & Esquilin, M. (2007). Racial microaggressions in everyday life. Implications for clinical practice. *American Psychologist, 62*, 271–286. doi:10.1037/0003-066X.62.4.271

Thorpe, R. J., Bell, C. N., Kennedy-Hendricks, A., Harvey, J., Smolen, J. R., Bowie, J. V., & LaVeist, T. A. (2015). Disentangling race and social context in understanding disparities in chronic conditions among men. *Journal of Urban Health, 92*, 83–92. doi: 10.1007/s11524-014-9900-9

Thorpe, R. J., McCleary, R., Smolen, J. R., Whitfield, K. E., Simonsick, E. M., & LaVeist, T. (2014). Racial disparities in disability among older adults: Findings from the Exploring health disparities in integrated communities study. *Journal of Aging Health, 26*, 1261–1279. doi:10.1177/0898264314534892

United States Census Bureau. (2012). Statistical abstract of the United States. Retrieved from http://www2.census.gov/library/publications/2011/compendia/statab/131ed/tables/pop .pdf

Van Dalen, H. P., Henkens, K., & Schippers, J. (2010). Productivity of older workers: Perceptions of employers and employees. *Population and Development Review, 36*(2), 309–330. doi:10.1111/ j.1728-4457.2010.00331.x

Van Wagenen, A., Driskell, J., & Bradford, J. (2013). "I'm still raring to go": Successful aging among lesbian, bisexual, and transgender older adults. *Journal of Aging Studies, 27,* 1–14. doi:10.1016/ j.jaging.2012.09.001

Viruell-Fuentes, E. A., Miranda, P. Y., & Abdulrahim, S. (2012). More than culture: Structural racism, intersectionality theory, and immigrant health. *Social Science & Medicine, 75,* 2099–2106. doi:10.1016/j.socscimed.2011.12.037

Wallace, S. P., Cochran, S. D., Durazo, E. M., & Ford, C. L. (2011). The health of aging lesbian, gay and bisexual adults in California. *Policy Brief UCLA Center for Health Policy Research,* 1–8. Retrieved from https://www.ncbi.nlm.nih.gov/pmc/articles/PMC3698220/pdf/nihms472438 .pdf

Walters, K. L., Evans-Campbell, T., Simoni, J. M., Ronquillo, T., & Bhuyan, R. (2006). "My spirit in my heart": Identity experiences and challenges among American Indian two-spirit women. *Journal of Lesbian Studies, 10,* 125–149. doi:10.1300/J155v10n01_07

*Williams, D. R., & Mohammed, S. A. (2009). Discrimination and racial disparities in health: Evidence and needed research. *Journal of Behavioral Medicine, 32,* 1–38. doi:10.1007/s10865-008 -9185-0

*Williams, K. N. (2004). Elderspeak: Impact on geriatric care. *Geriatrics and Aging, 7*(1), 57–60.

Williams, K. N. (2006). Improving outcomes of nursing home interactions. *Research in Nursing & Health, 29,* 121–133. doi:10.1002/nur.20117

Williams, K. N., Herman, R., Gajweski, B., & Wilson, K. (2009). Elderspeak communication: Impact on dementia care. *American Journal of Alzheimer's Disease and Other Dementias, 24,* 11–20. doi:10.1177/1533317508318472

Williams, M. E., & Fredriksen-Goldsen, K. I. (2014). Same-sex partnerships and the health of older adults. *Journal of Community Psychology, 42,* 558–570. doi:10.1002/Jcop.21637

Witten, T. M. (2009). Graceful exits: Intersection of aging, transgender identities, and the family/ community. *Journal of GLBT Family Studies, 5,* 36–62. doi:10.1080/15504280802595378

*Witten, T. M. (2016). Aging and transgender bisexuals: Exploring the intersection of age, bisexual sexual identity, and transgender identity. *Journal of Bisexuality, 16,* 58–80. doi:10.1080/1529971 6.2015.1025939

Woody, I. (2015). Lift every voice: Voices of African-American lesbian elders. *Journal of Lesbian Studies, 19,* 50–58. doi:10.1080/10894160.2015.972755

14

Aging and the Legal System

Sheri Gibson and Magdalene Lim

H ealth professionals are often called upon to intervene in complex ethical dilemmas that involve respecting an older adult's autonomy while also considering protective interventions to ensure safety. This chapter addresses the foundational ethical competencies for psychologists and geropsychologists including the unique challenges associated with surrogate decision making, legal, clinical, and psychosocial interventions specific to working with vulnerable older adults, ethical dilemmas that can emerge within various situations including assessment and integrated care settings, detection and intervention strategies in cases of elder abuse, neglect, and exploitation, and ethical approaches to research with older adults. Finally, the authors discuss the multicultural dimensions that influence how ethical and legal issues are conceptualized and addressed.

ETHICAL COMPETENCIES IN GEROPSYCHOLOGY

Psychologists make decisions every day involving fundamental beliefs and values about what is most appropriate in working with older adults, families, health care professionals, and within clinical or academic settings. A psychologist's comprehensive understanding of treatment is grounded in the ethical guidelines and principles of the American Psychological Association's (APA) Ethics Code (APA, 2017; www.apa.org/ethicscode/). The APA Ethics Code serves as a standard to direct the actions

---

*Key references in the References section are indicated by an asterisk.

and decision making of psychologists in their work with clients, families, communities, and colleagues with an emphasis on promoting advocacy for social change.

Within clinical geropsychology practice, the Geropsychology Knowledge and Skills Assessment Tool (Karel, Emery, Molinari, & CoPGTP Task Force on the Assessment of Geropsychology Competencies, 2010) captures the foundational competencies of geropsychology involving legal and ethical standards in four specific areas. Competencies include one's ability to

> . . . identify complex ethical and legal issues that arise in the care of older adults, analyze them accurately, and proactively address them, including: (a) tension between sometimes competing goals of promoting autonomy and protecting safety of at-risk older adults; (b) decision making capacity and strategies for optimizing older adults' participation in informed consent regarding a wide range of medical, residential, financial, and other life decisions; (c) surrogate decision making as indicated regarding a wide range of medical, residential, financial, end of life, and other life decisions; and (d) state and organizational laws and policies covering elder abuse, advance directives, conservatorship, guardianship, multiple relationships, and confidentiality (Karel et al., 2010, p. 117).

ADVANCE CARE PLANNING FOR OLDER ADULTS

Many of the ethical issues that psychologists face when working with older adults revolve around health care decisions and whether the older adult is capable of making his or her own health care decisions. There are several terms that are commonly used when discussing health care decision making. Advance directives, also known as living wills, are documents that specify a person's wishes for end-of-life care. Hospitals are typically required to present information on advance directives prior to admission in accordance with the Patient Self-Determination Act of 1990. Any individual older than the age of 18 can complete an advance directive, though research suggests that only about a quarter of U.S. adults have completed advance directives (Rao, Anderson, Lin, & Laux, 2013). Lack of awareness of advance directives is typically the most common reason for not completing one.

There are several pieces of information that are typically included in an advance directive. For the purposes for planning in the event of becoming unable to make decisions secondary to a disabling circumstance, individuals can specify their preference for medical treatment (full treatment vs. comfort-focused treatment), extraordinary measures (tube feeding, ventilator, etc.), and preferences for cardiopulmonary resuscitation (CPR), also known as a do-not-resuscitate (DNR) order. Individuals can also designate a health care surrogate to make decisions for them if they are unable to; this information may also be included in a medical power of attorney (POA) document, which is discussed in the next section. This person is sometimes referred to as a health care agent or health care proxy. If no surrogate is designated, the default surrogate is the next of kin, typically in the order of spouse/domestic partner, adult child, parent, sibling, or other relative. If no one is available to serve as the health care surrogate, the court may appoint a guardian to make the decisions. A guardian may also need to be appointed if the family is in conflict about the patient's wishes, though this is an ethical gray area. We revisit these issues later in the chapter when we discuss potential ethical problems around surrogate decision making.

Some advance directives include POA documents. A POA is a legal document that designates someone to make decisions on your behalf if you are deemed unable to make or express such decisions. With regard to older adults, a POA is typically designated for health care and/or financial matters. A financial POA is typically called a general POA, whereas a health care POA is typically called a medical POA. Individuals can choose whether a POA goes into effect immediately once it is signed (called a "durable POA") or whether it only goes into effect once the person is unable to make decisions, as verified by a health care professional (called a "springing POA"). Clinicians may be asked to help an older adult complete a living will or POA. It may be beneficial to choose a different person for the medical versus financial POA depending on who is most familiar with the older adult's views on life and death versus his or her financial affairs. Table 14.1 lists some example options that are typically included in forms that document treatment preferences. One example of this type of form that is used in California is the Physician Orders for Life-Sustaining Treatment (POLST). On the POLST, the patient can list their health care agent though the POLST does not include the level of detail regarding health care decisions that may present in a medical POA or advance directive. The POLST is freely available at www.capolst.org/polst-for-healthcare-providers/forms.

Table 14.1 Sample Questions Typically Used When Documenting Treatment Preferences

Decision	Description and Options
Cardiopulmonary resuscitation (CPR)	If the patient has no pulse and is not breathing Options: Administer CPR or not (DNR order)
Medical interventions	If patient has a pulse and/or is breathing Options: Full treatment—Prolong life using all medically effective means (for example, intubation, ventilation) Selective treatment—Treat medical conditions but do not intubate (for example, intravenous fluids or antibiotics). Avoid intensive care Comfort-focused treatment—Maximize comfort. Do not use full and selective treatments unless consistent with comfort goals. Examples include oxygen or suctioning
Artificially administered nutrition	Whether to offer food by mouth is feasible or desired Options: Long-term artificial nutrition, including feeding tubes Trial period of artificial nutrition, including feeding tubes No artificial means of nutrition, including feeding tubes
Health care proxy	Specify name and contact information of someone who can make decisions for you if you are unable to

DNR, do not resuscitate.

While the POLST is the form used in California, most states have similar forms that capture treatment preferences. For example, Colorado uses the Medical Orders for Scope of Treatment (MOST) form, which is freely available at www.coloradoadvancedirectives.com/most-in-colorado.

ETHICS IN LONG-TERM CARE

While the majority of older adults receive care from family members, approximately 14% of adults older than the age of 65 receive services in nursing home or long-term care settings, assisted living, or retirement communities (National Alliance for Caregiving [NAC], 2015). Results from the AARP/NAC study suggest that 16% of care recipients residing in retirement communities, assisted living, and skilled nursing facilities have dementia due to Alzheimer's disease or other causes. Ethical challenges can first emerge from the initial transition from independent living to a higher level of residential care.

For many of us, regardless of age, change can be difficult and typically requires time to adapt to any new circumstance or environment. You might recall events in your life which required changes that were anxiety provoking: the first day of high school; leaving home for college; starting a new job; moving to a new city or immigrating to a different country. Similar anxieties and fears are present for the older individual who may be faced with leaving a home and condensing a lifelong accumulation of sentimental possessions into a small room or apartment. Let us consider the following scenario:

Mr. Watsby, an 83-year-old widowed gentleman, was sent to the emergency department (ED) after he fell while showering in his single-family home. At the ED, he reported that it took him 2 hours to "crawl" from the bathroom to his phone to call for emergency help. He suffered bruises on his left arm and leg, but did not sustain a head injury. Prior to this injury, Mr. Watsby had undergone a left hip replacement for a fracture. He has lived alone for the past 3 years following his wife's death due to a motor vehicle accident. Mr. Watsby is treated for multiple medical conditions including congestive heart failure (CHF), atrial fibrillation, hypertension, diabetes, and chronic obstructive pulmonary disease (COPD). His two adult sons live out-of-state but each has offered him to live with them due to their increased concerns about his ability to continue living alone. Mr. Watsby had repeatedly declined their offer as well as their suggestion to move to an assisted living facility. His sons did not insist for him to move because they knew that their father's favorite pastime was to look at his wife's paintings, which were hung on every wall of the matrimonial family home. There would be too many paintings to bring to any other home.

On examination at the ED, Mr. Watsby was found to have back sores that had ulcerated and was poorly nourished with a weight of 125 pounds, down from 168 pounds the previous year. His mental status deteriorated rapidly on the second day of admission with delirium, but the agitation had resolved by the end of the week. A cognitive screen a week later indicated problems with memory, but Mr. Watsby denied any difficulties managing things on his own, including his medications. On the day of the hospital discharge, Mr. Watsby declined home-health services and stated he would be sure to carry his cell phone in his pocket to call for help when needed. He denied feeling depressed and expressed excitement at the thought of returning to the comfort of his own home. Mr. Watsby's sons had spoken to the attending physician and committed to taking turns to check in on their father by phone each day.

Three days after discharge, Mr. Watsby fell again in his home. This time, he fell in the kitchen and was found 9 hours later by paramedics with blood on his forehead. He was lying semiconscious on the floor close to his front door. Although he did not seem to have sustained any major injury, he was hospitalized and given intravenous fluids. The clinical team and one of Mr. Watsby's sons agreed that in the interest of maintaining his safety, he should be discharged to a subacute rehabilitation stay in a nursing home with plans to transition into long-term care. His sons shared responsibilities for his health care in a springing power of attorney (POA). Mr. Watsby reluctantly agreed but stated a preference to remain in his own home. After 20 days in the rehabilitation facility, his physician determined he was incapacitated and the medical durable POA was activated. Mr. Watsby was transferred to permanent long-term care. His physical and mental health conditions worsened over the next 5 months. The advance directive documents had not been completed and Mr. Watsby was placed on a feeding tube. In the days that followed, he had multiple episodes of breathlessness that required several resuscitation attempts that finally failed. Mr. Watsby died after living 5 months in the nursing home. On review of the admission chart record, he was noted as "depressed and disoriented."

In Mr. Watsby's case, several ethical and legal questions arise for psychologists and other health care professionals:

1. To what extent does the health care team promote Mr. Watsby's autonomy and independence versus implementing protective interventions to maintain his personal safety?

2. What more do we need to know about family dynamics and the strength of the relationship between Mr. Watsby and his two sons? Do his sons have the capacity to serve as surrogate decision makers? To what extent is it our role to ascertain this? If not them, then who? Do they know their father's values, preferences, and wishes for his care and end-of-life decisions?

3. How much weight do we place on Mr. Watsby's preference to return home in the face of declined physical functioning? What information do we need to gather to appreciate his refusal to receive care in a rehabilitation or skilled nursing setting?

4. And finally, who on the health care team is responsible for gathering relevant familial and psychosocial information and how is it shared with the family and the rest of the care team? Most importantly, how is the plan of care communicated with Mr. Watsby? Who should be involved in those discussions?

FOUNDATIONAL ETHICS OF DECISION MAKING

To appreciate the underpinnings of ethical dilemmas, clinicians must be familiar with the complexity and range of life events and decisions encountered by older adults, family members, and other health care professionals. Specific decisions have been identified (American Bar Association [ABA] & APA, 2008) and include the following: (a) medical decision making that can range from simple decisions—such as medication management—to complex decisions such as end of life or choosing a medical treatment (Karlawish, Quill, & Meier, 1999); (b) financial decision making ranging from balancing one's checkbook to managing investments and assets (Marson, 2001); (c) independent living decisions regarding the level of supervision or independence needed in one's living situation (Moye & Braun, 2007); (d) driving ability—for example, at what point does a person discontinue driving?; (e) decision making around sexual consent and relationships, particularly in situations where either one or both individuals have cognitive impairment; and finally, (f) the ability to make a will (referred to as *testamentary capacity*; Marson, Herbert, & Solomon, 2005). In addition, a psychologist may be called upon to evaluate the capacity to make a wide range of other decisions (e.g., capacity to marry, capacity to refuse or accept visitors in a hospice setting, etc.).

At the center of developing ethical competencies is the tension between autonomy, protection, and *beneficence—the intention to do good and no harm on behalf of the patient* (APA, 2010)—all of which must include appreciation for an individual's right to make life decisions and choices that are consistent with his or her beliefs and values. In most situations, those principles can be a guiding force in treatment planning, provision of education, and discussion with patients and families about interventions and best course of action for the patient. However, in some situations, conflict arises between what the patient wants and what the provider or family believes is best for the patient. A common challenge for professionals is discerning whether or not an older individual can be their own decision maker, particularly in situations where he or she is engaging in seemingly poor decision making. Such situations include neglecting one's health care needs (i.e., taking psychiatric or other chronic disease medications as prescribed, attending health care appointments, and general hygiene care), changing directives in a last will and testament, entering intimate partnerships or new relationships, or engaging in risky behaviors such as alcohol or substance use, and cigarette smoking.

AUTONOMY AND SURROGATE DECISION MAKING

In situations where others (health care professionals, friends, family, coworkers) question the type of decisions made by an older adult, concerns may be raised about whether the individual has the ability to make decisions and if not, what should be done to protect that individual from endangering himself or herself or others. Two core principles—autonomy and protection—are maximized when responding to these issues. Clinicians and physicians are often called to assess whether an individual has the cognitive capacity to function in any particular domain of decision making. Eight domains of capacity specific to older adults have been identified by

Moye and Marson (2007): (a) independent living; (b) financial management; (c) consent to treatment; (d) testamentary capacity; (e) consent to participate in research; (f) sexual consent; (g) voting; and (h) driving.

Capacity is delineated into either clinical capacity or legal capacity (also called competency). Clinical capacity is based on the judgment of health care professionals and usually revolves around whether the patient has the ability to express a choice, understand the risks and benefits of the decision, appreciate the significance of the decision, and state rational explanations for their decision (ABA & APA, 2008). Clinical capacity determinations are domain specific. As outlined in the eight domains of capacity, an older adult may lack capacity for financial decisions but capacity may be intact for medical decisions/consent to treatment. The assumption behind a capacity assessment is that the individual could possibly eventually regain capacity to make decisions in that area. For example, if the older adult is experiencing delirium due to various medications, the effects of this would be expected to clear over time.

Judgments about clinical decisional capacity are commonly made through informal information-gathering processes that involve interviewing persons within the familial and psychosocial network such as caregivers, family members, clinicians, attorneys, adult protective service caseworkers, and law enforcement. Neuropsychologists, psychologists, and physicians use various formal assessment measures for determining multiple domains of clinical capacity. If a patient is found to lack clinical capacity in a specific domain, the health care team may turn to the surrogate decision maker to provide insight into the person's wishes. The decisions made by a surrogate should be guided by two standards: (a) *substituted judgment* and (b) *best interests*. *Substituted judgment* involves the surrogate's understanding and appreciation for the individual's preferences, values, and wishes, to inform their decision making based on what the individual would have decided if he or she had the capacity to do so (Bush, Allen, & Molinari, 2017). In cases where there is insufficient information to make a substituted judgment, the surrogate's decision making should be guided by the *best interest* standard. In other words, the surrogate's decision would be considered in the best interest of the incapacitated person. Courts may become involved if the surrogate objects to a recommended treatment or if there is conflict within the family about what the patient would want.

The decision of clinical capacity is usually done through clinical interview without a formal measure. However, there are formal measures available that may assist in the interview process, although the ultimate decision about capacity should involve multiple informants and methods and not rely solely on one source of information. Formal measures of decisional capacity are typically domain specific and focus on areas such as the capacity to make medical and/or financial decisions. Instruments typically present hypothetical vignettes, which allow the clinician to understand the individual's reasoning process in how he or she approaches the vignette. Examples of these type of instruments for capacity to make medical decisions include the MacArthur Competence Assessment Tool for Treatment (Grisso & Appelbaum, 1998), the Hopemont Capacity Assessment Interview (Edelstein, 2000), and the Capacity to Consent to Treatment Instrument (Marson, Ingram, Cody, & Harrell, 1995). More information about these and other capacity assessment instruments is available in a handbook designed for psychologists, *Assessment of Older Adults with Diminished Capacity*, written jointly by the American Bar Association

Commission on Law and Aging and the APA (ABA & APA, 2008). This handbook, as well as handbooks designed for lawyers and judges, is freely available at www .apa.org/pi/aging/programs/assessment.

When older adults can no longer manage their affairs and there is no one available to act as surrogates, or the surrogates are in conflict, the court may need to appoint guardians or conservators. This decision is made by magistrates and judges. The judge decides about the level of supervision that may be needed to support or protect the older individual or their assets (Greene & Gibson, 2013). Although it varies by state, the following requirements are typically needed to file for a competency hearing: (a) a disabling condition (dementia, mental, or medical disorder), (b) a lack of cognitive ability to evaluate information and communicate preferences, (c) an inability to care for oneself without intervention, and (d) a determination that guardianship is the only feasible way to protect the person. Two forms of legal protections commonly used by courts are guardianship and conservatorship.

The responsibilities and duties associated with designated guardians or conservators vary from state to state. In most states, a guardian is a person who is legally responsible for someone who is unable to manage his or her own affairs, which can include domains of health care, personal affairs, and financial management. They are typically responsible for making sure that the individual receives appropriate services. A conservator is typically and primarily responsible for protecting and handling financial affairs for a person who is deemed incompetent. Federal laws do not govern guardianship practices; thus, duties or responsibilities associated with a guardianship role are left to individual states and jurisdictions to outline and uphold. Most determinations are made in probate court. Probate court is part of the state court system where cases involving wills and estates are presented to and ruled by a magistrate. In contrast, criminal courts are designated for criminal cases that typically involve a juried trial.

When a guardian or conservator is designated by the court, the older adult loses his or her right to make independent and autonomous decisions about living arrangements, medical treatment, selling or purchasing property, changing a will, driving, entering marriage or getting a divorce. Surrogate decisions can even be made and upheld despite objections from the incapacitated adult (Grisso, 2003). That said, the guardian or conservator is encouraged to always keep the older adult's preferences and values at the forefront of his or her decision making. Consider the following example:

Ms. Samson is a 78-year-old widowed, Caucasian woman who resides in an assisted-living facility following a stroke that resulted in cognitive, speech, and mobility impediments. Her sister-in-law, who is also widowed, is designated as Ms. Samson's guardian for all decision making around medical, personal, and financial affairs. Ms. Samson is a lifelong tobacco user. Her sister-in-law purchases cigarettes weekly and drops them off at the care facility. After the first of the year, the sister-in-law decides to quit smoking and simultaneously, stops bringing cigarettes to Ms. Samson. The facility staff notices increased negative behaviors such as agitation, bouts of crying, decreased attendance of activities, and isolation in her room. The facility administrator speaks to the sister-in-law about staff's observations and gently reminds her of Ms. Samson's preference to continue smoking. The sister-in-law agrees to purchase cigarettes and Ms. Samson's behavior returns to a pleasant and content baseline.

Recall that decisions made by surrogates should be guided by the standards of substituted judgment and the patient's best interests. In Ms. Samson's situation, the sister-in-law likely understood her preference to continue smoking although Ms. Samson was unable to effectively communicate her preferences. In the absence of knowing a person's preferences or wishes, surrogate decision makers base their decisions on what would be in the *best interest* of the individual. Again, in Ms. Samson's case, the surrogate substituted her own values (to quit smoking) for the values of Ms. Samson. This illustrates the risk that surrogate decision makers take, either intentionally or unintentionally, when making decisions for an incapacitated person. Hence, it is important for surrogate decision makers to evaluate their own biases and preferences regarding the individual's care so as to not pervert their decision-making processes.

The previous paragraphs focus mostly on a person's capacity to make medical decisions. As noted in the beginning of this section, there are other domains of capacity, some of which are encountered more often in working with older adults. If an older adult is giving money to someone or spending a lot of money in a potentially irresponsible way (i.e., gambling), a provider may begin to question the person's capacity to make financial decisions. As discussed earlier, a financial POA may need to be appointed if the person is found to lack capacity to make financial decisions. One formal measure of financial capacity, the Financial Capacity Instrument (Marson et al., 2000) enables a clinician to obtain more detailed information about an older adult's ability to understand financial activities such as cash transactions, checkbook management, and financial judgment. Other capacity assessment instruments such as the Hopemont Capacity Assessment Interview (Edelstein, 2000) or the Independent Living Scales (Loeb, 1996) include a section on financial decision making, which can be used to inform a decision about financial capacity. The Lichtenberg Financial Decision Rating and Screening Scales (Lichtenberg et al., 2016) provide a structured interview to assess an older adult's ability to make a sentinel financial decision, such as making a large donation or entering into an annuity.

Other areas of decisional capacity include whether an older adult has the capacity to enter into a sexual relationship or to continue driving. These types of decisions are often challenging for family and health care professionals. Most of the concerns around capacity to enter into sexual relationships center on patients with dementia. Consider a situation where two older adults are living in a long-term care setting and want to initiate a sexual relationship. There may be concern that one or both of the individuals are unable to understand the pros and cons of this type of relationship due to the dementia (Moye & Marson, 2007). Alternatively, consider a situation in which a person with dementia lives in a long-term care setting and his or her long-term partner lives in the community and does not have dementia. Would you have concerns about them continuing to have sexual intercourse, even as the person with dementia continues to experience cognitive decline?

Although sexual consent decisions are rarely a legal concern, it can become complicated due to balancing the principles of autonomy and to do no harm, while also considering the negative attitudes that exist regarding older adults' sexuality (Tarzia, Fetherstonhaugh, & Bauer, 2012). Lichtenberg and Strzepek (1990) suggest that an assessment of sexual consent capacity should include the patient's awareness of the relationship, the patient's ability to avoid exploitation, and the patient's awareness of potential risks such as sexually transmitted diseases. Any assessment of sexual consent capacity should include a review of medical records (including an assessment of conditions that may impact sexual functioning), a clinical interview to assess values around sex as well as understanding, reasoning, and choice, collateral interviews (i.e., family or nursing home staff), neuropsychological testing, and discussion with other team members at the facility (Syme & Steele, 2016). Even if the older adult is found to lack capacity to consent to sex, some researchers advocate that certain sexual behaviors may still be allowable based on a committee decision that includes nursing home staff and family members (Wilkins, 2015). This approach is suggested to avoid a condescending attitude toward sexual expression among older adults with dementia.

Determining an older adult's capacity to continue driving is also complex. For many individuals, the decision to stop driving has a major impact on perceived independence. However, family members may become concerned that an older adult with dementia lacks the judgment to continue driving, depending on the severity of the condition. In a longitudinal study of men with dementia, the decision to stop driving was often made abruptly after a physician recommendation (Adler & Kuskowski, 2003). Follow-up interviews 2 years later indicated that approximately half of the participants had stopped driving but the other half continued to drive up to 5 days per week.

Psychologists are often asked to assist with the decision to stop driving, either in terms of assessing the older adult's functioning with regard to skills involved in driving, or by initiating a discussion with the older adult around his or her views about driving and whether the individual has any concerns or motivation to reduce or stop driving. There are several components of a driving evaluation, including a medical exam, psychological exam, and an evaluation by a driving specialist (ABA & APA, 2008). Although the core part of the psychological exam should focus on cognitive functioning, it should also include assessment of symptoms of depression and anxiety, as these conditions can impair reaction time and lead to distraction when driving (ABA & APA, 2008). The evaluation by a driver specialist is critical because impairments observed in psychological testing may or may not impact driving skills.

Although this varies across jurisdictions, there are steps that health care professionals and family members can take if they are concerned about an older adult's ability to drive safely. In California, for example, physicians are required to report a medical condition, such as dementia, to the Department of Motor Vehicles (DMV), which will trigger a reexamination of driving ability. In some cases, based on the physician's report, the DMV may decide that the diagnosis is not severe enough yet to require a reexamination. Therefore, when a physician provides this information to the DMV, it does not necessarily mean that the person's license will be revoked. In some states, certain health care professionals are required to notify the DMV when certain conditions are diagnosed, whereas in other states, health care professionals are not allowed to share this type of private health information. In most states, family members can file a report with the DMV that will trigger a reexamination of driving ability.

ELDER MISTREATMENT, NEGLECT, AND EXPLOITATION

An important area where ethical and legal tensions arise is in cases of suspected or identified elder abuse and exploitation. According to the Centers for Disease Control and Prevention, elder abuse is defined as "an intentional act or failure to act by a caregiver or another person in a relationship involving an expectation of trust that causes or creates a risk of harm to an older adult" (Hall, Karch, & Crosby, 2016, p. 25). Various forms of elder abuse have been identified and include physical, sexual, emotional, caregiver and self-neglect, and financial exploitation. Important to note is that most states vary in their definitions of the various forms of abuse to older or at-risk adults, thus creating barriers for collecting and analyzing national data to describe the prevalence and incidence rates of elder mistreatment and exploitation. Some scholars have attempted to provide empirical evidence for the prevalence of elder abuse. The most recent prevalence study published by Acierno and colleagues (2010) used randomized telephone dialing methodology to survey 5,777 older adults. Results suggested that one in 10 respondents reported experiencing some form of abuse in the past year. The highest prevalence rate reported was financial abuse by a family member (5.2%), followed by potential neglect (5.1%), emotional abuse (4.6%), physical abuse (1.6%), and finally, sexual abuse (0.6%). The authors concluded that the most consistent correlates with abuse were low social support and previous exposure to a traumatic event.

Several risk factors increase older adults' vulnerability to mistreatment and exploitation. Factors include physical, cognitive, and sensory deficits, emotional instability (i.e., mental illness), physical and psychosocial isolation, a recent major life transition (i.e., widowhood), relocation, and/or poor access to resources such as medical care, mental health treatment, or spiritual/social activities. Several studies have investigated the association between dementia and older adult victimization. Aggregated findings suggest a higher prevalence of abuse among older individuals with a diagnosis of dementia (Cooper, Selwood, & Livingston, 2008) with upward of 50% of persons with dementia experiencing some form of abuse (Cooper et al., 2009). Another study, which surveyed caregivers of older adults with dementia, reported 47% of care recipients had been mistreated by their caregivers (Wigglesworth et al., 2010).

The ethical dilemmas in most cases of elder mistreatment, neglect, and exploitation return to the principles of autonomy and beneficence. As discussed earlier in the chapter, all persons are viewed to be competent unless determined otherwise by a physician or psychologist. Law enforcement and adult protective services—the human services agency commonly involved in investigating and intervening in cases of elder abuse—are sometimes confronted with an older adult's right to refuse services, particularly if the older person appears capable of understanding the consequences of doing so. Self-determination is an important component in intervention and can be a limitation to implementing services and resources. For example, a caseworker may determine that an at-risk adult may benefit from meal preparation services and home health care. The at-risk individual has the right to accept meal services yet refuse home health care. Unless there is a law, code, or ordinance prohibiting or limiting a person's choice, the at-risk adult has the right to make lifestyle choices that others may feel is objectionable or even dangerous, such as:

- Refusing medical treatment
- Refusing to take necessary medication
- Choosing to abuse alcohol or drugs
- Living in a dirty or cluttered home
- Continuing to live with a perpetrator
- Keeping a large number of pets
- Engaging in other behaviors that may not be safe (i.e., gambling, having multiple intimate partners)

Regardless of mental capacity, most states mandate health care professionals to report suspected or confirmed maltreatment; still, several states are not legally mandated to report and each state may have a different definition or criteria to identify an "at-risk adult." Health care professionals, including psychologists, need to be familiar with state laws guiding the reporting of mistreatment of older adults in their jurisdiction. A list of national resources for information about elder rights and protections can be found in Table 14.2. Familiarization can help psychologists identify a course of action to either protect or prevent abuse of an at-risk older adult (Bush et al., 2017).

Table 14.2 Resources for Information About Elder Rights and Protections

Organization	Website
Administration on Aging	https://www.acl.gov/about-acl/administration-aging
American Bar Association Commission on Law & Aging	https://www.americanbar.org/aba.html
Gerontological Society of America	www.geron.org
National Adult Protective Services Network	www.apsnetwork.org
National Center on Elder Abuse	www.ncea.acl.gov
National Clearinghouse on Abuse in Later Life	www.ncall.us
National Committee for the Prevention of Elder Abuse	www.preventelderabuse.org
Psychologists in Long-Term Care (PLTC)	www.pltcweb.org/index.php

RESPECTING CULTURAL DIFFERENCES IN CASES OF ELDER ABUSE

Cultural competence and respect for normative practices among all individuals from diverse backgrounds must be the first guiding principle when caring for older adults and when determining whether elder abuse has occurred. Introspection of any biases or awareness of any lack of knowledge of the relevant culture might be a helpful start in determining the course of action necessary to be a competent clinician. Culture and diversity in this context are not limited to understanding different racial and ethnic practices, but includes knowledge of how different groups embrace the meaning of being disabled, homosexual, or bisexual, gender role expectations, loyalty to family, caregiving, financial dependence, intergenerational communication, and perception of age or illness-related burden. This is obviously not an exhaustive list as every micro- and macrosystem of function brings with it different complexities as well as creativity for problem resolution and life celebrations. As in all clinical work, there are several ways to ensure that a reasonable amount of consideration has been made not to cause any additional harm to the older adult identified for protection. Any underestimation of the needs and efforts to clarify the situation from which elder abuse is suspected could be detrimental. Not only could it hurt the well-being of the identified older adult, it could also likely place a tremendous amount of emotional burden on that individual due to feelings of shame for being the cause of the family's additional hardship as imposed during investigations (Lee & Eaton, 2009).

It is prudent for clinicians to refer to the APA Ethics Code (2010) that clearly states under the general principles that psychologists "do no harm" (Principle A: Beneficence and Nonmaleficence), "exercise reasonable judgment and take precautions to ensure that their potential biases, the boundaries of their competence . . . do not lead to . . . unjust practices" (Principle D: Justice), and "respect the dignity and worth of all people, and the rights of individuals to . . . self-determination . . . are aware of and respect culture, individual and role differences . . ." (Principle E: Respect for People's Right and Dignity). Unless the older adult is determined through assessment to be clinically or legally incapacitated and therefore unable to self-protect or self-determine the desirable treatment from others, professionals who are often mandated to report elder abuse (psychologists and others) are encouraged to carefully navigate the terrain of varied and even conflicting information before taking any action.

Harbison and colleagues (2005) highlighted the tendency of elder abuse legislators to ignore the wishes of older adults, specifically those living in rural areas, by reporting elder abuse that would consequently subject the older adult to increased emotional turmoil such as shame and also fear of being further abused. They pointed to the possibility of achieving a more successful intervention outcome by attending to the specific culture of older adults living in rural settings. There are implications for professionals to more thoughtfully and collaboratively work with older adult victims. In so doing, mandated reporters and legislators could better help balance older adults' rights and wishes with what seems to be in the best interest of the victims. Other research involving different ethnic groups and individuals from diverse cultures also lends support to the need for an in-depth understanding of the context from which such important decisions pertaining to claims of elder abuse are usually made. Consider the following examples:

1. Financial/material exploitation:

An 85-year-old woman with end-stage cancer and fluctuating mental status lives at her oldest daughter's home. Although physically frail, she is still able to ambulate with some assistance. Her son visited and took her to the bank to transfer a substantial amount of money into his account because he recently lost his job. Her oldest daughter filed a report of elder abuse because her mother did not have enough funds needed for her medical treatment.

Cultural/ethical query: How would knowing the cultural background make a difference when understanding whether or not elder abuse had occurred?

2. Emotional abuse:

A 94-year-old man lives in his matrimonial home with his youngest son. Most friends and family are aware that he has an enmeshed relationship with his son. This enmeshment has been known to involve occasional arguments followed by reconciliations and mutual overprotection from the criticism of others. Alcohol abuse within the family has been a norm and altercations are frequent among male siblings and relatives after an evening of binge drinking together at the older adult's home. Such behaviors affect the older adult emotionally as his son yells vulgarities when intoxicated and then apologizes the next morning when sober. The older adult, when interviewed, denied any evidence of abuse despite noticeable bruises on his forearm.

Cultural/ethical query: Are there any specific ethnic groups that might tolerate such a pattern of coexistence whereby a report of elder abuse would bring more hardship to the older adult?

Although elder abuse is largely defined to include seven different types, mainly physical abuse, sexual abuse, emotional abuse, financial/material exploitation, neglect, abandonment, and self-neglect (Hall et al., 2016), the definition of "abuse" could be different for older adults in minority ethnic groups, especially when the concept could only be translated to mean "violence" or when disrespect could be considered "a major form of abuse" such as within the Chinese community (Bowes, Avan, & Macintosh, 2012). Lee and colleagues (2012) argue that the existing definition of financial abuse may be inaccurate because it is based on perceptions of supposedly highly educated professionals and policy makers, but not from older adults. In their study, for example, they found that Korean immigrants defined financial abuse as adult children either taking (stealing) possessions and/or assets from their parents or failing to financially support their parents.

Similarly, in an attempt to define elder abuse in culturally relevant terms, Parra-Cardona and colleagues (2007) sought to identify the "ecological framework" that could be at play for sustaining elder abuse and neglect among Latino older adults. They noted that acculturation status and differences in cultural beliefs and identity between the family caregiver and the older adult care recipient may be viewed as important factors for understanding elder abuse in Latino families. For example, the younger generation of Latinos are perceived to value traditional cultures less than their immigrant parents. This might explain their lack of awareness and also their likely different definition of elder abuse. Similarly, the family's financial standing and beliefs about aging should be considered when determining whether elder abuse or neglect has occurred because multiple ecological stressors could have been responsible for the outcome. Consequently, attending to these factors might help the development of interventions that would avoid placing blame solely on the abuser.

There remain many controversies regarding the meaning and definition of elder abuse and it is therefore not surprising that there is a lack of consensus and even confusion among health care professionals. Elder abuse is further made difficult to define due to the lack of training in geropsychology for psychologists, which would otherwise allow a greater appreciation of diversity issues in the competent care of older adults (Scheiderer, 2012). Koocher and Kieth-Spiegel (2016) proposed a six-item self-assessment as part of training in diversity to reflect upon one's biases and cultural competence. One item relevant for decision making in reporting elder abuse involves the question: "As I seek to protect myself, what are my ethical obligations when I notice a cultural incongruity in values between my professional association, my employer, legal obligations, and the people I serve?" (p. 132).

A review of the prevalence and risk factors for elder abuse in Asia (China, India, Singapore, Japan, and Korea) emphasized the need for sensitivity to the different normative definitions of elder abuse. They stressed the importance of establishing rapport with suspected older adult victims due to their unwillingness to share their experience of abuse that they likely perceive to be shameful or determine as a family affair to be kept private (Yan, Chan, & Tiwari, 2015). Hence, elder abuse might not simply be a matter of whether reporting is warranted, but rather, a term to be sensitively considered in the context of culture, diversity, and socioeconomic status. It is important to be mindful of different perceptions of older adults from minority groups and their sociocultural barriers to seeking help, such as lack of dominant language proficiency and isolation (Zannettino, Bagshaw, Wendt, & Adams, 2014).

ETHICS IN RESEARCH

Adhering to ethical standards when recruiting prospective research participants should be the standard practice of every researcher. Specifically, researchers are responsible for ensuring that best efforts are made to help participants understand as fully as possible the information depicted on informed consent forms. Older adults and individuals with lower education can be more vulnerable to inadequately understanding informed consent (Sugarman, McCrory, & Hubal, 1998). With the projected exponential increase in the geriatric population in the coming decades (see Chapter 1 and Ortman, Velkoff, & Hogan, 2014), it is expected that research on aging using older adults as participants will also increase accordingly. There have been concerns and fears over the unethical inclusion of older adults with cognitive impairment in research, but the exclusion could deprive them the opportunity to benefit from research where their well-being and quality of life could otherwise be improved.

These considerations bring rise to an important question of participants' varying levels of cognitive functioning. How might researchers ethically obtain consent from older adults who may present with impaired cognition without violating the ethical code to protect individuals from any potential harm as a research participant? As mentioned earlier, education level could also impact the understanding of informed consent information, but if cognition is also impaired, the challenge is much greater to warrant additional attention. One other important question is: Should the participants or the authorized representative consent to research when prospective participants are cognitively impaired? Several studies have attempted to provide guidance, which are summarized as follows.

Capacity to consent or decisions about who should provide consent on behalf of the older adult participant undoubtedly requires careful consideration. Specifically, it has been noted that ethical dilemmas begin at the level of capacity evaluation where the full range of contextual biopsychosocial information, including medical conditions, family relation, social function, and financial situation, need to be considered for accuracy of capacity judgment (Jimenez, Esplin, & Hernandez, 2015). Feliciano and colleagues (2011) explained how the capacity to consent for research participation is dependent on the older adult's cognitive ability and the study's complexity. They discussed the "principle of proportionality of the capacity to consent" wherein the amount of risk, time, and benefit involved in the study would determine how stringent the "standards of capacity to consent" should be (p. 477). That is, if a study involves more risk and time, the greater the importance to show adequate capacity to consent, whereas, if benefits are involved, the lesser the need to prove adequate capacity. In the same light, Bravo and colleagues (2003) found in their survey of older adults, informal caregivers, researchers, and institutional review board members, a unanimous opinion that for older adults with dementia, the need for a legal guardian's consent to participate in research becomes greater as the risks of the study increase. Despite the consensus, it was highlighted that many cognitively impaired older adults do not have a legal guardian. In a survey of older adults, informal caregivers, physicians, researchers, and research ethics board members, level of comfort with using proxy consent increased when risks to participants with dementia was lower (Dubois et al., 2011).

Some brief screening tools can assist a researcher in evaluating capacity to consent to research participation. Resnick and colleagues (2007) validated a five-item Evaluation to Sign Consent (ESC) measure in a randomized controlled trial using mainly European American nursing home residents aged 79 to 93 with a mean Mini Mental Status Examination (MMSE) score of 18. They found 63% of residents did not pass the ESC. As a comparison, a similar four-item capacity-to-consent screen was also validated for older adults in Korea using culturally and educationally appropriate questions (Lee, 2010). The majority (72%) had either no education or completed only elementary school. Lee demonstrated sensitivity to demographic backgrounds of participants by asking, "If you don't want to, do you have to be in the study?" versus Resnick and colleagues' directive, "Explain what he or she would do if he or she was experiencing distress or discomfort," which was more suitable for the study's predominantly White participants. Such attention to language when designing capacity measures is essential for protecting the rights and interests of research participants. While thoughtful planning is required when working with older adults with cognitive impairment, Gatz (2006) reminded researchers of the complexities of evaluating older adults' abilities to consent to participate in research or medical treatment. Gatz cautioned against the assumption that normal cognition equates to sound decision-making capacity because of the potential for cognitive changes in the older population and the existence of "a range of statuses between cognitive competence and decisional incapacity" (p. 468). Hence, it is important that researchers carefully weigh the risks and benefits of their study as well as attend to the nuances of capacity to consent that might not depend only on cognitive status at the time of recruitment. Researchers are also encouraged to observe legislative guidelines for research in their practice jurisdiction to ensure that prospective participants with impaired decision-making capacity are protected accordingly, such as whether proxy consent is absolutely required for research regardless of risks (Bravo, Duguet, Dubois, Delpierre, & Vellas, 2008).

CONCLUSION

As the U.S. older adult population grows, a number of ethical issues—only a few of which were discussed in this chapter—are increasingly coming into view for clinicians and health care providers. The micro- and macrosystems in which older adults live and thrive require a level of cultural sensitivity, an understanding of aging processes, and knowledge about professional ethics and legal standards involved in decision making. We have discussed the complexities of elder abuse and victimization, which involves complex judgments about capacity and potential surrogate decision making for an older adult. At the heart of ethical principles and guidelines is the challenge between autonomy and protection. We have also documented some of the real-world dilemmas faced by practitioners and families navigating long-term care placement and information sharing that occurs between providers, older adults, and the family. And finally, we addressed the ethical standards required for older adults to consent to participate in research—an important component to furthering the science and thus, expanding our knowledge and understanding of aging adults and families, and the communities in which we flourish together.

DISCUSSION QUESTIONS

1. Define the following terms and provide an example of when it would be useful to have each document: advance directive, power of attorney, health care surrogate.

2. Describe the difference between clinical capacity and legal capacity (competence), and discuss instruments used to assess capacity in older adults.

3. Define the domains of capacity discussed in the chapter and provide examples of ethical challenges that may be encountered in each domain.

4. Describe the concern when working with older adults about balancing the principles of autonomy and beneficence.

5. Discuss the prevalence of elder abuse and the cultural issues that are important to consider when determining the severity of elder abuse.

6. In the context of research with older adults, describe proxy consent and the ethical concerns about it.

REFERENCES

*Acierno, R., Hernandez, M., Amstadter, A., Resnick, H., Steve, K., Muzzy, W., & Kilpatrick, D. G. (2010). Prevalence and correlates of emotional, physical, sexual, and financial abuse and potential neglect in the United States: The National Elder Mistreatment Study. *American Journal of Public Health, 100,* 292–297.

Adler, G., & Kuskowski, M. (2003). Driving cessation in older men with dementia. *Alzheimer Disease and Associated Disorders, 17,* 68–71.

American Bar Association & American Psychological Association Assessment of Capacity in Older Adults Project Working Group. (2008). *Assessment of older adults with diminished capacity: A handbook for psychologists.* Washington, DC: Authors.

American Psychological Association. (2010). Ethical principles of psychologists and code of conduct: Including 2017 amendments. Retrieved from http://www.apa.org/ethics/code

Bowes, A., Avan, G., & Macintosh, S. B. (2012). Cultural diversity and the mistreatment of older people in black and minority ethnic communities: Some implications for service provision. *Journal of Elder Abuse & Neglect, 24,* 251–274. doi:10.1080/08946566.2011.653319

Bravo, G., Duguet, A. M., Dubois, M. F., Delpierre, C., & Vellas, B. (2008). Substitute consent for research involving the elderly: A comparison between Quebec and France. *Journal of Cross-Cultural Gerontology, 23,* 239–253. doi:10.1007/s10823-008-9070-x

*Bravo, G., Paquet, M., & Dubois, M. (2003). Opinions regarding who should consent to research on behalf of an older adult suffering from dementia. *Dementia, 2,* 49–65.

Bush, S. S., Allen, R. S., & Molinari, V. A. (2017). Ethical issues and decision making in geropsychology. In S. S. Bush, R. S. Allen, & V.A. Molinari (Eds.), *Ethical Practice in Geropsychology* (pp. 35–56). Washington DC: American Psychological Association.

Cooper, C., Selwood, A., Blanchard, M., Walker, Z., Blizard, R., & Livingston, G. (2009). Abuse of people with dementia by family carers: Representative cross sectional survey. *British Medical Journal, 338,* 480–485. doi:10.1136/bmj.b155

Cooper, C., Selwood, A., & Livingston, G. (2008). The prevalence of elder abuse and neglect: A systematic review. *Age and Ageing, 37,* 151–160. doi:10.1093/ageing/afm194

Dubois, M. F., Bravo, G., Graham, J., Wildeman, S., Cohen, C., Painter, K., & Bellemare, S. (2011). Comfort with proxy consent to research involving decisionally impaired older adults: Do type of proxy and risk-benefit profile matter? *International Psychogeriatrics, 23,* 1479–1488. doi:10.1017/S1041610211000433

*Edelstein, B. (2000). Challenges in the assessment of decision-making capacity. *Journal of Aging Studies, 14,* 423–437. doi:10.1016/S0890-4065(00)80006-7

*Feliciano, L., Yochim, B., Steers, M. E., Jay, A. A., & Segal, D. L. (2011). Research with older adults. In J. C. Thomas, & M. Hersen (Eds.), *Understanding research in clinical and counseling psychology* (2nd ed., pp. 457–484). New York, NY: Routledge/Taylor & Francis.

Gatz, M. (2006). Cognitive capacities of older adults who are asked to consent to medical treatment or to clinical research. *Behavioral Sciences & the Law, 24,* 465–468. doi:10.1002/bsl.694

Greene, E. & Gibson, S. C. (2013). The experiences of older adults in the legal system. In M. K. Miller and B.H. Bornstein (Eds.) *Stress, Trauma, and Wellbeing in the Legal System.* New York, NY: Oxford University Press.

*Grisso, T. (2003). *Evaluating competencies: Forensic assessments and instruments.* New York, NY: Kluwer Academic/Plenum.

Grisso, T., & Applebaum, P. S. (1998). *MacArthur competence assessment tool for treatment (MacCAT-T).* Sarasota, FL: Professional Resource Press/Professional Resource Exchange.

Hall, J. E., Karch, D. L., & Crosby, A. E. (2016). Elder abuse surveillance: Uniform definitions and recommended core data elements for use in elder abuse surveillance, Version 1.0. Retrieved from https://www.cdc.gov/violenceprevention/pdf/ea_book_revised_2016.pdf

Harbison, J., Coughlan, S., Karabanow, J., & Vanderplaat, M. (2005). A clash of cultures: Rural values and service delivery to mistreated and neglected older people in Eastern Canada. *Practice, 17*, 229–246. doi:10.1080/09503150500425091

Jimenez, X. F., Esplin, B. S., & Hernandez, J. O. (2015). Capacity consultation and contextual complexities: Depression, decisions, and deliberation. *Psychosomatics, 56*, 592–597. doi:10.1016/j.psym.2015.06.002

*Karel, M., Emery, E., Molinari, V., & the CoPGTP Task Force on the Assessment of Geropsychology Competencies. (2010). Development of a tool to evaluate geropsychology knowledge and skill competencies. *International Psychiatrics, 22*, 886–896. doi:10.1017/S1041610209991736

Karlawish, J. H., Quill, T. & Meier, D. (1999). A consensus-based approach to providing palliative care to patients who lack decision-making capacity. *Annals of Internal Medicine, 130*, 835–840.

Koocher, G. P., & Keith-Spiegel, P. (2016). *Ethics in psychology and the mental health professions: Standards and Cases.* New York, NY: Oxford University Press.

Lee, H. Y., & Eaton, C. K. (2009). Financial abuse in elderly Korean immigrants: Mixed analysis of the role of culture on perception and help-seeking intention. *Journal of Gerontological Social Work, 52*, 463–488. doi:10.1080/01634370902983138

Lee, H. Y., Lee, S. E., & Eaton, C. K. (2012). Exploring definitions of financial abuse in elderly Korean immigrants: The contribution of traditional cultural values. *Journal of Elder Abuse & Neglect, 24*, 293–311. doi:10.1080/08946566.2012.661672

Lee, M. (2010). The capacity to consent to research among older adults. *Educational Gerontology, 36*, 592–603. doi:10.1080/03601270903324461

Lichtenberg, P. A., Ficker, L., Rahman-Filipiak, A., Tatro, R., Farrell, C., Speir, J. J., . . . Jackman Jr., J. D. (2016). The Lichtenberg Financial Decision Screening Scale (LFDSS): A new tool for assessing financial decision making and preventing financial exploitation. *Journal of Elder Abuse & Neglect, 28*, 134–151, doi:10.1080/08946566.2016.1168333

Lichtenberg, P. A., & Strzepek, D. M. (1990). Assessments of institutionalized dementia patients' competencies to participate in intimate relationships. *Gerontologist, 30*, 117–120. doi:10.1093/geront/30.1.117

Loeb, P. A. (1996). *ILS: Independent living scales manual.* San Antonio, TX: Psychological Corporation.

*Marson, D. C. (2001). Loss of financial competency in dementia: Conceptual and empirical approaches. *Aging, Neuropsychology, and Cognition, 8*, 164–181.

Marson, D. C., Herbert, K., & Solomon, A. C. (2005). Assessing civil competencies in older adults with dementia: Consent capacity, financial capacity, and testamentary capacity. In G. J. Larrabee (Ed.), *Forensic neuropsychology casebook* (pp. 146–164). New York. NY: Guilford Press.

Marson, D. C., Ingram, K. K., Cody, H. A., & Harrell, L. E. (1995). Assessing the competency of patients with Alzheimer's disease under different legal standards: A prototype instrument. *Archives of Neurology, 52*, 949–954. doi:10.1001/archneur.1995.00540340029010

Marson, D. C., Sawrie, S. M., Snyder, S., McInturff, B., Stalvey, T., Boothe, A., . . . Harrell, L. E. (2000). Assessing financial capacity in patients with Alzheimer disease: A conceptual model and prototype instrument. *Archives of Neurology, 57*, 877–884. doi:10.1001/archneur.57.6.877

*Moye, J., & Braun, M. (2007). Assessment of medical consent capacity and independent living. In S. H. Qualls & M. A. Smyer (Eds.), *Changes in decision-making capacity in older adults: Assessment and interventions* (pp. 205–236). Hoboken, NJ: John Wiley.

*Moye, J., & Marson, D. C. (2007). Assessment of decision-making capacity in older adults: An emerging area of practice and research. *Journal of Gerontology: Psychological Sciences, 62B*, 3–11.

National Alliance for Caregiving. (2015). *Caregiving in the U.S. 2015.* Report conducted by National Alliance for Caregiving and AARP. Retrieved from http://www.caregiving.org/caregiving2015

Ortman, J. M., Velkoff, V. A., & Hogan, H. (2014). An aging nation: The older population in the United States, Current Population Reports. U.S. Census Bureau, Washington, DC. Retrieved from https://pdfs.semanticscholar.org/9e8d/9dc95a5130fa4fd0eb808b5c888e628c2023.pdf

Parra-Cardona, J. R., Meyer, E., Schiamberg, L., & Post, L. (2007). Elder abuse and neglect in Latino families: An ecological and culturally relevant theoretical framework for clinical practice. *Family Process, 46,* 451–470.

Rao, J. K., Anderson, L. A., Lin, F., & Laux, J. P. (2013). Completion of advance directives among U.S. consumers. *American Journal of Preventive Medicine, 46,* 65–70. doi:10.1016/j.amepre.2013.09.008

Resnick, B., Gruber-Baldini, A. L., Pretzer-Aboff, I., Galik, E., Buie, V. C., Russ, K., & Zimmerman, S. (2007). Reliability and validity of the evaluation to sign consent measure. *The Gerontologist, 47,* 69–77. doi:10.1093/geront/47.1.69

Scheiderer, E. M. (2012). Elder abuse: Ethical and related considerations for professionals in psychology. *Ethics & Behavior, 22,* 75–87. doi:10.1080/10508422.2012.638828

Sugarman, J., McCrory, D. C., & Hubal, R. C. (1998). Getting meaningful informed consent from older adults: A structured literature review of empirical research. *Journal of the American Geriatrics Society, 46,* 517–524.

Syme, M. L., & Steele, D. (2016). Sexual consent capacity assessment with older adults. *Archives of Clinical Neuropsychology, 31,* 495–505. doi:10.1093/arclin/acw046

Tarzia, L., Fetherstonhaugh, D., & Bauer, M. (2012). Dementia, sexuality and consent in residential aged care facilities. *Journal of Medical Ethics, 38,* 609–613. doi:10.1136/medethics-2011-100453

Wigglesworth, A., Mosqueda, L., Mulnard, R., Liao, S., Gibbs, L., & Fitzgerald, W. (2010). Screening for abuse and neglect of people with dementia. *Journal of the American Geriatrics Society, 3,* 493–500.

Wilkins, J. M. (2015). More than capacity: Alternatives for sexual decision making for individuals with dementia. *Gerontologist, 55,* 716–723. doi:10.1093/geront/gnv098

Yan, E., Chan, K.-L., & Tiwari, A. (2015). A systematic review of prevalence and risk factors for elder abuse in Asia. *Trauma, Violence & Abuse, 16,* 199–219. doi:10.1177/1524838014555033

Zannettino, L., Bagshaw, D., Wendt, S., & Adams, V. (2015). The role of emotional vulnerability and abuse in the financial exploitation of older people from culturally and linguistically diverse communities in Australia. *Journal of Elder Abuse & Neglect, 27,* 74–89. doi:10.1080/08946566.2014.976895

Index

AA. *See* Alzheimer's Association
ABPP. *See* American Board of Professional Psychology
accelerated cognitive decline, 185–186
access to mental health care, 136–137
 beliefs about mental health care, 136
 stigma, 136–137
acetylcholinesterase, 208. *See also* cholinesterase
active dying, 275
activities of daily living (ADL), 232, 238
ADA. *See* Americans With Disabilities Act (ADA)
ADEA. *See* Age Discrimination in Employment Act
ADL. *See* activities of daily living
adoption studies, 37
adult attachment style, 113–114
adult children as caregivers, 234–236
adult workforce, 251–253
adulthood, longitudinal studies of personality change in, 117–119
advance care planning, 276–278, 324–326
advanced glycation end products (AGE), 71
African Americans
 adult relationships, 113
 caregivers for their grandchildren, 233
 depression in, 236
 health care institutions and, 277
 life expectancy of, 8
 sleep problems and, 140–141
 stigma toward mental health services, 137
AGE. *See* advanced glycation end products (AGE)
age
 actual *versus* felt, 4
 chronological, 250
 cognitive reserve and, 186–187
 decrease in negative affect with, 121
 and emotional well-being, 119–122

 functional, 250
 late-life spousal loss and, 289
 old, 5
age change, 20
age differences, 20
Age Discrimination in Employment Act (ADEA), 172, 248, 250, 252, 254
age effects, 19
age-related changes
 to physiology of integumentary system, 51
 to physiology of musculoskeletal system, 53–54
age-related changes to the brain
 changes occurring with typical aging, 95–98
 methods of investigating, 87–95
age-related differences in emotion regulation, 125–127
age-related health conditions
 cardiovascular system, 61–64
 digestive system, 79–81
 endocrine system, 68–74
 immune system, 64–65
 integumentary system, 50–53
 musculoskeletal system, 53–55
 nervous system, 55–61
 reproductive system, 77–79
 respiratory system, 66–68
 urinary system, 75–77
age-related positivity effect, 122–124, 129
ageism, 249–251
aging
 challenges in research on genetics related to, 42
 free radicals and, 34–35
 genetics of, 37–39
 happy, 129
 international statistics on, 6–8
 negative perceptions of, 249
 U.S. statistics on, 6–8

CPSIA information can be obtained
at www.ICGtesting.com
Printed in the USA
BVHW062242100122
625897BV00005B/30